THE DEMOCRACY SOURCEBOOK

THE DEMOCRACY SOURCEBOOK

edited by Robert Dahl, Ian Shapiro, and José Antonio Cheibub

The MIT Press
Cambridge, Massachusetts
London, England

Excerpt from *The Liberal Tradition in America: An Interpretation of American Political Thought since the Revolution*, copyright © 1955 and renewed 1983 by Louis Hartz, reprinted by permission of Harcourt, Inc.

Every effort has been made to contact those who hold rights for each of the selections. Any rights holders not credited should contact the editors so a correction can be made in the next printing.

This book was set in Times New Roman on 3B2 by Asco Typesetters, Hong Kong, and was printed and bound in the United States of America.

Library of Congress Cataloging-in-Publication Data

The democracy sourcebook / Robert Dahl, Ian Shapiro, and José Antonio Cheibub, editors.
   p.   cm.
 Includes bibliographical references and index.
 ISBN 0-262-04217-7 (hc : alk. paper) — ISBN 0-262-54147-5 (pbk : alk. paper)
 1. Democracy. I. Dahl, Robert Alan, 1915– . II. Shapiro, Ian. III. Cheibub, José Antonio.
JC423.D4312   2003
321.8—dc21   2002045209

10 9 8 7 6 5 4 3 2 1

Contents

Contents

Contents

Introduction

This sourcebook is designed for undergraduate courses on democracy, though it will be useful for introductory graduate courses as well. It is not a textbook, but it could be a companion to many textbooks, and it could be used in courses on democracy that are taught without textbooks. The materials range over conceptual, normative, and empirical issues, giving students access, in one moderately priced volume, to classic arguments as well as the state of the art in contemporary scholarship. The materials draw on literature in American politics, comparative and international politics, and political philosophy. In this, they reflect an increasingly interconnected world and the increasingly interdisciplinary character of political science. The sourcebook is methodologically diverse and avoids unnecessarily technical or jargon-laden material. It also contains information providing vital statistics about the world's democracies.

The sourcebook is divided into nine self-contained chapters. In each, we combine edited selections from classic philosophical statements with more recent theoretical arguments and empirical applications.

Chapter 1, "Defining Democracy," is organized around the debates among proponents of procedural, deliberative, and substantive democracy. Procedural democrats emphasize practices and institutions that characterize democratic regimes, without specifying any outcome these regimes are supposed to bring about and without paying much attention to how preferences are formed. Deliberative democrats problematize preferences, arguing that appropriately deliberative procedures transform them in felicitous ways for democracy. Advocates of substantive democracy see procedures as necessary but insufficient to bring about democratic results. We begin with Joseph Schumpeter's influential assault on Jean-Jacques Rousseau and defense of his alternative "minimalist" conception of democracy. Then we turn to Adam Przeworski's recent elaboration and defense of a procedural view in light of the last several decades of litera-

ture in social choice theory. Excerpts from Amy Gutmann and Dennis Thompson, and James Fishkin, exemplify the deliberative alternative to proceduralism. We also include Larry Diamond's reformulation of the substantive view and Carole Pateman's theory of participatory democracy. We end with Robert Dahl's influential account of polyarchy, which synthesizes elements of these different views.

Chapter 2, "Sources of Democracy," guides students through debates about democracy and modernization, various macrohistorical arguments about the causes of democracy, and the literature on democratic transitions. The objective here is to illustrate the different arguments about why we observe democracies in some countries and not in others. We begin with the seminal defense of modernization theory by Seymour Martin Lipset. Observing a correlation between levels of economic development and democracy, he argues that development leads people to embrace values and attitudes that are friendly to democracy's emergence and viability. We then include various emendations of modernization theory, including Barrington Moore's argument about the importance of a bourgeoisie as summarized by Theda Skocpol, and an argument from Evelyne Huber, Dietrich Rueschmeyer, and John Stephens that emphasizes the presence of a working class. Then we turn to the literature on democratic transitions, where we include Przeworski's account of the relations between political and economic transitions, a discussion by Samuel Huntington of the three waves of democratic transitions, and a case study of the South African transition by Courtney Jung and Ian Shapiro. We conclude with a recent empirical evaluation of the modernization literature, which shows that although there is no relationship between modernization and the emergence of democracy, there is one between the level of economic development and the sustainability of democracy.

Chapter 3, "Democracy, Culture, and Society," explores debates about cultural and sociological preconditions for viable democracy with excerpts from *The Federalist Papers*, Louis Hartz, and the literature on pluralism and social cleavages. We then turn to the debate on consociationalism, beginning with Arend Lijphart's contention that divisions are so intense in some societies that majoritarian politics would be explosively dysfunctional. In such circumstances, he argues, minorities must be overrepresented, or even given veto rights over matters of intense importance to them. (In fact, this argument goes back to *The Federalist Papers* and accounts for such consociational elements in the U.S. Constitution as requiring concurrent majorities and supermajorities for constitutional reform, as well as overrepresentation of small states in the Senate.) This is followed by a critique of Lijphart by Donald Horowitz and a discussion by Shapiro about how to think about democratic institutional design in a world in which it is unclear how important culture and society are to democracy's viability. We then proceed to discussions of democracy and social capital prompted by Robert Putnam's *Bowling Alone*. This leads to consideration of debates about the role of "strong" civil society in sustaining democratic institutions that includes an article by Ronald Inglehart and Wayne Baker about the role of modernization in bringing about cultural change and an empirical assessment of arguments about social and cultural preconditions for democracy by Przeworski, José Antonio Cheibub, and Fernando Limongi.

Chapter 4, "Democracy and Constitutionalism," centers on the role of independent courts in the operation of democracies. It has long been an article of faith among legal theorists and liberal constitutionalists that bills of rights enforced through powers of judicial review are important guarantors of human freedom. We start with the relevant passages from *The Federalist Papers*, and then turn to Dahl's skeptical critique in *A Preface to Democratic Theory*. Then we turn to contemporary debates: Ronald Dworkin's defense of a bill of rights for Britain and Jeremy

Waldron's critique are followed by a recent comparative empirical assessment of the effects of bills of rights on the actual protection of human rights by Ran Hirschl, an analysis of the effect of constitutional courts on safeguarding rights by Dahl, and a discussion of types of judicial review that complement democracy rather than undermine it by Shapiro.

"Presidentialism versus Parliamentarism," chapter 5, deals with the relations between forms of democratic government and political stability. Presidential systems are hailed for their strong executives with popular mandates and comparatively inclusive legislatures. Parliamentary systems are touted as providing decisive governments and strong oppositions, where there is alternation in power between clearly defined political forces. We begin with an excerpt from Juan Linz's classic discussion of the relative advantages of parliamentary democracies. This is followed by Scott Mainwaring's modification of Linz's thesis, in which he argues that what matters for the functioning of democratic regimes is not presidentialism per se, but the combination of an independently elected president with a multiparty system. We then move to more recent scholarship that, in one way or another, modifies or refutes the thesis put forward by Linz. We include a discussion by Matthew Soberg Shugart and John Carey on the powers of the presidency and their impact on the instability of presidential regimes. They show that presidents differ significantly in the legislative and nonlegislative powers granted them by the constitution. They also suggest, still very much within the framework set up by Linz, that instability in presidential regimes is mostly due to the combination of a strong president (that is, one with a wide range of legislative and nonlegislative powers) and a strong congress. We also include an analysis by Cheibub in which he shows that minority presidents and deadlock situations are not as pervasive under presidentialism as many, since Linz, have believed, and that they do not affect the survival of democratic regimes.

This is followed by a piece by Kaare Strom in which he shows that minority governments under parliamentarism are not infrequent and, most significantly, that they are the product of political parties' calculus about the costs and benefits of participating in government, given that they are concerned not only with achieving office but also with the policies that are to be implemented by the government. Next, we include a discussion by Joe Foweraker in which he calls attention to the fact that coalition formation is an instrument available and frequently used by presidents to govern, and that this may mitigate the problems faced by presidents whose parties do not control a majority of seats in the legislature. Finally, we include an analysis of the Brazilian presidential system by Argelina Figueiredo and Fernando Limongi. They show that the president's legislative and agenda powers granted by Brazil's 1988 constitution, as well as the centralized organization of congress, work to neutralize the centripetal tendencies of the political system that are generated by the presidential form of government and the country's extremely permissive electoral and party legislation.

Chapter 6, "Representation," is concerned with debates over the fairest system of democratic accountability. We organize the selections around two debates: over whether democratic systems represent voters at all and over proportional versus majoritarian representation. We start with John Stuart Mill's argument that representative government is the best polity. Then we proceed to the locus classicus of the first debate: Condorcet's observation about cycling generalized by Kenneth Arrow in 1951. We will include a nontechnical summary of Arrow's theorem by William Riker, followed by excerpts from recent empirical work by Gerry Mackie and A. S. Tangian suggesting that the empirical likelihood of voting cycles is actually low. This suggests that the theoretical energy that has been directed at resolving the Arrow problem may not be warranted by its empirical importance. On majoritarianism versus proportionality, we include an excerpt from John Huber and G. Bingham Powell, Jr.'s discussion of proportionality as producing policies closer to those preferred by the median voter, Jung and Shapiro's account of the price paid for proportionality in terms of lost "loyal" opposition, and Douglas Rae's argument that although proportional representation may be more representative at the electoral stage, this is not necessarily the case at the government-formation stage. We conclude with a discussion by Anne Phillips about the representation of women in democracy.

Chapter 7, "Interest Groups," is organized around the debate over whether such groups are good or bad for democracy. We start by characterizing the pluralist view, according to which the influence of interest groups is positive. We use passages from David Truman to highlight the concepts of "latent groups" and "overlapping membership," central to the pluralist perspective on interest groups. We then turn to attacks on these arguments. We use Mancur Olson's criticism of how groups form, John Manley's defense of class analysis in view of pluralism's inability to account for existing political and economic inequality, George Stigler's demonstration of how interest group demands influence the regulatory process, and a text by Philippe Schmitter about the effect of corporatism on governability. Finally, we include a selection by Frank Sorauf about the relationship between money and politics as an illustration of the contemporary concerns about the role of interest groups on the democratic process.

In chapter 8, "Democracy's Effects," we turn to the effects of democracy on the economy and social life. The extracts on the economy are organized around the controversy over whether democracy is good or bad for economic growth. We include two types of negative arguments. One that is mostly made with respect to developing countries, represented by Karl de Schweinitz, Jr., emphasizes the negative impact of democracy on investment. The other, represented here by Ronald Wintrobe, emphasizes the propensity of politicians either to overregulate the economy or to extract rents by threatening to do so. We also include two arguments on the other side: Olson's contention that a good economy requires secure property rights that are better guaranteed by democracies than dictatorships, and Amartya Sen's argument that famines do not occur in democracies because democratic governments are forced by popular pressure to respond to crises. This is followed by an empirical selection from Przeworski et al., suggesting that democracy does not affect aggregate economic activity: it is neither a requirement nor a hindrance for a well-working economy. Turning to democracy's effects on social life, we start with Alexis de Tocqueville's claims about democracy as a cause of social leveling. This is followed by critiques of it with respect to the reduction of class inequality by John Roemer and Jennifer Hochschild, and of race and gender inequality by Rogers Smith.

Our final chapter, "Democracy and the Global Order," contains materials on the effects of democracy on international relations, as well as on the changing international system on democracies. With respect to the first, we start with Immanuel Kant's observation in *Perpetual Peace* that democracies tend not to fight one another. Next we have an excerpt from Bruce Russett, which updates Kant's observation and attempts to account for it empirically. This is followed by an empirically based critique by Donald Green et al., suggesting that democracy does not have a significant effect on the propensity to go to war (whether with democracies or nondemocracies). Turning to the effects of the global order on democracy, the focus is on the erosion of national sovereignty by transnational forces, illustrated by Russell Hardin's discussion of the loss of control over environmental policy. As Pippa Norris argues in our next selection, democratic theorists are more generally concerned with the creation of "democratic deficits" in transnational entities such as the European Union. David Held challenges this view in our

concluding selection. He makes the case that just as the centralization of national political authority was a precondition for the creation of national democracy, so the creation of effective systems of transnational authority must precede meaningful transnational democracy. On this view, those who bemoan the democratic deficit should see it as transitionally necessary—a positive development for the medium-term project of promoting European democracy.

In the appendix we include a discussion of the different measures of democracy that are commonly used in empirical research and information summarizing the distribution of democracies in the world across regions and over time.

1 DEFINING DEMOCRACY

The Social Contract
Jean-Jacques Rousseau

Capitalism, Socialism, and Democracy
Joseph Schumpeter

Minimalist Conception of Democracy: A Defense
Adam Przeworski

Democracy and Disagreement
Amy Gutmann and Dennis Thompson

The Voice of the People
James S. Fishkin

Defining and Developing Democracy
Larry Diamond

Participation and Democratic Theory
Carole Pateman

Polyarchal Democracy
Robert Dahl

The Social Contract

Jean-Jacques Rousseau

The Social Pact

I assume that men reach a point where the obstacles to their preservation in a state of nature prove greater than the strength that each man has to preserve himself in that state. Beyond this point, the primitive condition cannot endure, for then the human race will perish if it does not change its mode of existence.

Since men cannot create new forces, but merely combine and control those which already exist, the only way in which they can preserve themselves is by uniting their separate powers in a combination strong enough to overcome any resistance, uniting them so that their powers are directed by a single motive and act in concert.

Such a sum of forces can be produced only by the union of separate men, but as each man's own strength and liberty are the chief instruments of his preservation, how can he merge his with others' without putting himself in peril and neglecting the care he owes to himself? This difficulty, in terms of my present subject, may be expressed in these words:

"How to find a form of association which will defend the person and goods of each member with the collective force of all, and under which each individual, while uniting himself with the others, obeys no one but himself, and remains as free as before." This is the fundamental problem to which the social contract holds the solution.

The articles of this contract are so precisely determined by the nature of the act, that the slightest modification must render them null and void; they are such that, though perhaps never formally stated, they are everywhere the same, everywhere tacitly admitted and recognized; and

Excerpted from: Jean-Jacques Rousseau, *The Social Contract*. Translated by Maurice Cranston. London: Penguin Books, 1968. Reprinted by permission of the Estate of Maurice Cranston.

if ever the social pact is violated, every man regains his original rights and, recovering his natural freedom, loses that civil freedom for which he exchanged it.

These articles of association, rightly understood, are reducible to a single one, namely the total alienation by each associate of himself and all his rights to the whole community. . . .

If, then, we eliminate from the social pact everything that is not essential to it, we find it comes down to this: "Each one of us puts into the community his person and all his powers under the supreme direction of the general will; and as a body, we incorporate every member as an indivisible part of the whole."

Immediately, in place of the individual person of each contracting party, this act of association creates an artificial and corporate body composed of as many members as there are voters in the assembly, and by this same act that body acquires its unity, its common *ego*, its life and its will. The public person thus formed by the union of all other persons was once called the *city*, and is now known as the *republic* or the *body politic*. In its passive role it is called the *state*, when it plays an active role it is the *sovereign*; and when it is compared to others of its own kind, it is a *power*. Those who are associated in it take collectively the name of *a people*, and call themselves individually *citizens*, in that they share in the sovereign power, and *subjects*, in that they put themselves under the laws of the state. However, these words are often confused, each being mistaken for another; but the essential thing is to know how to recognize them when they are used in their precise sense.

The Sovereign

This formula shows that the act of association consists of a reciprocal commitment between society and the individual, so that each person, in making a contract, as it were, with himself, finds himself doubly committed, first, as a member of the sovereign body in relation to individuals, and secondly as a member of the state in relation to the sovereign. . . .

Now, as the sovereign is formed entirely of the individuals who compose it, it has not, nor could it have, any interest contrary to theirs; and so the sovereign has no need to give guarantees to the subjects, because it is impossible for a body to wish to hurt all of its members, and, as we shall see, it cannot hurt any particular member. The sovereign by the mere fact that it is, is always all that it ought to be.

But this is not true of the relation of subject to sovereign. Despite their common interest, subjects will not be bound by their commitment unless means are found to guarantee their fidelity.

For every individual as a man may have a private will contrary to, or different from, the general will that he has as a citizen. His private interest may speak with a very different voice from that of the public interest; his absolute and naturally independent existence may make him regard what he owes to the common cause as a gratuitous contribution, the loss of which would be less painful for others than the payment is onerous for him; and fancying that the artificial person which constitutes the state is a mere fictitious entity (since it is not a man), he might seek to enjoy the rights of a citizen without doing the duties of a subject. The growth of this kind of injustice would bring about the ruin of the body politic.

Hence, in order that the social pact shall not be an empty formula, it is tacitly implied in that commitment—which alone can give force to all others—that whoever refuses to obey the general will shall be constrained to do so by the whole body, which means nothing other than that he shall be forced to be free; for this is the necessary condition which, by giving each citizen to the nation, secures him against all personal dependence, it is the condition which shapes both the design and the working of the political machine, and which alone bestows justice on civil contracts —without it, such contracts would be absurd, tyrannical and liable to the grossest abuse. . . .

Whether the General Will Can Err

It follows from what I have argued that the general will is always rightful and always tends to the public good; but it does not follow that the deliberations of the people are always equally right. We always want what is advantageous to us but we do not always discern it. The people is never corrupted, but it is often misled; and only then does it seem to will what is bad.

There is often a great difference between the will of all [what all individuals want] and the general will; the general will studies only the common interest while the will of all studies private interest, and is indeed no more than the sum of individual desires. But if we take away from these same wills, the pluses and minuses which cancel each other out, the balance which remains is the general will.

From the deliberations of a people properly informed, and provided its members do not have any communication among themselves, the great number of small differences will always produce a general will and the decision will always be good. But if groups, sectional associations are formed at the expense of the larger association, the will of each of these groups will become general in relation to its own members and private in relation to the state; we might then say that there are no longer as many votes as there are men but only as many votes as there are groups. The differences become less numerous and yield a result less general. Finally, when one of these groups becomes so large that it can outweigh the rest, the result is no longer the sum of many small differences, but one great divisive difference; then there ceases to be a general will, and the opinion which prevails is no more than a private opinion.

Thus if the general will is to be clearly expressed, it is imperative that there should be no sectional associations in the state, and that every citizen should make up his own mind for himself—such was the unique and sublime invention of the great Lycurgus. But if there are sectional associations, it is wise to multiply their number and to prevent inequality among them, as Solon, Numa and Servius did. These are the only precautions which can ensure that the general will is always enlightened and the people protected from error....

Capitalism, Socialism, and Democracy

Joseph Schumpeter

The Classical Doctrine of Democracy

I. The Common Good and the Will of the People

The eighteenth-century philosophy of democracy may be couched in the following definition: the democratic method is that institutional arrangement for arriving at political decisions which realizes the common good by making the people itself decide issues through the election of individuals who are to assemble in order to carry out its will. Let us develop the implications of this.

It is held, then, that there exists a Common Good, the obvious beacon light of policy, which is always simple to define and which every normal person can be made to see by means of rational argument. There is hence no excuse for not seeing it and in fact no explanation for the presence of people who do not see it except ignorance—which can be removed—stupidity and anti-social interest. Moreover, this common good implies definite answers to all questions so that every social fact and every measure taken or to be taken can unequivocally be classed as "good" or "bad." All people having therefore to agree, in principle at least, there is also a Common Will of the people (= will of all reasonable individuals) that is exactly coterminous with the common good or interest or welfare or happiness. The only thing, barring stupidity and sinister interests, that can possibly bring in disagreement and account for the presence of an opposition is a difference of opinion as to the speed with which the goal, itself common to nearly all, is to be approached. Thus every member of the community, conscious of that goal, knowing his or her mind, discerning what is good and what is bad, takes part, actively and responsibly, in furthering the former and fighting the latter and all the members taken together control their public affairs.

It is true that the management of some of these affairs requires special aptitudes and techniques and will therefore have to be entrusted to specialists who have them. This does not affect the principle, however, because these specialists simply act in order to carry out the will of the people exactly as a doctor acts in order to carry out the will of the patient to get well. It is also true that in a community of any size, especially if it displays the phenomenon of division of labor, it would be highly inconvenient for every individual citizen to have to get into contact with all the other citizens on every issue in order to do his part in ruling or governing. It will be more convenient to reserve only the most important decisions for the individual citizens to pronounce upon—say by referendum—and to deal with the rest through a committee appointed by them— an assembly or parliament whose members will be elected by popular vote. This committee or body of delegates, as we have seen, will not represent the people in a legal sense but it will do so in a less technical one—it will voice, reflect or represent the will of the electorate. Again as a matter of convenience, this committee, being large, may resolve itself into smaller ones for the various departments of public affairs. Finally, among these smaller committees there will be a general-purpose committee, mainly for dealing with current administration, called cabinet or government, possibly with a general secretary or scapegoat at its head, a so-called prime minister.[1]

---

1. The official theory of the functions of a cabinet minister holds in fact that he is appointed in order to see to it that in his department the will of the people prevails.

Excerpted from: Joseph Schumpeter, *Capitalism, Socialism, and Democracy*. New York: Allen & Unwin, 1976.

As soon as we accept all the assumptions that are being made by this theory of the polity—or implied by it—democracy indeed acquires a perfectly unambiguous meaning and there is no problem in connection with it except how to bring it about. Moreover we need only forget a few logical qualms in order to be able to add that in this case the democratic arrangement would not only be the best of all conceivable ones, but that few people would care to consider any other. It is no less obvious however that these assumptions are so many statements of fact every one of which would have to be proved if we are to arrive at that conclusion. And it is much easier to disprove them.

There is, first, no such thing as a uniquely determined common good that all people could agree on or be made to agree on by the force of rational argument. This is due not primarily to the fact that some people may want things other than the common good but to the much more fundamental fact that to different individuals and groups the common good is bound to mean different things. This fact, hidden from the utilitarian by the narrowness of his outlook on the world of human valuations, will introduce rifts on questions of principle which cannot be reconciled by rational argument because ultimate values—our conceptions of what life and what society should be—are beyond the range of mere logic. They may be bridged by compromise in some cases but not in others. Americans who say, "We want this country to arm to its teeth and then to fight for what we conceive to be right all over the globe" and Americans who say, "We want this country to work out its own problems which is the only way it can serve humanity" are facing irreducible differences of ultimate values which compromise could only maim and degrade.

Secondly, even if a sufficiently definite common good—such as for instance the utilitarian's maximum of economic satisfaction[2]—proved acceptable to all, this would not imply equally definite answers to individual issues. Opinions on these might differ to an extent important enough to produce most of the effects of "fundamental" dissension about ends themselves. The problems centering in the evaluation of present versus future satisfactions, even the case of socialism versus capitalism, would be left still open, for instance, after the conversion of every individual citizen to utilitarianism. "Health" might be desired by all, yet people would still disagree on vaccination and vasectomy. And so on.

The utilitarian fathers of democratic doctrine failed to see the full importance of this simply because none of them seriously considered any substantial change in the economic framework and the habits of bourgeois society. They saw little beyond the world of an eighteenth-century ironmonger.

But, third, as a consequence of both preceding propositions, the particular concept of the will of the people or the *volonté générale* that the utilitarians made their own vanishes into thin air. For that concept presupposes the existence of a uniquely determined common good discernible to all. Unlike the romanticists the utilitarians had no notion of that semi-mystic entity endowed with a will of its own—that "soul of the people" which the historical school of jurisprudence made so much of. They frankly derived their will of the people from the wills of individuals. And unless there is a center, the common good, toward which, in the long run at least, *all* individual wills gravitate, we shall not get that particular type of "natural" *volonté générale*. The utilitarian center of gravity, on the one hand, unifies individual wills, tends to weld them

2. The very meaning of "greatest happiness" is open to serious doubt. But even if this doubt could be removed and definite meaning could be attached to the sum total of economic satisfaction of a group of people, that maximum would still be relative to given situations and valuations which it may be impossible to alter, or compromise on, in a democratic way.

by means of rational discussion into the will of the people and, on the other hand, confers upon the latter the exclusive ethical dignity claimed by the classic democratic creed. *This creed does not consist simply in worshiping the will of the people as such* but rests on certain assumptions about the "natural" object of that will which object is sanctioned by utilitarian reason. Both the existence and the dignity of this kind of *volonté générale* are gone as soon as the idea of the common good fails us. And both the pillars of the classical doctrine inevitably crumble into dust.

II. The Will of the People and Individual Volition

Of course, however conclusively those arguments may tell against this particular conception of the will of the people, they do not debar us from trying to build up another and more realistic one. I do not intend to question either the reality or the importance of the socio-psychological facts we think of when speaking of the will of a nation. Their analysis is certainly the prerequisite for making headway with the problems of democracy. It would however be better not to retain the term because this tends to obscure the fact that as soon as we have severed the will of the people from its utilitarian connotation we are building not merely a different theory of the same thing, but a theory of a completely different thing. We have every reason to be on our guard against the pitfalls that lie on the path of those defenders of democracy who while accepting, under pressure of accumulating evidence, more and more of the facts of the democratic process, yet try to anoint the results that process turns out with oil taken from eighteenth-century jars.

But though a common will or public opinion of some sort may still be said to emerge from the infinitely complex jumble of individual and group wise situations, volitions, influences,

actions and reactions of the "democratic process," the result lacks not only rational unity but also rational sanction. The former means that, though from the standpoint of analysis, the democratic process is not simply chaotic—for the analyst nothing is chaotic that can be brought within the reach of explanatory principles—yet the results would not, except by chance, be meaningful in themselves—as for instance the realization of any definite end or ideal would be. The latter means, since *that* will is no longer congruent with any "good," that in order to claim ethical dignity for the result it will now be necessary to fall back upon an unqualified confidence in democratic forms of government as such—a belief that in principle would have to be independent of the desirability of results. As we have seen, it is not easy to place oneself on that standpoint. But even if we do so, the dropping of the utilitarian common good still leaves us with plenty of difficulties on our hands.

In particular, we still remain under the practical necessity of attributing to the will of the *individual* an independence and a rational quality that are altogether unrealistic. If we are to argue that the will of the citizens *per se* is a political factor entitled to respect, it must first exist. That is to say, it must be something more than an indeterminate bundle of vague impulses loosely playing about given slogans and mistaken impressions. Everyone would have to know definitely what he wants to stand for. This definite will would have to be implemented by the ability to observe and interpret correctly the facts that are directly accessible to everyone and to sift critically the information about the facts that are not. Finally, from that definite will and from these ascertained facts a clear *and prompt* conclusion as to particular issues would have to be derived according to the rules of logical inference—with so high a degree of general efficiency moreover that one man's opinion could be held, without glaring absurdity, to be roughly as good as every other man's.[3] And all this the model citizen would have to perform for himself and independently of pressure groups and propaganda,[4] for volitions and inferences that are imposed upon the electorate obviously do not qualify for ultimate data of the democratic process. The question whether these conditions are fulfilled to the extent required in order to make democracy work should not be answered by reckless assertion or equally reckless denial. It can be answered only by a laborious appraisal of a maze of conflicting evidence.

Before embarking upon this, however, I want to make quite sure that the reader fully appreciates another point that has been made already. I will therefore repeat that even if the opinions and desires of individual citizens were perfectly definite and independent data for the democratic process to work with, and if everyone acted on them with ideal rationality and promptitude, it would not necessarily follow that the political decisions produced by that process from the raw material of those individual volitions would represent anything that could in any convincing sense be called the will of the people. It is not only conceivable but, whenever individual wills are much divided, very likely that the political decisions produced will not conform to "what people really want." Nor can it be replied that, if not exactly what they want, they will get a "fair compromise." This may be so. The chances for this to happen are greatest with those issues which are quantitative in nature or admit of gradation, such as the question how much is to be spent on unemployment relief provided everybody favors some expenditure for that purpose. But with qualitative issues, such as the question whether to persecute heretics or to enter upon a war, the result attained may well, though for different reasons, be equally distasteful to all the people whereas the decision imposed by a nondemocratic agency might prove much more acceptable to them....

... If results that prove in the long run satisfactory to the people at large are made the test of government *for* the people, then government *by* the people, as conceived by the classical doctrine of democracy, would often fail to meet it.

---

3. This accounts for the strongly equalitarian character both of the classical doctrine of democracy and of popular democratic beliefs. It will be pointed out later on how Equality may acquire the status of an ethical postulate. As a factual statement about human nature it cannot be true in any conceivable sense. In recognition of this the postulate itself has often been reformulated so as to mean "equality of opportunity." But, disregarding even the difficulties inherent in the word opportunity, this reformulation does not help us much because it is actual and not potential equality of performance in matters of political behavior that is required if each man's vote is to carry the same weight in the decision of issues.

It should be noted in passing that democratic phraseology has been instrumental in fostering the association of inequality of any kind with "injustice" which is so important an element in the psychic pattern of the unsuccessful and in the arsenal of the politician who uses him. One of the most curious symptoms of this was the Athenian institution of ostracism or rather the use to which it was sometimes put. Ostracism consisted in banishing an individual by popular vote, not necessarily for any particular reason: it sometimes served as a method of eliminating an uncomfortably prominent citizen who was felt to "count for more than one."

4. This term is here being used in its original sense and not in the sense which it is rapidly acquiring at present and which suggests the definition: propaganda is any statement emanating from a source that we do not like. I suppose that the term derives from the name of the committee of cardinals which deals with matters concerning the spreading of the Catholic faith, the *congregatio de propaganda fide*. In itself therefore it does not carry any derogatory meaning and in particular it does not imply distortion of facts. One can make propaganda, for instance, for a scientific method. It simply means the presentation of facts and arguments with a view to influencing people's actions or opinions in a definite direction.

Another Theory of Democracy

I. Competition for Political Leadership

I think that most students of politics have by now come to accept the criticisms leveled at the classical doctrine of democracy in the preceding chapter. I also think that most of them agree, or will agree before long, in accepting another theory which is much truer to life and at the same time salvages much of what sponsors of the democratic method really mean by this term. Like the classical theory, it may be put into the nutshell of a definition.

It will be remembered that our chief troubles about the classical theory centered in the proposition that "the people" hold a definite and rational opinion about every individual question and that they give effect to this opinion—in a democracy—by choosing "representatives" who will see to it that that opinion is carried out. Thus the selection of the representatives is made secondary to the primary purpose of the democratic arrangement which is to vest the power of deciding political issues in the electorate. Suppose we reverse the roles of these two elements and make the deciding of issues by the electorate secondary to the election of the men who are to do the deciding. To put it differently, we now take the view that the role of the people is to produce a government, or else an intermediate body which in turn will produce a national executive[1] or government. And we define: the democratic method is that institutional arrangement for arriving at political decisions in which individuals acquire the power to decide by means of a competitive struggle for the people's vote.

Defense and explanation of this idea will speedily show that, as to both plausibility of assumptions and tenability of propositions, it greatly improves the theory of the democratic process.

First of all, we are provided with a reasonably efficient criterion by which to distinguish democratic governments from others. We have seen that the classical theory meets with difficulties on that score because both the will and the good of the people may be, and in many historical instances have been, served just as well or better by governments that cannot be described as democratic according to any accepted usage of the term. Now we are in a somewhat better position partly because we are resolved to stress a *modus procedendi* the presence or absence of which it is in most cases easy to verify.[2]

For instance, a parliamentary monarchy like the English one fulfills the requirements of the democratic method because the monarch is practically constrained to appoint to cabinet office the same people as parliament would elect. A "constitutional" monarchy does not qualify to be called democratic because electorates and parliaments, while having all the other rights that electorates and parliaments have in parliamentary monarchies, lack the power to impose their choice as to the governing committee: the cabinet ministers are in this case servants of the monarch, in substance as well as in name, and can in principle be dismissed as well as appointed by him. Such an arrangement may satisfy the people. The electorate may reaffirm this fact by voting against any proposal for change. The monarch may be so popular as to be able to defeat any competition for the supreme office. But since no machinery is provided for making this competition effective the case does not come within our definition.

Second, the theory embodied in this definition leaves all the room we may wish to have for a proper recognition of the vital fact of leadership. The classical theory did not do this but, as we have seen, attributed to the electorate an

---

1. The insincere word "executive" really points in the wrong direction. It ceases however to do so if we use it in the sense in which we speak of the "executives" of a business corporation who also do a great deal more than "execute" the will of stockholders.

---

2. See however the fourth point below.

altogether unrealistic degree of initiative which practically amounted to ignoring leadership. But collectives act almost exclusively by accepting leadership—this is the dominant mechanism of practically any collective action which is more than a reflex. Propositions about the working and the results of the democratic method that take account of this are bound to be infinitely more realistic than propositions which do not. They will not stop at the execution of a *volonté générale* but will go some way toward showing how it emerges or how it is substituted or faked. What we have termed Manufactured Will is no longer outside the theory, an aberration for the absence of which we piously pray; it enters on the ground floor as it should.

Third, however, so far as there are genuine group-wise volitions at all—for instance the will of the unemployed to receive unemployment benefit or the will of other groups to help—our theory does not neglect them. On the contrary we are now able to insert them in exactly the role they actually play. Such volitions do not as a rule assert themselves directly. Even if strong and definite they remain latent, often for decades, until they are called to life by some political leader who turns them into political factors. This he does, or else his agents do it for him, by organizing these volitions, by working them up and by including eventually appropriate items in his competitive offering. The interaction between sectional interests and public opinion and the way in which they produce the pattern we call the political situation appear from this angle in a new and much clearer light.

Fourth, our theory is of course no more definite than is the concept of competition for leadership. This concept presents similar difficulties as the concept of competition in the economic sphere, with which it may be usefully compared. In economic life competition is never completely lacking, but hardly ever is it perfect. Similarly, in political life there is always some competition, though perhaps only a potential one, for the allegiance of the people. To simplify matters we have restricted the kind of competition for leadership which is to define democracy, to free competition for a free vote. The justification for this is that democracy seems to imply a recognized method by which to conduct the competitive struggle, and that the electoral method is practically the only one available for communities of any size. But though this excludes many ways of securing leadership which should be excluded,[4] such as competition by military insurrection, it does not exclude the cases that are strikingly analogous to the economic phenomena we label "unfair" or "fraudulent" competition or restraint of competition. And we cannot exclude them because if we did we should be left with a completely unrealistic ideal.[5] Between this ideal case which does not exist and the cases in which all competition with the established leader is prevented by force, there is a continuous range of variation within which the democratic method of government shades off into the autocratic one by imperceptible steps. But if we wish to understand and not to philosophize, this is as it should be. The value of our criterion is not seriously impaired thereby.

Fifth, our theory seems to clarify the relation that subsists between democracy and individual freedom. If by the latter we mean the existence of a sphere of individual self-government the boundaries of which are historically variable— *no* society tolerates absolute freedom even of

---

4. It also excludes methods which should not be excluded, for instance, the acquisition of political leadership by the people's tacit acceptance of it or by election *quasi per inspirationem*. The latter differs from election by voting only by a technicality. But the former is not quite without importance even in modern politics; the sway held by a party boss *within his party* is often based on nothing but tacit acceptance of his leadership. Comparatively speaking however these are details which may, I think, be neglected in a sketch like this.

5. As in the economic field, *some* restrictions are implicit in the legal and moral principles of the community.

conscience and of speech, *no* society reduces that sphere to zero—the question clearly becomes a matter of degree. We have seen that the democratic method does not necessarily guarantee a greater amount of individual freedom than another political method would permit in similar circumstances. It may well be the other way round. But there is still a relation between the two. If, on principle at least, everyone is free to compete for political leadership[6] by presenting himself to the electorate, this will in most cases though not in all mean a considerable amount of freedom of discussion *for all*. In particular it will normally mean a considerable amount of freedom of the press. This relation between democracy and freedom is not absolutely stringent and can be tampered with. But, from the standpoint of the intellectual, it is nevertheless very important. At the same time, it is all there is to that relation.

Sixth, it should be observed that in making it the primary function of the electorate to produce a government (directly or through an intermediate body) I intended to include in this phrase also the function of evicting it. The one means simply the acceptance of a leader or a group of leaders, the other means simply the withdrawal of this acceptance. This takes care of an element the reader may have missed. He may have thought that the electorate controls as well as installs. But since electorates normally do not control their political leaders in any way except by refusing to reelect them or the parliamentary majorities that support them, it seems well to reduce our ideas about this control in the way indicated by our definition. Occasionally, spontaneous revulsions occur which upset a government or an individual minister directly or else enforce a certain course of action. But they are not only exceptional, they are, as we shall see, contrary to the spirit of the democratic method.

Seventh, our theory sheds much-needed light on an old controversy. Whoever accepts the classical doctrine of democracy and in consequence believes that the democratic method is to guarantee that issues be decided and policies framed according to the will of the people must be struck by the fact that, even if that will were undeniably real and definite, decision by simple majorities would in many cases distort it rather than give effect to it. Evidently the will of the majority is the will of the majority and not the will of "the people." The latter is a mosaic that the former completely fails to "represent." To equate both by definition is not to solve the problem. Attempts at real solutions have however been made by the authors of the various plans for Proportional Representation.

These plans have met with adverse criticism on practical grounds. It is in fact obvious not only that proportional representation will offer opportunities for all sorts of idiosyncrasies to assert themselves but also that it may prevent democracy from producing efficient governments and thus prove a danger in times of stress.[7] But before concluding that democracy becomes unworkable if its principle is carried out consistently, it is just as well to ask ourselves whether this principle really implies proportional representation. As a matter of fact it does not. If acceptance of leadership is the true function of the electorate's vote, the case for proportional representation collapses because its premises are no longer binding. The principle of democracy then merely means that the reins of government should be handed to those who command more support than do any of the competing individuals or teams. And this in turn seems to assure the standing of the majority system within the logic of the democratic method, although we might still condemn it on grounds that lie outside of that logic. . . .

---

6. Free, that is, in the same sense in which everyone is free to start another textile mill.

7. The argument against proportional representation has been ably stated by Professor F. A. Hermens in "The Trojan Horse of Democracy," *Social Research*, November 1938.

Minimalist Conception of Democracy: A Defense

Adam Przeworski

Introduction

I want to defend a "minimalist," Schumpeterian, conception of democracy, by minimalist, Popperian, standards. In Schumpeter's (1942) conception, democracy is just a system in which rulers are selected by competitive elections. Popper (1962: 124) defends it as the only system in which citizens can get rid of governments without bloodshed. . . .

Since neither the position I wish to defend nor the claim in its favor are new, what do I defend them from? Perusing innumerable definitions, one discovers that democracy has become an altar on which everyone hangs his or her favorite *ex voto*. Almost all normatively desirable aspects of political, and sometimes even of social and economic, life are credited as intrinsic to democracy: representation, accountability, equality, participation, justice, dignity, rationality, security, freedom, . . . , the list goes on. We are repeatedly told that "unless democracy is x or generates x, . . ." The ellipsis is rarely spelled out, but it insinuates either that a system in which governments are elected is not worthy of being called "democracy" unless x is fulfilled or that democracy in the minimal sense will not endure unless x is satisfied.[2] The first claim is normative, even if it often hides as a definition. The second is empirical. . . .

Yet suppose this is all there is to democracy: that rulers are elected. Is it little? It depends on the point of departure.[24] If one begins with a vision of a basic harmony of interests, a common good to be discovered and agreed to by a ratio-nal deliberation, and to be represented as the view of the informed majority, the fact that rulers are elected is of no particular significance. Voting is just a time-saving expedient (Buchanan and Tullock 1962) and majority rule is just a technically convenient way of identifying what everyone would or should have agreed to. Yet if the point of departure is that in any society there are conflicts, of values and of interests, electing rulers appears nothing short of miraculous.

Let us put the consensualist view of democracy where it belongs—in the Museum of Eighteenth-century Thought—and observe that all societies are ridden with economic, cultural, or moral conflicts. True, as the modernization theory (notably Coser 1959) emphasized, these conflicts can be "cross-cutting": they need not pit class against class or religion against religion. They can be attenuated by an "overlapping consensus": consensus about practicalities compatible with differences of values (Rawls 1993). They may be also moderated by public discussion of both normative and technical reasons, although, as I have argued above, deliberation is a two-edged sword, for it may lead just to solidifying conflicting views. Yet in the end, when all the coalitions have been formed, the practical consensus has been elaborated, and all arguments have been exhausted, conflicts remain.

My defense of the minimalist conception proceeds in two steps. I take it as obvious that

---

2. Widely cited statements in this vein are Weffort 1992 and Schmitter and Karl 1991, but the phrase is ubiquitous. Here is Shapiro (1996: 108): "If democracy does not function to improve the circumstances of those who appeal to it, its legitimacy as a political system will atrophy." Even Kelsen (1988 [1929]: 38) poses the threat that "Modern democracy will not live unless the Parliament will show itself an instrument appropriate for the solution of the social questions of the hour."

24. Shapiro (1996: 82) also takes this position.

we want to avoid bloodshed, resolving conflicts through violence.[25] Starting with this assumption, I first argue that the mere possibility of being able to change governments can avoid violence. Secondly, I argue that being able to do it by voting has consequences of its own.

Popper's defense of democracy is that it allows us to get rid of governments peacefully. But why should we care about changing governments?[26] My answer is that the very prospect that governments may change can result in a peaceful regulation of conflicts. To see this argument in its starkest form, assume that governments are selected by a toss of a, not necessarily fair, coin: "heads" mean that the incumbents should remain in office, "tails" that they should leave. Thus, a reading of the toss designates "winners" and "losers." This designation is an *instruction* what the winners and the losers should and should not do: the winners should move into a White or Pink House or perhaps even a *palacio*; while there they can take everything up to the constitutional constraint for themselves and their supporters, and they should toss the same coin again when their term is up. The losers should not move into the House and should accept getting not more than whatever is left.

Note that when the authorization to rule is determined by a lottery, citizens have no electoral sanction, prospective or retrospective, and the incumbents have no electoral incentives to behave well while in office. Since electing governments by a lottery makes their chances of survival independent of their conduct, there are no reasons to expect that governments act in a representative fashion because they want to earn re-election: any link between elections and representation is severed.

Yet the very prospect that governments would alternate may induce the conflicting political forces to comply with the rules rather than engage in violence, for the following reason. Although the losers would be better off in the short run rebelling rather than accepting the outcome of the current round, if they have a sufficient chance to win and a sufficiently large payoff in the future rounds, they are better off continuing to comply with the verdict of the coin toss rather than fighting for power. Similarly, while the winners would be better off in the short run not tossing the coin again, they may be better off in the long run peacefully leaving office rather than provoking violent resistance to their usurpation of power. Regulating conflicts by a coin toss is then a self-enforcing equilibrium (Przeworski 1991: chap. 1). Bloodshed is avoided by the mere fact that, à la Aristotle, the political forces expect to take turns.

Suppose first that the winners of the coin toss get some predetermined part of the pie, $1/2 < x < 1$, while losers get the rest.[27] Winners decide at each time whether to hold elections at the next time and losers whether to accept defeat or to rebel. If democracy is repeated indefinitely from $t = 0$ on, the winner at $t = 0$ expects to get $D_W = x + V_W(e, x)$ and the loser at $t = 0$ expects to get $D_L = (1 - x) + V_L(1 - e, x)$, where V stands for the present value of continuing under democracy beyond the current round, e is the probability the current incumbent will win the next toss. Let "democratic equilibrium" stand for a pair of strategies in which the current winners always hold tosses if they expect losers to comply and the current losers always comply if they expect the winners to hold tosses. Then such an equilibrium exists if everyone is better off under democracy than under rebellion: if $D_W > R_W$ and $D_L > R_L$, where R stands for the expected values of violent conflict for each of the two parties.

---

25. I am not arguing against Locke that violence is never justified, just that a system that systematically avoids it is preferable to one that does not.

26. I want to thank Ignacio Sanchez-Cuenca for posing this question.

---

27. This analysis is based on joint work with James Fearon, still in progress.

Moreover, the prospect of alternation may induce moderation while in office. Suppose that the current incumbent can either manipulate the probability, e, of being re-elected or can decide what share of the pie, $x \in [0, 1]$, to take, or both. There are some initial values $\{e(0), x(0)\}$; at $t = 1$ the coin is tossed and it designates winners and losers. Whoever is the winner now chooses $\{e(1), x(1)\}$: the rules for this round, etc. Hence, rules are not given *ex ante*: the incumbent manipulates them at will. Yet there are conditions under which a democratic equilibrium exists in which the incumbents do not grab everything. If the cost of rebellion is sufficiently high for both, each incumbent will prefer to moderate its behavior while in office under democracy rather than provoke a rebellion by the current loser.

As Hardin (1989: 113) puts it, "for the constitutional case, the ultimate source [of stability] is the internal costs of collective action for re-coordination or, in Caesar's word, *mutiny*." Yet if the threat of mutiny were the only incentive to moderation, why would we ever adopt procedures that subject control over the exercise of rule to a lottery? If the relevant political actors knew what would happen as the result of an open conflict, they could just agree to a distribution that would have resulted from an open confrontation. Instead of a coin toss deciding who gets what, the distribution would be fixed to reflect the strength the conflicting political forces could muster in an open confrontation, x for one, $(1 - x)$ for the other. So why do we have democracy: an agreement to toss a coin with probabilities e and $(1 - e)$?

The reason, in my view, is that it would be impossible to write a dictatorial contract that would specify every contingent state of nature. In turn, leaving the residual control—control over issues not explicitly regulated by contract—to the dictator would generate increasing returns to power and undermine the contract. Endowed with residual control, the dictator could not commit itself not to use the advantage to under-

mine the strength of the adversaries in an open conflict. Hence, to avoid violence, the conflicting political forces adopt the following device: agree over those issues that can be specified and allow the residual control to alternate according to specified probabilities. In this sense, the constitution specifies x, the limits on incumbents, and e, their chances in electoral competition, but a random device decides who holds residual control.

Yet we do not use random devices; we vote. What difference does that make?

Voting is an imposition of a will over a will. When a decision is reached by voting, some people must submit to an opinion different from theirs or to a decision contrary to their interest.[28] Voting authorizes compulsion. It empowers governments, our rulers, to keep people in jail,[29] sometimes even to take their life, to seize money from some and give it to others, to regulate private behavior of consenting adults. Voting generates winners and losers, and it authorizes the winners to impose their will, even if within constraints, on the losers. This is what "ruling" is. Bobbio's (1984: 93) parenthetical addition bares a crucial implication of the Schumpeterian definition: "by 'democratic system'," Bobbio says, "I mean one in which supreme power (supreme in so far as it alone is authorized to use force as a last resort) is exerted in the name of and on behalf of the people by virtue of the procedure of elections."

It is voting that authorizes coercion, not reasons behind it. *Pace* Cohen (1997: 5), who claims that the participants "are prepared to cooperate in accordance with the results of such discussion,

---

28. This sentence is a paraphrase of Condorcet (1986 [1785]: 22): "il s'agit, dans une loi qui n'a pas été votée unanimement, de soumettre des hommes à une opinion qui n'est pas la leur, ou à une décision qu'ils croient contraire à leur intérêt."

29. Indeed, the oldest democracy in the world is also one that keeps more people in jail than any other country in the world.

treating those results as authoritative," it is the result of voting, not of discussion, that authorizes governments to govern, to compel. Deliberation may lead to a decision that is reasoned: it may illuminate the reasons a decision is or should not be taken. Further, these reasons may guide the implementation of the decision, the actions of the government. But if all the reasons have been exhausted and yet there is no unanimity, some people must act against their reasons. They are coerced to do so, and the authorization to coerce them is derived from counting heads, the sheer force of numbers, not from the validity of reasons.

What difference, then, does it make that we vote? One answer to this question is that the right to vote imposes an obligation to respect the results of voting. In this view, democracy persists because people see it as their duty to obey outcomes resulting from a decision process in which they voluntarily participated. Democracy is legitimate in the sense that people are ready to accept decisions of as yet undetermined content, as long as they can participate in the making of these decisions. I do not find this view persuasive, however, either normatively or positively. Clearly, this is not the place to enter into a discussion of a central topic of political theory (Dunn 1996a: chap. 4) but I stand with Kelsen (1998 [1929]: 21) when he observes that "The purely negative assumption that no individual counts more than any other does not permit to deduce the positive principle that the will of the majority should prevail," and I know no evidence to the effect that participation induces compliance.

Yet I think that voting does induce compliance, through a different mechanism. Voting constitutes "flexing muscles": a reading of chances in the eventual war. If all men are equally strong (or armed) then the distribution of vote is a proxy for the outcome of war. Referring to Herodotus, Bryce (1921: 25–6) announces that he uses the concept of democracy "in its old and strict sense, as denoting a government in

which the will of the majority of qualified citizens rules, taking qualified citizens to constitute the great bulk of the inhabitants, say, roughly three-fourths, *so that physical force of the citizens coincides (broadly speaking) with their voting power*" (italics supplied). Condorcet claims that this was the reason for adopting majority rule: for the good of peace and general welfare, it was necessary to place authority where lies the force.[30] Clearly, once physical force diverges from sheer numbers, when the ability to wage war becomes professionalized and technical, voting no longer provides a reading of chances in a violent conflict. But voting does reveal information about passions, values, and interests. If elections are a peaceful substitute for rebellion (Hampton 1994), it is because they inform everyone who would mutiny and against what. They inform the losers—"Here is the distribution of force: if you disobey the instructions conveyed by the results of the election, I will be more likely to beat you than you will be able to beat me in a violent confrontation"—and the winners—"If you do not hold elections again or if you grab too much, I will be able to put up a forbidding resistance." Dictatorships do not generate this information; they need secret police to find out. In democracies, even if voting does not reveal a unique collective will, it does indicate limits to rule. Why else would we interpret participation as an indication of legitimacy, why would we be concerned about support for extremist parties?

In the end, the miracle of democracy is that conflicting political forces obey the results of

---

30. "Lorsque l'usage de soumettre tous les individus à la volonté du plus grand nombre, s'introduisit dans les sociétes, et que les hommes convinrent de regarder la décision de la pluralité comme la volonté de tous, ils n'adoptèrent pas cette méthode comme un moyen d'éviter l'erreur et de se conduire d'aprés des décisions fondées sur la vérité: mais ils trouvèrent que, pour le bien de la paix et l'utilité générale, *il falloit placer l'autorité où etoit la force*" (Condorcet 1986 [1785]: 11; italics supplied).

voting. People who have guns obey those without them. Incumbents risk their control of governmental offices by holding elections. Losers wait for their chance to win office. Conflicts are regulated, processed according to rules, and thus limited. This is not consensus, yet not mayhem either. Just limited conflict; conflict without killing. Ballots are "paper stones," as Engels once observed.

Yet this miracle does not work under all conditions.[31] The expected life of democracy in a country with per capita income under $1,000 is about eight years.[32] Between $1,001 and $2,000, an average democracy can expect to endure eighteen years. But above $6,000, democracies last forever. Indeed, no democracy ever fell, regardless of everything else, in a country with a per capita income higher than that of Argentina in 1976: $6,055. Thus Lipset (1959: 46) was undoubtedly correct when he argued that "The more well-to-do a country, the greater the chance that it will sustain democracy."

Several other factors affect the survival of democracies but they all pale in comparison to per capita income. Two are particularly relevant. First, it turns out that democracies are more likely to fall when one party controls a large share (more than two-thirds) of seats in the legislature. Secondly, democracies are most stable when the heads of governments change not too infrequently, more often than once every five years (although not as often as less than every two years). Thus, democracy is more likely to survive when no single force dominates politics completely and permanently.

Finally, the stability of democracies does depend on their particular institutional arrangements: parliamentary democracies are much

more durable than pure presidential ones. The expected life of democracy under presidentialism is twenty-one years, while under parliamentarism it is seventy-two years. Presidential systems are less stable under any distribution of seats; indeed, they are less stable whatever variable is controlled for. The most likely reason presidential democracies are more fragile than parliamentary ones is that presidents rarely change because they are defeated in elections. Most of them leave office because they are obligated to do so by constitutionally imposed term limits. In turn, whenever incumbent presidents can run and do, two out of three win reelection (Cheibub and Przeworski 1996). Presidentialism thus appears to give an excessive advantage to incumbents when they are legally permitted to run for re-election and, in turn, to prevent the incumbents from exploiting this advantage, it obligates them to leave office whether or not voters want them to stay.

Here then are three facts: (1) democràcies are more likely to survive in wealthy countries; (2) they are more likely to last when no single political force dominates; and (3) they are more likely to endure when voters can choose rulers through elections. And these facts add up: democracy lasts when it offers an opportunity to the conflicting forces to advance their interests within the institutional framework.

In the end then, the Popperian posture is not sufficient, because democracy endures only under some conditions. Elections alone are not sufficient for conflicts to be resolved through elections. And while some of these conditions are economic, others are political and institutional. Thus, a minimalist conception of democracy does not alleviate the need for thinking about institutional design. In the end, the "quality of democracy," to use the currently fashionable phrase, does matter for its very survival. But my point is not that democracy can be, needs to be, improved, but that it would be worth defending even if it could not be.

---

31. The forthcoming paragraphs are based on Przeworski, Alvarez, Cheibub, and Limongi 1996, and Przeworski and Limongi 1997b.

32. Expected life is the inverse of the probability of dying. The income numbers are in purchasing power parity international dollars of 1985.

References

Bobbio, Norberto. 1984. *The Future of Democracy*. Minneapolis: University of Minnesota Press.

Bryce, James. 1921. *Modern Democracies*. New York: Macmillan.

Buchanan, James and Gordon Tullock. 1962. *The Calculus of Consent: Logical Foundations of Constitutional Democracy*. Ann Arbor: University of Michigan Press.

Cheibub, Jose Antonio and Adam Przeworski. 1996. "Democracy, elections, and accountability for economic outcomes." Revised paper presented at the Conference on Democracy and Accountability, New York University, 27–9 April.

Cohen, Joshua. 1997. "Procedure and substance in deliberative democracy." In Jon Elster (ed.), *Democratic Deliberation*. New York: Cambridge University Press.

Condorcet. 1986 (1785). "Essai sur l'application de l'analyse a la probabilité des décisions rendues a la pluralité des voix." In *Sur les élections et autres textes*. Textes choisis et revus par Olivier de Bernon. Paris: Fayard.

Coser, Lewis. 1959. *The Functions of Social Conflict*. Glencoe: Free Press.

Dunn, John. 1996a. *The History of Political Theory and other Essays*. Cambridge: Cambridge University Press.

Hampton, Jean. 1994. "Democracy and the rule of law." In Ian Shapiro (ed.), *NOMOS XXXVI: The Rule of Law*, pp. 13–45.

Hardin, Russell. 1989. "Why a constitution?" In Bernard Grofman and Donald Wittman (eds.), *The Federalist Papers and the New Institutionalism*, pp. 100–20. New York: Agathon Press.

Kelsen, Hans. 1988 (1929). *La Démocratie. Sa Nature—Sa Valeur*. Paris: Economica.

Lipset, Seymour Martin. 1959. "Some social requisites of democracy: economic development and political legitimacy." *American Political Science Review* 53: 69–105.

Popper, Karl. 1962. *The Open Society and Its Enemies*. London: Routledge and Kegan Paul.

Przeworski, Adam. 1986. *Capitalism and Social Democracy*. Cambridge: Cambridge University Press.

———. 1991. *Democracy and the Market*. New York: Cambridge University Press.

Przeworski, Adam, Mike Alvarez, Jose Antonio Cheibub, and Fernando Limongi. 1996. "What makes democracies endure?" *Journal of Democracy* 7: 39–55.

Przeworski, Adam and Fernando Limongi. 1997a. "Modernization: theories and facts." *World Politics* 49: 155–183.

———. 1997b. "Development and democracy." In Alex Hadenius (ed.), *Democracy's Victory and Crisis*. Cambridge: Cambridge University Press.

Rawls, John. 1993. "The domain of the political and overlapping consensus." In David Copp, Jean Hampton, and John H. Roemer (eds.), *The Idea of Democracy*. Cambridge: Cambridge University Press.

Schmitter, Philippe and Terry Lynn Karl. 1991. "What democracy is ... and what it is not". *Journal of Democracy* 2: 75–88.

Schumpeter, Joseph A. 1942. *Capitalism, Socialism, and Democracy*. New York: Harper & Brothers.

Shapiro, Ian. 1996. *Democracy's Place*. Ithaca: Cornell University Press.

Weffort, Francisco. 1992. *Qual Democracia?* Sao Paulo: Companhia das Letras.

Democracy and Disagreement

Amy Gutmann and Dennis Thompson

Introduction

Of the challenges that American democracy faces today, none is more formidable than the problem of moral disagreement. Neither the theory nor the practice of democratic politics has so far found an adequate way to cope with conflicts about fundamental values. We address the challenge of moral disagreement here by developing a conception of democracy that secures a central place for moral discussion in political life.

Along with a growing number of other political theorists, we call this conception deliberative democracy. The core idea is simple: when citizens or their representatives disagree morally, they should continue to reason together to reach mutually acceptable decisions. But the meaning and implications of the idea are complex....

Deliberative democracy involves reasoning about politics, and nothing has been more controversial in political philosophy than the nature of reason in politics. We do not believe that these controversies have to be settled before deliberative principles can guide the practice of democracy. Since on occasion citizens and their representatives already engage in the kind of reasoning that those principles recommend, deliberative democracy simply asks that they do so more consistently and comprehensively. The best way to prove the value of this kind of reasoning is to show its role in arguments about specific principles and policies, and its contribution to actual political debates. That is also ultimately the best justification for our conception of deliberative democracy itself....

Reprinted by permission of the publisher from *Democracy and Disagreement: Why Moral Conflict Cannot Be Avoided in Politics, and What Should Be Done about It* by Amy Gutmann and Dennis Thompson, pp. 1–5, 12–18, Cambridge, Mass.: The Belknap Press of Harvard University Press, Copyright © 1996 by the President and Fellows of Harvard College.

The aim of the moral reasoning that our deliberative democracy prescribes falls between impartiality, which requires something like altruism, and prudence, which demands no more than enlightened self-interest. Its first principle is reciprocity.... When citizens reason reciprocally, they seek fair terms of social cooperation for their own sake; they try to find mutually acceptable ways of resolving moral disagreements.

The precise content of reciprocity is difficult to determine in theory, but its general countenance is familiar enough in practice. It can be seen in the difference between acting in one's self-interest (say, taking advantage of a legal loophole or a lucky break) and acting fairly (following rules in the spirit that one expects others to adopt). In many of the controversies ... the possibility of any morally acceptable resolution depends on citizens' reasoning beyond their narrow self-interest and considering what can be justified to people who reasonably disagree with them. Even though the quality of deliberation and the conditions under which it is conducted are far from ideal in the controversies we consider, the fact that in each case some citizens and some officials make arguments consistent with reciprocity suggests that a deliberative perspective is not utopian.

... Citizens who reason reciprocally can recognize that a position is worthy of moral respect even when they think it morally wrong. They can believe that a moderate pro-life position on abortion, for example, is morally respectable even though they think it morally mistaken.... The presence of deliberative disagreement has important implications for how citizens treat one another and for what policies they should adopt. When a disagreement is not deliberative (for example, about a policy to legalize discrimination against blacks and women), citizens do not have any obligations of mutual respect toward their opponents. In deliberative disagreement (for example, about legalizing abortion), citizens should try to accommodate the moral convictions of their opponents to the greatest extent possible, without compromising their own moral convictions. We call this kind of accommodation an economy of moral disagreement, and believe that, though neglected in theory and practice, it is essential to a morally robust democratic life....

Some readers may still wonder why deliberation should have such a prominent place in democracy. Surely, they may say, citizens should care more about the justice of public policies than the process by which they are adopted, at least so long as the process is basically fair and at least minimally democratic. One of our main aims in this book is to cast doubt on the dichotomy between policies and process that this concern assumes. Having good reason as individuals to believe that a policy is just does not mean that collectively as citizens we have sufficient justification to legislate on the basis of those reasons. The moral authority of collective judgments about policy depends in part on the moral quality of the process by which citizens collectively reach those judgments. Deliberation is the most appropriate way for citizens collectively to resolve their moral disagreements not only about policies but also about the process by which policies should be adopted. Deliberation is not only a means to an end, but also a means for deciding what means are morally required to pursue our common ends....

The sound of moral argument in American democracy may be familiar, but the very familiarity has bred neglect, if not contempt. In the practice of our democratic politics, communicating by sound bite, competing by character assassination, and resolving political conflicts through self-seeking bargaining too often substitute for deliberation on the merits of controversial issues. In the standard theories of democracy — proceduralism and constitutionalism — deliberation likewise receives little attention. These theories are surprisingly silent about the need for ongoing discussion of moral disagreement in everyday political life. As a result, we suffer from a deliberative deficit not only in our democratic politics but also in our democratic theory. We are unlikely to lower the deficit in our politics if we do not also reduce it in our theory.

The conception of deliberative democracy that we defend here seeks to diminish that deficit in theory and in politics.[4] The conception consists of three principles—reciprocity, publicity, and accountability—that regulate the process of politics, and three others—basic liberty, basic opportunity, and fair opportunity—that govern the content of policies. It would promote extensive moral argument about the merits of public policies in public forums, with the aim of reaching provisional moral agreement and maintaining

4. For other discussions of the basis of deliberative democracy, see Seyla Benhabib, "Deliberative Rationality and Models of Democratic Legitimacy," *Constellations*, 1 (April 1994): 26–52; Joseph Bessette, *The Mild Voice of Reason: Deliberative Democracy and American National Government* (Chicago: University of Chicago Press, 1994), pp. 1–66; Joshua Cohen, "Deliberation and Democratic Legitimacy," in *The Good Polity: Normative Analysis of the State*, ed. Alan Hamlin and Philip Pettit (Oxford: Basil Blackwell, 1989), pp. 17–34; John S. Dryzek, *Discursive Democracy* (Cambridge: Cambridge University Press, 1990); David M. Estlund, "Who's Afraid of Deliberative Democracy? On the Strategic/Deliberative Dichotomy in Recent Constitutional Jurisprudence," *Texas Law Review*, 71 (June 1993): 1437–77; James Fishkin, *Democracy and Deliberation* (New Haven: Yale University Press, 1971); Charles Larmore, *Patterns of Moral Complexity* (Cambridge: Cambridge University Press, 1987), esp. pp. 59–66; Bernard Manin, "On Legitimacy and Political Deliberation," *Political Theory*, 15 (August 1987): 338–368; Jane Mansbridge, "Motivating Deliberation in Congress," in *Constitutionalism in America*, ed. Sarah Baumgartner Thurow, 3 vols. (Lanham, Md.: University Press of America, 1988), 2: 59–86; Jane Mansbridge, "A Deliberative Theory of Interest Representation," in *The Politics of Interests: Interest Groups Transformed*, ed. Mark P. Petracca (Boulder, Colo.: Westview Press, 1992), pp. 32–57; and Cass Sunstein, *The Partial Constitution* (Cambridge, Mass.: Harvard University Press, 1993), pp. 133–145.

mutual respect among citizens. In its most general form, the demand for deliberation has been a familiar theme in the American constitutional tradition. It is integral to the ideal of republican government as the Founders understood it. James Madison judged the design of political institutions in part by how well they furthered deliberation.[5]

Deliberation should not be confined to constitutional conventions, Supreme Court opinions, or their theoretical analogues. It should extend throughout the political process—to what we call the land of middle democracy. The forums of deliberation in middle democracy embrace virtually any setting in which citizens come together on a regular basis to reach collective decisions about public issues—governmental as well as nongovernmental institutions. They include not only legislative sessions, court proceedings, and administrative hearings at all levels of government but also meetings of grass roots organizations, professional associations, shareholders meetings, and citizens' committees in hospitals and other similar institutions.[6]

In defending this conception of deliberative democracy, we look at moral arguments already present in our political life, criticizing and extending them in light of other principles also present in our political culture.[7] The characteristics of moral arguments we find in actual political debate provide the basis for developing the normative principles with which we assess the ongoing debates. These features of moral disagreement themselves point toward a deliberative way of dealing with the disagreement.

What counts as a moral argument in deliberative democracy? The most rudimentary criterion—sometimes called generality—is one that deliberative democracy shares with most moral and political theories. The criterion of generality is so widely accepted that it is often identified with the moral point of view.[8] Moral arguments apply to everyone who is similarly

---

5. Madison favored political discussion, in which "minds [are] changing," in which "much [is] gained by a yielding and accommodating spirit," and in which no citizen is "obliged to retain his opinions any longer than he [is] satisfied of their propriety and truth." See "Jared Sparks: Journal," summarizing James Madison's views on the secret discussion in the Constitutional Convention and Congress, in *Records of the Federal Convention of 1787*, rev. ed., ed. Max Farrand, 4 vols. (New Haven: Yale University Press, 1966), 3: 479. The passage is quoted in a somewhat different form in Sunstein, *The Partial Constitution*, p. 164.

6. In the same spirit, Jürgen Habermas identifies deliberative democracy with the idea of a "decentered society" in "Three Normative Models of Democracy," *Constellations*, 1 (April 1994): 1–10. For discussions of neglected deliberative forums, see David Mathews, *Politics for People* (Urbana: University of Illinois Press, 1994); and Fishkin, *Democracy and Deliberation*.

7. Our view of deliberation should be distinguished from that presented by Bessette, who also looks at actual arguments in political debate, in particular those in the U.S. Congress. Although he also sees deliberative democracy as "reasoning on the merits of public policy" (*Mild Voice of Reason*, p. 46), one of his main arguments is that there is already more deliberation in Congress than most political scientists assume. Whether or not he is correct, we do not presume that the present state of deliberation in Congress and American politics generally is adequate, and in any case we do not focus, as he does, only on the need for deliberation among political elites and their role in preventing spontaneous or passionate judgments by the masses. Perhaps because he is content with deliberation among political elites, Bessette is skeptical about publicity and argues in favor of secrecy (pp. 208–209). In another respect, Bessette demands more of deliberation than we do. For him the "singular mark" of a deliberative process is that it must have "a real persuasive effect" and involve "some kind of change or development in the policymaker's understanding" (pp. 52–53). We do not insist that deliberation must change people's minds to be valuable.

8. See Kurt Baier, *The Moral Point of View* (Ithaca, N.Y.: Cornell University Press, 1958), pp. 187–213; and John Rawls, *A Theory of Justice* (Cambridge, Mass.: Harvard University Press, 1971), pp. 130–136.

situated in the morally relevant respects. The poor woman who seeks an abortion, the white male employee who fails to receive his promotion, the mother who needs prenatal care do not assert merely that they, or even only their friends, family, and associates, should receive the benefit; they maintain that all citizens similarly situated should receive it. Their claims, if fully developed, would impute rights and wrongs, or ascribe virtue and vice, to anyone who is similar in the respects that the argument assumes to be morally significant.

As these examples suggest, generality is not a purely formal standard. It always raises a substantive question: What are the morally relevant respects in which people are similarly situated? Does the same argument against preferential treatment for white males, for example, apply equally to preferential treatment of black Americans and white women? Generality forces us to take up substantive arguments ... which consider whether the differences between whites and blacks, and men and women, in this country are morally relevant in a way that would support a policy of preferential hiring.

In politics, however, substantive moral argument calls for more than merely satisfying the criterion of generality. Political decisions are collectively binding, and they should therefore be justifiable, as far as possible, to everyone bound by them. Three characteristics of moral arguments are especially important in politics. The first corresponds to our principle of reciprocity, a form of mutuality in the face of disagreement.... Citizens try to offer reasons that other similarly motivated citizens can accept even though they recognize that they share only some of one another's values. When our deliberations about moral disagreements in politics are guided by reciprocity, citizens recognize and respect one another as moral agents, not merely as abstract objects of others' moral reasoning.

Reciprocity asks us to appeal to reasons that are shared or could come to be shared by our fellow citizens.... It enables us, for example, mutually to respect one another as moral agents who share the goal of reaching deliberative agreement even when we disagree with one another's conclusions.

Reciprocity also applies to the empirical claims that often accompany moral arguments. Moral arguments take place in context, and they therefore depend at least implicitly on matters of fact, estimates of risk, suppositions about feasibility, and beliefs about human nature and social processes. Sometimes these assumptions are plausible but controversial: hiring and promoting simply on the basis of qualification will not end racial discrimination soon enough. Sometimes they are widely accepted but questionable: Arizona cannot afford both prenatal care and organ transplants because voters will not approve higher taxes. Sometimes the assumptions are obviously true: only women bear children. If technological advances and cultural changes were somehow to eliminate all the social and psychological effects of this biological fact, our moral attitudes and public policies might be different. But that possibility, even if realized in some other place or some other time, should not affect the moral argument for us now....

Reciprocity asks that our empirical claims in political argument be consistent with reliable methods of inquiry, as these methods are available to us here and now, not for all times and all places. Neither relativity nor uncertainty is grounds for abandoning the most reliable methods of inquiry at our collective disposal. By using the most reliable methods of inquiry, we demonstrate our mutual commitment to reach deliberative agreement in the empirical realms that are relevant to moral argument.

Once the fragments of moral argument with which this chapter began are put into context, they reveal two other characteristics of moral disagreement in politics. They take us beyond the nature of reasoning to the forums and the agents of the disagreement. Moral conflicts in politics typically take place in public forums or are intended for dissemination in public forums.... The principle of publicity ... captures this feature of moral disagreement in politics.

The third feature of this disagreement concerns the agents by whom and to whom the moral reasons are publicly offered. The agents are typically citizens and public officials who are accountable to one another for their political actions. One common way in which public officials offer an account of their actions is by responding to challenges from reporters such as Judy Woodruff, who put President Carter on the spot about subsidizing abortions for poor women. Accountability is ultimately to citizens, who not only vote for or against the president but also speak their minds between elections, often through organized groups and intermediary institutions. Accountability through moral disagreement in public forums extends not only to prominent elected officials such as the president but also to far less conspicuous officials, professionals, corporate executives, union leaders, employers and employees, and ordinary citizens when they act in a public capacity. The principle of accountability ... captures this characteristic of moral disagreement in politics.

These three features of moral disagreement, then, point to the need and at the same time provide the support for the three principles that refer to the process of deliberative democracy. Taken together the principles constitute a process that seeks deliberative agreement—on policies that can be provisionally justified to the citizens who are bound by them. Accountable agents reach out publicly to find reasons that others who are motivated to find deliberative agreement can also accept. When citizens and accountable officials disagree, and also recognize that they are seeking deliberative agreement, they remain willing to argue with one another with the aim of achieving provisionally justifiable policies that they all can mutually recognize as such.

Even when citizens find some provisionally justifiable principles, their disagreement over public policy may persist. In politics, disagreements often run deep. If they did not, there would be no need for argument. But if they ran too deep, there would be no point in argument. Deliberative disagreements lie in the depths between simple misunderstanding and immutable irreconcilability....

Some theorists would abstract from these moral disagreements and imagine a nearly ideal society in which some could be more readily resolved and many would not arise at all. In some familiar theories of justice, moral claims are constructed as hypothetical agreements among individuals who are not accountable to anyone and who are assumed to be living in a just society.[11] In such a society no one would need to argue for or against preferential hiring as a means of overcoming racial or gender discrimination because no such discrimination would exist in that society. Deliberative democracy, in contrast, admits reasons and principles that are suitable for actual societies, which all still suffer from discrimination and other kinds of injustice. Actual deliberation has an important advantage over hypothetical agreement: it encourages citizens to face up to their actual problems by listening to one another's moral claims rather than concluding (on the basis of only a thought experiment) that their fellow citizens *would* agree with them on all matters of justice if they were all living in an ideal society.

Deliberative democracy does not assume that the results of all actual deliberations are just. In fact, most of the time democracies fall far short of meeting the conditions that deliberative democracy prescribes. But we can say that the more nearly the conditions are satisfied, the

---

11. The most prominent contemporary example is Rawls, *A Theory of Justice*. See also Bruce Ackerman, *Social Justice in the Liberal State* (New Haven: Yale University Press, 1980).

more nearly justifiable are the results likely to be.[12] Even if, as one critic suggests, "all of the inequalities of society in general" were "replicated in the content of deliberation,"[13] it would not discredit deliberation. The process of deliberation as we understand it here is self-constraining; its own defining principles provide a basis for criticizing the unjust inequalities that affect the process. Deliberative democracy certainly does not accept as equally valid whatever reasons and principles citizens and public officials put forward in defense of their own interests.

Neither should we make deliberation the sovereign guide to resolving moral disagreements in politics, as some "discourse theorists" seem to suggest. Jürgen Habermas writes that "all contents, no matter how fundamental the action norm involved may be, must be made to depend on real discourses (or advocatory discourses conducted as substitutes for them)."[14] Habermas seems to imply that a provisionally justifiable resolution of moral conflicts in politics depends

solely on satisfying the conditions of deliberation. Principles such as basic liberty and opportunity therefore are valued only for their contribution to deliberation, not as constraints on what counts as a morally legitimate resolution of disagreement. If leaving "all concrete moral and ethical judgments to participants themselves"[15] means that principles such as liberty and opportunity should never constrain these judgments, then discourse theory does not adequately protect basic rights.[16]

Habermas and other discourse theorists try to avoid this implication by, in effect, building guarantees of basic liberty and opportunity into

---

12. In this respect the hypothetical approach may have a role in assessing deliberation, but only in combination with an empirical approach that examines the actual conditions under which deliberation takes place. Brian Barry shows how these approaches, when combined to evaluate a theory of justice, "provide a check on one another," in *Justice as Impartiality* (Oxford: Oxford University Press, 1995), pp. 195–199.

13. This critic, Frederick Schauer, concludes that deliberation is no "more likely to ameliorate than to exacerbate the existing inequalities in a society." The only alternative suggested by Schauer is a "more controlled communicative environment." Would the people who controlled communication do so without obtaining deliberative assent from citizens or their accountable representatives? If so, why should we think that they would be more egalitarian in their policies than people who are willing to subject their exercise of political power to the deliberative assent of citizens? See Frederick Schauer, "Discourse and Its Discontents," Working Paper no. 94–2, Joan Shorenstein Barone Center on the Press, Politics, and Public Policy, Cambridge, Mass., September 1994, p. 9.

14. Jürgen Habermas, "Discourse Ethics," in *Moral Consciousness and Communicative Action*, trans. Christian Lenhardt and Shierry Weber Nicholsen (Cambridge, Mass.: MIT Press, 1993), p. 94.

15. Thomas McCarthy, "Introduction" to Habermas, *Moral Consciousness and Communicative Action*, p. xi. McCarthy writes that this is why Habermas is critical of Rawls's two principles of justice. But one may criticize the two principles for going beyond what moral reasonableness demands while still recognizing the need for some principles of liberty and opportunity that give content to a common perspective and are not solely conditions of deliberation.

16. Another important deliberative democrat, Seyla Benhabib, argues that deliberation can ensure the legitimacy but not the rationality of outcomes: "We accept the will of the majority at the end of an electoral process that has been fairly and correctly carried out, but even when we accept the legitimacy of the process we may have grave doubts about the rationality of the outcome." If deliberation aims only at legitimacy, and legitimacy is defined as whatever "result[s] from the free and unconstrained public deliberation of all about matters of common concern," then deliberation may succeed (by definition) at ensuring legitimacy. Benhabib, "Deliberative Rationality," p. 26. But this concept of legitimacy has too little moral content to provide a robust defense of deliberative democracy. Why should we defend deliberation, so understood, over a conception of deliberative democracy that is dedicated both to respecting basic liberty and opportunity and to subjecting these principles to ongoing deliberation?

the ideal conditions of deliberation. They do so by qualifying what counts as a moral ideal of deliberation. The participants in practical deliberations must regard one another as "competent subjects"[17] and "moral and political equals."[18] Their deliberations not only must be free but also must be reasoned.[19] Deliberative outcomes, then, would have to respect basic liberty and opportunity as an ongoing condition of their own legitimacy.

This understanding still does not capture the value of basic rights. Citizens value basic liberty and opportunity, and their mutual recognition by fellow citizens, for reasons other than the role of these values in democratic deliberation. As we shall suggest, even in deliberative democracy, deliberation does not have priority over liberty and opportunity. The condition of honoring basic liberty and opportunity should still be

"reflexively" subject to deliberative understanding, as discourse theorists correctly insist.[20] But so should deliberation itself.

We do not assume that deliberative democracy can guarantee social justice either in theory or in practice. Our argument is rather that in the absence of robust deliberation in democracy, citizens cannot even provisionally justify many controversial procedures and constitutional rights to one another. Insofar as deliberation is missing in political life, citizens also lack a mutually justifiable way of living with their ongoing moral disagreements. When citizens deliberate in democratic politics, they express and respect their status as political equals even as they continue to disagree about important matters of public policy.

Before exploring how deliberative democracy deals with disagreement, we need first to examine the sources of that disagreement. Then we can better see why procedural and constitutional democracy can be only partial solutions to the problem of moral conflict, and how deliberative democracy provides a more nearly complete solution. . . .

---

17. Habermas, "Discourse Ethics," p. 100. See also Jürgen Habermas, "Reconciliation through the Use of Public Reason: Remarks on John Rawls's Political Liberalism," *Journal of Philosophy*, 92 (March 1995): 109–131.

18. Benhabib, "Deliberative Rationality," p. 27. Habermas writes that participants in deliberation must be "free and equal" and the discourse "inclusive and noncoercive" ("Reconciliation," pp. 109ff.). This description calls into question his earlier characterization of discourse ethics as offering "a rule of argumentation only" which "does not prejudge substantive regulations" ("Discourse Ethics," p. 94). Discourse ethics is "not compatible with all substantive legal and moral principles," as Habermas recognizes, partly because it is committed to a substantive view of what counts as ideal deliberation. The deliberative ideal lends itself to a stronger defense when it acknowledges the (partly) independent values of basic liberty and opportunity.

19. Benhabib, "Deliberative Rationality," pp. 30–35. Once content is given to reasoned discourse, a common perspective becomes far less purely procedural than Benhabib suggests: "Agreements in societies living with value-pluralism are to be sought for not at the level of substantive beliefs but at the level of procedures, processes, and practices for attaining and revising beliefs" (p. 34).

---

20. Habermas, "Discourse Ethics," p. 67.

The Voice of the People

James S. Fishkin

... The deliberative poll is unlike any poll or survey ever conducted. Ordinary polls model what the public is thinking, even though the public may not be thinking very much or paying much attention. A deliberative poll attempts to model what the public *would* think, had it a better opportunity to consider the questions at issue.

The idea is simple. Take a national random sample of the electorate and transport those people from all over the country to a single place. Immerse the sample in the issues, with carefully balanced briefing materials, with intensive discussions in small groups, and with the chance to question competing experts and politicians. At the end of several days of working through the issues face to face, poll the participants in detail. The resulting survey offers a representation of the considered judgments of the public—the views the entire country would come to if it had the same experience of behaving more like ideal citizens immersed in the issues for an extended period.

A deliberative poll is not meant to describe or predict public opinion. Rather it prescribes. It has a recommending force: these are the conclusions people would come to, were they better informed on the issues and had the opportunity and motivation to examine those issues seriously. It allows a microcosm of the country to make recommendations to us all after it has had the chance to think through the issues. If such a poll were broadcast before an election or a referendum, it could dramatically affect the outcome.

A deliberative poll takes the two technologies, polling and television, that have given us a superficial form of mass democracy, and harnesses them to a new and constructive purpose—giving

Excerpted from: James S. Fishkin, *The Voice of the People*. New Haven, Conn.: Yale University Press, 1995. © Yale University Press, 1995. Reprinted by permission of Yale University Press.

voice to the people under conditions where the people can think....

... The deliberative poll has not developed in a vacuum. It builds on important work in encouraging citizen deliberation. It also builds on the movement toward public journalism....

... We gathered the national random sample for the first deliberative poll, April 15–17, 1994, at the Granada Television Studio in Manchester, England. We attracted participants by paying their expenses, offering them a small honorarium, telling them they would be on national television, and advising them that they would be part of an important experiment in democracy....

What did the event accomplish? It demonstrated the viability of a different form of opinion polling and, in a sense, a different form of democracy. As we have seen, Americans have long struggled with how to adapt democracy to the large nation-state. Face-to-face democracy cannot be applied to large states. Even in Rhode Island, the anti-Federalists could not gather everyone together to hear all the arguments on either side. It was for this reason that the Federalists boycotted the referendum on the U.S. Constitution and said that the only appropriate method for making a decision was the elected state convention. A *representation* of the people, in the form of those elected to go to the convention, would be able to hear all the competing arguments and make an informed decision.

But recall the persistent anti-Federalist worry that no *elected* representation would be representative. Ordinary people like them—farmers, laborers, people without a great deal of education—would tend to get left out. The lawyers and judges and wealthy elite of the day would make the decisions. The elected microcosm, in other words, would not be a genuine microcosm —and might not consider or understand *their* interests.

Democracy, even in the elitist sense of the Founders, was only revived by the notion of elected representation. But another form of representation lay hidden in the dust of history. It was employed by the legislative commissions, citizens' juries and the Council in ancient Athens (the crucial body that set the agenda for meetings of the citizen Assembly). This other method was selection by lot or random sampling. In one sense the use of random sampling in politics was revived by opinion polling. After all, what is a random sample, at bottom, but a lottery? But in the ancient Greek form, and in the form employed in the deliberative poll, opinions are taken not from isolated citizens but from citizens meeting together, deliberating on common problems. These polls represent the considered judgments of the polity, not the top-of-the-head reactions of isolated citizens. Institutions that speak for the people need to be both representative and deliberative. The ancient Greek innovation was a random sample of citizens who deliberated together and in that way realized both values. And this is the form I propose to adapt to the television age.

If this new—and very old—form of democracy were employed in a general election, at the beginning of the primary season, or before a referendum, then the recommending force of the public's considered judgments, broadcast on national television, might well make a difference to the outcome. Recall Samuel Popkin's argument that voters are inclined to follow cues as arbitrary as President Ford's choking on a tamale in San Antonio. Surely, the cues formed from an elaborate deliberative process should be worth paying attention to. When broadcast on national television and disseminated in the press, the deliberative poll can affect the public's conclusions, but it can also affect the way that public frames and understands issues. If televised deliberative polls succeed in communicating the deliberative process, they can help transform the public agenda to the agenda of an engaged public— to an agenda citizens will care about, and be

attracted by, because it will be framed in terms that speak to their concerns in ordinary life....

Most ambitiously, the Deliberative Poll can be thought of as an actual sample for a hypothetical society—the deliberative and engaged society we do not have. Ideally, we should get everyone thinking and discussing the issues. But as we have seen the forces of rational ignorance are powerful. Yet although we cannot get everyone actively engaged under most conditions, through the deliberative poll we can do the experiment and get the microcosm engaged—and then broadcast the results to everyone else. Citizens in the microcosm are not subject to rational ignorance. Instead of one insignificant vote in millions each of them has an important role to play in a nationally televised event. With true engagement and attention from the microcosm this representation of the public's judgment becomes a voice worth listening to.

One of the key decisions we made in planning the British Deliberative Poll sheds light on the experiment's aspirations, both in Britain and in the United States. The problem was the seemingly simple issue of where in the schedule to place the small-group discussions. We struggled with two different models of how these discussions serve the deliberative process. One is by *absorption*, the other is by *activation*. In one model the respondents *absorb* information from competing experts, mull that information over in small groups, and form their conclusions. On this model the participants would spend a great deal of time listening to competing presentations of relevant factual materials and then they would process those materials in small group discussions.

In the second model, we attempt to do something far more ambitious. There, the small group discussions come first, before participants have any contact with experts or politicians. On this strategy, we facilitate the citizens' melding into groups first, identifying their key concerns first, establishing rapport among themselves first, setting the agenda of the questions and concerns they wish to raise first—and only then put them together with the competing experts and competing politicians. The second model, instead of absorbing its agenda from the experts, energizes a public voice coming *from* the citizens so that it can speak *to* the elites. This strategy was followed in the Manchester experiment, and it set an example for how we hope to conduct future deliberative polls. . . .

The logic is very simple. If we take a microcosm of the entire country and subject it to a certain experience, and if the microcosm (behaving in the way we would like ideal citizens to behave in seriously deliberating about the issues) then comes to different conclusions about those issues, our inference is simply that if, somehow, the entire country were subjected to the same experience as the microcosm, then hypothetically the entire country would also come to similar conclusions.

Of course, it is unlikely the entire country ever would approximate the experiences of a deliberative poll. Even when there is an intense debate, it may well be dominated by attack ads and misleading sound bites. But the point is that if, somehow, the public were enabled to behave more like ideal citizens, then the deliberative poll offers a representation of what the conclusions might look like. That representation should have a prescriptive value. It is an opportunity for the country, in microcosm, to make recommendations to itself through television under conditions where it can arrive at considered judgments.

Earlier I emphasized four democratic values—deliberation, nontyranny, political equality, and participation. I noted that efforts to fully realize all four have usually been unsuccessful. In particular, the move toward mass democracy—a move realized by increasing participation and political equality—has had a cost in deliberation. By transferring the effective locus of many decisions to the mass public, the system is far less deliberative than it would have been had those decisions been left in the hands of elites—elected representatives and party leaders. The deliber-

ative poll, however, offers a *representation* of a democracy that meets all four conditions. With a deliberative atmosphere of mutual respect, tyranny of the majority is unlikely. When all the citizens are effectively motivated to think through the issues, when each citizen's views count equally, and when every member of the microcosm participates, the other three values are realized as well. Fully realizing those values throughout the entire society may be hypothetical. But we can see, in microcosm, what deliberation, political equality, participation and non-tyranny would look like.

Suppose, hypothetically, that the new institution of Deliberative Polling somehow became as accepted a part of our public life as, say, conventional polling is today. Deliberative Polling at the state and local level need not be unusual or expensive. Transportation is a key component of the expense on the national level, and local deliberative polls would not face such a hurdle.

The experience of serious citizen deliberation seems to have a galvanizing effect on the participant's interest in public affairs. So far the evidence for this proposition has been largely anecdotal, but we hope to study this phenomenon systematically in follow-ups with participants in the British project. Suppose, for the sake of argument, that there is a *continuing* effect. In the same way that the citizen mentioned earlier was galvanized to read "every newspaper every day," we might imagine that he continues to be a far more engaged citizen—discussing public issues with others, being more aware of the media, and becoming more likely to participate in public or civic affairs. If Deliberative Polls ever became a staple of public life, we would end up with a society of more seriously engaged citizens—one which was not just a *representation* of how all four democratic values could be achieved but rather an *embodiment* of their achievement. Just as the apparatus of selection by lot in ancient Athens involved so many citizens, so often, that it seems to have galvanized an active citizenry, it is not inconceivable that selection by lot for Deliberative Polls could, someday, have the same effect on our country.

It is not inconceivable, but it is, admittedly, unlikely. Such a flourishing of a new institution is clearly utopian, even as a matter of aspiration. But the image helps clarify an ideal—a picture of the reconstructed role of citizen, not just on television but in actual life. At a minimum, the deliberative poll can articulate the considered judgments of an informed citizenry and broadcast those conclusions to the nation. It provides a different, and more thoughtful, public voice. Other innovations and other institutions would have to be relied on if we are to create a seriously engaged mass citizenry as a routine part of our national life. . . .

To make a democracy that works, we need citizens who are engaged, communities that function, and media that speak *for* us as well as *about* us. If we pay attention to the conditions under which citizens become reconnected to political life, we can create a public worthy of public opinion—and public judgment. It would indeed be "magic town" if we brought such a spirit to the entire country.

Defining and Developing Democracy

Larry Diamond

The basis of a democratic state is liberty.
—Aristotle, *The Politics*

Since April of 1974, when the Portuguese military overthrew the Salazar/Caetano dictatorship, the number of democracies in the world has multiplied dramatically. Before the start of this global trend, there were about forty democracies. The number increased moderately through the late 1970s and early 1980s as several states experienced transitions from authoritarian rule (predominantly military) to democratic rule. In the mid-1980s, the pace of global democratic expansion accelerated markedly. By the end of 1995, there were as many as 117 democracies or as few as 76, depending on how one counts....

The Best Form of Government

... The normative perspective underlying this book is that democratization is generally a good thing and that democracy is the best form of government. However, democracy is not an unmitigated blessing. Dating back to Aristotle (and to Plato, who had even less sympathy for democracy), the key shapers of democratic political thought have held that the best realizable form of government is mixed, or constitutional, government, in which freedom is constrained by the rule of law and popular sovereignty is tempered by state institutions that produce order and stability.[3] Aristotle saw that, in a state of pure democracy, "where the multitude have the supreme power, and supersede the law by their decrees ... demagogues spring up," and democracy degenerates into a form of despotism.[4]

Thus, as Locke, Montesquieu, and the American Federalists asserted, only a constitutional government, restraining and dividing the temporary power of the majority, can protect individual freedom. This fundamental insight (and value) gave birth to a tradition of political thought—liberalism—and to a concept—liberal democracy—that are central to this book. As elaborated below, I use the term *liberal* to mean a political system in which individual and group liberties are well protected and in which there exist autonomous spheres of civil society and private life, insulated from state control....

Even if we think of democracy as simply the rule of the people, as a system for choosing government through free and fair electoral competition at regular intervals, governments chosen in this manner are generally better than those that are not. They offer the best prospect for accountable, responsive, peaceful, predictable, good governance. And, as Robert Dahl cogently observes, they promote "freedom as no feasible alternative can."[6] ...

Up to a point consistent with the principles of constitutionalism and representative democracy, government is better when it is more democratic. This is not to argue that even electoral democracy is easily attainable in any country at any time.[7]

Excerpted from: Larry Diamond, *Developing Democracy: Toward Consolidation*, pp. 1–19. Baltimore: Johns Hopkins University Press, 1999. © 1999 The Johns Hopkins University Press. Reprinted with permission of The Johns Hopkins University Press.

3. Gabriel A. Almond, "Political Science: The History of the Discipline," in *A New Handbook of Political Science*, edited by Robert E. Goodin and Hans-Dieter Klingemann (Oxford: Oxford University Press, 1996), 53–61. See also David Held, *Models of Democracy* (Stanford: Stanford University Press, 1987), chaps. 1, 2.

4. Aristotle, *The Politics*, edited by Stephen Everson (Cambridge: Cambridge University Press, 1988), 1292.

6. Robert A. Dahl, *Democracy and Its Critics* (New Haven: Yale University Press, 1989), chap. 8; quotations at 88 and 89.

7. There are certain economic, social, and cultural conditions for democracy to be viable, but they are often overstated, and we should be cautious about

However, more democracy makes government more responsive to a wider range of citizens....

Normatively, I assume here that accountability of rulers to the ruled and government responsiveness to the diverse interests and preferences of the governed are basic goods. So also are the minimization of violence in political life and of arbitrary action by government. And so, above all, is liberty. Increasingly in the twentieth century, the freedoms of the individual to think, believe, worship, speak, publish, inquire, associate, and become informed, and the freedoms from torture, arbitrary arrest, and unlawful detention—not to mention enslavement and genocide—are recognized as universal and inalienable human rights....

Liberal democracy provides, by definition, comparatively good protection for human rights. However, there is no reason that electoral democracy and liberty must go together. Historically, liberty—secured through constitutional, limited government and a rule of law—came about before democracy both in England and, in varying degrees, in other European states. And today ... there are many illiberal democracies, with human rights abuses and civil strife. These two facts have rekindled intellectual interest in liberal autocracy as a better, safer, more stable form of government for many transitional societies.[11]

In times of very limited education and political consciousness, when the franchise could be confined to a narrow elite, liberal autocracy was possible. In today's world, it is an illusion, a historical anachronism. Save for two island states with populations of 100,000 each (Tonga; Antigua and Barbuda), there are no autocracies in the world that could possibly qualify as liberal.[12] And there will not be any significant ones in the future, for liberalism insists upon the sovereignty of the people to decide their form of government—and these days, according to Marc Plattner, "popular sovereignty can hardly fail to lead to popular government."[13] In an age of widespread communication and political consciousness, people expect political participation and accountability much more than they did in the eighteenth, nineteenth, and early twentieth centuries. The only way the demand for meaningful political participation and choice can be suppressed is to constrain liberty. Thus, as noted above, there is a powerful association between democracy and liberty: "countries that hold free elections are overwhelmingly more liberal than those that do not."[14] Indeed, the more closely countries meet the standards of electoral democracy (free and fair, multiparty elections by secret and universal ballot), the higher their human rights rating.[15] ...

---

positing them as "prerequisites." See Larry Diamond, "Economic Development and Democracy Reconsidered," in *Reexamining Democracy: Essays in Honor of Seymour Martin Lipset*, edited by Gary Marks and Larry Diamond (Newbury Park, Calif.: Sage, 1992), 93–139.

11. Fareed Zakaria, "The Rise of Illiberal Democracy," *Foreign Affairs* 76, no. 6 (1997): 22–43.

12. And even these governments are not very liberal, for the same reason that liberal autocracy is generally not possible: when Antiguans and Tongans demand real democracy, they are harassed by the state or the ruling party. Freedom House, *Freedom in the World: The Annual Survey of Political Rights and Civil Liberties, 1996–1997* (New York: Freedom House, 1997), 125, 488. As I explain in greater detail below, each year Freedom House rates countries on a scale from 1 to 7 on two measures, political rights and civil liberties (1 being most liberal). It also classifies all the countries in the world as to whether or not they are electoral democracies. Of the countries that are not electoral democracies, only the above two have scores of 3 on civil liberties (and none has better than 3).

13. Marc F. Plattner, "Liberalism and Democracy," *Foreign Affairs* 77, no. 2 (1998): 171–180; quotation on 175.

14. Ibid., 173.

15. Russell Bova, "Democracy and Liberty: The Cultural Connection," *Journal of Democracy* 8, no. 1 (1997): 115, table 1. The difference in average rating on the Humana human rights scale between countries that clearly have electoral democracy and those that clearly

The above positive benefits of democracy derive, as Russett notes with respect to interstate peace, from both the norms and the political institutions that characterize democracies. But which democracies? For peace and development and for the just treatment of minorities, is it enough that governments come to power through free, fair, and competitive elections? Or do these objectives require other features of democracy—a rule of law, free information, civil liberties, and a distribution of power that produces a horizontal accountability of rulers to one another? What do we mean by democracy?

Conceptualizing Democracy

Just as political scientists and observers do not agree on how many democracies there are in the world, so they differ on how to classify specific regimes, the conditions for making and consolidating democracy, and the consequences of democracy for peace and development. A key element in all these debates is lack of consensus on the meaning of *democracy*....

... By and large, most scholarly and policy uses of the term *democracy* today refer to a purely political conception of the term, and this intellectual shift back to an earlier convention has greatly facilitated progress in studying the dynamics of democracy, including the relationship between political democracy and various social and economic conditions.[31]

Where conceptions of democracy diverge today is on the range and extent of political properties encompassed by democracy. Minimalist definitions of what I call electoral democracy descend from Joseph Schumpeter, who defined democracy as a system "for arriving at political decisions in which individuals acquire the power to decide by means of a competitive struggle for the people's vote."[32] Huntington, among others, explicitly embraces Schumpeter's emphasis on competitive elections for effective power as the essence of democracy.[33] However, Schumpeter's

do not is enormous: 85 to 35. For a description of this 100-point scale (with 100 being the top score), see Charles Humana, *World Human Rights Guide*, 3d ed. (New York: Oxford University Press, 1992).

31. Severe, persistent socioeconomic inequality may well be (as some scholars find) a major threat to political democracy. But to establish this, we must first have a measure of democracy that is limited to features of the political system. For an effort exhibiting this approach (and finding), see Zehra F. Arat, *Democracy and Human Rights in Developing Countries* (Boulder, Colo.: Lynne Rienner, 1991). For a critique of the in-

corporation of socioeconomic criteria into the definition of democracy, see Terry Lynn Karl, "Dilemmas of Democratization in Latin America," *Comparative Politics* 23, no. 1 (1990): 2.

32. Joseph Schumpeter, *Capitalism, Socialism, and Democracy*, 2d ed. (New York: Harper, 1947), 269. For Schumpeter, Held explains, "the democratic citizen's lot was, quite straightforwardly, the right periodically to choose and authorize governments to act on their behalf" (*Models of Democracy*, 165). Schumpeter was clearly uneasy with direct political action by citizens, warning that "the electoral mass is incapable of action other than a stampede" (283). Thus, his "case for democracy can support, at best, only minimum political involvement: that involvement which could be considered sufficient to legitimate the right of competing elites to rule" (ibid., 168). This is, indeed, as spare a notion of democracy as one could posit without draining the term of meaning.

33. Huntington, *The Third Wave*, 5–13, esp. 6; Samuel P. Huntington, "The Modest Meaning of Democracy," in *Democracy in the Americas: Stopping the Pendulum*, edited by Robert A. Pastor (New York: Holmes and Meier, 1989), 15. For similar conceptions of democracy based on competitive elections, see Seymour Martin Lipset, *Political Man: The Social Bases of Politics* (Baltimore: Johns Hopkins University Press, 1981), 27; Lipset, "The Social Requisites of Democracy Revisited," *American Sociological Review* 59, no. 1 (1994): 1; Juan J. Linz, *The Breakdown of Democratic Regimes: Crisis, Breakdown, and Reequilibration* (Baltimore: Johns Hopkins University Press, 1978), 5–6; J. Roland Pennock, *Democratic Political Theory* (Princeton: Princeton University Press, 1979), 7–15; G. Bingham Powell, *Contemporary Democracies: Participation,*

concise expression has required periodic elaboration (or what Collier and Levitsky call "precising") to avoid inclusion of cases that do not fit the implicit meaning.

The seminal elaboration is Dahl's conception of *polyarchy*, which has two overt dimensions: opposition (organized contestation through regular, free, and fair elections) and participation (the right of virtually all adults to vote and contest for office). Yet embedded in these two dimensions is a third, without which the first two cannot be truly meaningful: civil liberty. Polyarchy encompasses not only freedom to vote and contest for office but also freedom to speak and publish dissenting views, freedom to form and join organizations, and alternative sources of information.[34] Both Dahl's original formulation and a later, more comprehensive effort to measure polyarchy take seriously the nonelectoral dimensions.[35]

Electoral Democracy

Minimalist conceptions of electoral democracy usually also acknowledge the need for minimum levels of freedom (of speech, press, organization,

and assembly) in order for competition and participation to be meaningful. But, typically, they do not devote much attention to them, nor do they incorporate them into actual measures of democracy. Thus (consistent with most other efforts to classify or measure regimes), Przeworski and his colleagues define democracy simply as "a regime in which governmental offices are filled as a consequence of contested elections" (with the proviso that real contestation requires an opposition with some nontrivial chance of winning office and that the chief executive office and legislative seats are filled by contested elections).[36] Such Schumpeterian conceptions (com-

Stability, and Violence (Cambridge: Harvard University Press, 1982), 3; Tatu Vanhanen, *The Process of Democratization: A Comparative Study of 147 States, 1980–88* (New York: Crane Russak, 1990), 17–18; Giuseppe Di Palma, *To Craft Democracies: An Essay on Democratic Transitions* (Berkeley: University of California Press, 1991), 16; Adam Przeworski, *Democracy and the Market: Political and Economic Reforms in Eastern Europe and Latin America* (Cambridge: Cambridge University Press, 1991), 10–11.

34. Dahl, *Polyarchy*, 2–3. Dahl uses the term *polyarchy* to distinguish these systems from a more ideal form of democracy, "one of the characteristics of which is the quality of being completely or almost completely responsive to all its citizens" (2).

35. Ibid., app. A; Michael Coppedge and Wolfgang H. Reinecke, "Measuring Polyarchy," in *On Measuring Democracy: Its Consequences and Concomitants*, edited by Alex Inkeles (New Brunswick, N.J.: Transaction, 1991), 47–68.

36. Adam Przeworski, Michael Alvarez, José Antonio Cheibub, and Fernando Limongi, "What Makes Democracies Endure?" *Journal of Democracy* 7, no. 1 (1996): 50–51. Their methodology is more comprehensively explained in Michael Alvarez, José Antonio Cheibub, Fernando Limongi, and Adam Przeworski, "Classifying Political Regimes for the ACLP Data Set," Working Paper 4, Chicago Center on Democracy, University of Chicago. Many other approaches to conceiving and measuring democracy in quantitative, cross-national analyses have also tended to rely on indicators of competition and participation (whether dichotomous, categorical, or continuous), but some of these were gravely flawed by their incorporation of substantively inappropriate indicators, such as voter turnout or political stability. (On this and other conceptual and measurement problems, see Kenneth A. Bollen, "Political Democracy: Conceptual and Measurement Traps," in Inkeles, *Measuring Democracy*, 3–20.)

As an alternative approach that explicitly includes the behavioral, noninstitutional dimensions of democracy, the combined Freedom House scales of political rights and civil liberties, described below, are increasingly being used in quantitative analysis. For examples, see Henry S. Rowen, "The Tide Underneath the 'Third Wave,'" *Journal of Democracy* 6, no. 1 (1995): 52–64; Surjit S. Bhalla, "Freedom and Economic Growth: A Virtuous Cycle?" in Hadenius, *Democracy's Victory and Crisis*, 195–241. While the Freedom House data is available annually, it goes back in time only to 1972, and the criteria for scoring have become stricter over time (particularly in the 1990s), creating problems for

mon among Western foreign policy makers as well) risk committing what Terry Karl calls the "fallacy of electoralism." This flawed conception of democracy privileges elections over other dimensions of democracy and ignores the degree to which multiparty elections (even if they are competitive and uncertain in outcome) may exclude significant portions of the population from contesting for power or advancing and defending their interests, or may leave significant arenas of decision making beyond the control of elected officials.[37] Philippe Schmitter and Terry Karl remind us that, "however central to democracy, elections occur intermittently and only allow citizens to choose between the highly aggregated alternatives offered by political parties, which can, especially in the early stages

of a democratic transition, proliferate in a bewildering variety."[38]

In recent years, electoral conceptions of democracy have expanded to rule out the latter element of ambiguity or misclassification; many now exclude regimes that suffer substantial reserved domains of military (or bureaucratic, or oligarchical) power that are not accountable to elected officials.[39] But still, such formulations may still fail to give due weight to political repression and marginalization, which exclude significant segments of the population—typically the poor or ethnic and regional minorities—from exercising their democratic rights. One of the most rigorous and widely used measures of democracy in cross-national, quantitative research—in the "polity" data sets—acknowledges civil liberties as a major component of democracy but, because of the paucity of data, does not incorporate them.[40]

---

interpreting changes in scores over time. The appeal of a simple dichotomous measure such as that used by Przeworski and his colleagues is precisely the relative simplification of data collection and regime classification and the ability to conduct a straightforward "event history" analysis that analyzes changes toward and away from democratic regime forms. Encouragingly, the Freedom House ratings and other measures of democracy are generally highly correlated with one another (Alex Inkeles, introduction to *Measuring Democracy*). In fact, Przeworski et al. report that the Freedom House combined ratings for 1972 to 1990 predict 93 percent of their regime classifications during this period ("What Makes Democracies Endure?" 52). However, as we see in chapter 2, since 1990 the formal properties and the liberal substance of democracy have increasingly diverged. Thus, the substantive validity of measures that focus mainly on formal competition may be particularly suspect after 1990.

37. Terry Lynn Karl, "Imposing Consent? Electoralism versus Democratization in El Salvador," in *Elections and Democratization in Latin America, 1980–1985*, edited by Paul Drake and Eduardo Silva (San Diego: Center for Iberian and Latin American Studies, Center for US/Mexican Studies, University of California at San Diego, 1986), 9–36; Karl, "Dilemmas of Democratization in Latin America," 14–15; Karl, "The Hybrid Regimes of Central America," *Journal of Democracy* 6, no. 3 (1995): 72–86.

38. Philippe C. Schmitter and Terry Lynn Karl, "What Democracy Is ... and Is Not," *Journal of Democracy* 2, no. 3 (1991): 78.

39. Collier and Levitsky, "Democracy with Adjectives." A seminal discussion of reserved domains appears in J. Samuel Valenzuela, "Democratic Consolidation in Post-Transitional Settings: Notion, Process, and Facilitating Conditions," in *Issues in Democratic Consolidation: The New South American Democracies in Comparative Perspective*, edited by Scott Mainwaring, Guillermo O'Donnell, and J. Samuel Valenzuela (Notre Dame: University of Notre Dame Press, 1992), 64–66. See also Huntington, *The Third Wave*, 10; Schmitter and Karl, "What Democracy Is," 81; Guillermo O'Donnell, "Illusions about Consolidation," *Journal of Democracy* 7, no. 2 (1996): 34–51; Juan J. Linz and Alfred Stepan, *Problems of Democratic Transition and Consolidation: Southern Europe, South America, and Post-Communist Europe* (Baltimore: Johns Hopkins University Press, 1996), 3–5.

40. On the Polity III data set, see Keith Jaggers and Ted Robert Gurr, "Tracking Democracy's Third Wave with the Polity III Data," *Journal of Peace Research* 32, no. 4 (1995): 469–482. On the Polity II data (which

Freedom exists over a continuum of variation. Rights of expression, organization, and assembly vary considerably across countries that do have regular, competitive, multiparty elections in which votes are (more or less) honestly counted and in which the winning candidates exercise (most of the) effective power in the country. How overtly repressed must a minority be for the political system to be disqualified as a polyarchy (a *liberal* democracy)? . . .

By the minimalist definition, Turkey, India, Sri Lanka, Colombia, and Russia qualify as democracies. But by the stricter conception of liberal democracy, all (except perhaps India as a whole) fall short. In fact, the gap between electoral and liberal democracy has grown markedly during the latter part of the third wave, forming one of its most significant but little-noticed features. As a result, human rights violations have become widespread in countries that are formally democratic.

Liberal Democracy

Electoral democracy is a civilian, constitutional system in which the legislative and chief executive offices are filled through regular, competitive, multiparty elections with universal suffrage. While this minimalist conception remains popular in scholarship and policy, it has been amplified, or precised, to various degrees by several scholars and theorists. This exercise has been constructive, but it has left behind a plethora of what Collier and Levitsky term "expanded procedural" conceptions, which do not clearly relate

to one another and which occupy intermediate locations in the continuum between electoral and liberal democracy.[41]

How does *liberal* democracy extend beyond these formal and intermediate conceptions? In addition to the elements of electoral democracy, it requires, first, the absence of reserved domains of power for the military or other actors not accountable to the electorate, directly or indirectly. Second, in addition to the vertical accountability of rulers to the ruled (secured mainly through elections), it requires the horizontal accountability of officeholders to one another; this constrains executive power and so helps protect constitutionalism, legality, and the deliberative process.[42] Third, it encompasses extensive pro-

---

41. Among the expanded procedural definitions that appear to bear a strong affinity to the conception of liberal democracy articulated here, but that are somewhat cryptic or ambiguous about the weight given to civil liberties, are Karl, "Dilemmas of Democratization in Latin America," 2; Dietrich Rueschemeyer, Evelyne Huber Stephens, and John D. Stephens, *Capitalist Development and Democracy* (Chicago: University of Chicago Press, 1992), 43–44, 46.

42. Obviously, the independent power of the legislature to "check and balance" executive power will differ markedly between presidential and parliamentary regimes. However, even in parliamentary regimes, democratic vigor requires striking a balance between disciplined parliamentary support for the governing party and independent capacity to scrutinize and question the actions of cabinet ministers and executive agencies. For the political quality of democracy, the most important additional mechanism of horizontal accountability is an autonomous judiciary, but crucial as well are institutionalized means (often in a separate, autonomous agency) to monitor, investigate, and punish government corruption at all levels. On the concept of lateral, or "constitutional," accountability and its importance, see Richard L. Sklar, "Developmental Democracy," *Comparative Studies in Society and History* 29, no. 4 (1987): 686–714; Sklar, "Towards a Theory of Developmental Democracy," in *Democracy and Development: Theory and Practice*, edited by Adrian Leftwich (Cambridge: Polity Press, 1996), 25–44. For the concept and theory of "horizontal

---

Polity III corrects and updates to 1994), see Ted Robert Gurr, Keith Jaggers, and Will H. Moore, "The Transformation of the Western State: The Growth of Democracy, Autocracy, and State Power since 1800," in Inkeles, *Measuring Democracy*, 69–104. Although it does not measure civil liberties, the democracy measure of the polity data sets goes beyond electoral competitiveness to measure institutional constraints on the exercise of executive power (the phenomenon of "horizontal accountability").

visions for political and civic pluralism as well as for individual and group freedoms, so that contending interests and values may be expressed and compete through ongoing processes of articulation and representation, beyond periodic elections.

Freedom and pluralism, in turn, can be secured only through a "rule of law," in which legal rules are applied fairly, consistently, and predictably across equivalent cases, irrespective of the class, status, or power of those subject to the rules. Under a true rule of law, all citizens have political and legal equality, and the state and its agents are themselves subject to the law.[43]

Specifically, liberal democracy has the following components:

• Control of the state and its key decisions and allocations lies, in fact as well as in constitutional theory, with elected officials (and not democratically unaccountable actors or foreign powers); in particular, the military is subordinate to the authority of elected civilian officials.

• Executive power is constrained, constitutionally and in fact, by the autonomous power of other government institutions (such as an independent judiciary, parliament, and other mechanisms of horizontal accountability).

• Not only are electoral outcomes uncertain, with a significant opposition vote and the presumption of party alternation in government, but no group that adheres to constitutional principles is denied the right to form a party and contest elections (even if electoral thresholds and other rules exclude small parties from winning representation in parliament).

• Cultural, ethnic, religious, and other minority groups (as well as historically disadvantaged majorities) are not prohibited (legally or in practice) from expressing their interests in the political process or from speaking their language or practicing their culture.

• Beyond parties and elections, citizens have multiple, ongoing channels for expression and representation of their interests and values, including diverse, independent associations and movements, which they have the freedom to form and join.[44]

• There are alternative sources of information (including independent media) to which citizens have (politically) unfettered access.

• Individuals also have substantial freedom of belief, opinion, discussion, speech, publication, assembly, demonstration, and petition.

• Citizens are politically equal under the law (even though they are invariably unequal in their political resources).

• Individual and group liberties are effectively protected by an independent, nondiscriminatory judiciary, whose decisions are enforced and respected by other centers of power.

• The rule of law protects citizens from unjustified detention, exile, terror, torture, and undue interference in their personal lives not only by

accountability," see Guillermo O'Donnell, "Delegative Democracy," *Journal of Democracy* 5, no. 1 (1994): 60–62, and "Horizontal Accountability and New Polyarchies," in Andreas Schedler, Larry Diamond, and Marc F. Plattner, eds., *The Self-Restraining State: Power and Accountability in New Democracies* (Boulder, Colo.: Lynne Rienner, forthcoming).

43. For an important explication of the rule of law and its related concepts, see Guillermo O'Donnell, "The (Un)Rule of Law in Latin America," in *The Rule of Law and the Underprivileged in Latin America*, edited by Juan Méndez, Guillermo O'Donnell, and Paulo Sérgio Pinheiro (Notre Dame: University of Notre Dame Press, forthcoming).

44. This is a particular emphasis of Schmitter and Karl, "What Democracy Is," 78–80, but it has long figured prominently in the work and thought of democratic pluralists such as Robert A. Dahl. In addition to his *Polyarchy*, see Dahl, *Who Governs?* (New Haven: Yale University Press, 1961); Dahl, *Dilemmas of Pluralist Democracy: Autonomy versus Control* (New Haven: Yale University Press, 1982).

the state but also by organized nonstate or anti-state forces.

These ten conditions imply an eleventh: if political authority is to be constrained and balanced, individual and minority rights protected, and a rule of law assured, democracy requires a constitution that is supreme. Liberal democracies in particular "are and have to be constitutional democracies. The lack of a constitutional spirit, of an understanding of the centrality of constitutional stability, is one of the weaknesses" of many illiberal third-wave democracies in the postcommunist world, as well as in the Third World.[45] . . .

Midrange Conceptions

Conceptual approaches are no longer easily dichotomized into electoral and liberal approaches. Some conceptions of democracy fall somewhere in between, explicitly incorporating basic freedoms of expression and association yet still allowing for constrictions in citizenship rights and a porous, insecure rule of law. The crucial distinction turns on whether freedoms are relevant mainly to the extent that they ensure meaningful electoral competition and participation or whether they are, instead, viewed as necessary for a wider range of democratic functions. . . .

The question of how extensive liberty must be before a political system can be termed a liberal democracy is a normative and philosophical one. The key distinction is whether the political process centers on elections or whether it encompasses a much broader and more continuous play of interest articulation, representation, and contestation. If we view the latter as an essential component of democracy, then there must be adequate freedoms surrounding that broader

process as well, and to use O'Donnell's language, individuals must be able to exercise their rights of citizenship not only in elections but also in obtaining "fair access to public agencies and courts," which is often denied in "informally institutionalized" polyarchies.

The distinction between political and civil freedom, on the one hand, and cultural freedom (or license), on the other, is often confused in the debate over whether democracy is inappropriate for Asia (or East Asia, or Confucian Asia, or simply Singapore) because of incompatible values. Liberal democracy does not require the comprehensively exalted status of individual rights that obtains in Western Europe and especially the United States. Thus, one may accept many of the cultural objections of advocates of the "Asian values" perspective (that Western democracies have shifted the balance too much in favor of individual rights and social entitlements over the rights of the community and the social obligations of the individual to the community) and still embrace the political and civic fundamentals of liberal democracy as articulated above.[55]

Pseudodemocracies and Nondemocracies

An appreciation of the dynamics of regime change and the evolution of democracy must allow for a third class of regimes, which are less than minimally democratic but still distinct from purely authoritarian regimes. This requires a second cutting point, between electoral democracies and electoral regimes that have multiple

45. Juan J. Linz, "Democracy Today: An Agenda for Students of Democracy," *Scandinavian Political Studies* 20, no. 2 (1997): 120–121.

55. For a perspective that does just this, see Joseph Chan, "Hong Kong, Singapore, and Asian Values: An Alternative View," *Journal of Democracy* 8, no. 2 (1997): 35–48. One can have a political system that meets the ten criteria of liberal democracy I outline but that is culturally conservative or restrictive in some policies. The key test is whether those who disagree with these policies have full civic and political freedom to mobilize to change them.

parties and many other constitutional features of electoral democracy but that lack at least one key requirement: an arena of contestation sufficiently fair that the ruling party can be turned out of power. Juan Linz, Seymour Martin Lipset, and I term these regimes *pseudodemocracies*, "because the existence of formally democratic political institutions, such as multiparty electoral competition, masks (often in part to legitimate) the reality of authoritarian domination."[56]

There is wide variation among pseudodemocracies. They include semidemocracies, which more nearly approach electoral democracies in their pluralism and competitiveness, as well as what Giovanni Sartori terms "hegemonic party systems," in which a relatively institutionalized ruling party makes extensive use of coercion, patronage, media control, and other features to deny formally legal opposition parties a fair and authentic chance to compete for power.[57] . . .

What distinguishes pseudodemocracies from other nondemocracies is that they tolerate legal alternative parties, which constitute at least somewhat real and independent opposition to the ruling party. Typically, this toleration is accompanied by more space for organizational pluralism and dissident activity in civil society than is the case in the most repressive authoritarian regimes. Invariably, pseudodemocracies are illiberal, but they vary in their repressiveness and in their proximity to the threshold of electoral democracy (which Mexico could well cross in its next presidential election, in the year 2000). Thus, pseudodemocracies tend to have somewhat higher levels of freedom than other authoritarian regimes.[58] . . .

This framework leaves a fourth, residual category, of authoritarian regimes. They vary in their level of freedom . . . , and they may even hold somewhat competitive elections (as in Uganda and other previously one-party African regimes). They may afford civil society and the judiciary some modest autonomy. Or they may be extremely closed and repressive, even totalitarian. But they all lack a crucial building block of democracy: legal, independent opposition parties. All the most repressive regimes in the world fall into this category.

This four-fold typology neatly classifies national political regimes, but political reality is always messier. Level of democracy may vary significantly across sectors and institutional arenas (as would be expected if democracy emerges in parts). It may also vary considerably across territories within the national state. . . .

With large countries, in particular, it is necessary to disaggregate to form a more sensitive picture of the quality and extent of democracy. . . .

---

56. Diamond et al., "What Makes for Democracy?" 8.

57. Giovanni Sartori, *Parties and Party Systems: A Framework for Analysis* (Cambridge: Cambridge University Press, 1976), 230–238.

58. . . . Taking seriously Collier and Levitsky's appeal to reduce the conceptual clutter in comparative democratic studies, we relate our categories here to similar concepts in other studies, particularly the "dimin-

ished subtypes" of democracy. Those subtypes that are missing the attribute of free elections or relatively fair multiparty contestation are pseudodemocracies. Those that have real and fair multiparty competition but with limited suffrage constitute exclusionary, or oligarchic, democracy, which is not relevant to the contemporary era of universal suffrage. Those regimes without adequate civil liberties or civilian control of the military may nevertheless be electoral democracies. Care is needed to empirically apply concepts, however. For example, Donald K. Emmerson's category of "illiberal democracy" would seem to be coincident with "electoral democracy" in my framework. However, as Emmerson applies the concept to what he calls "one-party democracy" in Singapore and Malaysia, the coincidence breaks down. Civil and political freedoms are so constrained in these two countries that the minimum criterion of electoral democracy (a sufficiently level electoral playing field to give opposition parties a chance at victory) is not met. See Emmerson, "Region and Recalcitrance: Rethinking Democracy through Southeast Asia," *Pacific Review* 8, no. 2 (1995): 223–248.

Democracy in Developmental Perspective

Even liberal democracies fall short of democratic ideals. At the less liberal end of the group, they may have serious flaws in their guarantees of personal and associational freedom. And certainly ongoing practices in Italy, Japan, Belgium, France, the United States, and most other industrialized democracies underscore that even long-established and well-institutionalized democracies with the most liberal average freedom scores of 1 or 1.5 are afflicted with corruption, favoritism, and unequal access to political power, not to mention voter apathy, cynicism, and disengagement.

There is not now and has never been in the modern world of nation-states a perfect democracy, one in which all citizens have roughly equal political resources and in which government is completely or almost completely responsive to all citizens. This is why Robert Dahl uses the term *polyarchy* to characterize the more limited form of democracy that has been attained to date. Important currents in democracy's third wave are the increased valorization of such limited political democracy as an end in itself and the growing tendency of intellectuals (even many who had once been on the Marxist left) to recognize the need for realism in what can be expected of democracy. Certainly, democracy does not produce all good things. As Linz observes, "political democracy does not necessarily assure even a reasonable approximation of what we would call a democratic *society*, a society with considerable equality of opportunity in all spheres."[64] As Schmitter and Karl argue, democracies are not necessarily more economically or administratively efficient, or more orderly and governable, than autocratic regimes.[65]

But by permitting widespread liberty and the real possibility of selecting alternative governments and policies, and by permitting disadvantaged groups to organize and mobilize politically, democracies (particularly liberal democracies) provide the best long-run prospects for reducing social injustices and correcting mistaken policies and corrupt practices.

It is important, then, not to take the existence of democracy, even liberal democracy, as cause for self-congratulation. Democracy should be viewed as a developmental phenomenon. Even when a country is above the threshold of electoral (or even liberal) democracy, democratic institutions can be improved and deepened or may need to be consolidated; political competition can be made fairer and more open; participation can become more inclusive and vigorous; citizens' knowledge, resources, and competence can grow; elected (and appointed) officials can be made more responsive and accountable; civil liberties can be better protected; and the rule of law can become more efficient and secure.[66] Viewed in this way, continued democratic development is a challenge for all countries, including the United States; all democracies, new and established, can become more democratic.

Obviously, the improvement and invigoration of democracy will not solve all social and economic problems that societies face. But widening the scope of public deliberation, empowering historically marginalized and alienated groups, and increasing citizen competence and government responsiveness—reforms that deepen and extend democracy—may increase the sophistication of mass publics and the legitimacy (and hence the governing capacity) of elected offi-

---

64. Linz, *The Breakdown of Democratic Regimes*, 97. Emphasis is mine.

65. Schmitter and Karl, "What Democracy Is," 85–87.

66. On civic competence and the challenges to improving it in contemporary, large-scale, complex, media-intensive, and information-saturated societies, see Robert A. Dahl, "The Problem of Civic Competence," *Journal of Democracy* 3, no. 4 (1992): 45–59.

cials.[67] Beyond this, increasing citizen competence and participation in the political process will spill over into other arenas of social life. Civic engagement, such as participation in voluntary associations and community networks, generates trust, reciprocity, and cooperation, which reduce cynicism, encourage political participation, and facilitate economic development, democratic stability, and the resolution of social problems. Increasingly, social scientists view such social capital as a critical resource for dealing with the seemingly intractable problems of poverty, alienation, and crime in the United States and other industrialized democracies. Otherwise, "mutual distrust and defection, vertical dependence and exploitation, isolation and disorder, criminality and backwardness [reinforce] one another in ... interminable vicious circles."[68]

Viewed from a developmental perspective, the fate of democracy is open-ended. The elements of liberal democracy emerge in various sequences and degrees, at varying paces in the different countries.[69] Democratic change can also move in differing directions. Just as electoral democracies can become more democratic—more liberal, constitutional, competitive, accountable, inclusive, and participatory—so they can also become less democratic—more illiberal, abusive, corrupt, exclusive, narrow, unresponsive, and unaccountable. And liberal democracies, too, can either improve or decline in their levels of political accountability, accessibility, competitiveness, and responsiveness. There is no guarantee that democratic development moves in only one direction, and there is much to suggest that all political systems (including democracies, liberal or otherwise) become rigid, corrupt, and unresponsive in the absence of periodic reform and renewal.[70] Democracy not only may lose its quality, it may even effectively disappear, not merely through the breakdown of formal institutions but also through the more insidious processes of decay....

70. Such a developmental perspective may help to inoculate democratic theory against the tendency toward teleological thinking that Guillermo O'Donnell discerns in the literature on democratic consolidation: that is, the underlying assumption that there is a particular natural path and end state of democratic development.

67. In their comparative study of the restructuring of property relations in postsocialist Eastern Europe, *Postsocialist Pathways* (Cambridge: Cambridge University Press, 1997), Laszlo Bruszt and David Stark argue that policy coherence, effectiveness, and sustainability are fostered when executives are constrained and reform policies are negotiated between governments and "deliberative associations."

68. Robert D. Putnam with Robert Leonardi and Raffaella Y. Nanetti, *Making Democracy Work: Civic Traditions in Modern Italy* (Princeton: Princeton University Press, 1993), 181; see also Putnam, "Bowling Alone: America's Declining Social Capital," *Journal of Democracy* 6, no. 1 (1995): 65–78. See also chapter 6, this volume.

69. Sklar, "Developmental Democracy."

Participation and Democratic Theory

Carole Pateman

... At the beginning of the century the size and complexity of industrialized societies and the emergence of bureaucratic forms of organisation seemed to many empirically minded writers on politics to cast grave doubts on the possibility of the attainment of democracy as that concept was usually understood. ...

But by the middle of the century even the ideal itself seemed to many to have been called in question; at least, "democracy" was still the ideal, but it was the emphasis on participation that had become suspect and with it the "classical" formulation of democratic theory. The collapse of the Weimar Republic, with its high rates of mass participation, into fascism, and the post-war establishment of totalitarian regimes based on mass participation, albeit participation backed by intimidation and coercion, underlay the tendency for "participation" to become linked to the concept of totalitarianism rather than that of democracy. The spectre of totalitarianism also helps explain the concern with the necessary conditions for stability in a democratic polity, and a further factor here was the instability of so many states in the post-war world, especially ex-colonial states that rarely maintained a democratic political system on Western lines.

If this background had led to great doubts and reservations about earlier theories of democracy, then the facts revealed by the post-war expansion of political sociology appear to have convinced most recent writers that these doubts were fully justified. Data from large-scale empirical investigations into political attitudes and behaviour, undertaken in most Western countries over the past twenty or thirty years, have revealed

that the outstanding characteristic of most citizens, more especially those in the lower socio-economic status (SES) groups, is a general lack of interest in politics and political activity and further, that widespread non-democratic or authoritarian attitudes exist, again particularly among lower socio-economic status groups. The conclusion drawn (often by political sociologists wearing political theorists' hats) is that the "classical" picture of democratic man is hopelessly unrealistic, and moreover, that in view of the facts about political attitudes, an increase in political participation by present non-participants could upset the stability of the democratic system.

There was a further factor that helped along the process of the rejection of earlier democratic theories, and that was the now familiar argument that those theories were normative and "value-laden," whereas modern political theory should be scientific and empirical, grounded firmly in the facts of political life. But even so, it may be doubted whether the revision of democratic theory would have been undertaken with such enthusiasm by so many writers if it had not been that this very question of the apparent contrast between the facts of political life and attitudes and their characterisation in earlier theories had not already been taken up, and answered, by Joseph Schumpeter. His extraordinarily influential book *Capitalism, Socialism and Democracy* (1943) was in fact written before the vast amounts of empirical information that we now have on politics became available, but nevertheless Schumpeter considered that the facts showed that "classical" democratic theory was in need of revision, and he provided just such a revised theory. More than that, however, and even more importantly for the theories that followed, he put forward a new, realistic *definition* of democracy. ...

The very great difference between [participatory] theories of democracy ... and the theories

Excerpted from: Carole Pateman, *Participation and Democratic Theory*. © Cambridge University Press, 1970. Cambridge: Cambridge University Press, 1970. Reprinted with the permission of Cambridge University Press.

of ... theorists of representative government makes it difficult to understand how the myth of one "classical" theory of democracy has survived so long and is so vigorously propagated. The theories of participatory democracy ... were not just essays in prescription as is often claimed, rather they offer just those "plans of action and specific prescriptions" for movement towards a (truly) democratic polity that it has been suggested are lacking. But perhaps the strangest criticism is that these earlier theorists were not, as Berelson puts it, concerned with the "general features necessary if the (political) institutions are to work as required," and that they ignored the political system as a whole in their work. It is quite clear that this is precisely what they were concerned with. Although the variable identified as crucial in those theories for the successful establishment and maintenance of a democratic political system, the authority structures of non-Governmental spheres of society, is exactly the same one that Eckstein indicates in his theory of stable democracy, the conclusions drawn from this by the earlier and later theorists of democracy are entirely different. In order that an evaluation of these two theories of democracy can be undertaken I shall now briefly set out (in a similar fashion to the contemporary theory of democracy above), a participatory theory of democracy. . . .

The theory of participatory democracy is built round the central assertion that individuals and their institutions cannot be considered in isolation from one another. The existence of representative institutions at national level is not sufficient for democracy; for maximum participation by all the people at that level socialisation, or "social training," for democracy must take place in other spheres in order that the necessary individual attitudes and psychological qualities can be developed. This development takes place through the process of participation itself. The major function of participation in the theory of participatory democracy is therefore an educative one, educative in the very widest sense, including both the psychological aspect and the gaining of practice in democratic skills and procedures. Thus there is no special problem about the stability of a participatory system; it is self-sustaining through the educative impact of the participatory process. Participation develops and fosters the very qualities necessary for it; the more individuals participate the better able they become to do so. Subsidiary hypotheses about participation are that it has an integrative effect and that it aids the acceptance of collective decisions.

Therefore, for a democratic polity to exist it is necessary for a participatory society to exist, i.e. a society where all political systems have been democratised and socialisation through participation can take place in all areas. The most important area is industry; most individuals spend a great deal of their lifetime at work and the business of the workplace provides an education in the management of collective affairs that it is difficult to parallel elsewhere. The second aspect of the theory of participatory democracy is that spheres such as industry should be seen as political systems in their own right, offering areas of participation additional to the national level. If individuals are to exercise the maximum amount of control over their own lives and environment then authority structures in these areas must be so organised that they can participate in decision making. A further reason for the central place of industry in the theory relates to the substantive measure of economic equality required to give the individual the independence and security necessary for (equal) participation; the democratising of industrial authority structures, abolishing the permanent distinction between "managers" and "men" would mean a large step toward meeting this condition.

The contemporary and participatory theories of democracy can be contrasted on every point of substance, including the characterisation of "democracy" itself and the definition of "political," which in the participatory theory is not confined to the usual national or local government sphere.

Again, in the participatory theory "participation" refers to (equal) participation in the making of decisions, and "political equality" refers to equality of power in determining the outcome of decisions, a very different definition from that in the contemporary theory. Finally, the justification for a democratic system in the participatory theory of democracy rests primarily on the human results that accrue from the participatory process. One might characterise the participatory model as one where maximum input (participation) is required and where output includes not just policies (decisions) but also the development of the social and political capacities of each individual, so that there is "feedback" from output to input.

Many of the criticisms of the so-called "classical" theory of democracy imply that the latter theory has only to be stated for it to become obvious that it is unrealistic and outmoded. With the participatory theory of democracy this is far from the case; indeed, it has many features that reflect some of the major themes and orientations in recent political theory and political sociology. For example, the fact that it is a model of a self-sustaining system might make it attractive to the many writers on politics who, explicitly or implicitly, make use of such models. Again, similarities between the participatory theory of democracy and recent theories of social pluralism are obvious enough, although these usually argue only that "secondary" associations should exist to mediate between the individual and the national polity and say nothing about the authority structures of those associations. The wide definition of the "political" in the participatory theory is also in keeping with the practice in modern political theory and political science. One of the advocates of the contemporary theory of democracy discussed above, Dahl (1963, p. 6), has defined a political system as "any persistent pattern of human relationships that involves to a significant extent power, rule or authority." All this makes it very odd that no recent writer on democratic theory appears to have reread the earlier theorists with these concerns in mind. Any explanation of this would, no doubt, include a mention of the widely held belief that (although these earlier theories are often said to be descriptive) "traditional" political theorists, especially theorists of democracy, were engaged in a largely prescriptive and "value-laden" enterprise and their work is thus held to have little direct interest for the modern, scientific, political theorist. . . .

Conclusions

Recent discussions of the theory of democracy have been obscured by the myth of the "classical doctrine of democracy" propagated so successfully by Schumpeter. The failure to re-examine the notion of a "classical" theory has prevented a proper understanding of the arguments of (some of) the earlier theorists of democracy about the central role of participation in the theory of democracy; prevented it even on the part of writers who wished to defend a participatory theory of democracy. This has meant that the prevailing academic orthodoxy on the subject, the contemporary theory of democracy, has not been subjected to substantive, rigorous criticism, nor has a really convincing case been presented for the retention of a participatory theory in the face of the facts of modern, large-scale political life.

The major contribution to democratic theory of those "classical" theorists whom we have called the theorists of participatory democracy is to focus our attention on the interrelationship between individuals and the authority structures of institutions within which they interact. This is not to say that modern writers are completely unaware of this dimension; clearly this is not so, as much political sociology, especially that dealing with political socialisation, confirms, but the implications of the findings on socialisation for the contemporary theory of democracy have not been appreciated. The link between these findings, particularly those on the development of the sense of political efficacy in adults and children, and the notion of a "democratic character" has been overlooked. Although many of the advocates of the contemporary theory of democracy argue that a certain type of character, or a set of psychological qualities or attitudes, is necessary for (stable) democracy—at least among a proportion of the population—they are far less clear on how this character could be developed or what the nature of its connection with the working of the "democratic method" itself really is. While most do not support Schumpeter's declaration that the democratic method and the democratic character are unconnected, nor do they take much trouble to examine the nature of the postulated relationship. Even Almond and Verba, after clearly showing the connection between a participatory environment and the development of a sense of political efficacy, show no realisation of the significance of this in their final, theoretical chapter.

However, this failure is only part of a more general, and striking, feature of much recent writing on democratic theory. Despite the stress most modern political theorists lay on the empirical and scientific nature of their discipline they display, at least so far as democratic theory is concerned, a curious reluctance to look at the facts in a questioning spirit. That is, they seem reluctant to see whether or not a theoretical explanation can be offered of why the political facts are as they are; instead they have taken it for granted that one theory which could possibly have yielded an explanation had already been shown to be outmoded, and so concentrated on uncritically building a "realistic" theory to fit the facts as revealed by political sociology.

The result of this one-sided procedure has been not only a democratic theory that has unrecognised normative implications, implications that set the existing Anglo-American political system as our democratic ideal, but it has also resulted in a "democratic" theory that in many respects bears a strange resemblance to the anti-democratic arguments of the last century. No longer is democratic theory centred on the participation of "the people," on the participation of the ordinary man, or the prime virtue of a democratic political system seen as the development of politically relevant and necessary qualities in the ordinary individual; in the contemporary theory of democracy it is the participation of the minority élite that is crucial and the non-participation of the apathetic, ordinary man lacking in the feeling of political efficacy, that is regarded as the main bulwark against instability. Apparently it has not occurred to recent theorists to wonder why there should be a positive correlation between apathy and low feelings of political efficacy and low socio-economic status. It would be more plausible to argue that the earlier democratic theorists were unrealistic in their notion of the "democratic character" and in their claim that it was, given a certain institutional setting, open to every individual to develop in this direction, if the persons today who do not measure up to this standard were to be found in roughly equal proportions in all sections of the community. The fact that they are not should surely cause empirical political theorists to pause and ask why.

Once it is asked whether there might not be institutional factors that could provide an explanation for the facts about apathy as suggested in the participatory theory of democracy, then the argument from stability looks far less securely based. Most recent theorists have been content to accept Sartori's assurance that the inactivity of the ordinary man is "nobody's fault" and to take the facts as given for the purpose of theory building. Yet we have seen that the evidence supports the arguments of Rousseau, Mill and Cole that we do learn to participate by participating and that feelings of political efficacy are more likely to be developed in a participatory environment. Furthermore, the evidence indicates that experience of a participatory authority structure might also be effective in diminishing tendencies toward non-democratic attitudes in the individual. If those who come newly into the political arena have been previously "educated" for it then their participation will pose no dangers to the stability of the system. Oddly enough, this evidence against the argument from stability should be welcomed by some writers defending the contemporary theory, for they occasionally remark that they deplore the low levels of political participation and interest that now obtain.

The argument from stability has only seemed as convincing as it has because the evidence relating to the psychological effects of participation has never been considered in relation to the issues of political, more specifically, democratic theory. Both sides in the current discussion of the role of participation in modern theory of democracy have grasped half of the theory of participatory democracy; the defenders of the earlier theorists have emphasised that their goal was the production of an educated, active citizenry and the theorists of contemporary democracy have pointed to the importance of the structure of authority in non-governmental spheres for political socialisation. But neither side has realised that the two aspects are connected or realised the significance of the empirical evidence for their arguments.

However, the socialisation aspect of the participatory theory of democracy is also capable of being absorbed into the general framework of the contemporary theory, providing the foundation for a more soundly based theory of stable democracy than those offered at present. The analysis of participation in the industrial context has made it clear that only a relatively minor modification of existing authority structures there may be necessary for the development of the sense of political efficacy. It is quite conceivable, given recent theories of management, that partial participation at the lower level may become widespread in well-run enterprises in the future because of the multiplicity of advantages it appears to bring for efficiency and the capacity of the enterprise to adapt to changing circumstances. Nevertheless, if the socialisation argu-

ment is compatible with either theory, the two theories of democracy remain in conflict over their most important aspect, over their respective definitions of a democratic polity. Is it solely the presence of competing leaders at national level for whom the electorate can periodically vote, or does it also require that a participatory society exist, a society so organised that every individual has the opportunity directly to participate in all political spheres? We have not, of course, set out to prove that it is one or the other; what we have been considering is whether the idea of a participatory society is as completely unrealistic as those writers contend who press for a revision of the participatory theory of democracy.

The notion of a participatory society requires that the scope of the term "political" is extended to cover spheres outside national government. It has already been pointed out that many political theorists do argue for just such an extension. Unfortunately this wider definition, and more importantly its implications for political theory, are usually forgotten when these same theorists turn their attention to democratic theory. Recognition of industry as a political system in its own right at once removes many of the confused ideas that exist about democracy (and its relation to participation) in the industrial context. Its rules out the use of "democratic" to describe a friendly approach by supervisors that ignores the authority structure within which this approach occurs, and it also rules out the argument that insists that industrial democracy already exists on the basis of a spurious comparison with national politics. There is very little in the empirical evidence on which to base the assertion that industrial democracy, full higher level participation, is impossible. On the other hand there is a great deal to suggest that there are many difficulties and complexities involved. . . .

The major difficulty in a discussion of the empirical possibilities of democratising industrial authority structures is that we do not have sufficient information on a participatory system that contains opportunities for participation at both the higher and lower levels to test some of the arguments of the participatory theory of democracy satisfactorily. . . .

Today, the question of economic efficiency is bound to loom very large in any discussion of the issues involved in democratising industrial authority structures; in particular how far the economic equality implied in a system of industrial democracy would be compatible with efficiency. Economic equality is often dismissed as of little relevance to democracy yet once industry is recognised as a political system in its own right then it is clear that a substantive measure of economic equality is necessary. If inequalities in decision-making power are abolished the case for other forms of economic inequality becomes correspondingly weaker. . . .

We have considered the possibility of establishing a participatory society with respect to one area only, that of industry, but because industry occupies a vitally important place in the theory of participatory democracy, that is sufficient to establish the validity, or otherwise of the notion of a participatory society. The analysis of the concept of participation presented here can be applied to other spheres, although the empirical questions raised by the extension of participation to areas other than industry cannot be considered. Nevertheless, it might be useful to indicate briefly some of the possibilities in this direction.

To begin, as it were, at the beginning, with the family. Modern theories of child-rearing . . . have helped to influence family life, especially among middle-class families, in a more democratic direction than before. But if the general trend is toward participation the educative effects arising from this may be nullified if the later experiences of the individual do not work in the same direction. The most urgent demands for more participation in recent years have come from the students and clearly these demands are very relevant to our general argument. With regard to the introduction of a participatory system in institutions of higher education, it is sufficient to note here that if the arguments for giving the

young worker the opportunity to participate in the workplace are convincing then there is a good case for giving his contemporary, the student, similar opportunities; both are the mature citizens of the future. One person whom the opportunities for participation in industry would pass by is the full-time housewife. She might find opportunities to participate at the local government level, especially if these opportunities included the field of housing, particularly public housing. The problems of running large housing developments would seem to give wide scope to residents for participation in decision making and the psychological effects of such participation might prove extremely valuable in this context. There is little point in drawing up a catalogue of possible areas of participation but these examples do give an indication of how a move might be made toward a participatory society.

A defender of the contemporary theory of democracy might object at this point that although the idea of a participatory society might not be completely unrealistic, this does not affect his definition of democracy. Even though authority structures in industry, and perhaps other areas, were democratised this would have little effect on the role of the individual; this would still be confined, our objector might argue, to a choice between competing leaders or representatives. The paradigm of direct participation would have no application even in a participatory society. . . . [W]ithin the industrial context, this objection is misplaced. Where a participatory industrial system allowed both higher and lower level participation then there would be scope for the individual directly to participate in a wide range of decisions while at the same time being part of a representative system; the one does not preclude the other.

If this is the case where the alternative areas of participation are concerned, there is an obvious sense in which the objection is valid at the level of the national political system. In an electorate of, say, thirty-five million the role of the individual must consist almost entirely of choosing representatives; even where he could cast a vote in a referendum his influence over the outcome would be infinitesimally small. Unless the size of national political units were drastically reduced then that piece of reality is not open to change. In another sense, however, this objection misses the point because it rests on a lack of appreciation of the importance of the participatory theory of democracy for modern, large scale, industrialised societies. In the first place it is only if the individual has the opportunity directly to participate in decision making and choose representatives in the alternative areas that, under modern conditions, he can hope to have any real control over the course of his life or the development of the environment in which he lives. Of course, it is true that exactly the same decisions are not made, for example, in the workplace as in the House of Commons or the Cabinet, but one may agree with Schumpeter and his followers in this respect at least: that it is doubtful if the average citizen will ever be as interested in all the decisions made at national level as he would in those made nearer home. But having said that, the important point is, secondly, that the opportunity to participate in the alternative areas would mean that one piece of reality would have changed, namely the context within which all political activity was carried on. The argument of the participatory theory of democracy is that participation in the alternative areas would enable the individual better to appreciate the connection between the public and the private spheres. The ordinary man might still be more interested in things nearer home, but the existence of a participatory society would mean that he was better able to assess the performance of representatives at the national level, better equipped to take decisions of national scope when the opportunity arose to do so, and better able to weigh up the impact of decisions taken by national representatives on his own life and immediate surroundings. In the context of a participatory society the significance of his vote to the individual would have changed; as well as being a private individual he would have multiple opportunities to become an educated, public citizen.

It is this ideal, an ideal with a long history in political thought, that has become lost from view in the contemporary theory of democracy. Not surprisingly perhaps when for some recent writers such a wide-ranging democratic ideal is regarded as "dangerous," and they recommend that we pitch our standards of what might be achieved in democratic political life only marginally above what already exists. The claim that the Anglo-American political system tackles difficult questions with distinction looks rather less plausible since, for example, the events in the American cities of the late 1960s or the discovery in Britain that in the midst of affluence many citizens are not only poor but also homeless, than it may have done in the late 1950s and early 1960s, but such a statement could have only seemed a "realistic" description then because questions were never asked about certain features of the system or certain aspects of the data collected, despite the much emphasised empirical basis of the new theory. In sum, the contemporary theory of democracy represents a considerable failure of the political and sociological imagination on the part of recent theorists of democracy.

When the problem of participation and its role in democratic theory is placed in a wider context than that provided by the contemporary theory of democracy, and the relevant empirical material is related to the theoretical issues, it becomes clear that neither the demands for more participation, nor the theory of participatory democracy itself, are based, as is so frequently claimed, on dangerous illusions or on an outmoded and unrealistic theoretical foundation. We can still have a modern, viable theory of democracy which retains the notion of participation at its heart.

Bibliography

Blumberg, P. (1968), *Industrial Democracy: The Sociology of Participation*, Constable, London.

Dahl, R. A. (1963), *Modern Political Analysis*, Prentice-Hall, New Jersey.

Schumpeter, J. A. (1943), *Capitalism, Socialism and Democracy*, Geo. Allen & Unwin, London.

Polyarchal Democracy

Robert Dahl

I

Examination of Madisonian and populistic theory suggests at least two possible methods one might employ to construct a theory of democracy. One way, the method of maximization, is to specify a set of goals to be maximized; democracy can then be defined in terms of the specific governmental processes necessary to maximize these goals or some among them.... Madisonian theory postulates a non-tyrannical republic as the goal to be maximized; populistic theory postulates popular sovereignty and political equality. A second way—this one might be called the descriptive method—is to consider as a single class of phenomena all those nation states and social organizations that are commonly called democratic by political scientists, and by examining the members of this class to discover, first, the distinguishing characteristics they have in common, and, second, the necessary and sufficient conditions for social organizations possessing these characteristics.

These are not, however, mutually exclusive methods. And we shall see that if we begin by employing the first method it will soon become necessary to employ something rather like the second as well.

II

... [T]he goals of populistic democracy and the simple Rule deduced from these goals do not provide us with anything like a complete theory. One basic defect of the theory is that it does no more than to provide a formal redefinition of

Excerpted from: Robert Dahl, *A Preface to Democratic Theory*. Chicago: University of Chicago Press, 1956. © 1956. The University of Chicago. Reprinted by permission.

one necessary procedural rule for the perfect or ideal attainment of political equality and popular sovereignty; but because the theory is no more than an exercise in axiomatics, it tells us nothing about the real world. However, let us now pose the key question in slightly different form: What are the necessary and sufficient conditions for maximizing democracy in the real world? I shall show that the words "in the real world" fundamentally alter the problem.

Let us begin, however, with a meticulous concern for precision of meaning. First, what do we mean by "maximizing democracy"? Evidently here, ... we must proceed by regarding democracy as a state of affairs constituting a limit, and all actions approaching the limit will be maximizing actions. But how shall we describe the state of affairs constituting the limit?

The model of populistic democracy suggests three possible characteristics that might be made operationally meaningful: (1) Whenever policy choices are perceived to exist, the alternative selected and enforced as governmental policy is the alternative most preferred by the members. (2) Whenever policy choices are perceived to exist, in the process of choosing the alternative to be enforced as government policy, the preference of each member is assigned an equal value. (3) The Rule: In choosing among alternatives, the alternative preferred by the greater number is selected.

To make the first of these operational we must either ignore the problem of different intensities of preference among individuals or find ourselves in so deep a morass of obstacles to observation and comparison that it would be very nearly impossible to say whether or not the characteristic in fact exists. I shall return to this problem in the next chapter. But if we ignore intensities, then in effect we adopt the second characteristic as our criterion: that the preference of each member is assigned an equal value. It would appear at first glance that the question whether the preference of each member of an organization is assigned an equal value is more or less susceptible of observation. Likewise the third characteristic, the Rule, should be observable. But since the Rule is deducible from the first two characteristics, would it not be enough simply to examine a social organization in order to discover the extent to which the Rule is or is not followed? That is, do we have in the Rule an adequate definition of the limit of democracy? Suppose we observe that a majority prefers x to y, and x happens to be selected as government policy. Yet it may be that among the majority is a dictator; if he were in the minority, then y would be selected. The condition of political equality evidently requires "interchangeability," i.e., the interchange of an equal number of individuals from one side to another would not affect the outcome of the decision. But how can we observe whether interchangeability is present? Evidently no single decision provides us with enough information, for at best a single decision can only reveal that the Rule is not being followed and that political equality therefore does not exist during that decision. We can infer interchangeability only by examining a large number of cases....

... If we take any specific action, such as the outcome of balloting, as a satisfactory index of preference, then no operational tests exist for determining political equality, other than those necessary for determining whether the Rule is or is not being followed. That is, given the expression of preferences as adequate, the only operational test for political equality is the extent to which the' Rule is followed in a number of cases.... What events must we observe in the real world in order to determine the extent to which the Rule is employed in an organization?

Unfortunately, the phrase "given the expression of preferences" harbors some serious difficulties. What kinds of activity shall we take as indices of preference? At one extreme we could rely on some overt act of choosing, such as casting a ballot or making a statement.[1] At the other extreme, through deep and careful probing we could search for psychological evidence. If the first is often naïve, the second is impossible on a sufficient scale. In practice most of us adopt a middle course and take our clues from the prevailing environment in which the particular preference is expressed. In one environment we accept the overt act of voting as an adequate if imperfect index; in another we reject it entirely....

III

The effect of the argument so far is to divide our key question into two: (1) What acts shall we consider sufficient to constitute an expression of individual preferences at a given stage in the decision process? (2) Taking these acts as an expression of preferences, what events must we observe in order to determine the extent to which the Rule is employed in the organization we are examining? We are still looking, let us remember, for a set of limiting conditions to be approached.

At a minimum, two stages need to be distinguished: the election stage[3] and the interelection stage. The election stage in turn consists of at least three periods which it is useful to distinguish: the voting period, the prevoting period, and the postvoting period....

During the voting period we would need to observe the extent to which at least three conditions exist:

1. Every member of the organization performs the acts we assume to constitute an expression

---

1. More accurately, in using votes and opinion polls we generally rely on some overt statements of individuals who compile the returns.

3. Election is used here in a broad sense. To apply the analysis to the internal operation of an organization that is itself constituted through elections, such as a legislative body, one would consider votes on measures as "the election stage."

of preference among the scheduled alternatives, e.g., voting.

2. In tabulating these expressions (votes), the weight assigned to the choice of each individual is identical.

3. The alternative with the greatest number of votes is declared the winning choice.

... [I]t is self-evident that we have thus far begged the first of our questions. A totalitarian plebiscite might meet—and indeed in practice evidently often has met—these three conditions better than a national election or legislative decision in countries that most Western political scientists would call democratic. The crux of the problem is in our first question, what we take to constitute an expression of individual preference. Can it not be truthfully said that the peasant who casts his ballot for the dictatorship is expressing his preferences among the scheduled alternatives as he sees them? For, perhaps, the alternatives he sees are either to vote for the dictatorship or to take a journey to Siberia....

What we balk at in accepting the vote of the Soviet citizen as an expression of preference is that he is not permitted to choose among all the alternatives that we, as outside observers, regard as in some sense potentially available to him....

What we have done, then, is to formulate a fourth limiting condition, one that must exist in the prevoting period governing the scheduling of alternatives for the voting period.

4. Any member who perceives a set of alternatives, at least one of which he regards as preferable to any of the alternatives presently scheduled, can insert his preferred alternative(s) among those scheduled for voting.

... [W]e must lay down a fifth condition operating in the prevoting period.

5. All individuals possess identical information about the alternatives.

...

At first glance it might be thought that these five conditions are sufficient to guarantee the operation of the Rule; but, at least in principle, it would be possible for a regime to permit these conditions to operate through the prevoting and voting periods and then simply to ignore the results. Consequently, we must postulate at least two more conditions for the postvoting period both of which are sufficiently obvious to need no discussion:

6. Alternatives (leaders or policies) with the greatest number of votes displace any alternatives (leaders or policies) with fewer votes.

7. The orders of elected officials are executed.

These, then, constitute our set of more or less observable limiting conditions which when present during the election stage will be taken as evidence for the maximal operation of the Rule, which in turn is taken as evidence for the maximal attainment of political equality and popular sovereignty. What of the interelection stage? If our argument so far is correct, then maximization of political equality and popular sovereignty in the interelection stage would require:

8.1. Either that all interelection decisions are subordinate or executory to those arrived at during the election stage, i.e., elections are in a sense controlling

8.2. Or that new decisions during the interelection period are governed by the preceding seven conditions, operating, however, under rather different institutional circumstances

8.3. Or both.

IV

I think it may be laid down dogmatically that no human organization—certainly none with more than a handful of people—has ever met or is ever likely to meet these eight conditions. It is true that the second, third, and sixth conditions are quite precisely met in some organizations, although in the United States corrupt practices sometimes nullify even these; the others are, at best, only crudely approximated....

Because human organizations rarely and perhaps never reach the limit set by these eight conditions, it is necessary to interpret each of the conditions as one end of a continuum or scale along which any given organization might be measured. Unfortunately there is at present no known way of assigning meaningful weights to the eight conditions. However, even without weights, if the eight scales could each be metricized, it would be possible and perhaps useful to establish some arbitrary but not meaningless classes of which the upper chunk might be called "polyarchies."

It is perfectly evident, however, that what has just been described is no more than a program, for nothing like it has, I think, ever been attempted. I shall simply set down here, therefore, the following observations. Organizations do in fact differ markedly in the extent to which they approach the limits set by these eight conditions. Furthermore, "polyarchies" include a variety of organizations which Western political scientists would ordinarily call democratic, including certain aspects of the governments of nation states such as the United States, Great Britain, the Dominions (South Africa possibly excepted), the Scandinavian countries, Mexico, Italy, and France; states and provinces, such as the states of this country and the provinces of Canada; numerous cities and towns; some trade-unions; numerous associations such as Parent-Teachers' Associations, chapters of the League of Women Voters, and some religious groups; and some primitive societies. Thus it follows that the number of polyarchies is large. (The number of egalitarian polyarchies is probably relatively small or perhaps none exist at all.) The number of polyarchies must run well over a hundred and probably well over a thousand. Of this number, however, only a tiny handful has been exhaus-

tively studied by political scientists, and these have been the most difficult of all, the governments of national states, and in a few instances the smaller governmental units....

... What are the necessary and sufficient conditions in the real world for the existence of these eight conditions, to at least the minimum degree we have agreed to call polyarchy?...

V

... ⌊W⌋e can set down some hypotheses for which considerable evidence exists.

... It would seem truistic that if all the members of an organization rejected the norms prescribing the eight conditions, then the conditions would not exist; or alternatively, the extent to which polyarchy exists must be related to the extent to which the norms are accepted as desirable. If we are willing to assume that the extent of agreement (consensus) on the eight basic norms is measurable, then we can formulate the following hypotheses, which have been commonplace in the literature of political science:

1. Each of the conditions of polyarchy increases with the extent of agreement (or consensus) on the relevant norm.

2. Polyarchy is a function of consensus on the eight norms, other things remaining the same.[11]

Unfortunately for the simplicity of the hypotheses, consensus possesses at least three dimensions: the number of individuals who agree, the intensity or depth of their belief, and the extent to which overt activity conforms with belief....

The extent of agreement, in turn, must be functionally dependent upon the extent to which the various processes for social training are employed on behalf of the norms by the family,

---

11. Appendix E to this chapter raises some questions about treating polyarchy as positive and increasing with both consensus and political activity.

schools, churches, clubs, literature, newspapers, and the like. Again, if it were possible to measure the extent to which these processes are used, our hypotheses could be stated as:

3. The extent of agreement (consensus) on each of the eight norms increases with the extent of social training in the norm.

4. Consensus is therefore a function of the total social training in all the norms.

It also follows from the preceding hypotheses that:

5. Polyarchy is a function of the total social training in all the norms.[12]

... It is reasonable to suppose that the less the agreement on policy choices, the more difficult it will be in any organization to train members in the eight norms. For then, although the operation of the rules may confer benefits on some members, it will impose severe restraints on others. If the results are severe for relatively large numbers, then it is reasonable to suppose that those who suffer from the operation of the rules will oppose them and hence resist training in them. Thus:

6. Social training in the eight norms increases with the extent of consensus or agreement on choices among policy alternatives.

From 5 and 6 it follows that:

7. One or more of the conditions of polyarchy increases with consensus on policy alternatives.

Hypothesis 6 suggests, moreover, that the reverse of Hypothesis 4 is also valid. We would expect that the extent to which social training in the norms is indulged in is itself dependent upon the amount of agreement that already exists on the norms. The more disagreement there is about the norms, the more likely it is that some of the means of social training—the family and the school in particular—will train some individuals in conflicting norms. The relationship between social training and consensus is thus a perfect instance of the hen-and-egg problem. Hence:

8. The extent of social training in one of the eight norms also increases with the extent of agreement on it.

...

Now the extent of agreement cannot be considered entirely independently of the extent of political activity in an organization. The extent to which some of the conditions for polyarchy—1, 4, and 5—are met is also a measure of the political activity of members, that is, the extent to which they vote in elections and primaries, participate in campaigns, and seek and disseminate information and propaganda. Thus by definition:

9. Polyarchy is a function of the political activity of the members.[18]

A good deal is now known about the variables with which political activity is associated.... At present we know that political activity, at least in the United States, is positively associated to a significant extent with such variables as income, socio-economic status, and education, and that it is also related in complex ways with belief systems, expectations, and personality structures. We now know that members of the ignorant and unpropertied masses which Madison and his colleagues so much feared are considerably less active politically than the educated and well-to-do. By their propensity for political passivity the

---

12. For a "Summary of the hypothetical functions relating polyarchy to its preconditions" see Appendix C to this chapter.

18. For an important complexity in this hypothetical function, see Appendix E to this chapter, "A note on the relation between agreement and political activity."

poor and uneducated disfranchise themselves.[19] Since they also have less access than the wealthy to the organizational, financial, and propaganda resources that weigh so heavily in campaigns, elections, legislative, and executive decisions, anything like equal control over government policy is triply barred to the members of Madison's unpropertied masses. They are barred by their relatively greater inactivity, by their relatively limited access to resources, and by Madison's nicely contrived system of constitutional checks.

VI

... Because we are taught to believe in the necessity of constitutional checks and balances, we place little faith in social checks and balances. We admire the efficacy of constitutional separation of powers in curbing majorities and minorities, but we often ignore the importance of the restraints imposed by social separation of powers. Yet if the theory of polyarchy is roughly sound, it follows that in the absence of certain social prerequisites, no constitutional arrangements can produce a nontyrannical republic. The history of numerous Latin-American states is, I think, sufficient evidence. Conversely, an increase in the extent to which one of the social prerequisites is present may be far more important in strengthening democracy than any particular constitutional design. Whether we are concerned with tyranny by a minority or tyranny by a majority, the theory of polyarchy suggests that the first and crucial variables to which political scientists must direct their attention are social and not constitutional....

19. Cf. especially B. R. Berelson, P. F. Lazarsfeld, and W. N. McPhee, [*Voting* (Chicago: Chicago University Press, 1954)]; S. M. Lipset *et al.*, "The Psychology of Voting: An Analysis of Political Behavior," *Handbook of Social Psychology* (Cambridge: Addison-Wesley, 1954).

2 SOURCES OF DEMOCRACY

Political Man: The Social Bases of Politics
Seymour Martin Lipset

Social Revolutions in the Modern World
Theda Skocpol

The Impact of Economic Development on Democracy
Evelyne Huber, Dietrich Rueschemeyer, and John D. Stephens

Democracy and the Market: Political and Economic Reforms in Eastern Europe and Latin America
Adam Przeworski

Democracy's Third Wave
Samuel P. Huntington

South Africa's Negotiated Transition: Democracy, Opposition, and the New Constitutional Order
Courtney Jung and Ian Shapiro

Economic Development and Political Regimes
Adam Przeworski, Michael E. Alvarez, José Antonio Cheibub, and Fernando Limongi

Political Man: The Social Bases of Politics

Seymour Martin Lipset

Economic Development and Democracy

Democracy in a complex society may be defined as a political system which supplies regular constitutional opportunities for changing the governing officials, and a social mechanism which permits the largest possible part of the population to influence major decisions by choosing among contenders for political office....

Perhaps the most common generalization linking political systems to other aspects of society has been that democracy is related to the state of economic development. The more well-to-do a nation, the greater the chances that it will sustain democracy....

To test this hypothesis concretely, I have used various indices of economic development—wealth, industrialization, urbanization, and education—and computed averages (means) for the countries which have been classified as more or less democratic in the Anglo-Saxon world and Europe, and in Latin America. In each case, the average wealth, degree of industrialization and urbanization, and level of education is much higher for the more democratic countries.... If I had combined Latin America and Europe ... the differences would have been even greater.[9]

The main indices of *wealth* used are per capita income, number of persons per motor vehicle and thousands of persons per physician, and the number of radios, telephones, and newspapers per thousand persons. The differences are striking on every score.... In the more democratic European countries, there are 17 persons per motor vehicle compared to 143 for the less democratic. In the less dictatorial Latin-American countries there are 99 persons per motor vehicle versus 274 for the more dictatorial.[10] Income differences for the groups are also sharp, dropping from an average per capita income of $695

9. Lyle W. Shannon has correlated indices of economic development with whether a country is self-governing or not, and his conclusions are substantially the same. Since Shannon does not give details on the countries categorized as self-governing and nonself-governing, there is no direct measure of the relation between "democratic" and "self-governing" countries. All the countries examined in this chapter, however, were chosen on the assumption that a characterization as "democratic" is meaningless for a nonself-governing country, and therefore, presumably, all of them, whether democratic or dictatorial, would fall within Shannon's "self-governing" category. Shannon shows that underdevelopment is related to lack of self-government; my data indicate that once self-government is attained, development is still related to the character of the political system. See the book edited by Shannon, *Underdeveloped Areas* (New York: Harper & Bros., 1957), and also his article, "Is Level of Development Related to Capacity for Self-Government?" *American Journal of Economics and Sociology*, 17 (1958), pp. 367–382. In the latter paper Shannon constructs a composite index of development, using some of the same indices, such as inhabitants per physician, and derived from the same United Nations sources, as appear in the tables to follow. Shannon's work did not come to my attention until after this chapter was first prepared, so that the two analyses can be considered as separate tests of comparable hypotheses.

10. It must be remembered that these figures are means, compiled from census figures for the various countries. The data vary widely in accuracy, and there is no way of measuring the validity of compound calculated figures such as those presented here. The consistent direction of all these differences, and their large magnitude, is the main indication of validity.

Excerpted from: Seymour Martin Lipset, *Political Man: The Social Bases of Politics*, pp. 33–53. Baltimore: The Johns Hopkins University Press, 1981. © 1959, 1960, 1981 by Seymour Martin Lipset. Reprinted by permission of The Johns Hopkins University Press.

for the more democratic countries of Europe to $308 for the less democratic; the corresponding difference for Latin America is from $171 to $119. The ranges are equally consistent, with the lowest per capita income in each group falling in the "less democratic" category, and the highest in the "more democratic."

Industrialization, to which indices of wealth are of course clearly related, is measured by the percentage of employed males in agriculture and the per capita commercially produced "energy" being used in the country (measured in terms of tons of coal per person per year). Both of these show equally consistent results. The average percentage of employed males working in agriculture and related occupations was 21 in the "more democratic" European countries and 41 in the "less democratic"; 52 in the "less dictatorial" Latin-American countries and 67 in the "more dictatorial." The differences in per capita energy employed are equally large.

The degree of *urbanization* is also related to the existence of democracy.[11] Three different indices of urbanization are available from data compiled by International Urban Research (Berkeley, California): the percentage of the population in communities of 20,000 and over, the percentage in communities of 100,000 and over, and the percentage residing in standard

metropolitan areas. On all three of these indices the more democratic countries score higher than the less democratic for both of the areas under investigation.

Many people have suggested that the higher the *education* level of a nation's population, the better the chances for democracy, and the comparative data available support this proposition. The "more democratic" countries of Europe are almost entirely literate: the lowest has a rate of 96 percent; while the "less democratic" nations have an average rate of 85 percent. In Latin America the difference is between an average rate of 74 percent for the "less dictatorial" countries and 46 percent for the "more dictatorial."[12] The educational enrollment per thousand total population at three different levels—primary, post-primary, and higher educational—is equally consistently related to the degree of democracy. The tremendous disparity is shown by the extreme cases of Haiti and the United States. Haiti has fewer children (11 per thousand) attending school in the primary grades than the United States has attending colleges (almost 18 per thousand).

The relationship between education and democracy is worth more extensive treatment since an entire philosophy of government has seen increased education as the basic requirement of democracy.[13] As James Bryce wrote, with special

---

11. Urbanization has often been linked to democracy by political theorists. Harold J. Laski asserted that "organized democracy is the product of urban life," and that it was natural therefore that it should have "made its first effective appearance" in the Greek city states, limited as was their definition of "citizen." See his article "Democracy" in the *Encyclopedia of the Social Sciences* (New York: Macmillan, 1937), Vol. V, pp. 76–85. Max Weber held that the city, as a certain type of political community, is a peculiarly Western phenomenon, and traced the emergence of the notion of "citizenship" from social developments closely related to urbanization. For a partial statement of his point of view, see the chapter on "Citizenship" in *General Economic History* (Glencoe: The Free Press, 1950), pp. 315–338.

12. The pattern indicated by a comparison of the averages for each group of countries is sustained by the ranges (the high and low extremes) for each index. Most of the ranges overlap; that is, some countries which are in the "less democratic" category are higher on any given index than some which are "more democratic." It is noteworthy that in both Europe and Latin America, the nations which are lowest on any of the indices presented in the table are also in the "less democratic" category. Conversely, almost all countries which rank at the top of any of the indices are in the "more democratic" class.

13. See John Dewey, *Democracy and Education* (New York: Macmillan, 1916).

reference to South America, "education, if it does not make men good citizens, makes it at least easier for them to become so."[14] Education presumably broadens man's outlook, enables him to understand the need for norms of tolerance, restrains him from adhering to extremist doctrines, and increases his capacity to make rational electoral choices.

The evidence on the contribution of education to democracy is even more direct and strong on the level of individual behavior *within* countries than it is in cross-national correlations. Data gathered by public opinion research agencies which have questioned people in different countries about their beliefs on tolerance for the opposition, their attitudes toward ethnic or racial minorities, and their feelings for multi-party as against one-party systems have showed that the most important single factor differentiating those giving democratic responses from the others has been education. The higher one's education, the more likely one is to believe in democratic values and support democratic practices.[15] All the rele-

vant studies indicate that education is more significant than either income or occupation.

These findings should lead us to anticipate a far higher correlation between national levels of education and political practice than we in fact find. Germany and France have been among the best educated nations of Europe, but this by itself did not stabilize their democracies.[16] It may be, however, that their educational level has served to inhibit other antidemocratic forces.

If we cannot say that a "high" level of education is a *sufficient* condition for democracy, the available evidence suggests that it comes close to being a *necessary* one. In Latin America, where widespread illiteracy still exists, only one of all the nations in which more than half the population is illiterate—Brazil—can be included in the "more democratic" group. . . .

Although the evidence has been presented separately, all the various aspects of economic development—industrialization, urbanization,

14. James Bryce, *South America: Observations and Impressions* (New York: Macmillan, 1912), p. 546. Bryce considered several classes of conditions in South America which affected the chances for democracy, some of which are substantially the same as those presented here. The physical conditions of a country determined the ease of communications between areas, and thus the ease of formation of a "common public opinion." By "racial" conditions Bryce really meant whether there was ethnic homogeneity or not, with the existence of different ethnic or language groups preventing that "homogeneity and solidarity of the community which are almost indispensable conditions to the success of democratic government." Economic and social conditions included economic development, widespread political participation, and literacy. Bryce also detailed the specific historical factors which, over and above these "general" factors, operated in each South American country. See James Bryce, *op. cit.*, pp. 527–533 and 580 ff. See also Karl Mannheim, *Freedom, Power and Democratic Planning* (New York: Oxford University Press, 1950).

15. See G. H. Smith, "Liberalism and Level of Information," *Journal of Educational Psychology*, 39 (1948), pp. 65–82; Martin A. Trow, *Right Wing Radicalism and Political Intolerance* (Ph.D. thesis, Department of Sociology, Columbia University, 1957), p. 17; Samuel A. Stouffer, *Communism, Conformity, and Civil Liberties* (New York: Doubleday & Co., Inc., 1955); Kotaro Kido and Masataka Sugi, "A Report of Research on Social Stratification and Mobility in Tokyo" (III), *Japanese Sociological Review*, 4 (1954), pp. 74–100. This point is also discussed in Chap. 4.

16. Dewey has suggested that the character of the educational system will influence its effect on democracy, and this may shed some light on the sources of instability in Germany. The purpose of German education, according to Dewey, writing in 1916, was one of "disciplinary training rather than of personal development." The main aim was to produce "absorption of the aims and meaning of existing institutions," and "thoroughgoing subordination" to them. This point raises issues which cannot be entered into here, but indicates the complex character of the relationship between democracy and closely related factors, such as education. See John Dewey, *op. cit.*, pp. 108–110.

wealth, and education—are so closely inter-related as to form one major factor which has the political correlate of democracy.[18] ...

Economic development, producing increased income, greater economic security, and widespread higher education, largely determines the form of the "class struggle," by permitting those in the lower strata to develop longer time perspectives and more complex and gradualist views of politics. A belief in secular reformist gradualism can be the ideology of only a relatively well-to-do lower class. Striking evidence for this thesis may be found in the relationship between the patterns of working-class political action in different countries and the national income, a correlation that is almost startling in view of the many other cultural, historical, and juridical factors which affect the political life of nations.

In the two wealthiest countries, the United States and Canada, not only are communist parties almost nonexistent but socialist parties have never been able to establish themselves as major forces. Among the eight next wealthiest countries—New Zealand, Switzerland, Sweden, United Kingdom, Denmark, Australia, Norway, Belgium, Luxembourg and Netherlands—all of whom had a per capita income of over $500 a year in 1949 (the last year for which standardized United Nations statistics exist), moderate socialism predominates as the form of leftist politics. In none of these countries did the Communists secure more than 7 percent of the vote, and the actual Communist party average among them has been about 4 percent. In the eight European countries which were below the $500 per capita income mark in 1949—France, Iceland, Czechoslovakia, Finland, West Germany, Hungary, Italy, and Austria—and which have had at least one postwar democratic election in which both communist and noncommunist parties could compete, the Communist party has had more than 16 percent of the vote in six, and an over-all average of more than 20 percent in the eight countries as a group. The two low-income countries in which the Communists are weak—Germany and Austria—have both had direct experience with Soviet occupation.[24]

Leftist extremism has also dominated working-class politics in two other European nations which belong to the under $500 per capita income group—Spain and Greece. In Spain before Franco, anarchism and left socialism were much stronger than moderate socialism; while in Greece, whose per capita income in 1949 was only $128, the Communists have always been much stronger than the socialists, and fellow-traveling parties have secured a large vote in recent years.[25]

---

18. This statement is a "statistical" statement, which necessarily means that there will be many exceptions to the correlation. Thus we know that poorer people are more likely to vote for the Democratic or Labor parties in the U.S. and England. The fact that a large minority of the lower strata vote for the more conservative party in these countries does not challenge the proposition that stratification position is a main determinant of party choice.

---

24. It should be noted that before 1933–34, Germany had one of the largest Communist parties in Europe; while the Socialist party of Austria was the most left-wing and Marxist European party in the Socialist International.

25. Greece, economically the poorest political democracy in Europe, "is now the only country in Europe where there is no socialist party. The Socialist party (ELD), established in 1945 by individuals who collaborated with the Communists during the Occupation, dissolved itself in August 1953, a victim of its fickle and pro-Communist policy. The whole field was then surrendered to the Communists with the justification that conditions were not mature enough for the development of a socialist movement!" Manolis Korakas, "Grecian Apathy," *Socialist Commentary*, May 1957, p. 21; in the elections of May 11, 1958, the "Communist directed" Union of the Democratic Left won 78 out of 300 parliamentary seats and is now the second largest party in the country. See *New York Times*, May 16, 1958, p. 3, col. 4.

The inverse relationship between national economic development as reflected by per capita income and the strength of Communists and other extremist groups among Western nations is seemingly stronger than the correlations between other national variables like ethnic or religious factors.[26] Two of the poorer nations with large Communist movements—Iceland and Finland—are Scandinavian and Lutheran. Among the Catholic nations of Europe, all the poor ones except Austria have large Communist or anarchist movements. The two wealthiest Catholic democracies—Belgium and Luxembourg—have few Communists. Though the French and Italian cantons of Switzerland are strongly affected by the cultural life of France and Italy, there are almost no Communists among the workers in these cantons, living in the wealthiest country in Europe.

The relation between low per capita wealth and the precipitation of sufficient discontent to provide the social basis for political extremism is supported by a recent comparative polling survey of the attitudes of citizens of nine countries. Among these countries, feelings of personal security correlated with per capita income (.45) and with per capita food supply (.55). If satisfaction with one's country, as measured by responses to the question, "Which country in the world gives you the best chance of living the kind of life you would like to live?" is used as an index of the amount of discontent in a nation, then the relationship with economic wealth is even higher. The study reports a rank order correlation of .74 between per capita income and the degree of satisfaction with one's own country.[27]

This does not mean that economic hardship or poverty *per se* is the main cause of radicalism. There is much evidence to sustain the argument that stable poverty in a situation in which individuals are not exposed to the possibilities of change breeds, if anything, conservatism.[28] Individuals whose experience limits their significant communications and interaction to others on the same level as themselves will, other conditions being equal, be more conservative than people who may be better off but who have been exposed to the possibilities of securing a better way of life.[29] The dynamic in the situation would seem to be exposure to the possibility of a better way of life rather than poverty as such. As Karl Marx put it in a perceptive passage: "A house may be large or small; as long as the surrounding houses are equally small it satisfies all social demands for a dwelling. But if a palace arises beside the little house, the little house shrinks into a hut."[30]

With the growth of modern means of communication and transportation both within and among countries, it seems increasingly likely that the groups in the population that are poverty-stricken but are isolated from knowledge of better ways of life or unaware of the possibilities for

---

26. The relationship expressed above can be presented in another way. The seven European countries in which Communist or fellow-traveling parties have secured large votes in free elections had an average per capita income in 1949 of $330. The ten European countries in which the Communists have been a failure electorally had an average per capita income of $585.

27. William Buchanan and Hadley Cantril, *How Nations See Each Other* (Urbana: University of Illinois Press, 1953), p. 35.

28. See Emile Durkheim, *Suicide: A Study in Sociology* (Glencoe: The Free Press, 1951), pp. 253–254; see also Daniel Bell, "The Theory of Mass Society," *Commentary*, 22 (1956), p. 80.

29. There is also a considerable body of evidence which indicates that those occupations which are economically vulnerable and those workers who have experienced unemployment are prone to be more leftist in their outlook. See Chap. 7, pp. 242–249.

30. Karl Marx, "Wage-Labor and Capital," in *Selected Works*, Vol. I (New York: International Publishers, 1933), pp. 268–269. "Social tensions are an expression of unfulfilled expectations," Daniel Bell, *op. cit.*, p. 80.

improvement in their condition are becoming rarer and rarer, particularly in the urban areas of the Western world. One may expect to find such stable poverty only in tradition-dominated societies.

Since position in a stratification system is always relative and gratification or deprivation is experienced in terms of being better or worse off than other people, it is not surprising that the lower classes in all countries, regardless of the wealth of the country, show various signs of resentment against the existing distribution of rewards by supporting political parties and other organizations which advocate some form of redistribution.[31] The fact that the form which these political parties take in poorer countries is more extremist and radical than it is in wealthier ones is probably more related to the greater degree of inequality in such countries than to the fact that their poor are actually poorer in absolute terms. A comparative study of wealth distribution by the United Nations "suggest[s] that the richest fraction of the population (the richest 10th, 5th, etc.) generally receive[s] a greater proportion of the total income in the less developed than in the more developed countries."[32] The

gap between the income of professional and semiprofessional personnel on the one hand and ordinary workers on the other is much wider in the poorer than in the wealthier countries. Among manual workers, "there seems to be a greater wage discrepancy between skilled and unskilled workers in the less developed countries. In contrast the leveling process, in several of the developed countries at least, has been facilitated by the over-all increase of national income ... not so much by reduction of the income of the relatively rich as by the faster growth of the incomes of the relatively poor."[33]

The distribution of consumption goods also tends to become more equitable as the size of national income increases. The wealthier a country, the larger the proportion of its population which owns automobiles, telephones, bathtubs, refrigerating equipment, and so forth. Where there is a dearth of goods, the sharing of such goods must inevitably be less equitable than in a country in which there is relative abundance. For example, the number of people who can

---

31. A summary of the findings of election studies in many countries shows that, with few exceptions, there is a strong relationship between lower social position and support of "leftist" politics. There are, of course, many other characteristics which are also related to left voting, some of which are found among relatively well paid but socially isolated groups. Among the population as a whole, men are much more likely to vote for the left than women, while members of minority religious and ethnic groups also display a leftist tendency. . . .

32. *United Nations Preliminary Report on the World Social Situation* (New York: 1952), pp. 132–133. Gunnar Myrdal, the Swedish economist, has recently pointed out: "It is, indeed, a regular occurrence endowed almost with the dignity of an economic law that the poorer the country, the greater the difference between poor and rich." *An International Economy* (New York: Harper & Bros., 1956), p. 133.

33. *United Nations Preliminary Report . . . , ibid.* (See also Table II.) A recently completed comparison of income distribution in the United States and a number of western European countries concludes that "there has not been any great difference" in patterns of income distribution among these countries. These findings of Robert Solow appear to contradict those reported above from the U.N. Statistics Office, although the latter are dealing primarily with differences between industrialized and underdeveloped nations. In any case, it should be noted that Solow agrees that the relative position of the lower strata in a poor as compared with a wealthy country is quite different. As he states, "in comparing Europe and America, one may ask whether it makes sense to talk about relative income inequality independently of the absolute level of income. An income four times another income has different content according as the lower income means malnutrition on the one hand or provides some surplus on the other." Robert M. Solow, *A Survey of Income Inequality Since the War* (Stanford: Center for Advanced Study in the Behavioral Sciences, 1958, mimeographed), pp. 41–44, 78.

afford automobiles, washing machines, decent housing, telephones, good clothes, or have their children complete high school or go to college still represents only a small minority of the population in many European countries. The great national wealth of the United States or Canada, or even to a lesser extent the Australasian Dominions or Sweden, means that there is relatively little difference between the standards of living of adjacent social classes, and that even classes which are far apart in the social structure will enjoy more nearly similar consumption patterns than will comparable classes in Southern Europe. To a Southern European, and to an even greater extent to the inhabitant of one of the "underdeveloped" countries, social stratification is characterized by a much greater distinction in ways of life, with little overlap in the goods the various strata own or can afford to purchase. It may be suggested, therefore, that the wealthier a country, the less is status inferiority experienced as a major source of deprivation.

Increased wealth and education also serve democracy by increasing the lower classes' exposure to cross-pressures which reduce their commitment to given ideologies and make them less receptive to extremist ones. The operation of this process will be discussed in more detail in the next chapter, but it means involving those strata in an integrated national culture as distinct from an isolated lower-class one.

Marx believed that the proletariat was a revolutionary force because it had nothing to lose but its chains and could win the whole world. But Tocqueville, analyzing the reasons why the lower strata in America supported the system, paraphrased and transposed Marx before Marx ever made his analysis by pointing out that "only those who have nothing to lose ever revolt."[34]

Increased wealth also affects the political role of the middle class by changing the shape of the stratification structure from an elongated pyramid, with a large lower-class base, to a diamond with a growing middle class. A large middle class tempers conflict by rewarding moderate and democratic parties and penalizing extremist groups.

The political values and style of the upper class, too, are related to national income. The poorer a country and the lower the absolute standard of living of the lower classes, the greater the pressure on the upper strata to treat the lower as vulgar, innately inferior, a lower caste beyond the pale of human society. The sharp difference in the style of living between those at the top and those at the bottom makes this psychologically necessary. Consequently, the upper strata in such a situation tend to regard political rights for the lower strata, particularly the right to share power, as essentially absurd and immoral. The upper strata not only resist democracy themselves; their often arrogant political behavior serves to intensify extremist reactions on the part of the lower classes.

The general income level of a nation also affects its receptivity to democratic norms. If there is enough wealth in the country so that it does not make too much difference whether some redistribution takes place, it is easier to accept the idea that it does not matter greatly which side is in power. But if loss of office means serious losses for major power groups, they will seek to retain or secure office by any means available. A certain amount of national wealth is likewise necessary to ensure a competent civil service. The poorer the country, the greater the emphasis on nepotism—support of kin and friends. And this in turn reduces the opportunity to develop the efficient bureaucracy which a modern democratic state requires.[35]

---

34. Alexis de Tocqueville, *Democracy in America*, Vol. I (New York: Alfred A. Knopf, Vintage ed., 1945), p. 258.

35. For a discussion of this problem in a new state, see David Apter, *The Gold Coast in Transition* (Princeton: Princeton University Press, 1955), esp. Chaps. 9 and 13. Apter shows the importance of efficient bureaucracy, and the acceptance of bureaucratic values and behavior patterns for the existence of a democratic political order.

Intermediary organizations which act as sources of countervailing power seem to be similarly associated with national wealth. Tocqueville and other exponents of what has come to be known as the theory of the "mass society"[36] have argued that a country without a multitude of organizations relatively independent of the central state power has a high dictatorial as well as revolutionary potential. Such organizations serve a number of functions: they inhibit the state or any single source of private power from dominating all political resources; they are a source of new opinions; they can be the means of communicating ideas, particularly opposition ideas, to a large section of the citizenry; they train men in political skills and so help to increase the level of interest and participation in politics. Although there are no reliable data on the relationship between national patterns of voluntary organization and national political systems, evidence from studies of individual behavior demonstrates that, regardless of other factors, men who belong to associations are more likely than others to give the democratic answer to questions concerning tolerance and party systems, to vote, or to participate actively in politics. Since the more well-to-do and better educated a man is, the more likely he is to belong to voluntary organizations, the propensity to form such groups seems to be a function of level of income and opportunities for leisure within given nations.[37]

. . .

It is obvious that the conditions related to stable democracy discussed here are most readily found in the countries of northwest Europe and their English-speaking offspring in America and Australasia; and it has been suggested, by Weber

36. See Emil Lederer, *The State of the Masses* (New York: Norton, 1940); Hannah Arendt, *Origins of Totalitarianism* (New York: Harcourt, Brace & Co., 1951); Max Horkheimer, *Eclipse of Reason* (New York: Oxford University Press, 1947); Karl Mannheim, *Man and Society in an Age of Reconstruction* (New York: Harcourt, Brace & Co., 1940); Philip Selznick, *The Organizational Weapon* (New York: McGraw-Hill Book Co., 1952), José Ortega y Gasset, *The Revolt of the Masses* (New York: Norton, 1932); William Kornhauser, *The Politics of Mass Society* (Glencoe: The Free Press, 1959).

37. See Edward Banfield, *The Moral Basis of a Backward Society* (Glencoe: The Free Press, 1958), for an excellent description of the way in which abysmal poverty serves to reduce community organization in southern Italy. The data which do exist from polling surveys conducted in the United States, Germany, France, Great Britain, and Sweden show that somewhere between 40 and 50 per cent of the adults in these countries belong to voluntary associations, without lower rates of membership for the less stable democracies, France and Germany, than among the more stable ones, the United States, Great Britain, and Sweden. These results seemingly challenge the general proposition, although no definite conclusion can be made, since most of the studies employed noncomparable categories. This point bears further research in many countries. For the data on these countries see the following studies.

For France, see Arnold Rose, *Theory and Method in the Social Sciences* (Minneapolis, University of Minnesota Press, 1954), p. 74 and O. R. Gallagher, "Voluntary Associations in France," *Social Forces*, 36 (1957), pp. 154–156; for Germany see Erich Reigrotzki, *Soziale Verflechtungen in der Bundesrepublik* (Tübingen: J. D. B. Mohr, 1956), p. 164; for the U.S. see Charles L. Wright and Herbert H. Hyman, "Voluntary Association Memberships of American Adults: Evidence from National Sample Surveys," *American Sociological Review*, 23 (1958), p. 287, J. C. Scott, Jr., "Membership and Participation in Voluntary Associations," *American Sociological Review*, 22 (1957), pp. 315–326 and Herbert Maccoby, "The Differential Political Activity of Participants in a Voluntary Association," *American Sociological Review*, 23 (1958), pp. 524–533; for Great Britain see Mass Observation, *Puzzled People* (London: Victor Gollancz, 1947), p. 119 and Thomas Bottomore, "Social Stratification in Voluntary Organizations," in David Glass, ed., *Social Mobility in Britain* (Glencoe: The Free Press, 1954), p. 354; for Sweden see Gunnar Heckscher, "Pluralist Democracy: The Swedish Experience," *Social Research*, 15 (1948), pp. 417–461.

among others, that a historically unique concatenation of elements produced both democracy and capitalism in this area. Capitalist economic development, the basic argument runs, had its greatest opportunity in a Protestant society and created the burgher class whose existence was both a catalyst and a necessary condition for democracy. Protestantism's emphasis on individual responsibility furthered the emergence of democratic values in these countries and resulted in an alignment between the burghers and the throne which preserved the monarchy and extended the acceptance of democracy among the conservative strata. Men may question whether any aspect of this interrelated cluster of economic development, Protestantism, monarchy, gradual political change, legitimacy, and democracy is primary, but the fact remains that the cluster does hang together.[44] ...

---

44. In introducing historical events as part of the analysis of factors *external* to the political system, which are part of the causal nexus in which democracy is involved, I am following in good sociological and even functionalist tradition. As Radcliffe-Brown has well put it: "... one 'explanation' of a social system will be its history, where we know it—the detailed account of how it came to be what it is and where it is. Another 'explanation' of the same system is obtained by showing ... that it is a special exemplification of laws of social psychology or social functioning. The two kinds of explanation do not conflict but supplement one another." A. R. Radcliffe-Brown, "On the Concept of Function in Social Science," *American Anthropologist*, New Series, 37 (1935), p. 401; see also Max Weber, *The Methodology of the Social Sciences* (Glencoe: The Free Press, 1949), pp. 164–188, for a detailed discussion of the role of historical analysis in sociological research.

Social Revolutions in the Modern World

Theda Skocpol

I. Social Origins: An Analytic Summary[5]

A. The Moral of the Story

[Barrington Moore's] *Social Origins of Dictatorship and Democracy* is not organized or written in the style of a scientist trying to elaborate clearly and minutely justify a falsifiable *theory* of comparative modernization. It is, rather, like a giant mural painted in words, in which a man who has contemplated the modern histories of eight major nations seeks to convey in broad strokes the moral and factual discoveries that he personally has made, about the various routes to the "world of modern industry" traveled by his "subject" countries, about the roles of landed upper classes and peasantries in the politics of that transformation, and about the consequences of each route for human freedom and societal rationality. For Professor Moore's purpose in writing *Social Origins* is as much moral as theoretical—and it is important that he sees no contradiction between these purposes....

... Professor Moore argues in *Social Origins* that because in

any society the dominant groups are the ones with the most to hide about the way the society works.... [V]ery often ... truthful analyses are bound to have a critical ring, to seem like exposures rather than objective statements, as the term is conventionally used [to denote "mild-mannered statements in favor of the *status quo* ..."].... For all students of human society, sympathy with the victims of historical processes and

skepticism about the victors' claims provide essential safeguards against being taken in by the dominant mythology. A scholar who tries to be objective needs these feelings as part of his ordinary working equipment.[7]

What is the particular truthful message with a critical ring that *Social Origins* attempts to convey? I believe it is the conclusion that "the evidence from the comparative history of modernization" tells us that "the costs of moderation have been at least as atrocious as those of revolution, perhaps a great deal more."[8] This conclusion is argued by Moore in several ways. First, in assessing the evidence of British history, he emphasizes the *legal* violent suffering inflicted on peasants by the enclosure movements; second, in discussing the Indian case, Moore emphasizes the costs in popular suffering of "democratic stagnation," or modernization forgone. Finally, and I believe most important, Moore organizes *Social Origins* around three main "Routes to the modern world," and devotes considerable effort to demonstrating that each has contained a roughly equivalent measure of popular suffering and large-scale collective violence. "A pox on all their houses" is the message about modes of modernization, and the organizing framework of *Social Origins* functions more to facilitate the exposition of this moral conclusion than to clarify or test the (basically Marxist) conceptions of social change and political process which informed Moore's interpretation of "the facts," which to him dictated that moral conclusion.

Excerpted from: Theda Skocpol, *Social Revolutions in the Modern World*. Cambridge: Cambridge University Press, 1994. © Cambridge University Press, 1994. Reprinted with the permission of Cambridge University Press.

5. Reading the following analytic summary is no substitute for reading *Social Origins* itself. The summary presupposes acquaintance with the book.

7. Pp. 522–523. All page number references for quotes are to Barrington Moore, Jr., *Social Origins of Dictatorship and Democracy* (Boston: Beacon Press, 1966). A paperback edition was published by Beacon Press in 1967; pagination is the same as in the hardback edition.

8. Ibid., p. 505.

B.   The Theoretical Argument

Social Origins, in the words of its author,

endeavors to explain the varied political roles played
by the landed upper classes and the peasantry in the
transformation from agrarian societies ... to modern
industrial ones.... [I]t is an attempt to discover the
range of historical conditions under which either or
both of these rural groups have become important
forces behind the emergence of Western parliamentary
versions of democracy, and dictatorships of the right
and the left, that is, fascist and communist regimes.[9]

The book is organized around the discussion of
three distinct Routes to the modern world, each
culminating in one of the three societal political
outcomes that interest Moore: Western democracy, fascism, and communist dictatorship.[10]
The class structures of "agrarian states" under-
going the initial stages of economic modernization are linked to alternate political outcomes via
critical political events analyzed as class struggles: "bourgeois revolution" in the case of the
three societies that ended up as Western parliamentary democracies (Britain, France, the
U.S.A.); "revolution from above" in the case of
societies that ended up as fascist dictatorships

(Germany, Japan); and "peasant revolution" in
the case of the societies (Russia, China) that became Communist dictatorships. Two of Moore's
Routes—the Communist and the "Capitalist
Reactionary (or Fascist)"—represent genuine
theoretical constructs in that they identify patterns of (a) initial class structure, (b) revolutionary political conflict, *and* (c) ultimate systemic
political outcome that Moore argues apply to
both of the two societies classified in each Route.
The "Bourgeois Route," on the other hand, is
actually a residual category defined only by the
twentieth-century political system ("Western
democracy") common to its "members." Britain,
France, and the United States, as Moore
emphasizes, started the modernizing process
with very different social structures; and the political upheavals these societies underwent during modernization—the English Civil War, the
French Revolution, and the American Civil
War—were characterized by very different concrete patterns of class struggle. Moore labels
each of these conflicts "bourgeois revolution,"
but admits that he does so in each case primarily
because the conflict in question contributed crucially to the eventual establishment of "bourgeois democracy," not because any one of them
constituted simply or mainly a political offensive
of a "rising bourgeoisie." Insofar as any theoretically significant common causal pattern is
identified as characteristic of the three "bourgeois revolutions," it is "the development of a
group in society with an independent economic
base, which attacks obstacles to a democratic
version of capitalism that have been inherited
from the past."[11] In this respect, Moore emphasizes the role of commercial agrarians—gentry
in the English Civil War, rich peasants in the
French Revolution, and commercial farmers in
the American Civil War.

Moore (rather nonsystematically) elaborates
and interrelates *three key variables* in order to
explain (a) differences among the sequences

---

9. Ibid., p. xi.

10. India does not fit well into the theoretical analysis
that Moore presents for the three main Routes; hence,
I shall have little to say about that case account in
this essay. Both India's inclusion in the book, and its
classification as a "democracy" seem dubious to me.
And Moore's conclusions about India are entirely
equivocal.

Since the United States was never an agrarian bureaucracy or a feudal society, it does not fit well into
the overall explanatory scheme of *Social Origins* either.
I believe that Moore badly twisted the facts of American history in order to present the Civil War as a
"bourgeois revolution." Lee Benson has made a basically sound (though overly rancorous) argument to this
effect in his *Toward the Scientific Study of History*
(Philadelphia: J. B. Lippincott, 1972), chap. 8, and I
will not repeat what would be a similar argument in
this essay.

11. *Social Origins*, p. xv.

characteristic of the major Routes, and (b) differences among the "Bourgeois Revolution" cases. His overall "explanation sketch" seems so nonsystematic not only because he fails to define variables and spell out their roles in explaining sequences of structures and events, but also because so much of *Social Origins* is taken up by case accounts for individual countries. This fact has even led one reviewer to assert that Moore's method is "idiographic"! However, appearances can be very deceptive: what Moore really does in the case analyses is to interpret available secondary materials in a way that makes his explanatory and moral concepts seem plausible. It is those concepts that I am attempting to make explicit in this review.

The first key variable is the strength of a bourgeois or commercial impulse. Some degree of commercialization—which for Moore seems to mean *growth of urban-based commodity markets*—is asserted to be operating to undermine and destabilize each agrarian state that Moore discusses. Just as a "rising bourgeoisie" is the prime mover, itself not moved, in virtually every Marxist account of European modernization, so in *Social Origins*, commercialization is an unexplained given. But degrees of strength of the commercial or bourgeois impulse are differentiated and function as the one variable which both cuts across and differentiates all three Routes. According to Moore, "Bourgeois Revolution" countries (seventeenth-century England, eighteenth-century France, nineteenth-century U.S.) are characterized by the presence of a "strong" bourgeois impulse at an early stage of modernization (though the "strong" bourgeois impulse is weakest in France); the bourgeois impulse is of "medium" strength in early modernizing (late eighteenth–mid-nineteenth century) Germany and Japan; and is "weak" in late nineteenth-century China and Russia (and twentieth-century India).

An old-fashioned Marxist might proceed directly from assertions about the strength of the bourgeoisie in relation to other classes to the

explanation of patterns and outcomes of class-conflict political struggles (e.g., strong bourgeois impulse → politically aggressive bourgeoisie → bourgeois revolution). But, for Moore, agrarian strata are the strategic actors in the political revolutions from above or below which create the conditions for the development of various forms of political institutions in industrial societies. Therefore, he must identify variables which can explain agrarian strata's (a) political propensities (pro- or anti-liberal/democratic) and (b) opportunities for extra-agrarian class alliances.

The one general pattern of cross-class alliance that Moore discusses is alliance between agrarian and urban upper classes:

The coalitions and countercoalitions that have arisen ... across these two groups have constituted and in some parts of the world still constitute the basic framework and environment of political action, forming the series of opportunities, temptations, and impossibilities within which political leaders have had to act.[12]

Here the critical thing seems to be the "strength" of the bourgeoisie: if it is "strong," it will set the cultural and political "tone" of any coalition with a landed upper class (i.e., as in England, according to Moore) *no matter who actually holds political office*; if it is only of "medium" strength, the landed upper class will set the tone.

As for the political propensities and capacities of agrarian strata, Moore's elaboration and application to case analyses of two remaining key variables—(1) the form of commercial agriculture: "labor-repressive" versus "market," and (2) "peasant revolutionary potential"—constitute the core of *Social Origins'* analyses of the politics of modernization.

For any Marxist:

It is always the direct relationship of the owners of the conditions of production to the direct producers ... [t]he specific form in which unpaid surplus labor is

_____

12. Ibid., p. 423.

pumped out of the direct producers ... which reveals the innermost secret, the hidden basis of the entire social structure, and with it the political form of the relation of sovereignty and dependence, in short, the corresponding specific form of the state.[13]

Yet Marx himself concentrated on analyzing the capitalist-proletarian relationship, and most Marxist writers since have been content to contrast the exploitative relationship under capitalism (capitalist-worker) with a generic "feudal" lord-peasant exploitative relationship, without attempting to come to grips with the various producer-surplus-controller relationships found in commercial agricultures. It is this task that Moore tackles by drawing a distinction between "labor-repressive" and "market" forms of commercial agriculture:

The form of commercial agriculture ... [is] just as important as commercialization itself....[14]

There are certain forms of capitalist transformation in the countryside that may succeed economically, in the sense of yielding good profits, but which are for fairly obvious reasons unfavorable to the growth of free institutions of the nineteenth-century Western variety....

The distinction I am trying to suggest is one between the *use of political mechanisms* (using the term "political" broadly ... [to include "traditional relationships and attitudes" used by landlords]) on the one hand and *reliance on the labor market*, on the other hand, to ensure an adequate labor force for working the soil and the creation of an agricultural surplus for consumption by other classes.[15]

The "labor-repressive"- versus "market"-commercial agriculture distinction stands at the heart of the explanation of different patterns and outcomes of modernization offered in *Social Origins*. "Market" commercialization created crucial agrarian political allies for "strong" bourgeoisies in England and the (Northern)

United States. In contrast, "labor-repressive agrarian systems provide[d] an unfavorable soil for the growth of democracy and [if peasant revolution failed and a moderately strong bourgeoisie existed] an important part of the institutional complex leading to fascism."[16] Why? Moore gives us two main reasons: First:

While a system of labor-repressive agriculture may be started in opposition to the central authority, it is likely to fuse with the monarchy at a later point in search of political support. This situation can also lead to the preservation of a military ethic among the nobility in a manner unfavorable to the growth of democratic institutions.[17]

Second:

At a later stage in the course of modernization, a new and crucial factor is likely to appear in the form of a rough working coalition between influential sectors of the landed upper classes and the emerging commercial and manufacturing interests.[18]

Industrial development may proceed rapidly under such auspices. But the outcome, after a brief and unstable period of democracy has been fascism.[19]

Finally, let me introduce the third key variable, "peasant revolutionary potential." "Reactionary Capitalist" modernization is possible,

---

13. Karl Marx, *Capital*, Vol. 3 (New York: International Publishers, 1967; originally published, 1894), p. 791.

14. *Social Origins*, p. 420.

15. Ibid., pp. 433–434, italics added. Moore explicitly *excludes* from the category "labor-repressive" agriculture: (1) family farming; (2) "a system of hired agricultural laborers where the workers ... [have] considerable real freedom to refuse jobs and move about ..."; and (3) "precommercial and pre-industrial agrarian systems ... if there is a rough balance between the overlord's contribution to justice and security and the cultivators' contribution in the form of crops" (pp. 434–435). Strictly speaking, it seems to me, (3) should not even be relevant, since the "labor-repressive" versus "market" distinction refers only to commercial agricultures.

16. Ibid., p. 435.

17. Ibid.

18. Ibid., p. 436.

19. Ibid., p. xvi.

Table 2.1
Categories and explanatory variable clusters in Barrington Moore's *Social Origins of Dictatorship and Democracy*

	Route one "Bourgeois revolution"		Route two "Reactionary capitalism"	Route three "Communism"
Common starting point* (except U.S.A.)	Agrarian bureaucracy		Agrarian bureaucracy	Agrarian bureaucracy
Key variable clusters				
Bourgeois impulse	Strong	Strong	Medium-strength	Weak
Mode of commercial agriculture	Market	Labor-repressive	Labor-repressive	Labor-repressive
Peasant revolutionary potential	Low	High	Low	High
Critical political event	Bourgeois revolution		Revolution from above	Peasant revolution
Major systemic political outcome	Democratic capitalism		Fascism	Communist dictatorship
Cases	Britain U.S.A.	France	Germany Japan	Russia China

*[P]owerful central governments that we can loosely call royal absolutisms or agrarian bureaucracies established themselves in the sixteenth and seventeenth centuries in all the major countries examined in connection with this study (except of course the United States).... [T]he fact forms a convenient if partly arbitrary peg upon which to hang the beginnings of modernization" (*Social Origins*, p. 417).

according to Moore's analysis, only if both "bourgeois" and peasant revolution from below fail to occur. Peasants provide much of the insurrectionary force in both types of revolution. This leads Moore to ask: "what kinds of social structure and historical situations produce peasant revolutions and which ones inhibit or prevent them[?]"[20] A very basic condition for any social revolution, he concludes, is that "commercialization" in an agrarian state must be of such a (moderate or low) strength and form as to leave peasant society basically intact, but "impaired." Beyond that, the interaction of several factors determines whether the peasantry will have a "strong or weak revolutionary potential." Factors conducive[21] to strong potential are: weak and "exploitative"[22] ties to a landed upper class

which is not making (or promoting) a successful transition to modern industrialism; and a "radical" form of peasant community solidarity (where "institutional arrangements are such as to spread grievances through the peasant community...").[23] Factors tending to produce weak revolutionary potential are: strong ties to the

20. Ibid., p. 453.

21. *All* "conducive factors" need not be present in any particular case of peasant revolution, according to Moore's argument.

22. On pp. 470–473 of *Social Origins*, Moore develops what I consider to be a naive functionalist definition of "exploitation" in landlord-peasant relationships. He holds that one can objectively measure whether lords (in precommercial agrarian systems) are performing valuable services for "the community" in return for the surpluses they claim. But Moore overlooks the fact that any upper class quite *un*manipulatively creates through its own existence and activities many of the problems that it simultaneously overcomes in "service" to "the community." Thus, if feudal lords had not been wont to fight among themselves, "their" peasants would not have needed the protection for which they supposedly "gave" their surpluses in "fair exchange"!

23. Ibid., p. 475.

landed upper class, and weak peasant community solidarity, or else a "conservative" form of solidarity (which ties "those with actual and potential grievances into the prevailing social structure").[24] Finally, Moore points out that potentially revolutionary peasants must have non-peasant allies to succeed, but he is not able to provide a general formula for ascertaining who they might be. Still, what made the French Revolution "bourgeois," according to Moore's analysis, was the fact that a peasantry with a significant rich peasant element was able to find Third Estate allies; combined rich peasant and Third Estate interest in promoting private property precluded a collectivist outcome.[25]

Now that an analytic summary has been provided of the Routes and the key variables that Moore uses to explain differences among and within them, it may be helpful to the reader to provide at this point a schematic summary of what has been presented (table 2.1):

A word should be said about the kind of explanation that Moore appears to be attempting in *Social Origins*. Robert Somers aptly labels it "sequence analysis ... the systematic study of particular kinds of sequences of events that are assumed to have some kind of causal connection."[26]

The essence of ... [Moore's] argument [ ] ... is that certain combinations of factors make certain subsequent events more likely.... One wants to know: what are the antecedents or consequences of structure X? Weber has referred to the notion that once certain structures appear, the "die is cast," making it more likely that certain events will occur on the next roll of the dice.[27]

Significantly, Moore does not attain *complete* explanation (or anything approaching it): he tends to *assume* commercialization-flowing-into-industrialization, and focuses on determinants of political institutional outcomes. This really means that he does not explain the *process* of economic development per se, but instead identifies what seem to him probable sequences of three types of states or events—agrarian bureaucratic social structures, revolutions (from above or below), and "modern" political arrangements—with economic development assumed as the continuous process connecting and activating the sequence of structures and events....

---

24. Ibid., p. 476.

25. I am not going to have much to say about Moore's discussion of "peasant revolutionary potential" in the critical remarks which follow. For three reasons: first, I think Moore is basically on the right track in refusing to focus on peasants alone, or as an aggregate mass; instead, he considers both peasant community social structures and peasant ties to upper strata. Second, what differences I have with Moore on the peasant question stem from my alternative approach to social revolutions, viewed holistically, and those differences are spelled out in a paper delivered at the August 1973 meetings of the American Sociological Association in New York City. Finally, for the theoretical purposes of this paper, it is more important to criticize the way Moore handles upper-class relations to political processes.

26. Robert Somers, "Applications of an Expanded Survey Research Model to Comparative Institutional Studies," in Ivan Vallier, ed., *Comparative Methods in Sociology* (Berkeley and Los Angeles: University of California Press, 1971), p. 392.

27. Ibid., p. 389.

The Impact of Economic Development on Democracy

Evelyne Huber, Dietrich Rueschemeyer, and John D. Stephens

Methods, Theory, and Major Results

Any account of the social and economic conditions of democracy must come to terms with the central finding of the cross-national statistical research: a sturdy (though not perfect) association between economic development and democracy. But these correlations do not validate the theoretical accounts that have often been associated with them, in particular modernization theory. Nor do cross-sectional correlations allow us to make adequate inferences about causal sequence. Similar outcomes might be produced by a variety of factors and causal sequences.

To tackle these questions of causation, we adopted a strategy of analytic induction based on comparative historical research. This strategy is a case-based method of study, which builds on a theoretical framework that takes past research into account, and then proceeds by analyzing successive individual histories. In this way, this method gains information on historical sequence and can do justice to the particular historical context of each factor analyzed. Each case may modify both the specific hypotheses used in earlier analyses and the broader theoretical framework. The result is a range of cases interpreted by a single set of theoretical propositions and a progressively modified theory that is consistent with the cases studied. . . .

Our central thesis, and indeed our most basic finding, can now be stated in stark fashion: Capitalist development is related to democracy because it shifts the balance of class power, because it weakens the power of the landlord

Excerpted from: Evelyne Huber, Dietrich Rueschemeyer, and John D. Stephens, "The Impact of Economic Development on Democracy." *Journal of Economic Perspectives* 7, no. 3 (1993): 71–86. Reprinted by permission.

class and strengthens subordinate classes. The working and the middle classes—unlike other subordinate classes in history—gain an unprecedented capacity for self-organization due to such developments as urbanization, factory production, and new forms of communication and transportation.

This thesis negates other explanations. The primary link between capitalist development and democracy is not found in an expansion of the middle classes. Nor can the relationship be explained by the argument that more complex societies require a differentiated and flexible form of government, as modernization theory suggested. And finally democracy is not the creation of the bourgeoisie, the new dominant class of capital owners, as was claimed by both liberal and Marxist political theory. The bourgeoisie made important contributions to the move towards democracy by insisting on its share in political power in the form of parliamentary control of the state, but the bourgeoisie was also hostile to further democratization when its interests seemed threatened. In fact, one of the more important findings of our comparative research, which we did not fully anticipate, is that—especially in Latin America—the economically dominant classes accepted democracy only where their political interests were effectively protected by large parties of a conservative or non-ideological character. It is also important to note that the bourgeoisie often comes around to support democracy once it turns out that its interests can be protected within the system. . . .

The fact that class interests are historically constructed has crucial consequences for the analysis. It raises interclass relations to critical importance. One class may exercise hegemonic influence over another, and this will affect the alliance options among classes. The interests actually pursued by peasants and even by urban middle classes are often profoundly shaped by landlords, the bourgeoisie, and the state as well as state-affiliated churches. The alliance developments at the top—among landlords, bourgeoisie, and the state—can be decisive for the alliance options of other classes. This is of critical importance for the chances of democracy because the working class, even the European working class, was too weak on its own to succeed in the final push toward democracy with universal suffrage.

Democratic Transition and Breakdown in Europe and South America

In 1870, only one European country, Switzerland, was a democracy. Many countries frequently thought to be democratic at this time such as Britain, Netherlands, and Belgium, had parliamentary government and competitive party systems, but the electorate was limited by income or property qualifications. By contrast, by 1920, almost all Western European countries were fully democratic. This period of transition to democracy in Europe was also marked by the arrival of the organized working class. The change in the underlying class structure as indicated by labor force figures is significant enough: between 1870 and 1910, the non-agricultural workforce grew by one-third to one-half, eventually reaching an average of 61 percent of the total workforce in the 13 European countries we studied. The change at the level of class formation and class organization was even more significant: in 1870, in no country were the socialists a significant mass-based party, and the trade unions organized a minuscule proportion of the labor force. By the eve of World War I, the major socialist and labor parties garnered an average of 26 percent of the vote (despite suffrage restrictions in a number of countries) and the trade unions organized an average of 11 percent of the non-agricultural labor force. In the immediate postwar elections, the socialists' electoral share increased to an average of

32 percent, while trade union organizations grew spectacularly, increasing two and a half times. The organized working class was also the most consistently pro-democratic force in the period under consideration: at the onset of World War I, European labor movements had converged on an ideology which placed the achievement of universal suffrage and parliamentary government at the center of their program (Zolberg, 1986)....

Does Latin America show similar developments? Patterns for large land-holding and the existence of a powerful class of landlords with a need for a large cheap labor force also posed significant problems for democracy in South America. Breakthroughs to full democracy before the 1970s, even if temporary, were only possible where the large landowners were primarily engaged in ranching and thus had lower labor needs (Argentina and Uruguay), or where their economic power was undermined or counterbalanced by the presence of a strong mining export sector (Venezuela and Bolivia).

Like its counterpart in Europe, the bourgeoisie was not a promoter of full democracy in South America. As in Europe, the forces pushing for democracy were the organized segments of the subordinate classes, but the leadership roles were reversed. In South America the middle classes were the driving force, but they mainly promoted their own inclusion and thus often accepted restricted forms of democracy. For full democracy to be installed, the middle classes had to be dependent on working class support in their push for democracy, and they had to receive support from a working class which had some measure of strength....

The political history of 20th century Latin America is characterized by numerous breakthroughs to restricted or full democracies, then followed by breakdowns of democracy. Essentially, the economically dominant classes tolerated democracy only as long as what they perceived to be their vital interests were protected. Where the capacity of the state or political parties to channel and contain militant action of subordinate classes declined, economic elites turned to the military in search of allies to replace the democratic with authoritarian regimes.

... The position of South American countries in the world economy as late and dependent developers, with imported technology, resulted in small industrial working classes compared to Europe at similar levels of economic development, and thus in class structures inimical to democratization. Economic dependence further meant high vulnerability to fluctuations in world markets, and the resulting economic instability made stabilization and legitimization of regimes difficult, whether those regimes were authoritarian or democratic....

Central America and the West Indies

The West Indies and the Central American countries share a number of socioeconomic characteristics that have been shown to be inimical to democracy.[2] Their economies were traditionally plantation economies, with some mining and industrialization—and tourism in the West Indies—superimposed in the post–World War II period. The corresponding societies were traditionally very hierarchical and their economies highly dependent on foreign trade and foreign investment. Low economic development, extremely high dependence, high inequality, a small working class, and rapid social change all have been found to be unfavorable for the installation and consolidation of democratic regimes, and they all characterized Caribbean Basin countries in the post–World War II period.

2. The term "West Indies" refers to the English-speaking Caribbean countries (the larger ones are Jamaica, Barbados, Trinidad, and Guyana); the term "Caribbean" includes them along with Spanish, French, and Dutch-speaking countries; the term "Caribbean Basin" refers to Caribbean and Central American countries.

Not surprisingly, then, all but two of the Spanish-speaking countries in the Caribbean basin were ruled by authoritarian regimes in the 1960s and 1970s, and during the 1970s, economic elites and the military establishment resorted to increasingly violent repression of both revolutionary movements and democratic reformist forces. The exceptions were Costa Rica and, from 1978 on, the Dominican Republic. In contrast, all but two of the English-speaking Caribbean countries had democratic regimes from the time of their independence in the 1960s throughout the 1970s.[3] How do we explain these contrasting political developments?

The antecedents of the contrasts in the 1960s and 1970s lie in the developments of the 1930s. The Depression brought great disruptions to the extremely export-dependent societies in the region. In response to decreasing real wages and increasing unemployment, attempts at labor organization and labor protests emerged in virtually all countries throughout this region. The reactions of the economic elites to these protests and organizing attempts were universally negative, but the reaction of the state varied widely. British colonialism was important here, because it was an alternative to the Central American pattern of landlord or military control of the state, and thus an alternative to the use of the coercive forces of the state to repress both the protests and the emerging labor unions and allied political parties. Consequently, the '30s marked the beginning of organized political life, and opened the way for the subsequent consolidation of civil society in the West Indies, whereas in Central America they solidified the pattern of the primacy of the coercive apparatus of the state and of state control over the repression of civil society, exercised either by landowner-

3. Racially polarized Guyana and tiny Grenada were the exceptions, but analysis of these two countries would take us too far afield here; the interested reader should see Rueschemeyer, Stephens and Stephens (1992, pp. 251–258).

military coalitions or the military alone. Costa Rica, the deviant case in Central America, resembled the West Indies insofar as the large landowners were not in firm control of the state apparatus (though for different reasons, as we shall see in a moment) and consequently unions and political parties were allowed to consolidate their organizations.

In sum, the growth of democracy cannot be read off from the economic development and its effect on the development of the class structure alone. Both Central American and Caribbean countries started from roughly similar levels of development, similar economic structures, and similar world market niches. What emerges as critical in this comparison of the emergence of democracy in the West Indies and its absence in Central America is the nature of state-class relations, especially the critical contribution of British colonialism.

Similarly, the development of a strong military state or its absence cannot be explained by internal factors alone. The third power cluster, transnational structures of power, must be brought in to complete the explanation. The United States' economic and geopolitical interests, along with political alignments within the United States, led it to support the build-up of the coercive apparatus of the Central American states. In Britain, by contrast, the colonies were increasingly viewed as an expense which a declining power could ill afford and which the social democratic forces, which were far stronger in Britain, no longer desired.

This analysis of the West Indies and Central America leads to a reinterpretation of our evidence on Europe, as one would expect in this strategy of analytic induction. In the discussion of Europe, we attributed the authoritarian trajectory of four of the countries—Germany, Italy, Austria-Hungary, and Spain—to the strength of the landed upper classes in those countries. The West Indian cases indicate that this strength had to be complemented with a structure of state power which was open to strong landlord influ-

ence and could be turned to coercive purposes on a national scale. Such a state had been created across the European continent in the course of the centuries-long consolidation of the European states, largely as a result of warfare between the states. As Tilly (1975, pp. 40–44) points out, the coalition of large landlords with the central state was a militarily strong one and was frequently victorious in these centuries of war. Moreover, the state-building process in these countries generally resulted in the landed upper classes having a strong foothold in the military, which made recourse to authoritarian politics more attractive since landlords and their allies could rely on the military to exercise the coercion necessary to maintain or install authoritarian rule.

Questions, Method, and Applications

Our program of comparative historical research confirmed the conclusion of the cross-national statistical analyses of the correlates of political democracy: The level of economic development is causally related to the development of political democracy. However, the underlying reason for the connection, in our view, is that capitalist development transforms the class structure, enlarging the working and middle classes and facilitating their self-organization, thus making it more difficult for elites to exclude them politically. Simultaneously, development weakens the landed upper class, democracy's most consistent opponent. The development of the class structure hardly accounts for all national differences in democratic development, as the contrasting political development in the Spanish-speaking Central American countries and the English-speaking Caribbean islands demonstrates, but it is of central importance.

Some readers may be familiar with the argument that the bourgeoisie played an important role as the agents of democratic reform, and thus may be surprised at how little weight we give this factor. Surely, leading businessmen in contemporary advanced capitalist countries are rightly regarded as supporters of democracy. However, most of their predecessors in 19th century Europe and 20th century Latin America were not, because they feared that extending suffrage to workers would represent a threat to their material interests. As democracy was established during the 20th century and these fears proved to be exaggerated, the bourgeoisies of advanced capitalist societies gradually came to accept and then strongly to support democratic institutions. A similar process occurred in the West Indies in the post–World War II period, and one can hope that contemporary South America is experiencing the same phenomenon. . . .

We conclude with a few observations about the implications of our analysis for the future of democracy in the contemporary Third World. Across the less developed countries, most U.S. intervention since World War II (at least) was primarily motivated by geopolitical competition with the former Soviet Union, rather than by direct defense of economic interests. Concerns for national security were invariably invoked to justify support for authoritarian regimes. The end of the Cold War both alleviates these concerns and greatly weakens them as a basis for foreign policy towards Latin America. The discrediting of the Soviet model has also dealt a mortal blow to Leninist socialism as a model for opposition movements and a basis for legitimization of authoritarian regimes in the Third World. These factors at least open the door for a more unambiguously pro-democratic policy towards the Third World on the part of the United States and the other developed countries, all of which are now democracies.

But other factors lead to less optimism about the chances for democracy in the Third World. In the case of both workers and businessmen, our analysis shows that their political posture toward democratic institutions was motivated in no small part by their perception of how democracy would affect their material interests. On this account, one can say that the current economic problems in the Third World, economic stagnation and the crushing debt, are also a problem for democracy. There is no doubt that rapid economic growth, or a growing economic pie, facilitates compromise between capital and labor and that, conversely, slow growth makes it almost impossible to satisfy both parties. Under such conditions, demands for mere economic betterment on the part of workers become a threat to business.

The analysis leads us to expect some countries within the Third World to have better prospects for democratization than others. Most obviously, the prospects are brighter for those countries at higher levels of economic development. However, as our analysis made clear, it is not the mere rise in per capita income (created, for example, by mineral wealth) that is of greatest importance, but rather the changes in the class and social structure caused by industrialization and urbanization which are most consequential for democracy. In addition, the analysis of agrarian class relations leads us to the conclusion that democratic prospects are much better in Third World countries without a significant group of large landholders and with a significant agrarian middle class.

References

Rueschemeyer, Dietrich, Evelyne Huber Stephens, and John D. Stephens, *Capitalist Development and Democracy*. Cambridge. Polity Press, and Chicago: Chicago University Press, 1992.

Tilly, Charles, "Reflections on the History of European State-making." In Tilly, Charles ed., *The Formation of National States in Western Europe*. Princeton: Princeton University Press, 1975, 3–83.

Zolberg, Aristide R., "How Many Exceptionalisms?" In Katznelson, Ira, and Aristide Zolberg, eds., *Working Class Formation: Nineteenth Century Patterns in Western Europe and the United States*. Princeton: Princeton University Press, 1986, 397–455.

Democracy and the Market: Political and Economic Reforms in Eastern Europe and Latin America

Adam Przeworski

Transitions to Democracy

Democratization

Introduction

The problem that thrusts itself to the center of the political agenda once a dictatorship breaks down is whether any institutions that will allow open-ended, even if limited, contestation will be accepted by the relevant political forces. And as soon as these institutions are in place, the question arises whether they will evoke spontaneous compliance; that is, whether, willing to subject their interests to the uncertainty of competition and to comply with its outcomes, they will absorb the relevant political forces as participants.

To organize the analysis, note that the conflicts inherent in transitions to democracy often occur on two fronts: between the opponents and defenders of the authoritarian regime about democracy and among the proto-democratic actors against one another for the best chance under democracy. The image of the campaign for democracy as a struggle of the society against the state is a useful fiction during the first period of transition, as a unifying slogan of the forces opposed to the current authoritarian regime. But societies are divided in many ways, and the very essence of democracy is the competition among political forces with conflicting interests. This situation creates a dilemma: to bring about democracy, anti-authoritarian forces must unite against authoritarianism, but to be victorious under democracy, they must compete with each

Excerpted from: Adam Przeworski, *Democracy and the Market: Political and Economic Reforms in Eastern Europe and Latin America*. New York: Cambridge University Press, 1991. © Cambridge University Press, 1991. Reprinted with the permission of Cambridge University Press.

other. Hence, the struggle for democracy always takes place on two fronts: against the authoritarian regime for democracy and against one's allies for the best place under democracy.

Thus, even if they sometimes coincide temporally, it is useful to focus separately on the two different aspects of democratization: extrication from the authoritarian regime and the constitution of a democratic one. The relative importance of extrication and constitution depends on the place within the authoritarian regime of those political forces that control the apparatus of repression, most often the armed forces.[22] Wherever the military remains cohesive in defense of the regime, elements of extrication dominate the process of transition. Chile and Poland are the paradigmatic cases of extrication, but extrication also overshadowed the transitions in Spain, Brazil, Uruguay, South Korea, and Bulgaria. In contrast, wherever military cohesion disintegrated because of a failed foreign adventure—Greece, Portugal, and Argentina—and in regimes where the military were effectively subjected to civilian control—all the other Eastern European countries—the process of constituting a new regime was less affected by elements of extrication.

Extrication

Since extrication has been extensively studied, I proceed schematically. First, let me follow O'Donnell (1979) and O'Donnell and Schmitter (1986) in distinguishing four political actors:

---

22. These need not be monolithic. Note that, as a legacy of the Stalin era, in Eastern Europe there have been two organized forces of repression: the armed forces for external defense under the control of the Ministry of Defense, and the army for internal order under the control of the Ministry of Interior. The autonomy of the secret police varied from country to country and period to period.

Hardliners and Reformers (who may or may not have been Liberalizers) inside the authoritarian bloc and Moderates and Radicals in the opposition. Hardliners tend to be found in the repressive cores of the authoritarian bloc: the police, the legal bureaucracy, censors, among journalists, and so on. Reformers tend to be recruited from among politicians of the regime and from some groups outside the state apparatus: sectors of the bourgeoisie under capitalism, and some economic managers under socialism.[23] Moderates and Radicals may but need not represent

different interests. They may be distinguished only by risk aversion. Moderates may be those who fear Hardliners, not necessarily those who have less radical goals.[24]

Extrication can result only from understandings between Reformers and Moderates. Extrication is possible if (1) an agreement can be reached between Reformers and Moderates to establish institutions under which the social forces they represent would have a significant political presence in the democratic system, (2) Reformers can deliver the consent of Hardliners or neutralize them, and (3) Moderates can control Radicals.

The last two conditions are logically prior, since they determine the set of possible solutions for Reformers and Moderates. Whatever agreement they reach, it must induce Hardliners to go along with Reformers and dissuade Radicals from mobilizing for a more profound transformation. When can these conditions be satisfied?

If the armed forces control extrication, they must either opt for reforms or be cajoled into cooperation, or at least passivity, by Reformers. Moderates must pay the price. But if Reformers are a viable interlocutor for Moderates only when they can control or deliver the armed forces, Moderates have no political importance unless they can restrain Radicals. Moderate gentlemen in cravats may lead civilized negotiations in government palaces, but if streets are filled with crowds or factories are occupied by workers calling for the necks of their interlocutors, their moderation is irrelevant. Hence, Moderates must either deliver terms tolerable to Radicals or, if they cannot obtain such terms from Reformers, they must leave enough power in the hands of the apparatus of repression to intimidate Radicals. On the one hand, Moderates need Radicals to be able to put pressure on Reformers; on the other, Moderates fear that

---

23. The attitudes of the bourgeoisie toward authoritarian regimes belie facile generalizations. The reason is the following. The bourgeoisie has three ways of defending its interests: (1) Under democracy, it can organize itself as a party and compete; (2) under any regime, it can organize itself as a pressure group and use privileged channels of access to the state; (3) under any regime, decentralized pursuit of profit constitutes a constraint on the actions of the state directed against its interests ("structural dependence of the state on capital" see Przeworski and Wallerstein 1988). Now, contrary to Marx, the last constraint may turn out to be insufficient to protect the bourgeoisie from the state. In fact, several military regimes in Latin America did enormous damage to some sectors of the bourgeoisie: Martínez de Hoz destroyed one-half of Argentine firms, and the Brazilian military built a state sector that competed with private firms. This is why by 1978 the leading sectors of the Paulista bourgeoisie saw the military regime as a threat. Thus, at least in Brazil, the anti-authoritarian posture arose from economic liberalism. (For interpretations of this posture, see Bresser Pereira 1978 and Cardoso 1983.) In turn, in countries where popular mobilization is feeble, the bourgeoisie can compete quite well under democratic conditions. This seems to be the case in Ecuador, where the autonomy of the technobureaucrats—the style rather than the substance of economic policy making, according to Conaghan (1983)—turned the bourgeoisie against the military government and where the bourgeoisie did not fear electoral competition.

Similarly, in the socialist countries some factory managers saw relatively early the possibility of converting their political power into economic power (Hankiss 1989) and supported democratization.

---

24. In fact, in Poland in 1981 moderates were those who perceived Soviet intervention as imminent; radicals, those who saw it as unlikely.

Table 2.2

		Moderates ally with	
		Radicals	Reformers
Reformers ally with	Hardliners	Authoritarian regime survives in old form: 2,1	Authoritarian regime holds, with concessions: 4,2
	Moderates	Democracy without guarantees: 1,4	Democracy with guarantees: 3,3

Radicals will not consent to the deal they work out with Reformers. No wonder the feasible set is often empty.

When can an agreement that satisfies all these constraints be reached? Reformers face a strategic choice of remaining in an authoritarian alliance with Hardliners or seeking a democratic alliance with Moderates. Moderates, in turn, can seek all-out destruction of the political forces organized under the authoritarian regime by allying with Radicals, or they can seek an accommodation by negotiating with Reformers. Suppose the structure of the situation is as in table 2.2.[25]

If Reformers ally with Hardliners and Moderates with Radicals, two opposing coalitions are formed, and they fight it out. If Reformers ally with Moderates and Moderates with Reformers, the outcome is democracy with guarantees. The off-diagonal outcomes should be read as follows: When Moderates ally with Radicals and Reformers with Moderates, Reformers are accepting the democracy without guarantees that results from the Radical–Moderate coalition. When Reformers ally with Hardliners and Moderates with Reformers, Moderates are accepting

liberalization. They are entering in the sense used above.

Under such conditions, Reformers have a dominant strategy, namely, always to ally with Hardliners. If Moderates ally with Radicals, the opposition is defeated and the authoritarian bloc survives intact, which is better for Reformers than democracy brought about by a coalition of Moderates and Radicals that offers no guarantees. If Moderates seek an alliance with Reformers, some concessions are made, to the cost of Hardliners. These concessions are better for Reformers than democracy even with guarantees. Hence, potential Reformers are always better off defending the authoritarian regime in alliance with Hardliners.

The defining feature of this situation is that Reformers have no political strength of their own and thus no prospect of being politically successful under democracy. Without special guarantees, they will do very badly under democracy, and even with guarantees they are still better off under the protection of their authoritarian allies. This was the case of Poland in 1980–1.[26] Any solution had to satisfy two conditions: (1) The opposition insisted on the principle of open electoral competition, and (2) the party wanted to have a guarantee that it could win the electoral competition. The opposition was willing to have the party win; it did not de-

25. The first number in each cell represents the value of this outcome to Reformers; the second number, to Moderates (4 is better than 3, and so on). These numbers are not interpersonally comparable; they only rank the alternatives. Hence, Moderates may be miserable under their second-worst option, while Reformers may be quite happy with theirs.

26. The Polish situation was analyzed in game theoretic terms by Stefan Nowak in *Polityka*, Warsaw, September 1981.

Table 2.3

		Moderates ally with	
		Radicals	Reformers
Reformers ally with	Hardliners	Authoritarian regime survives in old form: 2,1	Authoritarian regime holds, with concessions: 3,2
	Moderates	Democracy without guarantees: 1,4	Democracy with guarantees: 4,3

mand a chance to win but only to compete. The party did not object to elections but wanted to have a good chance of winning.[27] But in clandestine polls, the party was running at about 3 percent in voting intentions. No way was found to overcome this impediment. If the party had been getting 35 percent, it would have been child's play to invent an electoral system that would be competitive and give it a good chance of winning. But not at 3 percent. No institutions existed to satisfy the constraints imposed by the interests and outside opportunities of the conflicting political forces.[28] Under such conditions, Reformers could not venture into a democratic alliance with Moderates.

Suppose that Reformers do have sufficient political strength to be able to compete under democratic conditions if they are given institutional guarantees. Is this sufficient for them to opt for democracy? Consider table 2.3. Here Reformers have political weight independent of Hardliners: They can get some support under competitive conditions, and they prefer democracy with guarantees over other alternatives. Yet the outcome for Reformers depends on the actions of Moderates. If Moderates opt for guarantees, Reformers are better off under democracy, but if Moderates ally with Radicals, Reformers lose.[29] And Moderates prefer democracy without guarantees. Examine this structure of conflict in the extensive form; that is, assume that first Reformers decide what to do, anticipating the reaction of Moderates (see figure 2.1). Reformers analyze the situation as follows: If they ally with Hardliners, the result will be the status quo, which is the second-best outcome. They would be better off under democracy with guarantees. But if they decide to negotiate

---

27. This general posture was put forth rather directly by Jakub Berman, number-two man in Poland during the Stalinist period, in a 1981 interview. Referring to the postwar election, Berman said: "To whom were we supposed to yield power? Perhaps Mikołajczyk [leader of the Peasant party]? Or perhaps those standing even farther to the right of Mikołajczyk? Or who the hell knows who else? You will tell me immediately that this would represent respect for democracy. So what? Who needs such democracy! Now, by the way, we cannot have free elections either, even less now than ten or twenty years ago, because we would lose. There is no doubt about this. So what is the sense of such elections? Unless we would want to show ourselves to be such super-democrats, such gentlemen, that we would take top hats off our heads, bow down and say: 'Be welcome, we are retiring, take power for yourself'" (interview in Torańska 1985: 290).

28. The same strategic situation was solved in March 1989 by a stroke of genius. Someone suggested creating an upper chamber of the parliament and having completely free elections to this chamber while guaranteeing the Communist party and its allies a majority in the lower house and hence the right to form the government.

29. In this game there is no equilibrium in pure strategies.

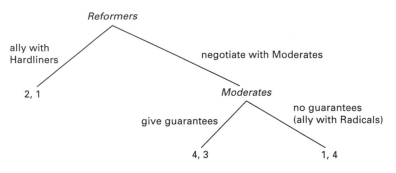

Reformers

ally with
Hardliners

negotiate with Moderates

2, 1

Moderates

give guarantees

no guarantees
(ally with Radicals)

4, 3   1, 4

Figure 2.1

with Moderates, the latter will opt for an alliance with Radicals, which will result in the worst outcome for Reformers. Hence, Reformers stay with the regime.

Will not democracy come about nevertheless, as a result of repetitions of this situation?[30] Imagine everyone knows that this strategic situation is almost certain to be repeated forever. Moderates know that if they respond to the opening by embracing the demands of Radicals, Reformers will ally with Hardliners next time around. Hence, the payoff to Moderates from defecting on the first round will be $\{4, 1, 1, \ldots\}$ or another mixture of 4s and 1s, depending on the punishment strategy chosen by Reformers.[31] But if Moderates decide to give guarantees on the first round, Reformers will respond in kind, and the payoff to Moderates will be $\{3, 3, 3, \ldots\}$. It is easy to see that there are many Reformers' punishment strategies that should persuade

Moderates to cooperate. Hence, if the original situation is to be repeated, democracy can evolve spontaneously.

But I do not think that situations in which regime change is at stake are repeatable. These are unique situations; something cracks in the authoritarian power apparatus; a group begins to feel that perhaps it would prefer to share power with consent rather than monopolize it by force, decides to make a move, and turns to eventual partners outside the regime in quest of assurances about its role under democracy. Once Reformers decide to make a move, *alea iacta est*—they cannot go back to the status quo. Payoffs for the future change as a result of actions chosen now. To go back is to admit the failure of the strategy of democratic opening and to meet with the wrath of Hardliners. Reformers who decide to go back almost never survive their failure; they are playing for broke.[32] This does not mean that an opening may not be tried again in the future by new Reformers; this is what did happen in South Korea and in Poland. But these are new forces, facing new circumstances. And if the Reformers' strategy is successful and democracy is institutionalized, the payoffs change as well. The devolution of power to democratic

30. The paragraphs that follow result from a heated discussion with Jon Elster, who, as always, forced me to decide what I really think.

31. Tit for tat, the strategy people tend to choose in experimental situations, does maximize overtime payoff, but it is not a strategy for perfect equilibrium. In turn, there are a very large number of strategies that support the cooperative outcome. On this and many other technicalities involved here, see the excellent textbook by Rasmusen 1989.

32. I say "almost" because of Brazil, where the architects of the failed "decompression" of 1974 succeeded in regrouping and trying again.

institutions is irreversible even if democracy can be subverted anew.[33]

Does this argument imply that democracy is never established as an equilibrium but can only result from a normative commitment to democracy? No; it is sufficient to tinker with the payoffs to see that there can exist unique situations in which the equilibrium outcome is democracy. There are two possibilities. One is that Radicals will accept democracy with guarantees; the other, that Moderates will continue to be protected by the existence of autonomous armed forces.

The first possibility—that Radicals will cease being radical—is not so farfetched as it may first appear. Until democracy is established, forces that seek profound political or economic transformation have no alternative to channeling their actions into streets and factories; there are no political institutions where their demands will not meet with violent repression. Yet once a competitive democratic framework is established because of an agreement between Moderates and Reformers, Radicals find that they too can play the game, participate. They tend to be wary of democratic institutions, distrustful of

their chances, and skeptical that their victories will ever be tolerated. Yet the attraction of an open-ended democratic interplay is irresistible, and Radicals find that to abstain is to forsake popular support. As the history of Socialist parties in Western Europe demonstrates, all political forces face the alternatives of joining or vanishing, and, except for the Anarchists, who persevered in resisting "the siren song of elections," they all joined (see Przeworski 1985: ch. 1).

If Radicals refuse to participate in the institutions forged by Moderates and Reformers, Moderates' interests may still be such that they prefer a democracy in which the forces in the civil society represented by Reformers have a significant presence to one that is dominated by Radicals.[34] Under such conditions, the payoffs in the game tree above will be interchanged: Moderates will prefer democracy with guarantees for Reformers to an alliance with Radicals. What this often means is that some sectors associated with the authoritarian regime continue to enjoy the protection of the armed forces. If Reformers have some political strength of their own and if Moderates prefer an institutional arrangement in which the armed forces remain autonomous as a counterbalance to the demands of Radicals, then Reformers have little to fear from democracy. Under such conditions, the equilibrium outcome will be democracy, but a democracy in which the armed forces will remain free of civilian control and will exercise tutelage over the democratic process.[35]

---

33. This is why I do not think that evolutionary theories of institutions (Schotter 1981, 1986) can explain transitions to democracy.

Some technical issues are involved here. The results concerning the emergence of cooperation in repeated games govern only those situations that are repeated exactly; specifically, with the same payoffs. To the best of my knowledge, we know little about games in which component subgames change somewhat from one round to the next. Benhabib and Radner (1988) analyzed a labor–capital game in which payoffs change and discovered that if they change greatly from one subgame to the next, the equilibrium is noncooperative; if they change somewhat, the path of the equilibria moves monotonically to cooperative equilibrium, which reigns once the game becomes stationary. This result makes intuitive sense, so the relevant question is how much payoffs change from one situation to the next. My argument is that, at least for the Reformers, they change drastically.

34. In Figure 2.1, let the payoff to Moderates in a democracy with guarantees be 4, with no. 3.

35. I realize that the game is in fact more complicated than my analysis suggests, since I take the behavior of Hardliners as parametric. Yet Hardliners may, for example, provoke Radicals in order to undermine the agreement between Moderates and Reformers. In many cases of transition, there emerge shadowy groups that appear to be Radicals but may be Provocateurs: GRAPO in Spain provides one illustration; the Tablada affair in Argentina another.

But why would Moderates tolerate military autonomy? Why would they consent to military tutelage that restricts the possible range of democratic outcomes, at times humiliates civilian politicians, and introduces a source of instability into the democratic system?[36]

Except in Poland, the communist systems of Eastern Europe produced civilian regimes. The military and most of the forces of order were subject to minute political control, which extended even to operational matters.[37] Hence, it should not be surprising that in conflicts over the leading role of the Communist parties, the armed forces in all Eastern European countries placed themselves squarely on the side of those who wanted to abolish the communist monopoly on power. "The army wants to serve not a party but the nation"—this has been the generals' paradigmatic declaration. From a Latin American perspective, this noble sentiment sounds ominous: not a pledge to democratic values but an assertion of independence.

In most Latin American countries, the military have preserved their autonomy and have continued to exercise tutelage over the political system, not only in countries where the transition to democracy was a result of negotiations, but even in Argentina, where the armed forces suffered a humiliating external defeat. The specter of military intervention is a permanent constraint on the political process, and the eventual reaction of the military is a consideration that permeates everyday political life in the new democracies. The Argentine experience is par-

Table 2.4

	Probability that a coup will occur	
	Immediately	Eventually but not now
With tutelage	0.20	0.60
With civilian control	0.80	0.01

ticularly poignant, since the impunity enjoyed by kidnappers, torturers, and murderers has a profoundly demoralizing effect on all political life. Among the recent transitions to democracy, Spain and Greece are the only countries where democratic governments succeeded in establishing effective civilian control over the military and freed themselves from this tutelage.

One obvious answer is that Moderates fear that any attempt to impose civilian control will immediately provoke exactly what it is intended to eliminate: military intervention. The strategic calculus involved must be the following. First, the probability of an immediate coup after any attempt to establish civilian control must be seen as higher than when the military are left alone. Hence, even if civilian control, once established, would greatly reduce the likelihood of military intervention, the probability that the coup will ever occur is lower without civilian control. Consider table 2.4. The probability that the military will step in now or in the future if they continue to exercise tutelage over the political system is 68 percent, while the probability that they will undertake a coup if the government seeks to impose civilian control is 80.2 percent.[38]

---

36. In October 1987, the Brazilian government raised military pay by more than 100 percent overnight in reaction to a takeover of a city hall by a small military unit stationed in a provincial town—this after the minister of finance had publicly committed himself not to do it.

37. The secret police are a different matter. Conflicts between the secret police and Communist parties have punctuated much of the political life of communist regimes. The secret police are the group that had the most to lose from the dismantling of communism, and they were the target of popular ire in several countries.

---

38. Let p be the probability of an immediate coup under tutelage, and t the probability of an eventual coup in the same case. Let q be the probability of an immediate coup if the government imposes civilian control, and c the probability of an eventual coup. Then the total probability of a coup under tutelage is $p + (1 - p)t$, and under attempted civilian control it is $q + (1 - q)c$.

This is not the end of the difficulty, for not all coups are the same. One argument for punishing violations of human rights is that the effect of punishment is dissuasive: The military will think twice before stepping in again because they know that once out of power they will be punished. That may be true, but if this argument is valid, it also implies that if the military are not deterred by the threat of punishment from stepping in, it will be less likely to give up power because of this threat. Thus, imposition of civilian control may lower the probability of a coup but increase the conditional probability that, once it occurs, the coup will be highly repressive, a *golpe duro*.

Thus, if a government is intent on not provoking a coup and not risking repression, it may swallow its moral outrage and its democratic ideals and accept the limits set by military tutelage.[39] But I suspect that this reasoning is not sufficient to explain the behavior of civilian politicians vis-à-vis the military. There are two reasons why democratic politicians may not want to dismantle the threat from the military even if they could.

First, Fontana (1984: 121) observed that in 1981 the Argentine political parties feared that if the threat from the military was removed, a new wave of popular mobilization would push them, as in 1973, farther to the left than they wanted: They feared radicals. To paraphrase an expression Ernest Bevin once used about the Labour party, they "did not want to be put in the position of having to listen to their own people." If the military can be counted on to repress popular mobilizations, their tutelage is a bulwark for established political parties.

Second, the problem in many countries with a long tradition of military intervention is the absence of institutional models through which civilian control over the military can be exercised.[40] Through the chain of command, the military are responsible directly to the president rather than to parliamentary committees and civilian bureaus that supervise particular aspects of their conduct. Without such an apparatus of civilian control, the choice faced by democratic governments may be one of either tolerating military autonomy or destroying the military altogether.[41] And here, I suspect, nationalism plays a role: No president can afford to commit himself or herself to actions that will undermine the ability of the nation to defend itself. Perhaps when the choice of strategy vis-à-vis the military appears to be one of leaving it intact or dismantling it altogether, the perpetuation of military domination turns out to be a lesser evil for nationalistic politicians.

The issue of civilian control over the military is thus not only whether it is prudent to attempt it but also who wants to have it.[42] Military tutelage may be preferred by some civilian

---

39 In a 1987 article entitled "La política militar del gobierno constitucional argentino," Fontana stresses that in 1983 the government did not have a good picture of the situation in the armed forces, that it believed erroneously that the military would purify itself if given a chance, and that it repeatedly underestimated the solidarity among military generations. All of this may be true, but what strikes me is that the article fails to demonstrate that the government had any military policy.

40. This observation is due to José Murilo de Carvalho.

41. For example, Delich (1984: 135) presents as follows the choice available to the Argentine democratic government. Since the atrocities committed by the military constituted acts sanctioned by the military as an institution, under written orders and under control by the military command, the democratic government could only either condemn the armed forces as a whole or forget the whole matter.

42. This is how in October 1987 José Murilo de Carvalho (1987: 18) characterized the attitudes of the Brazilian political forces in the Constituent Assembly: "It is more difficult to visualize a surge of solid political will to construct the hegemony of civil power. As we have seen, such a will certainly does not exist in the political action of the actual occupant of the presidency of the Republic, and it does not manifest itself in an

political forces as a protection from demands for greater representation, to ward off pressure from those who seek a social as well as a political revolution.[43]

Extrications thus leave institutional traces. Just note the price extorted by Pinochet for his consent to free elections: (1) permanent office for the current commanders in chief of the armed forces and the police, (2) protection of the "prestige of members of the military and the police," (3) an "energetic struggle against terrorism," (4) respect for the opinions of a national security council to be formed of four military representatives and four civilians, (5) maintenance of the amnesty covering political crimes

committed between 1973 and 1978, (6) abstention by the political authorities from intervening in the definition and application of defense policies, including not modifying the powers of military courts, the command structure, and the military budget and not interfering in the promotion of generals (normally a presidential prerogative), (7) the right to name nine members to the Senate, (8) autonomy of the central bank, the president of which was chosen by the military, (9) acceptance of privatizations conducted during the last months of the military regime without investigation of how they were conducted, and (10) automatic allocation of 20 percent of copper revenues to the military budget. When the armed forces themselves are the Reformers and the resistance comes from bureaucrats, the situation is simpler, even if at moments dramatic.[44] Yet note that in Poland, where the impetus for reforms came from the head of the armed forces, the regime also succeeded in exacting several guarantees: (1) The Communist party was guaranteed 35 percent of the seats in the more important house of the parliament (Sejm), and its then allies were given another 30 percent: in principle, ample support to form a government; (2) it was understood that the opposition would not block the election of General Jaruzelski as president; and (3) matters of external defense and internal order were left under the control of communists.

Hence, the optimal strategy of extrication is inconsistent. The forces pushing for democracy must be prudent ex ante, and they would like to be resolute ex post. But decisions made ex ante create conditions that are hard to reverse ex post,

---

unambivalent way in the majority party, the PMDB. It is not even necessary to say that there are no traces of such will in the PFL, the PTB, etc. Whoever observes the political scene in the new Republic has the impression that military tutelage is something normal and that it should continue to be exercised."

It should not be surprising, therefore, that the *Latin American Weekly Report* of 15 September 1988 (WR–88–36) could report, under the title "Brazil's Military Gain Quietly What Pinochet Demands Loudly," that "as some Brazilian military men have readily admitted in private, whereas elsewhere civilians have worried how much autonomy they could or should grant the military, in Brazil the military have carefully dosed [prescribed] the autonomy of the civilians."

43. José Antonio Cheibub (personal communication) offered the following criticism of this hypothesis. "The explanation based on the elite's fear of popular mobilization is not good for two reasons. First, because leaders of countries that face a problem of civilian control over the military learned (or should have learned) that the protection the military offers (from one perspective) is also a threat (from another perspective). In other words, their job as politicians is also threatened by the very tutelage they want to maintain to protect them from popular mobilization.... Second, it seems to me that this explanation may be ... transformed into an argument that assumes the political elite in those countries to be inherently conservative; that it always prefers the risk of a military coup to a greater representativeness of the regime."

44. The program of political reforms proposed by General Jaruzelski at the party plenum in January 1989 failed to win a majority. At that moment, the general (who was the commander in chief), the minister of defense, and the minister of interior (both also generals) offered their resignations and walked out of the meeting. Only then did the Central Committee deem desirable the turn toward negotiations with the opposition.

since they preserve the power of forces associated with the ancien régime. Ex post the democratic forces regret their prudence, but ex ante they have no choice but to be prudent.[45]

Yet the conditions created by transitions negotiated with the ancien régime are not irreversible. The essential feature of democracy is that nothing is decided definitively. If sovereignty resides with the people, the people can decide to undermine all the guarantees reached by politicians around a negotiating table. Even the most institutionalized guarantees give at best a high degree of assurance, never certainty.[46]

---

45. Since democracy has been consolidated in a number of countries, some North American intellectuals now advise us that the protagonists in the struggles against authoritarianism should have been more radical in pushing for social and economic transformation. For a fantasy of this kind, see Cumings 1989.

46. Moreover, this entire analysis assumes more knowledge than the protagonists normally have or can have. In Poland, everyone miscalculated at several points: The party got so little electoral support in the first round of elections in June 1989 that the legitimacy of the negotiated deal was undermined, the heretofore loyal allies of the communists decided to venture out on their own, and the whole carefully designed plan of transition unraveled. The opposition had to make last-minute additional concessions to keep the reformers in the game. I suspect that if the party had known what would happen, it would not have agreed to elections; if the opposition had anticipated what happened, it would not have made the concessions.

Party strategists cited all kinds of reasons why Solidarity would do badly in the elections of June 1989. An eminent reformer assured me that party candidates would win a majority in the elections to the Senate. (In fact, they received 15.8 percent of the vote; see Ostrowski 1989.) But the other side was equally surprised. When asked whether political developments followed his plan, Wałęsa responded: "My project was different from what happened. With regard to politics, I wanted to stop at the conquests of the round table: make a pause and occupy ourselves with the economy and the society. But, by a stroke of bad luck, we won the elections" (interview in *Le Figaro*, Paris, 26 September 1989, p. 4).

True, in Chile, South Korea, and Pakistan attempts to modify the constitutions left as the authoritarian legacy have thus far been abortive, and in Uruguay a referendum failed to reverse the auto-amnesty declared by the military. In Poland, the initial agreement concluded in April 1989 unraveled immediately as a result of the elections of June 1989, and its remains were gradually destroyed. Transition by extrication generates incentives for the democratic forces to remove the guarantees left as the authoritarian legacy. Hence, it leaves an institutional legacy that is inherently unstable. . . .

The Political Dynamics of Economic Reform

Introduction

The goal of recent economic reforms, undertaken in several countries around the globe, is to organize an economy that rationally allocates resources and in which the state is financially solvent.

These are market-oriented reforms. Rationalizing the allocation of resources requires organizing new markets, deregulating prices, attenuating monopolies, and lowering protection. Making the state solvent entails reducing public expenditures, increasing revenues, and at times selling public assets.

Such reforms necessarily cause a temporary fall in aggregate consumption. They are socially costly and politically risky. Perhaps in the long run reforms do accomplish all one former Polish minister of the economy announced they would: motivate, generate market clearing, and satisfy social justice (Baka 1986: 46). Yet meanwhile they hurt large social groups and evoke opposition from important political forces. And if that happens, democracy may be undermined or reforms abandoned, or both.

Even if governments that launch such reforms often hate to admit it, a temporary economic deterioration is inevitable. Inflation must flare up when prices are deregulated. Unemployment of capital and labor must increase when competition is intensified. Allocative efficiency must temporarily decline when the entire economic structure is being transformed. Structural transformations of economic systems are costly.

Can such transformations be accomplished under democratic conditions?[1] The question about the relationship of democracy and reforms concerns transitional effects. The reason is the following: Even if the post-reform system would be more efficient—more, even if the new steady state would be Pareto-superior to the status quo, that is, no one would be worse off in the new system and someone would be better off— a transient deterioration of material conditions may be sufficient to undermine either democracy or the reform process....

Structural economic transformations are being undertaken in many countries, South and East, under nascent democratic institutions. Four outcomes may occur under such conditions: (1) Reforms may advance under democratic conditions, (2) reforms may be forced through by a dictatorship, (3) democracy may survive by abandoning reforms, and (4) both reforms and democracy may be undermined....

---

1. By posing the question in this manner, I do not want to imply that they would in fact be accomplished under a dictatorship. Remmer (1986) provides persuasive evidence that the rate of success of the IMF's Standby Agreements, albeit not very high, was slightly higher for democratic than for authoritarian regimes in Latin America between 1954 and 1984. Haggard (1986) found that among the thirty cases of Extended Fund Facility programs he examined, IMF disbursements were interrupted or canceled for noncompliance in all the democratic countries except for the special case of India, but the rate of success among the "weak" authoritarian regimes he considered was not different. In turn, Stallings and Kaufman (1989) found in their analysis of nine Latin American countries that whereas "established democracies" did about as well as authoritarian regimes with regard to stabilization, only the latter progressed with regard to both stabilization and structural reform.

One way to think about reforms is in the traditional terms of international financial institutions,[11] distinguishing stabilization, structural adjustment, and privatization. Stabilization consists of short-term measures designed to slow down inflation, reduce the balance-of-payments deficit, and cut the government deficit. Structural adjustment is the set of measures designed to make the economy competitive. It is the most heterogeneous category, comprising everything from trade liberalization to price deregulation to tax reform. Privatization is self-explanatory....

Conclusion

Whatever their long-term consequences, in the short run reforms are likely to cause inflation, unemployment, and resource misallocation as well as to generate volatile changes in relative incomes. These are not politically popular consequences anywhere. And under such conditions, democracy in the political realm works against economic reforms. In Comisso's (1988) words, a hierarchy may reemerge because the market failed to deliver efficient results.

Political Dynamics of Reforms: A Model

Both political reactions to reform and their eventual success or failure depend not only on their economic effects but also on political conditions. In November 1987 a program of reforms failed to win majority support in a referendum organized by the communist government in Poland. Yet economic reforms by the postcommunist government enjoyed overwhelming support. The program was almost the same; it was the government that changed. Hence, the question is not only how deep and wide is the valley of transition but also which political forces are

---

11. I say "traditional" because recently the World Bank has become much more concerned about income distribution and, hence, taxation and poverty. See the 1989 *Development Report*.

most apt to traverse it. This is the question examined here.

Three somewhat stylized facts organize this analysis. First, it seems that reforms are almost invariably launched by surprise. Second, they often generate widespread initial support that erodes as social costs set in. Last, reforms tend to follow a stop-and-go pattern. . . .

Political Consequences of Economic Reforms

If reforms are to proceed under democratic conditions, distributional conflicts must be institutionalized; all groups must channel their demands through democratic institutions and abjure other tactics. Regardless of how pressing their needs may be, the politically relevant groups must be willing to subject their interests to the verdict of democratic institutions. They must be willing to accept defeat and to wait, confident that these institutions will continue to offer opportunities the next time around. They must adopt the institutional calendar as the temporal horizon of their actions, thinking in terms of forthcoming elections, contract negotiations, or at least fiscal years.[53] They must assume the stance put forth by John McGurk, chairman of the British Labour party, in 1919: "We are either constitutionalists or we are not constitutionalists. If we are constitutionalists, if we believe in the efficacy of the political weapon (and we do, or why do we have a Labour Party?) then it is both unwise and undemocratic because we fail to get a majority at the polls to turn around and demand that we should substitute industrial action" (Miliband 1975: 69).

Reforms can progress under two polar conditions of the organization of political forces: The latter have to be very strong and support the reform program, or they have to be very weak and unable to oppose it effectively. Reforms are least likely to advance when political forces— in particular, opposition parties and unions—are strong enough to be able to sabotage them and not large enough to internalize the entire cost of arresting them. As Haggard and Kaufman (1989: 269) put it, "The greatest difficulty comes in intermediate cases where labor is capable of defensive mobilization, but uncertain about its long-term place in the political system."[54] To put it bluntly, reform-oriented governments face a choice of either cooperating with opposition parties and unions, as did the Spanish Socialist government, or destroying them, as did the Bolivian government of Paz Estenssoro with regard to unions.

The role of unions is crucial for two reasons. On the one hand, they organize the people whose demands are the potential source of wage pressure. If workers and salaried employees have market power, they can exercise this power to push for wage increases. And during reforms, wage pressure is a source of inertial inflation; it slows down the recovery and results in increasing differentials among different sectors and occupations. Wage restraint is a necessary condition for the success of reforms. On the other hand, union federations can control the behavior of their constituents. Whether by using coercive powers delegated by the state or by relying on their persuasive powers, the leadership of a union can persuade the rank and file to wait for reforms to bear fruit. Unions have what is best described by the Spanish term *poder convocatorio*: the power to discipline the behaviors of their constituents in the collective interest.

---

53. This notion of institutional time is due to Norbert Lechner.

54. The best example of unions that are neither strong enough nor large enough comes, again, from Argentina. As I am writing this text, the Argentine Union Federation (CGT) has called for price controls on all basic consumer goods, imposition of exchange controls, an end to the government's plans for privatization, abandonment of the plans to streamline public administration, and massive wage increases (*Latin American Weekly Report*, WR–90–11, 22 March 1990).

To function as partners, unions must constitute encompassing, centralized organizations and must trust in the good faith of the government. Such organizations must be encompassing: They must associate large parts of their potential constituencies. And they must be centralized: They must be able to control the behavior of their constituents. Finally, they must have confidence in the government: They must trust that the government will not be unfair in distributing the costs and the benefits of reforms and that it will be competent in conducting reforms.

This assertion is supported not only by extensive evidence from the developed countries, where encompassing, centralized unions are willing to restrain their wage demands when social democratic parties are in office, but also by the experience of some newly democratic countries. In post-1976 Spain, a Socialist government has advanced a program of industrial modernization under conditions of very high unemployment—until recently with the consent of the unions. In Poland, Solidarność offered a striking moratorium to facilitate the reforms initiated by the postcommunist government. In Brazil, a movement of "results-oriented unionism" was willing to do the same, and it is significant that its general secretary is the first union leader to become a minister of labor.[55]

Political parties represent more heterogeneous interests, and their impact is potentially wider. They play the central role in presenting alternatives and molding attitudes with regard to particular governments as well as with regard to the very project of structural transformation. Yet parties, at least modern noncommunist parties, do not have the same power to discipline their

constituents as do unions. They may refuse to process demands they find untimely or inappropriate, but they face competition from other parties and the threat that popular mobilization will assume extraparliamentary forms.

In sum, to advance reforms, governments must either seek the broadest possible support from unions, opposition parties, and other encompassing and centralized organizations, or they must work to weaken these organizations and try to make their opposition ineffective. Obviously, the latter strategy raises the question of democracy. Is a government that resorts to a state of siege to counter opposition to reforms democratic? Moreover, if a government adopts the strategy of forcing reforms against popular opposition, the posture of the armed forces becomes relevant. This posture largely defines whether nondemocratic alternatives are perceived as feasible, either by those who are tempted to force reforms against democratically organized opposition or by the groups that are determined to defend their interests in any way possible against a democratically organized proreform majority. When the armed forces are independent of civilian control and are present as a political actor, various groups in the civil society engage in what Huntington (1968) termed praetorian politics: strategies such as "If you do not moderate your demands, we will ask the military to intervene" or "If you do not concede to our demands, we will create a disorder which will provoke the military to intervene." The competitive political process in the presence of an autonomous military creates the permanent possibility of military intervention.

Responding to this bipolar choice, the new democratic governments can pursue two contrasting political strategies to control economic conflicts, placing different emphases on economic logic and on participation. Reform-oriented governments can insulate themselves from popular demands and impose economic policies from above. Or, trying to mobilize support for reform programs, they can seek to or-

---

55. Antonio Rogerio Magri broke ranks with Brazilian unionism when, as president of the Electrical Workers, he made statements such as "All we workers want is that firms invest, so that the economy will expand. There is no better guarantee of employment than economic expansion" (*Journal da Tarde*, São Paulo, 27 July 1987, p. 12).

chestrate consensus by engaging in widespread concertation with parties, unions, and other organizations. Hence, governments face the choice of either involving a broad range of political forces in the shaping of reforms, thus compromising their economic soundness, or of trying to undermine all opposition to the program. Confronted with this dilemma and the resistance that the social costs of reforms inherently engender, governments tend to vacillate between the technocratic political style inherent in market-oriented reforms and the participatory style required to maintain consensus.

Market-oriented economic reforms are an application of a technical economic blueprint based on theories developed inside the walls of North American universities and often forced on governments by the international lending agencies. They are based on a model of economic efficiency that is highly technical. They involve choices that are not easy to explain to the general public and decisions that do not always make sense to popular opinion. Moreover, they call for some measures that are most successful if they are introduced by surprise.[56]

From the political point of view, reforms are thus a strategy of control from above. The particular measures implement technicians' ideas; they are adopted without consultation and sometimes announced by surprise. A reform policy is not one that emerges from broad participation, from a consensus among all the affected interests, from compromises. As we have seen, parties that want to complete structural transformation have an incentive to manipulate the agenda in such a way as to push the electorate to accept radical reforms. And the success of

the bitter-pill strategy depends on its initial brutality, on proceeding as quickly as possible with the most radical measures, on ignoring all the special interests and all immediate demands. Any government that is resolute must proceed in spite of the clamor of voices that call for softening or slowing down the reform program. Since reformers know what is good and since they are eager to go ahead as fast as possible, political conflicts seem just a waste of time. Hence, market-oriented reforms are introduced by decree or are rammed through legislatures. . . .

. . . At the same time, reforms require political support from individuals at the polls, from unions and professional associations in the workplaces, and at times from opposition parties in the legislature. And since they engender transitional costs, reforms inevitably provoke resistance. Voices are raised to the effect that social costs are excessive and the program should be moderated. Others point out that their situation is in some way special and that they should be accorded special treatment. In this situation, governments are tempted to seek consensus, to explain and justify their program, to listen and to compromise. They seek to involve opposing parties, unions, and employers' associations in economic policy making, hoping that this will reduce conflicts and induce economic actors to behave in ways consistent with continuation of at least the basic lines of the reform program.

The social pacts that are sought in bargaining typically consist of the granting of wage restraint by the unions in return for some welfare programs together with economic policies that control inflation and encourage investment and employment.[58] . . . Yet there are several reasons why such pacts seem unlikely to succeed in most new democracies.

---

56. If everyone knows that the price of a particular commodity will be deregulated, there will be a rush on it before the measure is adopted; if everyone knows that wages and prices will be frozen on a particular day, they will be pushed as high as possible before the freeze takes place; if everyone knows savings will be frozen, money will be withdrawn from the banks.

---

58. The economic logic and the political preconditions of such pacts are discussed by Lechner (1985) and Przeworski (1987b). Reviews of experience from various countries include Cordova 1985, Pappalardo 1985, and dos Santos 1987.

(1) Social pacts are always exclusive....

(2) Unions will participate in such pacts only if they are strong: encompassing, centralized, and politically influential. Otherwise they have no reason to expect that they will benefit in future from the present underutilization of their power....

(3) Even if unions in the private sector may be willing to participate in a pact, public sector unions have no incentive to do so. In the profit sector, unions trade wage restraint for employment and investment, but neither employment nor investment in public services depends on their employees' wage rates. Hence, public sector unions face neither the stick of unemployment nor the carrot of investment. Moreover, reforms normally involve measures to reduce public spending, a threat to the public sector unions.

These obstacles are so overwhelming that most of the time attempts to conclude social pacts collapse. And even when such pacts are ceremoniously signed, they are rarely observed.

Since a temporary deterioration of material conditions is inherent in any reform process, neither decrees nor concertation generate immediate economic improvement. Governments learn that decrees evoke opposition and pacts do not result in what they wanted to achieve by decree. They discover, in the words of a former Argentine vice-minister of the economy, that "requirements of participation conflict with those of competence."[60] And as pressures mount, governments begin to vacillate between *decretismo* and *pactismo* in search of a peaceful resolution of conflicts. Since the idea of resolving conflicts by agreement is alluring, they turn to making bargains when opposition against reforms mounts; they turn back to the technocratic style when the compromises involved in

pacts imperil reforms. They promise consultation and shock the eventual partners with decrees;[61] they pass decrees and hope for consensus. As a result, governments appear to lack a clear conception of reforms and the resolve to pursue them. The state begins to be perceived as the principal source of economic instability.[62] Then comes the time for sorcerers with yet another magic formula. Once confidence in reforms is eroded, each new government tries to make a clean break with the past by doing something that people have not yet learned to distrust. Reforms are addictive; a stronger dosage is needed each time to soothe the accumulated desperation. Market-oriented reforms may be based on sound economics. But they breed voodoo politics.

The effect of this style is to undermine representative institutions. When candidates hide their economic programs during election campaigns or when governments adopt policies diametrically opposed to their electoral promises, they systematically educate the population that elections have no real role in shaping policies. When governments announce vital policies by decree or ram them through legislatures without debate, they teach parties, unions, and other representative organizations that they have no role to play in policy making. When they revert to bargaining only to orchestrate support for policies already chosen, they breed distrust and bitterness.

Democracy is thus weakened. The political process is reduced to elections, executive decrees, and sporadic outbursts of protest. The government rules by decree, in an authoritarian fashion

---

60. Juan Carlos Torre, speaking at the seminar Transição política: Necessidades e limites da negociação at the University of São Paulo in June 1987. See Guilhon Albuquerque and Durham 1987.

---

61. The Pacote Bresser was announced on the eve of a meeting that was designed to investigate the feasibility of a social pact at the personal instigation of President Sarney.

62. For complaints about the inconstancy of government policies, see the presentations by both representatives of employers' associations and union leaders during the São Paulo seminar on social pacts (Guilhon Albuquerque and Durham 1987).

but often without much repression. All the power in the state is concentrated in the executive, which is nevertheless ineffectual in managing the economy. People get a regular chance to vote, but not to choose. Participation declines. Political parties, unions, and other representative organizations face a choice between passive consent and extraparliamentary outbursts.

These consequences are perhaps not inevitable. Indeed, the reason why the whole pattern of stop–go reforms sets in is that democracy is incomplete to begin with. In a country with constitutional provisions that force the executive to seek formal approval for policies before they are launched, with effective representative institutions and widespread political participation, governments could not set out on the path of reform independent of the support they could muster. Reforms would have to emerge from widespread consultation channeled through the representative institutions and ratified by elections. The Spanish Socialist government did proceed in this fashion and succeeded in conducting the country through a painful program of industrial reconversion with widespread support (Maravall 1990).[63] But this seems an exceptional case among new democracies.

Once democracy is weakened, pursuit of reforms may become politically destabilizing. At some point, the alternative may become either to abandon reforms or to discard the representative institutions altogether. Authoritarian temptations are inevitable. The clamor of discordant voices, the delay caused by having to follow procedures, and the seeming irrationality of conflicts inescapably cause impatience and intolerance among the proponents of reforms. For them, reforms are obviously needed and transparently rational: Doubts, oppositions, insistence on procedures appear to be symptoms of irrationality. Technocracy hurls itself against democracy and breeds the inclination to proceed against popular resistance: to suppress *glasnost* in order to continue with *perestroika*. And, on the other side, as suffering persists, confidence erodes, and the government seems less and less competent, temptations are born to defend one's interests at any cost, even at the cost of democracy.

References

Baka, Władysław. 1986. *Czas reformy.* Warsaw: Ksiazka i Wiedza.

Benhabib, Jeff, and Roy Radner. 1988. "Joint Exploitation of a Productive Asset: A Game-Theoretic Approach." Manuscript, New York University and A.T.&T.

Bresser Pereira, Luiz Carlos. 1978. *O colapso de uma alianca de classes.* São Paulo: Editora Brasiliense.

Cardoso, Fernando Henrique. 1983. "O papel dos empresarios no proceso de transição: O caso brasileiro." *Dados* 26: 9–27.

Comisso, Ellen. 1988. "Market Failures and Market Socialism: Economic Problems of the Transition." *Eastern European Politics and Societies* 2: 433–465.

Conaghan, Catherine M. 1983. "Industrialists and the Reformist Interregnum: Dominant Class Political Behavior and Ideology in Ecuador, 1972–1979." Ph.D. dissertation, Yale University.

Córdova, Efrén. 1985. *Pactos sociais; Experiência internacional, tipologia e modelos.* Brasilia: Instituto Brasileiro de Relacoes do Trabalho.

Cumings, Bruce. 1989. "The Abortive Abertura: South Korea in the Light of Latin American Experience." *New Left Review* 173: 5–33.

Delich, Francisco. 1984. "Estado, sociedad y fuerzas armadas en la transición argentina." In *Transición a la democracia.* Augusto Varas, ed. Santiago: Associatión Chilena de Investigaciones para la Paz.

dos Santos, Mario R. 1987. *Concertación política-social y democratización.* Buenos Aires: CLACSO.

Fontana, Andres. 1984. "Fuerzas armadas, partidos políticos y transición a la democracia en la Argentina."

63. Note that when the Italian Communist party decided in 1976 to support the austerity policy of the government, it processed one million workers through evening school for a course in economics that explained the need for austerity.

In *Transición a la democracia*. Augusto Varas, ed. Santiago: Associación Chilena de Investigaciones para la Paz.

Guilhon Albuquerque, José A., and Eunice Ribeiro Durham, eds. 1987. *Transição política: Necessidades e limites da Negociaciao*. São Paulo: Universidade de São Paulo.

Haggard, Stephan. 1986. "The Politics of Adjustment: Lessons from the IMF's Extended Fund Facility." In *The Politics of International Debt*, pp. 157–186. Miles Kahler, ed. Ithaca, N.Y.: Cornell University Press.

Haggard, Stephan and Robert Kaufman. 1989. "The Politics of Stabilization and Structural Adjustment." In *Developing Country Debt and the World Economy*, pp. 263–274. Jeffrey D. Sachs, ed. Chicago: University of Chicago Press.

Hankiss, Elemer. 1989. *East European Alternatives: Are There Any?* Budapest: Institute of Sociology, Hungarian Academy of Sciences.

Huntington, Samuel P. 1968. *Political Order in Changing Societies*. New Haven, Conn.: Yale University Press.

Latin American Weekly Report. Published by Latin American Newsletters, London.

Lechner, Norbert. 1985. "Pacto social nos processos de democratização: A experiência latino-americana." *Novos Estudos* 13: 29–44.

Maravall, José María. 1990. "Economic Reforms in New Democracies: The Southern European Experience." University of Chicago, ESST Working Papers, no. 2.

Miliband, Ralph. 1975. *Parliamentary Socialism: A Study in the Politics of Labour*. 2d ed. London: Merlin Press.

Murilo de Carvalho, José. 1987. "Militares e civis: Um debate alem da contituinte." Paper presented at the Eleventh Annual Meeting of ANPOCS, Aguas de São Pedro.

O'Donnell, Guillermo. 1979. "Notas para el estudio de procesos de democratización a partir del estado burocrático-autoritario." *Estudios CEDES* 5.

O'Donnell, Guillermo, and Philippe C. Schmitter. 1986. *Transitions from Authoritarian Rule: Tentative Conclusions about Uncertain Democracies*. Baltimore: Johns Hopkins University Press.

Ostrowski, Krzysztof. 1989. "The Decline of Power and Its Effects on Democratization: The Case of the Polish United Workers Party." In *Eastern Europe and Democracy: The Case of Poland*, pp. 15–28. New York: Institute for East–West Security Studies.

Pappalardo, Adriano. 1985. *ll governo del salario nelle democrazie industriali*. Milan: Franco Agneli.

Przeworski, Adam. 1985. *Capitalism and Social Democracy*. Cambridge: Cambridge University Press.

———. 1987b. "Capitalismo, democracia, pactos." In *Transição política: Necessidades e limites da negociaciao*. José A. Guilhon Albuquerque and Eunice Ribeiro Durham, eds. São Paulo: Universidade de São Paulo.

Przeworski, Adam, and Michael Wallerstein. 1982. "The Structure of Class Conflicts under Democratic Capitalism." *American Political Science Review* 76: 215–238.

Rasmusen, Eric. 1989. *Games and Information: An Introduction to Game Theory*. Oxford: Blackwell Publisher.

Remmer, Karen L. 1986. "The Politics of Economic Stabilization." *Comparative Politics* 19: 1–24.

Schotter, Andrew. 1981. *The Economic Theory of Social Institutions*. Cambridge: Cambridge University Press.

Stallings, Barbara, and Robert Kaufman. 1989. "Debt and Democracy in the 1980s: The Latin American Experience." In *Debt and Democracy in Latin America*, pp. 201–223. Barbara Stallings and Robert Kaufman, eds. Boulder, Colo.: Westview.

Torańska, Teresa. 1985. *Oni*. London: Aneks.

Democracy's Third Wave

Samuel P. Huntington

Between 1974 and 1990, at least 30 countries made transitions to democracy, just about doubling the number of democratic governments in the world. Were these democratizations part of a continuing and ever-expanding "global democratic revolution" that will reach virtually every country in the world? Or did they represent a limited expansion of democracy, involving for the most part its reintroduction into countries that had experienced it in the past?

The current era of democratic transitions constitutes the third wave of democratization in the history of the modern world. The first "long" wave of democratization began in the 1820s, with the widening of the suffrage to a large proportion of the male population in the United States, and continued for almost a century until 1926, bringing into being some 29 democracies. In 1922, however, the coming to power of Mussolini in Italy marked the beginning of a first "reverse wave" that by 1942 had reduced the number of democratic states in the world to 12. The triumph of the Allies in World War II initiated a second wave of democratization that reached its zenith in 1962 with 36 countries governed democratically, only to be followed by a second reverse wave (1960–1975) that brought the number of democracies back down to 30.

At what stage are we within the third wave? Early in a long wave, or at or near the end of a short one? And if the third wave comes to a halt, will it be followed by a significant third reverse wave eliminating many of democracy's gains in the 1970s and 1980s? Social science cannot provide reliable answers to these questions, nor can any social scientist. It may be possible, however, to identify some of the factors that will affect the

Excerpted from: Samuel P. Huntington, "Democracy's Third Wave." *Journal of Democracy* 2, no. 2 (1991): 12–34. © The Johns Hopkins University Press and National Endowment for Democracy.

future expansion or contraction of democracy in the world and to pose the questions that seem most relevant for the future of democratization.

One way to begin is to inquire whether the causes that gave rise to the third wave are likely to continue operating, to gain in strength, to weaken, or to be supplemented or replaced by new forces promoting democratization. Five major factors have contributed significantly to the occurrence and the timing of the third-wave transitions to democracy:

(1) The deepening legitimacy problems of authoritarian regimes in a world where democratic values were widely accepted, the consequent dependence of these regimes on successful performance, and their inability to maintain "performance legitimacy" due to economic (and sometimes military) failure.

(2) The unprecedented global economic growth of the 1960s, which raised living standards, increased education, and greatly expanded the urban middle class in many countries.

(3) A striking shift in the doctrine and activities of the Catholic Church, manifested in the Second Vatican Council of 1963–65 and the transformation of national Catholic churches from defenders of the status quo to opponents of authoritarianism.

(4) Changes in the policies of external actors, most notably the European Community, the United States, and the Soviet Union.

(5) "Snowballing," or the demonstration effect of transitions earlier in the third wave in stimulating and providing models for subsequent efforts at democratization.

I will begin by addressing the latter three factors, returning to the first two later in this article.

Historically, there has been a strong correlation between Western Christianity and democracy. By the early 1970s, most of the Protestant countries in the world had already become democratic. The third wave of the 1970s and 1980s was overwhelmingly a Catholic wave.…

The Role of External Forces

During the third wave, the European Community (EC) played a key role in consolidating democracy in southern Europe. In Greece, Spain, and Portugal, the establishment of democracy was seen as necessary to secure the economic benefits of EC membership, while Community membership was in turn seen as a guarantee of the stability of democracy. In 1981, Greece became a full member of the Community, and five years later Spain and Portugal did as well.…

The withdrawal of Soviet power made possible democratization in Eastern Europe. If the Soviet Union were to end or drastically curtail its support for Castro's regime, movement toward democracy might occur in Cuba. Apart from that, there seems little more the Soviet Union can do or is likely to do to promote democracy outside its borders. The key issue is what will happen within the Soviet Union itself. If Soviet control loosens, it seems likely that democracy could be reestablished in the Baltic states. Movements toward democracy also exist in other republics. Most important, of course, is Russia itself. The inauguration and consolidation of democracy in the Russian republic, if it occurs, would be the single most dramatic gain for democracy since the immediate post-World War II years.…

During the 1970s and 1980s the United States was a major promoter of democratization. Whether the United States continues to play this role depends on its will, its capability, and its attractiveness as a model to other countries.… What might happen, however, if the American model ceases to embody strength and success, no longer seems to be the winning model? At the end of the 1980s, many were arguing that "American decline" was the true reality. If people around the world come to see the United States as a fading power beset by political stagnation, economic inefficiency, and social chaos, its perceived failures will inevitably be seen as the failures of democracy, and the worldwide appeal of democracy will diminish.

Snowballing

The impact of snowballing on democratization was clearly evident in 1990 in Bulgaria, Romania, Yugoslavia, Mongolia, Nepal, and Albania. It also affected movements toward liberalization in some Arab and African countries. In 1990, for instance, it was reported that the "upheaval in Eastern Europe" had "fueled demands for change in the Arab world" and prompted leaders in Egypt, Jordan, Tunisia, and Algeria to open up more political space for the expression of discontent.[1]

The East European example had its principal effect on the leaders of authoritarian regimes, not on the people they ruled.…

If a country lacks favorable internal conditions, however, snowballing alone is unlikely to bring about democratization. The democratization of countries A and B is not a reason for democratization in country C, unless the conditions that favored it in the former also exist in the latter.…

A Third Reverse Wave?

By 1990 at least two third-wave democracies, Sudan and Nigeria, had reverted to authoritarian rule; the difficulties of consolidation could lead to further reversions in countries with unfavorable conditions for sustaining democracy. The first and second democratic waves, however, were followed not merely by some backsliding

---

1. *New York Times.* 28 December 1989. A13: *International Herald Tribune*, 12–13 May 1990. 6.

but by major reverse waves during which most regime changes throughout the world were from democracy to authoritarianism. If the third wave of democratization slows down or comes to a halt, what factors might produce a third reverse wave?

Among the factors contributing to transitions away from democracy during the first and second reverse waves were:

(1) the weakness of democratic values among key elite groups and the general public;

(2) severe economic setbacks, which intensified social conflict and enhanced the popularity of remedies that could be imposed only by authoritarian governments;

(3) social and political polarization, often produced by leftist governments seeking the rapid introduction of major social and economic reforms;

(4) the determination of conservative middle-class and upper-class groups to exclude populist and leftist movements and lower-class groups from political power;

(5) the breakdown of law and order resulting from terrorism or insurgency;

(6) intervention or conquest by a nondemocratic foreign power;

(7) "reverse snowballing" triggered by the collapse or overthrow of democratic systems in other countries. . . .

The overwhelming majority of transitions from democracy, however, took the form either of military coups that ousted democratically elected leaders, or executive coups in which democratically chosen chief executives effectively ended democracy by concentrating power in their own hands, usually by declaring a state of emergency or martial law. . . . Although the causes and forms of the first two reverse waves cannot generate reliable predictions concerning the causes and forms of a possible third reverse wave, prior experiences do suggest some potential causes of a new reverse wave.

First, systemic failures of democratic regimes to operate effectively could undermine their legitimacy. . . .

Second, a shift to authoritarianism by any democratic or democratizing great power could trigger reverse snowballing. . . .

If a nondemocratic state greatly increased its power and began to expand beyond its borders, this too could stimulate authoritarian movements in other countries. . . .

Finally, as in the 1920s and the 1960s, various old and new forms of authoritarianism that seem appropriate to the needs of the times could emerge. . . .

Obstacles to Democratization

Another approach to assessing democracy's prospects is to examine the obstacles to and opportunities for democratization where it has not yet taken hold. As of 1990, more than one hundred countries lacked democratic regimes. Most of these countries fell into four sometimes overlapping geocultural categories:

(1) Home-grown Marxist-Leninist regimes, including the Soviet Union, where major liberalization occurred in the 1980s and democratic movements existed in many republics;

(2) Sub-Saharan African countries, which, with a few exceptions, remained personal dictatorships, military regimes, one-party systems, or some combination of these three;

(3) Islamic countries stretching from Morocco to Indonesia, which except for Turkey and perhaps Pakistan had nondemocratic regimes;

(4) East Asian countries, from Burma through Southeast Asia to China and North Korea, which included communist systems, military regimes, personal dictatorships, and two semi-democracies (Thailand and Malaysia).

The obstacles to democratization in these groups of countries are political, cultural, and economic. One potentially significant political obstacle to future democratization is the virtual absence of experience with democracy in most countries that remained authoritarian in 1990....

Another obstacle to democratization is likely to disappear in a number of countries in the 1990s. Leaders who found authoritarian regimes or rule them for a long period tend to become particularly staunch opponents of democratization. Hence some form of leadership change within the authoritarian system usually precedes movement toward democracy....

One serious impediment to democratization is the absence or weakness of real commitment to democratic values among political leaders in Asia, Africa, and the Middle East....

Even when Asian, African, and Middle Eastern leaders have more or less abided by the rules of democracy, they often seemed to do so grudgingly....

Culture

It has been argued that the world's great historic cultural traditions vary significantly in the extent to which their attitudes, values, beliefs, and related behavior patterns are conducive to the development of democracy. 'A profoundly antidemocratic culture would impede the spread of democratic norms in the society, deny legitimacy to democratic institutions, and thus greatly complicate if not prevent the emergence and effective functioning of those institutions. The cultural thesis comes in two forms. The more restrictive version states that only Western culture provides a suitable base for the development of democratic institutions and, consequently, that democracy is largely inappropriate for non-Western societies....

A less restrictive version of the cultural obstacle argument holds that certain non-Western cultures are peculiarly hostile to democracy. The two cultures most often cited in this regard are Confucianism and Islam. Three questions are relevant to determining whether these cultures now pose serious obstacles to democratization. First, to what extent are traditional Confucian and Islamic values and beliefs hostile to democracy? Second, if they are, to what extent have these cultures in fact hampered progress toward democracy? Third, if they have significantly retarded democratic progress in the past, to what extent are they likely to continue to do so in the future?

Confucianism

Almost no scholarly disagreement exists regarding the proposition that traditional Confucianism was either undemocratic or antidemocratic. The only mitigating factor was the extent to which the examination system in the classic Chinese polity opened careers to the talented without regard to social background. Even if this were the case, however, a merit system of promotion does not make a democracy. No one would describe a modern army as democratic because officers are promoted on the basis of their abilities. Classic Chinese Confucianism and its derivatives in Korea, Vietnam, Singapore, Taiwan, and (in diluted fashion) Japan emphasized the group over the individual, authority over liberty, and responsibilities over rights. Confucian societies lacked a tradition of rights against the state; to the extent that individual rights did exist, they were created by the state. Harmony and cooperation were preferred over disagreement and competition. The maintenance of order and respect for hierarchy were central values. The conflict of ideas, groups, and parties was viewed as dangerous and illegitimate. Most important, Confucianism merged society and the state and provided no legitimacy for autonomous social institutions at the national level.

In practice Confucian or Confucian-influenced societies have been inhospitable to democracy. In East Asia only two countries, Japan and the Philippines, had sustained experience with democratic government prior to 1990. In both cases, democracy was the product of an American presence. The Philippines, moreover, is overwhelmingly a Catholic country. In Japan, Confucian values were reinterpreted and merged with autochthonous cultural traditions. . . .

Islamic doctrine . . . contains elements that may be both congenial and uncongenial to democracy. In practice, however, the only Islamic country that has sustained a fully democratic political system for any length of time is Turkey, where Mustafa Kemal Ataturk explicitly rejected Islamic concepts of society and politics and vigorously attempted to create a secular, modern, Western nation-state. And Turkey's experience with democracy has not been an unmitigated success. Elsewhere in the Islamic world, Pakistan has made three attempts at democracy, none of which lasted long. While Turkey has had democracy interrupted by occasional military interventions, Pakistan has had bureaucratic and military rule interrupted by occasional elections. . . .

The Limits of Cultural Obstacles

Strong cultural obstacles to democratization thus appear to exist in Confucian and Islamic societies. There are, nonetheless, reasons to doubt whether these must necessarily prevent democratic development. First, similar cultural arguments have not held up in the past. At one point many scholars argued that Catholicism was an obstacle to democracy. Others, in the Weberian tradition, contended that Catholic countries were unlikely to develop economically in the same manner as Protestant countries. Yet in the 1960s, 1970s, and 1980s Catholic countries became democratic and, on average, had higher rates of economic growth than Protestant countries. . . .

Second, great cultural traditions like Islam and Confucianism are highly complex bodies of ideas, beliefs, doctrines, assumptions, and behavior patterns. Any major culture, including Confucianism, has some elements that are compatible with democracy, just as both Protestantism and Catholicism have elements that are clearly undemocratic. . . .

Third, cultures historically are dynamic, not stagnant. The dominant beliefs and attitudes in a society change. While maintaining elements of continuity, the prevailing culture of a society in one generation may differ significantly from what it was one or two generations earlier. . . .

Economics

Few relationships between social, economic, and political phenomena are stronger than that between the level of economic development and the existence of democratic politics. Most wealthy countries are democratic, and most democratic countries—India is the most dramatic exception—are wealthy. The correlation between wealth and democracy implies that transitions to democracy should occur primarily in countries at the mid-level of economic development. In poor countries democratization is unlikely; in rich countries it usually has already occurred. In between there is a "political transition zone": countries in this middle economic stratum are those most likely to transit to democracy, and most countries that transit to democracy will be in this stratum. As countries develop economically and move into the transition zone, they become good prospects for democratization. . . .

Economic Development and Political Leadership

History has proved both optimists and pessimists wrong about democracy. Future events will probably do the same. Formidable obstacles to the expansion of democracy exist in many societies. The third wave, the "global democratic revolution" of the late twentieth century, will not last forever. It may be followed by a new surge of authoritarianism sustained enough to constitute a third reverse wave. That, however, would not preclude a fourth wave of democratization developing some time in the twenty-first century. Judging by the record of the past, the two most decisive factors affecting the future consolidation and expansion of democracy will be economic development and political leadership.

Most poor societies will remain undemocratic so long as they remain poor. Poverty, however, is not inevitable. In the past, nations such as South Korea, which were assumed to be mired in economic backwardness, have astonished the world by rapidly attaining prosperity. In the 1980s, a new consensus emerged among developmental economists on the ways to promote economic growth. The consensus of the 1980s may or may not prove more lasting and productive than the very different consensus among economists that prevailed in the 1950s and 1960s. The new orthodoxy of neo-orthodoxy, however, already seems to have produced significant results in many countries.

Yet there are two reasons to temper our hopes with caution. First, economic development for the late, late, late developing countries—meaning largely Africa—may well be more difficult than it was for earlier developers because the advantages of backwardness come to be outweighed by the widening and historically unprecedented gap between rich and poor countries. Second, new forms of authoritarianism could emerge in wealthy, information-dominated, technology-based societies. If unhappy possibilities such as these do not materialize, economic development should create the conditions for the progressive replacement of authoritarian political systems by democratic ones. Time is on the side of democracy.

Economic development makes democracy possible; political leadership makes it real. For democracies to come into being, future political elites will have to believe, at a minimum, that democracy is the least bad form of government for their societies and for themselves. They will also need the skills to bring about the transition to democracy while facing both radical oppositionists and authoritarian hard-liners who inevitably will attempt to undermine their efforts. Democracy will spread to the extent that those who exercise power in the world and in individual countries want it to spread. For a century and a half after Tocqueville observed the emergence of modern democracy in America, successive waves of democratization have washed over the shore of dictatorship. Buoyed by a rising tide of economic progress, each wave advanced further—and receded less—than its predecessor. History, to shift the metaphor, does not sail ahead in a straight line, but when skilled and determined leaders are at the helm, it does move forward.

South Africa's Negotiated Transition: Democracy, Opposition, and the New Constitutional Order

Courtney Jung and Ian Shapiro

Few seasoned observers of South African politics ever expected to see Nelson Mandela inaugurated as the country's president. When this happened in May of 1994, it would have been difficult not to interpret it as a major democratic achievement. The April elections caught the world's imagination. Democrats everywhere applauded as the apartheid regime began fading into history, and the African National Congress took over the reins of power. In a country and on a continent where democracy has seldom fared well historically, the achievement seemed all the more remarkable. In an astonishingly short time South Africa had been transformed from a pariah nation, vilified around the world, into a progressive multicultural democracy, identified in the Western press as a model throughout Africa and a symbol of hope for struggling democratizers elsewhere.[1]

No less noteworthy than the result was the process that led to it. Despite considerable violence there was no civil war, no military coup, and the cooperation among the players whose cooperation was needed was impressive. Starting in 1990, after the National Party (NP) government's decision to release all political prisoners, legalize all opposition parties, and begin genuine negotiations with them on the shape of the new South Africa, it was clear that real change was in the offing. Multiparty negotiations for a new constitution seemed to exemplify both the letter and spirit of a democratic transition to democracy. Even when the all-party CODESA negotiations failed and were replaced by more circumscribed elite negotiations, the fact that the entire process commanded agreement among the principal players was widely heralded as an encouraging portent for the future.

The widespread popular enthusiasm for South Africa's democratic transition is in line with much recent academic orthodoxy in political science. Negotiated transitions to democracy are seen as desirable, if not necessary for democratic survival. "Pacts are not always likely or possible," Guillermo O'Donnell and Philippe Schmitter tell us, "but where they are a feature of the transition they are desirable—that is they enhance the possibility that the process will lead to a viable political democracy."[3] "How were democracies made?" asks Huntington of the third wave of democratic transformations between 1974 and 1990. His answer is that they "were made by the methods of democracy, there was no other way. They were made through negotiations, compromises and agreements."[4] Przeworski reiterates the view that democracy "cannot be dictated; it emerges from bargaining."[5] From the vantage point of these opinions, South Africa is a textbook case of a well-crafted transition; despite various fits and starts, the principals made no serious mistakes and shepherded the country safely through its first democratic elections.

The worldwide attention to the South African transition, and to transition negotiations elsewhere, has not been matched by comparable

Excerpted from: Courtney Jung and Ian Shapiro, "South Africa's Negotiated Transition: Democracy, Opposition, and the New Constitutional Order." *Politics and Society* 23(3): 269–308. © 1995 by Sage Publications. Reprinted by permission of Sage Publications.

1. See, e.g., *New York Times*, June 21, 1994, pp. A1, A8.

3. Guillermo O'Donnell and Philippe Schmitter, *Transitions from Authoritarian Rule* (Baltimore: Johns Hopkins University Press, 1986), p. 39.

4. Samuel P. Huntington, *The Third Wave: Democratization in the Late Twentieth Century* (Norman: University of Oklahoma Press, 1991), p. 164.

5. Adam Przeworski, *Democracy and the Market* (New York: Cambridge University Press, 1991), p. 80.

scrutiny of what the parties to the transition negotiations agreed to or why. Yet there are serious questions as to whether constitutional orders that emerge from negotiations facilitate democratic politics in the medium term. In particular, South Africa's transitional constitution lacks a system of opposition institutions that any healthy democracy requires. Although terms such as *group rights*, *consociationalism*, and *minority vetoes* are anathema in the South African political vocabulary, the political order that has been created is consociational in many critical respects; as such it is designed to give every powerful player a say in government. The electoral system, the rules of parliamentary control, and the powers and composition of the cabinet and the executive all reinforce this reality. The result is that there are no powerful actors to play the role of "loyal" opponents to the new government and its policies. A system designed to involve every player of political consequence in government leaves no institutional space for a loyal opposition.

... [W]e examine the disquieting possibility that the new South Africa's lack of these basic ingredients of a viable democracy is a direct result of the transition's having been negotiated between reformers in the NP government and the moderate leadership of the ANC. We explore and evaluate the conjecture that the dynamics of negotiated transitions such as South Africa's make it virtually impossible for the principal players to converge on an agreement that includes provision for effective opposition forces in the new democratic order. If our analysis is persuasive, then it leads to the conclusion that although the interim constitution may well have been the best possible device to end apartheid without a civil war, it should not be replicated in the permanent constitution.[6] This means that the advice of such analysts as Arend Lijphart, who makes the contrary recommendation, should be ignored....

Those who negotiate transitions to democracy all bring to the bargaining table interests that will lead them to see the costs and benefits of various institutional outcomes differently. Negotiators representing a party that expects to be in the minority in the new democratic order should be expected to prefer a power-sharing arrangement in which they are guaranteed some of the spoils of office and veto powers on measures that affect their critical interests. Leaders of parties that expect to alternate in government and opposition in the new regime might reasonably take a more mixed view of things: when they are in government, they will want the power to govern but when they are in opposition they will want to be able to frustrate as much of the government's agenda as possible. Parties that anticipate being able to win a majority can be expected to prefer an oppositional model that will give them the power and authority to govern and to enact as much of their agenda as they can. Consequently, they should be expected to push for a majority system during the transition negotiations and to be more resistant than any of the other players

---

6. The National Assembly and the Senate jointly form the Constitutional Assembly, which was required to adopt a final constitution with a two-thirds majority by May 1996. This constitution comes into operation only if the Constitutional Court certifies that it complies with the constitutional principles laid down in the provisional constitution. These include a democratic system of government, universal franchise, regular elections, a multiparty system, one class of citizenship for all, recognition of individual rights, antidiscrimination provisions, equality before the law, separation of powers, three levels of government (national, provincial, and local), and an entrenched constitution that—as interpreted by the Constitutional Court—is the supreme law of the land. This last feature was a notable change from the old British-style system of the supremacy of parliament. Other features of the interim arrangements, such as the boundaries of the provinces, could not be changed in the final constitution. There was no requirement, however, that the interim system of constitutionally mandated power sharing (the central focus of this chapter) be retained in the final document. See *South Africa 1995* (Johannesburg: South Africa Foundation, 1995), pp. 14–15.

to power sharing and other consociational arrangements.

The story of the South African transition partly belies these expectations. As anticipated, the National Party insisted on a consociational outcome throughout the negotiations and eventually prevailed, making few concessions. But the ANC, with its overwhelming grass roots support and its well-founded expectation that it would hold an absolute majority in the new parliament, made concession after concession, eventually accepting constitutionally mandated power sharing, for the rest of the century at least, almost without a whimper. As power sharing had been anathema to the ANC as late as mid-1992 and as most observers inside and outside South Africa seemed to think that the ANC held most of the cards, this outcome needs an explanation. . . .

The Dynamics of Transition Negotiations

Transplacements, as Huntington describes negotiated transitions,[29] should be expected to occur only when two conditions are present. First, dominant groups in both government and opposition must bargain with one another while recognizing that neither party is capable of determining the future unilaterally. Second, at critical junctures reformers must appear to be stronger than standpatters in the government while moderates seem stronger than extremists in the opposition.[30] Elites who negotiate transitions are thus subject to constraints that arise both out of the negotiations and out of their relations with their own grass roots constituencies. The negotiating partners are concerned to maximize power along two dimensions. First, each tries to maximize power in relation to the other in the negotiations. Because both sides expect to lead parties that will compete in the new democratic regime,

each has an interest in trying to get the upper hand in the negotiations to secure the result most favorable to its future political fortunes. Second, the negotiating partners (the reformers in the government and the moderates in the opposition) have incentives to maximize grass roots support for themselves (thereby continuing to marginalize standpatters and extremists) while causing their negotiating partner merely to satisfice with respect to its grass roots supporters. Each wants the other to retain enough constituent support—but no more—to be able to deliver an agreement, and each seeks to achieve this result in an evolving context. Thus negotiators are bound by three constraints as they move toward an agreement: time, their respective constituencies, and the changing demands of the other party. . . .

Negotiations begin in earnest once negotiating elites on both sides realize that they are approaching the point of no return: when retreat from the negotiations would be followed by a collapse of support from which political recovery is unlikely. Both leaderships, and perhaps their political parties as well, will by then have become so identified with the negotiated transition that, if the negotiations collapse, they will lose their leadership positions, presumably to standpatters and radicals. From this point on, political survival for reformers and moderates depends on concluding a successful agreement. This is most likely to occur if negotiators on both sides come to believe that their leverage to force concessions from the other side has reached its maximum or begun to diminish and that replacement and transformation continue not to be viable options. These beliefs will give both sides strong incentives to make the compromises necessary to reach an agreement, once they face what appears to them to be secular erosion of their own grass roots support.

A transplacement, or negotiated transition, differs from a Huntingtonian replacement in that in the former the authoritarian regime does not cede control of the armed forces until after the

---

29. Huntington, *Third Wave*, pp. 113–114. . . .

30. Huntington, *Third Wave*, pp. 124, 152.

agreement has been concluded. Both government reformers and opposition moderates know, therefore, that there are hard-liners in the military who will insist on security guarantees and also that grass roots support for government reformers is likely to be critically reliant on their being able credibly to claim that they can guarantee their constituents' physical security. Thus the government reformers have a structural advantage over the opposition moderates throughout the negotiations, as we have noted. It also suggests that, if an agreement is reached, in the end it will involve more substantial concessions from the opposition than from the government because the government retains control of the means of coercion. Once the opposition moderates realize that they have passed their point of no return, so that their political survival is contingent on reaching an agreement, they can be expected to accept demands rejected earlier. Even if the government reformers have passed their own point of no return, both sides are likely to assume that, in the event of a terminal collapse of negotiations, government reformers will turn control over to (or be pushed aside by) standpatters rather than accept the complete loss of control suggested by replacement or civil war.

The government will have an incentive not to force too many concessions out of the opposition moderates, however. It needs them to satisfice, to retain enough support among their grass roots to be able to sell the agreement and continue to marginalize the radical opposition elites waiting in the wings. The government must, therefore, simultaneously reassure its own constituent base, give the opposition just enough to crow about to its supporters, and claim as credibly as possible to undecided potential voters to have made the deal that is in their best interest. Opposition moderates confront the no less delicate task of convincing their core supporters that they have made the best possible bargain and concurrently presenting their concessions to others as evidence of their moderation and lack of partisanship.

In short, in negotiated transitions government reformers have more valuable cards going in than do the opposition moderates, deriving from their monopoly control of the state's coercive institutions. They may lack the power to impose what Huntington describes as a transformation, but by the same token the opposition lacks the power to impose a replacement. (Were this not so, negotiations would, presumably, not begin; and should it not remain so, they would not continue to an agreement.) The test of the government reformers' negotiating skill is how successfully they manage to use their structural advantage to get the opposition moderates to concede the maximum possible while forcing them to satisfice with respect to their grass roots constituency. They must do this in a way that alienates as few of the government's own potential supporters as possible. The test for the opposition moderates is how successfully they can undermine the government's structural advantage, reach an agreement with which their core supporters can live, and make themselves attractive to as many other potential voters as possible. How these interacting imperatives were played out in the South African transition between 1990 and 1994 is the subject to which we now turn.

South Africa's Negotiated Transition

The National Party's grand design for apartheid ran into trouble almost as soon as its leaders began to implement it when they came to power in 1948. When basic tenets of separate racial and ethnic development proved unworkable, parts of the strategy were abandoned and others were redesigned.[32] With various liberalizing fits and starts, South Africa was thus an unstable au-

---

32. See Hermann Giliomee, *The Parting of the Ways: South African Politics, 1976–1982* (Cape Town: Philip, 1982), and Heribert Adam and Hermann Giliomee, *The Rise and Crisis of Afrikaner Power* (Cape Town: Philip, 1979).

thoritarian regime for some forty-two years before the NP government of F. W. De Klerk decided, in 1990, to dismantle the apartheid regime and create a new multiracial political order....

Prenegotiations

The National Party Reformers

Yet many observers were caught off guard by the speed and decisiveness with which change came in February 1990. President De Klerk, a conservative Afrikaner by history and reputation who had been one of the mainstays of apartheid in previous cabinets, surprised both the South African opposition and the world by unbanning the ANC, the Pan-Africanist Congress (PAC), and the South African Communist Party (which had been illegal since 1960). He simultaneously announced plans to release all political prisoners, including Nelson Mandela, and to begin negotiations toward democracy. Given the NP's history of relentlessly demonizing these groups while sustaining the apartheid order behind a veil of cosmetic adjustments, these decisions left little room for doubt that fundamental change was at hand.

The government's decision to act suddenly and release Mandela before his role within the ANC had been agreed upon seemed calculated to promote and capitalize on the ANC's disorganization and to enable the NP to structure the terms of future negotiations as much as possible....

The ANC was reluctant to let the negotiations move rapidly. Whereas the NP pressed for a substantive agreement on a postapartheid government, the ANC focused on reaching agreement on a procedure by which a democratic government could be formed.[37] To this end,

it sought partly to remain a liberation movement, demanding an interim government and an elected constituent assembly to write the first constitution. ANC leaders sought to undermine the legitimacy and strategic advantage of the NP by challenging its role as legitimate government and primary negotiator. An interim government would assume (some undefined degree of) responsibility for governing while the two sides negotiated on what the ANC termed "a more level playing field." Additionally, ANC leaders argued that only an elected constituent assembly would lead to a democratic process in which the constitution would be drafted by democratically elected delegates. Confident that they would win a majority in elections for a constituent assembly, they expected that they would then have a free rein to draft the new constitution and control the new government.[38]

The Central Issue: Majority Rule

The debate over majority rule plagued discussions even in the prenegotiating phase.... The NP proposed that minority parties with significant support be assured of cabinet representation, that the presidency rotate among three to five members, and that decisions be based on consensus in both bodies.[40]

Power sharing had been anathema to the ANC for its entire history. It seemed too obviously to be a euphemism for "group rights," in turn little more than a smoke screen for apartheid by another name. Given this history and the ANC's knowledge of the extent of its own grass roots support, it is not surprising that initially the ANC regarded all talk of power sharing as taboo. In his early campaigning and international travels, Mandela heaped scorn on assertions by the government that South Africa was unique in its ethnic and racial composition and that as a result it needed a political system

---

37. [Hermann Giliomee and Johannes Rantete, "Transition to Democracy through Transaction? Bilateral Negotiations between the ANC and the NP in South Africa," *African Affairs* no. 91 (1992)], p. 526.

---

38. Ibid., p. 527.

40. [Ibid.], p. 523.

tailored to its idiosyncrasies. The ANC rejected all such claims, insisting that they wanted no more—but also no less—than an "ordinary democracy."[41]

Negotiations Begin

Early in 1992, a series of Conservative Party wins in local by-elections in former NP strongholds served to warn reformers in the NP that substantial numbers of whites might not support a transition. De Klerk responded by calling a referendum, held in March 1992, in which white voters were asked whether they supported negotiations. In so doing, he took a substantial political risk. Had the referendum results been negative, he would certainly have had to reverse policy, and he would likely have been deposed as leader of the NP and head of the government. But he won a resounding two-thirds majority, revealing the white-right electoral threat to be chimerical....

De Klerk was quick to declare that the referendum result was a mandate to negotiate a settlement, and he insisted throughout the remainder of the negotiating process and the 1994 election campaign that everything he agreed to had been outlined in the referendum and thus previously endorsed by an overwhelming majority of the whites.[43] His freedom in this regard was not unlimited, however. Although the referendum gave De Klerk the political leverage he needed to negotiate a settlement on behalf of

the white population, it committed him to some version of power sharing. This had been explicit in the referendum campaign, in effect making the referendum a contract between De Klerk and the white minority that he would not devolve all power to the black majority.[44] Had he ventured beyond the terms of this contract, his support would have fragmented and the far right would likely have reemerged as a serious force. Within the constraints implied by the contract, however, De Klerk was now free to begin genuine negotiations with the moderate leadership of the ANC.

The ANC leadership's incentive and capacity to negotiate emerged gradually. In the June 1992 Boipatong massacre, thirty-nine unarmed ANC supporters were killed by apparent Inkatha members while South African police and vehicles stood idly by. Mandela immediately pulled out of the talks in protest against the security forces' unwillingness to stem so-called black-on-black violence as well as Inkatha attacks against the ANC, precipitating the end of the all-party round-table negotiations.[45] The ANC backed up its dramatic walkout by calling for mass action and popular protest. The leadership used this, its most valuable extra-institutional bargaining chip, to demonstrate that it retained the capacity to mobilize its following against the govern-

41. In 1990, Mandela wrote in his best-selling autobiography that there would be no peace until majority rule was fully implemented; see Nelson Mandela, *The Struggle Is My Life* (London: IDAF Publications, 1990), p. 206. As late as April 1992 he was still insisting at press conferences that the ANC could never accept the various "fancy proposals" for power sharing that were on offer from the government: "We want an ordinary democracy as practiced elsewhere in the world." ANC press conference, *BBC Summary of World Broadcasts*, April 9, 1992.

43. *SAPA* (Johannesburg), June 8, 1993.

44. De Klerk launched the referendum campaign by saying, "We will not say yes to a suicide plan. We will once again reiterate the importance that in such a new constitution, whether it be a first phase or a fully encompassing constitution, how important we regard it that there must be effective protection against domination of minorities"; *SABC Network* (Johannesburg), February 24, 1992. After his victory, De Klerk said, "We want to share power, we want a new dispensation, we want it to be fair, we want it to be equitable"; ibid., March 19, 1992.

45. These negotiations had been stalled for some time over the percentage of votes needed for acceptance of the constitution, with the ANC advocating two-thirds, which it thought it might be able to win outright, and the government insisting on 75 percent.

ment.... Although Mandela called repeatedly for peaceful demonstrations, South Africa's highest levels of transitional violence occurred in the month after Boipatong.[46]

Three months after Boipatong, the Ciskei government opened fire on a group of ANC followers marching in support of the mass-action campaign at Bisho. This event in particular made the human cost of the transition graphically evident to the ANC leadership....

At the same time as social unrest was threatening to spiral out of the ANC leadership's control, De Klerk was greatly increasing the stakes for both sides by threatening to play the transformation card. Having faced down the hard right, he was now approaching his point of no return; now he needed to get a settlement. During this period he declared repeatedly that he would negotiate with anyone or no one, that he would arrange the transition by himself if need be, but that, no matter what, it would occur....

The dual triggers of Boipatong and Bisho, and their repercussions, seem to have caused the ANC leadership to look into the abyss and realize that time for a negotiated settlement over which they could have substantial influence was running out.[52] In any event, ANC leaders returned to bilateral talks with the government immediately after the Ciskei massacre, and the real negotiations began. Unlike the two earlier CODESA round-table negotiations, which had been public events adorned by many marginal players, the post-Boipatong talks involved the government and the ANC only, they were held

in secret, and both sides appeared determined to fix the main terms of their agreement before multilateral talks would again be allowed to begin. These terms were announced in the Record of Understanding, made public in February 1993, between the ANC and the government.[53]

From "Ordinary Democracy" to Power Sharing

Once the ANC leaders became convinced that all the alternatives to a relatively quick negotiated settlement were worse, they faced [a] Hobson's choice ... and the government's structural advantage in the negotiations became manifest. De Klerk's commitment to power sharing was nonnegotiable; this meant that the ANC would make the principal concessions. A successful agreement thus came to hinge on whether the moderate ANC leadership could move itself tactically and ideologically into a position where it could accept power sharing before its core constituency support was lost. The leadership had to shift its policy to accept power sharing and marginalize other elites inside and outside the ANC who might challenge its position as the principal representative of the opposition. The government, which had been ready to negotiate seriously since mid-1992 but needed a serious partner, did everything it could to help with the second matter. Once the bilateral talks began in September, government ministers began to mute public criticism of the ANC leaders (who responded in kind), and the government began trying to marginalize opposition groups that were in competition with the ANC—most notably the IFP. This marked a distinct change in government strategy. As late as May of 1992 the government had seemed bent on pumping up non-ANC opposition groups through such actions as meeting with the PAC (which was then boycotting CODESA) outside the country and disputing ANC claims about its own grass roots

46. In that month, there were 1,535 incidents of political violence with 240 deaths, the highest number to that date; *Southern Africa Report*, May 14, 1993, p. 3. That number was to be exceeded only in the final weeks before the April 1994 elections.

52. It is hard to believe that the daily news of civil war and ethnic slaughter in Bosnia and the recent memories of what had happened in Angola had no impact, though it would be difficult to determine just what that impact was.

53. *New York Times*, February 19, 1993, pp. A1, A7.

support (insisting, for example, that the IFP had more substantial support than the ANC among the Zulu in Natal). The old strategy of seeking to divide the opposition as much as possible—consistent with a transformative strategy—was now shelved in favor of finding, and to some extent even creating, a negotiating partner with whom a deal could be made.

By the end of 1992, the government and the ANC leadership were being criticized from the left and the right in ways that suggested that the alliance necessary for transplacement to occur was close to being cemented in place.... Both sides had managed to marshal sufficient support to sustain the negotiation process, and both sides seemed aware that this support would not last indefinitely. Each side had maneuvered itself into a position from which it could afford to reach an agreement *and* from which the costs of failing to reach one were growing all the time.[54]

The other essential ingredient was that the ANC leadership subdue its radical wing and get its core supporters to accept power sharing....

The fight over power sharing within the ANC lasted several months. It was not clear that the radical wing had been subdued until the end of a fractious three-day debate in February 1993. The issue was whether the Congress's one hundred-member governing committee would endorse the agreement that had been negotiated with the government.... The agreement called for a legally mandated five-year government of national unity regardless of the election outcome, with cabinet representation for all parties that won at least 5 percent of the vote, and a share of executive power for the strongest minority party. The government made marginal concessions on the size of supermajority thresholds and agreed

for the first time to defer some questions about regional powers to the next parliament.[57] But on the central question of majority rule, the ANC reversed its decades-old policy and accepted a strong consociational arrangement, at least for the rest of the century.

However accurate the militants' portrayal of the agreement as a sellout might have been, they were unable to secure the votes on the ANC's governing committee for a nationwide membership conference to debate the issue.[58] The agreement that had been negotiated was approved, and from that point through the elections, the ANC leadership faced no serious threat from its left. Although multiparty talks began the following month, the bilateral agreement of February 1993 set the basic terms of the constitution that was adopted by the white parliament in its final act in December of that year. In October, an act was passed creating the Transitional Executive Council (TEC), a multiparty executive body designed to oversee the government in the run-up to the elections of April 1994.[59] Although the act limited the TEC's powers to matters having to do with ensuring a level playing field for the elections, the TEC quickly became a kind of supercabinet. When the TEC successfully ordered the military to go into Bophuthatswana to put down a white separatist group that was supporting the local black leader in opposing the coming elections, two things became clear for the first time: the army was loyal to the TEC, and the transition to multiracial government in South Africa was a fait accompli before a single black vote had been cast.

54. The impression that these shifts in strategy had occurred is based on interviews with people close to the principal negotiating partners, conducted during visits to South Africa in May and December 1992.

57. The changes on regional powers were not really concessions because they mattered more to white separatists and the IFP, neither of whom were serious players by this time, than to the government, which never considered abandoning the concept of a unitary state once negotiations began.

58. *New York Times*, February 19, 1993, pp. A1, A7.

59. "Transitional Executive Council Act," Act no. 151 (1993), *Government Gazette*, October 27, 1993.

The Absence of Democratic Opposition

Huntington advises the leaders of authoritarian regimes who are engaged in negotiated transitions to begin planning for politics in opposition.[60] Not only did De Klerk fail to take this advice, he could not have taken it while still negotiating a transition to a multiracial state with the ANC moderate leadership. The necessary condition for his marginalizing the standpatters to his right was that he commit to a power-sharing model that would ensure the white minority a role, if a junior one, in the next government. Once the moderate ANC leaders had passed their point of no return and needed an agreement, they had to accept this reality as well—hence the mutual convergence on power sharing. Beyond these constraints, the negotiating principals had few incentives to pay attention to opposition institutions in the new order because at no time did either of them intend not to be in the next government. Whether either would have found a different model more attractive had they considered the longer term turned out to be irrelevant; both were prisoners of the myopia that, in the last analysis, became the minimum price of a negotiated transition.

As they moved closer together, the government and the ANC leadership developed a common interest in marginalizing all opposition to their joint venture, so that there was no dissent, for example, when the TEC made the ominous decision to suspend the planned abolition of Section 29 of the Internal Security Act permitting detention without trial, which had been inherited from the apartheid regime.[61] During the heady final months of the transition negotiations and the run-up to the elections, co-opting or marginalizing opposition seemed desirable to the principals and to most observers. This is understandable because the opposition being expressed was opposition to the end of the apartheid regime. But because the principals expected to be major players in the new political order, they were engaged in more than regime building. And in ensuring that there could be no serious opposition to the new order they were creating, they also ensured that there would be little scope for democratic opposition within it. . . .

---

60. Huntington, *Third Wave*, p. 162.

61. *Southscan*, February 11, 1994.

Economic Development and Political Regimes

Adam Przeworski, Michael E. Alvarez, José Antonio Cheibub, and Fernando Limongi

Introduction

Any casual glance at the world will show that poor countries tend to have authoritarian regimes, and wealthy countries democratic ones. The question is why. What are the conditions that determine whether democracy or dictatorship prevails? What causes political regimes to rise, endure, and fall? Can their transformations be explained generally, or are they caused by circumstances idiosyncratic to each country or period? Are they driven by economic development or by other factors, such as the preceding political history, cultural traditions, political institutions, or the international political climate? . . .

Development and Democracy

First advanced in 1959, S. M. Lipset's observation that democracy is related to economic development has generated the largest body of research on any topic in comparative politics. It has been supported and contested, revised and extended, buried and resuscitated. And yet, though several articles in the *Festschrift* honoring Lipset (Marks and Diamond 1992) proclaim conclusions, neither the theory nor the facts are clear.

Aggregate patterns . . . show that the relationship between the level of economic development

Excerpted from: Adam Przeworski, Michael E. Alvarez, José Antonio Cheibub, and Fernando Limongi, *Democracy and Development: Political Institutions and Well-Being in the World, 1950–1990*. Cambridge: Cambridge University Press, 2000. © Adam Przeworski, Michael E. Alvarez, José Antonio Cheibub, and Fernando Limongi, 2000. Reprinted with the permission of Cambridge University Press.

and the incidence of democratic regimes is strong and tight. Indeed, one can correctly predict 77.5 percent of the 4,126 annual observations of regimes just by looking at per capita income.[1] What remains controversial, however, is the relative importance of the level of development as compared with other factors, such as the political legacy of a country, its past history, its social structure, its cultural traditions, the specific institutional framework, and, last but not least, the international political climate. . . .

. . . [T]he level of economic development, as measured by per capita income, is by far the best predictor of political regimes. Yet there are countries in which dictatorships persist when all the observable conditions indicate they should not; there are others in which democracies flourish in spite of all the odds. Thus some factors influencing the incidence of the different kinds of regimes are not identified by this analysis.

---

1. These predictions are derived from probit, a form of non-linear regression, in which the probability that a country i will have had a dictatorial (as opposed to democratic) regime at time t is modeled as $\Pr(\text{REG}_{it} = \text{Dictatorship}) = F(X_{it}\beta)$, where $F(\cdot)$ is the cumulative distribution function (c.d.f.) of the normal distribution. A fair amount of ink has been spilled over the issue whether or not the relationship between development and democracy is linear (Jackman 1973; Arat 1988). We now know better. Democracy, however it is measured, is a qualitative or limited variable (it assumes the value of 0 or 1 under our measurement, it ranges from 2 to 14 on the Freedom House scale, from 0 to 100 on the Bollen scale, and so on). Hence, no predicted index of democracy can become negative as the level of development tends to zero, and no predicted index of democracy can exceed whatever is the maximum value of a particular scale as the level gets very large. Only a non-linear function, such as the normal or logistic (as suggested by Dahl 1971), can satisfy these constraints. This is why we use probit throughout.

Regime Dynamics

There are two distinct reasons that the incidence of democracy may be related to the level of economic development: Democracies may be more likely to emerge as countries develop economically, or, having been established for whatever reasons, democracies may be more likely to survive in developed countries. We call the first explanation "endogenous" and the second "exogenous."

Because we are dealing with only two kinds of regimes, democracies emerge whenever dictatorships die.[6] Hence, to assert that democracies emerge as a result of economic development is the same as saying that dictatorships die as countries ruled by them become economically developed. Democracy thus is said to be secreted out of dictatorships by economic development. A story told about country after country is that as a country develops, its social structure becomes complex, new groups emerge and organize, labor processes require the active cooperation of employees, and, as a result, the system can no longer be effectively run by command: The society is too complex, technological change endows the direct producers with autonomy and private information, civil society emerges, and dictatorial forms of control lose their effectiveness. Various groups, whether the bourgeoisie, workers, or just the amorphous "civil society," rise against the dictatorial regime, and it falls.

The endogenous explanation is a "modernization" theory. The basic assumption of this theory is that there is one general process, of which democratization is but the final facet. Modernization consists of a gradual differentiation and specialization of social structures culminating in a separation of the political from other structures, and making democracy possible. The specific

causal chains consist in sequences of industrialization, urbanization, education, communication, mobilization, political incorporation, and innumerable other "-ations": a progressive accumulation of social changes that make a society ready to proceed to the final one, democratization.

Modernization may be one reason that the incidence of democracy is related to economic development, and this is the reading imputed to Lipset by most commentators (Diamond 1992: 125; Huber, Rueschemeyer, and Stephens 1993: 711). His most influential critic, O'Donnell (1973: 3), paraphrases Lipset's thesis as saying that "if other countries become as rich as the economically advanced nations, it is highly probable that they will become political democracies." Democracy is endogenous, because it results from economic development under authoritarianism. The hypothesis is that if authoritarian countries develop, they become democratic. The sequence of events we would thus expect to observe is one of poor authoritarian countries developing and becoming democratic once they reach some level of development, a "threshold."

Yet suppose, just suppose, that dictatorships are equally likely to die, and democracies to emerge, at any level of development. They may die for so many different reasons that development, with all its modernizing consequences, plays no privileged role. After all, as Therborn (1977) emphasized, many European countries became democratized because of wars, not because of "modernization," a story repeated by the Argentine defeat in the Malvinas and elsewhere. Some dictatorships have fallen in the aftermath of the death of the founding dictator, such as a Franco, uniquely capable of maintaining the authoritarian order. Some have collapsed because of economic crises, some because of foreign pressures, and perhaps some for purely idiosyncratic reasons.

If dictatorships die and democracies emerge randomly with regard to economic develop-

---

6. This is not quite true of our data set, because different countries enter and exit the sample at different moments. For the moment, we consider the population of countries as fixed.

ment, is it still possible that there should be more democracies among wealthy countries than among poor countries? If one is to judge Lipset (1959: 56) by his own words—"The more well-to-do a nation, the greater the chances it will sustain democracy"—then even if the emergence of a democracy is independent of the level of development, the chance that this regime will survive will be greater if it is established in an affluent country. We would thus expect democracies to appear randomly with regard to levels of development, and then to die in the poorer countries and to survive in the wealthier countries. And because every time a dictatorship happened to die in an affluent country democracy would be there to stay, history should gradually accumulate wealthy democracies. This is no longer a modernization theory, because the emergence of democracy is not brought about by development. Democracy appears exogenously, deus ex machina. It tends to survive if a country is "modern," but it is not a product of "modernization.". . .

Thus, to decide which mechanism generates the relationship between development and democracy, we need to determine how the respective transition probabilities change with the level of development. . . .

Level of Economic Development and Regime Dynamics

Examine first some descriptive patterns. . . . If the theory according to which the emergence of democracy is a result of economic development is true, transitions to democracy should be more likely when authoritarian regimes reach higher levels of development. In fact, dictatorships survive almost invariably in the very poor countries, those whose per capita incomes are under $1,000, or at least they succeed one another and the regime remains the same. They are less stable in countries with incomes between $1,001 and

$4,000, and even less so between $4,001 and $7,000. But if income reaches the level of $7,000, the trend reverses and they become more likely to survive. . . . [T]ransitions to democracy are less likely in poor countries and in rich ones, but they are more likely at the intermediate income levels. If we take all the dictatorships, their probability of dying during any year is 0.0198; for those with incomes over $1,000, this probability is 0.0280, over $5,000 it is 0.0526, over $6,000 it is 0.0441, and over $7,000 it is 0.0286; the two very wealthy dictatorships with incomes above $8,000 still survived in 1990. Hence, it appears that Huntington was correct, albeit only with regard to authoritarian regimes, when he argued that one should expect to observe "a bell-shaped pattern of instability" (1968: 43). Economic development seems to destabilize dictatorships in countries at intermediate levels of income, but not in those that are poor nor in those that are wealthy.

Indeed, dictatorships survived for years in countries that were wealthy by comparative standards. Whatever the threshold at which development is supposed to dig the grave for an authoritarian regime, it is clear that many dictatorships must have passed it in good health. . . .

Conversely, many dictatorships fell in countries with low income levels. . . .

Yet this may not be a fair test of modernization theory. After all, this theory supposes that countries develop over a longer period, so that all the modernizing consequences have time to accumulate. Let us therefore examine more closely those countries that did develop under authoritarian regimes and that at some time became "modern," which we will take somewhat arbitrarily to mean that they had a per capita income of $4,115. . . .

Twenty dictatorships (to remind, out of 123) did develop over longer periods of time and reached "modernity." Gabon, Mexico, Syria, and Yugoslavia developed continuously for at least a decade, reached the level at which democracy would be expected to be the more likely regime, and, having remained under dictatorships, experienced a series of economic crises. Singapore and Malaysia developed over a long period, became wealthy, and remained dictatorships. In East Germany, Taiwan, the Soviet Union, Spain, Bulgaria, and Hungary competitive elections eventually took place, but at very different levels of income. Given its 1974 income level, Uruguay should have never been a dictatorship. The economic history of the Chilean dictatorship is convoluted: Its income in 1974 was $3,561; it climbed with downs and ups to $4,130 by 1981, collapsed to $3,199 by 1983, recovered to surpass the 1974 level only by 1986, and passed the threshold of $4,115 in 1989, exactly the year of transition. The history of Poland is similar: By our criteria, it reached the threshold of democracy in 1974; it experienced an economic crisis in 1979 and a mass movement for democracy in 1980, passed the threshold again in 1985, and became a democracy in 1989. In turn, Brazil, Czechoslovakia, Portugal, and perhaps even South Korea and Greece are the dream cases for a modernization theorist. Those countries developed under dictatorships, became wealthy, and threw off their dictatorships more or less when their levels of development would have predicted. But they are few.

This is not to say that democracy did not emerge in some countries when they became modern. Indeed, perhaps in those countries that did develop over a long period, the very thought of democracy appeared on the political agenda because they were too modern—not only in those countries that became democratic just when our model predicts but also those that waited much longer: Taiwan, the Soviet Union, Spain, and Bulgaria. Modernization may create the "prerequisites" for political conflict over the form of regime. But the manner in which these conflicts will develop remains unpredictable. When conflicts over regimes are examined at a micro level, by looking at the political actors involved, their motives and their beliefs, it becomes apparent that these are situations laden with uncertainty (O'Donnell and Schmitter 1986; Przeworski 1991). Game-theoretic analyses of transitions to democracy make it apparent that the actors involved often do not know each other's preferences, the relationships of physical forces, or the outcomes of eventual conflicts (Wantchekon 1996; Zielinski 1997). And under such conditions, various equilibria can prevail: Whereas transition to democracy is one feasible outcome, so is the perpetuation of the dictatorial status quo, or even a solidification of dictatorship. Hence, even if modernization may generate conflicts over democracy, the outcomes of such conflicts are open-ended.

But if modernization theory is to have any predictive power, there must be some level of income at which one can be relatively sure that the country will throw off its dictatorship. And one is hard put to find this level: Even among the countries that satisfy the premise of the modernization theory . . . the range of incomes at which dictatorships survived is very wide. Few authoritarian regimes have developed over a long period, and even if most of them should eventually become democracies, no level of income can predict when that should occur.

Moreover, even if to predict is not the same as to explain, "explaining" can easily entail an expost fallacy. Take Taiwan, which in 1952 had a per capita income of $968. It developed rapidly, passing by 1979 our threshold of $4,115; it had a probability of 0.10 of being a dictatorship in 1990, and in 1995, for the first time, elected its president in contested elections. Suppose that during all that time the Taiwanese dictatorship had faced each year a probability of 0.02 of dying, for reasons not related to development. It thus would have had a cumulative chance of about 50 percent of not being around by 1995 even if it had not developed at all. Thus we might erroneously attribute to development what may have been just a cumulation of random hazards.[9] And, indeed, the Taiwanese dictatorship most likely democratized to mobilize international support against the threat from China: for geopolitical reasons, not for economic reasons.

In sum, the causal power of economic development in bringing down dictatorships appears paltry. The level of development, at least as measured by per capita income, gives little information about the chances of transition to democracy.

On the other hand, per capita income has a strong impact on the survival of democracies.... Indeed, no democracy has ever been subverted, not during the period we studied nor ever before nor after, regardless of everything else, in a country with a per capita income higher than that of Argentina in 1975: $6,055. There is no doubt that democracy is stable in affluent countries....

Huntington (1968: 1) was concerned with stability and did not care whether regimes were democratic or authoritarian. "The most important political distinction among countries," he thought, "concerns not their form of government but their degree of government." Hence, the United States, the United Kingdom, and the Soviet Union were all systems in which "the government governs." Whether it was the Politburo, the cabinet, or the president mattered little. "The problem," he insisted, "was not to hold elections but to create organizations." Indeed, we were told, "the primary problem is not liberty but the creation of a legitimate public order" (1968: 7). Though never explicitly referring to Lipset, Huntington (1968: 35–36) observed that "in actuality, only some of the tendencies encompassed in the concept of 'political

modernization' characterized the 'modernizing' areas. Instead of a trend toward competitiveness and democracy, there was an 'erosion of democracy' and a tendency to autocratic military regimes and one-party regimes. Instead of stability, there were repeated coups and revolts." We should expect "a bell-shaped pattern of political instability" (p. 43) among democratic as well as authoritarian regimes.

O'Donnell dragged Lipset over the coals for various methodological transgressions. Reflecting on his criticisms in retrospect, he observed that "Chapter I is now an archeological remnant—testimony of a debate that in 1971 had recently begun and today is finished: it is no longer necessary to lead the reader through tedious series of data to demonstrate that 'socio-economic development' does not foster 'democracy and/or political stability'" (1979: 204). What the data show, O'Donnell asserted, is that "in contemporary South America, the higher and the lower levels of modernization are associated with non-democratic political systems, while political democracies are found at intermediate levels of modernization." Hence, at least within the range observed by O'Donnell, we should observe that democracies fall as economies develop.

Is there some level of development beyond which democracies are more likely to die than they were earlier? We have already seen ... that the probability of a democracy dying declines monotonically with per capita income. Although O'Donnell did cite a countercase against Lipset, his account of the rise of bureaucratic authoritarianism does not undermine Lipset's theory.[10] O'Donnell studied a country that turns out to be a distant outlier.... Thus, Lipset was right in

9. An analogy may be useful. Suppose that a woman runs a risk of 0.01 of dying from accidental causes during each year of her life, and then at the age of 78 she gets hit by a falling brick. To attribute her death to development would be to conclude that she died of old age.

10. O'Donnell was careful not to make general claims: His purpose was to explain the downfall of democracies in the Southern Cone. But his theory of "bureaucratic authoritarianism" captured the imaginations of scholars all around the world, who treated it as applicable almost everywhere.

thinking that the richer the country, the more likely it is to sustain democracy.

Clearly, this fact cries for an explanation. One possible account for the durability of democracies in wealthy countries, proposed already by Lipset, is that, through various sociological mechanisms, wealth lowers the intensity of distributional conflicts. An alternative explanation is that income is just a proxy for education, and more highly educated people are more likely to embrace democratic values. Education, specifically accumulated years of education for an average member of the labor force, does increase the probability of survival of democracy at each level of income.[11] The probability that a democracy will die in a country where the average member of the labor force has fewer than three years of formal education is 0.1154; it is 0.0620 when the level of education is between three and six years, 0.0080 when it is six to nine years, and zero when the average worker has more than nine years of education. The highest level of education under which a country experienced a transition to dictatorship was 8.36 years in Sri Lanka in 1977, but that was an outlier. The next highest level of education when democracy fell was 6.85 years in Uruguay.

But income is not a proxy for education. Even though these two variables are highly correlated (0.78), their effects are to a large measure independent.... [W]hereas at each income level the probability of democracy falling decreases with increasing education, the converse is also true: At each level of education, the probability of democracy dying decreases with income. Hence, for reasons that are not easy to identify,

wealth does make democracies more stable, independently of education.

Finally, we find no evidence of "consolidation." Democracies become "consolidated" if the conditional probability that a democratic regime will die during a particular year given that it has survived thus far (the "hazard rate") declines with its age, so that, as Dahl (1990) has argued, democracies are more likely to survive if they have lasted for some time. Examining the ages at which democracies die indicates that this is true, but once the level of development is taken into account, the hazard rates become independent of age, meaning that for a given level of development, democracies are about equally likely to die at any age.... These findings indicate that the hazard rates uncorrected for the level of development decline because countries develop, not because a democracy that has long been around is more likely to continue.

The conclusion reached thus far is that whereas economic development under dictatorship has at most a non-linear relationship to the emergence of democracies, once they are established, democracies are much more likely to endure in more highly developed countries. Yet because our systematic observations begin in 1950, the question arises whether or not these patterns also characterize the earlier period. Studies in the Lipset tradition have assumed that they do: They have inferred the historical process from cross-sectional observations. Yet the validity of such inferences is contested by followers of Moore (1966), who claimed that the Western European route to democracy was unique, not to be repeated. Note that when Rustow (1970) pointed out that the levels of development at which different countries permanently established democratic institutions varied widely, Lipset's rejoinder (1981) was that the thresholds at which democracy was established were lower for the early democracies. Is that true?

Although economic data for the pre-war period are not comparable to those at our disposal after 1950, Maddison (1995) reconstructed

---

11. We have data only for 2,900 country-years of education. The mean is 4.85 years, and the standard deviation is 3.12, with a minimum of 0.03 (Guinea in 1966) and a maximum of 12.81 (United States in 1985); 27.6% of the sample had educational levels lower than three years, 64.4% lower than six years, and 90.8% lower than nine years. Only 13.0% of the sample had education levels higher than Sri Lanka in 1977, and 26.1% higher than Uruguay in 1973.

per capita income series for several countries going back to the nineteenth century.... The levels at which democracies were established before 1950 vary as widely as they do for the later period; indeed, they cover almost the entire range of incomes observed....

To conclude, there is no doubt that democracies are more likely to be found in the more highly developed countries. Yet the reason is not that democracies are more likely to emerge when countries develop under authoritarianism, but that, however they do emerge, they are more likely to survive in countries that are already developed....

References

Almond, Gabriel A., and Sidney Verba. 1963. *The Civic Culture: Political Attitudes and Democracy in Five Nations.* Princeton, NJ: Princeton University Press.

Arat, Zehra F. 1988. Democracy and Economic Development: Modernization Theory Revisited. *Comparative Politics* 21(1): 21–36.

Dahl, Robert A. 1971. *Polyarchy.* New Haven, CT: Yale University Press.

———. 1990. Transitions to Democracy. Paper read at the symposium Voices of Democracy, March 16–17, University of Dayton Center for International Studies.

Diamond, Larry. 1992. Economic Development and Democracy Reconsidered. In *Reexamining Democracy: Essays in Honor of Seymour Martin Lipset*, edited by G. Marks and L. Diamond, pp. 93–139. Newbury Park, CA: Sage Publications.

Eisenstadt, S. N. 1968. The Protestant Ethic Theses in the Framework of Sociological Theory and Weber's Work. In *The Protestant Ethic and Modernization: A Comparative View*, edited by S. N. Eisenstadt, pp. 3–45. New York: Basic Books.

Gellner, Ernest. 1991. Civil Society in Historical Context. *International Social Science Journal* 129: 495–510.

Huber, Evelyne, Dietrich Rueschemeyer, and John D. Stephens. 1993. The Impact of Economic Development on Democracy. *Journal of Economic Perspectives* 7(3): 71–86.

Huntington, Samuel P. 1968. *Political Order in Changing Societies.* New Haven, CT: Yale University Press.

———. 1993. The Clash of Civilizations? *Foreign Affairs* 72(3): 22–49.

Jackman, Robert W. 1973. On the Relation of Economic Development to Democratic Performance. *American Journal of Political Science* 17: 611–621.

Lewis, Bernard. 1993. Islam and Liberal Democracy. *Atlantic Monthly* 271(2): 89–98.

Lipset, Seymour Martin. 1959. Some Social Requisites of Democracy: Economic Development and Political Legitimacy. *American Political Science Review* 53(1): 69–105.

———. 1960. *Political Man: The Social Bases of Politics.* Garden City, NY: Doubleday.

———. 1981. *Political Man: The Social Bases of Politics*, expanded edition. Baltimore: Johns Hopkins University Press.

Maddison, Angus. 1995. *Monitoring the World Economy, 1820–1992.* Paris: Organization for Economic Co-operation and Development.

Marks, Gary, and Larry Diamond (eds.). 1992. *Reexamining Democracy: Essays in Honor of Seymour Martin Lipset.* Newbury Park, CA: Sage Publications.

Montesquieu. 1995. *The Spirit of the Laws*, translated by Thomas Nugent. New York: Hafner Press. (Originally published 1748.)

Moore, Barrington, Jr. 1966. *Social Origins of Dictatorship and Democracy: Lord and Peasant in the Making of the Modern World.* Boston: Beacon Press.

O'Donnell, Guillermo. 1979. Postscript: 1979. In *Modernization and Bureaucratic-Authoritarianism: Studies in South American Politics.* Berkeley: Institute of International Studies, University of California.

O'Donnell, Guillermo, and Philippe C. Schmitter. 1986. *Transitions from Authoritarian Rule: Tentative Conclusions about Uncertain Democracies.* Baltimore: Johns Hopkins University Press.

Przeworski, Adam. 1991. *Democracy and the Market.* Cambridge University Press.

Przeworski, Adam, José Antonio Cheibub, and Fernando Limongi. 1997. Culture and Democracy. In *World Culture Report*, pp. 157–187. Paris: UNESCO.

Rustow, Dankwart A. 1970. Transitions to Democracy: Toward a Dynamic Model. *Comparative Politics* 2(3): 337–364.

Therborn, Goran. 1977. The Rule of Capital and the Rise of Democracy. *New Left Review* 103 (May–June): 3–41.

Wantchekon, Leonard. 1996. Political Coordination and Democratic Instability. Unpublished manuscript, Yale University.

Weber, Max. 1958. *The Protestant Ethic and the Spirit of Capitalism*. New York: Scribner. (Originally published 1904.)

Zielinski, Jakub. 1997. The Polish Transition to Democracy: A Game-Theoretic Approach. *European Archives of Sociology* 36: 135 158.

3 DEMOCRACY, CULTURE, AND SOCIETY

The Federalist No. 10

James Madison

To the People of the State of New York

Among the numerous advantages promised by a well-constructed Union, none deserves to be more accurately developed than its tendency to break and control the violence of faction. The friend of popular governments never finds himself so much alarmed for their character and fate, as when he contemplates their propensity to this dangerous vice. He will not fail, therefore, to set a due value on any plan which, without violating the principles to which he is attached, provides a proper cure for it. The instability, injustice, and confusion introduced into the public councils, have, in truth, been the mortal diseases under which popular governments have everywhere perished; as they continue to be the favorite and fruitful topics from which the adversaries to liberty derive their most specious declamations. The valuable improvements made by the American constitutions on the popular models, both ancient and modern, cannot certainly be too much admired; but it would be an unwarrantable partiality, to contend that they have as effectually obviated the danger on this side, as was wished and expected. Complaints are everywhere heard from our most considerate and virtuous citizens, equally the friends of public and private faith, and of public and personal liberty, that our governments are too unstable; that the public good is disregarded in the conflicts of rival parties; and that measures are too often decided, not according to the rules of justice and the rights of the minor party, but by the superior force of an interested and overbearing major-ity.[11] However anxiously we may wish that these complaints had no foundation, the evidence of known facts will not permit us to deny that they are in some degree true. It will be found, indeed, on a candid review of our situation, that some of the distresses under which we labor have been erroneously charged on the operation of our governments; but it will be found, at the same time, that other causes will not alone account for many of our heaviest misfortunes; and, particularly, for that prevailing and increasing distrust of public engagements, and alarm for private rights, which are echoed from one end of the continent to the other. These must be chiefly, if not wholly, effects of the unsteadiness and injustice with which a factious spirit has tainted our public administrations.

By a faction, I understand a number of citizens, whether amounting to a majority or minority of the whole, who are united and actuated by some common impulse of passion, or of interest, adverse to the rights of other citizens, or to the permanent and aggregate interests of the community.[12]

There are two methods of curing the mischiefs of faction: the one, by removing its causes; the other, by controlling its effects.

There are again two methods of removing the causes of faction: the one, by destroying the liberty which is essential to its existence; the other,

Excerpted from: Alexander Hamilton, James Madison, and John Jay, *The Federalist Papers: A Collection of Essays Written in Support of the Constitution of the United States*, second edition. Edited by Roy P. Fairfield. Garden City: Anchor, 1966.

11. Compare with Jefferson's *First Inaugural:* "... that though the will of the majority is in all cases to prevail, that will, to be rightful, must be reasonable ..." See Herbert McClosky, "The Fallacy of Absolute Majority Rule," *Journal of Politics* (Nov. 1949), 637–654, and Wilmoore Kendall's response, *ibid.* (Nov. 1950), 694–713.

12. Both Federalists and anti-Federalists used "faction" and "party" synonymously. And, as J. Allen Smith pointed out, English conservatives had the same objections to factions; *The Spirit of American Government* (N.Y., 1912), 205.

by giving to every citizen the same opinions, the same passions, and the same interests.

It could never be more truly said than of the first remedy, that it is worse than the disease. Liberty is to faction what air is to fire, an aliment without which it instantly expires. But it could not be less folly to abolish liberty, which is essential to political life, because it nourishes faction, than it would be to wish the annihilation of air, which is essential to animal life, because it imparts to fire its destructive agency.[13]

The second expedient is as impracticable as the first would be unwise. As long as the reason of man continues fallible, and he is at liberty to exercise it, different opinions will be formed. As long as the connection subsists between his reason and his self-love, his opinions and his passions will have a reciprocal influence on each other; and the former will be objects to which the latter will attach themselves. The diversity in the faculties of men, from which the rights of property originate, is not less an insuperable obstacle to a uniformity of interests. The protection of these faculties is the first object of government. From the protection of different and unequal faculties of acquiring property, the possession of different degrees and kinds of property immediately results; and from the influence of these on the sentiments and views of the respective proprietors, ensues a division of the society into different interests and parties.

The latent causes of faction are thus sown in the nature of man; and we see them everywhere brought into different degrees of activity, according to the different circumstances of civil society. A zeal for different opinions concerning religion, concerning government, and many other points, as well of speculation as of practice; an attachment to different leaders ambitiously

contending for pre-eminence and power; or to persons of other descriptions whose fortunes have been interesting to the human passions, have, in turn, divided mankind into parties, inflamed them with mutual animosity, and rendered them much more disposed to vex and oppress each other than to co-operate for their common good.[14] So strong is this propensity of mankind to fall into mutual animosities, that where no substantial occasion presents itself, the most frivolous and fanciful distinctions have been sufficient to kindle their unfriendly passions and excite their most violent conflicts. But the most common and durable source of factions has been the various and unequal distribution of property.[15] Those who hold and those who are without property have ever formed distinct interests in society. Those who are creditors, and those who are debtors, fall under a like discrimination. A landed interest, a manufacturing interest, a mercantile interest, a moneyed interest, with many lesser interests, grow up of necessity in civilized nations, and divide them into different classes, actuated by different sentiments and views.[16] The regulation of these various and

13. Contrast with *Federalist, No. 9*, in which Hamilton, arguing for union, says that, "The utility of a Confederacy, as well to suppress faction and to guard the internal tranquillity of States . . is in reality not a new idea."

14. Adair points to this sentence as a compression of "the greater part of Hume's essay on factions." Adair, ["That Politics May Be Reduced to a Science." *Huntington Library Quarterly* (Aug. 1957), pp. 343–360], 358.

15. Harold Laski, stressing Madison's economic determinism, misquoted this passage as follows: "the only durable source of faction is property." *The Grammar of Politics* (London, 1925), 162.

16. For Marxist comparisons other than Beard's, see Saul K. Padover, ed., *The Complete Madison*, 14–15, and Jacques Barzun, *Darwin, Marx, Wagner* (Garden City, 1958), 146. For scholarly evaluations of the Marxist interpretation, see Diamond, ["Democracy and *The Federalist*: A Reconsideration of the Framers' Intent." *American Political Science Review* 53(1): 52–68, March 1959], 65–66; Adair, "The Tenth Federalist Revisited," *Wm. & Mary Quarterly* (Jan. 1951), 48–67; Wright, ["*The Federalist* on the Nature of Political Man." *Ethics* 59, no. 2 (Jan. 1949), pp. 1–31], 17. . . .

interfering interests forms the principal task of modern legislation, and involves the spirit of party and faction in the necessary and ordinary operations of the government....

The inference to which we are brought is, that the *causes* of faction cannot be removed, and that relief is only to be sought in the means of controlling its *effects*.

If a faction consists of less than a majority, relief is supplied by the republican principle, which enables the majority to defeat its sinister views by regular vote. It may clog the administration, it may convulse the society; but it will be unable to execute and mask its violence under the forms of the Constitution. When a majority is included in a faction, the form of popular government, on the other hand, enables it to sacrifice to its ruling passion or interest both the public good and the rights of other citizens. To secure the public good and private rights against the danger of such a faction, and at the same time to preserve the spirit and the form of popular government, is then the great object to which our inquiries are directed....

From this view of the subject it may be concluded that a pure democracy, by which I mean a society consisting of a small number of citizens, who assemble and administer the government in person, can admit of no cure for the mischiefs of faction.[17] A common passion or interest will, in almost every case, be felt by a majority of the whole; a communication and concert result from the form of government itself; and there is nothing to check the inducements to sacrifice the weaker party or an obnoxious individual. Hence it is that such democracies have ever been spectacles of turbulence and contention; have ever been found incompatible with personal security or the rights of property; and have in general been as short in their lives as they have been violent in their deaths. Theoretic politicians, who have patronized this species of government, have erroneously supposed that by reducing mankind to a perfect equality in their political rights, they would, at the same time, be perfectly equalized and assimilated in their possessions, their opinions, and their passions.

A republic, by which I mean a government in which the scheme of representation takes place, opens a different prospect, and promises the cure for which we are seeking....

The two great points of difference between a democracy and a republic are: first, the delegation of the government in the latter to a small number of citizens elected by the rest; secondly, the greater number of citizens and greater sphere of country over which the latter may be extended.

The effect of the first difference is, on the one hand, to refine and enlarge the public views, by passing them through the medium of a chosen body of citizens,[18] whose wisdom may best discern the true interest of their country, and whose

---

17. Democracy had a bad name from early times. Plato condemned it in *The Republic* (Book VIII), Aristotle in *Politics* (Book IV). In more recent times, Montesquieu, who had a great impact upon the fathers, attacked it in *Spirit of Laws* (I, Book VIII). For an account of the conservative-democratic controversy in the 1763–87 period, see Merrill Jensen, *The Articles of Confederation* and *The New Nation*; for a few typical eighteenth-century views of democracy, see Richard Hofstadter, *The American Political Tradition* (N.Y., 1948), 4. As Ralph Ketcham points out, ["Notes on James Madison's Sources," *Midwest Journal of Political Science* (May 1957)], 25, "... there was almost universal agreement in the eighteenth century that 'democracy' was a nasty word—it meant tumult, violence, instability, mob rule, and bloody revolution."

(By permission of the Wayne State University Press.) For two other valuable historical and philosophical views, see Harold Laski's essay on the concept in the *Encyclopedia of the Social Sciences* (N.Y., 1931), V, 76–84, and Henry B. Mayo, *An Introduction to Democratic Theory* (N.Y., 1960).

18. A variation on a theme? Also, see Jay's reliance upon Providence in *No. 2*. Other "chosen people" concepts: Hebrew, England's Whig oligarchy, New England's theocratic oligarchy, etc. Suggested by B. C. Rodick, *American Constitutional Custom* (N.Y., 1953), 136.

patriotism and love of justice will be least likely to sacrifice it to temporary or partial considerations. Under such a regulation, it may well happen that the public voice, pronounced by the representatives of the people, will be more consonant to the public good than if pronounced by the people themselves, convened for the purpose. On the other hand, the effect may be inverted. Men of factious tempers, of local prejudices, or of sinister designs, may by intrigue, by corruption, or by other means, first obtain the suffrages, and then betray the interests of the people. The question resulting is, whether small or extensive republics are more favorable to the election of proper guardians of the public weal; and it is clearly decided in favor of the latter by two obvious considerations.

In the first place, it is to be remarked that, however small the republic may be, the representatives must be raised to a certain number in order to guard against the cabals of a few; and that, however large it may be, they must be limited to a certain number in order to guard against the confusion of a multitude. Hence, the number of representatives in the two cases not being in proportion to that of the two constituents, and being proportionally greater in the small republic, it follows that, if the proportion of fit characters be not less in the large than in the small republic, the former will present a greater option and consequently a greater probability of a fit choice.

In the next place, as each representative will be chosen by a greater number of citizens in the large than in the small republic, it will be more difficult for unworthy candidates to practise with success the vicious arts by which elections are too often carried; and the suffrages of the people being more free, will be more likely to centre in men who possess the most attractive merit and the most diffusive and established characters.

It must be confessed that in this, as in most other cases, there is a mean, on both sides of which inconveniences will be found to lie. By enlarging too much the number of electors, you render the representative too little acquainted with all their local circumstances and lesser interests: as by reducing it too much, you render him unduly attached to these, and too little fit to comprehend and pursue great and national objects. The federal Constitution forms a happy combination in this respect; the great and aggregate interests being referred to the national, the local and particular to the State legislatures.

The other point of difference is, the greater number of citizens and extent of territory which may be brought within the compass of republican than of democratic government; and it is this circumstance principally which renders factious combinations less to be dreaded in the former than in the latter. The smaller the society, the fewer probably will be the distinct parties and interests composing it; the fewer the distinct parties and interests, the more frequently will a majority be found of the same party; and the smaller the number of individuals composing a majority, and the smaller the compass within which they are placed, the more easily will they concert and execute their plans of oppression. Extend the sphere, and you take in a greater variety of parties and interests; you make it less probable that a majority of the whole will have a common motive to invade the rights of other citizens; or if such a common motive exists, it will be more difficult for all who feel it to discover their own strength and to act in unison with each other. Besides other impediments, it may be remarked that, where there is a consciousness of unjust or dishonorable purposes, communication is always checked by distrust in proportion to the number whose concurrence is necessary.[19]

---

19. It might be asked, Where does Madison acquire his faith in the magic of numbers? Does he come to grips with the problem of the demagogue? And does he discuss comprehensively the fact that the impediments eliminating the dire effects of faction might also prevent positive action? Is Louis Hartz correct when he claims that Madison did not solve the problem of faction as related to economic factors? *The Liberal Tradition in America* (N.Y., 1955), 84–85.

Hence, it clearly appears that the same advantage which a republic has over a democracy in controlling the effects of faction is enjoyed by a large over a small republic,—is enjoyed by the Union over the States composing it.[20] Does the advantage consist in the substitution of representatives whose enlightened views and virtuous sentiments render them superior to local prejudices and to schemes of injustice? It will not be denied that the representation of the Union will be most likely to possess these requisite endowments. Does it consist in the greater security afforded by a greater variety of parties, against the event of any one party being able to outnumber and oppress the rest? In an equal degree does the increased variety of parties comprised within the Union, increase this security. Does it, in fine, consist in the greater obstacles opposed to the concert and accomplishment of the secret wishes of an unjust and interested majority? Here, again, the extent of the Union gives it the most palpable advantage.

The influence of factious leaders may kindle a flame within their particular States, but will be unable to spread a general conflagration through the other States. A religious sect may degenerate into a political faction in a part of the Confederacy; but the variety of sects dispersed over the entire face of it must secure the national councils against any danger from that source. A rage for paper money, for an abolition of debts, for an equal division of property, or for any other improper or wicked project, will be less apt to pervade the whole body of the Union than a particular member of it; in the same proportion as such a malady is more likely to taint a particular county or district, than an entire State.

In the extent and proper structure of the Union, therefore, we behold a republican remedy for the diseases most incident to republican government. And according to the degree of pleasure and pride we feel in being republicans, ought to be our zeal in cherishing the spirit and supporting the character of Federalists.

PUBLIUS

---

20. Aristotle said that "the size of a state . . . should be determined by the range of a man's voice," quoted by Cousins, ["World Citizenship—When?" in Lyman Bryson, ed. *Approaches to World Peace* (New York: Harper, 1944)], 523. And such remained the thought and experience of the eighteenth century, that a republic was feasible only in a small geographic area. Thus it is not surprising to find the anti-Federalists attacking the concept of the extensive republic found in the Constitution and *Federalist, No. 10*; Ford, *Essays*, 4, 74, 76, 91, 255–256.

Adair, tracing the sources for *No. 10*, suggests that Madison may have been "electrified" by the following comments in Hume:

In a large government, which is modelled with masterly skill, there is compass and room enough to refine the democracy, from the lower people, who may be admitted into the first elections or first concoction of the commonwealth, to the higher magistrates, who direct all the movements. At the same time, the parts are so distant and remote, that it is very difficult, either by intrigue, prejudice, or passion, to hurry them into any measure against the public interest. Op. cit., 351.

The Federalist No. 14

James Madison

To the People of the State of New York

We have seen the necessity of the Union, as our bulwark against foreign danger, as the conservator of peace among ourselves, as the guardian of our commerce and other common interests, as the only substitute for those military establishments which have subverted the liberties of the Old World, and as the proper antidote for the diseases of faction, which have proved fatal to other popular governments, and of which alarming symptoms have been betrayed by our own. All that remains, within this branch of our inquiries, is to take notice of an objection that may be drawn from the great extent of country which the Union embraces. A few observations on this subject will be the more proper, as it is perceived that the adversaries of the new Constitution are availing themselves of the prevailing prejudice with regard to the practicable sphere of republican administration, in order to supply, by imaginary difficulties, the want of those solid objections which they endeavor in vain to find.

The error which limits republican government to a narrow district has been unfolded and refuted in preceding papers. I remark here only that it seems to owe its rise and prevalence chiefly to the confounding of a republic with a democracy, applying to the former reasonings drawn from the nature of the latter. The true distinction between these forms was also adverted to on a former occasion. It is, that in a democracy, the people meet and exercise the government in person; in a republic, they assemble and administer it by their representatives and agents. A democracy, consequently, will be confined to a small spot. A republic may be extended over a large region.

To this accidental source of the error may be added the artifice of some celebrated authors, whose writings have had a great share in forming the modern standard of political opinions. Being subjects either of an absolute or limited monarchy, they have endeavored to heighten the advantages, or palliate the evils of those forms, by placing in comparison the vices and defects of the republican, and by citing as specimens of the latter the turbulent democracies of ancient Greece and modern Italy. Under the confusion of names, it has been an easy task to transfer to a republic observations applicable to a democracy only; and among others, the observation that it can never be established but among a small number of people living within a small compass of territory.

Such a fallacy may have been the less perceived, as most of the popular governments of antiquity were of the democratic species; and even in modern Europe, to which we owe the great principle of representation, no example is seen of a government wholly popular, and founded at the same time wholly on that principle. If Europe has the merit of discovering this great mechanical power in government, by the simple agency of which the will of the largest political body may be concentred, and its force directed to any object which the public good requires, America can claim the merit of making the discovery the basis of unmixed and extensive republics. It is only to be lamented that any of her citizens should wish to deprive her of the additional merit of displaying its full efficacy in the establishment of the comprehensive system now under her consideration.

As the natural limit of a democracy is that distance from the central point which will just

Excerpted from: Alexander Hamilton, James Madison, and John Jay, *The Federalist Papers: A Collection of Essays Written in Support of the Constitution of the United States*, second edition. Edited by Roy P. Fairfield. Garden City: Anchor, 1966.

permit the most remote citizens to assemble as often as their public functions demand, and will include no greater number than can join in those functions; so the natural limit of a republic is that distance from the centre which will barely allow the representatives to meet as often as may be necessary for the administration of public affairs. Can it be said that the limits of the United States exceed this distance? It will not be said by those who recollect that the Atlantic coast is the longest side of the Union, that during the term of thirteen years the representatives of the States have been almost continually assembled, and that the members from the most distant States are not chargeable with greater intermissions of attendance than those from the States in the neighborhood of Congress.

That we may form a juster estimate with regard to this interesting subject, let us resort to the actual dimensions of the Union. . . .

. . . [I]t is to be remembered that the general government is not to be charged with the whole power of making and administering laws. Its jurisdiction is limited to certain enumerated objects which concern all the members of the republic, but which are not to be attained by the separate provisions of any. The subordinate governments, which can extend their care to all those other objects which can be separately provided for, will retain their due authority and activity. Were it proposed by the plan of the convention to abolish the governments of the particular States, its adversaries would have some ground for their objection; though it would not be difficult to show that if they were abolished the general government would be compelled, by the principle of self-preservation, to reinstate them in their proper jurisdiction.

A second observation to be made is that the immediate object of the federal Constitution is to secure the union of the thirteen primitive States, which we know to be practicable; and to add to them such other States as may arise in their own bosoms or in their neighborhoods, which we cannot doubt to be equally practicable. The

arrangements that may be necessary for those angles and fractions of our territory which lie on our northwestern frontier, must be left to those whom further discoveries and experience will render more equal to the task.

Let it be remarked, in the third place, that the intercourse throughout the Union will be facilitated by new improvements. Roads will everywhere be shortened and kept in better order; accommodations for travellers will be multiplied and meliorated; an interior navigation on our eastern side will be opened throughout, or nearly throughout, the whole extent of the thirteen States. The communication between the Western and Atlantic districts, and between different parts of each, will be rendered more and more easy by those numerous canals with which the beneficence of nature has intersected our country, and which art finds it so little difficult to connect and complete.

A fourth and still more important consideration is, that as almost every State will on one side or other be a frontier, and will thus find, in a regard to its safety, an inducement to make some sacrifices for the sake of the general protection; so the States which lie at the greatest distance from the heart of the Union, and which, of course, may partake least of the ordinary circulation of its benefits, will be at the same time immediately contiguous to foreign nations, and will consequently stand, on particular occasions, in greatest need of its strength and resources. It may be inconvenient for Georgia, or the States forming our western or northeastern borders, to send their representatives to the seat of government; but they would find it more so to struggle alone against an invading enemy, or even to support alone the whole expense of those precautions which may be dictated by the neighborhood of continual danger. If they should derive less benefit, therefore, from the Union in some respects than the less distant States, they will derive greater benefit from it in other respects, and thus the proper equilibrium will be maintained throughout.

I submit to you, my fellow-citizens, these considerations, in full confidence that the good sense which has so often marked your decisions will allow them their due weight and effect; and that you will never suffer difficulties, however formidable in appearance, or however fashionable the error on which they may be founded, to drive you into the gloomy and perilous scene into which the advocates for disunion would conduct you. Hearken not to the unnatural voice which tells you that the people of America, knit together as they are by so many cords of affection, can no longer live together as members of the same family; can no longer continue the mutual guardians of their mutual happiness; can no longer be fellow-citizens of one great, respectable, and flourishing empire. Hearken not to the voice which petulantly tells you that the form of government recommended for your adoption is a novelty in the political world;[21] that it has never yet had a place in the theories of the wildest projectors; that it rashly attempts what it is impossible to accomplish. No, my countrymen, shut your ears against this unhallowed language. Shut your hearts against the poison which it conveys; the kindred blood which flows in the veins of American citizens, the mingled blood which they have shed in defence of their sacred rights, consecrate their Union and excite horror at the idea of their becoming aliens, rivals, enemies. And if novelties are to be shunned, believe me, the most alarming of all novelties, the most wild of all projects, the most rash of all attempts, is that of rending us in pieces in order to preserve our liberties and promote our happiness. But why is the experiment of an extended republic to be rejected, merely because it may comprise what is new? Is it not the glory of the people of America, that, whilst they have paid a decent regard to the opinions of former times and other nations, they have not suffered a blind veneration for antiquity, for custom, or for names to overrule the suggestions of their own good sense, the knowledge of their own situation, and the lessons of their own experience? To this manly spirit posterity will be indebted for the possession, and the world for the example, of the numerous innovations displayed on the American theatre in favor of private rights and public happiness. Had no important step been taken by the leaders of the Revolution for which a precedent could not be discovered, no government established of which an exact model did not present itself, the people of the United States might at this moment have been numbered among the melancholy victims of misguided councils, must at best have been laboring under the weight of some of those forms which have crushed the liberties of the rest of mankind. Happily for America, happily, we trust, for the whole human race, they pursued a new and more noble course. They accomplished a revolution which has no parallel in the annals of human society. They reared the fabrics of governments which have no model on the face of the globe. They formed the design of a great Confederacy which it is incumbent on their successors to improve and perpetuate. If their works betray imperfections, we wonder at the fewness of them. If they erred most in the structure of the Union, this was the work most difficult to be executed; this is the work which has been new modelled by the act of your convention, and it is that act on which you are now to deliberate and to decide.

PUBLIUS

---

21. Diamond, *op. cit.*, 60, argues that the novelty "consisted in solving the problems of popular government by means which yet maintain the government 'wholly popular.'"

The Concept of a Liberal Society

Louis Hartz

1. America and Europe

The analysis which this book contains is based on what might be called the storybook truth about American history: that America was settled by men who fled from the feudal and clerical oppressions of the Old World. If there is anything in this view, as old as the national folklore itself, then the outstanding thing about the American community in Western history ought to be the nonexistence of those oppressions, or since the reaction against them was in the broadest sense liberal, that the American community is a liberal community. We are confronted, as it were, with a kind of inverted Trotskyite law of combined development, America skipping the feudal stage of history as Russia presumably skipped the liberal stage. I know that I am using broad terms broadly here. "Feudalism" refers technically to the institutions of the medieval era, and it is well known that aspects of the decadent feudalism of the later period, such as primogeniture, entail, and quitrents, were present in America even in the eighteenth century. "Liberalism" is an even vaguer term, clouded as it is by all sorts of modern social reform connotations, and even when one insists on using it in the classic Lockian sense, as I shall insist here, there are aspects of our original life in the Puritan colonies and the South which hardly fit its meaning. But these are the liabilities of any large generalization, danger points but not insuperable barriers. What in the end is more interesting is the curious failure of American historians, after repeating endlessly that America was grounded in escape from the European past, to interpret our history in the

Excerpted from: Louis Hartz, *The Liberal Tradition in America: An Interpretation of American Political Thought Since the Revolution*. New York: Harcourt, Brace & World, 1955. Reprinted by permission.

light of that fact. There are a number of reasons for this which we shall encounter before we are through, but one is obvious at the outset: the separation of the study of American from European history and politics. Any attempt to uncover the nature of an American society without feudalism can only be accomplished by studying it in conjunction with a European society where the feudal structure and the feudal ethos did in fact survive. This is not to deny our national uniqueness, one of the reasons curiously given for studying America alone, but actually to affirm it. How can we know the uniqueness of anything except by contrasting it with what is not unique? The rationale for a separate American study, once you begin to think about it, explodes the study itself....

2. "Natural Liberalism": The Frame of Mind

One of the central characteristics of a nonfeudal society is that it lacks a genuine revolutionary tradition, the tradition which in Europe has been linked with the Puritan and French revolutions: that it is "born equal," as Tocqueville said. And this being the case, it lacks also a tradition of reaction: lacking Robespierre it lacks Maistre, lacking Sydney it lacks Charles II. Its liberalism is what Santayana called, referring to American democracy, a "natural" phenomenon. But the matter is curiously broader than this, for a society which begins with Locke, and thus transforms him, stays with Locke, by virtue of an absolute and irrational attachment it develops for him, and becomes as indifferent to the challenge of socialism in the later era as it was unfamiliar with the heritage of feudalism in the earlier one. It has within it, as it were, a kind of self-completing mechanism, which insures the universality of the liberal idea.... It is not accidental that America which has uniquely lacked a feudal tradition has uniquely lacked also a socialist tradition. The hidden origin of socialist thought everywhere in the West is to be found in the feudal ethos. The *ancien régime* inspires Rousseau; both inspire Marx.

Which brings us to the substantive quality of the natural liberal mind.... And yet if we study the American liberal language in terms of intensity and emphasis, if we look for silent omissions as well as explicit inclusions, we begin to see a pattern emerging that smacks distinctively of the New World. It has a quiet, matter of fact quality, it does not understand the meaning of sovereign power, the bourgeois class passion is scarcely present, the sense of the past is altered, and there is about it all, as compared with the European pattern, a vast and almost charming innocence of mind.... America has presented the world with the peculiar phenomenon, not of a frustrated middle class, but of a "frustrated aristocracy"—of men, Aristotelian-like, trying to break out of the egalitarian confines of middle class life but suffering guilt and failure in the process. The South before the Civil War is the case par excellence of this, though New England of course exemplifies it also....

Surely, then, it is a remarkable force: this fixed, dogmatic liberalism of a liberal way of life. It is the secret root from which have sprung many of the most puzzling of American cultural phenomena. Take the unusual power of the Supreme Court and the cult of constitution worship on which it rests. Federal factors apart, judicial review as it has worked in America would be inconceivable without the national acceptance of the Lockian creed, ultimately enshrined in the Constitution, since the removal of high policy to the realm of adjudication implies a prior recognition of the principles to be legally interpreted....

... [L]aw has flourished on the corpse of philosophy in America, for the settlement of the ultimate moral question is the end of speculation upon it.... The moral unanimity of a liberal society reaches out in many directions.

At bottom it is riddled with paradox. Here is a Lockian doctrine which in the West as a whole is the symbol of rationalism, yet in America the devotion to it has been so irrational that it has not even been recognized for what it is: liberalism. There has never been a "liberal movement" or a real "liberal party" in America: we have only had the American Way of Life, a nationalist articulation of Locke which usually does not know that Locke himself is involved; and we did not even get that until after the Civil War when the Whigs of the nation, deserting the Hamiltonian tradition, saw the capital that could be made out of it. This is why even critics who have noticed America's moral unity have usually missed its substance. Ironically, "liberalism" is a stranger in the land of its greatest realization and fulfillment. But this is not all. Here is a doctrine which everywhere in the West has been a glorious symbol of individual liberty, yet in America its compulsive power has been so great that it has posed a threat to liberty itself....

I believe that this is the basic ethical problem of a liberal society: not the danger of the majority which has been its conscious fear, but the danger of unanimity, which has slumbered unconsciously behind it: the "tyranny of opinion" that Tocqueville saw unfolding as even the pathetic social distinctions of the Federalist era collapsed before his eyes. But in recent times this manifestation of irrational Lockianism, or of "Americanism," to use a favorite term of the American Legion, one of the best expounders of the national spirit that Whiggery discovered after the Civil War, has neither slumbered nor been unconscious. It has been very much awake in a red scare hysteria which no other nation in the West has really been able to understand. And this suggests a very significant principle: that when a liberal community faces military and ideological pressure from without it transforms eccentricity into sin, and the irritating figure of the bourgeois gossip flowers into the frightening figure of an A. Mitchell Palmer or a Senator McCarthy. Do we not find here, hidden away at the base of the American mind, one of the reasons why its legalism has been so imperfect a barrier against the violent moods of its mass Lockianism? If the latter is nourished by the former, how can we expect it to be strong? . . .

The decisive domestic issue of our time may well lie in the counter resources a liberal society can muster against this deep and unwritten tyrannical compulsion it contains. They exist. Given the individualist nature of the Lockian doctrine, there is always a logical impulse within it to transcend the very conformitarian spirit it breeds in a Lockian society: witness the spirit of Holmes and Hand. Given the fact, which we shall study at length later, that "Americanism" oddly disadvantages the Progressive despite the fact that he shares it to the full, there is always a strategic impulse within him to transcend it: witness the spirit of Brandeis, Roosevelt, and Stevenson. In some sense the tragedy of these movements has lain in the imperfect knowledge they have had of the enemy they face, above all in their failure to see their own unwitting contribution to his strength. . . .

But the most powerful force working to shatter the American absolutism is, paradoxically enough, the very international involvement which tensifies it. This involvement is complex in its implications. If in the context of the Russian Revolution it elicits a domestic redscare, in the context of diplomacy it elicits an impulse to impose Locke everywhere. The way in which "Americanism" brings McCarthy together with Wilson is of great significance and it is, needless to say, another one of Progressivism's neglected roots in the Rousseauan tide it often seeks to stem. Thus to say that world politics shatters "Americanism" at the moment it intensifies it is to say a lot: it is to say that the basic horizons of the nation both at home and abroad are drastically widened by it. . . .

Historically the issue here is one for which we have little precedent. It raises the question of whether a nation can compensate for the uniformity of its domestic life by contact with alien cultures outside it. It asks whether American liberalism can acquire through external experience that sense of relativity, that spark of philosophy which European liberalism acquired through an internal experience of social diversity and social conflict. But if the final problem posed by the American liberal community is bizarre, this is merely a continuation of its historic record. That community has always been a place where the common issues of the West have taken strange and singular shape.

3. The Dynamics of a Liberal Society

So far I have spoken of natural liberalism as a psychological whole, embracing the nation and inspiring unanimous decisions. We must not assume, however, that this is to obscure or to minimize the nature of the internal conflicts which have characterized American political life. We can hardly choose between an event and its context, though in the study of history and politics there will always be some who will ask us to do so. What we learn from the concept of a liberal society, lacking feudalism and therefore socialism and governed by an irrational Lockianism, is that the domestic struggles of such a society have all been projected with the setting of Western liberal alignments. And here there begin to emerge, not a set of negative European correlations, but a set of very positive ones which have been almost completely neglected.

We can thus say of the right in America that it exemplifies the tradition of big propertied liberalism in Europe, a tradition familiar enough though, as I shall suggest in a moment, much still remains to be done in studying it along transnational lines. . . . Similarly the European "petit-bourgeois" tradition is the starting point for an understanding of the American left. Here, to be sure, there are critical problems of identification, since one of the main things America did was to expand and transform the European "petit-bourgeois" by absorbing both the peasantry and the proletariat into the structure of his personality....

One of the reasons these European liberal correlations have gone neglected is quite obvious once you try to make them. America represents the liberal mechanism of Europe functioning without the European social antagonisms, but the truth is, it is only through these antagonisms that we recognize the mechanism. We know the European liberal, as it were, by the enemies he has made: take them away in American fashion and he does not seem like the same man at all.... After 1840, when the American Whig gives up his Hamiltonian elitism and discovers the Horatio Alger ethos of a liberal society, discovers "Americanism," the task of identification is even harder. For while it is true that the liberals of England and France ultimately accepted political democracy, Algerism and "Americanism" were social ideologies they could hardly exploit. So that the continuing problem of a missing Toryism, which is enough to separate the American Republicans from the reactionary liberals of Victorian England and the Neo-Girondins of the Third Republic, is complicated further by the unique ideological shape that the Whig tradition is destined to take in a liberal society.

The American democrat, that "petit-bourgeois" hybrid of the American world, raises even more intricate questions. To take away the Social Republic from the French Montagnards changes their appearance just about as much as taking away the feudal right from the English Whigs. But the American democrat, alas, deviated sharply from the Montagnards to begin with, since in addition to being "petit-bourgeois" in their sense he was a liberal peasant and a liberal proletarian as well: indeed the whole of the nation apart from the Whig, a condition hardly vouchsafed to the Montagnards. And yet even in the face of such tremendous variations, comparative analysis can continue. We have to tear the giant figure of Jackson apart, sorting out not only the "petit-bourgeois" element of the man

but those rural and urban elements which the American liberal community has transformed. Ultimately, as with the Whigs, for all of the magical chemistry of American liberal society, we are dealing with social materials common to the Western world.

That society has been a triumph for the liberal idea, but we must not assume that this ideological victory was not helped forward by the magnificent material setting it found in the New World. The agrarian and proletarian strands of the American democratic personality, which in some sense typify the whole of American uniqueness, reveal a remarkable collusion between Locke and the New World. Had it been merely the liberal spirit alone which inspired the American farmer to become capitalistically oriented, to repudiate save for a few early remnants the village organization of Europe, to produce for a market and even to enter capitalist occupations on the side such as logging and railroad building, then the difficulties he encountered would have been greater than they were. But where land was abundant and the voyage to the New World itself a claim to independence, the spirit which repudiated peasantry and tenantry flourished with remarkable ease. Similarly, had it merely been an aspect of irrational Lockianism which inspired the American worker to think in terms of the capitalist setup, the task would have been harder than it was.

But social fluidity was peculiarly fortified by the riches of a rich land, so that there was no small amount of meaning to Lincoln's claim in 1861 that the American laborer, instead of "being fixed to that condition for life," works for "a while," then "saves," then "hires another beginner" as he himself becomes an entrepreneur.[1] And even when factory industrialism gained sway after the Civil War, and the old artisan and cottage-and-mill mentality was definitely gone, it

---

1. L. Hacker, *The Triumph of American Capitalism* (New York, 1940), p. 279.

was still a Lockian idea fortified by material resources which inspired the triumph of the job mentality of Gompers rather than the class mentality of the European worker. The "petit-bourgeois" giant of America, though ultimately a triumph for the liberal idea, could hardly have chosen a better material setting in which to flourish.

But a liberal society does not merely produce old Whig and new democrat, does not merely cast a strange set of lights and shadows on them. More crucially it shapes the outcome of the struggle in which they engage....

Firstly America, by making its "petit-bourgeois" hybrid the mass of the nation, makes him unconquerable, save in two instances: when he is disorganized, as prior to Jefferson and Jackson, or when he is enchanted with the dream of becoming a Whig himself, as prior to the crash of 1929. Which is merely another way of saying that the historic Whig technique of *divide et impera* which comes out perhaps most vividly at the time of the First Reform Act and the July Revolution—of playing the mass against the *ancien régime*, the *ancien régime* against the mass, and the mass against itself—cannot work in a society where the mass embraces everything but Whiggery. This is what the Hamiltonian Federalists, who actually tried to pursue this course in America, ultimately had to learn. And this is also why, when they learned it, even their existing resemblance to European Whiggery disappeared and they became distinctively American operators. What they learned was the Alger mechanism of enchanting the American democrat and the "Americanistic" mechanism of terrifying him, which was the bounty they were destined to receive for the European strategies of which they were deprived. For the defeat of Hamilton, so long as the economy boomed, they were bound to get the victory of McKinley. One might call this the great law of Whig compensation inherent in American politics. The record of its functioning takes up a large part of American history.

So one cannot say of the liberal society analysis that by concentrating on national unities it rules out the meaning of domestic conflict. Actually it discovers that meaning, which is obscured by the very Progressive analysis that presumably concentrates on conflict. You do not get closer to the significance of an earthquake by ignoring the terrain on which it takes place. On the contrary, that is one of the best ways of making sure that you will miss its significance. The argument over whether we should "stress" solidarity or conflict in American politics misleads us by advancing a false set of alternatives.

4. The Problem of a Single Factor

It will be said that this is a "single factor" analysis of American history and politics, and probably the only way of meeting this charge is to admit it. Technically we are actually dealing with two factors: the absence of feudalism and the presence of the liberal idea. The escape from the old European order could be accompanied by other ideas, as for instance the Chartist concept which had some effect in the settlement of Australia.* But in terms of European history it-

---

* What is needed here is a comparative study of new societies which will put alongside the European institutions left behind the positive cultural concepts brought to the various frontier settings. There are an infinite variety of combinations possible, and an infinite variety of results. Veblen, in a sentence he never followed up, caught some of the significance of this problem when he said that "it was the fortune of the American people to have taken their point of departure from the European situation when the system of Natural Liberty was still 'obvious and simple,'" while other colonial enterprises "have had their institutional point of departure blurred with a scattering of the holdovers that were brought in again by the return wave of reaction in Europe, as well as by these later-come stirrings of radical discontent that have questioned the eternal fitness of the system of Natural Liberty itself." *What Veblen Taught*, ed. W. Mitchell (New York, 1947), pp. 368–369.

self the abstraction of the feudal force implies the natural development of liberalism, so that for all practical purposes we are dealing with a single factor....

Viewed in these terms the feudal issue is one whose consideration in American history is long overdue. This is not only because of the chain of insights it yields, as long as the course of our national development itself, but also because without it other elements have been burdened with work which it alone can do. Consider that ancient question: the early triumph of American democracy. Turner's frontier, of course, has been advanced to explain this phenomenon but, discovering alas that frontiers are to be found in Canada where feudalism was originally imported and in Russia, historians have revolted against the Turner approach. Actually, as I have suggested on the basis of the comparative European data, the speedy victory of manhood suffrage in America was dictated by the inevitable frustration of elitist Whiggery in a liberal context. Which suggests that Turner was not wrong but, in a way he scarcely understood, half right, for how could American liberalism flourish as it did without a frontier terrain free of Old World feudal burdens?[2] By claiming its own, in other words, the liberal society concept puts the frontier in proper perspective, dissolving both the exaggerated enthusiasms and the exaggerated hostilities that it has engendered.

It does the same thing with other factors, as for example capitalist growth. Reacting against Turner (to continue with the democratic illustration) some recent historians have pointed to the growth of industrialism and an Eastern urban proletariat to explain the swift appearance of American manhood suffrage. Certainly there were pressures here. But if we do not find them in Canada and Russia prior to Jackson, we do

in England and France, and on a larger scale, so that the theory advanced to supplant Turner fares no better than his own. Indeed if we check back to the comparative analysis yielded by the liberal society concept we see that it was the nonproletarian outlook of the early American working class, the fact that it did not frighten the mass of small property owners above it, as the Social Republic frightened the French Mountain in 1848, which saved the democratic forces of the nation from being split to the advantage of Whiggery, as they so often were in Europe. Or take the explanation from capitalist growth of the national Alger ideology after the Civil War. Capitalism was surely related to Alger, but if it produced him, why did it not do so in Germany where it was booming at the same time or in England where it boomed earlier? Actually the Alger spirit is the peculiar instinct of a Lockian world, and what capitalist growth did, once the Whigs began to articulate it, was to fortify their case....

These sample instances illustrate the utility of the liberal society concept in relation to familiar problems. Though concerned with a "single factor," its effect is actually to balance distorted emphases that we have traditionally lived with in the study of American history and politics.

5. Implications for Europe

If Europe provides data for checking America, America provides data for checking Europe: we are dealing with a two-way proposition. So that the liberal society analysis, at the same moment it stresses the absence of the feudal factor in America, stresses its presence abroad. Modern European historians have never evolved an interpretation of their subject from precisely this point of view. To some extent, no doubt, this is because they have been no more transatlantic in their orientation than their American brethren. But there is also a superficial logical reason for this: if modern history begins with liberalism,

2. See the brilliant comments of B. F. Wright in "Political Institutions and the Frontier," *Sources of American Culture*, ed. D. R. Fox (New York, 1934), pp. 15–39.

why stress feudalism, which after all is "medieval history"? And yet, quite apart from the lessons of the American experience, is not the fallacy of this reasoning patent? Merely to state that the feudal structure was the target of modern forces is to affirm the fact, by any sophisticated logic, that it determined the shape these forces took. One hardly needs to read Mannheim to realize that the status quo determines the categories of revolution, or Hegel to realize that the thesis is not unrelated to the sort of antithesis that arises. If the feudal factor is the mother factor of modern life, how can its influence be anything less than permanent and inescapable? . . .

. . . [T]he American experience suggests that a study of modern European history from the feudal angle might yield interesting results. One of these, curiously enough, is a point of departure, not merely for the comparative study of America and Europe, but for the comparative study of European nations themselves. With the crystallization of national states, the European nations have been studied almost as independently as America itself, the idea being apparently that since the "medieval unity" had broken down there was no use preserving it in historical study. The result is that many of the most primitive correlations among the European countries, in economics and politics, have not been made. But if the "medieval unity" is found actually to be a decisive factor in the epoch that followed it, the basis for these correlations automatically appears. Now this is not to suggest that national differences in Western Europe are not crucial. As in the case of America we must be careful to avoid useless debate over a situation and its context. To stress feudalism in Europe is no more to deny that wide variations take place within it than to stress liberalism in America is to deny that wide variations take place within that. One can still emphasize the differences between Burke and Haller, or Jaurès and Bernstein, just as one can still emphasize the differences between Bryan and William Howard Taft. Indeed, were it not for the fact that a uniform liberalism

does not see itself at all, while a uniform feudalism sees itself considerably by virtue of the antagonisms it engenders, one might even argue for a certain similarity between America and Europe on this very score. Here Locke has been so basic that we have not recognized his significance, there Filmer. And the two issues dovetail: to discover the one yields the perspective for discovering the other. . . .

Pluralism and Social Choice

Nicholas R. Miller

This article considers together two theoretical traditions in political analysis—pluralist theory and social choice theory, argues that there is an implicit normative contradiction between the two, and attempts to resolve that contradiction. I believe that the argument is of some significance for political theory generally and for a theoretical understanding of the bases of political stability in particular. The argument may be summarized as follows.

Pluralist political theory identifies certain patterns of political preferences (reflecting certain social and economic structures) as promoting the "stability" of democratic political systems; conversely, it identifies other patterns as threatening to such stability. Social choice theory likewise identifies certain patterns of political preferences as leading to "stability" in social choice under majority rule and related collective choice rules; conversely, it identifies other patterns as leading to unstable social choice. In the context of each theory, stability is characterized—at least implicitly—as desirable. Thus on the face of things, the two theoretical traditions appear to run in parallel, and in a sense they do—but in opposite directions, because the preference patterns identified by pluralist theory as promoting desired stability are essentially those identified by social choice theory as entailing instability. Conversely, the preference patterns identified by social choice theory as leading to stable choice are essentially those identified by pluralist theory as destabilizing for the system. Thus, not only are the notions of stability associated with the two theories logically distinct—a point that

Excerpted from: Nicholas R. Miller, "Pluralism and Social Choice." *American Political Science Review* 77, no. 3 (1983): 734–747. © American Political Science Association, 1983. Reprinted with the permission of the American Political Science Association and Cambridge University Press.

is reasonably evident (but I think sometimes missed)—but they are very close to being logically incompatible. The existence of one kind of stability typically entails the nonexistence of the other kind. Thus, also, the (explicit or implicit) normative criteria in the two theories are incompatible. Finally, this incompatibility suggests that the social choice ideal of collective rationality may not be one that we should endorse. Indeed, the generic instability of the pluralist political process, and its consequent collective irrationality, may in fact contribute to the relative stability of pluralist political systems....

Pluralist Theory and Political Stability

Pluralism as Dispersed Preferences

The variant of pluralist theory that is of concern to us here relates the pattern of group affiliations and conflict in society with patterns of political preferences and in turn relates these preference patterns to the stability of the political system, i.e., whether there is widespread acceptance of existing constitutional arrangements or whether the political system is threatened by such factors as civil war, revolution, separatism, widespread discontent, organized violence, and deep alienation.

The fundamental postulates of this variant of pluralism theory are that (1) all societies are divided along one or more lines of fundamental conflict or cleavage that partition its members into different sets, and (2) the preferences of members of society, with respect to alternative public policies, are largely determined by the set to which those members belong—individuals in the same set having (more or less) the same political preferences and individuals in different sets having (in one respect or other) conflicting preferences. We can refer to these sets, therefore, as *preference clusters*.

All societies are divided to some degree. But some societies, especially larger and more complex ones, are divided by a pluralism of cleavages that are often related to one another in a crosscutting rather than reinforcing pattern. The superposition of this multiplicity of crosscutting partitions is a fine partition of society into a large number of relatively small preference clusters. Two random individuals, therefore, most likely belong to different preference clusters and, if so, have conflicting preferences with respect to one or more issues but almost certainly agree on many issues as well. (For a far more extended and precise discussion along these lines, see Rae & Taylor, 1970.) ...

... There are, I think, at least four different arguments—logically distinct but by no means mutually exclusive—supporting the proposition that pluralistic preferences lead to political stability. Three of these arguments are standard in academic political science literature and are summarized below. The fourth is merely noted below and is then developed further in the last part of this essay.

Pluralism Causes Moderate Attitudes

The first argument is that, in a pluralist society, individuals tend to have more moderate or less intense preferences than in a nonpluralist society. This moderation results from the cross-pressure mechanism operating at the level of individual attitudes and interactions....

Pluralism Causes Moderate Behavior

Even if a pluralist society is not characterized by moderate preferences, its structure generates incentives for moderate political behavior on the part of both individuals and organized groups....

Pluralism Distributes Political Satisfaction

... In a pluralist society, crosscut by many cleavages and partitioned into a multiplicity of preference clusters, political satisfaction is dis-tributed much more equally. No majority-sized preference cluster can exist....

Pluralism Encourages Political Strategems

That the prevalence of such political maneuvers as logrolling, vote trading, coalition building and splitting, agenda manipulation, strategic voting, patronage, and pork barrel constitutes an important feature of political life, and especially so in pluralist systems, is often noted. Although the prevalence of such political strategems is not usually associated with political stability in the academic literature,[3] I believe that such a connection can be made. But before doing this, we must turn our attention to the second theoretical tradition with which this article is concerned.

Social Choice Theory and Collective Rationality

The "Problem" of Cyclical Majorities

It is now fairly well known to political scientists —although it was not a few decades ago—that, even if every individual in a group has a consistent preference ordering over a set of alternatives (e.g., candidates, policies, platforms), majority preference may be inconsistent or intransitive— that is, alternative X may be preferred by a majority to alternative Y, Y may be preferred by a majority to Z, and yet Z may be preferred by a majority to X. This "paradox of voting" was evidently first discovered some 200 years ago by

---

3. The function of such strategems in promoting political stability seems to be more clearly implied in the writings of some political figures who draw on their practical experience (e.g., Savile, First Marquess of Halifax, 1700; Burke, 1790; Smith, 1940), or in biographies of such figures (e.g., Oliver, 1930, on Sir Robert Walpole; Foxcroft, 1946, on the First Marquis of Halifax) and some broader histories (e.g., Plumb, 1967), and in some political novels (e.g., Trollope, 1869). I am indebted to Lewis Dexter for impressing this point on me and for providing references.

the French philosopher, the Marquis de Condorcet, and it was then alternately forgotten and rediscovered until about thirty-five years ago....

By about 1960, the paradox of cyclical majority preference had been clearly embedded into the consciousness of a small group of political scientists and economists concerned with social choice. And the paradox was—I think it is fair to say—almost universally regarded as a "problem" by those who were aware of it....

The Consequences of Cyclical Majorities

Cyclical majority preference has these more specific and concrete consequences in varying political contexts.

1. *The "core" of the political process is empty.* This is the most fundamental consequence: for every possible political outcome, there is some coalition of actors who jointly prefer some other outcome and have the power to get it....

2. *Electoral competition between two power-oriented political parties or candidates cannot lead to equilibrium....* No matter what platform or set of policies one party selects, it can always be defeated, and the outcome of electoral competition—even if modelled under the assumption of complete information—is intrinsically indeterminate and unpredictable, and the resulting electoral victories and attendant outcomes are thus arbitrary.

3. *Noncooperative voting decisions depend on what particular (majoritarian) voting procedure is used, on whether voting is sincere or sophisticated, and (if the procedure is sequential) on the order in which alternatives are voted on....*

4. *Social choices from varying agendas vary in an erratic and unreasonable fashion....*

Escape from Paradox

All conditions on preference profiles that logically preclude the paradox of majority cycles necessarily say that only a subset of all logically possible profiles are admissible. At least roughly, such conditions can be divided into three categories. With respect to social choice from finite sets of discrete alternatives, most attention has focused on conditions in the first (especially) and second categories, which in different ways point to the advantage of social homogeneity in avoiding cycles.

1. *Exclusion conditions* simply prohibit certain combinations of orderings from ever occurring. The best known of these is Black's (1958) single-peakedness condition. This is also the most plausible such condition, although its reverse, single-troughedness or single-cavedness (Vickrey, 1960, p. 514), also precludes majority cycles and may be plausible in certain contexts. Both conditions require that voters commonly perceive alternatives to be arrayed over a single dimension and evaluate them accordingly....

2. *Popularity conditions* point out that preference profiles exhibiting sufficient consensus, even if exclusion conditions are violated, map into transitive social preference under majority rule. Most obviously, perfect consensus (all orderings are identical) precludes majority cycles (but such consensus satisfies all exclusion conditions as well). Hardly less obviously, so does majority consensus (a majority of orderings are identical).

3. *Balance conditions* do not exclude any combination of orderings or require any level of consensus but require a certain symmetry of disagreement, as it were, so that opposing preferences "balance out." For example, if in a given profile all individual orderings but one can be paired (assume n is odd) so that the orderings in each pair are the opposite of each other, then majority preference is transitive, since the majority vote between each pair of alternatives is everywhere a tie broken by the one remaining unpaired ordering, and majority preference is identical to that ordering (and hence transitive)....

Pluralist Preferences versus Collective Rationality

We now consider the two theoretical traditions —pluralism and social choice—together. The fundamental point that quickly becomes evident is that pluralistic preference profiles and preference profiles entailing collective rationality under majority rule are virtually disjoint sets.

Thus, in effect, pluralist theory argues that cyclical majority preference is desirable because such preference profiles are associated with the stability of political systems. Of course, writers in the pluralist tradition have not directly argued that majority cycling is desirable. Indeed, it is almost certain that only a very few of them have been aware of the phenomenon.... But they have argued that certain preference patterns promote, and others threaten, political stability, and it turns out that the former typically entail, whereas the latter preclude, majority cycling. That is, *the sorts of conditions identified in formal social choice theory as sufficient to avoid majority cycles are just those sorts of patterns viewed unfavorably in the pluralist literature.* Conversely, *pluralistic preference patterns are those that most typically result in cyclical majorities.*

Let us review the situation. The most obvious condition that assures transitivity of majority rule is the popularity condition of majority consensus, i.e., one preference cluster includes more than half the population. Such a condition would be fulfilled in a dualist society, and it would result in what Madison (1787) and others would call *majority faction* or even *majority tyranny* and which typically (although not as a logical necessity) entails a large set of universal losers likely to be deeply alienated from the political system. It is, in any case, a nonpluralistic pattern, resulting from a single cleavage or from multiple reinforcing cleavages.

Next, the exclusion condition of single-peaked preferences assures transitive majority preference. But the most plausible translation of single-

peakedness into substantive political terms of a systemwide nature is politics fought out on a single left-right (or other) ideological dimension. This also is a circumstance condemned in pluralist theory, although for a population to be arrayed over a one-dimensional ideological continuum (especially in a unimodal fashion) would be viewed as preferable to polarization of the population into two totally opposed ideological camps.

As we have seen, reinforcing divisions of a population into majority and minority groups (on different issues) preclude the possibility of cyclical majority preference, regardless of the distribution of intensity. On the other hand, crosscutting divisions of the population into majority and minority groups (on different issues) permit cyclical majorities, which will actually occur if intensity is distributed appropriately. Consider, for example, the diagrams shown in figure 3.1, each of which shows a population divided 60%–40% on two issues, one in a more or less reinforcing fashion and one in a more or less crosscutting fashion (cf. the diagrams in Schattschneider, 1960, pp. 62ff). The table below each diagram shows the partition of the population into clusters in terms of first preferences for both issues (from which last preferences can be inferred).[4] The diagrams, and a fortiori the concept of reinforcing versus cross-cutting cleavages, do not allow us to infer the second (and third) preferences, which are determined by "intensity" (i.e., for each individual, which issue he would rather get his way on, given that he can get his way on only one). But, whatever the unspecified preferences, majority preference is transitive in the reinforcing case, there being a majority faction. On the other hand, in the crosscutting case, majority preference may be cyclical—and indeed is, if most voters (precisely, 70% of them) in the two middle clusters care more about the issue in terms of which they are in the minority than about the issue in terms of which they are in the

---

4. This again assumes "separability." ...

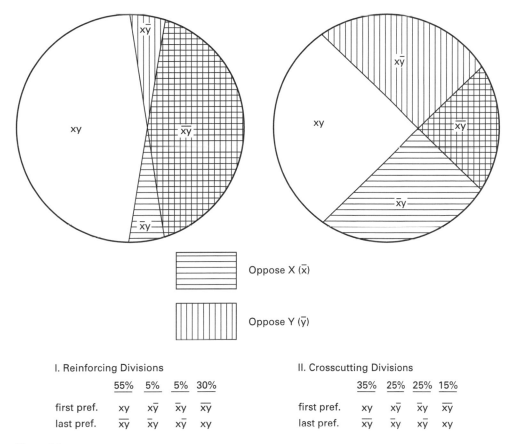

Oppose X ($\bar{x}$)

Oppose Y ($\bar{y}$)

I. Reinforcing Divisions				
	55%	5%	5%	30%
first pref.	xy	x$\bar{y}$	$\bar{x}$y	$\bar{x}\bar{y}$
last pref.	$\bar{x}\bar{y}$	$\bar{x}$y	x$\bar{y}$	xy

II. Crosscutting Divisions				
	35%	25%	25%	15%
first pref.	xy	x$\bar{y}$	$\bar{x}$y	$\bar{x}\bar{y}$
last pref.	$\bar{x}\bar{y}$	$\bar{x}$y	x$\bar{y}$	xy

Figure 3.1

majority. However, if there is (contrary to the subsidiary theme in pluralist theory identified earlier) a consensus of intensities—put otherwise, if the majorities on the respective issues are "passionate" (cf. Downs, 1957, pp. 64ff)—no coalition of minorities can form, and majority transitivity is assured.[5]

More generally, given multiple issues and separable preferences, cyclical majorities exist if and only if logrolling situations exist (Kadane, 1972; Miller, 1975, 1977b; Oppenheimer, 1972;

---

5. There is some reason to believe that majorities are usually not "passionate" and coalitions of minorities are often effective. Many political issues are essentially (re)distributive, and others have a significant distributive component. Insofar as dichotomous issues have a

distributive component, losers, being fewer in number, lose more per capita than winners win. (If, as public choice theorists often suggest, redistributive transfers are typically inefficient, the argument is reinforced.) This argument can only be suggestive, for the relevant comparison is not between majority versus minority intensity on a given issue, but between issues for given voters.

Schwartz, 1977). Thus, Dahl's (1956) well-known assertion that "specific policies tend to be products of 'minorities rule'" (p. 128), justifying the conclusion that "majority tyranny is mostly a myth, . . . for if the majority cannot rule, surely it cannot be tyrannical" (p. 133), is an assertion that cyclical majorities are prevalent.

Although a single ideological dimension, implying single-peaked preferences, precludes cyclical majorities, the existence of two or more ideological dimensions almost guarantees. . . .

Next, it was demonstrated long ago that purely allocative or distributive issues (such as patronage, spoils division, and pork barrel) of the sort often associated with pluralist politics and political stability entail massive majority cycles (Ward, 1961; cf. Miller, 1982b; Schofield, 1982). . . .

Finally, we may note that pluralism implies a large number of distinct preference clusters (i.e., entities with distinct preference orderings), as well as a complex political environment (i.e., many alternatives for political choice); and, according to the probabilistic literature on social choice, both factors—a larger number of individuals and a larger number of alternatives—make cyclical majorities more likely. . . .

Paradox Welcomed: Autonomous Politics and a Critique of Collective Rationality

The conclusion of the previous section was that pluralistic preference patterns entail cyclical majority preference, and conversely, that those conditions that assure or make more likely majority transitivity virtually always entail nonpluralistic preferences. Thus, if pluralist theory is correct that pluralistic preference patterns entail—and nonpluralistic preferences threaten—political stability, there is a clear conflict between the value of collective rationality (transitivity of social preference and stable social choice) and the value of political stability (widespread acceptance of existing constitutional arrangements).

Nothing in the previous section, of course, bears on what choice we should make between these evidently conflicting values. On the whole, it seems clear that we should choose political stability, although we must recognize that collective rationality is not a merely technical condition, but one that has important implications, both normative (i.e., for the terms in which we can justify democracy; cf. Nelson, 1980, especially chap. 4; Riker, 1978, 1982) and empirical (discussed above). This section partially justifies such a choice by arguing further that cyclical majority preference is not merely an otherwise undesirable phenomenon that happens to come along with pluralistic preference patterns and that we must accept as the unavoidable cost of achieving the great benefit of political stability, but that the "generic instability" (cf. Schofield, 1978a) of the pluralist political process is itself an important contributing factor to the stability of pluralist political systems.[6]

Politics is important—it is played for high stakes. Politics concerns how the coercive power of government is to be used in the "authoritative allocation of values for a society" (Easton, 1953, p. 129). And the values at stake are not merely material. For various reasons, political conflicts are inevitably overlaid with powerful symbols, emotions, and loyalties, making the stakes even higher than they would otherwise be.

Political conflict inevitably produces losers as well as winners. A fundamentally important question (and *the* question of political stability) is how to induce losers to continue to play the political game, to continue to work within the system rather than to try to overthrow it. . . .

Elections likewise arouse passions and likewise inevitably produce both winners and losers. And the losers (both politicians and their followers) can likewise console themselves with the thought: "Wait till the next election." But once again this prospect is comforting to the losers

---

6. My reading of Riker (1982, especially chap. 8) was very important in developing the thoughts expressed below.

only insofar as there is some reasonable prospect that the next election may produce a different outcome with different winners and losers.[10]

Commonly in pluralist democracies, there is indeed fairly regular alternation of winners and losers in successive elections. *It is very important to try to understand what brings about this alternation.*

The most obvious answer is that there are substantial shifts in the distribution of political preferences over time. Although the assertion involves great methodological and conceptual complexities, I am inclined to argue that empirical research on public opinion generally supports the conclusion that *the distribution of political preferences—as that term is used in social choice theory,* i.e., complete preference orderings or utility functions over all alternatives—*changes only slowly over time* (mostly as a result of generational replacement) and does not account for alternation in electoral victories.

Suppose, in any case, that the distribution of political preferences is essentially constant from election to election. Then, if collective rationality holds and preference profiles map into stable social choice, all elections would have the same outcome,[11] and the thought "wait till the next election" would offer no solace to the losers.

This argument can be extended and related more closely to our earlier discussion. Let us think of politics as a series of dichotomous issues. Given a majoritarian constitution, if preferences are nonpluralistically distributed, the same people will tend to win and others lose across successive issues. If preferences are pluralistically distributed, then—*whether or not this distribution entails cyclical majority preference*—different people will win and lose on different issues. Thus, as argued earlier, political disaffection plausibly is reduced.

But now we can make this further argument. If preferences are pluralistically distributed, then—as argued in the previous section—majority preference is typically cyclical and, *if this distribution does entail cyclical majority preference,* the present losers on a particular issue can yet hope to become winners *on the same issue*—perhaps by entering into some new alliance, by trading away their votes on some other issue, or generally by engaging in the kinds of political stratagems identified at the end of the second section as associated with pluralist politics, and which are efficacious only given cyclical majorities, i.e., in the absence of collective rationality. Precisely because social choice is *not* stable, i.e., not uniquely determined by the distribution of preferences, there is some range for autonomous politics to hold sway, and pluralist politics offers almost everybody hope of victory....

Thus, a pluralist political system does *not* authoritatively allocate values in a stable fashion. Rather, it sets political competitors—who might otherwise be bashing heads instead of (repeatedly) counting them (and seemingly getting different counts each time)—running around "one of Escher's stairways leading always up yet always coming back to its own foundation" (to use Rae's metaphor; 1980, p. 454). Not only does each competitor "win some and lose some," but most wins and losses are themselves reversible. Thus the competitors can never be confident of their victories, nor need they resign themselves to their defeats. Of course, since considerable resources are devoted to this competitive treadmill, pluralist politics is

---

10. An even more fundamental requirement, of course, is that there is a reasonable prospect of *having* a next election. And a corollary is that results of a one-shot election to determine the political future of a nation apparently for all time, or of a referendum to decide some essentially irreversible question, are less likely to be accepted by the losers.

11. At least the winning platform would remain constant. In the established formal theory of electoral competition (without party loyalty), the two parties, having fully "converged," would alternate victories in a random manner. But if there were *any* degree of party loyalty in the electorate, unequally distributed, the same party would always win.

somewhat inefficient in economic terms. But the state of affairs associated with severe political instability is far more profoundly inefficient.

Conclusion

The argument of this essay has been that the pluralist political process leads to unstable political choice, and that such instability of choice in fact fosters the stability of pluralist political systems.

The question remains of whether political outcomes in a pluralist democracy are "arbitrary" and unrelated to public opinion. If so, this might be a high price to pay for political stability.

In this connection, it is significant that a variety of recent results in positive political theory have suggested plausible ways in which the outcomes of a competitive political process are likely to be restricted or bounded in a "reasonable" fashion even in the face of massive or all-inclusive majority cycles. These notions include the "minmax set" (Kramer, 1977), the "competitive solution" (McKelvey et al., 1978), the "admissible set" (McKelvey & Ordeshook, 1976) and the related "uncovered set" (Miller, 1980), as well as various probabilistic notions (e.g., Ferejohn, McKelvey & Packel, 1981). All these notions have the common characteristic of setting reasonable bounds on social choice, yet preserving some more or less large range of indeterminacy within which autonomous politics can hold sway. It is also worth noting that experimental studies (e.g., Fiorina & Plott, 1978; McKelvey et al., 1978) do not show outcomes randomly scattered about the entire alternative space. Finally, of course, most of us would view political outcomes in the real world of pluralism as considerably unpredictable but clearly confined within certain bounds of "political feasibility."

In conclusion, I should emphasize that the argument presented here needs to be further developed. First, greater technical precision is clearly needed at several points. Second and more important, the argument at present is very abstract and needs more concrete specification in terms of recognizable political phenomena. For example, a distinction should be made between micro-level politics (e.g., a legislative assembly considering a particular bill or set of proposals) and macro-level politics (e.g., the broad structure of electoral politics over time). There are a variety of reasons why potential instabilities are likely to be submerged at the micro-level (cf. Shepsle, 1979; Shepsle & Weingast, 1981; Tullock, 1981). My sense is that the present argument pertains primarily at the macro-level and could profitably be linked with the established literature on critical realignment and electoral dynamics (e.g., Burnham, 1970; Key, 1955; cf. Riker, 1982, chap. 9).

References

Black, D. *The theory of committees and elections.* Cambridge: Cambridge University Press, 1958.

Burke, E. *Reflections on the revolution in France.* New York: Library of Liberal Arts, 1955. (Originally published, 1790.)

Burnham, W. D. *Critical elections and the mainsprings of American politics.* New York: W. W. Norton, 1970.

Dahl, R. A. *A preface to democratic theory.* Chicago: University of Chicago Press, 1956.

Downs, A. *An economic theory of democracy.* New York: Harper & Row, 1957.

Easton, D. *The political system.* New York: Alfred A. Knopf, 1953.

Ferejohn, J. A., McKelvey, R. D., & Packel, E. W. Limiting distributions for continuous state Markov voting models. Social Science Working Paper No. 394, California Institute of Technology, July, 1981.

Fiorina, M. P., & Plott, C. R. Committee decisions under majority rule: An experimental study. *American Political Science Review*, 1978, *72*, 575–598.

Foxcroft, H. C. *A character of the trimmer: Being a short life of the first Marquis of Halifax.* Cambridge: Cambridge University Press, 1946.

Kadane, J. B. On division of the question. *Public Choice*, 1972, *13*, 47–54.

Kent, F. R. *The great game of politics*. Garden City, N.Y.: Doubleday, 1923.

Key, V. O., Jr. A theory of critical elections. *Journal of Politics*, 1955, *17*, 3–18.

Kramer, G. A. A dynamical model of political equilibrium. *Journal of Economic Theory*, 1977, *16*, 310–334.

Madison, J. Federalist Paper No. 10, 1787.

McKelvey, R. D., & Ordeshook, P. C. Symmetric spatial games without majority rule equilibria. *American Political Science Review*, 1976, *70*, 1172–1184.

McKelvey, R. D., Ordeshook, P. C., & Winer, M. The competitive solution for *n*-person games without transferable utility, with an application to committee games. *American Political Science Review*, 1978, *72*, 599–615.

Miller, N. R. Logrolling and the Arrow paradox: A note. *Public Choice*, 1975, *21*, 107–110.

Miller, N. R. Logrolling, vote trading, and the paradox of voting: A game-theoretical overview. *Public Choice*, 1977b, *30*, 51–75.

Miller, N. R. A new solution set for tournaments and majority voting: Further graph-theoretical approaches to the theory of voting. *American Journal of Political Science*, 1980, *24*, 68–96.

Miller, N. R. The complete structure of majority rule on distributive politics. Paper presented at the Annual Meeting of the Public Choice Society, San Antonio, Texas, March, 1982.

Nelson, W. N. *On justifying democracy*. London: Routledge & Kegan Paul, 1980.

Oliver, F. S. *The endless adventure*. London: Macmillan, 1930.

Oppenheimer, J. A. Relating coalitions of minorities to the voters' paradox or putting the fly in the democratic pie. Paper presented at the Annual Meeting of the Southwest Political Science Association, San Antonio, Texas, March–April 1972.

Plumb, J. H. *The origins of political stability: England, 1675–1725*. Boston: Houghton Mifflin, 1967.

Rae, D. An altimeter for Mr. Escher's stairway: A comment on William H. Riker's "Implications from the disequilibrium of majority rule for the study of institutions." *American Political Science Review*, 1980, *74*, 451–455.

Rae, D., & Taylor, M. *The analysis of political cleavages*. New Haven, Conn.: Yale University Press, 1970.

Riker, W. H. A confrontation between the theory of social choice and the theory of democracy. Paper presented at the Annual Meeting of the American Political Science Association, New York, September, 1978.

Riker, W. H. *Liberalism against populism: A confrontation between the theory of democracy and the theory of social choice*. San Francisco: Freeman, 1982.

Schattschneider, E. E. *The semisovereign people*. New York: Holt, Rinehart and Winston, 1960.

Schofield, N. Generic instability of voting games. Paper presented at the Annual Meeting of the Public Choice Society, New Orleans, March, 1978a.

Schofield, N. Instability and development in the political economy. In P. C. Ordeshook & K. A. Shepsle (Eds.), *Political equilibrium*. Boston: Kluwer-Nijhoff, 1982.

Schwartz, T. Collective choice, separation of issues and vote trading. *American Political Science Review*, 1977, *71*, 999–1010.

Shepsle, K. A. Institutional arrangements and equilibrium in multidimensional voting models. *American Journal of Political Science*, 1979, *23*, 27–59.

Shepsle, K. A., & Weingast, B. R. Structure-induced equilibrium and legislative choice. *Public Choice*, 1981, *37*, 503–519.

Smith, T. V. *The legislative way of life*. Chicago: University of Chicago Press (Midway Reprint), 1940.

Trollope, A. *Phineas Finn: The Irish member*. Oxford: Oxford University Press, 1951. (Originally published, 1869.)

Tullock, G. Why so much stability? *Public Choice*, 1981, *37*, 189–202.

Vickrey, W. Utility, strategy, and social decision rules. *Quarterly Journal of Economics*, 1960, *74*, 507–535.

Ward, B. Majority rule and allocation. *Journal of Conflict Resolution*, 1961, *5*, 379–389.

Consociational Democracy

Arend Lijphart

Fragmented but Stable Democracies

... The political stability of a system can apparently not be predicted solely on the basis of the two variables of political culture and role structure. According to the theory of crosscutting cleavages, one would expect [countries] with subcultures divided from each other by mutually reinforcing cleavages, to exhibit great immobilism and instability. But they do not. These deviant cases of fragmented but stable democracies will be called "consociational democracies."[14] In general, deviant case analysis can lead to the discovery of additional relevant variables, and in this particular instance, a third variable can account for the stability of the consociational democracies: the behavior of the political elites. The leaders of the rival subcultures may engage in competitive behavior and thus further aggravate mutual tensions and political instability, but they may also make *deliberate efforts to counteract the immobilizing and unstabilizing effects of cultural fragmentation*. As a result of such overarching cooperation at the elite level, a country can, as Claude Ake states, "achieve a degree of political stability quite out of proportion to its social homogeneity."[15] ...

The desire to avoid political competition may be so strong that the cartel of elites may decide to extend the consociational principle to the electoral level in order to prevent the passions aroused by elections from upsetting the carefully constructed, and possibly fragile, system of cooperation. This may apply to a single election or to a number of successive elections....

Consociational democracy violates the principle of majority rule, but it does not deviate very much from normative democratic theory. Most democratic constitutions prescribe majority rule for the normal transaction of business when the stakes are not too high, but extraordinary majorities or several successive majorities for the most important decisions, such as changes in the constitution. In fragmented systems, many other decisions in addition to constituent ones are perceived as involving high stakes, and therefore require more than simple majority rule. Similarly, majority rule does not suffice in times of grave crisis in even the most homogeneous and consensual of democracies. Great Britain and Sweden, both highly homogeneous countries, resorted to grand coalition cabinets during the Second World War. Julius Nyerere draws the correct lesson from the experience of the Western democracies, in which, he observes, "it is an accepted practice in times of emergency for opposition parties to sink their differences and join together in forming a national government."[20] And just as the formation of a national unity government is the appropriate response to an external emergency, so the formation of a grand coalition cabinet or an alternative form of elite cartel is the appropriate response to the internal crisis of fragmentation into hostile subcultures.

Excerpted from: Arend Lijphart, "Consociational Democracy." *World Politics* 21, no. 2 (1969): 207–225. © Center of International Studies, Princeton University. Reprinted by permission of The Johns Hopkins University Press.

14. Cf. Johannes Althusius' concept of *consociatio* in his *Politica Methodice Digesta*, and the term "consociational" used by David E. Apter, *The Political Kingdom in Uganda: A Study in Bureaucratic Nationalism* (Princeton 1961), 24–25.

15. Claude Ake, *A Theory of Political Integration* (Homewood 1967), 113. This possibility exists not only in the fragmented democracies, but also in fragmented predemocratic or nondemocratic systems, of course. See also Arend Lijphart, *The Politics of Accommodation: Pluralism and Democracy in the Netherlands* (Berkeley 1968), 1–15, 197–211.

20. Nyerere, "One-Party Rule," in Paul E. Sigmund, Jr., ed., *The Ideologies of the Developing Nations* (New York 1963), 199.

Furthermore, the concept of consociational democracy is also in agreement with the empirical "size principle," formulated by William H. Riker. This principle, based on game-theoretic assumptions, states: "In social situations similar to *n*-person, zero-sum games with side-payments [private agreements about the division of the payoff], participants create coalitions just as large as they believe will ensure winning and no larger." The tendency will be toward a "minimum winning coalition," which in a democracy will be a coalition with bare majority support— but only under the conditions specified in the size principle. The most important condition is the zero-sum assumption: "only the direct conflicts among participants are included and common advantages are ignored."[21] Common advantages will be completely ignored only in two diametrically opposite kinds of situations: (1) when the participants in the "game" do not perceive any common advantages, and when, consequently, they are likely to engage in unlimited warfare; and (2) when they are in such firm agreement on their common advantages that they can take them for granted. In the latter case, politics literally becomes a game. In other words, the zero-sum condition and the size principle apply only to societies with completely homogeneous political cultures and to societies with completely fragmented cultures. To the extent that political cultures deviate from these two extreme conditions, pressures will exist to fashion coalitions and other forms of cooperation that are more inclusive than the bare "minimum winning coalition" and that may be all-inclusive grand coalitions. . . .

Factors Conducive to Consociational Democracy

Consociational democracy means government by elite cartel designed to turn a democracy with

a fragmented political culture into a stable democracy. Efforts at consociationalism are not necessarily successful, of course: consociational designs failed in Cyprus and Nigeria, and Uruguay abandoned its Swiss-style consociational system. Successful consociational democracy requires: (1) That the elites have the ability to accommodate the divergent interests and demands of the subcultures. (2) This requires that they have the ability to transcend cleavages and to join in a common effort with the elites of rival subcultures. (3) This in turn depends on their commitment to the maintenance of the system and to the improvement of its cohesion and stability. (4) Finally, all of the above requirements are based on the assumption that the elites understand the perils of political fragmentation. These four requirements are logically implied by the concept of consociational democracy as defined in this paper. Under what conditions are they likely to be fulfilled? An examination of the successful consociational democracies in the Low Countries, Switzerland, Austria, and Lebanon suggests a number of conditions favorable to the establishment and the persistence of this type of democracy. These have to do with inter-subcultural relations at the elite level, inter-subcultural relations at the mass level, and elite-mass relations within each of the subcultures.

Relations among the Elites of the Subcultures

It is easier to assess the probability of continued success of an already established consociational democracy than to predict the chance of success that a fragmented system would have if it were to attempt consociationalism. In an existing consociational democracy, an investigation of the institutional arrangements and the operational code of inter-elite accommodation can throw light on the question of how thorough a commitment to cooperation they represent and how effective they have been in solving the problems caused by fragmentation. *The length of time a consociational democracy has been in*

---

21. William H. Riker, *The Theory of Political Coalitions* (New Haven 1962), 29, 32–33.

operation is also a factor of importance. As inter-elite cooperation becomes habitual and does not represent a deliberate departure from competitive responses to political challenges, consociational norms become more firmly established. And, as Gerhard Lehmbruch states, these norms may become an important part of "the political socialization of elites and thus acquire a strong degree of persistence through time."[23]

There are three factors that appear to be strongly conducive to the establishment or maintenance of cooperation among elites in a fragmented system. The most striking of these is the existence of *external threats* to the country. In all of the consociational democracies, the cartel of elites was either initiated or greatly strengthened during periods of international crisis, especially the First and Second World Wars.... In all cases, the external threats impressed on the elites the need for internal unity and cooperation. External threats can also strengthen the ties among the subcultures at the mass level and the ties between leaders and followers within the subcultures.

A second factor favorable to consociational democracy, in the sense that it helps the elites to recognize the necessity of cooperation, is a *multiple balance of power among the subcultures* instead of either a dual balance of power or a clear hegemony by one subculture. When one group is in the majority, its leaders may attempt to dominate rather than cooperate with the rival minority. Similarly, in a society with two evenly matched subcultures, the leaders of both may hope to achieve their aims by domination rather than cooperation, if they expect to win a major-ity at the polls. Robert Dahl argues that for this reason it is doubtful that the consociational arrangement in Colombia will last, because "the temptation to shift from coalition to competition is bound to be very great."[24] When political parties in a fragmented society are the organized manifestations of political subcultures, a multiparty system is more conducive to consociational democracy and therefore to stability than a two-party system. This proposition is at odds with the generally high esteem accorded to two-party systems. In an already homogeneous system, two-party systems may be more effective, but a moderate multiparty system, in which no party is close to a majority, appears preferable in a consociational democracy....

Consociational democracy presupposes not only a willingness on the part of elites to cooperate but also a capability to solve the political problems of their countries. Fragmented societies have a tendency to immobilism, which consociational politics is designed to avoid. Nevertheless, decision-making that entails accommodation among all subcultures is a difficult process, and consociational democracies are always threatened by a degree of immobilism. Consequently, a third favorable factor to inter-elite cooperation is a *relatively low total load on the decision-making apparatus*. The stability of Lebanon is partly due to its productive economy and the social equilibrium it has maintained so far, but it may not be able to continue its successful consociational politics when the burdens on the system increase....

Inter-Subcultural Relations at the Mass Level

The political cultures of the countries belonging to Almond's Continental European type and to the consociational type are all fragmented, but the consociational countries have even clearer boundaries among their subcultures. Such *dis-*

23. Lehmbruch, "A Non-Competitive Pattern of Conflict Management in Liberal Democracies: The Case of Switzerland, Austria and Lebanon" (paper presented at the Seventh World Congress of the International Political Science Association, Brussels, 1967), 6. See also Lehmbruch, *Proporzdemokratie: Politisches System und politische Kultur in der Schweiz und in Österreich* (Tübingen 1967).

24. Dahl, *Political Oppositions in Western Democracies* (New Haven 1966), 337.

tinct lines of cleavage appear to be conducive to consociational democracy and political stability. The explanation is that subcultures with widely divergent outlooks and interests may coexist without necessarily being in conflict; conflict arises only when they are in contact with each other. As Quincy Wright states: "Ideologies accepted by different groups within a society may be inconsistent without creating tension; but if ... the groups with inconsistent ideologies are in close contact ... the tension will be great."[29] David Easton also endorses the thesis that good social fences may make good political neighbors, when he suggests a kind of voluntary *apartheid* policy as the best solution for a divided society: "Greater success may be attained through steps that conduce to the development of a deeper sense of mutual awareness and responsiveness among *encapsulated cultural units*." This is "the major hope of avoiding stress."[30] And Sidney Verba follows the same line of reasoning when he argues that political and economic modernization in Africa is bringing "differing subcultures into contact with each other and *hence* into conflict."[31]

This argument appears to be a direct refutation of the overlapping-memberships proposition, but by adding two amendments to this proposition the discrepancy can be resolved. In the first place, the basic explanatory element in the concept of consociational democracy is that political elites may take joint actions to counter the effects of cultural fragmentation. This means that the overlapping-memberships propositions may become a self-denying hypothesis under

certain conditions. Secondly, the view that any severe discontinuity in overlapping patterns of membership and allegiance is a danger to political stability needs to be restated in more refined form. A distinction has to be made between essentially homogeneous political cultures, where increased contacts are likely to lead to an increase in mutual understanding and further homogenization, and essentially heterogeneous cultures, where close contacts are likely to lead to strain and hostility. This is the distinction that Walker Connor makes when he argues that "increased contacts help to dissolve regional cultural distinctions within a state such as the United States. Yet, if one is dealing not with minor variations of the same culture, but with two quite distinct and self-differentiating cultures, are not increased contacts between the two apt to increase antagonisms?"[32] This proposition can be refined further by stating both the degree of homogeneity and the extent of mutual contacts in terms of continua rather than dichotomies. In order to safeguard political stability, the volume and intensity of contacts must not exceed the commensurate degree of homogeneity. Karl W. Deutsch states that stability depends on a "balance between transaction and integration" because "the number of opportunities for possible violent conflict will increase with the volume and range of mutual transactions."[33] Hence, it may be desirable to keep transactions among antagonistic subcultures in a divided society— or, similarly, among different nationalities in a multinational state—to a minimum.

Elite-Mass Relations within the Subcultures

Distinct lines of cleavage among the subcultures are also conducive to consociational democracy because they are likely to be concomitant with a

29. Wright, "The Nature of Conflict," *Western Political Quarterly*, IV (June 1951), 196.

30. Easton, *A Systems Analysis of Political Life* (New York 1965), 250–51 (italics added). See also G. H. Scholten, "Het vergelijken van federaties met behulp van systeem-analyse," *Acta Politica*, II (1966–67), 51–68.

31. Verba, "Some Dilemmas in Comparative Research," *World Politics*, XX (October 1967), 126 (italics added).

32. Connor, "Self-Determination: The New Phase," *World Politics*, XX (October 1967), 49–50.

33. Deutsch, *Political Community at the International Level* (Garden City 1954), 39.

high degree of *internal political cohesion of the subcultures*. This is vital to the success of consociational democracy. The elites have to cooperate and compromise with each other without losing the allegiance and support of their own rank and file. When the subcultures are cohesive political blocs, such support is more likely to be forthcoming. As Hans Daalder states, what is important is not only "the extent to which party leaders are more tolerant than their followers" but also the extent to which they "are yet able to carry them along."[34]

A second way in which distinct cleavages have a favorable effect on elite-mass relations in a consociational democracy is that they make it more likely that the parties and interest groups will be the organized representatives of the political subcultures. If this is the case, the political parties may not be the best aggregators, but there is at least an *adequate articulation of the interests of the subcultures*. Aggregation of the clearly articulated interests can then be performed by the cartel of elites....

A final factor which favors consociational democracy is *widespread approval of the principle of government by elite cartel*. This is a very obvious factor, but it is of considerable importance and deserves to be mentioned briefly. For example, Switzerland has a long and strong tradition of grand coalition executives, and this has immeasurably strengthened Swiss consociational democracy. On the other hand, the grand coalition in Austria was under constant attack by critics who alleged that the absence of a British-style opposition made Austrian politics "undemocratic." This attests to the strength of the British system as a normative model even in fragmented political systems, where the model is inappropriate and undermines the attempt to achieve political stability by consociational means....

---

34. [Hans Daalder, "Parties, Elites, and Political Developments in Western Europe," in Joseph La-Palombara and Myron Weiner, eds., *Political Parties and Political Development* (Princeton: Princeton University Press, 1996)], 69.

The Contest of Ideas

Donald Horowitz

If there is a subject called constitutional design, then there must be alternative constitutional *designs*. Assuredly there are, but even now most constitutional drafters and reformers are, at best, only vaguely informed by anything resembling an articulate theory of their enterprise. Most act on the basis of inchoate and partially worked-out ideas, such as the notion that assuring legislative representation for minorities is the crucial step in inter-group accommodation: a notion that has animated many judicial and legislative determinations under the Voting Rights Act in the United States. Politicians have their own ideas, and these are not so easily dislodged, even with the growth of constitutional design and various sub-fields, such as electoral-system design, as matters for experts. Individual politicians can still make their influence felt, even in very large countries.[3] Before we even reach the contest of explicitly stated theories, we need to recognize the more significant, albeit often subliminal, contest between explicit theories and the more influential, implicit theories espoused by practitioners. The inarticulate theories call out for study. As of now, we lack a theory of their theories.

We also lack a consensus emerging from the articulate theories, whether these relate to electoral systems, presidential or parliamentary structure, or the costs and benefits of centralized or devolved power. Lack of consensus is the first obstacle.

No treatment of the contest of ideas can avoid an encounter with consociational democracy. There is much to admire in the efforts of Arend Lijphart in behalf of managing inter-group conflict, most notably his realism about group divisions (they are not to be wished away) and his optimism (they do not need to produce civil war). Yet Lijphart ... is right to identify me as a dissenter from the consociational approach, although, as I shall point out, completely wrong to identify me as an opponent of either power-sharing or territorial devolution. I want to move on to a brief statement of a more promising approach and to a fuller treatment of the gap between constitutional design and the constitutions that actually emerge from processes of constitutional innovation, but I need first to state why I think consociational theory is not a fruitful path for constitutional designers.

To avoid restating objections to consociationalism that I have advanced in several previous publications (Horowitz 1985: 568–576; 1991: 137–145, 167–171; 1997: 439–440; 2000: 256–259), I shall resort to a list of the main objections.

1. The consociational approach is motivationally inadequate. Lijphart (1977: 53, 165) identifies statesmanship as the reason elites will form a cartel across group lines to resolve inter-ethnic differences. In his view, leaders are motivated by a desire to avert the danger of mutual destruction. But why should majority-group leaders, with 60 percent support, and the ability to gain all of political power in a majoritarian democracy, be so self-abnegating as to give some of it away to minority-group leaders? There may be instances of this sort of generosity, in the face of the attractiveness of a less-than-maximal coalition (see Riker 1962: 32–33), but the motive of avoiding ultimate mutual destruction is based on a time horizon longer than that employed by

Excerpted from: Donald Horowitz, "Constitutional Design: Proposals versus Processes." In *The Architecture of Democracy: Constitutional Design*. Edited by Andrew Reynolds. Oxford. Oxford University Press, 2002. Reprinted by permission of Oxford University Press.

3. I am thinking here of the singular part played by Viktor Shaynis, a parliamentarian, in designing the Russian electoral system.

most political leaders, who, in any case, are apt to think that retaining control for themselves is the best way to avoid disaster. On this point, Lijphart . . . now contends that the motive is not statesmanship but the desire to enter into a coalition. This, of course, does not account for the motives of leaders of majorities, who do not need coalitions, much less the all-inclusive or grand coalitions that Lijphart (1977) specifies as a central element of the consociational prescription.[4] The failure to make the elementary distinction between the different incentives of majorities and minorities, to which I shall return, is crucial. Even states that start out multipolar, with several ethnic groups, can become bipolar and bifurcated—witness the growth of northern versus southern groups in many African states— thus obviating the need for a coalition across group lines for the group that is slightly larger. In general, bipolar states, with a majority and a minority, are the more seriously conflicted. A theory of conflict reduction that cannot cope with hard cases is of limited utility.[5]

2. To the extent that the imputed motive is still statesmanship rather than self-interest, the assumption that elites in divided societies are likely to be more tolerant of other ethnic groups or less inclined to pursue advantage for their own group is extremely dubious. Studies of ethnocentrism show educated elites in some countries to be less ethnocentric than their followers, in others more, in some others neither less nor more, and in still others more with respect to some groups and less or the same with respect to other groups (see Horowitz 1997: 457 n. 31; 1991: 140–141 nn. 44–50). It is very risky to count on statesmanship (see Reilly and Reynolds 1999: 13).

3. When leaders compromise across ethnic lines in the face of severe divisions, there is usually a high price to pay. Counter-elites arise who make an issue of the compromise, referring to it as a sell-out. Consociational theory assumes the existence of "group leaders," but, even when groups begin with a single set of leaders, compromise across group lines is likely to show those leaders to be merely party leaders opposed by leaders of other parties seeking the support of the same group. The centrifugal competition for group allegiance is an enormous constraint on compromise across group lines, and it renders the grand coalition, under conditions of free elections, a contradiction in terms. Not one of the four developing countries cited by Lijphart (1977) as consociational—Lebanon, Malaysia, Surinam, and the Netherlands Antilles—had a grand coalition. Each had an inter-ethnic coalition of some parties, opposed by other parties representing the same groups. Some of the four also violated other core conditions of consociational theory, such as proportionality in allocations, proportionality in executive participation, and cultural autonomy, but were claimed for the theory nonetheless. For reasons I shall enumerate later, it is not amiss to refer to consociational *elements* or consociational *practices*, but consociational regimes in the developing world are, to be generous about it, few and far between.[6]

---

4. Lijphart sometimes includes and sometimes omits the grand-coalition requirement. The tendency to shift ground about the indispensable requisites of the theory is one of the main reasons why consociationalism attracts such strong criticism (see, for example, Dixon 1997; Halpern 1986).

In the actual experience of constitutional innovators, there are some examples of motivation to accept consociational arrangements, but these are idiosyncratic and cannot be assumed to be widely distributed. Motivation always needs to be treated as an issue, not a given.

5. The claim that the bipolar (60–40) problem is rare (which Lijphart made in an earlier version of the paper published in this volume) cannot be sustained. In many developing countries, bipolar alignments emerge as a result of the amalgamation of group identities.

---

6. The tendency to shift the goal posts and to claim countries for the theory is palpable. Whenever a divided society seems to be more or less democratic and more or less lacking in the most severe forms of con-

Consociational theory exaggerates the latitude enjoyed by leaders in ethnically divided societies where free elections prevail.

4. If the grand coalition, proportional resource allocations and shares of executive power, and the minority veto all encounter the motivational problem mentioned earlier, cultural autonomy encounters a different problem. Presumably, groups are to find satisfaction—and power—in the ability to manage their own affairs, and that will contribute to stable democracy (Lijphart 1977: 42 . . .). But those who work on the sources of conflict in ethnically-divided societies know there is more to it than that. Cultural matters, such as the designation of official languages and official religions, and educational issues, such as languages of instruction, the content of curricula, and the official recognition of degrees from various educational streams associated with various ethnic groups, are habitually divisive issues in severely divided societies. These issues go straight to the heart of the conflict in three of its most important respects. To accord equal recognition to all cultures, religions, and languages is to concede equal ownership of the state, contrary to what groups are very often willing to concede (see Wimmer 1997). To accord equal recognition is also to concede another core issue: the issue of group superiority, which is contested by reference to disputes over cultural

superiority and primacy. To accord equal recognition is, finally, to concede the issue of the identity of who will get ahead, which otherwise would be regulated by limitations on languages and educational streams associated with competitors. In short, cultural autonomy, with its implication of equality, is the product of the reduction of inter-ethnic conflict, not an ingredient of a conflict-regulating prescription at the threshold.

5. Lijphart fails to make a critical distinction between pre-electoral and post-electoral coalitions. The coalitions recommended by consociational theory are post-electoral coalitions, which no doubt entail compromise over the division of cabinet portfolios, but typically not compromise over divisive inter-ethnic issues. A better analysis of Lebanon and Malaysia during their most accommodative periods would have put the emphasis on the need of candidates, parties, and coalitions to attract votes across group lines, rather than on post-electoral compromise. In those cases and others, pre-electoral coalitions across group lines required compromise on ethnic issues. The combination of list-system proportional representation and political parties based on ethnic-group support does nothing to foster compromise on ethnic issues. The zero-sum relation of party lists to each other translates into a zero-sum electoral competition between ethnic groups (see Horowitz 1991: 167–176).

These criticisms suggest that when consociational arrangements are adopted a conflict is probably already on the wane, and they also point the way towards alternative power-sharing prescriptions. Certainly, to conflate consociation with all of power-sharing is completely unwarranted.[7] . . .

---

flict, the reason must be that it is consociational. India, the leading example of adversary democracy in Asia—and adversary democracy is the form of democracy to which consociationalism is juxtaposed as an alternative—is said to be consociational (Lijphart 1996). If South Africa settles its differences peacefully and electorally, even if it lacks central elements of consociationalism, such as minority vetoes, then South Africa must be consociational (Lijphart 1994b).

To be perfectly clear at the outset, it is not possible to identify states that have adopted an incentives approach—or any other coherent, conflict-reducing approach—across the board either. The difficulty of adopting constitutional designs in toto is precisely the point of this chapter.

---

7. Others have also pointed out that the appropriation of the term "power-sharing" to refer exclusively to the consociational approach is confusing and conceptually constricting (see, for example, Dixon 1997: 23, 32).

Several points follow from what has already been said. If it is true that inter-group conflict involves a conflict for control and ownership of the state, for group superiority, and for group success, all measured in relative terms, then compromise will be difficult to achieve. The divisive issues are not easy to compromise. No single formula will assure the reduction of conflict. Progress will be, in most cases, incremental and, in many of these, reversible. When electorates are alert to ethnic issues, as they typically are, exhortations to leaders to compromise are likely to be futile in the absence of rewards for compromise. Attention needs to be devoted, therefore, to maximizing incentives for accommodative behaviour. For elected politicians, those incentives are likely to be found in the electoral system. Electoral systems that reward inter-ethnic accommodation can be identified and can be made to work more or less as intended (see Reilly 1997; see also International Crisis Group 1998; 1999). Where electoral rewards are present, they can provide the motivation ethnic leaders otherwise lack, they can operate even in the presence of ethnocentrism, and they can offset electoral losses that leaders anticipate as a result of making concessions to other groups. Where these rewards are present, they typically operate by means of vote-pooling arrangements: the exchange of votes by ethnically-based parties that, because of the electoral system, are marginally dependent for victory on the votes of groups other than their own and that, to secure those votes, must behave moderately on the issues in conflict. The electoral rewards provided to a moderate middle compensate for the threat posed by opposition from those who can benefit from the aversion of some group members to inter-ethnic compromise.

Where vote pooling takes place, as it did in Lebanon and Malaysia, it promotes pre-electoral coalitions, coalitions that need to compromise in order to attract voters across group lines but that may be opposed by ethnic parties on the flanks.

A recent instance in which a vote-pooling electoral system was used successfully to induce the formation of a multi-ethnic coalition that won the election was the alternative vote (AV), adopted in the 1997 Fijian constitution. The electoral incentives in Fiji were weak, but they had a powerful effect.[8] A severely divided society, Fiji elected a thoroughly multi-ethnic government, led by its first-ever Indian prime minister (see Lal 1999). A year later, that government was overthrown, but not because the incentives did not work.

Incentives, then, are the key to accommodation in difficult conditions, but the difficult conditions imply that the incentives approach will not be attractive to everyone or attractive at all times. Some times are more propitious than others, and the problem of motives does not disappear by invoking the incentives approach. The incentives approach has had no more success in securing full-blown acceptance than has any other. . . .

If political leaders are likely to be more willing to compromise under some electoral systems than under others, it follows that the electoral system is the central feature of the incentives approach to accommodation. Indeed, differing electoral logics can create differing ethnic outcomes, reversing even favourable and unfavourable starting points, an argument I have made in a comparison of Sri Lanka, which began with a relatively easy ethnic problem, and Malaysia, which began with a very difficult one (Horowitz 1989a).

Vote pooling is the major, but not the only, goal of the incentives approach. As the difficulty of reconciling majorities to nonmajoritarian institutions suggests, multipolar fluidity makes inter-ethnic accommodation easier, since, by definition, it lacks a majority. The presence of

---

8. By way of disclosure, I should report that I served as a consultant to the Fijian Constitution Review Commission that recommended the AV system (see FCRC 1996). Arend Lijphart was also consulted by the Commission.

many groups, no one of which can lay claim to majority status, in Tanzania and India is conducive to the mitigation of conflict. But group identities can change: as I mentioned earlier, a large number of groups can consolidate into a smaller number, and the formal institutional structure can facilitate the change from multipolar fluidity to bipolar opposition. Where multipolarity prevails, another purpose of the electoral system is to preserve it against consolidating tendencies. Among others, the Lebanese system did this for a long time. By acknowledging the plasticity of group identities, which consociational theory completely neglects, the incentives approach can prevent the crystallization of identities and the emergence of more severe conflict.

It is not usually recognized, however, that territory can act in aid of or in lieu of electoral mechanisms for such purposes. Territory can partition groups off from each other and direct their political ambitions at one level of government rather than another. Federalism, and especially the proliferation of federal units, or regional autonomy can act in effect as an electoral reform and can preserve multipolar fluidity. There is very good evidence of this in the case of the proliferation of Nigerian federal units.

Federalism and regional autonomy have other conflict-reducing functions as well. If the units are homogeneous, they may foster intra-group competition, at the expense of an exclusive focus on inter-group competition. If the units are heterogeneous, they may provide an experience in political socialization for politicians of different groups who become habituated to dealing with each other at lower levels before they need to do so at the centre.

Does devolution lead to secession, as central-level politicians so often fear? The intervening variables here are timing and the ties woven with the centre. Early, generous devolution, coupled with carefully crafted connections of the regional population with the centre, is likely to avert rather than produce separatism. Late, grudging devolution, coupled with a view at the centre that members of a group residing in the autonomous territory should henceforth look exclusively to the regional unit for their satisfaction, is far more likely to encourage departure from the state. Hesitation about devolution creates a self-fulfilling prophecy. Because of hesitation, devolution often comes too late.

The incentives approach is as difficult as, or more difficult than, the consociational to adopt, but, once adopted, it has an important advantage. Consociation is certainly easier to understand: one size fits all. But, even if adopted, consociation is far from self-executing, because compromise is not likely to be rewarded by the electorate. The matter will not be left in elite hands. By contrast, politicians who benefit from electoral incentives to moderation have continuing reason to try to reap those rewards, whatever their beliefs and whatever their inclination to toleration and statesmanship. Politicians who are merely exhorted to behave moderately may be left with mere exhortations.

References

Dixon, Paul (1997). "Consociationalism and the Northern Ireland Peace Process: The Glass Half Full or Half Empty?" *Nationalism and Ethnic Politics*, 3/3: 20–36.

FCRC (Fiji Constitution Review Commission, "Reeves Commission") (1996). *Towards A United Future: Report of the Fiji Constitution Review Commission* (Parliamentary Paper 13). Suva: FCRC.

Halpern, Sue (1986). "The Disorderly Universe of Consociational Democracy." *West European Politics*, 9/2: 181–197.

Horowitz, Donald L. (1985). *Ethnic Groups in Conflict*. Berkeley: University of California Press.

——— (1989a). "Incentives and Behaviour in the Ethnic Politics of Sri Lanka and Malaysia." *Third World Quarterly*, 11/4: 18–35.

——— (1991). *A Democratic South Africa? Constitutional Engineering in a Divided Society*. Berkeley: University of California Press.

—— (1997a). "Self-Determination: Politics, Philosophy, and Law." *NOMOS*, 39: 421–463.

—— (2000). "Constitutional Design: An Oxymoron?" *NOMOS*, 42: 253–284.

International Crisis Group (1998). "Changing the Logic of Bosnian Politics: Discussion Paper on Electoral Reform." Brussels (10 March).

—— (1999). "Breaking the Mould: Electoral Reform in Bosnia and Herzegovina." Brussels (4 March).

Lal, Brij (1993). "Chiefs and Indians: Elections and Politics in Contemporary Fiji." *The Contemporary Pacific: A Journal of Island Affairs*, 5: 275–301.

—— (1999a). "Towards a United Future: Report of the Fiji Constitution Review Commission." *Journal of Pacific History*, 32: 71–84.

—— (1999b). "The Voice of the People: Ethnic Identity and Nation Building in Fiji." *Journal of the Pacific Society*, 22/3/4: 1–12.

—— (1999c). *A Time to Change: The Fiji General Elections of 1999* (Discussion Paper 23). Canberra: Department of Political and Social Change, The Australian National University.

Lijphart, Arend (1969). "Consociational Democracy." *World Politics*, 21: 207–225.

—— (1977). *Democracy in Plural Societies: A Comparative Exploration*. New Haven: Yale University Press.

—— (1994b). "Prospects for Power-Sharing in the New South Africa," in Andrew Reynolds (ed.), *Election '94 South Africa*. London: James Currey.

—— and Waisman, Carlos (1996). *Institutional Design in New Democracies*. Boulder, CO: Westview Press.

Reilly, Ben (1997). "Preferential Voting and Political Engineering: A Comparative Study." *Journal of Commonwealth and Comparative Politics*, 35/1: 1–19.

—— and Reynolds, Andrew (1999). *Electoral Systems and Conflict in Divided Societies*. Washington, DC: National Academy Press.

Riker, William H. (1962). *The Theory of Political Coalitions*. New Haven: Yale University Press.

Wimmer, Andreas (1997). "Who Owns the State? Understanding Ethnic Conflict." *Nations and Nationalism: Journal of the Association for the Study of Ethnic Conflict*, 3: 631–665.

The State of Democratic Theory

Ian Shapiro

Even if democracy might in principle operate anywhere, it becomes plain from the literature on its durability ... that this does not mean democracy is easily instituted, or, once installed, destined to survive. These, too, are subjects about which empirically well-supported generalizations are hard to come by ... notwithstanding the confident assertions of various commentators, we are mainly in the dark about the cultural and institutional factors that influence democracy's viability. Little is known about which democratic institutional arrangements are best, and, although prudence suggests that it is wise to try to inculcate support for democracy among those who operate it, it is far from clear how important this is or how to achieve it....

Electoral systems are potential instruments for undermining ethnic conflict in the service of promoting competitive politics, but ... it is unclear how effective they can be. Assuming opinion to be at least partly mobilized and shaped from above, a logical place to start is the incentives facing candidates for office. In a Schumpeterian spirit the goal should be to avoid encouraging aspiring leaders to foment group-based hatred as they seek power. From this perspective we can array electoral systems on an ethnic engineering continuum, ranging from *reactive* systems that cater to ethnic difference, through *reflective* systems that are neutral with respect to existing preferences, to *proactive* that seek to alter it in ways that promote competitive democracy. Secession or partition anchors the reactive pole. Next to it come apartheid and consociationalism ... where the aspiration is to achieve functional partition within a unified

polity. Further along are systems that engineer around ethnic differences to produce diversity in legislatures, as is the case with gerrymandering to create majority minority districts in the American south. These reactive responses all take ethnic difference as given, hoping to work around it. Toward the center of the continuum we come to reflective responses: those that are sensitive to ethnic difference but neutral in the sense of being biased neither in favor nor against it. The various cumulative voting schemes discussed by Lani Guinier fit this description.[32] Here the principle is to give each voter as many votes as there are seats. If a state is to have eight congressional representatives, every voter gets eight votes that can be cast however they wish: all for one candidate or spread among several. If there are intense minority ethnic preferences, members of a particular group can cast all eight votes for "their" representative; if not, not. Unlike racial gerrymandering and consociationalism, reflective schemes respond to ethnic preferences without doing anything to produce or reinforce them. As a result, they avoid the critique of reactive systems that they promote balkanization. Yet by the same token cumulative voting does nothing to ameliorate or undermine potentially polarizing forms of aspirational difference where these are present.

For engineered responses aimed at reducing such conflicts we move to the proactive part of the continuum: arrangements that supply would-be leaders with incentives to avoid mobilizing

---

Excerpted from: Ian Shapiro, "The State of Democratic Theory." *Political Science: The State of the Discipline*. Edited by Ira Katznelson and Helen Milner. Washington, D.C.: American Political Science Association, 2001. © APSA. Reprinted by permission.

32. For Guinier's proposals see Guinier (1991: 1077–1154; 1994a: 109–137). On the battle over her confirmation as Assistant Attorney General for Civil Rights, which she lost for her advocacy of this scheme, see Guinier (1994b). Her fate suggests a criterion, in addition to representative fairness, for evaluating proposed decision rules: whether they can be widely understood and perceived as democratic.

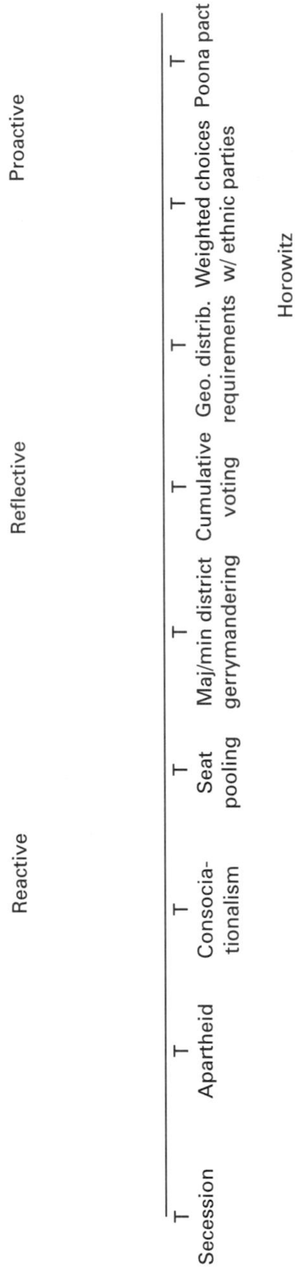

Figure 3.2
Ethnic engineering continuum.

support in ways that exacerbate cultural competition and to devise, instead, ideologies that can appeal across the divisions of relevant groups. Hence Donald Horowitz's contention that, when group-based antipathies are strong, electoral systems are needed that give elites incentives to compete for votes among politicized groups other than their own, and so promote accommodation rather than exclusionary politics (Horowitz 1991: 155; 1985). He describes a successful example of this kind from Malaysia, in which Malay and Chinese politicians were forced to rely in part on votes delivered by politicians belonging to the other ethnic group....

Another possible device is geographical distribution requirements, such as the Nigerian formula for presidential elections employed in 1979 and 1983, in which the winning candidate had to get both the largest number of votes and at least 25 percent of the vote in two thirds of the then-nineteen states of the Nigerian Federation. This type of system would not work in countries like South Africa, however, given the territorial dispersion of politicized groups. In such circumstances, the two most promising candidates are proportional representation utilizing the single transferable vote system, and an alternative vote rule that also lists more than one ordered preference, but declares elected only candidates who receive a majority, rather than a plurality, of votes. Both systems require politicians to cater to voters' choices other than their first preferences, assuming heterogeneous constituencies, so that the politicians' incentives work in the appropriate moderating directions. This will be further accentuated by the alternative vote system, assuming that parties proliferate (Horowitz 1985: 184, 166, 187–196). In many circumstances such vote-pooling systems are more likely to achieve interethnic political cooperation than consociational arrangements or systems, whether first-past-the-post or proportional, that merely require seat-pooling by politicians in coalition governments. As reactive systems, they do nothing to moderate group antipathies. On the contrary, they give politicians incentives to maximize their ex-ante bargaining position by increasing what economists might describe as their group's reservation price for cooperation.

Proactive incentives to avoid appealing to inter-group antipathies will not always work. Parties might proliferate within politicized groups in ways that undermine this dimension of the logic behind weighted vote schemes.[33] Moreover, some of the worst of what often (misleadingly) gets labeled inter-ethnic violence is actually intra-ethnic violence that results when different parties seek to mobilize support from the same ethnic group.... There are limits to the degree that intra-ethnic competition of this sort can be ameliorated by weighted vote mechanisms. If parties have incentives to mobilize support in more than one ethnic constituency, they should avoid campaigning as ethnic parties any more than they have to. In practice, however, parties ... whose *raison d'être* is ethnic—may have little scope to campaign on any other basis. Accordingly, they may resist—perhaps violently—any inroads into their "traditional" sources of support. They can only play a zero-sum ethnic game.

When relying on the logic of cross-group mobilization does not lead to ethnic accommodation, it may be possible to move further along the continuum and become more explicitly proactive, as in the 1931 Poona Pact in India. It requires that Untouchables be the representative in 148 designated constituencies, a number corresponding roughly to their proportion in the population (Van Parijs 1996: 111–112). This both ensures that the specified number of Untouchables become parliamentary representatives and it gives aspirants for office an incentive to seek support from all sectors of heterogeneous constituencies, not merely "their own" ethnic group.... Attractive as such solutions can be in some circumstances, they involve manifestly paternalistic institutional design that is unlikely to win legitimacy unless there is widespread acknowledgment that a minority has been unjustly treated over a long time and that it will not otherwise be represented.[35] Even then, such proposals will likely be attacked on many of the same grounds as are reverse discrimination and affirmative action. They can also be expected to provoke the charge, if from a different ideological quarter, that those competing for the designated minority spots will lack the incentive to represent the relevant minority interests....

The further institutional designers try to move along the continuum toward explicit proactive systems that force integration in exclusionary and racist societies, the more they will learn about how much redesign of ethnic antipathy is feasible in them. At present the only statement that can be made with much confidence is that there is no particular reason to think any society inherently incapable of Schumpeterian electoral competition. As the Indian and Japanese examples underscore, even societies with profoundly inegalitarian cultures and undemocratic histories have adapted to the demands of democratic politics in ways that many would have insisted was impossible before the fact. South Africa might turn out to be another such case in the making, though the jury must remain out until ANC hegemony faces a serious challenge.

References

Guinier, Lani. 1991. "The Triumph of Tokenism: The Voting Rights Act and the Theory of Black Educational Success." *Michigan Law Review* 89. 1077–1154.

———. 1994a. "(E)racing Democracy: The Voting Rights Cases." *Harvard Law Review* 108. 109–137.

---

33. For elaboration of these and related difficulties confronting Horowitz's proposals, see Shapiro (1993: 145–147).

35. According to Nagel (1993: 11), a comparable solution operates with respect to four seats reserved for New Zealand's Maoris, who are also geographically dispersed.

————. 1994b. *The Tyranny of the Majority: Fundamental Fairness in Representative Democracy.* New York: Free Press.

Horowitz, Donald L. 1985. *Ethnic Groups in Conflict.* Berkeley and Los Angeles: University of California Press.

————. 1991. *A Democratic South Africa? Constitutional Engineering in a Divided Society.* Berkeley and Los Angeles: University of California Press.

Nagel, Jack. 1993. "Lessons of the impending electoral reform in New Zealand." *PEGS Newsletter* 3(1): 9–10.

Shapiro, Ian. 1993. "Democratic Innovation: South Africa in Comparative Context." *World Politics* 46: 121–150.

Van Parijs, Philippe. 1996. "Justice and democracy: Are they incompatible?" *Journal of Political Philosophy* 4(2): 101–117.

Democracy

Robert D. Putnam

... That democratic self-government requires an actively engaged citizenry has been a truism for centuries.... I consider both the conventional claim that the health of American democracy requires citizens to perform our *public* duties and the more expansive and controversial claim that the health of our *public* institutions depends, at least in part, on widespread participation in *private* voluntary groups—those networks of civic engagement that embody social capital.

The ideal of participatory democracy has deep roots in American political philosophy....

Many of America's Founding Fathers, however, didn't think much of voluntary associations. They were famously opposed to political parties and local political committees, as well as to any other group whose members might combine to threaten political stability....

Echoing Tocqueville's observations, many contemporary students of democracy have come to celebrate "mediating" or "intermediary" associations, be they self-consciously or only indirectly political, as fundamental to maintaining a vibrant democracy.[9] Voluntary associations and the social networks of civil society that we have been calling "social capital" contribute to democracy in two different ways: they have "external" effects on the larger polity, and they have "internal" effects on participants themselves.

Externally, voluntary associations, from churches and professional societies to Elks clubs and reading groups, allow individuals to express their interests and demands on government and to protect themselves from abuses of power by their political leaders. Political information flows through social networks, and in these networks public life is discussed....

When people associate in neighborhood groups, PTAs, political parties, or even national advocacy groups, their individual and otherwise quiet voices multiply and are amplified.... Citizen connectedness does not require formal institutions to be effective. A study of the democracy movement in East Germany before the collapse of the Berlin Wall, for example, found that recruitment took place through friendship networks and that these informal bonds were more important than ideological commitment, fear of repression, or formal organizing efforts in determining who joined the cause.[12]

Internally, associations and less formal networks of civic engagement instill in their members habits of cooperation and public-spiritedness, as well as the practical skills necessary to partake in public life. Tocqueville observed that "feelings and ideas are renewed, the heart enlarged, and the understanding developed only by the reciprocal action of men one upon another."[13] Prophylactically, community bonds keep individuals from falling prey to extremist groups that target isolated and untethered individuals. Studies of political psychology over the last forty years have suggested that "people divorced from community, occupation, and association are first and foremost among the supporters of extremism."[14]

More positively, voluntary associations are places where social and civic skills are learned—

Reprinted with the permission of Simon & Schuster from *Bowling Alone: The Collapse and Revival of American Community* by Robert D. Putnam. Copyright © 2000 by Robert D. Putnam.

9. See, for example, Peter L. Berger and Richard John Neuhaus, *To Empower People: From State to Civil Society* (Washington, D.C.: AEI Press, 1977; 1996).

12. Karl-Dieter Opp and Christiane Gern, "Dissident Groups, Personal Networks, and Spontaneous Cooperation: The East German Revolution of 1989," *American Sociological Review* 58 (1993): 659–680.

13. Tocqueville, *Democracy in America*, 515.

14. William Kornhauser, *The Politics of Mass Society* (Glencoe, Ill.: Free Press, 1959), 73.

"schools for democracy." Members learn how to run meetings, speak in public, write letters, organize projects, and debate public issues. . . .

The most systematic study of civic skills in contemporary America suggests that for working-class Americans voluntary associations and churches offer the best opportunities for civic skill building, and even for professionals such groups are second only to the workplace as sites for civic learning. Two-thirds or more of the members of religious, literary, youth, and fraternal/service organizations exercised such civic skills as giving a presentation or running a meeting.[17] Churches, in particular, are one of the few vital institutions left in which low-income, minority, and disadvantaged citizens of all races can learn politically relevant skills and be recruited into political action.[18] The implication is vitally important to anyone who values egalitarian democracy: without such institutions, the class bias in American politics would be much greater.[19]

Just as associations inculcate democratic habits, they also serve as forums for thoughtful deliberation over vital public issues. Political theorists have lately renewed their attention to the promise and pitfalls of "deliberative democracy."[20] Some argue that voluntary associations best enhance deliberation when they are micro-cosms of the nation, economically, ethnically, and religiously.[21] Others argue that even homogeneous organizations can enhance deliberative democracy by making our public interactions more inclusive. When minority groups, for example, push for nondiscrimination regulations and mandatory inclusion of ethnic interests in school curricula and on government boards, they are in effect widening the circle of participants.[22]

Voluntary associations may serve not only as forums for deliberation, but also as occasions for learning civic virtues, such as active participation in public life.[23] A follow-up study of high school seniors found that regardless of the students' social class, academic background, and self-esteem, those who took part in voluntary associations in school were far more likely than nonparticipants to vote, take part in political campaigns, and discuss public issues two years after graduating.[24] Another civic virtue is trustworthiness. Much research suggests that when people have repeated interactions, they are far less likely to shirk or cheat.[25] A third civic virtue acquired

17. Verba, Schlozman, Brady, *Voice and Equality*, 378.

18. Frederick C. Harris, "Religious Institutions and African American Political Mobilization," in Paul Peterson, ed., *Classifying by Race* (Princeton, N.J.: Princeton University Press, 1995), 299. The evidence suggests that churches organized congregationally, such as Protestant denominations, tend to provide more opportunities for parishioners to build civic skills than do hierarchically organized churches, including Catholic and evangelical denominations. Protestants are three times as likely as Catholics to report opportunities to exercise civic skills. Verba, Schlozman, Brady, *Voice and Equality*, 321–322, 329.

19. Verba, Schlozman, Brady, *Voice and Equality*, 385.

20. Jon Elster, ed., *Deliberative Democracy* (Cambridge, UK: Cambridge University Press, 1998); Amy Gutmann and Dennis Thompson, *Democracy and Disagreement* (Cambridge, Mass.: Harvard University Press, 1996): J. Bohman, *Public Deliberation* (Cambridge, Mass.: MIT Press, 1996); C. Nino, *The Constitution of Deliberative Democracy* (New Haven, Conn.: Yale University Press, 1996).

21. Gutmann "Freedom of Association," 25.

22. See, for example, Will Kymlicka, "Ethnic Associations and Democratic Citizenship," in Gutmann, *Freedom of Association*, 177–213.

23. See Michael Walzer, "The Civil Society Argument," in Ronald Beiner, ed., *Theorizing Citizenship* (Albany: State University of New York Press, 1995).

24. Michael Hanks, "Youth, Voluntary Associations, and Political Socialization," *Social Forces* 60 (1981): 211–223.

25. David Sally, "Conversation and Cooperation in Social Dilemmas: A Meta-Analysis of Experiments from 1958 to 1992," *Rationality and Society* 7, no. 1 (1995): 58–92.

through social connectedness is reciprocity.... [T]he more people are involved in networks of civic engagement (from club meetings to church picnics to informal get-togethers with friends), the more likely they are to display concern for the generalized other—to volunteer, give blood, contribute to charity, and so on. To political theorists, reciprocity has another meaning as well—the willingness of opposing sides in a democratic debate to agree on the ground rules for seeking mutual accommodation after sufficient discussion, even (or especially) when they don't agree on what is to be done.[26] Regular connections with my fellow citizens don't *ensure* that I will be able to put myself in their shoes, but social isolation virtually guarantees that I will not.

On the other hand, numerous sensible critics have raised doubts about whether voluntary associations are necessarily good for democracy.[27] Most obviously, some groups are overtly antidemocratic—the KKK is everyone's favorite example. No sensible theorist has ever claimed that *every* group works to foster democratic values. But even if we restrict our attention to groups that act within the norms of democracy, one common concern is that associations—or interest groups—distort governmental decision making. From Theodore Lowi's *End of Liberalism* in the 1960s to Jonathan Rauch's *Demosclerosis* in the 1990s, critics of American pluralism have argued that the constant and conflicting pleas of ever more specialized lobbies have paralyzed even well-intentioned public officials and stifled efforts to cut or improve ineffective government programs.[28] This complaint is reminiscent of Madison's worry that mischievous

"factions" would profit at the expense of the commonweal. Contrary to the pluralists' ideal, wherein bargaining among diverse groups leads to the greatest good for the greatest number, we end up instead with the greatest goodies for the best-organized few.

A second concern is that associational ties benefit those who are best equipped by nature or circumstance to organize and make their voices heard. People with education, money, status, and close ties with fellow members of their community of interest will be far more likely to benefit politically under pluralism than will the uneducated, the poor, and the unconnected.[29] In our words, social capital is self-reinforcing and benefits most those who already have a stock on which to trade. As long as associationalism is class biased, as virtually every study suggests it is,[30] then pluralist democracy will be less than egalitarian. In the famous words of the political scientist E. E. Schattschneider: "The flaw in the pluralist heaven is that the heavenly chorus sings with a strong upper-class accent."[31]

Finally, critics of pluralism have suggested that it can trigger political polarization and cynicism. Political scientists concerned about the decline in mass political parties as forces for organizing politics argue that citizen group poli-

26. Gutmann and Thompson, *Democracy and Disagreement*, 52–53.

27. See, for example, Nancy Rosenblum, *Membership and Morals* (Princeton, N.J.: Princeton University Press, 1998); Daniel Schulman, "Voluntary Organization Involvement and Political Participation," *Journal of Voluntary Action Research* 7 (1978): 86–105.

28. Theodore J. Lowi, *The End of Liberalism: Ideology, Policy, and the Crisis of Public Authority* (New York: Norton, 1969); Jonathan Rauch, *Demosclerosis: The Silent Killer of American Government* (New York: Times Books, 1994).

29. Michael Walzer, "The Civil Society Argument," in Ronald Beiner, ed., *Theorizing Citizenship* (Albany: State University of New York Press, 1995)

30. See, for example, Hausknecht, *The Joiners*; Verba, Scholzman, Brady, *Voice and Equality*; and David Horton Smith, "Determinants of Voluntary Association Participation and Volunteering: A Literature Review," *Nonprofit and Voluntary Sector Quarterly* 23, no. 3 (fall 1994): 243–263.

31. E. E. Schattschneider, *The Semisovereign People: A Realist's View of Democracy in America* (New York: Holt, Rinehart & Winston, 1960).

tics is almost by nature extremist politics, since people with strongly held views tend to be the leaders and activists. Evidence from the Roper Social and Political Trends archives indeed suggests that ideological extremism and civic participation are correlated, although as we shall shortly see, that fact turns out to have unexpected implications for our current predicament.

If participation and extremism are linked, there are a number of important repercussions. First, voluntary organizations that are ideologically homogeneous may reinforce members' views and isolate them from potentially enlightening alternative viewpoints.[32] In some cases such parochialism may nurture paranoia and obstruction. In a polarized voluntary group universe, reasonable deliberation and bargaining toward a mutually acceptable compromise is well nigh impossible, as each side refuses "on principle" to give ground. Moreover, political polarization may increase cynicism about government's ability to solve problems and decrease confidence that civic engagement makes any difference.[33]

These are all serious concerns. Voluntary associations are not everywhere and always good. They can reinforce antiliberal tendencies; and they can be abused by antidemocratic forces. Further, not everyone who participates will walk away a better person: some people who join self-help groups, for example, will learn compassion and cooperation, while others will become more narcissistic. In the words of political theorist Nancy Rosenblum: "The moral uses of associational life by members are indeterminate."[34]

Voluntary groups are not a panacea for what ails our democracy. And the absence of social capital—norms, trust, networks of association—does not eliminate politics. But without social capital we are more likely to have politics of a certain type. American democracy evolved historically in an environment unusually rich in social capital, and many of our institutions and practices—such as the unusual degree of decentralization in our governmental processes, compared with that of other industrialized countries—represent adaptations to such a setting. Like a plant overtaken by climatic change, our political practices would have to change if social capital were permanently diminished. How might the American polity function in a setting of much lower social capital and civic engagement?

A politics without face-to-face socializing and organizing might take the form of a Perot-style electronic town hall, a kind of plebiscitary democracy. Many opinions would be heard, but only as a muddle of disembodied voices, neither engaging with one another nor offering much guidance to decision makers. TV-based politics is to political action as watching *ER* is to saving someone in distress. Just as one cannot restart a heart with one's remote control, one cannot jump-start republican citizenship without direct, face-to-face participation. Citizenship is not a spectator sport.

Politics without social capital is politics at a distance. Conversations among callers to a studio in Dallas or New York are not responsible, since these "participants" need never meaningfully engage with opposing views and hence learn from that engagement. Real conversations—the kind that take place in community meetings about crack houses or school budgets—are more "realistic" from the perspective of democratic problem solving. Without such face-to-face interaction, without immediate feedback, without being forced to examine our

32. Seymour Martin Lipset, *Political Man: The Social Bases of Politics* (Garden City, N.Y.: Doubleday, 1960); Samuel Stouffer, *Communism, Conformity and Civil Liberties* (New York: Doubleday, 1955); Sheri Berman, "Civil Society and the Collapse of the Weimar Republic," *World Politics* 49 (April 1997): 401–429.

33. Samuel P. Huntington, "The Democratic Distemper," *The Public Interest* 41 (fall 1975): 9–38.

34. Rosenblum, *Membership and Morals*, 155.

opinions under the light of other citizens' scrutiny, we find it easier to hawk quick fixes and to demonize anyone who disagrees. Anonymity is fundamentally anathema to deliberation.

If participation in political deliberation declines—if fewer and fewer voices engage in democratic debate—our politics will become more shrill and less balanced. When most people skip the meeting, those who are left tend to be more extreme, because they care most about the outcome. Political scientist Morris Fiorina describes, for example, how a generally popular proposal to expand a nature reserve in Concord, Massachusetts, where he lived, became bogged down in protracted and costly controversy perpetuated by a tiny group of environmentalist "true believers."[35]

The Roper Social and Political Trends surveys show that Fiorina's experience is typical: Americans at the political poles are more engaged in civic life, whereas moderates have tended to drop out. Controlling for all the standard demographic characteristics—income, education, size of city, region, age, sex, race, and job, marital, and parental status—Americans who describe themselves as "very" liberal or "very" conservative are more likely to attend public meetings, write Congress, be active in local civic organizations, and even attend church than their fellow citizens of more moderate views. Moreover, this correlation between ideological "extremism" and participation strengthened over the last quarter of the twentieth century, as people who characterize themselves as being "middle of the road" ideologically have disproportionately disappeared from public meetings, local organizations, political parties, rallies, and the like.[36]

In the 1990s self-described middle-of-the-roaders were about *one-half* as likely to participate in public meetings, local civic organizations, and political parties as in the mid-1970s. Participation by self-described "moderate" liberals or conservatives declined by about *one-third*. The declines were smallest—averaging less than *one-fifth*—among people who described themselves as "very" liberal or "very" conservative. Writing to a newspaper, writing to Congress, or even giving a speech declined by a scant 2 percent among people who described themselves as "very" liberal or conservative, by about 15 percent among people who described themselves as "moderately" liberal or conservative, and by about 30 percent among self-described "middle-of-the-roaders."[37]

35. Morris P. Fiorina, "Extreme Voices: The Dark Side of Civic Engagement," in Skocpol and Fiorina, eds., *Civic Engagement in American Democracy.* Fiorina's anecdote is insightful, and his concluding call for more civic engagement is correct. Unfortunately, some passages of his essay confuse a) a high degree of citizen participation in a community with b) a system of representation or a decision-making process that privileges citizen participation, however few the participants may be. The former is a behavioral characteristic, the latter an institutional one. (The two may be linked causally or historically, but they are not the same thing.) Confusingly, Fiorina uses the term *civic engagement* to refer to both, but his essay demonstrates the "dark side" of b), not the dark side of a). Contrary to the essay's title, his evidence shows the dark side of civic *dis*engagement.

36. Generalizations in this and the following paragraph are drawn from the author's analysis of Roper Social and Political Trends archives. Ideological self-description is based on this question: "Now, thinking politically and socially, how would you describe your general outlook—as being very conservative, moderately conservative, middle-of-the-road, moderately liberal, or very liberal?"

37. I have calculated the linear trend between 1974 and 1994 for each of the twelve basic forms of participation for each of the five categories of ideological self-identification and expressed the net change over the twenty-one years as a fraction of the participation rate in 1974. This approach is less sensitive to annual outliers than other possible measures and allows easier comparisons across the different forms of participation, but any reasonable metric yields the same conclusion: The more extreme the self-declared ideological position, the smaller the relative decline in participation rates over these two decades.

Ironically, more and more Americans describe their political views as middle of the road or moderate, but the more polarized extremes on the ideological spectrum account for a bigger and bigger share of those who attend meetings, write letters, serve on committees, and so on. The more extreme views have gradually become more dominant in grassroots American civic life as more moderate voices have fallen silent. In this sense civic disengagement is exacerbating the classic problem of "faction" that worried the Founders.

Just as important as actual engagement is psychic engagement. Social capital is also key here. Surveys show that most of our political discussions take place informally, around the dinner table or the office water cooler. We learn about politics through casual conversation. You tell me what you've heard and what you think, and what your friends have heard and what they think, and I accommodate that new information into my mental database as I ponder and revise my position on an issue. In a world of civic networks, both formal and informal, our views are formed through interchange with friends and neighbors. Social capital allows political information to spread.[38]

However, as political scientists Cathy J. Cohen and Michael C. Dawson have pointed out, these informal networks are not available to everyone. African Americans who live in clusters of poverty in American inner cities suffer not only from economic deprivation, but also from a dearth of political information and opportunity. Their study of Detroit neighborhoods with concentrated poverty found that even residents not themselves destitute are far less likely to attend church, belong to a voluntary organization, attend public meetings, and talk about politics than similar people in more advantaged neighborhoods.[39] People in high-poverty neighborhoods feel cut off from their political representatives and see political and community engagement as futile. In part a realistic assessment of the nation's long-standing inattention to the truly disadvantaged, this alienated apathy also reflects the fact that inner-city neighborhoods often lack institutions to mobilize citizens into political action. In other words, people don't participate because they're not mobilized, and not mobilized, they can never savor the fruits of participation.

But perhaps face-to-face mobilization isn't necessary for effective democracy. It is sufficient, the argument goes, for large national membership groups, such as the American Association of Retired Persons, the Audubon Society, and the NAACP, to represent the interests of their diffuse membership. Just as you and I hire a mechanic to fix our cars and money managers to husband our wealth, so, too, one might argue, it is simply a sensible division of labor for us to hire the AARP to defend our interests as prospective retirees, the Audubon Society our environmentalist views, the NAACP our sympathies on racial issues, and so on. "This is not Tocquevillian democracy," concedes Michael Schudson, "but these organizations may be a highly efficient use of civic energy. The citizen who joins them may get the same civic payoff for less personal hassle. This is especially so if we conceive of politics as a set of public policies. The

38. Gabriel Weimann, "On the Importance of Marginality: One More Step in the Two-Step Flow of Communication," *American Sociological Review* 47 (December 1982): 764–773; Gabriel Weimann. "The Strength of Weak Conversational Ties in the Flow of Information and Influence," *Social Networks* 5 (1983): 245–267; Matthew A. Crenson, "Social Networks and Political Processes in Urban Neighborhoods," *American Journal of Political Science* 22, no. 3 (August 1978): 578–594. Michael MacKuen and Courtney Brown, "Political Context and Attitude Change," *American Political Science Review* 81 (June 1987): 471–490; Robert Huckfeldt and John Sprague, *Citizens, Politics, and Social Communication: Information and Influence in an Election Campaign* (New York: Cambridge University Press, 1995).

39. Cathy J. Cohen and Michael C. Dawson, "Neighborhood Poverty and African American Politics," *American Political Science Review* 87 (1993): 286–302.

citizen may be able to influence government more satisfactorily with the annual membership in the Sierra Club or the National Rifle Association than by attending the local club luncheons."[40] To some intellectuals, citizenship by proxy has a certain allure.[41]

But if we have a broader conception of politics and democracy than merely the advocacy of narrow interests, then the explosion of staff-led, professionalized, Washington-based advocacy organizations may not be as satisfactory, for it was in those local luncheons that civic skills were honed and genuine give-and-take deliberation occurred. . . .

Peter Skerry has argued that broad national membership organizations tend to be dominated not by member input—which is, after all, usually just a check sent in for their dues—but by headquarters staff. These people are inevitably pulled toward the wishes of their major patrons: wealthy individuals, foundations, even the government agencies that indirectly fund many of them. Because the voluntary organizations' members are geographically dispersed, these organizations also tend to rely on media strategies to push their agendas. Media strategies to generate more contributions often emphasize threats from the group's "enemies" and in the process give us a politics fraught with posturing and confrontation, rather than reasoned debate.[43]

There is another reason why large "tertiary" organizations are no substitute for more personal forms of political engagement: Most political decision making does not take place in Washington. To be effective, therefore, political activity cannot be confined to mailing one's dues to an inside-the-Beltway interest group. For example, economist James T. Hamilton discovered that neighborhoods where people owned their homes and voted were (holding constant many other factors) less likely to get hazardous waste plants than neighborhoods where people rented and rarely voted. He concluded that in deciding where to locate, hazardous waste companies look to locate in places in which they can expect the least locally organized opposition.[44] In this way, civic disengagement at the local level undermines neighborhood empowerment. Of course, the reverse is true as well, for disengagement and disempowerment are two sides of the same coin.

Social capital affects not only what goes into politics, but also what comes out of it. The best illustration of the powerful impact of civic engagement on government performance comes not from the United States, but from an investigation that several colleagues and I conducted on the seemingly arcane subject of Italian regional government.[45]

Beginning in 1970, Italians established a nationwide set of potentially powerful regional governments. These twenty new institutions were virtually identical in form, but the social, economic, political, and cultural contexts in which they were implanted differed dramatically, ranging from the preindustrial to the postindustrial, from the devoutly Catholic to the ardently Communist, from the inertly feudal to the frenetically modern. Just as a botanist might investigate plant development by measuring the growth of genetically identical seeds sown in different plots, we sought to understand government performance by studying how these new institutions evolved in their diverse settings. As we expected, some of the new govern-

40. Michael Schudson, "What If Civic Life Didn't Die?" *The American Prospect* 25 (1996): 17–20, quotation at 18.

41. Tarrow, *Power in Movement*, 133.

43. Peter Skerry, "The Strange Politics of Affirmative Action," *Wilson Quarterly* (Winter 1997): 39–46.

44. James T. Hamilton, "Testing for Environmental Racism: Prejudice, Profits, Political Power?," *Journal of Policy Analysis and Management* 14, no. 1 (1995): 107–132.

45. Robert D. Putnam with Robert Leonardi and Raffaella Nanetti, *Making Democracy Work: Civic Traditions in Modern Italy* (Princeton, N.J.: Princeton University Press, 1993).

ments proved to be dismal failures—inefficient, lethargic, and corrupt. Others were remarkably successful, however, creating innovative day care programs and job training centers, promoting investment and economic development, pioneering environmental standards and family clinics—managing the public's business efficiently and satisfying their constituents.

What could account for these stark differences in quality of government? Some seemingly obvious answers turned out to be irrelevant. Government organization was too similar from region to region for that to explain the contrasts in performance. Party politics or ideology made little difference. Affluence and prosperity had no direct effect. Social stability or political harmony or population movements were not the key. None of these factors was correlated with good government as we had anticipated. Instead the best predictor is one that Alexis de Tocqueville might have expected. Strong traditions of civic engagement—voter turnout, newspaper readership, membership in choral societies and literary circles, Lions Clubs, and soccer clubs—were the hallmarks of a successful region.

Some regions of Italy, such as Emilia-Romagna and Tuscany, have many active community organizations. Citizens in these regions are engaged by public issues, not by patronage. They trust one another to act fairly and obey the law. Leaders in these communities are relatively honest and committed to equality. Social and political networks are organized horizontally, not hierarchically. These "civic communities" value solidarity, civic participation, and integrity. And here democracy works.

At the other pole are "uncivic" regions, like Calabria and Sicily, aptly characterized by the French term *incivisme*. The very concept of citizenship is stunted there. Engagement in social and cultural associations is meager. From the point of view of the inhabitants, public affairs is somebody else's business—that of *i notabili*, "the bosses," "the politicians"—but not theirs. Laws, almost everyone agrees, are made to be broken,

but fearing others' lawlessness, everyone demands sterner discipline. Trapped in these interlocking vicious circles, nearly everyone feels powerless, exploited, and unhappy. It is hardly surprising that representative government here is less effective than in more civic communities.

The historical roots of the civic community are astonishingly deep. Enduring traditions of civic involvement and social solidarity can be traced back nearly a millennium to the eleventh century, when communal republics were established in places like Florence, Bologna, and Genoa, exactly the communities that today enjoy civic engagement and successful government. At the core of this civic heritage are rich networks of organized reciprocity and civic solidarity—guilds, religious fraternities, and tower societies for self-defense in the medieval communes; cooperatives, mutual aid societies, neighborhood associations, and choral societies in the twentieth century.

Civic engagement matters on both the demand side and the supply side of government. On the demand side, citizens in civic communities expect better government, and (in part through their own efforts) they get it. As we saw earlier in the hazardous waste study, if decision makers expect citizens to hold them politically accountable, they are more inclined to temper their worst impulses rather than face public protests. On the supply side, the performance of representative government is facilitated by the social infrastructure of civic communities and by the democratic values of both officials and citizens. In the language of economics, social capital lowers transaction costs and eases dilemmas of collection action. Where people know one another, interact with one another each week at choir practice or sports matches, and trust one another to behave honorably, they have a model and a moral foundation upon which to base further cooperative enterprises. Light-touch government works more efficiently in the presence of social capital. Police close more cases when citizens monitor neighborhood comings and goings. Child welfare departments do a better job of "family preservation" when neighbors and relatives provide social support to troubled parents. Public schools teach better when parents volunteer in classrooms and ensure that kids do their homework. When community involvement is lacking, the burdens on government employees—bureaucrats, social workers, teachers, and so forth—are that much greater and success that much more elusive.

Civic traditions seem to matter in the United States as well.... [I]n the 1950s political scientist Daniel Elazar did a pathbreaking study of American "political cultures."[46] He concluded that there were three cultures: a "traditionalistic" culture in the South; an "individualistic" culture in the mid-Atlantic and western states; and a "moralistic" culture concentrated in the Northeast, upper Midwest, and Pacific Northwest. Strikingly, Elazar's political-culture map looks much like the distribution of social capital .... The traditionalistic states, where politics tends to be dominated by elites resistant to innovation, are also the states that tend to be lowest in social capital. The individualistic states, where politics is run by strong parties and professional politicians and focused on economic growth, tend to have moderate levels of social capital. The moralistic states—in which "good government," issue-based campaigning, and social innovation are prized—tend to have comparatively high levels of social capital. The correlation between the political-culture index derived from Elazar's study[47] and our Social Capital Index is strikingly large.[48]

Do civic traditions also predict the character of governments in the United States? Suggestive studies have found that the social capital–rich "moralistic" states tend to be unusually innovative in public policy and to have merit systems governing the hiring of government employees. Politics in these states is more issue oriented, focused on social and educational services, and apparently less corrupt. Preliminary studies suggest that states high in social capital sustain governments that are more effective and innovative.[49]

At the municipal level, too, research has found that high levels of grass-roots involvement tend to blunt patronage politics[50] and secure a fairer distribution of federal community development grants.[51] And cities that have institu-

46. Daniel Elazar, *American Federalism: A View from the States* (New York: Crowell, 1966).

47. Ira Sharkansky, "The Utility of Elazar's Political Culture," *Polity* 2 (1969): 66–83.

48. The Pearson's r correlation coefficient is 0.77, where 1.0 signifies a perfect linear relationship.

49. Charles A. Johnson, "Political Culture in American States: Elazar's Formulation Examined," *American Journal of Political Science* 20 (1976): 491–509; Ira Sharkansky, *Regionalism in American Politics* (Indianapolis, Ind.: Bobbs-Merrill, 1970); Richard A. Joslyn, "Manifestations of Elazar's Political Subcultures: State Public Opinion and the Content of Political Campaign Advertising," John Kincaid. "Political Culture and the Quality of Urban Life," and Susan Welch and John G. Peters, "State Political Culture and the Attitudes of State Senator Toward Social, Economic Welfare, and Corruption Issues," all in *Political Culture, Public Policy and the American States*, John Kincaid, ed. (Philadelphia: Institute for the Study of Human Issues, 1982), 59–80; 121–149; 151–159; Tom W. Rice and Alexander F. Sumberg, "Civic Culture and Government Performance in the American States," *Publius* 27 (1997): 99–114; Maureen Rand Oakley, "Explaining the Adoption of Morality Policy Innovations: The Case of Fetal Homicide Policy," paper presented at the Annual Meeting of the American Political Science Association (Atlanta, Ga., September 1999).

50. Patronage politics are often based on bonding social capital. While they may lead to inefficient government and reinforce ethnic cleavages, they are often highly effective at political mobilization.

51. Margaret Weir, "Power, Money, and Politics in Community Development," in Ronald F. Ferguson and William T. Dickens, eds., *Urban Problems and Community Development* (Washington, D.C.: Brookings Institution Press, 1999).

tionalized neighborhood organizations, such as Portland (Oregon) and St. Paul (Minnesota), are more effective at passing proposals that local people want. These cities also enjoy higher levels of support for and trust in municipal government.[52]

The connection between high social capital and effective government performance begs an obvious question: Is there a similar link between declining social capital and declining trust in government? Is there a connection between our democratic discontent and civic disengagement? It is commonly assumed that cynicism toward government has caused our disengagement from politics, but the converse is just as likely: that we are disaffected because as we and our neighbors have dropped out, the real performance of government has suffered. As Pogo said, "We have met the enemy and he is us."

Social capital affects government in many ways. We all agree that the country is better off when everyone pays the taxes they owe. Nobody wants to subsidize tax cheats. The legitimacy of the tax system turns in part on the belief that we all do our share. Yet we know that the IRS cannot possibly audit everyone, so rational citizens have every reason to believe that if they pay their share, they will indeed be subsidizing those who are not so honor bound. It is a recipe for disillusionment with the IRS and the tax system in general.

Yet not everyone is equally disillusioned. It turns out that in states where citizens view other people as basically honest, tax compliance is higher than in low-social-capital states.... If we consider state differences in social capital, per capita income, income inequality, racial composition, urbanism, and education levels, *social capital is the only factor that successfully predicts tax compliance*.[53] Similarly, surveys have found that individual taxpayers who believe that others

are dishonest or are distrustful of government are more likely themselves to cheat.[54] My willingness to pay my share depends crucially on my perception that others are doing the same. In effect, in a community rich in social capital, government is "we," not "they." In this way social capital reinforces government legitimacy: I pay my taxes because I believe that most other people do, and I see the tax system as basically working as it should. Conversely, in a community that lacks bonds of reciprocity among its inhabitants, I won't feel bound to pay taxes voluntarily, because I believe that most people cheat, and I will see the tax system as yet another broken government program, instituted by "them," not "us."

In this context it is not surprising that one of the best predictors of cooperation with the decennial census is one's level of civic participation. Even more striking is the finding that communities that rank high on measures of social capital, such as turnout and social trust, provide significantly higher contributions to public broadcasting, even when we control for all the other factors that are said to affect audience preferences and expenditures—education, affluence, race, tax deductibility, and public spend-

---

52. Jeffrey M. Berry, Kent E. Portney, and Ken Thomson, *The Rebirth of Urban Democracy* (Washington, D.C.: Brookings Institution Press, 1993).

53. In a regression analysis predicting compliance rates across states, only the Social Capital Index proved to be a statistically significant variable. Other variables—per capita income, income inequality, racial composition, urbanism, education—were not significant. On the role of social capital and trust in undergirding compliance, see Tyler, "Trust and Democratic Governance."

54. Young-dahl Song and Tinsley E. Yarbrough, "Tax Ethics and Taxpayer Attitudes: A Survey," *Public Administration Review* 38 (1978): 442–452; Steven M. Sheffrin and Robert K. Triest, "Can Brute Deterrence Backfire: Perceptions and Attitudes in Taxpayer Compliance," in *Why People Pay Taxes: Tax Compliance and Enforcement*, Joel Slemrod, ed. (Ann Arbor: University of Michigan Press, 1992), 193–222; Scholz and Lubell, "Trust and Taxpaying," and Scholz, "Trust, Taxes, and Compliance."

ing.[55] Public broadcasting is a classic example of a public good—I obtain the benefit whether or not I pay, and my contribution in itself is unlikely to keep the station on the air. Why should any rational, self-interested listener, even one addicted to Jim Lehrer, send off a check to the local station? The answer appears to be that, at least in communities that are rich in social capital, civic norms sustain an expanded sense of "self-interest" and a firmer confidence in reciprocity. Thus if our stocks of social capital diminish, more and more of us will be tempted to "free-ride," not merely by ignoring the appeals to "viewers like you," but by neglecting the myriad civic duties that allow our democracy to work.

Similarly, research has found that military units are more effective when bonds of solidarity and trust are high, and that communities with strong social networks and grassroots associations are better at confronting unexpected crises than communities that lack such civic resources.[56] In all these instances our collective interest requires actions that violate our immediate self-interest and that assume our neighbors will act collectively, too. Modern society is replete with opportunities for free-riding and opportunism. Democracy does not require that citizens be selfless saints, but in many modest ways it does assume that most of us much of the time will resist the temptation to cheat. Social capital, the evidence increasingly suggests, strengthens our better, more expansive selves. The performance of our democratic institutions depends in measurable ways upon social capital.

55. Martha E. Kropf and Stephen Knack, "Viewers Like You: Community Norms and Contributions to Public Broadcasting," unpub. ms. (Kansas City: University of Missouri, Kansas City Department of Political Science, 1999).

56. Jennifer M. Coston, Terry Cooper, and Richard A. Sundeen, "Response of Community Organizations to the Civil Unrest in Los Angeles," *Nonprofit and Voluntary Sector Quarterly* 22 (1993): 357, and Krzysztof Kaniasty and Fran H. Norris, "In Search of Altruistic Community: Patterns of Social Support Mobilization Following Hurricane Hugo," *American Journal of Community Psychology*, 23 (1995): 447–477. The literature on small-group solidarity and military effectiveness is enormous, and much of it is directly relevant to social-capital theory. See Edward A. Shils and Morris Janowitz, "Cohesion and Disintegration in the Wehrmacht in World War II," *Public Opinion Quarterly* 12 (1948): 280–315; Samuel A. Stouffer et al., *The American Soldier* (Princeton, N.J.: Princeton University Press, 1949); and Anthony Kellett, *Combat Motivation: The Behavior of Soldiers in Battle* (Boston: Kluwer-Nijhoff, 1982).

Modernization, Cultural Change, and the Persistence of Traditional Values

Ronald Inglehart and Wayne E. Baker

The last decades of the twentieth century were not kind to modernization theory, once widely considered a powerful tool for peering into the future of industrial society. . . .

Nevertheless, a core concept of modernization theory seems valid today: Industrialization produces pervasive social and cultural consequences, from rising educational levels to changing gender roles. Industrialization is seen as the central element of a modernization process that affects most other elements of society. . . .

Our thesis is that economic development has systematic and, to some extent, predictable cultural and political consequences. These consequences are not iron laws of history; they are probabilistic trends. Nevertheless, the probability is high that certain changes will occur, once a society has embarked on industrialization. We explore this thesis using data from the World Values Surveys. These surveys include 65 societies and more than 75 percent of the world's population. They provide time-series data from the earliest wave in 1981 to the most recent wave completed in 1998, offering new and rich insights into the relationships between economic development and social and political change.

Modernization or the Persistence of Traditional Values?

In recent years, research and theory on socioeconomic development have given rise to two contending schools of thought. One school emphasizes the *convergence* of values as a result of "modernization"—the overwhelming economic and political forces that drive cultural change.

This school predicts the decline of traditional values and their replacement with "modern" values. The other school of thought emphasizes the *persistence* of traditional values despite economic and political changes. This school assumes that values are relatively independent of economic conditions (DiMaggio 1994). Consequently, it predicts that convergence around some set of "modern" values is unlikely and that traditional values will continue to exert an independent influence on the cultural changes caused by economic development. . . .

The central claim of modernization theory is that economic development is linked with coherent and, to some extent, predictable changes in culture and social and political life. Evidence from around the world indicates that economic development tends to propel societies in a roughly predictable direction: Industrialization leads to occupational specialization, rising educational levels, rising income levels, and eventually brings unforeseen changes—changes in gender roles, attitudes toward authority and sexual norms; declining fertility rates: broader political participation; and less easily led publics. Determined elites in control of the state and the military can resist these changes, but in the long run, it becomes increasingly costly to do so and the probability of change rises.[1]

Excerpted from: Ronald Inglehart and Wayne E. Baker, "Modernization, Cultural Change, and the Persistence of Traditional Values." *American Sociological Review* 65 (Feb. 2000): 19–51. Reprinted by permission.

---

1. Paradoxically, modernization can actually strengthen traditional values. Elites in underdeveloped nations who attempt to mobilize a population for social change often use traditional cultural appeals, as in Japan's Meiji Restoration. More recently, radical reformist groups in Algeria used Islam to gain peasant support, but as an unintended result strengthened fundamentalist religious values (Stokes and Marshall 1981). Thus, cultural identity can be used to promote the interests of a group (Bernstein 1997) and in the process may strengthen cultural diversity. Generally, "[a]s global integration intensifies, the currents of multiculturalism swirl faster. Under these conditions, which include the juxtaposition of ethnically distinct

But cultural change does not take the simple linear path envisioned by Marx, who assumed that the working class would continue to grow until a proletarian revolution brought an end to history. In 1956, the United States became the world's first society to have a majority of its labor force employed in the service sector. During the next few decades, practically all OECD (Organization for Economic Cooperation and Development) countries followed suit, becoming "post-industrial" societies, in Bell's (1973) terms. These changes in the nature of work had major political and cultural consequences (Bell 1973, 1976; Dahrendorf 1959). In marked contrast to the growing materialism linked with the industrial revolution, the unprecedented existential security of advanced industrial society gave rise to an intergenerational shift toward postmaterialist and postmodern values (Inglehart 1977, 1990, 1997). While industrialization was linked with an emphasis on economic growth at almost any price, the publics of affluent societies placed increasing emphasis on quality-of-life, environmental protection, and self-expression. Bell emphasized changes in the nature of work, while Inglehart emphasized the consequences of economic security; but they and others agreed that cultural change in postindustrial society was moving in a new direction. Accordingly, we suggest that economic development gives rise to not just one, but two main dimensions of cross-cultural differentiation: a first dimension linked with early industrialization and the rise of the working class; a second dimension that reflects the changes linked with the affluent conditions of advanced industrial society and with the rise of the service and knowledge sectors. . . .

Different societies follow different trajectories even when they are subjected to the same forces of economic development, in part because situation-specific factors, such as cultural heritage, also shape how a particular society develops. Weber ([1904] 1958) argued that traditional religious values have an enduring influence on the institutions of a society. Following this tradition. Huntington (1993, 1996) argues that the world is divided into eight major civilizations or "cultural zones" based on cultural differences that have persisted for centuries. These zones were shaped by religious traditions that are still powerful today, despite the forces of modernization. The zones are Western Christianity, the Orthodox world, the Islamic world, and the Confucian, Japanese, Hindu, African, and Latin American zones.

Scholars from various disciplines have observed that distinctive cultural traits endure over long periods of time and continue to shape a society's political and economic performance. For example, Putnam (1993) shows that the regions of Italy in which democratic institutions function most successfully today are those in which civil society was relatively well developed in the nineteenth century and even earlier. Fukuyama (1995) argues that a cultural heritage of "low-trust" puts a society at a competitive disadvantage in global markets because it is less able to develop large and complex social institutions. Hamilton (1994) argues that, although capitalism has become an almost universal way of life, civilizational factors continue to structure the organization of economies and societies. . . . Thus, there are striking cross-cultural variations in the organization of capitalist production and associated managerial ideologies (DiMaggio 1994; Guillén 1994). . . .

Findings and Discussion

Global Cultural Map, 1995–1998

Figure 3.3 shows the location of 65 societies on the two dimensions. . . . The vertical axis on our global cultural map corresponds to the polarization between traditional authority and secular-

---

labor forces and communities, the politics of identity tends to substitute for the civic (universalist) politics of nation-building" (McMichael 1996: 42).

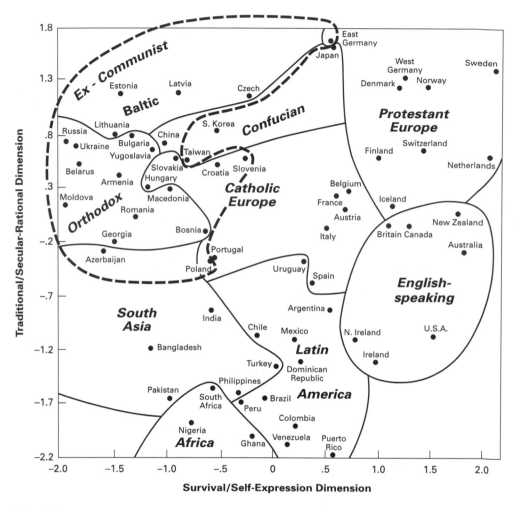

Figure 3.3
Locations of 65 societies on two dimensions of cross-cultural variation: world values surveys, 1990 to 1991 and 1995 to 1998. Note: The scales on each axis indicate the country's factor scores on the given dimension. The positions of Columbia and Pakistan are estimated from incomplete data.

rational authority associated with the process of industrialization. The horizontal axis depicts the polarization between survival values and self-expression values related to the rise of post-industrial society.[5] The boundaries around groups of countries in figure 3.3 are drawn using Huntington's (1993, 1996) cultural zones as a guide.[6]

Cross-cultural variation is highly constrained. As the traditional/secular-rational dimension's loadings indicate ... if the people of a given society place a strong emphasis on religion, that society's relative position on many other variables can be predicted—from attitudes toward abortion, level of national pride (highly religious nations rank high on national pride), the desirability of more respect for authority (religious nations place much more emphasis on respect for authority), to attitudes toward childrearing. The survival/self-expression dimension reflects another wide-ranging but tightly correlated cluster of variables involving materialist values (such as maintaining order and fighting inflation) versus postmaterialist values (such as freedom and self-expression), subjective well-being, interpersonal trust, political activism, and tolerance of outgroups (measured by acceptance or rejection

of homosexuality, a highly sensitive indicator of tolerance toward outgroups in general).

Economic development seems to have a powerful impact on cultural values: The value systems of rich countries differ systematically from those of poor countries. Figure 3.3 reflects a gradient from low-income countries in the lower left quadrant, to rich societies in the upper right quadrant. Figure 3.4 redraws figure 3.3 showing the economic zones into which these 65 societies fall. All 19 societies with an annual per capita gross national product over $15,000 rank relatively high on both dimensions and fall into a zone at the upper right-hand corner. This economic zone cuts across the boundaries of the Protestant, ex-Communist, Confucian, Catholic, and English-speaking cultural zones. All societies with per capita GNPs below $2,000 fall into a cluster at the lower left of figure 3.4, in an economic zone that cuts across the African, South Asian, ex-Communist, and Orthodox cultural zones. The remaining societies fall into two intermediate cultural-economic zones. Economic development seems to move societies in a common direction, regardless of their cultural heritage. Nevertheless, distinctive cultural zones persist two centuries after the industrial revolution began.

GNP per capita is only one indicator of a society's level of economic development. As Marx argued, the rise of the industrial working class was a key event in modern history. Furthermore, the changing nature of the labor force defines three distinct stages of economic development: agrarian society, industrial society, and postindustrial society (Bell 1973, 1976). Thus, another set of boundaries could be superimposed on the societies in figure 3.3: Societies with a high percentage of the labor force in agriculture would fall near the bottom of the map, societies with a high percentage of industrial workers would fall near the top, and societies with a high percentage in the service sector would be located near the right-hand side of the map.

---

5. This cultural map is consistent with an earlier one by Inglehart (1997: 334–337) based on the 1990–1991 World Values Surveys. Although our Figure 3.3 is based on a factor analysis that uses less than half as many variables as Inglehart used (1997), and adds 22 societies that were not included in the earlier map, the overall pattern is strikingly similar to the cultural maps in Inglehart (1997, chaps. 3 and 11). These similarities demonstrate the robustness of the two key dimensions of cross-cultural variation. The same broad cultural zones appear in essentially the same locations, even though some zones now contain many more societies.

6. An alternative strategy would be to use one of the many available clustering techniques to identify groups of nations and draw boundaries. We prefer to use the theoretical classifications proposed by Huntington and then test for their explanatory power.

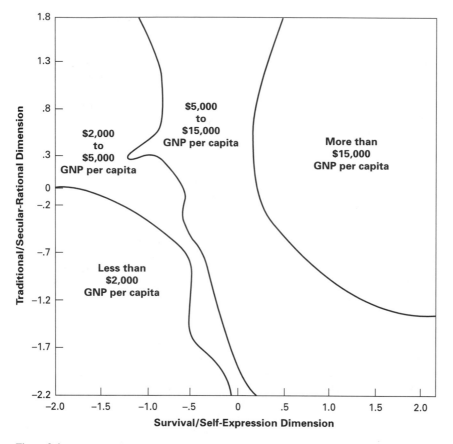

Figure 3.4
Economic zones for 65 societies superimposed on two dimensions of cross-cultural variation. Note: All but one of the 65 societies shown in figure 3.3 fit into the economic zones indicated here; only the Dominican Republic is mislocated. Source: GNP per capita is based on the World Bank's purchasing power parity estimates as of 1995, in U.S. dollars (World Bank 1997: 214–215).

The traditional/secular-rational dimension is associated with the transition from agrarian society to industrial society. Accordingly, this dimension shows a strong positive correlation with the percentage in the industrial sector ($r = .65$) and a negative correlation with the percentage in the agricultural sector ($r = -.49$) but it is weakly linked with the percentage in the service sector ($r = .18$). Thus, the shift from an agrarian mode of production to industrial production seems to bring with it a shift from traditional values toward increasing rationalization and secularization. Nevertheless, a society's cultural heritage also plays a role. Thus, all four of the Confucian-influenced societies have relatively secular values, regardless of the proportion of their labor forces in the industrial sector. The former Communist societies also rank relatively high on this secularization dimension, despite varying degrees of industrialization. Conversely, the historically Roman Catholic societies display relatively traditional values when compared with Confucian or ex-Communist societies with the same proportion of industrial workers.

The survival/self-expression dimension is linked with the rise of a service economy: It shows a .73 correlation with the relative size of the service sector, but is unrelated to the relative size of the industrial sector ($r = .03$). While the traditional/secular-rational values dimension and the survival/self-expression values dimension reflect industrialization and the rise of post-industrial society, respectively, this is only part of the story. Virtually all of the historically Protestant societies rank higher on the survival/self-expression dimension than do all of the historically Roman Catholic societies, regardless of the extent to which their labor forces are engaged in the service sector. Conversely, virtually all of the former Communist societies rank low on the survival/self-expression dimension. Changes in GNP and occupational structure have important influences on prevailing worldviews, but traditional cultural influences persist.

Religious traditions appear to have had an enduring impact on the contemporary value systems of 65 societies, as Weber, Huntington, and others have argued. But a society's culture reflects its entire historical heritage. A central historical event of the twentieth century was the rise and fall of a Communist empire that once ruled one-third of the world's population. Communism left a clear imprint on the value systems of those who lived under it. East Germany remains culturally close to West Germany despite four decades of Communist rule, but its value system has been drawn toward the Communist zone. And although China is a member of the Confucian zone, it also falls within a broad Communist-influenced zone. Similarly Azerbaijan, though part of the Islamic cluster, also falls within the Communist superzone that dominated it for decades.

The influence of colonial ties is apparent in the existence of a Latin American cultural zone. Former colonial ties also help account for the existence of an English-speaking zone. All seven of the English-speaking societies included in this study show relatively similar cultural characteristics. Geographically, they are halfway around the world from each other, but culturally Australia and New Zealand are next-door neighbors of Great Britain and Canada. The impact of colonization seems especially strong when reinforced by massive immigration from the colonial society—thus, Spain, Italy, Uruguay, and Argentina are all near each other on the border between Catholic Europe and Latin America: The populations of Uruguay and Argentina are largely descended from immigrants from Spain and Italy. Similarly, Rice and Feldman (1997) find strong correlations between the civic values of various ethnic groups in the United States, and the values prevailing in their countries of origin—two or three generations after their families migrated to the United States.

Figure 3.3 indicates that the United States is not a prototype of cultural modernization for other societies to follow, as some modernization writers of the postwar era naively assumed. In fact, the United States is a deviant case, having a much more traditional value system than any other advanced industrial society. On the traditional/secular-rational dimension, the United States ranks far below other rich societies, with levels of religiosity and national pride comparable to those found in developing societies. The phenomenon of American exceptionalism has been discussed by Lipset (1990, 1996). Baker (1999), and others; our results support their argument. The United States does rank among the most advanced societies along the survival/self-expression dimension, but even here, it does not lead the world, as the Swedes and the Dutch seem closer to the cutting edge of cultural change than do the Americans....

Modernization theory implies that as societies develop economically, their cultures tend to shift in a predictable direction, and our data fit the implications of this prediction. Economic differences are linked with large and pervasive cultural differences (see figure 3.4). Nevertheless, we find clear evidence of the influence of long-established cultural zones. Using data from the latest available survey for each society, we created dummy variables to reflect whether a given society is predominantly English-speaking, ex-Communist, and so on for each of the clusters outlined in figure 3.3. Empirical analysis of these variables shows that the cultural locations of given societies are far from random.... Eight of the nine zones outlined on figure 3.3 show statistically significant relationships with at least one of the two major dimensions of cross-cultural variation....

Do these cultural clusters simply reflect economic differences? For example, do the societies of Protestant Europe have similar values simply because they are rich? The answer is no.... [A] society's Catholic or Protestant or Confucian or Communist heritage makes an independent contribution to its position on the global cultural map. The influence of economic development is pervasive. GDP per capita shows a significant impact in five of the eight multiple regressions predicting traditional/secular-rational values, and in all of the regressions predicting survival/

self-expression values. The percentage of the labor force in the industrial sector seems to influence traditional/secular-rational values even more consistently than does GDP per capita, showing a significant impact in seven of the eight regressions. The percentage of the labor force in the service sector has a significant impact in six of the eight regressions predicting survival/self-expression....

The impact of a society's historical-cultural heritage persists when we control for GDP per capita and the structure of the labor force. Thus, the ex-Communist dummy variable shows a strong and statistically significant impact on traditional/secular-rational values, controlling for economic development. The secularizing effect of Communism is even greater than that of the relative size of the industrial sector and almost as great as that for GDP per capita. The ex-Communist dummy variable also has a strong significant ($p < .001$) negative impact on survival/self-expression values. Similarly, the Protestant Europe dummy variable has strong and significant impacts on both of the major cultural dimensions. English-speaking culture has a strong and significant impact on the traditional/secular-rational dimension: Controlling for level of development, it is linked with a relatively *traditional* outlook. But although the English-speaking societies are clustered near the right-hand pole of the survival/self-expression dimension, this tendency disappears when we control for the fact that they are relatively wealthy and have a high percentage of the work force in the service sector. All but one of the dummy variables for cultural zones ... show a statistically significant impact on at least one of the two dimensions....

When we combine the clusters shown in figure 3.3 into broader cultural zones with large sample sizes, we generate variables having even greater explanatory power....

To illustrate the coherence of these clusters, we examine one of the key variables in the literature on cross-cultural differences—interpersonal trust (one component of the survival/self-expression dimension). Coleman (1990), Almond and Verba (1963), Putnam (1993), and Fukuyama (1995) argue that interpersonal trust is essential for building the social structures on which democracy depends and for creating the complex social organizations on which large-scale economic enterprises are based. Figure 3.5 demonstrates that most historically Protestant societies rank higher on interpersonal trust than do most historically Catholic societies. This holds true even after controlling for levels of economic development: Interpersonal trust is significantly correlated with a society's level of GDP per capita ($r = .60$), but even rich Catholic societies rank lower than equally prosperous historically Protestant societies. A heritage of Communist rule also has an impact on interpersonal trust, with virtually all ex-Communist societies ranking relatively low (in italic type in figure 3.5): thus, the historically Protestant societies that had experienced Communist rule (e.g., East Germany and Latvia) show relatively low levels of interpersonal trust. Of the 19 societies in which more than 35 percent of the public believe that most people can be trusted, 14 are historically Protestant, three are Confucian-influenced, one (India) is predominantly Hindu, and only one (Ireland) is historically Catholic. Of the 10 societies ranking lowest on trust in figure 3.5, 8 are historically Catholic and none is historically Protestant.

Within given societies, Catholics rank about as high on interpersonal trust as do Protestants. The shared historical experience of given nations, not individual personality, is crucial. As Putnam (1993) argues, horizontal, locally controlled organizations are conducive to interpersonal trust, whereas rule by large, hierarchical, centralized bureaucracies seems to corrode interpersonal trust. Historically, the Roman Catholic Church was the prototype of a hierarchical, centrally controlled institution; Protestant churches were relatively decentralized and more open to local control. The contrast between local control and domination by a remote hierarchy

has important long-term consequences for interpersonal trust. Clearly, these cross-cultural differences do not reflect the contemporary influence of the respective churches. The Catholic church has changed a great deal in recent decades, and in many countries, especially Protestant ones, church attendance has dwindled to the point where only a small minority of the population attends church regularly. While the majority of individuals have little or no contact with the church today, the impact of living in a society that was historically shaped by once-powerful Catholic or Protestant institutions persists today, shaping everyone—Protestant, Catholic, or other—to fit into a given national culture.

The individual-level data provide additional insights concerning the transmission of religious traditions today. There are two main possibilities: (1) that contemporary religious institutions instill distinctively Protestant, Catholic, or Islamic values in their respective followers within each society; or (2) that given religious traditions have historically shaped the national culture of given societies, but that today their impact is transmitted mainly through nationwide institutions, to the population of that society as a whole—even to those who have little or no contact with religious institutions. As figure 3.6 indicates, the empirical evidence clearly supports the latter interpretation. Although historically Catholic or Protestant or Islamic societies show distinctive values, the differences between Catholics and Protestants or Muslims within given societies are relatively small. In Germany, for example, the basic values of German Catholics resemble those of German Protestants more than they resemble Catholics in other countries. This is true in the United States, Switzerland, The Netherlands, and other religiously mixed societies: Catholics tend to be slightly more traditional than their Protestant compatriots, but they do not fall into the historically Catholic cultural zone. Rather surprisingly, this also holds true of the differences between Hindus and Muslims in

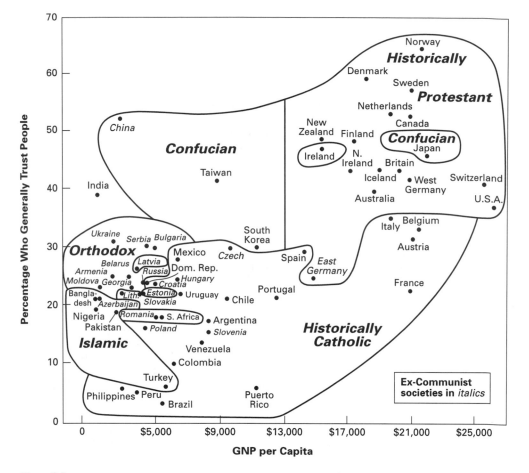

Figure 3.5
Locations of 65 societies on dimensions of interpersonal trust and economic development, by cultural/religious tradition. Note: GNP per capita is measured by World Bank purchasing power parity estimates in 1995 U.S. dollars. Trust is correlated with GNP per capita at r = .60 (p < .001).

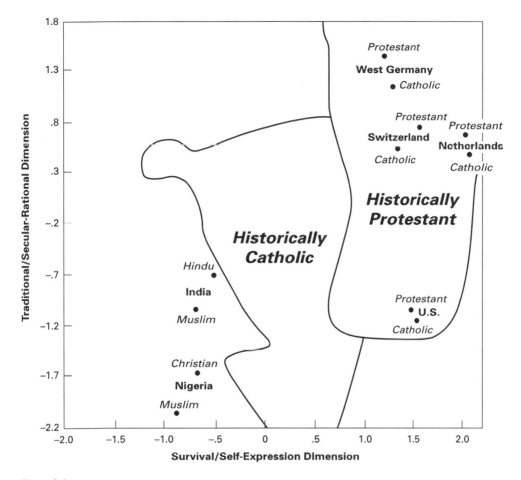

Figure 3.6
Differences between the religious groups within religiously mixed societies on two dimensions of cross-cultural variation.

India, and between Christians and Muslims in Nigeria: The basic values of Nigerian Muslims are closer to those of their Christian compatriots than they are to those of Indian Muslims. On questions that directly evoked Islamic or Christian identity, this would probably not hold true; but on these two dimensions of basic values as measured in the World Values Surveys, the cross-national differences dwarf within-nation differences.

Protestant or Catholic societies display distinctive values today mainly because of the historical impact their respective churches had on their societies, rather than through their contemporary influence. For this reason, we classify Germany, Switzerland, and The Netherlands as historically Protestant societies—historically, Protestantism shaped them, even though today (as a result of immigration, relatively low Protestant birth rates, and higher Protestant rates of secularization) they may have more practicing Catholics than practicing Protestants.

These findings suggest that, once established, the cross-cultural differences linked with religion have become part of a national culture that is transmitted by the educational institutions and mass media of given societies to the people of that nation. Despite globalization, the nation remains a key unit of shared experience, and its educational and cultural institutions shape the values of almost everyone in that society.

The persistence of distinctive value systems suggests that culture is path-dependent. Protestant religious institutions gave rise to the Protestant Ethic, relatively high interpersonal trust, and a relatively high degree of social pluralism—all of which may have contributed to earlier economic development in Protestant countries than in the rest of the world. Subsequently, the fact that Protestant societies were (and still are) relatively prosperous has probably shaped them in distinctive ways. Although they have experienced rapid social and cultural change, historically Protestant and Catholic (and Confucian, Islamic, Orthodox, and other) societies remain

distinct to a remarkable degree. Identifying the specific mechanisms through which these path-dependent developments have occurred would require detailed historical analyses that we will not attempt here, but survey evidence from societies around the world supports this conclusion.

More detailed regression analyses that control for the structure of the work force and simultaneously test the impact of various cultural zones, provide additional support for the conclusion that a society's value system is systematically influenced by economic development—but that a Protestant or Catholic or Confucian or ex-Communist heritage also exerts a persistent and pervasive influence on contemporary values and beliefs....

Conclusion

Evidence from the World Values Surveys demonstrates both massive cultural change and the persistence of distinctive traditional values. Economic development is associated with pervasive, and to some extent predictable, cultural changes. Industrialization promotes a shift from traditional to secular-rational values, while the rise of postindustrial society brings a shift toward more trust, tolerance, well-being, and postmaterialist values. Economic collapse tends to propel societies in the opposite direction. If economic development continues, we expect a continued decline of institutionalized religion. The influence of traditional value systems is unlikely to disappear, however, as belief systems exhibit remarkable durability and resilience. Empirical evidence from 65 societies indicates that values can and do change, but also that they continue to reflect a society's cultural heritage.

Modernization theorists are partly right. The rise of industrial society is linked with coherent cultural shifts away from traditional value systems, and the rise of postindustrial society is linked with a shift away from absolute norms and values toward a syndrome of increasingly rational, tolerant, trusting, postindustrial values. But values seem to be path dependent: A history of Protestant or Orthodox or Islamic or Confucian traditions gives rise to cultural zones with distinctive value systems that persist after controlling for the effects of economic development. Economic development tends to push societies in a common direction, but rather than converging, they seem to move on parallel trajectories shaped by their cultural heritages. We doubt that the forces of modernization will produce a homogenized world culture in the foreseeable future.

We propose several modifications of modernization theory. First, modernization does not follow a linear path. The rise of the service sector and the transition to a knowledge society are linked with a different set of cultural changes from those that characterized industrialization. Moreover, protracted economic collapse can reverse the effects of modernization, resulting in a return to traditional values, as seems to be happening in the former Soviet Union.

Second, the secularization thesis is oversimplified. Our evidence suggests that it applies mainly to the industrialization phase—the shift from agrarian society to industrial society that was completed some time ago in most advanced industrial societies. This shift was linked with major declines in the role of the church, which led Marx and others to assume that, in the long run, religious beliefs would die out. The shift from agrarian to urban industrial society reduces the importance of organized religion, but this is counterbalanced by growing concerns for the meaning and purpose of life. Religious beliefs persist, and spiritual concerns, broadly defined, are becoming more widespread in advanced industrial societies.

Third, cultural change seems to be path dependent. Economic development tends to bring pervasive cultural changes, but the fact that a society was historically shaped by Protestantism or Confucianism or Islam leaves a cultural heritage with enduring effects that influence subsequent development. Even though few people attend church in Protestant Europe today, historically Protestant societies remain distinctive across a wide range of values and attitudes. The same is true for historically Roman Catholic societies, for historically Islamic or Orthodox societies, and for historically Confucian societies.

Fourth, it is misleading to view cultural change as "Americanization." Industrializing societies in general are *not* becoming like the United States. In fact, the United States seems to be a deviant case, as many observers of American life have argued (Lipset 1990, 1996)—its people hold much more traditional values and beliefs than do those in any other equally prosperous society (Baker 1999). If any societies exemplify the cutting edge of cultural change, it would be the Nordic countries.

Finally, modernization is probabilistic, not deterministic. Economic development tends to transform a given society in a predictable direction, but the process and path are not inevitable. Many factors are involved, so any prediction must be contingent on the historical and cultural context of the society in question.

Nevertheless, the central prediction of modernization theory finds broad support: Economic development is associated with major changes in prevailing values and beliefs: The worldviews of rich societies differ markedly from those of poor societies. This does not necessarily imply cultural convergence, but it does predict the general direction of cultural change and (in so far as the process is based on intergenerational population replacement) even gives some idea of the rate at which such change is likely to occur.

References

Almond, Gabriel and Sidney Verba. 1963. *The Civic Culture*. Princeton, NJ: Princeton University Press.

Baker, Wayne E. 1999. *North Star Falling: The American Crisis of Values at the New Millennium*. School of Business, University of Michigan, Ann Arbor, MI. Unpublished manuscript.

Bell, Daniel. 1973. *The Coming of Post-Industrial Society*. New York: Basic Books.

———. 1976. *The Cultural Contradictions of Capitalism*. New York: Basic Books.

Bernstein, Mary. 1997. "Celebration and Suppression: The Strategic Uses of Identity by the Lesbian and Gay Movement." *American Journal of Sociology* 103: 531–565.

Coleman, James S. 1990. *Foundations of Social Theory*. Cambridge, MA: Harvard University Press.

Dahrendorf, Ralf. 1959. *Class and Class Conflict in Industrial Society*. Stanford, CA: Stanford University Press.

DiMaggio, Paul. 1994. "Culture and Economy." Pp. 27–57 in *The Handbook of Economic Sociology*, edited by N. J. Smelser and R. Swedberg. Princeton, NJ: Princeton University Press.

Fukuyama, Francis. 1995. *Trust: The Social Virtues and the Creation of Prosperity*. New York: Free Press.

Guillén, Mauro. 1994. *Models of Management: Work, Authority, and Organization in a Comparative Perspective*. Chicago, IL: University of Chicago Press.

Hamilton, Gary G. 1994. "Civilizations and Organization of Economies." Pp. 183–205 in *The Handbook of Economic Sociology*, edited by N. J. Smelser and R. Swedberg. Princeton, NJ: Princeton University Press.

Huntington, Samuel P. 1993. "The Clash of Civilizations?" *Foreign Affairs* 72(3): 22–49.

———. 1996. *The Clash of Civilizations and the Remaking of World Order*. New York: Simon and Schuster.

Inglehart, Ronald. 1977. *The Silent Revolution: Changing Values and Political Styles in Advanced Industrial Society*. Princeton, NJ: Princeton University Press.

———. 1990. *Culture Shift in Advanced Industrial Society*. Princeton, NJ: Princeton University Press.

———. 1997. *Modernization and Postmodernization: Cultural, Economic, and Political Change in 43 Societies*. Princeton, NJ: Princeton University Press.

Lipset, Seymour Martin. 1990. "American Exceptionalism Reaffirmed." *Toqueville Review* 10: 23–45.

———. 1996. *American Exceptionalism*. New York: Norton.

McMichael, Philip. 1996. "Globalization: Myths and Realities." *Rural Sociology* 61: 25–56.

Putnam, Robert. 1993. *Making Democracy Work: Civic Traditions in Modern Italy*. Princeton NJ: Princeton University Press.

Rice, Tom W. and Jan L. Feldman. 1997. "Civic Culture and Democracy from Europe America." *Journal of Politics* 59: 1143–72.

Rokeach, Milton. 1968. *Beliefs, Attitudes, and Values*. San Francisco: Jossey-Bass.

Rokeach, Milton. 1973. *The Nature of Human Values*. New York: Free Press.

Schuman, Howard and Jacqueline Scott. 1989. "Generations and Collective Memories. *American Sociological Review* 54: 359–81.

Smith, Tom. 1999. "Church Attendance Declining in the U.S." National Opinion Center press release, June 8, 1999.

Spier, Fred. 1996. *The Structure of Big History: From the Big Bang until Today*. Amsterdam, Holland: Amsterdam University Press.

Stokes, Randall G. and Susan Marshall. 1981. "Tradition and the Veil: Female Status in Tunisia and Algeria." *Journal of Modern African Studies* 19: 625–46.

U.S. Census Bureau. 1996. *World Population Profile: 1996*. Washington, DC: U.S. Census Bureau.

Wallerstein, Immanuel. 1974. *The Modern World System*. Vol. 1. New York: Academic Press.

———. 1976. "Modernization: Requiescat in Pace." Pp. 131–135 in *The Uses of Controversy in Sociology*, edited by L. A. Coser and O. N. Larsen. New York: Free Press.

Watson, James, ed. 1998. *Golden Arches East: McDonald's in East Asia*. Stanford, CA: Stanford University Press.

Weber, Max. [1904] 1958. *The Protestant Ethnic and the Spirit of Capitalism*. Translated by T. Parsons. Reprint, New York: Charles Scribner's Sons.

Weiner, Myron, ed. 1966. *Modernization: The Dynamics of Growth*. New York: Basic.

Williams, Rhys H., ed. 1997. *Cultural Wars in American Politics*. New York: Aldine de Gruyter.

World Bank. 1997. *World Development Report*. New York: Oxford University Press.

Wuthnow, Robert. 1998. *After Heaven: Spirituality in America Since the 1950s*. Berkeley, CA: University of California Press.

Culture and Democracy

Adam Przeworski, José Antonio Cheibub, and Fernando Limongi

Democracy and a "Democratic Culture"

Does democracy have to rely on a "democratic culture" in order to exist and endure? And, if so, are particular cultural patterns either more or less compatible with such a "democratic culture" and accordingly conductive or counter to democracy?

In one view, i.e. "non-culturalist," culture exerts no causal power with regard to democracy. No democratic culture is needed for a country to establish democratic institutions and none to sustain them. In the "weakly culturalist" view, a democratic culture is required for democracy to emerge or to endure, but the question of the compatibility of this democratic culture with the traditions of particular societies is moot, since these traditions are malleable, subject to being invented and reinvented. Thus, the democratic culture can flourish even in those cultural settings that appear hostile to it. Finally, in the "strongly culturalist" view, some cultures are simply incompatible with democracy. Different countries, therefore, must seek different political arrangements.

What is thus at stake is whether democratic institutions can function in all cultural environments or whether we must accept that some cultures are compatible only with various forms of authoritarianism.

This is a hard question to answer. It is subject to strongly held conflicting beliefs and the evidence required to adjudicate between them is difficult to come by. All we can do is to reconstruct these rival views and to cite some facts.

Excerpted from: Adam Przeworski, José Antonio Cheibub, and Fernando Limongi, "Culture and Democracy." *World Culture Report: Culture, Creativity, and Markets.* Paris: UNESCO Publishing, 1998. © UNESCO 1998. Reproduced by permission of UNESCO.

Our general conclusion is sceptical. We think that economic and institutional factors are sufficient to generate a convincing explanation of the dynamic of democracies without any recourse to culture. And we find empirically that at least the most obvious cultural traits, such as the dominant religion, have little relevance for the emergence and durability of democracies. Hence, while there may be good reasons one should expect cultures to matter, the available empirical evidence provides little support for the view that democracy requires a democratic culture.

We begin with a brief history of culturalist views and then analyse them more systematically. The question here is whether democracy can emerge and endure only if it is supported by some definite cultural patterns. Are some specific aspects of culture necessary for democracy and, if so, which and how? We also develop an explanation that does not rely on culture and show that this explanation is supported by some facts. Later, we ask whether particular cultures can be assessed to be more or less compatible with democracy and then examine empirically whether these cultures, crudely identified in terms of dominant national religions, affect the emergence and the survival of democratic regimes. A discussion of some normative issues closes the chapter....

What Is It about Culture That Matters, and How?

... [T]he view that democracy requires a definite cultural basis has many lives. Something about culture seems necessary for democracy to emerge or endure. But what? Montesquieu thought it was an irrational motive force ("les passions humaines qui le font mouvoir," *EL*, III, 1)—fear; honour, virtue—which, in turn, reflect religions, mores and manners. Stage theorists looked for feelings, habits, as well as for a rational sense of public utility. Mill was more systematic, distinguishing between a preference for democracy, the temperamental characteristics necessary to sustain it and a sense of community. Almond and Verba looked at beliefs, affects and evaluations of the political process and political outcomes. Inglehart wanted to know whether people are satisfied with their lives, whether they trust each other, and whether they like revolutionary changes. Other survey researchers inquired whether people value democracy per se, regardless of the conditions with which it has to cope and the outcomes it generates.

This ambiguity, and the confusions it engenders, are most apparent in Weingast's (1997) attempt to reconcile apparently rival explanations of democratic stability. Weingast set himself to demonstrate that for democracy to be stable, citizens must adopt a shared view of what constitutes illegitimate actions by the state and must be prepared to act against the transgressions of these limits were they to occur....

What, then, is the role of culture in supporting this democratic equilibrium? Weingast (p. 253) is careful to emphasize that his is not a causal story, in which values would make democracy stable, nor the reverse. A particular culture and democratic stability are just different aspects of situations in which a society resolves its co-ordination dilemmas. But what exactly are the aspects of culture that support these situations? At the first level, two are prominent: a consensus about the limits of legitimate state actions and a common sense of "duty" to defend it.[3] ...

Yet if culturalist views are to furnish a compelling explanation of the origins and life of de-

mocracy, they must specify what it is about culture that matters and how. Let us first distinguish different aspects of culture that may matter.[4]

First, people value democracy per se, regardless of the outcomes it generates.... They believe that democracy is unconditionally the best (or the least bad) system of government, they say so when asked, or act as if they so believed.

Second, people see it as their duty to obey outcomes resulting from rules to which they "agreed."[5] We put "agree" in quotation marks, since the agreement in question can be putative: people would have chosen these rules had they been consulted. Democracy is then legitimate in the sense that people are ready to accept decisions of as yet undetermined content, as long as these decisions result from applying the rules. Even if they do not like them, people comply with the outcomes of the democratic interplay

---

3. Weingast assumes implicitly that the state is a potential threat to everyone: the possibility of a stable alliance between the state and particular classes is ruled out. As a result, he misinterprets his own conclusions when he says that citizens act out of a sense of "duty" when they oppose the state. What kind of "duty" is it that is driven only by self-interest?

4. A new fashion among game theorists is to interpret culture as "out-of-equilibrium" beliefs: beliefs about what would happen if something that never happens actually transpired. Suppose the bourgeoisie is considering whether to accede to workers' demands or to turn to the military with the request to suppress them. The bourgeoisie believes that the military would not suppress and, therefore, accedes to workers' demands. Hence, the belief that the military is non-political, an out-of-equilibrium belief, underlies democratic stability. Or suppose that workers believe that the military would suppress them if requested to do so by the bourgeoisie: then the bourgeoisie, knowing that workers would moderate their demands out of the fear of military intervention, would not turn to the military. Now it is workers' out-of-equilibrium belief that the military are prone to intervention that supports democracy. The problem with such explanations is that while equilibrium beliefs can be based on observations of past events, and can be thus updated rationally, out-of-equilibrium beliefs are completely arbitrary. Hence, 'culture' becomes just a name for the black box of beliefs. This does not seem to us a fruitful line of investigation.

5. On the difficulties of this conception as a positive theory of action, see Dunn (1996, Chap. 4).

because they result from applying rules they accept.... "Participatory culture" is then the key to democratic stability.

Third, people have values and perhaps temperamental characteristics ("democratic personality," in the language of the 1950s) that support it.... These characteristics may include 'republican virtue', trust,[6] empathy, tolerance, moderation, or patience. People may love the collectivity above themselves; they may trust that the government will not take an unfair advantage of them even if it is in the hands of their adversaries; they may be ready to respect the validity of views and interests different from theirs; they may be willing to accept that others should also have rights; or they may be willing to wait for their turn.

Fourth, what may matter for democracy to be possible is not so much what people share but that they do: "consensus."[7] ... Unless people share basic characteristics, such as language, religion, or ethnicity, they do not have enough in common to sustain democracy. But homogeneity with regard to such basic characteristics is not sufficient: "agreement" about some basic values, rules of the game, or what not is required for democracy to function (Dahl 1956; Lipset 1959; Eckstein 1961).[8] ...

Clearly, these cultural underpinnings of democracy need not be mutually exclusive. Even if some may be more important in bringing de-

mocracy about and others in making it last, any or all of them may be necessary for people to struggle for democracy when they live under dictatorship and to support it actively once it is established. But if culturalist views are to have an explanatory power, they must distinguish and specify. Otherwise, it will never be possible to conclude that culture does not matter.

The second issue concerns causality. For even if all the enduring democracies were found to share a definite "democratic culture," this observation would not be sufficient to determine which, if either, comes first: democratic culture or democratic institutions. At the risk of being pedantic, we need to distinguish causal chains that may connect economic development, cultural transformations, and political institutions.

First, culture causes both development and democracy, whatever the causal connection between the latter two elements. This is what we mean by a "strongly culturalist" view....

Second, both development and culture are needed independently for democracy to be possible. And even if development generates some cultural transformations, these transformations are not sufficient to generate the democratic culture, which is, in turn, necessary for democracy to emerge and survive. This was the view of Almond and Verba, discussed above, still a strongly culturalist view.

Third, a particular culture is necessary for democracy to be possible, but this culture is automatically generated by economic development.... Clearly, in this view cultures, in plural, are sufficiently malleable to become "modernized" along with other aspects of societies as an effect of economic development. Thus, the causal chain goes from development, through culture, to democracy. This is a "weakly culturalist" view.

Fourth, a particular culture is necessary for democracy to endure but this culture emerges as an effect of democratic institutions once they are in place.... In this view, we should expect all enduring democracies to have the same political

---

6. Trust is the recent fashion of democratic theorists. But one might wonder if democratic citizens should trust their governments too much: should they not, instead, monitor what governments are doing and sanction them appropriately?

7. Such a consensus may be "overlapping" (Rawls, 1993) in the sense that the reasons people accept the particular institutional framework may be different among groups holding different "fundamental" values.

8. Eckstein (1961), as well as Eckstein and Gurr (1975), are among those who claim that democratic politics also require democratic value to permeate less inclusive social units such as families, communities or workplaces. For a contrary view, see Linz (1996).

culture, and for such culture to emerge as a consequence of democratic institutions and support them in turn.

Fifth, in the non-culturalist view, democracy emerges and endures independently of culture. Democracy may or may not generate cultural homogeneity but culture has no causal impact on the durability of democratic institutions.

Given the paucity of data about culture, the first three explanations cannot be tested systematically for a large number of countries. However, the non-culturalist explanations can indeed be.

A Non-Culturalist Explanation

The non-culturalist view is strongly supported by evidence. In this view, democracy persists because the relevant political forces are better off, in terms of pure self-interest, complying with its verdicts rather than doing anything else. Even if the losers in the democratic competition would be better off in the short run rebelling rather than accepting the outcome of the current round, they face sufficiently large benefits in the future rounds and a sufficient chance to win and are therefore better off continuing to comply with the democratic verdicts. Similarly for the winners. Democracy is then an equilibrium because the conflicting political forces find it in their best interest to comply with its verdicts (Przeworski, 1991, Chap. 1).[10] . . .

Examine now some empirical patterns concerning almost all democracies that existed at any time between 1950 and 1990.[12]

The most striking fact is that no democracy ever fell, during the period under our scrutiny, regardless of everything else, in a country with a per capita income higher than that of Argentina in 1976.

The probability that democracy survives increases monotonically with per capita income. . . .

Several other factors affect the survival of democracies but they all pale in comparison with per capita income. Two are particularly relevant for the rational choice perspective. First, it turns out that democracies are more likely to endure when no party controls a large share of legislative seats, i.e. more than two-thirds. Secondly, democracies are most stable when the heads of governments change every so often, more frequently than once in five but less frequently than once in two years. These two observations—and both are statistically justified in multivariate analyses—add up to the second fact: democracy is more likely to survive when no political force dominates completely and permanently. When one party has unchecked control over the legislature or when chief executives stay in office for a long time, democracies are less stable.

Finally, the instances in which democracies were subverted follow the pattern predicted by the model: poor democracies (those under $1,000 per capita income) are overthrown by incumbents as well as by those out of power, democracies in countries with incomes between $1,000 and $6,000 are much more likely to be subverted

---

10. For a technical reader, we need to raise a caveat. In most situations, there are several equilibria. One is "war": the winner expects the loser to rebel, the loser expects the winner not to hold elections, and they fight it out. Another is dictatorship without a war: the dictator does not put down so much as provoke the opposition and the opposition finds that it is better off acquiescing to the dictatorship than fighting. Thus, a democratic equilibrium, if one exists, is just one of several, which means that Weingast (1997) is correct to emphasize the importance of co-ordination. Yet if the choice of equilibrium depends on economic development, then culture plays no role in this choice.

---

12. All the statistical results presented here are based on Przeworski et al. (in preparation). Published results include Przeworski et al. (1996) and Przeworski and Limongi (1997). The data cover 135 countries and a total of 4,126 years. Among them, there were 100 democracies which together lasted 1,645 years. All the income figures are expressed in 1985 purchasing power parity United States dollars.

by outsiders, and wealthy democracies are not overthrown by anyone.[14] ...

Finally, we find no evidence of habituation to democracy. The fact that a democracy has been around does not increase its chances of remaining around.... [E]ven if habituation to democracy generates a democratic culture, it is wealth that keeps democracies going, not culture.

As a glance at table 3.1 indicates, economic factors do not have an equally strong effect on the survival of dictatorships and thus on transitions to democracy. The probability that a democracy is established increases as countries become wealthier but then declines again once they become wealthy enough. Economic crises have a weaker effect on the survival of dictatorships. Indeed, statistical analyses indicate that transitions to democracy are almost impossible to predict, even with the entire panopticum of observable factors, economic or cultural. Dictatorships just seem to run many risks and to die for a broad variety of reasons....

Hence, the evidence in favour of economic factors is overwhelming. No recourse to culture is necessary to reproduce the actually observed patterns of regime dynamics. True, one could still defend the culturalist view by claiming that some culture, say "market culture," is what causes development in the first place and that the ultimate explanation is thus still cultural. That may well be, but this line of inquiry leads to infinite regress, since one could ask in turn what

causes the "market culture" to emerge, and so forth. Hence, we stop here.

Cultures, the Democratic Culture, and Democracy

Are particular, otherwise identifiable cultures, conducive or detrimental to the rise and durability of democratic institutions? The question is the following: Suppose we were to observe that, independently of their wealth and other factors, all countries with a high proportion of Protestants are democracies and no countries with a low proportion of Protestants are. We would then have prima facie evidence that, whatever the "democratic culture" is, Protestantism furnishes its necessary ingredients. But note that if we fail to find such patterns, it may be for two distinct reasons: either because the rise and durability of democracy need not call for a particular set of cultural patterns or because, while democracy does have cultural requisites and cultural barriers, all cultures are, or at least can be made, compatible with these patterns.

We first discuss the issue of compatibility of particular cultures, in plural, with the democratic culture. Then we examine some empirical patterns.

Cultures and the Democratic Culture

Historically, the discussion of this topic revolved mainly around cultures identified by dominant religions....

There are several reasons to doubt that cultures, or civilizations, as Mazrui (1997, p. 118) prefers to think of Islam, furnish requisites for or constitute irremovable barriers to democracy. First, the arguments relating civilizations to democracy appear terribly *ex-post*: if many countries dominated by Protestants are democratic, we look for features of Protestantism that promote democracy; if no Muslim countries are

---

14. Transitions to dictatorship are coded differently in table 3.4 and in table 3.3. In table 3.3, regimes in which the incumbents perpetuated an *autogolpe* at any time during their tenure in office are classified as dictatorships throughout. In table 3.2, such regimes are classified as democracies until the *autogolpe* occurred. Hence, the transitions in table 3.4 include all those in table 3.3 plus the transitions by incumbents. For details see Alvarez et al. (1996). Note that what we observe are the outcomes of conflicts rather than their initiation: hence, an inference is entailed in interpreting these results.

Table 3.1
Observed rates of transitions (by lagged per capita income and lagged rate of economic growth)

Level growth	All			Dictatorships			Democracies		
	PJK	TJK	N	PAD	TAD	N	PDA	TDA	N
−1000	0.0147	15	1019	0.0063	6	945	0.1216	9	74
G ≤ 0	0.0193	9	467	0.0091	4	440	0.1852	5	27
G > 0	0.0109	6	552	0.0040	2	505	0.0851	4	47
1001–2000	0.0321	32	997	0.0242	18	745	0.0556	14	252
G ≤ 0	0.0447	14	313	0.0313	7	224	0.0787	7	89
G > 0	0.0263	18	684	0.0211	11	521	0.0429	7	163
2001–3000	0.0325	16	493	0.0261	8	306	0.0428	8	187
G ≤ 0	0.0522	7	134	0.0341	3	88	0.0870	4	46
G > 0	0.0251	9	359	0.0229	5	218	0.0284	4	141
3001–4000	0.0201	7	349	0.0146	3	205	0.0278	4	144
G ≤ 0	0.0303	3	99	0.0172	1	58	0.0488	2	41
G > 0	0.0160	4	250	0.0136	2	147	0.0194	2	103
4001–5000	0.0339	8	236	0.0469	6	128	0.0185	2	108
G ≤ 0	0.0500	3	60	0.0588	2	34	0.0385	1	26
G > 0	0.0284	5	176	0.0426	4	94	0.0122	1	82
5001–6000	0.0308	6	195	0.0595	5	84	0.0090	1	111
G ≤ 0	0.0541	2	37	0.0952	2	21	0.0000	0	16
G > 0	0.0253	4	158	0.0476	3	63	0.0105	1	95
6001–7000	0.0190	3	158	0.0606	2	33	0.0080	1	125
G ≤ 0	0.0857	3	35	0.3333	2	6	0.0345	1	29
G > 0	0.0000	0	123	0.0000	0	27	0.0000	0	96
7001–	0.0015	1	679	0.0286	1	35	0.0000	0	644
G ≤ 0	0.0000	0	120	0.0000	0	3	0.0000	0	117
G > 0	0.0018	1	559	0.0313	1	32	0.0000	0	527
Total	0.0213	88	4126	0.0198	49	2481	0.0237	39	1645
G ≤ 0	0.0324	41	1265	0.0240	21	874	0.0512	20	391
G > 0	0.0164	47	2861	0.0174	28	1607	0.0152	19	1254

Key: "Level" stands for per capita income, in 1985 purchasing power parity US$. PJK is the probability of transitions, TJK is their total number, N is the number of annual observations, PAD is the probability of transitions from authoritarianism to democracy and TAD their number, PDA is the probability of transitions from democracy to authoritarianism and TDA their number.

Table 3.2

Cases when democracy was overthrown (by per capita income and the perpetuators)

Income	Number of transitions		
	Total	By incumbents	Not by incumbents
−1000	17	10	7
1001–3000	29	12	17
3001–6055	9	1	8
6066–	0	0	0
Total	55	23	32

democratic, obviously there must be something about Islam that is anti-democratic. Eisenstadt (1968), for example, finds that the Indian civilization has what it takes but Confucianism and Islam do not, and one wonders what he would have found if China were democratic and India not.[16]

Secondly, one can find elements in every culture, Protestantism included, that appear compatible and others that seem incompatible with democracy. Protestant legitimation of economic inequality, not to speak of the very ethic of self-interest, offer a poor moral basis for living together and resolving conflicts in a peaceful way. Other cultures are authoritarian but egalitarian, hierarchical but respectful of the right of rebellion, communal but tolerant of diversity, and so forth. So one can pick and choose.[17]

Thirdly, each of the religious traditions has been historically compatible with a broad range of practical political arrangements. This range is not the same for different religious traditions, but broad enough in each case to demonstrate

that these traditions are quite flexible with regard to the political arrangements with which they can be made compatible.

Finally, and most importantly, traditions are not given once and for all: they are continually invented and reinvented (Hobsbawm and Ranger, 1983), a point stressed by Eickelman and Piscatori (1996) in their analysis of Islam. In fact, the very analyses of the Confucian tradition cited above are best seen as attempts to invent a democratic Confucianism. Cultures are made of cloth but the fabric of culture drapes differently in the hands of different tailors....

Empirical Evidence

What, then, is the empirical evidence concerning the impact of religions on the dynamic of political regimes? Protestants, and Catholics, are more frequent in democracies; Moslems and others in dictatorships. But this prima facie observation does not suffice to establish a causal link....

Hence, to test the importance of religions for regime dynamics, we calculated the impact of different variables on the probabilities that democracy will be established and that it will collapse. We considered first the three variables that made our non-cultural model: per capita income, its rate of growth, and the rate of turnover of heads of government accumulated during the life of the regime.[18] As table 3.3 shows, all these variables are statistically significant. The wealthier a democracy, the less likely it is to collapse; while wealthier dictatorships are somewhat more likely to collapse. Both regimes are much less likely to collapse if their economy grew during the preceding year. Democracies in which heads of government change more frequently are somewhat more likely to collapse, while dictatorships are much more likely to die under such conditions.

---

16. The *ex-post* method is even more apparent in cultural analyses of economic growth. See Sen (1997).

17. Thus Nathan and Shi (1993) find elements of democratic culture in China, while Gibson, Duch and Tedin (1992) discover them in Russia.

---

18. The proportion of legislative seats held by the largest party is not significant in statistical analyses.

Table 3.3
Religions and regime transitions: Dynamic probit model

Log-likelihood	−355.9044
Restricted (Slopes = 0) Log-L.	−2685.421
Chi-squared (13)	4659.033
Significance level	0.0000000

	Transitions to dictatorship			Transitions to democracy		
Variable	Coefficient	t-ratio	Prob |t| ≥ x	Coefficient	t-ratio	Prob |t| ≥ x
Constant	−0.53859	−5.676	0.00000	−2.46014	−11.762	0.00000
Income	−0.84880E−04	−3.935	0.00008	0.102732E−03	1.814	0.06961
Growth	−0.16626E−01	−2.942	0.00327	−0.222413E−01	−3.764	0.00017
Turnover	0.17583	1.938	0.05262	0.636220	3.585	0.00034
Catholic	0.83732E−03	0.781	0.43487	0.497148E−02	1.941	0.05221
Protestant	−0.84245E−03	−0.418	0.67630	−0.512016E−02	−0.962	0.33593
Muslim	0.18935E−02	1.360	0.17386	−0.186515E−02	−0.657	0.51107

Frequencies of actual and predicted outcomes.
Predicted outcome has maximum probability.

	Predicted		
Actual	DEM	DIC	Total
DEM	1546	49	1595
DIC	38	2358	2396
Total	1584	2407	3991

Key: Coefficients are partial derivatives of the respective probabilities with regard to the variables, evaluated at the mean. DEM represents democracy, and DIC dictatorship.

When added to this non-culturalist model, the frequency of the three religions for which we have data—Catholics, Protestants and Moslems—in the population of each country has no impact whatever on the durability of democracy and only Catholicism has some—negative—impact on the stability of dictatorships. Moreover, when other variables are introduced into the analysis—the colonial legacy, religious and ethnic heterogeneity, or the proportion of countries in the world that are democracies during the particular year—none of the religions matter for anything.

To test the hypothesis about the impact of cultural heterogeneity, we used indices of ethnolinguistic and religious fractionalization.[19] Ethnolinguistic fractionalization makes democracies less likely to survive: this much confirms com-

19. Fractionalization indices measure the probability that two randomly chosen individuals do not belong to the same group. The index of ethnolingistic fractionalization is taken from Easterly and Levine (1997; from the Web). Their data set also contains indices measuring the percentage of the population not speaking the official and the most widely used language. These two indices have no effect on regime stability.

Table 3.4

Ethnolinguistic fractionalization and regime transitions: Dynamic probit model

Log-likelihood	−306.7057
Restricted (Slopes = 0) Log-L.	−2382.604
Chi-squared (13)	4151.797
Significance level	0.0000000

Variable	Transitions to dictatorship			Transitions to democracy		
	Coefficient	t-ratio	Prob $|t| \geq x$	Coefficient	t-ratio	Prob $|t| \geq x$
Constant	−1.4462	−5.822	0.00000	−2.08905	−11.480	0.00000
Income	−0.22950E−03	−4.090	0.00004	0.11891E−03	1.567	0.11709
Growth	−0.43770E−01	−2.750	0.00596	−0.25457E−01	−3.565	0.00036
Turnover	0.53737	2.273	0.02305	0.53882	3.428	0.00061
Elf60	0.90067	2.517	0.01185	0.16581	2.390	0.01684
Newc	0.20553E−01	0.060	0.95183	−0.85350	−2.106	0.03517
Britcol	−0.47802	−1.402	0.16103	0.35732	0.303	0.76211

Frequencies of actual and predicted outcomes.
Predicted outcome has maximum probability.

Actual	Predicted		
	DEM	DIC	Total
DEM	1475	43	1518
DIC	36	1924	1960
Total	1511	1967	3478

Key: ELF60 stands for ethnolinguistic fractionalization, as of 1960. NEWC is a dummy variable, indicating that the country was not independent as of 1945. BRITCOL is a dummy variable indicating that it was a British colony. Coefficients are partial derivatives of the respective probabilities with regard to the variables, evaluated at the mean.

mon wisdom. But, when the colonial legacy of a country is considered, it makes dictatorships less likely to survive as well. Hence, it seems that ethnolinguistic heterogeneity just makes political regimes less stable and, indeed, its effects on both regimes vanish when controlled for past political instability. Thus, the claim that common values are needed to support democracy reduces to the observation that regime transitions are more frequent in heterogeneous countries. In turn, religious heterogeneity has no effect on the stability of either regime.

This is scant evidence, but cultures just do not lend themselves to simple classifications. Hence, the opportunity for statistical analyses is limited. We would have obviously liked to be able to classify cultures as hierarchical or egalitarian, universalistic and particularistic, religious and secular, consensual or conflictuous, and so on. But the evidence we do have does not support the claim that some cultures are incompatible with democracy. They seem to have little effect on whether democracy is established and none on whether it endures.

References

Dahl, R. 1956. *A Preface to Democratic Theory*. Chicago, University of Chicago Press.

Dunn, J. 1996. *The History of Political Theory and Other Essays*. Cambridge, Cambridge University Press.

Eckstein, H. 1961. *A Theory of Stable Democracy*. Princeton, New Jersey, Princeton University Center for International Studies.

Eckstein, H.; Gurr, T. R. 1975. *Patterns of Inquiry: A Structural Basis for Political Inquiry*. New York, Wiley.

Eickelman, D. F.; Piscatori, J. 1996. *Muslim Politics*. Princeton, Princeton University Press.

Eisenstadt, S. N. 1968. The Protestant Ethic Theses in the Framework of Sociological Theory and Weber's Work. In: S. N. Eisenstadt (ed.), *The Protestant Ethic and Modernization: A Comparative View*, pp. 3–45. New York, Basic Books.

Gibson, J. L.; Duch, R. M.; Tedin, K. L. 1992. Democratic Values and the Transformation of the Soviet Union. *Journal of Politics*, No. 54.

Hobsbawm, E.; Ranger, T. (eds.). 1983. *The Invention of Tradition*. Cambridge, Cambridge University Press.

Lipset, S. M. 1959. Some Social Requisites of Democracy: Economic Development and Political Legitimacy. *American Political Science Review*, No. 53, pp. 69–105.

Mazrui, A. A. 1997. Islamic and Western Values. *Foreign Affairs*, Vol. 76, No. 5, pp. 118–132.

Nathan, A. J.; Shi, T. 1993. Cultural Requisites for Democracy in China: Findings from a Survey. *Dedalus*, No. 122.

Przeworski, A. 1991. *Democracy and the Market*. New York, Cambridge University Press.

Przeworski, A.; Alvarez, M.; Cheibub, J. A.; Limongi, F. 1996. What Makes Democracy Endure? *Journal of Democracy*, Vol. 7, No. 1, pp. 39–56.

Przeworski, A.; Limongi, F. 1997. Modernization: Theories and Facts. *World Politics*, No. 49, pp. 155–184.

Rawls, J. 1993. The Domain of the Political and Overlapping Consensus. In: D. Copp, J. Hampton and J. E. Roemer (eds.), *The Idea of Democracy*. Cambridge, Cambridge University Press.

Sen, A. 1997. *Culture and Development: Global Perspectives and Constructive Criticism*. (Paper prepared for UNESCO's *World Culture Report 1998*.)

Weingast, B. R. 1997. Political Foundations of Democracy and the Rule of Law. *American Political Science Review*, No. 91, pp. 245–263.

4 DEMOCRACY AND CONSTITUTIONALISM

The Federalist No. 23

Alexander Hamilton

To the People of the State of New York

The necessity of a Constitution, at least equally energetic with the one proposed, to the preservation of the Union, is the point at the examination of which we are now arrived.

This inquiry will naturally divide itself into three branches—the objects to be provided for by the federal government, the quantity of power necessary to the accomplishment of those objects, the persons upon whom that power ought to operate. Its distribution and organization will more properly claim our attention under the succeeding head.

The principal purposes to be answered by union are these—the common defence of the members; the preservation of the public peace, as well against internal convulsions as external attacks; the regulation of commerce with other nations and between the States; the superintendence of our intercourse, political and commercial, with foreign countries.

The authorities essential to the common defence are these: to raise armies; to build and equip fleets; to prescribe rules for the government of both; to direct their operations; to provide for their support. These powers ought to exist without limitation, *because it is impossible to foresee or define the extent and variety of national exigencies, or the correspondent extent and variety of the means which may be necessary to satisfy them.* The circumstances that endanger the safety of nations are infinite, and for this reason no constitutional shackles can wisely be imposed on the power to which the care of it is committed. This power ought to be co-extensive with all the possible combinations of such circumstances; and ought to be under the direction of the same councils which are appointed to preside over the common defence. . . .

Every view we may take of the subject, as candid inquirers after truth, will serve to convince us, that it is both unwise and dangerous to deny the federal government an unconfined authority, as to all those objects which are intrusted to its management. It will indeed deserve the most vigilant and careful attention of the people, to see that it be modelled in such a manner as to admit of its being safely vested with the requisite powers. If any plan which has been, or may be, offered to our consideration, should not upon a dispassionate inspection be found to answer this description, it ought to be rejected. A government, the constitution of which renders it unfit to be trusted with all the powers which a free people *ought to delegate to any government*, would be an unsafe and improper depositary of the NATIONAL INTERESTS. Wherever THESE can with propriety be confided, the coincident powers may safely accompany them. This is the true result of all just reasoning upon the subject. . . .

. . . If we embrace the tenets of those who oppose the adoption of the proposed Constitution as the standard of our political creed, we cannot fail to verify the gloomy doctrines which predict the impracticability of a national system pervading entire limits of the present Confederacy.

PUBLIUS

Excerpted from: Alexander Hamilton, James Madison, and John Jay. *The Federalist Papers: A Collection of Essays Written in Support of the Constitution of the United States*, second edition. Edited by Roy P. Fairfield. Garden City: Anchor, 1966.

The Federalist No. 47

James Madison

To the People of the State of New York

... The accumulation of all powers, legislative, executive, and judiciary, in the same hands, whether of one, a few, or many, and whether hereditary, self-appointed, or elective, may justly be pronounced the very definition of tyranny. Were the federal Constitution, therefore, really chargeable with the accumulation of power, or with a mixture of powers having a dangerous tendency to such an accumulation, no further arguments would be necessary to inspire a universal reprobation of the system. I persuade myself, however, ... that the charge cannot be supported, and that the maxim on which it relies has been totally misconceived and misapplied. In order to form correct ideas on this important subject, it will be proper to investigate the sense in which the preservation of liberty requires that the three great departments of power should be separate and distinct.

The oracle who is always consulted and cited on this subject is the celebrated Montesquieu....

On the slightest view of the British Constitution, we must perceive that the legislative, executive, and judiciary departments are by no means totally separate and distinct from each other. The executive magistrate forms an integral part of the legislative authority. He alone has the prerogative of making treaties with foreign sovereigns, which, when made, have, under certain limitations, the force of legislative acts. All the members of the judiciary department are appointed by him, can be removed by him on the address of the two Houses of Parliament, and

form, when he pleases to consult them, one of his constitutional councils. One branch of the legislative department forms also a great constitutional council to the executive chief as ... it is the sole depositary of judicial power in cases of impeachment, and is invested with the supreme appellate jurisdiction in all other cases. The judges, again, are so far connected with the legislative department as often to attend and participate in its deliberations, though not admitted to a legislative vote.

From these facts, by which Montesquieu was guided, it may clearly be inferred that, in saying "There can be no liberty where the legislative and executive powers are united in the same person, or body of magistrates," or, "if the power of judging be not separated from the legislative and executive powers" [sic], he did not mean that these departments ought to have no *partial agency* in, or no *control* over, the acts of each other.[61] His meaning ... can amount to no more than this, that where the *whole* power of one department is exercised by the same hands which possess the *whole* power of another department, the fundamental principles of a free constitution are subverted....

The reasons on which Montesquieu grounds his maxim are a further demonstration of his meaning. "When the legislative and executive

---

61. Montesquieu actually said:

When the legislative and executive powers are united in the same person or in the same body of magistrates, there can be no liberty, because apprehensions may arise, lest the same monarch or senate should enact tyrannical laws, to execute them in a tyrannical manner. Were it joined with the legislative, the life and liberty of the subject would be exposed to arbitrary control; for the judge would then be the legislator. Were it joined to the executive power, the judge might behave with violence and oppression.

Nugent translation (London, 1894), I, 163. Madison provided the italics.

Excerpted from: Alexander Hamilton, James Madison, and John Jay. *The Federalist Papers: A Collection of Essays Written in Support of the Constitution of the United States,* second edition. Edited by Roy P. Fairfield. Garden City: Anchor, 1966.

powers are united in the same person or body,"
says he, "there can be no liberty, because apprehensions may arise lest *the same* monarch or
senate should *enact* tyrannical laws to *execute*
them in a tyrannical manner." ...

In citing these cases in which the legislative,
executive, and judiciary departments have not
been kept totally separate and distinct, I wish
not to be regarded as an advocate for the particular organizations of the several State governments. I am fully aware that among the many
excellent principles which they exemplify, they
carry strong marks of the haste, and still stronger
of the inexperience, under which they were
framed. It is but too obvious that in some instances the fundamental principle under consideration has been violated by too great a mixture,
and even an actual consolidation, of the different
powers; and that in no instance has a competent
provision been made for maintaining in practice the separation delineated on paper. What
I have wished to evince is, that the charge
brought against the proposed Constitution, of
violating the sacred maxim of free government,
is warranted neither by the real meaning
annexed to that maxim by its author, nor by the
sense in which it has hitherto been understood in
America.

The Federalist No. 48

James Madison

To the People of the State of New York

It was shown in the last paper that the political apothegm there examined does not require that the legislative, executive, and judiciary departments should be wholly unconnected with each other. I shall undertake, in the next place, to show that unless these departments be so far connected and blended as to give to each a constitutional control over the others, the degree of separation which the maxim requires, as essential to a free government, can never in practice be duly maintained.

It is agreed on all sides that the powers properly belonging to one of the departments ought not to be directly and completely administered by either of the other departments. It is equally evident that none of them ought to possess, directly or indirectly, an overruling influence over the others in the administration of their respective powers....

Will it be sufficient to mark with precision the boundaries of these departments in the constitution of the government, and to trust to these parchment barriers against the encroaching spirit of power? This is the security which appears to have been principally relied on by the compilers of most of the American constitutions. But experience assures us that the efficacy of the provision has been greatly overrated; and that some more adequate defence is indispensably necessary for the more feeble, against the more powerful, members of the government....

[I]n a representative republic, where the executive magistracy is carefully limited, both in the extent and the duration of its power; and where the legislative power is exercised by an assembly, which is inspired, by a supposed influence over the people, with an intrepid confidence in its own strength; which is sufficiently numerous to feel all the passions which actuate a multitude, yet not so numerous as to be incapable of pursuing the objects of its passions, by means which reason prescribes; it is against the enterprising ambition of this department that the people ought to indulge all their jealousy and exhaust all their precautions.

The legislative department derives a superiority in our governments from other circumstances. Its constitutional powers being at once more extensive and less susceptible of precise limits, it can with the greater facility mask under complicated and indirect measures the encroachments which it makes on the coördinate departments. It is not unfrequently a question of real nicety in legislative bodies, whether the operation of a particular measure will, or will not, extend beyond the legislative sphere. On the other side, the executive power being restrained within a narrower compass and being more simple in its nature, and the judiciary being described by landmarks still less uncertain, projects of usurpation by either of these departments would immediately betray and defeat themselves. Nor is this all; as the legislative department alone has access to the pockets of the people, and has in some constitutions full discretion, and in all a prevailing influence, over the pecuniary rewards of those who fill the other departments, a dependence is thus created in the latter, which gives still greater facility to encroachments of the former.

I have appealed to our own experience for the truth of what I advance on this subject. Were it necessary to verify this experience by particular proofs, they might be multiplied without end. I might find a witness in every citizen who has

Excerpted from: Alexander Hamilton, James Madison, and John Jay. *The Federalist Papers: A Collection of Essays Written in Support of the Constitution of the United States*, second edition. Edited by Roy P. Fairfield. Garden City: Anchor, 1966.

shared in, or been attentive to, the course of public administrations. I might collect vouchers in abundance from the records and archives of every State in the Union. But as a more concise, and at the same time equally satisfactory, evidence, I will refer to the example of two States, attested by two unexceptionable authorities....

The conclusion which I am warranted in drawing from these observations is, that a mere demarcation on parchment of the constitutional limits of the several departments, is not a sufficient guard against those encroachments which lead to a tyrannical concentration of all the powers of government in the same hands.

PUBLIUS

The Federalist No. 62

James Madison

To the People of the State of New York

I. The qualifications proposed for senators, as distinguished from those of representatives, consist in a more advanced age and a longer period of citizenship. A senator must be thirty years of age at least; as a representative must be twenty-five. And the former must have been a citizen nine years; as seven years are required for the latter. The propriety of these distinctions is explained by the nature of the senatorial trust, which, requiring greater extent of information and stability of character, requires at the same time that the senator should have reached a period of life most likely to supply these advantages; and which, participating immediately in transactions with foreign nations, ought to be exercised by none who are not thoroughly weaned from the prepossessions and habits incident to foreign birth and education....

II. It is equally unnecessary to dilate on the appointment of senators by the State legislatures....

III. The equality of representation in the Senate is another point, which, being evidently the result of compromise between the opposite pretensions of the large and the small States, does not call for much discussion....

In this spirit it may be remarked, that the equal vote allowed to each State is at once a constitutional recognition of the portion of sovereignty remaining in the individual States, and an instrument for preserving that residuary sovereignty....

Excerpted from: Alexander Hamilton, James Madison, and John Jay. *The Federalist Papers: A Collection of Essays Written in Support of the Constitution of the United States*, second edition. Edited by Roy P. Fairfield. Garden City: Anchor, 1966.

Another advantage accruing from this ingredient in the constitution of the Senate is the additional impediment it must prove against improper acts of legislation. No law or resolution can now be passed without the concurrence, first, of a majority of the people, and then, of a majority of the States....

IV. The number of senators and the duration of their appointment come next to be considered. In order to form an accurate judgment on both these points, it will be proper to inquire into the purposes which are to be answered by a senate; and in order to ascertain these, it will be necessary to review the inconveniences which a republic must suffer from the want of such an institution.

First. It is a misfortune incident to republican government, though in a less degree than to other governments, that those who administer it may forget their obligations to their constituents and prove unfaithful to their important trust. In this point of view, a senate, as a second branch of the legislative assembly, distinct from and dividing the power with a first, must be in all cases a salutary check on the government....

Secondly. The necessity of a senate is not less indicated by the propensity of all single and numerous assemblies to yield to the impulse of sudden and violent passions, and to be seduced by factious leaders into intemperate and pernicious resolutions....

Thirdly. Another defect to be supplied by a senate lies in a want of due acquaintance with the objects and principles of legislation....

A good government implies two things: first, fidelity to the object of government, which is the happiness of the people; secondly, a knowledge of the means by which that object can be best attained....

Fourthly. The mutability in the public councils arising from a rapid succession of new members, however qualified they may be, points out, in the strongest manner, the necessity of some stable institution in the government. . . .

In the first place, it forfeits the respect and confidence of other nations and all the advantages connected with national character. . . .

The internal effects of a mutable policy are still more calamitous. It poisons the blessing of liberty itself. . . .

Another effect of public instability is the unreasonable advantage it gives to the sagacious, the enterprising, and the moneyed few over the industrious and uninformed mass of the people. . . .

In another point of view, great injury results from an unstable government. The want of confidence in the public councils damps every useful undertaking, the success and profit of which may depend on a continuance of existing arrangements. . . .

But the most deplorable effect of all is that diminution of attachment and reverence which steals into the hearts of the people towards a political system which betrays so many marks of infirmity, and disappoints so many of their flattering hopes. No government, any more than an individual, will long be respected without being truly respectable; nor be truly respectable, without possessing a certain portion of order and stability.

PUBLIUS

The Federalist No. 70

Alexander Hamilton

To the People of the State of New York

... The ingredients which constitute energy in the Executive are, first, unity; secondly, duration; thirdly, an adequate provision for its support; fourthly, competent powers.

The ingredients which constitute safety in the republican sense are, first, a due dependence on the people; secondly, a due responsibility.

Those politicians and statesmen who have been the most celebrated for the soundness of their principles and for the justice of their views have declared in favor of a single Executive and a numerous legislature. They have with great propriety considered energy as the most necessary qualification of the former, and have regarded this as most applicable to power in a single hand; while they have with equal propriety considered the latter as best adapted to deliberation and wisdom, and best calculated to conciliate the confidence of the people and to secure their privileges and interests.

That unity is conducive to energy will not be disputed. Decision, activity, secrecy, and despatch will generally characterize the proceedings of one man in a much more eminent degree than the proceedings of any greater number; and in proportion as the number is increased, these qualities will be diminished....

Upon the principles of a free government, inconvenience ... must necessarily be submitted to in the formation of the legislature; but it is unnecessary, and therefore unwise, to introduce them into the constitution of the Executive. It is here too that they may be most pernicious. In the

Excerpted from: Alexander Hamilton, James Madison, and John Jay. *The Federalist Papers: A Collection of Essays Written in Support of the Constitution of the United States*, second edition. Edited by Roy P. Fairfield. Garden City: Anchor, 1966.

legislature promptitude of decision is oftener an evil than a benefit. The differences of opinion and the jarrings of parties in that department of the government, though they may sometimes obstruct salutary plans, yet often promote deliberation and circumspection, and serve to check excesses in the majority. When a resolution too is once taken, the opposition must be at an end. That resolution is a law, and resistance to it punishable. But no favorable circumstances palliate or atone for the disadvantages of dissension in the executive department. Here, they are pure and unmixed. There is no point at which they cease to operate. They serve to embarrass and weaken the execution of the plan or measure to which they relate, from the first step to the final conclusion of it. They constantly counteract those qualities in the Executive which are the most necessary ingredients in its composition, —vigor and expedition, and this without any counterbalancing good. In the conduct of war, in which the energy of the Executive is the bulwark of the national security, everything would be to be apprehended from its plurality....

But one of the weightiest objections to a plurality in the Executive ... is that it tends to conceal faults and destroy responsibility. Responsibility is of two kinds—to censure and to punishment. The first is the more important of the two, especially in an elective office. Man, in public trust, will much oftener act in such a manner as to render him unworthy of being any longer trusted, than in such a manner as to make him obnoxious to legal punishment. But the multiplication of the Executive adds to the difficulty of detection in either case. It often becomes impossible, amidst mutual accusations, to determine on whom the blame or the punishment of a pernicious measure, or series of pernicious measures, ought really to fall. It is shifted from one to another with so much dexterity and under such plausible appearances, that the public opinion is left in suspense about the real author. The circumstances which may have led to any national miscarriage of misfortune are sometimes so complicated that, where there are a number of actors who may have had different degrees and kinds of agency, though we may clearly see upon the whole that there has been mismanagement, yet it may be impracticable to pronounce to whose account the evil which may have been incurred is truly chargeable. . . .

It is evident from these considerations, that the plurality of the Executive tends to deprive the people of the two greatest securities they can have for the faithful exercise of any delegated power: *first*, the restraints of public opinion, which lose their efficacy, as well on account of the division of the censure attendant on bad measures among a number, as on account of the uncertainty on whom it ought to fall; and, *secondly*, the opportunity of discovering with facility and clearness the misconduct of the persons they trust, in order either to effect their removal from office or . . . their actual punishment in cases which admit of it. . . . I will only add that, prior to the appearance of the Constitution, I rarely met with an intelligent man from any of the States, who did not admit, as the result of experience, that the UNITY of the executive of this State was one of the best of the distinguishing features of our constitution.

Publius

The Federalist No. 78

Alexander Hamilton

To the People of the State of New York

We proceed now to an examination of the judiciary department of the proposed government.

In unfolding the defects of the existing Confederation, the utility and necessity of a federal judicature have been clearly pointed out....

The manner of constituting it seems to embrace these several objects: 1st. The mode of appointing the judges. 2d. The tenure by which they are to hold their places. 3d. The partition of the judiciary authority between different courts, and their relations to each other.

First. As to the mode of appointing the judges; this is the same with that of appointing the officers of the Union in general, and has been so fully discussed in the two last numbers, that nothing can be said here which would not be useless repetition.

Second. As to the tenure by which the judges are to hold their places: this chiefly concerns their duration in office; the provisions for their support; the precautions for their responsibility.

According to the plan of the convention, all judges who may be appointed by the United States are to hold their offices *during good behavior*; which is conformable to the most approved of the State constitutions, and among the rest, to that of this State. Its propriety having been drawn into question by the adversaries of that plan, is no light symptom of the rage for objection, which disorders their imaginations and judgments. The standard of good behavior for the continuance in office of the judicial magistracy is certainly one of the most valuable of the modern improvements in the practice of government. In a monarchy it is an excellent barrier to the despotism of the prince; in a republic it is a no less excellent barrier to the encroachments and oppressions of the representative body. And it is the best expedient which can be devised in any government to secure a steady, upright, and impartial administration of the laws.

Whoever attentively considers the different departments of power must perceive, that, in a government in which they are separated from each other, the judiciary, from the nature of its functions, will always be the least dangerous to the political rights of the Constitution; because it will be least in a capacity to annoy or injure them. The Executive not only dispenses the honors, but holds the sword of the community. The legislature not only commands the purse, but prescribes the rules by which the duties and rights of every citizen are to be regulated. The judiciary, on the contrary, has no influence over either the sword or the purse;[97] no direction either of the strength or of the wealth of the society; and can take no active resolution whatever. It may truly be said to have neither FORCE nor WILL, but merely judgment; and must ultimately depend upon the aid of the executive arm even for the efficacy of its judgments.

This simple view of the matter suggests several important consequences. It proves incontestably that the judiciary is beyond comparison

Excerpted from: Alexander Hamilton, James Madison, and John Jay. *The Federalist Papers: A Collection of Essays Written in Support of the Constitution of the United States*, second edition. Edited by Roy P. Fairfield. Garden City: Anchor, 1966.

97. Hamilton's judgment seemed to be borne out a half century later when Andrew Jackson, disagreeing with the court in Worcester *v.* Georgia (1832), allegedly remarked, "John Marshall has made his decision, now let him enforce it." Mason and Leach, [*In Quest of Freedom: American Political Thought and Practice.* Englewood Cliffs, N.J.: Prentice-Hall, 1959], 262. The 1954–55 desegregation decisions and their subsequent application continue to raise questions about the relationships between the Executive and judiciary.

the weakest of the three departments of power [*sic*];[98] that it can never attack with success either of the other two; and that all possible care is requisite to enable it to defend itself against their attacks. It equally proves that though individual oppression may now and then proceed from the courts of justice, the general liberty of the people can never be endangered from that quarter; I mean so long as the judiciary remains truly distinct from both the legislature and the Executive. For I agree, that "there is no liberty, if the power of judging be not separated from the legislative and executive powers."[99] And it proves, in the last place, that as liberty can have nothing to fear from the judiciary alone, but would have every thing to fear from its union with either of the other departments; that as all the effects of such a union must ensue from a dependence of the former on the latter, notwithstanding a nominal and apparent separation; that as, from the natural feebleness of the judiciary it is in continual jeopardy of being overpowered, awed, or influenced by its coördinate branches; and that as nothing can contribute so much to its firmness and independence as permanency in office, this quality may therefore be justly regarded

---

98. At this point in the text Hamilton ran a footnote: "The celebrated Montesquieu, speaking of them, says: 'Of the three powers above mentioned, the judiciary is next to nothing.' 'Spirit of Laws,' vol. i., page 186.— PUBLIUS" A close check of the Nugent text, which Hamilton used, reveals that Montesquieu actually said, "Of the three powers above mentioned, the judiciary is *in some measure* next to nothing." (Edinburgh edition, 1772; I, 193.) I have provided the italics to indicate that Montesquieu made a *qualified* judgment about the power of the judiciary, not an unqualified one, as Hamilton indicated. A few pages later Montesquieu did say that "the national judges are no more than the mouth that pronounces the words of the law, mere passive beings, incapable of moderating either its force or rigour" (197). He seemed to regard the power of judging with some awe, referring to it as "... a power so terrible to mankind ..." (166).

99. This quote is accurate. *Ibid.*, 165.

as an indispensable ingredient in its constitution, and, in a great measure, as the citadel of the public justice and the public security.

The complete independence of the courts of justice is peculiarly essential in a limited Constitution. By a limited Constitution, I understand one which contains certain specified exceptions to the legislative authority; such, for instance, as that it shall pass no bills of attainder, no *ex-post-facto* laws, and the like. Limitations of this kind can be preserved in practice no other way than through the medium of courts of justice, whose duty it must be to declare all acts contrary to the manifest tenor of the Constitution void. Without this, all the reservations of particular rights or privileges would amount to nothing.

Some perplexity respecting the rights of the courts to pronounce legislative acts void, because contrary to the constitution, has arisen from an imagination that the doctrine would imply a superiority of the judiciary to the legislative power. It is urged that the authority which can declare the acts of another void must necessarily be superior to the one whose acts may be declared void. As this doctrine is of great importance in all the American constitutions, a brief discussion of the ground on which it rests cannot be unacceptable.[100]

---

100. Next to *No. 10*, this essay has probably been studied more than any other because it sets forth a systematic argument for the doctrine of judicial review. Marshall gave it living force in Marbury v. Madison (1803) and other precedent-forming decisions, and it remains today among the most discussed American judicial practices. Even the Europeans, long skeptical of the doctrine, seem to be considering it more seriously; see Arnold J. Zurcher, ed., *Constitutions and Constitutional Trends since World War II* (N.Y., 1951), 20–22, 216.

Although it is generally agreed that Sir Edward Coke probably originated the doctrine in the *Dr. Bonham Case* (1610), there is controversy as to whether or not the founding fathers intended to include judicial review in the new system of government. Serious students of this question, as well as other problems per-

There is no position which depends on clearer principles than that every act of a delegated authority, contrary to the tenor of the commission under which it is exercised, is void. No legislative act, therefore, contrary to the Constitution, can be valid. To deny this would be to affirm that the deputy is greater than his principal; that the servant is above his master; that the representatives of the people are superior to the people themselves; that men acting by virtue of powers may do not only what their powers do not authorize, but what they forbid.

If it be said that the legislative body are themselves the constitutional judges of their own powers, and that the construction they put upon them is conclusive upon the other departments, it may be answered that this cannot be the natural presumption where it is not to be collected from any particular provisions in the Constitution. It is not otherwise to be supposed that the Constitution could intend to enable the representatives of the people to substitute their *will* to that of their constituents. It is far more rational to suppose that the courts were designed to be an intermediate body between the people and the legislature, in order, among other things, to keep the latter within the limits assigned to their authority. The interpretation of the laws is the proper and peculiar province of the courts. A constitution is, in fact, and must be regarded by the judges, as a fundamental law. It therefore belongs to them to ascertain its meaning, as well as the meaning of any particular act proceeding from the legislative body. If there should happen to be an irreconcilable variance between the two, that which has the superior obligation and validity ought, of course, to be preferred; or, in other words, the Constitution ought to be preferred to the statute, the intention of the people to the intention of their agents.[101]

Nor does this conclusion by any means suppose a superiority of the judicial to the legislative power. It only supposes that the power of the people is superior to both; and that where the will of the legislature, declared in its statutes, stands in opposition to that of the people, declared in the Constitution, the judges ought to be governed by the latter rather than the former. They ought to regulate their decisions by the fundamental laws, rather than by those which are not fundamental.

This exercise of judicial discretion, in determining between two contradictory laws, is exemplified in a familiar instance. It not uncommonly happens that there are two statutes existing at one time, clashing in whole or in part with each other, and neither of them containing any repealing clause or expression. In such a case, it is the province of the courts to liquidate and fix their meaning and operation. So far as they can, by any fair construction, be reconciled to each other, reason and law conspire to dictate that this should be done; where this is impracticable, it becomes a matter of necessity to give effect to one in exclusion of the other. The rule which has obtained in the courts for determining their relative validity is, that the last in order of time shall

---

taining to judicial review, will not only wish to consult the bibliography in Beloff's ed. of the *Federalist*, 483, but they will also find the following helpful: Robert K. Carr, *The Supreme Court and Judicial Review* (N.Y., 1942), 54–55; Gottfried Dietze, *The Federalist*; Farrand, *Records*, II, 73–80; Crosskey, *op. cit.*, II, 941–945; Miller, *op. cit.*, 204; Robert J. Harris, "The Decline of Judicial Review," *Journal of Politics* (Feb. 1948), 1–19, Corwin's survey in *Encyclopedia of the Social Sciences*, VIII, 456, and Corwin, *Court over Constitution* (Princeton, 1938). Also see "Luther Martin's Letter," Elliot, *Debates*, I, 380, in which Martin said, "Whether ... any laws or *regulations* of the Congress, any acts of *its President or other officers*, are contrary to, or not warranted by, the Constitution, rests only with the judges, who are appointed by Congress, to determine; by whose determinations every state must *be bound*."

101. For Justice David Brewer's famous statement indicating the way in which the court employs the Constitution as a higher law, see Ralph Gabriel, *The Course of American Democratic Thought* (N.Y., 1940), 233.

be preferred to the first. But this is a mere rule of construction, not derived from any positive law but from the nature and reason of the thing. It is a rule not enjoined upon the courts by legislative provision but adopted by themselves, as consonant to truth and propriety for the direction of their conduct as interpreters of the law. They thought it reasonable, that between the interfering acts of an *equal* authority, that which was the last indication of its will should have the preference.

But in regard to the interfering acts of a superior and subordinate authority, of an original and derivative power, the nature and reason of the thing indicate the converse of that rule as proper to be followed. They teach us that the prior act of a superior ought to be preferred to the subsequent act of an inferior and subordinate authority; and that accordingly, whenever a particular statute contravenes the Constitution, it will be the duty of the judicial tribunals to adhere to the latter and disregard the former.

It can be of no weight to say that the courts, on the pretence of a repugnancy, may substitute their own pleasure to the constitutional intentions of the legislature. This might as well happen in the case of two contradictory statutes; or it might as well happen in every adjudication upon any single statute. The courts must declare the sense of the law; and if they should be disposed to exercise WILL instead of JUDGMENT, the consequence would equally be the substitution of their pleasure to that of the legislative body. The observation, if it prove any thing, would prove that there ought to be no judges distinct from that body.

If, then, the courts of justice are to be considered as the bulwarks of a limited Constitution against legislative encroachments, this consideration will afford a strong argument for the permanent tenure of judicial offices, since nothing will contribute so much as this to that independent spirit in the judges which must be essential to the faithful performance of so arduous a duty.

This independence of the judges is equally requisite to guard the Constitution and the rights of individuals from the effects of those ill humors, which the arts of designing men or the influence of particular conjunctures sometimes disseminate among the people themselves; and which, though they speedily give place to better information and more deliberate reflection, have a tendency, in the meantime, to occasion dangerous innovations in the government, and serious oppressions of the minor party in the community. Though I trust the friends of the proposed Constitution will never concur with its enemies[102] in questioning that fundamental principle of republican government, which admits the right of the people to alter or abolish the established Constitution whenever they find it inconsistent with their happiness; yet it is not to be inferred from this principle that the representatives of the people, whenever a momentary inclination happens to lay hold of a majority of their constituents, incompatible with the provisions in the existing Constitution, would, on that account, be justifiable in a violation of those provisions; or that the courts would be under a greater obligation to connive at infractions in this shape, than when they had proceeded wholly from the cabals of the representative body. Until the people have by some solemn and authoritative act annulled or changed the established form, it is binding upon themselves collectively, as well as individually; and no presumption, or even knowledge, of their sentiments, can warrant their representatives in a departure from it, prior to such an act. But it is easy to see that it would require an uncommon portion of fortitude in the judges to do their duty as faithful guardians of the Constitution, where legislative invasions of it had been instigated by the major voice of the community.

---

102. Hamilton's footnote: "*Vide* 'Protest of the Minority of the Convention of Pennsylvania,' Martin's Speech, etc.—PUBLIUS" The former may be found in McMaster and Stone, *op. cit.*, 454–82; the latter, Elliot's *Debates*, I, 344–89.

But it is not with a view to infractions of the Constitution only that the independence of the judges may be an essential safeguard against the effects of occasional ill humors in the society. These sometimes extend no farther than to the injury of the private rights of particular classes of citizens by unjust and partial laws. Here also the firmness of the judicial magistracy is of vast importance in mitigating the severity and confining the operation of such laws. It not only serves to moderate the immediate mischiefs of those which may have been passed, but it operates as a check upon the legislative body in passing them; who, perceiving that obstacles to the success of iniquitous intention are to be expected from the scruples of the courts, are in a manner compelled by the very motives of the injustice they meditate to qualify their attempts. This is a circumstance calculated to have more influence upon the character of our governments, than but few may be aware of. The benefits of the integrity and moderation of the judiciary have already been felt in more States than one; and though they may have displeased those whose sinister expectations they may have disappointed, they must have commanded the esteem and applause of all the virtuous and disinterested. Considerate men of every description ought to prize whatever will tend to beget or fortify that temper in the courts; as no man can be sure that he may not be tomorrow the victim of a spirit of injustice by which he may be a gainer today. And every man must now feel that the inevitable tendency of such a spirit is to sap the foundations of public and private confidence, and to introduce in its stead universal distrust and distress.

That inflexible and uniform adherence to the rights of the Constitution and of individuals, which we perceive to be indispensable in the courts of justice, can certainly not be expected from judges who hold their offices by a temporary commission. Periodical appointments, however regulated or by whomsoever made, would, in some way or other, be fatal to their necessary independence. If the power of making them was

committed either to the Executive or legislature, there would be danger of an improper complaisance to the branch which possessed it; if to both, there would be an unwillingness to hazard the displeasure of either; if to the people or to persons chosen by them for the special purpose, there would be too great a disposition to consult popularity, to justify a reliance that nothing would be consulted but the Constitution and the laws.

There is yet a further and a weightier reason for the permanency of the judicial offices, which is deducible from the nature of the qualifications they require. It has been frequently remarked, with great propriety, that a voluminous code of laws is one of the inconveniences necessarily connected with the advantages of a free government. To avoid an arbitrary discretion in the courts, it is indispensable that they should be bound down by strict rules and precedents, which serve to define and point out their duty in every particular case that comes before them; and it will readily be conceived from the variety of controversies which grow out of the folly and wickedness of mankind, that the records of those precedents must unavoidably swell to a very considerable bulk, and must demand long and laborious study to acquire a competent knowledge of them. Hence it is, that there can be but few men in the society who will have sufficient skill in the laws to qualify them for the stations of judges. And making the proper deductions for the ordinary depravity of human nature, the number must be still smaller of those who unite the requisite integrity with the requisite knowledge. These considerations apprise us that the government can have no great option between fit character; and that a temporary duration in office, which would naturally discourage such characters from quitting a lucrative line of practice to accept a seat on the bench, would have a tendency to throw the administration of justice into hands less able, and less well qualified, to conduct it with utility and dignity. In the present circumstances of this country and in those in which it is likely to be for a long time to come, the disadvantages on this score would be greater than they may at first sight appear; but it must be confessed that they are far inferior to those which present themselves under the other aspects of the subject.

Upon the whole, there can be no room to doubt that the convention acted wisely in copying from the models of those constitutions which have established *good behavior* as the tenure of their judicial offices, in point of duration; and that so far from being blamable on this account, their plan would have been inexcusably defective if it had wanted this important feature of good government. The experience of Great Britain affords an illustrious comment on the excellence of the institution.

PUBLIUS

Madisonian Democracy

Robert Dahl

I

Democracy, it is frequently said, rests upon compromise. But democratic theory itself is full of compromises—compromises of clashing and antagonistic principles. What is a virtue in social life, however, is not necessarily a virtue in social theory.

What I am going to call the "Madisonian" theory of democracy is an effort to bring off a compromise between the power of majorities and the power of minorities, between the political equality of all adult citizens on the one side, and the desire to limit their sovereignty on the other. As a political system the compromise, except for one important interlude, has proved to be durable. What is more, Americans seem to like it. As a political theory, however, the compromise delicately papers over a number of cracks without quite concealing them. It is no accident that preoccupation with the rights and wrongs of majority rule has run like a red thread through American political thought since 1789. For if most Americans seem to have accepted the legitimacy of the Madisonian political system, criticism of its rather shaky rationale never quite dies down; and as a consequence, no doubt, the Madisonian theses must themselves be constantly reiterated or even, as with Calhoun, enlarged upon. . . .

The central proposition of the Madisonian theory is partly implicit and partly explicit, namely:

Hypothesis 1:   If unrestrained by external checks, any given individual or group of individuals will tyrannize over others.

Excerpted from: Robert Dahl, *A Preface to Democratic Theory.* Chicago: University of Chicago Press, 1956. © 1956 by the University of Chicago. Reprinted by permission.

This proposition in turn presupposes at least two implied definitions:

Definition 1:   An "external check" for an individual consists of the application of rewards and penalties, or the expectation that they will be applied, by some source other than the given individual himself.[1]

Definition 2:   "Tyranny" is every severe deprivation of a natural right.

Three comments need to be made about the definition of tyranny supplied here. First, it is not the same as Madison's explicit definition of tyranny in *The Federalist*, No. 47, where he states that "the accumulation of all powers, legislative, executive, and judiciary, in the same hands, whether of one, a few, or many, may justly be pronounced the very definition of tyranny."[2] It seems to me that Madison's explicit definition has been derived from Definition 2 by the insertion of an empirical premise, i.e., the accumulation of all powers in the same hands would lead to severe deprivations of natural rights and hence to tyranny. It seems reasonable, therefore, to reconstruct Madison's explicit argument into the following Madisonian reasoning:

1. Hypothesis 1 and Definition 1 are a paraphrase, but I think a reasonably accurate paraphrase, of numerous references in Madison's writings. My language may be more modern, but the ideas are, I think, expressed by Madison, e.g., in his "Observations" of April, 1787, in *The Complete Madison, His Basic Writings*, ed. Saul K. Padover (New York: Harper & Bros., 1953), pp. 27–29. Cf. also his letter to Jefferson, October 24, 1787, pp. 40–43.

2. *The Federalist*, ed. Edward Mead Earle ("The Modern Library" [New York: Random House, n.d.]), p. 313. For another analysis of Madison see Mark Ashin, "The Argument of Madison's 'Federalist' No. 10," *College English*, XV (October, 1953), 37–45.

Hypothesis 2:   The accumulation of all powers, legislative, executive, and judiciary in the same hands implies the elimination of external checks (empirical generalization).

The elimination of external checks produces tyranny (from Hypothesis 1).

Therefore the accumulation of all powers in the same hands implies tyranny.

. . .

. . . [T]he natural rights are not clearly specified. Among Madison's contemporaries as among his predecessors there was by no means a perfect agreement as to what "rights" are "natural rights." . . . As will be seen, the absence of an agreed definition of natural rights is one of the central difficulties of the Madisonian theory.

. . . I have used the expression "severe deprivation" to cover an ambiguity in the thought of Madison and his contemporaries. How far could governments go in limiting natural rights without becoming tyrannical? Here again, neither Madison nor any other Madisonian, so far as I am aware, has provided wholly satisfactory criteria. However, Madison no doubt agreed with his contemporaries that, at a minimum, any curtailment of natural rights without one's "consent" was a sufficiently severe deprivation to constitute tyranny.[4] . . .

As corollaries of Hypothesis 1 two additional hypotheses need to be distinguished:

Hypothesis 3:   If unrestrained by external checks, a minority of individuals will tyrannize over a majority of individuals.

Hypothesis 4:   If unrestrained by external checks, a majority of individuals will tyrannize over a minority of individuals.

. . .

---

4. [Clinton Rossiter, *Seedtime of the Republic* (New York: Harcourt Brace, 1953)], p. 383. Rossiter describes the consensus on this point.

II

Clearly Hypothesis 1 is an empirical proposition. Its validity can therefore be tested only by experience. Madison's own methods of validating the hypothesis seem to be representative of the widespread American style of thought that in this book is called "Madisonian." Madison's first method of proof is to enumerate historical examples drawn, for example, from the history of Greece and Rome.[6] His second method of proof is to derive the hypothesis from certain psychological axioms that were widely accepted in his day—and perhaps are now. These axioms are Hobbesian in character and run something like this: Men are instruments of their desires. They pursue their desires to satiation if given the opportunity. One such desire is the desire for power over other individuals, for not only is power directly satisfying but it also has great instrumental value because a wide variety of satisfactions depend upon it. . . .

III

If Hypothesis 1 is accepted as validated by these two methods (or others), then Hypotheses 3 and 4, which are merely derived from Hypothesis 1, are also valid. Nevertheless, Hypothesis 4 seems to play a special role in Madisonian thought.[11]

---

6. E.g., Madison's remarks at the Convention, [*The Debates in the Several State Conventions on the Adoption of the Federal Constitution as Recommended by the General Convention at Philadelphia, in 1787, Together with the Journal of Federal Convention* . . . , ed. Jonathan Elliot (2nd ed.; Philadelphia: Lippincott, 1941), V], p. 162.

11. For example, see Padover, *op. cit.*, pp. 28, 37–38, 41, 45–47. But see also Madison's "comment" in 1833, *ibid.*, p. 49. In later years Madison seems to have had a more tender regard for the majority principle. Like most Americans, Madison seems never to have felt any logical contradiction in his position.

Neither at the Constitutional Convention nor in the "Federalist Papers" is much anxiety displayed over the dangers arising from minority tyranny; by comparison, the danger of majority tyranny appears to be a source of acute fear. The "Federalist Papers," for example, reveal no deep-seated distrust of the executive branch, which was regarded by the authors (wrongly, as it turned out) as the strong point for the minority of wealth, status, and power.[12] By contrast, a central theme of Madison's is the threat from the legislature, supposedly the stronghold of the majority....

And it follows from Definition 2, as well as from Madison's own explicit definition of tyranny, that legislative or majority tyranny is not any less tyrannical than executive or minority tyranny. They are equally undesirable....

Both majorities and minorities, then, are weighed on the same scales. For the objective test of non-tyranny is not the size of the ruling group; it is whether the ruling group, whatever its size, imposes severe deprivations on the "natural rights" of citizens.

IV

So far, the propositions in the Madisonian system are definitional or empirical. With the admission of one more definition, it now becomes possible to state the goals to be used in guiding the choice among possible political systems.

What is needed at this point is a definition of "democracy." However, in Madison's day the term "democracy" was less common than in ours. To some extent it was associated with radical equalitarianism; it was also ambiguous because many writers had defined it to mean what we today would call "direct" democracy, i.e., non-representative democracy. The term "republic" was frequently used to refer to what we would be more inclined to call "representative" democracy.[16] It will do no harm, therefore, to adhere to Madison's own term "republic," which he defined as follows:

Definition 3: A republic is a government which (a) derives all of its powers directly or indirectly from the great body of the people and (b) is administered by persons holding their office during pleasure, for a limited period, or during good behavior.[17]

It is now possible to state the central ethical goal of the Madisonian system, which can conveniently be called the Madisonian axiom:

The goal that ought to be attained, at least in the United States, is a non-tyrannical republic.

This goal was taken as a postulate. Because it was not seriously questioned at the Constitutional Convention or elsewhere and has never been seriously questioned in this country since that time, the goal has pretty much remained an unexamined axiom.[18] ...

---

12. Hamilton appears to have written the relevant papers, Nos. 67–77; given his political views, he might be expected to deprecate the dangers of tyranny from this branch. Moreover, it must never be forgotten that the "Federalist Papers" were polemical and propagandistic writing, reflecting a highly partisan viewpoint.

16. On this question, however, see the comment of Elisha P. Douglas, *Rebels and Democrats* (Chapel Hill: University of North Carolina Press, 1955), p. viii.

17. *The Federalist*, No. 39. "It is *essential* to such a government that it is derived from the great body of society, not from an unconsiderable proportion, or a favored class of it.... It is *sufficient* for such a government that the persons administering it be appointed, either directly or indirectly, by the people; and that they hold their appointments by either of the tenures just specified...."

18. Cf. Louis Hartz, "The Whig Tradition in America and Europe," *American Political Science Review*, XLVI (December, 1952), 989–1002.

V

... What conditions are necessary for attaining the goal of a non-tyrannical republic?

Hypothesis 5: At least two conditions are necessary for the existence of a non-tyrannical republic:

First Condition: The accumulation of all powers, legislative, executive, and judiciary, in the same hands, whether of one, a few, or many, and whether hereditary, self-appointed, or elective, must be avoided.[19]

Second Condition: Factions must be so controlled that they do not succeed in acting adversely to the rights of other citizens or to the permanent and aggregate interests of the community.[20]

VI

In attempting to prove that the first condition is an essential prerequisite of every non-tyrannical republic, the Madisonian system becomes so deeply ambiguous that it is difficult to know precisely how to do justice to the argument.

We are faced at the outset with two alternative possibilities. The first I rejected a moment ago as essentially trivial. For if we accept Madison's explicit definition of tyranny, and if we postulate that tyranny is to be avoided, then the first condition is necessary merely by definition: (1) Tyranny means the accumulation of all powers, etc. (definition). (2) Tyranny is undesirable (axiom). (3) Therefore the accumulation of all powers, etc., is undesirable. Yet to solve the problem by definition leaves open many major questions....

Another possibility, therefore, is to accept Madison's implicit definition that tyranny is

19. *The Federalist*, No. 47, p. 313.
20. *The Federalist*, No. 10, pp. 57 ff.

every severe deprivation of natural rights and to propose the empirical hypothesis that the accumulation of all powers, etc., will eliminate external checks (Hypothesis 2) and hence produce tyranny (by Hypothesis 1 and Definition 2).

Yet if we now attempt to retrieve the Madisonian system from a trivial argument by the addition of these implicit hypotheses and definitions, we are faced with a dilemma. For if by "power" we mean constitutionally prescribed authority, then the First Condition is demonstrably false, for it is pretty clearly not necessary to every non-tyrannical republic, as an examination of parliamentary, but certainly non-tyrannical, democratic systems like that of Great Britain readily prove. Let us suppose, then, that by "power" we mean to describe a more realistic relationship, such as A's capacity for acting in such a manner as to control B's responses. Then it is plain that "legislative, executive, and judiciary" by no means comprise all the power relations or control processes in a society. For example, electoral processes make it possible for some individuals to control others; certainly they assist non-leaders in controlling leaders. Hence it is not obvious that the mere accumulation of legislative, executive, and judicial power must lead to tyranny, in the sense of severe deprivation of rights. Popular elections (and competing parties) might be sufficient to prevent such invasions of basic rights. That is, Madison's argument now seems to require proof of at least one additional hypothesis, namely:

Hypothesis 6: Frequent popular elections will not provide an external check sufficient to prevent tyranny.

For if this last hypothesis is false, and frequent popular elections will provide an external check sufficient to prevent tyranny, then Madison's argument about the need to keep the legislative, executive, and judicial powers constitutionally or otherwise separate in order to prevent tyranny is also patently false....

The Federalist, No. 49,[22] to be sure, does attempt to prove that the check provided by electoral processes is inadequate to prevent all powers, legislative, executive, and judiciary, from accumulating in the same hands. Two observations can be made about this argument. First, even if the proposition is valid, it cannot establish the necessity of the First Condition except by the trivial definitional route rejected above. For, except by definition, it does not follow that the accumulation of "all powers, legislative, executive, and judiciary" leads to tyranny. Second, the specific arguments in support of the proposition in *The Federalist*, No. 49, seem to me patently invalid or highly inconclusive. They are (1) that frequent appeals would indicate defects in government and so weaken the veneration necessary to stability; (2) that public tranquillity would be dangerously disturbed by interesting public passions too strongly; (3) that being few in number, members of the executive and judiciary can be known only to a small part of the electorate; the judiciary are far removed, the executive are objects of jealousy and unpopularity. By contrast, members of the legislature dwell among the people and have connections of blood and friendship. Hence the contest for power would be an unequal one in which the legislature would swallow up the others.[23]

I am afraid, then, that the validity of the First Condition is not established.

---

22. Although the authorship of this paper was once contested, it is now established that Madison, not Hamilton, was the author. (Irving Brant, *James Madison*, Vol. III: *Father of the Constitution, 1787–1800* [New York: Bobbs-Merrill Co., 1950], p. 184.)

23. Madison also appends an argument more common among antidemocrats, namely, that issues in popular elections would not be decided on "the true merits of the question" but on a partisan basis. Unlike the first three, which seem to me plainly false, this one is merely meaningless—at least without a very considerable philosophical and empirical inquiry not attempted by Madison. Cf. *The Federalist*, No. 49, pp. 327–332.

Yet the necessity for this condition for a nontyrannical republic is an article of faith in the American political credo. From it Madison, and successors who out-Madisoned Madison, have deduced the necessity for the whole complicated network of constitutional checks and balances: the separate constituencies for electing President, senators, and representatives; the presidential veto power; a bicameral Congress; presidential control over appointments, senatorial confirmation; and, in part, federalism. Over the years still other checks and balances within the political system have developed and have been rationalized by the same arguments: judicial review, decentralized political parties, the Senate filibuster, senatorial "courtesy," the power of committee chairmen, and indeed almost every organizational technique that promises to provide an additional external check on any identifiable group of political leaders.

VII

Let us now turn to the Second Condition: Factions must be so controlled that they do not succeed in acting adversely to the rights of other citizens or to the permanent and aggregate interests of the community.

How is this state of affairs to be attained? In answering this question, Madison produced one of the most lucid and compact sets of political propositions ever set forth by an American: the now familiar argument of *The Federalist*, No. 10.[24] I shall here attempt no more than to set forth the bare skeleton of his argument.

Obviously a definition is needed at the outset:

Definition 4:   A faction is "a number of citizens, whether amounting to a majority or a minority of the whole, who are united and

---

24. This represents a refinement of ideas Madison had already expounded at the Convention and earlier. Cf., for example, *Elliot's Debates*, V, 242–243.

actuated by some common impulse of passion, or of interest, adverse to the rights of other citizens, or to the permanent and aggregate interests of the community."[25]

Given this definition, it is easy to show from Hypothesis 1 that a faction will produce tyranny if unrestrained by external checks. Thus the Second Condition is proved to be necessary.

How, then, can factions be controlled? In brief, Madison argues with elegant rigor and economy that the latent causes of faction are sown in the nature of man: they stem from differences of opinion based on the fallibility of man's reason, from attachments to different leaders, and from differences in property, that are in turn a result of "the diversity in the faculties of men." If people cannot be made alike, the causes of faction could be controlled only by destroying liberty—a solution obviously barred to anyone seeking a non-tyrannical republic. Hence it follows that factions cannot be controlled by eliminating their causes. In this fashion Madison proves the validity of

Hypothesis 7:   If factions are to be controlled and tyranny is to be avoided, this must be attained by controlling the effects of faction.

Can the effects of faction be controlled so as to avoid tyranny? Yes, Madison tells us, provided two further conditions are present:

Hypothesis 8:   If a faction consists of less than a majority, it can be controlled by the operation of "the republican principle" of voting in the legislative body, i.e., the majority can vote down the minority.

Hypothesis 9:   The development of majority faction can be limited if the electorate is numerous, extended, and diverse in interests.

The validity of Hypothesis 8 must have seemed self-evident to Madison, for he made no effort to prove it. . . .

25. *The Federalist*, No. 10, p. 54.

Hypothesis 9 is proved by an argument that contains a number of exceedingly doubtful statements and some that, if true, raise serious questions as to the validity of other basic hypotheses in the Madisonian system. Madison argues that there are only two possible ways of controlling the effects of a majority faction. First, the existence of the same passion or interest in a majority at the same time must be prevented. But because in this case no majority faction would exist, Madison seems to have reversed his earlier argument that the causes of faction cannot be controlled. Second, even though a majority faction exists, its members must be made incapable of acting together effectually.

Both ways of controlling the effects of a majority faction, Madison argues, are provided by a large republic. There ensues an extremely dubious and probably false set of propositions purporting to show that representation in a large republic will provide "better" politicians and reduce the probability of success of "the vicious arts by which elections are too often carried." Then Madison states a final and exceptionally important proposition. . . . Let us then paraphrase Madison:

Hypothesis 10:   To the extent that the electorate is numerous, extended, and diverse in interests, a majority faction is less likely to exist, and if it does exist, it is less likely to act as a unity.

VIII

. . .

The first hypothesis, it will be recalled, is implicit rather than explicit in the Madisonian argument. . . .

Inter alia, the first hypothesis implies:

1. That control over others by means of governmental processes is a highly valued goal, i.e., such control is believed to be either directly or indirectly rewarding to those who exercise it.

2. That it is impossible by social training to create through conscience a self-restraint sufficient to inhibit impulses to tyranny among political leaders....

3. That the range of sympathetic identification of one individual with another is too narrow to eliminate impulses to tyranny.

Many political theorists prior to Madison placed heavy emphasis on the role of social indoctrination and habituation in creating attitudes, habits, and even personality types requisite to a given type of political system....

... [P]resent evidence suggests that "internal checks"—the conscience (super-ego), attitudes, and basic predispositions—are crucial in determining whether any given individual will seek to tyrannize over others; that these internal checks vary from individual to individual, from social group to social group, and from time to time; and that the probability of tyranny emerging in a society is a function of the extent to which various types of internalized responses are present among members of that society.

Yet we should make Madison and his present-day followers seem fools if we were to assume that they were oblivious to these or similar facts.... Thus we might try to save one of Madison's basic implicit hypotheses by casting it in probability terms:

Hypothesis 1′: The probability that any given individual or group will tyrannize over others if unrestrained by external checks is sufficiently high so that if tyranny is to be avoided over a long period, the constitutionally prescribed machinery of any government must maintain some external checks on all officials.

That is, it seems reasonable to propose that even if internal checks might frequently inhibit impulses to tyranny, they may not always do so with all individuals likely to be in a position to tyrannize. Hence, if tyranny is to be avoided, external checks are required. And these external checks must be constitutionally prescribed.

IX

... What kinds of external checks does the Madisonian have in mind as restraints on tyranny?

... Madison evidently had in mind a basic concept, namely, that of reciprocal control among leaders. But in several ways, the Madisonian argument is inadequate:

1. It does not show, and I think cannot be used to show, that reciprocal control among leaders, sufficient to prevent tyranny, requires constitutionally prescribed separation of powers, as in the American Constitution.

2. Either the significance of constitutional prescription as an external check is exaggerated or the argument misunderstands the psychological realities implied by the concept of a check on, or control over, behavior. And the inferences from either type of incorrect premise to propositions about political behavior or the requisites of a non-tyrannical democracy are false.

3. The Madisonian argument exaggerates the importance, in preventing tyranny, of specified checks to governmental officials by other specified governmental officials; it underestimates the importance of the inherent social checks and balances existing in every pluralistic society. Without these social checks and balances, it is doubtful that the intragovernmental checks on officials would in fact operate to prevent tyranny; with them, it is doubtful that all of the intragovernmental checks of the Madisonian system as it operates in the United States are necessary to prevent tyranny.

X

In the preceding discussion I have assumed that "tyranny" in the Madisonian system is a meaningful term. By assuming it to be meaningful, it has been possible to show that Hypothesis 1 leads to false conclusions. Now, however, we must ask whether the concept of "tyranny" implicit in the Madisonian system, and basic to the usual rationale of the American constitutional framework, has any operational meaning. . . .

It is self-evident that the definition of tyranny would be entirely empty unless natural rights could somehow be defined. It can be shown, I think, that we must specify a process by which specific natural rights can be defined in the context of some political society. To specify this process creates some dilemmas for the Madisonian.

If a natural right were defined, rather absurdly, to mean the right of every individual to do what he wishes to do, then every form of government must be tyrannical; for every government restrains at least some individuals from doing what they wish to do. . . .

It follows that tyranny must be defined to mean that severe penalties are inflicted only on some kinds of behavior. How are these kinds of behavior, which it is tyrannical to restrain, to be specified in practice? . . .

The typical political situation is one in which individuals in a group or a society disagree as to the desirability of penalizing or rewarding certain kinds of behavior. Governmental processes are then employed to adjudicate the dispute. But when individuals disagree, what rule is to be employed to determine whether the punishing of some specified act would or would not be tyrannical? One possibility is to permit the majority to decide. . . . Yet since this operating rule is precisely what Madison meant to prevent, and moreover would make the concept of majority tyranny meaningless, we must reject it. The only remaining possibility, then, is that some specified group in the community, not defined as the majority, but not necessarily always in opposition to it, would be empowered to decide. But if Hypothesis 1 is correct, then any group in the community with such a power would use it to tyrannize over other individuals in the community. Hence, in practice, no one could

have the power to decide this question. Hence this definition of tyranny seems to have no operational meaning in the context of political decision-making.[33] And, of course, it follows further that, if tyranny has no operational meaning, then majority tyranny has no operational meaning. . . .

XI

If we turn to Madison's explicit concept of faction, we find that it suffers from the same difficulties as the implicit concept of tyranny. It would hardly be worth while to examine Madison's explicit concept of faction, however, if it were not for the fact that some such thought is implicit in many other attempts to defend the idea of constitutionally prescribed checks on "majorities."[34] . . .

The difficulty with this definition of a faction is similar to the difficulty encountered with "tyranny." How can one use this concept? . . .

XII

It is not part of my purpose to examine every detailed aspect of the Madisonian viewpoint. Yet one more major point is worth considering.

Protection against factions and therefore against tyranny, it will be recalled, requires two conditions:

---

33. It might be said that each individual would decide himself, upon consulting his own value system, whether or not a given act was tyrannical. But this is merely a prescription for individual behavior and provides no rule for a collective decision.

34. The quotation marks reflect my belief that in the usual sense intended, majorities rarely, if ever, rule in any country or social organization at any time. Thus the fear of majority rule, as well as the advocacy of it, is founded upon a misconception of the probabilities permitted by political reality. . . .

Hypothesis 8:   If a faction consists of less than a majority, it can be controlled by the operation of "the republican principle" of voting in the legislative body, i.e., the majority can vote down the minority.

Hypothesis 9:   The development of majority faction can be limited if the electorate is numerous, extended, and diverse in interests.

Because, as we have seen, the terms "factions" and "tyranny" have been given no specific meaning, as they stand these two hypotheses also have no specific meaning, i.e., no conceivable way exists by which we can test their validity. Hence they remain mere untestable assertions....

XIII

Hypothesis 9 asserts that the effects of majority faction can be controlled if the electorate is numerous, extended, and diverse in interests. Here again, the absence of any definite meaning of the word faction is an obstacle to testing the prediction. Yet if we examine the arguments that Madison himself used to prove the validity of this hypothesis, it is clear that the hypothesis must be read to mean that the effectiveness of any majority whatsoever is severely limited if the electorate is numerous, extended, and diverse in interests. Whether or not the majority is factional is irrelevant to the operation of the restrictions imposed by the existence of a numerous, extended, and diverse electorate. Furthermore, so far as I am aware, no modern Madison has shown that the restraints on the effectiveness of majorities imposed by the facts of a pluralistic society operate only to curtail "bad" majorities and not "good" majorities; and I confess I see no way by which such an ingenious proposition could be satisfactorily established.

Hence the net effect of Hypothesis 9 seems to be this: because majorities are likely to be unstable and transitory in a large and pluralistic

society, they are likely to be politically ineffective; and herein lies the basic protection against their exploitation of minorities. This conclusion is of course scarcely compatible with the preoccupation with majority tyranny that is the hallmark of the Madisonian style of thought.

XIV

The absence of specific meaning for terms like "majority tyranny" and "faction" coupled with the central importance of these concepts in the Madisonian style of thinking has led to a rather tortuous political theory that is explicable genetically rather than logically. Genetically the Madisonian ideology has served as a convenient rationalization for every minority that, out of fear of the possible deprivations of some majority, has demanded a political system providing it with an opportunity to veto such policies.[37] ...

Nevertheless, as political science rather than as ideology the Madisonian system is clearly inadequate. In retrospect, the logical and empirical deficiencies of Madison's own thought seem to have arisen in large part from his inability to reconcile two different goals. On the one hand, Madison substantially accepted the idea that all the adult citizens of a republic must be assigned equal rights, including the right to determine the general direction of government policy. In this sense majority rule is "the republican principle." On the other hand, Madison wished to erect a political system that would guarantee the liberties of certain minorities whose advantages of status, power, and wealth would, he thought, probably not be tolerated indefinitely by a

---

37. Calhoun's transparent defense of the southern slavocracy by his doctrine of concurrent majorities seems to me prone to all the weaknesses of the Madisonian system, which in many respects it parallels. But I have not tried to deal specifically with Calhoun's special variant on Madison. Cf. his *Disquisition on Government*, ed. R. K. Cralle (New York: Peter Smith, 1943), esp. pp. 28–38.

constitutionally untrammeled majority. Hence majorities had to be constitutionally inhibited. Madisonianism, historically and presently, is a compromise between these two conflicting goals. I think I have shown that the explicit and implicit terms of the compromise do not bear careful analysis. Perhaps it is foolish to expect them to. . . .

A Bill of Rights for Britain

Ronald Dworkin

When the eminent French historian François Furet came recently to Britain to lecture on the occasion of the bicentennial of the French Revolution, he said that the signal triumph of democracy in our time is the growing acceptance and enforcement of a crucial idea: that democracy is not the same thing as majority rule, and that in a real democracy liberty and minorities have legal protection in the form of a written constitution that even Parliament cannot change to suit its whim or policy. Under that vision of democracy, a bill of individual constitutional rights is part of fundamental law, and judges, who are not elected and who are therefore removed from the pressures of partisan politics, are responsible for interpreting and enforcing that Bill of Rights as they are for all other parts of the legal system.

The United States was born committed to that idea of democracy, and now every member of the European Community but Britain accepts it, and so do the great majority of other mature democracies, including India, Canada, and almost all the other democratic Commonwealth nations. Britain stands alone in insisting that Parliament must have absolutely unlimited legal power to do anything it wishes.

British constitutional lawyers once bragged that a constitutional Bill of Rights was unnecessary because in Britain the people can trust the rulers they elect. But now a great many people—more than ever before—believe that this is no longer true, and that the time has come for Britain to join other democracies and put its Parliament under law. Charter 88, an organisation created to press that argument, has attracted impressive support at every level of British society. Would a charter of constitutional rights help

Excerpted from: Ronald Dworkin, *A Bill of Rights for Britain*. London: Chatto & Windus, 1990. Used by permission of The Random House Group Ltd.

to restore the British culture of liberty? Learned Hand, a great American constitutional judge, said that when the spirit of freedom dies in a people, no constitution or Supreme Court can bring it back to life. And it is true that many nations with formal constitutional guarantees, including some of the European nations that have made the European Convention of Human Rights part of their own law, fail fully to honour their constitutional rights in practice. But though a written constitution is certainly not a sufficient condition for liberty to thrive again in Britain, it may well be a necessary one....

Of course the idea of a Bill of Rights is rejected by many of the people you might expect to reject it: the leading politicians of both of the two great parties whose power, when in office, would be curtailed if people enjoyed constitutional rights as individuals. Most Tory politicians, in spite of the shambles they have made of liberty in recent years, think that their government is too much rather than too little hedged in by judges. They howl whenever judges find the actions of ministers and officials illegal, as judges have done several times in recent years, and they call for Parliament to change the law to keep the judges off their backs. The Labour Party, too, has so far been adamantly opposed to a constitutional Bill of Rights, in spite of its own historical concern for individual liberty. Fortunately, there are now indications that Labour has changed its mind and will support a Bill of Rights. But most of the pressure has come from the bottom rather than the top, from people demanding the rights and liberties that in other countries belong to them, not to the politicians.

How could a Bill of Rights be enacted? One way would be remarkably simple. As I said earlier, Britain is already committed by international treaty to a charter of constitutional rights called the European Convention. With very little procedural fuss Parliament could enact a statute providing that the principles of that convention are henceforth part of the law of Britain, enforceable by British judges in British courts. A statute to that effect has been introduced in Parliament on three occasions in recent years; it was actually debated, as a private member's Bill, in 1986, though it did not obtain the necessary majority for closure to permit a vote....

In theory, then, Britain already has a constitution of individual rights, enforceable by a court in Strasbourg, which Parliament is powerless to abridge except in a case of emergency. But the European Convention is no substitute for a domestic Bill of Rights interpreted and enforced by British judges trained in British traditions. A private citizen who feels his rights under the Convention have been violated must first exhaust whatever remedies might be thought to be available at home, and then prepare and argue a case first before the European Commission and then, if matters go that far, before the European Court. The process is fearsomely expensive (there is, for all practical purposes, no legal aid available) and takes on average six years, by which time, particularly in cases involving censorship, the issue is almost always academic.

Two thirds of European countries, including all the other major ones, have made the Convention part of their domestic law, so that it can be raised and its benefit claimed in national courts. But Britain has not done so....

If Parliament made the European Convention part of British law, on the other hand, judges could decide on their own whether some official action or parliamentary statute violated the Convention. They could decide that question in the same way they decide any other issue of law. So the broadcasting ban, and all the other tawdry acts of censorship that violate Britain's solemn obligations under the treaty, could be challenged at once and not five or six years later when the government's aim or stopping public access to information has long since been achieved anyway. Official denials of privacy, or of the right of legitimate protest, or of the rights of people accused of crimes, could be challenged at once, and not years later when the damage was done and long past undoing.

If the judges used this new authority well, the most important and immediate benefit would be a revitalisation of the liberty and dignity of the people. Government and officials would no longer be so free to keep secrets from the people they are supposed to serve, or to ignore rights the nation has a solemn obligation to respect. Other, more speculative but in the long run equally important, benefits might then follow....

If British judges began to create as well as follow constitutional jurisprudence in that way, their decisions would be bound to influence the Commission and Court in Strasbourg, as well as the courts of the other nations who have signed the Convention, and, indeed, of all the other nations across the globe who are now wrestling with the problem of making abstract human rights concrete. Incorporation would put the special skills of British lawyers and judges, and the heritage of British legal principle, at the service of the civilised world. Britain could become once again a leader in defining and protecting individual freedom, instead of a sullen defendant giving ground to liberty only when ordered to do so by a foreign court....

The European Convention is not a perfect Bill of Rights for Britain. It was a compromise drafted to accommodate a variety of nations with different legal systems and traditions; it is in many ways weaker than the American Bill of Rights; and it is hedged about with vague limitations and powerful escape clauses of different sorts. The Convention does protect liberty better than it is now protected by Parliament alone, however, as recent history shows. It protects freedom of speech, religion and expression, privacy, and the most fundamental rights of accused criminals, and it grants in an indirect but effective way rights against discrimination. Since Britain is already subject to the Convention as a matter of both moral obligation and international law, it would plainly be easier to enact that charter into British law, substantially as it is, perhaps with clarifying changes and additions from other international covenants Britain has also signed, than to begin drafting and debating a wholly new Bill of Rights. Even if it were possible to adopt an entirely new set of rights, perhaps modelled on the American Constitution, the European Convention would remain law enforceable in Strasbourg, and the potential conflict between the two fundamental charters of rights would be a source of wasteful confusion.

So those who love liberty should unite in supporting the incorporation of the Convention. But how can this be done, and in what form should it be done? . . . [T]he popular argument that there is no way Parliament can impose a constitutional Bill of Rights on a later Parliament is at least dubious. But notice that I have so far been discussing what might be called a *strong* form of incorporation, which provides that any statute inconsistent with the Convention is null and void. Several influential supporters of a Bill of Rights . . . have proposed that in the first instance incorporation should take what is technically a weaker form: the incorporating statute should provide that an inconsistent statute is null and void unless Parliament has expressly stated that it *intends* the statute to override the Convention. In practice this technically weaker version of incorporation would probably provide almost as much protection as the stronger one. If a government conceded that its statute violated the Convention, it would have no defence before the Commission or Court in Strasbourg. In any case, quite apart from that practical point, no respectable government would wish to announce that it did not care whether its legislation or decisions violated the country's domestic promises and international obligations. If a government felt itself able to make such an announcement, except in the most extraordinary circumstances, the spirit of liberty would be dead anyway, beyond the power of any constitution to revive.

At least in the first instance, therefore, proponents should press for the weaker version of incorporation. If they succeed, then unless Parliament has expressly provided to the contrary any citizen will have the right in British courts to challenge a law or an official decision on the ground that it is offensive to the Convention's principles. Some European nations have established special courts to hear constitutional challenges. But it would be better, at least in Britain, to allow any division of the High Court to entertain such a challenge. Constitutional issues are not so arcane or specialised that ordinary judges, assisted by counsel in the normal way, could not master them. . . .

That is the case for incorporating the European Convention into domestic British law. It is no mystery that powerful politicians are reluctant to accept that case. . . .

The politicians say that the very idea of a Bill of Rights restricting the power of Parliament is hostile to the British tradition that Parliament and Parliament alone should be sovereign. That supposed tradition seems less appealing now, when a very powerful executive and well-disciplined political parties mean less effective power for backbench MPs than it did before these developments. The tradition has already been compromised in recent decades, moreover. It was altered by the European Communities Act, for example, under which judges have the power to override parliamentary decisions in order to enforce directly effective Community rules.

In any case, quite apart from these considerations, incorporating the European Convention would not diminish Parliament's present power in any way that could reasonably be thought objectionable. Parliament is *already* bound by international law to observe the terms of that Convention. If the Convention were incorporated in what I have called the strong form, under which a future Parliament would not have the legal power to violate the Convention even if it expressly said it intended to do so, then the power of Parliament might be somewhat more limited than it is now, because British judges might develop a special British interpretation of the Convention that in some cases recognised individual constitutional rights the Strasbourg Court would not. . . .

The argument for parliamentary supremacy would be irrelevant, moreover, if the Convention were incorporated in the weaker form I suggested should be the initial goal. For then Parliament could override the Convention by mere majority vote, provided it was willing expressly to concede its indifference about doing so. No doubt that condition would, in practice, prevent a government from introducing legislation it might otherwise enact. That is the point of incorporation, even in the weak form. But forcing Parliament to make the choice between obeying its international obligations and admitting that it is violating them does not limit Parliament's supremacy, but only its capacity for duplicity. Candour is hardly inconsistent with sovereignty. . . .

The argument for parliamentary supremacy is often thought to rest on a more important and fundamental argument, however, according to which Britain should not have subscribed to the European Convention in the first place. This is the argument: that it is undemocratic for appointed judges rather than an elected Parliament to have the last word about what the law is. People who take that view will resist incorporation, because incorporation enlarges the practical consequences of what they regard as the mistake of accepting the Convention. They will certainly resist the idea that domestic judges should have the power to read the Convention more liberally and so provide more protection than Strasbourg requires.

Their argument misunderstands what democracy is, however. In the first place, it confuses democracy with the power of elected officials. There is no genuine democracy, even though

officials have been elected in otherwise fair elections, unless voters have had access to the information they need so that their votes can be knowledgeable choices rather than only manipulated responses to advertising campaigns. Citizens of a democracy must be able to participate in government not just spasmodically, in elections from time to time, but constantly through informed and free debate about their government's performance between elections. Those evident requirements suggest what other nations have long ago realised: that Parliament *must* be constrained in certain ways in order that democracy be genuine rather than sham. The argument that a Bill of Rights would be undemocratic is therefore not just wrong but the opposite of the truth. . . .

This seems to me a decisive answer to the argument that incorporation would be undemocratic. I hope and believe that a different but equally decisive answer can also be made in Britain now: that the argument is self-defeating because the great majority of British people themselves rejects the crude statistical view of democracy on which the argument is based. Even people who do not think of themselves as belonging to any minority have good reasons for insisting that a majority's power to rule should be limited. Something crucially important to them—their religious freedom or professional independence or liberty of conscience, for example—might one day prove inconvenient to the government of the day. Even people who cannot imagine being isolated in that way might prefer to live in a genuine political community, in which everyone's dignity as an equal is protected, rather than just in a state they control. . . .

A Right-Based Critique of Constitutional Rights

Jeremy Waldron

1 Introduction

... Should we embody our rights in legalistic formulae and proclaim them in a formal Bill of Rights? Or should we leave them to evolve informally in dialogue among citizens, representatives and officials? How are we to stop rights from being violated? Should we rely on a general spirit of watchfulness in the community, attempting to raise what Mill called "a strong barrier of moral conviction" to protect our liberty?[4] Or should we also entrust some specific branch of government—the courts, for example—with the task of detecting violations and with the authority to overrule any other agency that commits them?

The advantages of this last approach continue to attract proponents of constitutional reform in the United Kingdom. Ronald Dworkin, for example, has argued that it would forge a decisive link between rights and legality, giving the former much greater prominence in public life. By throwing the authority of the courts behind the idea of rights, the legal system would begin to play "a different, more valuable role in society"....

In this paper, I shall question that assumption. I want to develop four main lines of argument. The first is a negative case: I shall show that there is no necessary inference from a right-based position in political philosophy to a commitment to a Bill of Rights as a political institution along with an American-style practice of judicial review.

Secondly, I shall argue that political philosophers should be more aware than other proponents of constitutional reform of the difficulty, complexity, and controversy attending the idea of basic rights. I shall argue that they have reason—grounded in professional humility—to be more than usually hesitant about the enactment of any canonical list of rights, particularly if the aim is to put that canon beyond the scope of political debate and revision.

Thirdly, I shall argue that philosophers who talk about rights should pay much more attention than they do to the processes by which decisions are taken in a community under circumstances of disagreement. Theories of rights need to be complemented by theories of authority, whose function it is to determine how decisions are to be taken when the members of a community disagree about what decision is right. Since we are to assume a context of moral disagreement, a principle such as "Let the right decision be made" cannot form part of an adequate principle of authority. It follows from this that, if people disagree about basic rights (and they do), an adequate theory of authority can neither include nor be qualified by a conception of rights as "trumps" over majoritarian forms of decision-making.

Finally, I shall argue that, in a constitutional regime of the sort envisaged by proponents of Charter 88, the courts will inevitably become the main forum for the revision and adaptation of basic rights in the face of changing circumstances and social controversies. (This of course is an extrapolation from the experience of constitutional politics in the United States.) I shall argue that a theorist of rights should have grave misgivings about this prospect. Some of us think that people have a right to participate in the democratic governance of their community, and that this right is quite deeply connected to the values of autonomy and responsibility that are

Excerpted from Jeremy Waldron, "A Right Based Critique of Constitutional Rights." *Oxford Journal of Legal Studies* 13, no. 1 (1993): 18–51. Reprinted by permission of Oxford University Press.

4. John Stuart Mill, *On Liberty*, ch 1, para 15 (Indianapolis: Bobbs-Merrill, 1955), 18.

celebrated in our commitment to other basic liberties. We think moreover that the right to democracy is a right to participate on equal terms in social decisions on issues of high principle and that it is not to be confined to interstitial matters of social and economic policy. I shall argue that our respect for such democratic rights is called seriously into question when proposals are made to shift decisions about the conception and revision of basic rights from the legislature to the courtroom, from the people and their admittedly imperfect representative institutions to a handful of men and women, supposedly of wisdom, learning, virtue and high principle who, it is thought, alone can be trusted to take seriously the great issues that they raise? . . .

For these reasons, then, the proponent of a given right may be hesitant about embodying it in a constitutionally entrenched Bill of Rights. She may figure that the gain, in terms of an immunity against wrongful legislative abrogation, is more than offset by the loss in our ability to evolve a free and flexible discourse.

But the deepest reasons of liberal principle have yet to be addressed. When a principle is entrenched in a constitutional document, the claim-right (to liberty or provision) that it lays down is compounded with an immunity against legislative change. Those who possess the right now get the additional advantage of its being made difficult or impossible to alter their legal position. That can sound attractive; but as W. N. Hohfeld emphasized, we should always look at both sides of any legal advantage.[30] The term correlative to the claim-right is of course the duty incumbent upon officials and others to respect and uphold the right. And the term correlative to the constitutional immunity is what Hohfeld would call a disability: in effect, a disabling of the legislature from its normal functions of revision, reform and innovation in the law. To think that a constitutional immunity is

called for is to think oneself justified in disabling legislators in this respect (and thus, indirectly, in disabling the citizens whom they represent). It is, I think, worth pondering the attitudes that lie behind the enthusiasm for imposing such disabilities.

To embody a right in an entrenched constitutional document is to adopt a certain attitude towards one's fellow citizens. That attitude is best summed up as a combination of self-assurance and mistrust: self-assurance in the proponent's conviction that what she is putting forward really *is* a matter of fundamental right and that she has captured it adequately in the particular formulation she is propounding; and mistrust, implicit in her view that any alternative conception that might be concocted by elected legislators next year or the year after is so likely to be wrong-headed or ill-motivated that *her own* formulation is to be elevated immediately beyond the reach of ordinary legislative revision.

This attitude of mistrust of one's fellow citizens does not sit particularly well with the aura of respect for their autonomy and responsibility that is conveyed by the substance of the rights which are being entrenched in this way. The substantive importance of a given right may well be based on a view of the individual person as essentially a thinking agent, endowed with an ability to deliberate morally and to transcend a preoccupation with her own particular or sectional interests. For example, an argument for freedom of speech may depend on a view of people as "political animals" in Aristotle's sense, capable of evolving a shared and reliable sense of right and wrong, justice and injustice, in their conversations with one another.[31] If *this* is why one thinks free speech important, one cannot simply turn round and announce that the products of any deliberative process are to be mistrusted.

If, on the other hand, the desire for entrenchment is motivated by a predatory view of human

---

30. Wesley N. Hohfeld, *Fundamental Legal Conceptions* (New Haven: Yale University Press, 1923).

31. See Aristotle, *Politics*, Bk I, ch 2, 1253al–18 (3).

nature and of what people will do to one another when let loose in the arena of democratic politics, it will be difficult to explain how or why people are to be viewed as essentially bearers of rights. For in order to develop a theory of rights, we need some basis for distinguishing those interests which are characteristic of human dignity from those which are relatively unimportant in a person's activity and desires. If our only image of man is that of a self-seeking animal who is not to be trusted with a concern for the interests of others, we lack the conception of dignified moral autonomy on which such discriminations of interest might be based.

These are not intended as knock-down arguments against constitutionalization. All I have tried to show so far is that there is nothing obvious about combining a respect for rights with a profound mistrust of people in their democratic and representative capacities. Accordingly there is nothing perverse in saying: "The reasons which make me think of the human individual as a bearer of rights are the very reasons that allow me to trust her as the bearer of political responsibilities. It is precisely because I see each person as a potential moral agent, endowed with dignity and autonomy, that I am willing to entrust the people *en masse* with the burden of self-government." Once we see *this* as an intelligible set of attitudes, we might be more hesitant in expressing our enthusiasm for rights in terms of the disabling of representative institutions....

5   Doing Philosophy

... American-style judicial review is often defended by pointing to the possibility that democratic majoritarian procedures may yield unjust or tyrannical outcomes. And so they may. But so may *any* procedure that purports to solve the problem of social choice in the face of disagreements about what counts as injustice or what counts as tyranny. The rule that the Supreme Court should make the final decision (by majority voting among its members)[44] on issues of fundamental rights is just such a procedural rule. It too may (and sometimes has) yielded egregiously unjust decisions.[45] Anyone whose theory of authority gives the Supreme Court power to make decisions must—as much as any democrat—face up to the paradox that the option she thinks is just may not be the option which, according to her theory of authority, should be followed....

10   Imperfect Democracy

... [T]he enactment of a Bill of Rights need not involve the entrenchment of one particular view of individual rights beyond the reach of challenge or reform. A Bill of Rights can specify procedures for amendment; and certainly one upshot of the argument I have made is that we should insist on such opportunities for constitutional revision, for they give a politically empowered people the chance to think afresh about their understanding of individual rights.[64] However, even if the efforts of rights-proponents fall short of absolute entrenchment, there is a temptation to make the amendment process as difficult as possible, a temptation often motivated by the same self-assured mistrust of one's fellow citizens that I have been criticizing throughout

44. So it is a little misleading to describe the democratic objection to judicial review in the US as "the counter-majoritarian difficulty"—cf Alexander Bickel, *The Least Dangerous Branch: the Supreme Court at the Bar of Politics* (New Haven: Yale University Press, 1962), 16. The US Supreme Court is a majoritarian institution; the problem is the very small number of participants in its majoritarian decision-making.

45. For an uncontroversial example of an egregiously unjust decision, see the *"Dred Scott"* decision, *Scott v Sandford* 60 US (19 How) 393 (1857).

64. The opportunity for constitutional amendment is celebrated, in the American context, in Bruce Ackerman, "The Storrs Lectures: Discovering the Constitution," (1984) 93 *Yale Law Journal* 1013.

this paper. At the very least, it is thought appropriate that any amendment to a Bill of Rights should require a super-majority, and often the procedural obstacles that are proposed are much more formidable than that.

The point of such super-majoritarian requirements is, presumably, to reduce the probability that any amendment will be successful. To the extent that that is the aim, one needs to ask: how is the Bill of Rights to be made responsive to changing circumstances and different opinions in the community over time about the rights we have and the way they should be formulated? Are the formulations of one generation to be cast in stone, and given precedence over all subsequent revisions, save for the rare occasion on which the obstacles to amendment can be surmounted? Or are there to be, in effect, other and even less democratic procedures for constitutional revision than these?

The experience of the United States indicates the importance of the latter possibility. For, of course, *there* it would be quite misleading to suggest that the formal amendment procedure exhausts the possibilities for constitutional revision. In addition to the processes specified in Article V of the US Constitution, changes in the American Bill of Rights have come about most often through the exercise of judicial power. The Supreme Court is not empowered to alter the written terms of the Bill of Rights. But the justices do undertake the task of altering the way in which the document is interpreted and applied, and the way in which individual rights are authoritatively understood—in many cases with drastic and far-reaching effects....

Members of the higher judiciary in the United States have the power to revise the official understanding of rights for that society and, when they do, their view prevails. The ordinary electors and their state and Congressional representatives do not have that power, at least in any sense that counts. A proposal to establish a Bill of Rights for Britain, judicially interpreted and

enforced, is a proposal to institute a similar situation: to allow in effect routine constitutional revision by the courts and to disallow routine constitutional revision by Parliament. I hope it is easy to see ... why this arrogation of judicial authority, this disabling of representative institutions, and above all this quite striking political inequality, should be frowned upon by any right-based theory that stresses the importance of democratic participation on matters of principle by ordinary men and women.

Responses to this critique take three forms. First, it is argued that the judicial power of interpretation and revision is simply unavoidable. After all, it is the job of the courts to apply the law. They cannot do that except by trying to understand what the law says, and that involves interpreting it....

However, the inescapability of judicial interpretation does not settle the issue of whether *other* institutions should not also have the power to revise the official understanding of rights. On any account of the activity of the US Supreme Court over the past century or so, the inescapable duty to interpret the law has been taken as the occasion for serious and radical revision. There may not be anything wrong with that, but there is something wrong in conjoining it with an insistence that the very rights which the judges are interpreting and revising are to be put beyond the reach of *democratic* revision and reinterpretation.

In the end, either we believe in the need for a cumbersome amendment process or we do not. If we do, then we should be disturbed by the scale of the revisions in which the judges engage (inescapably, on Dworkin's account). They find themselves routinely having to think afresh about the rights that people have, and having to choose between rival conceptions of those rights, in just the way that traditional arguments for making amendment difficult are supposed to preclude. It is no answer to this that the amendment process focuses particularly on changes in constitutional *wording*, and that the judges are not assuming the power to make verbal alterations. For one thing, judicial doctrine in the US has yielded catch-phrases (such as "clear and present danger," or "substantive due process," or "strict scrutiny") which have become as much a part of the verbalism of the American constitutional heritage as anything in the Constitution itself. For another thing, it cannot be that the *words* matter more—and so need more protection from change—than our substantive understanding of the content of the rights themselves.

If, on the other hand, we think it desirable that a Bill of Rights should be treated as "a living organism ... capable of growth—of expansion and of adaptation to new conditions,"[67] then we do have to face the question of authority: who should be empowered to participate in this quotidian organic process? Now, if Dworkin is right, the question is not "Who?" but "The judges and who else?," for the judges' participation is inescapable. But if it is really thought to be necessary for society "to adapt canons of right to situations not envisaged by those who framed them, thereby facilitating their evolution and preserving their vitality,"[68] it is difficult to see why the ordinary people and their representatives should be excluded from this process. Or rather—and more disturbingly—it is all too easy to see why: those who want an adaptive constitution do not trust the people to participate in its adaptation. That distrust, it seems to me, is something we should recoil from, on the same right-based ground as we recoil from any attempt to exclude people from the governance of the society in which they live.

A second response is to appeal, not to the inescapability of judicial power, but to its demo-

cratic credentials. Judicial review, it may be said, *is* a form of democratic representation, albeit a rather indirect form. In the US, justices are nominated to the Supreme Court by the President and their appointment is ratified by the Senate, and in the United Kingdom appointments to the higher judiciary are made on the advice of the Prime Minister, who is of course head of the elected government. To that extent, the authority of a judge is an upshot of the exercise of elected representative power, and recent American experience shows that occasionally something of an electoral issue can be made of who a Presidential candidate's Supreme Court nominees are likely to be.

But it is not enough to show, as this argument does, a scintilla of democratic respectability in the constitution of judicial power. For that does not show that the courts should have prerogatives that the people and their directly elected representatives lack, nor does it establish that when judicial authority clashes with parliamentary authority, the former ought to prevail. The sponsors of a piece of legislation struck down by a court can also point to a democratic pedigree. They can say, moreover, that if the people disagree with their legislation, they can hold them accountable for it at the next election, throw them out of office, and elect MPs who are pledged to repeal it, and so on. Nothing like that can be said in behalf of the judges.

In other words, the second response goes wrong by failing to see that the issue is essentially a *comparative* one. If a majority of judges in the House of Lords, for example, strikes down legislation passed by majoritarian processes in parliament, then the voting powers of a few judges are being held to prevail over the voting powers of the people's representatives. To provide a *democratic* justification for the judges' prevailing, one has to show not only that they have democratic credentials but that they have a *better* democratic claim than that asserted in the legislative action in question. I don't know of

67. Justice Brandeis, quoted in William Brennan, "Why Have a Bill of Rights?" (1989) 9 *OJLS* 426.

68. Brennan, "Why Have a Bill of Rights?" 426. (These are Brennan's own words now, not those of Brandeis.)

any jurist who can maintain that (with a straight face).[69]

Consider, moreover, how artificial this line of argument is. It is true that judges are appointed by elected officials. But the courts are not, either in their ethos or image, elective institutions, whereas parliament—whatever its imperfections—obviously is. Both in theory and in political practice, the legislature is thought of as the main embodiment of popular government: it is where responsible representatives of the people engage in what they would proudly describe as the self-government of the society. Now there are lots of dignified ways of describing the judiciary, but "locus of representative authority" is unlikely to be one of them. Since my argument is in part about the respect and honour we accord to the people in our constitutional structures, it is important to understand that when a court strikes down a piece of legislation, a branch of the government that neither thinks of itself, nor is thought of, as a representative institution is striking down the act of an institution that is seen in more or less precisely that way.

Thirdly and perhaps most insidiously, it is argued that the objection to judicial power is a weak one, since both legislative and plebiscitary channels are rather imperfect forms of democracy. Now it is certainly true that the processes of election, representation, and legislation, as they actually exist in the United Kingdom, are quite imperfect by democratic standards. The executive dominates the House of Commons, leaving it weak as an independent institution; small or new parties are squeezed out by the plurality system; voters have to choose between whole packages of policies and cannot vote

issue by issue; and as for deliberation, Prime Minister's Question-time and party political broadcasts on television hardly answer to the high-minded account of participation that we developed in Section 8. It is all very well to say that Parliament has a democratic self-image. What are we to say about the numerous ways in which the corrupt reality falls short of this ideal?

We must remember, once again, what that argument is seeking to justify—the disempowerment of ordinary citizens, on matters of the highest moral and political importance. No one ever thought that the imperfection of existing representative institutions was a justification for not enfranchising women, or that in the United States it could be an argument to continue denying political rights to Americans of African descent. If someone were to meet *those* participatory demands with an argument like the one we are currently considering, the move would be rejected immediately as an insult. . . .

The other thing to note about the argument from the imperfections of democracy is that it is still not an argument in favour of judicial power. The imperfection of one institution, by democratic standards, goes no way towards justifying the imperfection of another. One cannot, for example, legitimize the power of the monarchy or the unelected second chamber by pointing to the democratic imperfections of the House of Commons (egregious though they are); for the Lords and the monarchy are even *worse* from a democratic point of view. To empower those institutions is to compound rather than mitigate the imperfections of British democracy. The same applies to the courts. Even if we agree that parliament is not the epitome of democratic decision-making, the question is whether allowing parliamentary decisions to be overridden by the courts makes matters better or worse from a democratic point of view.

Ronald Dworkin has argued that "[i]f we give up the idea that there is a canonical form of democracy, then we must also surrender the idea that judicial review is wrong because it inevitably

---

69. I shall not waste time with the argument that since judges live in the same community as the rest of us and read the newspapers, etc, their views about rights are therefore "informally" in tune with, and representative of, the views prevalent in the community. Even if this is true, the same might be said of any dictator who inhabits the society that she dominates.

compromises democracy."[70] Certainly there is no canonical form of democracy—no final or transcendently given set of answers to the question of what institutions can best embody the popular aspiration to self-government. But the argument against judicial reform does not depend on our access to a democratic canon. It depends solely on the point that, *whatever you say* about your favourite democratic procedures, decision-making on matters of high importance by a small elite that disempowers the people or their elected and accountable representatives is going to score lower than decision-making by the people or their elected and accountable representatives. It *may* score higher in terms of the substantive quality of the decision. But it will not score higher in terms of the respect accorded to ordinary citizens' moral and political capacities.

11 Democratic Self-Restraint

If a Bill of Rights is incorporated into British law it will be because parliament (or perhaps the people in a referendum) will have voted for incorporation. Ronald Dworkin has argued that this fact alone is sufficient to dispose of the democratic objections we have been considering. The objections, in his view, are self-defeating because polls reveal that more than 71 percent of people believe that British democracy would be improved by the incorporation of a Bill of Rights.[71]

However, the matter cannot be disposed of so easily. For one thing, the fact that there is popular support, even overwhelming popular support, for an alteration in constitutional procedures does not show that such alteration therefore makes things more democratic. Certainly, my arguments entail that if the people want a regime of constitutional rights, then that is what they should have: democracy requires

that. But we must not confuse the reason for carrying out a proposal with the character of the proposal itself. If the people wanted to experiment with dictatorship, principles of democracy might give us a reason to allow them to do so. But it would not follow that dictatorship is democratic. Everyone agrees that it is possible for a democracy to vote itself out of existence; that, for the proponents of constitutional reform, is one of their great fears. My worry is that popular support for the constitutional reforms envisaged by Dworkin and other members of Charter 88 amounts to exactly that: voting democracy out of existence, at least so far as a wide range of issues of political principle is concerned.

There *is* a debate going on in Britain about these issues. Citizens are deliberating about whether to limit the powers of parliament and enhance the powers of the judiciary along the lines we have been discussing. One of the things they are considering in this debate is whether such moves will make Britain more or less democratic. This article is intended as a contribution to that debate: I have offered grounds for thinking that this reform will make Britain less of a democracy. What the participants in that debate do *not* need to be told is that constitutional reform will make Britain more democratic if they think it does. For they are trying to work out *what to think* on precisely that issue.

Dworkin also suggests that the democratic argument against a Bill of Rights is self-defeating in a British context, "because a majority of British people themselves rejects the crude statistical view of democracy on which the argument is based."[72] But although democracy connotes the idea of popular voting, it is not part of the concept of democracy that its own content be fixed by popular voting. If a majority of the British people thought a military dictatorship was democratic (because more in tune with the "true spirit of the people" or whatever), that would not show that it was, nor would it provide

---

70. Dworkin, *A Matter of Principle*, 70.

71. Dworkin, *A Bill of Rights for Britain*, 36–37.

72. Ibid., 36.

grounds for saying that democratic arguments against the dictatorship were "self-defeating." If Dworkin wants to make a case against "the crude statistical view" as a conception of democracy, he must argue for it: that is, he must *show* that a system in which millions of votes cast by ordinary people are actually *counted*, and actually *count* for something when decisions are being made against a background of disagreement, is a worse conception of the values set out in section 8 than a model in which votes count only when they accord with a particular theory of what citizens owe one another in the way of equal concern and respect.

However, Dworkin's comments do point the way to what is perhaps a more sophisticated answer to the democratic objection. We are familiar in personal ethics with the idea of "pre-commitment"—the idea that an individual may have reason to impose on herself certain constraints so far as her future decision-making is concerned. Ulysses, for example, decided that he should be bound to the mast in order to resist the charms of the sirens, and he instructed his crew that "if I beg you to release me, you must tighten and add to my bonds."[73] Similarly, a smoker trying to quit may hide her own cigarettes, and a heavy drinker may give her car keys to a friend at the beginning of a party with strict instructions not to return them when they are requested at midnight. These forms of pre-commitment strike us as the epitome of self-governance rather than as a derogation from that ideal. So, similarly, it may be said, an electorate could decide collectively to bind itself in advance to resist the siren charms of rights-violations in the future. Aware, as much as the smoker or the drinker, of the temptations of wrong or irrational action under pressure, the people of a society might in a lucid moment put themselves under certain constitutional disabilities—disabilities which serve the same function in relation to democratic values as strategies like hiding the cigarettes or handing the car keys to a friend serve in relation to the smoker's or the drinker's autonomy.[74]

The analogy is an interesting one, but it is not ultimately persuasive. In the cases of individual pre-commitment, the person is imagined to be quite certain, in her lucid moments, about the actions she wants to avoid and the basis of their undesirability. The smoker knows that smoking is damaging her health and she can give a clear explanation in terms of the pathology of addiction of why she still craves a smoke notwithstanding her possession of that knowledge. The drinker knows at the beginning of the evening that her judgment at midnight about her own ability to drive safely will be seriously impaired. But the case *we* are dealing with is that of a society whose members disagree, even in their "lucid" moments, about what rights they have, how they are to be conceived, and what weight they are to be given in relation to other values. They need not appeal to aberrations in rationality to explain these disagreements; they are, as we have seen, sufficiently explained by the subject-matter itself. A pre-commitment in these circumstances, then, is not the triumph of pre-emptive rationality that it appears to be in the smoker's or in the drinker's case. It is rather the artificially sustained ascendancy of one view in the polity over other views whilst the philosophical issue between them remains unresolved. . . .

Upholding another's pre-commitment may be regarded as a way of respecting her autonomy only if a clear line can be drawn between the aberrant mental phenomena the pre-commitment was supposed to override, on the one hand, and genuine uncertainty, changes of mind, conversions, etc, on the other hand. In the drunk driver case, we can draw such a line; in the theological case, we have much more difficulty, and that is why respecting the pre-commitment seems like taking sides in an inter-

---

73. Quoted in Jon Elster, *Ulysses and the Sirens: Studies in Rationality and Irrationality* (Cambridge: Cambridge University Press, 1984), 36.

---

74. I am grateful to Eric Rakowski for these analogies.

nal dispute between two factions warring on roughly equal terms.

Clearly there are dangers in *any* simplistic analogy between the rational autonomy of individuals and the democratic governance of a community. The idea of a society binding itself against certain legislative acts in the future is particularly problematic in cases where the members of that society disagree with one another about the need for such bonds, or if they agree abstractly about the need, disagree about their content or character. It is particularly problematic where such disagreements can be expected to persist and to develop and change in unpredictable ways. If, moreover, the best explanation of these persisting disagreements is that the issues the society is addressing are just *very difficult issues*, then we have no justification whatever for regarding the temporary ascendancy of one or other party to the disagreement as an instance of full and rational pre-commitment on the part of the entire society. In these circumstances, the logic of pre-commitment must simply be put aside, and we must leave the members of the society to work out their differences and to change their minds in collective decision-making over time, the best way they can.

---

13   Conclusion

It is odd that people expect theorists of rights to support the institutionalization of a Bill of Rights and the introduction of American-style practices of judicial review. All modern theories of rights claim to respect the capacity of ordinary men and women to govern their own lives on terms that respect the equal capacities of others. It is on this basis that we argue for things like freedom of worship, the right to life and liberty, free speech, freedom of contract, the right to property, freedom of emigration, privacy and reproductive freedoms. It would be curious if nothing followed from these underlying ideas

so far as the governance of the community was concerned. Most theories of rights commit themselves also to democratic rights: the right to participate in the political process through voting, speech, activism, party association, and candidacy. I have argued that these rights are in danger of being abrogated by the sort of proposals put forward by members of Charter 88 in the United Kingdom.

The matter is one of great importance. People fought long and hard for the vote and for democratic representation. They wanted the right to govern themselves, not just on mundane issues of policy, but also on high matters of principle. They rejected the Platonic view that the people are incapable of thinking through issues of justice. Consider the struggles there have been, in Britain, Europe and America—first for the abolition of property qualifications, secondly for the extension of the franchise to women, and thirdly, for bringing the legacy of civil rights denials to an end in the context of American racism. In all those struggles, people have paid tribute to the democratic aspiration to self-governance, without any sense at all that it should confine itself to the interstitial quibbles of policy that remain to be settled after some lawyerly elite have decided the main issues of principle.

These thoughts, I have argued, are reinforced when we consider how much room there is for honest and good faith disagreement among citizens on the topic of rights. Things might be different if principles of right were self-evident or if there were a philosophical elite who could be trusted to work out once and for all what rights we have and how they are to be balanced against other considerations. But the consensus of the philosophers is that these matters are not settled, that they are complex and controversial, and that certainly in the seminar room the existence of good faith disagreement is undeniable. Since that is so, it seems to me obvious that we should view the disagreements about rights that exist among citizens in exactly the same light, unless there is compelling evidence to the contrary. It is no doubt possible that a citizen or an elected politician who disagrees with my view of rights is motivated purely by self-interest. But it is somewhat uncomfortable to recognize that she probably entertains exactly the same thought about me. Since the issue of rights before us remains controversial, there seems no better reason to adopt my view of rights as definitive and dismiss her opposition as self-interested, than to regard me as the selfish opponent and her as the defender of principle.

Of course such issues have got to be settled. If I say P has a right to X and my opponent disagrees, some process has got to be implemented to determine whether P is to get X or not. P and people like her cannot be left waiting for our disagreements to resolve themselves. One of us at least will be dissatisfied by the answer that the process comes up with, and it is possible that the answer may be wrong. But the existence of that possibility—which is, as we have seen, an important truth about all human authority—should not be used, as it is so often, exclusively to discredit the democratic process. There is always something bad about the denial of one's rights. But there is nothing specially bad about the denial of rights at the hands of a majority of one's fellow citizens.

In the end, I think, the matter comes down to this. If a process is democratic and comes up with the correct result, it does no injustice to anyone. But if the process is non-democratic, it inherently and necessarily does an injustice, in its operation, to the participatory aspirations of the ordinary citizen. And it does *this* injustice, tyrannizes in *this* way, whether it comes up with the correct result or not.

One of my aims in all this has been to "disaggregate" our concepts of democracy and majority rule. Instead of talking in grey and abstract terms about democracy, we should focus our attention on the individuals—the millions of men and women—who claim a right to a say, on equal terms, in the processes by which they are governed. Instead of talking impersonally about

"the counter-majoritarian difficulty," we should distinguish between a court's deciding things by a majority, and lots and lots of ordinary men and women deciding things by a majority. If we do this, we will see that the question "Who gets to participate?" always has priority over the question "How do they decide, when they disagree?"

Above all, when we think about taking certain issues away from the people and entrusting them to the courts, we should adopt the same individualist focus that we use for thinking about any other issue of rights. Someone concerned about rights does not see social issues in impersonal terms: she does not talk about "the problem of torture" or "the problem of censorship" but about the predicament of each and every individual who may be tortured or silenced by the State. Similarly, we should think not about "the people" or "the majority," as some sort of blurred quantitative mass, but of the individual citizens, considered one by one, who make up the polity in question.

If we are going to defend the idea of an entrenched Bill of Rights put effectively beyond revision by anyone other than the judges, we should try and think what we might say to some public-spirited citizen who wishes to launch a campaign or lobby her MP on some issue of rights about which she feels strongly and on which she has done her best to arrive at a considered and impartial view. She is not asking to be a dictator; she perfectly accepts that her voice should have no more power than that of anyone else who is prepared to participate in politics. But—like her suffragette forebears—she wants a vote; she wants her voice and her activity to count on matters of high political importance.

In defending a Bill of Rights, we have to imagine ourselves saying to her: "You may write to the newspaper and get up a petition and organize a pressure group to lobby Parliament. But even if you succeed, beyond your wildest dreams, and orchestrate the support of a large number of like-minded men and women, and manage to prevail in the legislature, your measure may be challenged and struck down because your view of what rights we have does not accord with the judges' view. When their votes differ from yours, theirs are the votes that will prevail." It is my submission that saying this does not comport with the respect and honour normally accorded to ordinary men and women in the context of a theory of rights.

The Political Origins of Judicial Empowerment through Constitutionalization: Lessons from Four Constitutional Revolutions

Ran Hirschl

The constitutionalization of rights has recently become a booming industry. Many countries and several supranational entities (e.g., the European Union) have engaged in fundamental constitutional reform over the past three decades.[1] Significantly, nearly every recently adopted constitution or constitutional revision contains a bill of rights and establishes some form of active judicial review.[2] In most countries in which a constitutional bill of rights has been recently enacted, there has been an increasing intrusion of the judiciary into the prerogatives of legislatures and executives and a corresponding acceleration of the process whereby political agendas have been judicialized, thus bringing about a growing reliance on adjudicative means for clarifying and settling crucial public policy issues and normative debates (Tate and Vallinder 1995).[3] These global trends have been described by scholars as "one of the most significant developments in comparative politics" (Gibson, Caldeira, and Baird 1998, 343) and

Excerpted from: Ran Hirschl, "The Political Origins of Judicial Empowerment through Constitutionalization: Lessons from Four Constitutional Revolutions." *Law and Social Inquiry: Journal of the American Bar Foundation* 25, no. 1 (2000): 91–149. © 2000 American Bar Foundation. Reprinted by permission.

1. A partial list of countries that have undergone fundamental constitutional reform since the early 1970s includes new democracies in Eastern Europe (e.g., Hungary 1990, Romania 1991, Bulgaria 1991, Poland 1992, the Czech Republic 1993, Russia 1993, Slovakia 1993); new democracies in Southern Europe (e.g., Greece 1975, Portugal 1976; Spain 1978, Turkey 1982); new democracies in Africa (e.g., Mozambique 1990, Zambia 1991, Uganda 1992, Ghana 1993, Ethiopia 1995, South Africa 1993 and 1996); new independent countries in Africa (e.g., Zimbabwe 1980, Namibia 1990, Eritrea 1993); other African countries (e.g., Egypt 1980); Asian countries and territories (e.g., Sri Lanka 1978, the Philippines 1987; Hong Kong 1991, Vietnam 1992, Cambodia 1993); Pacific Islands (e.g., Papua New-Guinea 1975, Solomon Islands 1978, Cook Islands 1981, Niue 1994, Fiji 1998); Latin American countries (e.g., Chile 1980, Nicaragua 1987, Brazil 1988, Colombia 1991, Peru 1993, Bolivia 1994); and industrialized democracies (e.g., Sweden 1975, Canada 1982, Israel 1992, New Zealand 1990 and 1993). For comprehensive surveys see Maddox (1995); and Blaustein and Flanz (1998).

2. E.g., Canada adopted a Charter of Rights in 1982. Brazil adopted a Bill of Rights in 1988. New Zealand adopted a Bill of Rights in 1990, and Hong Kong did so in 1991. Almost all the new democracies in Eastern Europe adopted bills of basic rights as part of their new constitutions. Israel adopted Basic Laws on human rights in 1992. Peru adopted a Bill of Rights in 1993. Denmark adopted the European Convention on Human Rights in 1993, and Sweden did so in 1995. South Africa adopted a Bill of Rights as part of its new constitution in 1993. Even Britain, the last bastion of the Westminster system, has embarked on a comprehensive overhaul of its political institutions. This overhaul is most notably marked by the newly elected Labour Government's consideration of a bill of rights to formally incorporate the provisions of the European Convention for the Protection of Human Rights and Fundamental Freedoms into British constitutional law. On November 9, 1998, the proposed Human Rights Act gained royal assent. This enshrined the act in law and marked the first rights legislation to be introduced in the United Kingdom in 300 years.

3. Substantive judicial review is almost always related to the existence of a justiciable bill of rights. If the constitution does not provide rights for individuals against the state, judicial review is often confined to procedural matters. Ordinarily, the probability of intervention by the judiciary into highly political, or politicized, issues is rather low in these circumstances. The existence of a constitutional bill of rights in a polity, on the other hand, provides the necessary institutional conditions for judicial review to expand its boundaries to encompass substantive political issues central to that polity. The rise of a "politics of rights" following the constitutionalization of rights further facilitates the process whereby political disputes are judicialized.

as "one of the most significant trends in late-twentieth and early-twenty-first-century government" (Tate and Vallinder 1995, 5).

Despite the fact that judicial power has recently been expanded in many countries through the constitutional entrenchment of rights and the establishment of judicial review, very few studies have thoroughly examined the political vectors behind the recent global wave of judicial empowerment....

Three broad categories of constitutionalization have been most common in the past three decades. In some countries constitutionalization was part of a dual transition to democracy and market economy (e.g., countries in the Eastern Bloc). In other countries, constitutionalization of rights and the expansion of judicial power were byproducts of a transition to democracy (e.g., South Africa, several Latin American countries in the 1980s, and a number of southern European countries in the late 1970s). In many other countries, the constitutionalization of rights has neither been accompanied by, nor has resulted from, fundamental changes in political or economic regime (e.g., Canada 1982, Belgium 1985, New Zealand 1990, and Israel 1992). Most if not all constitutional revolutions of the two latter types have taken place in societies deeply divided along political, economic, or ethnic lines.[5] This article seeks to offer a coherent explanation for the seemingly counterintuitive, voluntary delegation of policymaking authority from legislatures and executives to judiciaries through constitutionalization of rights in internally fragmented polities....

5. To these three common constitutionalization one might add, of course, the domestic constitutionalization of rights through supranational treaties and its impact upon constitutional reforms in member countries of such supranational regimes (as in the recent enactment in the United Kingdom of the Human Rights Act, 1998, or the incorporation of the ECHR provisions into domestic law in Denmark in 1993 and in Sweden in 1995).

Since judiciaries and national high courts possess neither military nor financial power and do not bring much leverage to negotiations with the other branches of government, the question arises of how we can explain judicial empowerment in relatively open polities that were not subject to comprehensive changes in the political or economic regimes. The removal of policymaking authority from legislatures and executives and its investiture in the courts through the enactment of constitutional catalogues of rights and the establishment of judicial review seems, prima facie, to run counter to the interests of power holders in legislatures and executives.

I suggest that neither the institutional fortification of judiciaries nor the accelerated judicialization of politics that often follows it develop in isolation from the central political struggles and interests that structure political systems. Political power holders usually attempt to shape the institutional structure within which they operate so that it best suits their interests. Since institutions such as bills of rights and judiciaries do not possess independent enforcement power but nonetheless limit the flexibility of decision makers, those who establish such institutions must generally think it serves their interests to abide by the limits imposed by them. In other words, those who are eager to pay the price of judicial empowerment assume that their position vis-a-vis other political forces would be improved under a "juristocracy."

Hence, the process of judicial empowerment through the constitutionalization of rights may accelerate when the hegemony of ruling elites in majoritarian decision-making arenas is threatened by "peripheral" groups. As such threats become severe, hegemonic elites who possess disproportionate access to and influence upon the legal arena may initiate a constitutional entrenchment of rights in order to transfer power to the courts. This process of conscious judicial empowerment in relatively open, rule-of-law polities is likely to occur when the judiciary's public reputation for political impartiality and rectitude is relatively high and when the courts are likely to rule, by and large, in accordance with the cultural propensities of the hegemonic community. In other words, judicial empowerment through the constitutional fortification of rights may provide an efficient institutional way for hegemonic sociopolitical forces to preserve their hegemony and to secure their policy preferences even when majoritarian decision-making processes are not operating to their advantage. . . .

II. The Hegemonic Preservation Thesis

My explanation for judicial empowerment as based on the struggle for hegemony suggests that legal innovators, that is, politicians, representing cultural and economic elites, in cooperation with the legal elite, determine the timing, extent, and nature of constitutional reforms. Legal innovations are, in other words, products of the interplay between hegemonic elites (and their political representatives) and the legal profession. Political actors representing hegemonic social and economic forces usually attempt to shape the legal system to suit their interests. To do so effectively in rule-of-law societies, they must secure the cooperation of the legal elite to whom the political elite often have close social ties. The changes that emerge reflect a combination of political and economic preferences and professional interests. To be sure, demands for constitutional change often emanate from various groups within the body politic, but if hegemonic political and economic elites, their parliamentary representatives, and the legal elite do not forecast gain from a proposed change, the change is likely to be blocked (Horowitz 1994, 251; Watson 1983).

Moreover, because institutions such as judicial review (and other semi-autonomous institutions such as central banks, transnational trade organizations, international monetary funds, and supranational tribunals) limit the flexibility of decision makers, and because such institutions carry no arms and hold no independent purse strings, it must be in the interest of actors who establish such institutions and protect their autonomy to abide by the limits imposed by those institutions. When the establishment of judicial review is initiated by those whose prima facie decision-making flexibility it is likely to limit, the most plausible assumption is that those who initiated the reform, or who consciously refrained from blocking it despite having the power to do so, estimate that the reform will enhance their relative power vis-a-vis other elements in the political system.[15] Thus, political actors who establish self-enforcing institutions such as constitutions and judicial review, and the hegemonic elites who actively support or refrain from blocking such reforms, assume that their costs under the new institutional structure will prove less expensive than the limits the new institutional structure will impose on rival political elements.[16]

15. The now classic argument of North and Weingast (1989) illustrates this point. According to them, the self-constraining of a ruler's arbitrary authority to confiscate wealth was the key political factor underpinning economic growth and the development of markets in early capitalist Europe. Making credible commitments through self-enforcing institutional mechanisms (such as developing private property rights enforceable in parliament and removing the ruler's control of the judiciary) established the legal security of expectations and allowed rulers to borrow capital from lenders who were protected by law from arbitrary seizure of their capital. In other words, by constraining themselves by establishing new institutions that limited, prima facie, their flexibility, rulers were able to maintain their long-term economic survival.

16. My argument here finds striking parallels in the literature regarding the political sources of empowerment of other semi-autonomous institutions similar in nature to the judicial review of bills of rights, such as central banks and supranational tribunals. For example, in her study of the political sources of central bank authority in developing countries, Sylvia Maxfield (1994, 1997) argues that the interests and capacities of

When their hegemony is increasingly challenged in majoritarian decision-making arenas, powerful elites and their political representatives may deliberately initiate and support a constitutionalization of rights in order to transfer power to supreme courts, where they assume, based primarily on the courts' record of adjudication and on the justices' ideological preferences, that their policy preferences will be less contested. In other words, increasing judicial intrusion into the prerogatives of the legislature and the executive following the enactment of constitutional bills of rights may provide an efficient institutional solution for influential sociopolitical groups who seek to preserve their hegemony vis-a-vis marginalized minority groups and who, given an erosion in their popular support, may find strategic drawbacks in adhering to majoritarian decision-making processes.

The judicialization of politics through the constitutionalization of rights and the empowerment of courts may serve the interests of political power holders in at least four principal ways. First, hegemonic elites, as well as political and economic power holders who possess dispropor-

tionate access to and influence upon the legal environment, may promote their interests by transferring political disputes from majoritarian decision-making arenas, in which particularistic interests are often attributed to individual participants, to the professional judiciary, whose actions seem to be circumscribed by objective rules. These transfers take advantage of the expertise, rectitude, and political impartiality often attributed to courts.

The second way that political power holders may profit from an increasing judicialization of politics is that politicians may encourage a transfer of power to the judiciary in order to divert responsibility to the court. This institutional transfer reduces the possible costs of their own involvement in potential public blunders as well as the risk that their policy preferences will be challenged in majoritarian policymaking arenas. From the politicians' point of view, the courts may be an effective means of reducing the risk to themselves and to the institutional apparatus within which they operate. Delegating policymaking to courts may become even more attractive for political power holders when disputes arise that most of them would rather not address publicly, either because they present "no-win" dilemmas, such as the dispute about abortion policy in the United States (Graber 1993) or because politicians regard public disputes in majoritarian policymaking fora as likely to put their own policy preferences at risk. Under such conditions, empowering national high courts may serve the interests of the political status quo by transferring public responsibility for policymaking and by insulating policymaking from popular political pressures.

Third, as specific groups (primarily economic elites) that possess disproportionate access to the legal environment discover the potential usefulness of the courts to maximize their objectives, they become more enthusiastic about expanding the legal understanding of human rights to include interests that may appear to some to be only remotely connected to any constitutional

---

early central banking institutions in such countries are shaped by the financial interests of those in a position to delegate authority to central banks: government politicians and private banks. Another example is the "intergovernmentalist" thesis, which suggests that member states are the central institution builders of the European Community and that they provide autonomy to the European Court of Justice to serve their own purposes. According to this approach, member states choose to create (and selectively abide by the limits imposed by) supranational institutions, because these institutions help them surmount problems raised by the need for collective action and overcome domestic political problems. The political power version of this thesis suggests that national governments from the EU member states have not been passive and unwilling victims of European legal integration. They consciously delegated power to the European Court of Justice, and where the court has been pro-active, the member governments have supported this. See Garrett et al. (1998); Garrett (1992).

foundation in a formal bill of rights.[17] Influential coalitions of domestic neoliberal economic forces (e.g., powerful industrialists and economic conglomerates given added impetus by global economic trends) may view constitutionalization of rights (especially property, mobility, and occupational rights) as a means to promote economic deregulation and to fight what its members often understand to be harmful "large government" policies of the encroaching state.

The delegation of power to the courts may also serve both the interests of a professional legal elite seeking to enhance its symbolic power and the interests of a supreme court seeking to enhance its political influence and international profile. National high courts may primarily be seekers of legal policy, but they are also sophisticated and strategic actors who may realize when the changing preferences of other influential political actors as well as changes in the institutional context allow them to strengthen their institutional position by widening and deepening their involvement in crucial policymaking arenas. As recent studies have shown (Epstein and Knight 1998; Epstein and Walker 1995), landmark decisions of the U.S. Supreme Court, for example, have not merely been apolitical jurisprudence or a reflection of its justices' ideological preferences but also a reflection of their strategic behavior as rational actors who

seek to preserve or improve the Court's institutional position vis-a-vis other major national decision-making bodies. The striving of the legal elite and the judiciary to enhance their power is especially likely to be an important factor in instituting a judicial review in a polity whose legal establishment and political personnel are drawn from the same social groups. Moreover, the constitutionalization of rights may support the interests of a supreme court seeking to increase its symbolic power by fostering its alignment with the growing community of liberal democratic nations engaged in rights-based discourse.

Having shown that there are distinct groups whose ability to gain or maintain power and influence for themselves is contingent upon judicial empowerment through the constitutionalization of rights, it is clear that my interest-based hegemonic struggle explanation does not depend upon the existence of any systemic social need. Nor does this movement assume any necessary evolution in a progressive direction. Such movement is not deterministic but is actor oriented and, unlike extant microfoundational theories of judicial independence, it does not depend upon the competitiveness of the party system.

III. The "Constitutional Revolution" in Israel as an Illustrative Case

The 1992 constitutional revolution in Israel presents a nearly ideal illustration of my explanation of judicial empowerment. The hands that guided the constitutionalization of rights and the establishment of judicial review in Israel are entirely visible. They were driven by purely political interests not by their subordination to some invisible evolutionist or structural forces or by the devotion of politicians to some elevated vision of human rights or national unity.

The 1992 constitutional entrenchment of rights and the establishment of judicial review in Israel were initiated and supported by politicians representing Israel's secular bourgeoisie,

---

17. E.g., the extension of some constitutional human rights protections (e.g., freedom of expression, property rights, search and seizure, due process rights, occupational rights, and mobility rights) to business corporations, which often draw upon those rights in challenging various governmental regulatory measures (e.g., claims for protection of commercial speech under freedom of expression constitutional provisions, claims against taxation in general and income tax in particular based on constitutional provisions protecting property rights, claims against state monitoring and licensing of various professions or against regulatory environmental laws based on freedom of occupation constitutional provisions, claims against marketing quotas based on freedom of occupation and freedom of movement constitutional provisions).

whose political hegemony in the majoritarian policymaking arena had become increasingly threatened. The political representatives of this group found the delegation of policymaking authority to the court an efficient way to overcome the growing popular backlash against its ideological hegemony and, perhaps more importantly, an efficient way to avoid the potentially negative consequences of its continuously declining control over the majoritarian decision-making arena.

The intentional empowerment of the judiciary by the secular bourgeoisie in Israel was also supported by neoliberal economic forces in Israeli society (mainly powerful industrialists and economic conglomerates) who have used basic law litigation since 1992 to promote their own material interests (Hirschl 1998; Gross 1998; Marmor 1997). These forces joined the representatives of the (mainly) Ashkenazi secular high-income group to create an influential coalition that initiated and advocated the delegation of policymaking authority to the judiciary.[18] While the secular bourgeoisie was motivated by serious popular challenges to its political and cultural hegemony and by its parliamentary representatives' growing political dependence upon representatives of marginalized groups in the Israeli society, the economic elite supported the delegation of power to courts as a means to fight what its members understood to be the regulated market, large government, and policies of the encroaching state (Hirschl 1999)....

Although the judicialization of politics in Israel began in the mid-1980s, it accelerated significantly in the aftermath of the constitutional revolution of 1992. Until 1992, the Knesset retained formal legislative powers that only a few parliaments in democratic countries (e.g., the United Kingdom and New Zealand) still held

during the same period; after the enactment of the new Basic Laws in 1992, however, the balance of powers between the branches changed, enabling the Supreme Court to begin scrutinizing legislative and administrative acts.

The seemingly counterintuitive voluntary delegation of authority from the Knesset to the judiciary through the entrenchment of rights and the establishment of judicial review decreased the significance of majoritarian politics in determining the public policy agenda and gradually transferred the locus of political struggle to a seemingly apolitical arena, where the ideology of the "enlightened public"—the ruling elite of Israel and its Ashkenazi, secular bourgeois constituency—has traditionally enjoyed a clear dominance. This alliance between the Supreme Court, the neoliberal economic elite, and the secular bourgeoisie initiated the constitutional revolution and the transition to "juristocracy," not as a means for protecting human rights in Israel or as a solution to a systemic ungovernability crisis but simply as a way to protect its hegemony and to promote the policies favored by its members.

IV. Factors Facilitating the Delegation of Power to Courts

In general, two factors may facilitate conscious judicial empowerment and *reduce the short-term risk* of those who voluntarily hand policymaking authority over to the judiciary. The first condition is a sufficient level of certainty among those initiating the transition to juristocracy that the judiciary in general and the supreme court in particular are likely to produce decisions that, by and large, will better serve their interests and reflect their ideological preferences. In this regard, a growing body of literature tends to refute the proposition that supreme courts are simply guardians of the rule of law without any other complementary or contradictory political interests. According to this body of literature, supreme courts are inclined to rule in accordance

---

18. Also among the forces that publicly supported Israel's constitutional revolution were the country's major economic organizations, such as the Chambers of Commerce and Manufacturing, and leading economic figures.

with national metanarratives, prevailing ideological and cultural propensities, and the interests of ruling elites (Smith 1997; Knight and Epstein 1996; Epstein and Walker 1995; Mishler and Sheehan 1993; Koh 1988; Tushnet 1988; Dahl 1957). There is quite decisive evidence showing that the U.S. Supreme Court, for example, has been inclined to adapt itself to hegemonic ideological and cultural propensities.[34] As Robert Dahl observes, "it is unrealistic to suppose that a Court whose members are recruited in the fashion of the Supreme Court justices would long hold to norms of justice that are substantially at odds with the rest of the political elite" (Dahl 1957, 291). The Court may be "the forum of principle" in American life, as Ronald Dworkin argues (1990), but the principles that justices articulate, Dahl and others point out, are likely to be those favored by members of the existing lawmaking majority (Graber 1993, 36). The adjudication of the Israeli Supreme Court is, to say the least, no exception to this pattern....

A second condition that *reduces the short-term risk* for those who voluntarily hand power over to courts is the existence of widespread public trust in the political impartiality of the judiciary. The appearance of political dependence would collapse the distinction between law and politics on which the fundamental legitimacy of separation of powers system depends (Gibson, Caldeira, and Baird 1998; Mishler and Sheehan 1993)....

V. Some Possible Unintended Consequences of Intentional Judicial Empowerment

Having discussed two factors that may encourage conscious judicial empowerment by reducing the short-term risk of those who voluntarily hand over policymaking authority to national high courts, an important caveat should be entered. Political power holders tend to be myopic, seeking to advance their particularistic short-term interests even at the expense of potentially unfavorable long-term consequences to the institutional apparatus within which they operate. Moreover, political power holders tend to underestimate the unfavorable long-term consequences of the policies they advocate, especially when their immediate gain from adopting these policies is significant. Politics, however, is an ongoing, multidimensional, and reflective environment that may yield unintended consequences even for carefully designed institutions and policies. At least two such possible *unintended long-term consequences* of the judicialization of politics through the constitutionalization of rights and the establishment of judicial review come to mind.

First, while the delegation of policymaking authority to courts increases the courts' formal capacity for active participation in the political arena in the short term, the abrupt change in the balance of power between the judicial branch and other branches of government may have a negative long-term effect on the popular legitimacy accorded to the courts' decisions. Courts have historically enjoyed professional autonomy and a large measure of protection from political interference; however, as they exercise their newly awarded authority, they may come to be seen as active political bodies trying to forward their own political agendas, rather than neutral arbiters. The delegation of power to courts may therefore pose a long-term threat to the legitimacy, impartiality, and independence of the judiciary.

The negative impact of the judicialization of politics in Israel on its Supreme court's legitimacy is not merely theoretical. Over the past five years, there has been an increasing erosion of the public image of the Israeli Supreme Court as an autonomous and politically impartial arbiter as the political representatives of minority groups have come to realize that political arrangements

---

34. The literature on this issue is too vast to cite. Two recent examples are Smith (1997) and Kairys (1998).

and public policies agreed upon in majoritarian decision-making arenas are likely to be thoroughly reviewed by an often hostile Supreme Court. As a result, the court and its judges are increasingly viewed by a considerable portion of the Israeli public as pushing forward their own political agenda, one identified primarily with the secular-liberal segment of the Israeli society (Avnon 1996, Hofnung 1996b). . . .

A second possible unintended long-term consequence of judicial empowerment through the establishment of judicial review that myopic and threatened elites are likely to underestimate is the irreversibility of the constitutionalization process in rule-of-law democracies. As the history of constitutionalism teaches us, constitutions are difficult to amend or reform after their enactment, so that an entrenched constitution seems to acquire a "life of its own." The delegation of power to courts through constitutionalization may prove to be an irreversible process. While increasing judicial intrusion into the prerogatives of the legislature and the executive through the constitutionalization of rights and the fortification of judicial review may provide a short-term institutional solution for influential elites—who, given an erosion in their popular support, may find strategic drawbacks in adhering to majoritarian decision-making processes—it may also establish long-term limitations on the institutional room for maneuvering that political power holders possess. Hence, intentional judicial empowerment through constitutionalization may create an undesirable institutional setting for the ruling elites and their constituencies in the long term. Minority groups may learn to draw upon the new constitutional framework to advance their policy preferences by presenting them as rights claims. But perhaps more important, it may bring about an embedded institutional obstacle to the reduction of the court's significance as a major national policymaking body, which may pose problems if the political incentive structure that encouraged the delegation of power to the judiciary changes.

In summary, the empowerment of courts in Israel through the constitutional revolution of 1992 marked an abrupt change in the balance of power between the judiciary, the legislature, and the executive. While the legislative and executive branches of government enjoyed clear dominance as Israel's most important policymaking arenas until the late-1980s, in Israel's post-constitutional revolution era there is hardly a public policy question that does not sooner or later turn into a judicial question (to paraphrase de Tockville's often-cited observation regarding the American political system). At first glance, this shift may seem to run counter to the interests of the legislature and the executive. In practice, however, a coalition of Knesset members representing a relatively coherent social class composed of Israel's political, cultural, and economic elites initiated and promoted the entrenchment of rights and the establishment of judicial review in Israel in 1992. The primary motivation for this initiative, as I have shown, was a strong interest in preserving the political and cultural hegemony of the ruling elite and its secular bourgeois constituency. Indeed, the constitutional revolution of 1992 generated an extensive judicialization of politics in Israel and enhanced values and policies favored by those who initiated the reform at the expense of ideological and policy preferences of peripheral groups. Relying, on the one hand, on the Israeli Supreme Court's reputation for rectitude and political impartiality and, on the other hand, on the court's inclination to rule in accordance with the values of the "enlightened public," the forces behind Israel's constitutional revolution were able to transfer sensitive political and cultural issues to the legal arena and reduce some of the growing costs they were forced to pay when complying with the rules of the game of proportional political representation. While the delegation of policymaking authority to the judiciary bought short-term political relief for Israel's ruling elite and its bourgeois constituency, the unprecedented judicialization of politics also brought about a gradual politicization of the law and hence unintentionally planted the seeds of a long-term erosion of the judiciary's legitimacy, as well of the ruling elite's future institutional room for political maneuvering.

VI. The Hegemonic Preservation Thesis in Other Politics

My explanation for the conscious judicial empowerment in Israel may shed light on the political rationale behind judicial empowerment through constitutionalization in other polities as well. In the following pages I briefly demonstrate the contribution of the "hegemonic struggle" thesis to the understanding of constitutional politics in Canada, New Zealand, and South Africa.

Canada

The Canadian Constitution Act of 1982 includes a bill-of-rights-type document titled the Charter of Rights and Freedoms. The enactment of the Constitution Act marked the official patriation of the Canadian constitution from the authority of the British Crown after a 115-year-long process, which started with the enactment of the Constitution Act in 1867. The adoption of the Charter of Rights and Freedoms, which constitutes the first 34 sections of the Constitution Act, also marked a dramatic change in the *de jure* status of rights and liberties in Canada and provided the necessary institutional framework for an extensive judicialization of politics in Canada over the past 15 years (Manfredi 1997; Bakan 1997; Mandel 1994; Bogart 1994). Since the enactment of the charter in 1982, the Canadian Supreme Court has become one of the most important decision-making fora with regard to the contentious issues of Canadian politics—the rights of indigenous people, language politics, gender equality, and the political and cultural status of Quebec. In 1992, 10 years after the charter came into force, Chief Justice Lamer of the Canadian Supreme Court declared that "the

introduction of the Charter has been nothing less than a revolution on the scale of the introduction of the metric system, the great medical discoveries of Louis Pasteur, and the invention of penicillin and the laser" (Lamer 1992, A11)....

As in Israel, the delegation of authority to the Canadian Supreme Court has also depended on the court's inclination to rule, by and large, in accordance with hegemonic ideological and cultural propensities. On the basis of a customary constitutional convention, the judges of the Canadian Supreme Court are nominated to the bench according to a "provincially representative" key, whereby three justices represent Ontario, three come from Quebec, two from the western provinces (one is usually from British Columbia), and one from the Maritime provinces. The selection and nomination process itself, however, is controlled exclusively by the federal government and by the prime minister. The judges selected through this explicitly political nomination process are not likely to hold policy preferences substantially at odds with those held by the rest of the political elite.

Indeed, in its federalism jurisprudence over the past decades, the Supreme Court of Canada tended, by and large, to adopt values and policies favored by the national government at the expense of undermining the policy autonomy of the provinces. Moreover, as recent analyses of the interpretations of the charter by the Canadian Supreme Court point out, the chief beneficiaries of charter politics and litigation have been hegemonic ideas of formal equality, "negative" liberty, and social atomism rather than "peripheral" interests and ideas (Hirschl 2000; Bakan 1997; Beatty 1997; Hutchinson 1995; Bogart 1994; Mandel 1994; Scott and Macklem 1992). In sum, despite the dissimilarities between the Canadian and Israeli sociopolitical scenes and legacies of constitutional politics, there are striking parallels in the political rationales that supported judicial empowerment through constitutionalization in the two countries.

New Zealand

Only 15 years ago, New Zealand's political system was described by leading political scientists as "a virtually perfect example of the Westminster model of democracy" and as "the only example of the British majoritarian democracy system left" (Lijphart 1984, 19). The enactment of the New Zealand Bill of Rights Act in 1990 marked an abrupt change in the balance of power between, on the one hand, the judiciary and, on the other, the legislature and the executive (which were important policymaking arenas until the late-1980s) and symbolized the demise of the "last Westminster system" (Lijphart 1987). The driving force behind the 1990 constitutionalization of rights in New Zealand was a coalition of the disparate sections of a threatened elite seeking to preserve its power and economic actors who were pushing for neoliberal economic reforms. . . .

Although the Bill of Rights does not formally empower the courts to nullify legislation inconsistent with its provisions, the courts are required to interpret ambiguous laws in a manner consistent with the act, and there are clear signs that the New Zealand Court of Appeal may simply be giving it a de facto entrenched status.[67] Moreover, it has acquired a de facto constitutional status as a politically, if not legally, entrenched document and has therefore become an important catalyst for the judicialization of politics in New Zealand. Thus, the Bill of rights has been recognized by scholars as finally establishing an effective guarantee for the protection of New Zealand residents' individual rights and liberties (Richardson 1995; Rishworth 1995, 1996; Joseph 1996). Perhaps this is why Sir Ivor Richardson of the Court of Appeal of New Zealand has recently declared that "[f]uture historians may recognize the Bill of Rights as one of the most important statutes ever enacted in New Zealand" (Richardson 1995, 75).

Following the enactment of the NZBOR, New Zealand's judiciary in general, and the court of appeal in particular, have gradually become important political actors dealing with the salient political issues on New Zealand's public agenda (e.g., Maori rights and land claims, immigration policy, and the extensive privatization of public services). This appears to match the expectation of the act's author (Geoffrey Palmer) that the Bill of Rights, though nonentrenched, would gradually acquire sufficient legal and political authority to allow the courts to exercise at least some of the powers of scrutiny and control that they would have had under a system of full-scale judicial review (Joseph 1998).

In sum, the enactment of the NZBOR, along with other new laws such as the Human Rights Act of 1993 and the Privacy Act of 1993,[68] was intended to elevate the traditional set of classic civil liberties to the status of prime constitutional rights and to empower New Zealand's judiciary by delegating policymaking authority from Parliament to the Court of Appeal.[69] Not surprisingly then, the judicial elite and the oligarchy of

---

67. In a recent verdict, the court observed that lack of entrenchment and constitutional status "makes no difference to the strength of the Bill of Rights where it is to be applied." See *Simpson v. Attorney General* (1994) 3 NZLR 667, 706. This and other recent decisions of the Court of Appeal indicate that the Bill of Rights, though unentrenched, may gradually gain sufficient legal and political authority to allow the courts to practically exercise most of the powers of scrutiny and control they would have had under a system of full-scale judicial review.

68. The Human Rights Act 1993 prohibits discrimination on the basis of sex, marital status, religious belief, ethical belief, color, race, ethnic or national origin, disability, age, political opinion, employment status or family status. The Privacy Act 1993 aims to protect individuals by regulating the disclosure of information about them. For a detailed discussion of the new legal regime protecting rights and liberties in New Zealand, see the essays in Rishworth (1995).

69. For a comprehensive discussion of the bill's operational provisions and a survey of the adjudication related to the bill, see Joseph (1996).

wealth and political power, seeking to preserve their hegemony and to increase their impact on policymaking outcomes, quickly endorsed the constitutional change, while opposition to the enactment of the NZBOR came mainly from leftist opponents of privatization and from Maori activists who perceived the enactment as a threat to the status of the Treaty of Waitangi and to the success of future Maori land claims.[70]

South Africa

Yet another confirmation of the hegemonic preservation thesis is the struggle of South Africa's white ruling elite during the late-1980s and early-1990s to ensure the inclusion of an entrenched bill of rights and active constitutional court in the postapartheid political pact in South Africa.[71] Prior to the enactment of the 1993 interim Bill of Rights (replaced by the final Bill of Rights in 1996), there was perhaps no other country in the postwar world in which the gap between popular will and constitutional arrangements was quite so wide. Up until that

year, South Africa excluded over 80% of its population from participation in the democratic political game, while parliamentary sovereignty was strictly adhered to. Calls for entrenched rights and for the establishment of active judicial review were strongly and consistently opposed by the ruling elites of South Africa throughout the twentieth century. Throughout the early-1980s, for example, the National Party leaders insisted that a bill of rights should not form part of any future constitutional order in South Africa, arguing that an emphasis on "individual interests" would be inconsistent with the political and religious tradition of Afrikaanerdom which preferred to emphasize "the State" over "individual interests." The strong anti-judicial-review position of the ruling elites echoed President Kruger's famous declaration that the power of the courts to test legislation was "a principle invented by the Devil!" (Cockrell 1997, 518).

But when it became obvious in the late-1980s that the apartheid regime could not be sustained by repression, the incentive structure of the white minority rapidly changed, and a sudden conversion to the supposed virtues of a bill of rights occurred. Not surprisingly, the idea of instituting a bill of rights came from its old enemies—the National Party Government and other political representatives of the white minority, who suddenly "rediscovered" judicial review. Conscious judicial empowerment through constitutionalization followed....

---

70. The Treaty of Waitangi (1840, amended 1975) has been an important symbolic source for New Zealand's constitutional law. The beginning of constitutional government is commonly said to be the signing of the Treaty of Waitangi in 1840. In that year, New Zealand became a British colony and the Parliament in Westminster could make laws that applied in New Zealand. Thus, the Treaty of Waitangi is often claimed to be a "founding document," a "fundamental charter," which brought about the foundation of the state. The Maori perception, in particular, is that the treaty is a "basic document" since it recognizes the rights of the indigenous people of New Zealand (and thus its alleged breach by the colonizers is the legal basis for Maori land claims). For many Maori, the entrenchment of the Treaty of Waitangi would have demeaned the document and exposed it to change through the bill's amending procedure (a 75% majority vote of the members of the House of Representatives or a referendum).

71. The literature dealing with the constitutional aspects of the abolition of apartheid in South Africa is too vast to cite. For a broad survey of the road to general suffrage in South Africa see "South Africa—Recent History," in *Africa South of the Sahara* (1999, 974). For two general accounts of the struggle over the new constitution in South Africa see Gloppen (1997), Worden (1995), and Sisk (1995). On the political origins and likely consequences of South Africa's "negotiated transition" to democracy see Jung and Shapiro (1995).

Conclusion

As my analysis of the 1992 constitutional revolution in Israel and my brief discussion of other constitutional reforms suggest, the constitutional entrenchment of rights and the establishment of judicial review do not develop in isolation from the central political struggles and economic interests that structure political systems. To best serve their own interests, hegemonic political, economic, and judicial elites attempt to shape the institutional structure within which they operate. Constitutional reform is one such arena in which these power struggles occur. Because entrenched rights and judicial review (like other semi-autonomous, professional policymaking institutions such as central banks, electoral committees, transnational trade organizations, supranational financial bodies and judicial tribunals) are self-enforcing institutions that limit, by and large, the flexibility of political decision makers, the actors who voluntarily establish such institutions must have an interest in abiding by their limits. Moreover, because bills of rights and judiciaries lack the a priori independent power to enforce their mandates, their authority depends mainly on the degree to which elites find judicial empowerment beneficial to their own political, economic and cultural hegemony.

The governing elites in divided, rule-of-law polities face a constant struggle to preserve their hegemony. Such elites are likely to advocate a delegation of power to the judiciary (a) when their hegemony is increasingly challenged in majoritarian decision-making arenas by peripheral minority groups; (b) when the judiciary in that polity enjoys a relatively high reputation for rectitude and political impartiality; and (c) when the courts in that polity are inclined, by and large, to rule in accordance with hegemonic ideological and cultural propensities. Moreover, in many countries (e.g., Israel, Canada, New Zealand, and South Africa) the intentional empowerment of the judiciary by threatened but still dominant political powers was strongly supported by influential coalitions of domestic neoliberal economic forces (mainly powerful industrialists and economic conglomerates given added impetus by global economic trends) who viewed the constitutionalization of rights as a means to promote economic deregulation, as well as by national high courts seeking to enhance their political influence and international profile.

The causal mechanisms behind the trend toward constitutionalization and judicialization in divided polities have not been adequately delineated by the major theories of constitutional transformation. As I have shown in this article, the "consociational," evolutionist, systemic need-based (or the "ungovernability"), "new institutionalist," and electoral markets models cannot explain, for example, the recent history of constitutional entrenchment of rights and judicial review in Israel, Canada, New Zealand, and South Africa (to mention only the four cases I have examined in this paper). My brief analysis of constitutional politics in the above polities reveals that the wave of constitutionalization in these countries can be more productively understood, on the basis of an interest-based hegemonic struggle approach, as a conscious strategy undertaken by threatened political and economic elites seeking to preserve their hegemony through the insulation of policymaking from the democratic menace of popular political pressures. Moreover, what I have called the "hegemonic preservation" thesis serves as a reminder that seemingly humanitarian constitutional reforms often mask an essentially self-serving agenda. The constitutionalization of rights, in other words, is often not so much the cause or a reflection of a progressive revolution in a given polity, as it is a means by which preexisting and ongoing sociopolitical struggles in that polity are carried out.

References

Avnon, Dan. 1996. The Enlightened Public: Jewish and Democratic or Liberal and Democratic (in Hebrew). *Mishpat U'Mimshal* 3: 113–149.

Baaklini, Abdo, and Helen Desfosses. 1997. *Designs for Democratic Stability: Studies in Viable Constitutionalism.* Armonk, N.Y.: M. E. Sharpe.

Bakan, Joel. 1997. *Just Words: Constitutional Rights and Social Wrongs.* Toronto: University of Toronto Press.

Beatty, David. 1997. The Canadian Charter of Rights: Lessons and Laments. *Modern Law Review* 60: 481–498.

Blaustein, Albert, and G. H. Flanz. eds. 1998. *Constitutions of the Countries of the World.* Dobbs Ferry, N.Y.: Oceana Publications.

Bogart, William A. 1994. *Courts and Country: The Limits of Litigation and the Social and Political Life of Canada.* New York: Oxford University Press.

Cockrell, Alfred. 1997. The South African Bill of Rights and the "Duck/Rabbit." *Modern Law Review* 60: 513–537.

Dahl, Robert. 1957. Decision-Making in a Democracy: The Supreme Court as a National Policy-Maker. *Journal of Public Law* 6: 279–295.

Epstein, Lee, and Jack Knight. 1998. *The Choices Justices Make.* Washington, D.C.: CQ Press.

Epstein, Lee, and Gary Walker. 1995. The Role of the Supreme Court in American Society: Playing the Reconstructing Game. In *Contemplating Courts*, ed. Lee Epstein. Washington: D.C.: CQ Press.

Garrett, Geoffrey. 1992. International Cooperation and Institutional Choice: The European Community's Internal Market. *International Organization* 46: 533–560.

Garrett, Geoffrey, R. Daniel Keleman, and Heiner Schulz. 1998. The European Court of Justice, National Governments, and Legal Integration in the European Union. *International Organization* 52: 149–176.

Gibson, James L., Gregory A. Caldeira, and Vanessa Baird. 1998. On the Legitimacy of National High Courts. *American Political Science Review* 92: 343–358.

Gloppen, Siri. 1997. *South Africa: The Battle over the Constitution.* Aldershot, United Kingdom: Ashgate.

Graber, Mark. 1993. The Nonmajoritarian Difficulty: Legislative Deference to the Judiciary. *Studies in American Political Development* 7: 35–73.

Gross, Aeyal. 1998. The Politics of Rights in Israeli Constitutional Law. *Israel Studies* 3: 80–119.

Hirschl, Ran. 1998. Israel's "Constitutional Revolution": The Legal Interpretation of Entrenched Civil Liberties in an Emerging Neo-Liberal Economic Order. *American Journal of Comparative Law* 46: 427–452.

———. 1999. The Great Economic-Juridical Transformation: The Legal Arena and the Transformation of Israel's Economic Order. In Shafir and Peled 1999.

———. 2000. "Negative" Rights vs. "Positive" Entitlements: A Comparative Study of Judicial Interpretations of Rights in an Emerging Neo-Liberal Economic Order. *Human Rights Quarterly* 22: 1060–1098.

———. 1996b. The Unintended Consequences of Unplanned Constitutional Reform: Constitutional Politics in Israel. *American Journal of Comparative Law* 44: 585–604.

Horowitz, Donald. 1994. The Qur'an and the Common Law: Islamic Law Reform and the Theory of Legal Change. *American Journal of Comparative Law* 42: 233–293.

Hutchinson, Allan. 1995. *Waiting for Coraf: A Critique of Law and Rights.* Toronto: University of Toronto Press.

Joseph, Philip, ed. 1995. *Essays on the Constitution.* Wellington, New Zealand: Brooker's.

———. 1996. The New Zealand Bill of Rights Act 1990. *Public Law Review* 7: 76–92.

———. 1998. Constitutional Review Now. *New Zealand Law Review* [1998]: 85–128.

Jung, Courtney, and Ian Shapiro. 1995. South Africa's Negotiated Transition: Democracy, Opposition, and the New Constitutional Order. *Politics and Society* 23: 269–308.

Kairys, David. Ed. 1998. *The Politics of Law.* New York: Basic Books.

Knight, Jack, and Lee Epstein. 1996. On the Struggle for Judicial Supremacy. *Law and Society Review* 30: 87–120.

Koh, Harold H. 1988. Why the President (Almost) Always Wins in Foreign Affairs. *Yale Law Journal* 97: 1255–1342.

Lamer, Antonio. 1992. How the Charter Changes Justice. *Globe and Mail* (Toronto), 17 April 1992, A11.

Lijphart, Arendt. 1984. *Democracies: Patterns of Majoritarian and Consensus Government in Twenty-One Countries.* New Haven, Conn.: Yale University Press.

———. 1987. The Demise of the Last Westminster System? *Electoral Studies* 6: 2–26.

Maddox, Robert. 1995. *Constitutions of the World.* Washington D.C.: Congressional Quarterly.

Mandel, Michael. 1994. *The Charter of Rights and the Legalization of Politics in Canada.* Toronto: Thompson.

Marmor, Andrei. 1997. Judicial Review in Israel (in Hebrew). *Mishpat U'Mimshal* 4: 133–160.

Maxfield, Sylvia. 1994. Financial Incentives and Central Bank Authority in Industrializing Nations. *World Politics* 46: 556–588.

———. 1997. *Gatekeepers of Growth.* Princeton, N.J.: Princeton University Press.

Mishler, William, and Robert Sheehan. 1993. The Supreme Court as Countermajoritarian Institution? The Impact of Public Opinion on Supreme Court Decisions. *American Political Science Review* 87: 87–101.

North, Douglas, and Barry Weingast. 1989. Constitutions and Commitment: The Evolution of Institutions Governing Public Choice in Seventeenth-Century England. *Journal of Economic History* 49: 803–832.

Richardson, Ivor. 1995. "Rights Jurisprudence—Justice for All?" In Joseph 1995.

Rishworth, Paul. 1995. The Birth and Rebirth of the Bill of Rights." In *Rights and Freedoms: The New Zealand Bill of Rights Act and the Human Rights Act 1993,* ed. Grant Huscroft and Paul Rishworth. Wellington, New Zealand: Brooker's.

———. 1996. Human Rights and the Bill of Rights. *New Zealand Law Review* [1996]: 298–324.

Scott, Craig, and Patrick Macklem. 1992. Constitutional Ropes of Sand of Judicial Guarantees? Social Rights in a New South African Constitution. *University of Pennsylvania Law Review* 141: 1–141.

Shafir, Gershon, and Yoav Peled. 1999. *The New Israel.* Boulder, Colo.: Westview Press.

Sisk, T. D. 1995. *Democratization in South Africa.* Princeton, N.J.: Princeton University Press.

Smith, Rogers. 1997. *Civic Ideals: Conflicting Visions of Citizenship in U.S. History.* New Haven, Conn.: Yale University Press.

Tate, C. Neal, and Torbjorn Vallinder. 1995. *The Global Expansion of Judicial Power.* New York: New York University Press.

Tushnet, Mark. 1988. *Red, White, and Blue: A Critical Analysis of Constitutional Law.* Cambridge: Harvard University Press.

Watson, Alan. 1983. Legal Change: Sources of Law and Legal Culture. *University of Pennsylvania Law Review* 131: 1121–1187.

Worden, Nigel. 1995. *The Making of Modern South Africa.* Oxford, Eng.: Blackwell.

Decision Making in a Democracy: The Supreme Court as a National Policymaker

Robert Dahl

To consider the Supreme Court of the United States strictly as a legal institution is to underestimate its significance in the American political system. For it is also a political institution, an institution, that is to say, for arriving at decisions on controversial questions of national policy. As a political institution, the Court is highly unusual, not least because Americans are not quite willing to accept the fact that it is a political institution and not quite capable of denying it; so that frequently we take both positions at once. This is confusing to foreigners, amusing to logicians, and rewarding to ordinary Americans who thus manage to retain the best of both worlds. . . .

II

In determining and appraising the role of the Court, two different and conflicting criteria are sometimes employed. These are the majority criterion and the ceriterion of Right or Justice.

Every policy dispute can be tested, at least in principle, by the majority criterion, because (again: in principle) the dispute can be analyzed according to the numbers of people for and against the various alternatives at issue, and therefore according to the proportions of the citizens or eligible members who are for and against the alternatives. Logically speaking, except for a trivial case, every conflict within a given society must be a dispute between a majority of those eligible to participate and a minority or minorities; or else it must be a dispute between or among minorities only.[2] Within certain limits, both possibilities are independent of the number of policy alternatives at issue, and since the argument is not significantly affected by the number of alternatives, it is convenient to assume that each policy dispute represents only two alternatives.[3]

If everyone prefers one of two alternatives, then no significant problem arises. But a case will hardly come before the Supreme Court unless at least one person prefers an alternative that is opposed by another person. Strictly speaking, then, no matter how the Court acts in determining the legality or constitutionality of one alternative or the other, the outcome of the Court's

Excerpted from: Robert Dahl, "Decision Making in a Democracy: The Supreme Court as a National Policymaker." In *Toward Democracy: A Journey, Reflections 1940–1997*. Berkeley: Institute of Governmental Studies Press, 1997. Reprinted with permission of Institute of Governmental Studies Press, University of California Berkeley.

2. Provided that the total membership of the society is an even number, it is technically possible for a dispute to occur that divides the membership into two equal parts, neither of which can be said to be either a majority or minority of the total membership. But even in the instances where the number of members is even (which should occur on the average only half the time), the probability of an exactly even split, in any group of more than a few thousand people, is so small that it may be ignored.

3. Suppose the number of citizens, or members eligible to participate in collective decisions, is *n*. Let each member indicate his "most preferred alternative." Then it is obvious that the maximum number of most preferred alternatives is *n*. It is equally obvious that if the number of preferred alternatives is more than or equal to $n/2$, then no majority is possible. But for all practical purposes those formal limitations can be ignored, for we are dealing with a large society where the number of alternatives at issue before the Supreme Court is invariably quite small. If the number of alternatives is greater than two, it is theoretically possible for preferences to be distributed so that no outcome is consistent with the majority criterion even where all members can rank all the alternatives and where there is perfect information as to their preferences, but this difficulty does not bear on the subsequent discussion, and it is disregarded. For an examination of this problem, consult Arrow, *Social Choice and Individual Values* (1951).

decision must either (1) accord with the preferences of a minority of citizens and run counter to the preferences of a majority; (2) accord with the preferences of a majority and run counter to the preferences of a minority; or (3) accord with the preferences of one minority and run counter to the preferences of another minority, the rest being indifferent.

In a democratic system with a more or less representative legislature, it is unnecessary to maintain a special court to secure the second class of outcomes. A case might be made out that the Court protects the rights of national majorities against local interests in federal questions, but so far as I am aware, the role of the Court as a policymaker is not usually defended in this fashion; in what follows, therefore, I propose to pass over the ticklish question of federalism and deal only with "national" majorities and minorities. The third kind of outcome, although relevant according to other criteria, is hardly relevant to the majority criterion, and may also be passed over for the moment.

One influential view of the Court, however, is that it stands in some special way as a protection of minorities against tyranny by majorities. In the course of its 167 years, in 78 cases, the Court has struck down 86 different provisions of federal law as unconstitutional,[4] and by interpreta-

Table 4.1

Type of congressional action after Supreme Court decisions holding legislation unconstitutional within four years after enactment (including new deal legislation)

Congressional action	Major policy	Minor policy	Total
Reverses Court's policy	17	2	19
None	0	12	12
Other	6*	1	7
Total	23	15	38

*[This table] includes the NRA legislation affected by the *Schechter Poultry* case.

tion it has modified a good many more. It might be argued, then, that in all or in a very large number of these cases the Court was, in fact, defending the rights of some minority against a "tyrannical" majority. There are, however, some exceedingly serious difficulties with this interpretation of the Court's activities. . . .

The entire record of the duel between the Court and the lawmaking majority, in cases where the Court has held legislation unconstitutional within four years after enactment, is summarized in table 4.1.

Thus the application of the majority criterion seems to show the following: First, if the Court did in fact uphold minorities against national majorities, as both its supporters and critics often seem to believe, it would be an extremely anomalous institution from a democratic point of view. Second, the elaborate "democratic" rationalizations of the Court's defenders and the hostility of its "democratic" critics are largely

---

4. Actually, the matter is somewhat ambiguous. There appear to have been 78 cases in which the Court has held provisions of federal law unconstitutional. Sixty-four different acts in the technical sense have been construed, and 86 different provisions in law have been in some respects invalidated. I rely here on the figures and the table given in Library of Congress Legislative Reference Service, Provisions of Federal Law Held Unconstitutional By the Supreme Court of the United States 95, 141–47 (1936), to which I have added United States v. Lovett, 328 U.S. 303 (1946), and United States ex rel. *Toth v. Quarles*, 350 U.S. 11 (1955). There are some minor discrepancies in totals (not attributable to the differences in publication dates) between this volume and Acts of Congress Held Unconstitutional in Whole or in Part by the Supreme Court of the United States, in Library of Congress,

Legislative Reference Service, The Constitution of the United States of America, Analysis and Interpretation (Corwin, ed. 1953). The difference is a result of classification. The latter document lists 73 acts held unconstitutional (to which *Toth v. Quarles*, supra, should be added), but different sections of the same act are sometimes counted separately.

irrelevant, for lawmaking majorities generally have had their way. Third, although the Court seems never to have succeeded in holding out indefinitely, in a very small number of important cases it has delayed the application of policy up to as much as 25 years.

How can we appraise decisions of the third kind just mentioned? Earlier I referred to the criterion of Right or Justice as a norm sometimes invoked to describe the role of the Court. In accordance with this norm, it might be argued that the most important policy function of the Court is to protect rights that are in some sense basic or fundamental. Thus (the argument might run) in a country where basic rights are, on the whole, respected, one should not expect more than a small number of cases where the Court has had to plant itself firmly against a lawmaking majority. But majorities may, on rare occasions, become "tyrannical"; and when they do, the Court intervenes; and although the constitutional issue may, strictly speaking, be technically open, the Constitution assumes an underlying fundamental body of rights and liberties that the Court guarantees by its decisions.

Here again, however, even without examining the actual cases, it would appear, on political grounds, somewhat unrealistic to suppose that a Court whose members are recruited in the fashion of Supreme Court justices would long hold to norms of Right or Justice substantially at odds with the rest of the political elite. Moreover, in an earlier day it was perhaps easier to believe that certain rights are so natural and self-evident that their fundamental validity is as much a matter of definite knowledge, at least to all reasonable creatures, as the color of a ripe apple. To say that this view is unlikely to find many articulate defenders today is, of course, not to disprove it; it is rather to suggest that we do not need to elaborate the case against it in this essay.

In any event the best rebuttal to the view of the Court suggested above will be found in the record of the Court's decisions. Surely the six

cases referred to a moment ago, where the policy consequences of the Court's decisions were overcome only after long battles, will not appeal to many contemporary minds as evidence for the proposition under examination. A natural right to employ child labor in mills and mines? To be free of income taxes by the federal government? To employ longshoremen and harbor workers without the protection of workmen's compensation? The Court itself did not rely upon such arguments in these cases, and it would be no credit to their opinions to reconstruct them along such lines.

So far, however, our evidence has been drawn from cases in which the Court has held legislation unconstitutional within four years after enactment. What of the other 40 cases? Do we have evidence in these that the Court has protected fundamental or natural rights and liberties against the dead hand of some past tyranny by the lawmakers? The evidence is not impressive. In the entire history of the Court there is not one case arising under the First Amendment in which the Court has held federal legislation unconstitutional. If we turn from these fundamental liberties of religion, speech, press and assembly, we do find a handful of cases—something less than 10—arising under Amendments Four to Seven in which the Court has declared acts unconstitutional that might properly be regarded as involving rather basic liberties.[25] An inspection of these cases leaves the impression that, in all of them, the lawmakers and the Court were not very far apart; moreover, it is doubtful that the

25. The candidates for this category would appear to be *Boyd v. United States*, 116 U.S. 616 (1886), *Rassmussen v. United States*, 197 U.S. 516 (1905); *Wong Wing v. United States*, 163 U.S. 228 (1896); *United States v. Moreland*, 258 U.S. 433 (1922); *Kirby v. United States*, 174 U.S. 47 (1899); *United States v. Cohen Grocery Co.*, 255 U.S. 81 (1921); *Weeds, Inc. v. United States*, 255 U.S. 109 (1921); *Justices of the Supreme Court v. United States ex rel Murray*, 9 Wall. (U.S.) 274 (1870); *United States ex rel. Toth v. Quarles*, 350 U.S. 11 (1955).

fundamental conditions of liberty in this country have been altered by more than a hair's breadth as a result of these decisions. However, let us give the Court its due; it is little enough.

Over against these decisions we must put the 15 or so cases in which the Court used the protections of the Fifth, Thirteenth, Fourteenth, and Fifteenth Amendments to preserve the rights and liberties of a relatively privileged group at the expense of the rights and liberties of a submerged group: chiefly slaveholders at the expense of slaves,[26] white people at the expense of colored people,[27] and property holders at the expense of wage earners and other groups.[28] These cases, unlike the relatively innocuous ones of the preceding set, all involved liberties of genuinely fundamental importance, where an opposite policy would have meant thoroughly basic shifts in the distribution of rights, liberties, and opportunities in the United States—where, moreover, the policies sustained by the Court's action have since been repudiated in every civilized nation of the western world, including our own. Yet, if our earlier argument is correct, it is futile—precisely because the basic distribution of privilege was at issue—to suppose that the Court could have possibly acted much differently in these areas of policy from the way in which it did in fact act.

26. Dred Scott v. Sandford, 19 How. (U.S.) 393 (1857).

27. United States v. Reese, 92 U.S. 214 (1876); United States v. Harris, 106 U.S. 629 (1883); United States v. Stanley (Civil Rights Cases), 109 U.S. 3 (1883); Baldwin v. Franks, 120 U.S. 678 (1887); James v. Bowman, 190 U.S. 127 (1903); Hodges v. United States, 203 U.S. 1 (1906); Butts v. Merchants & Miners Transportation Co., 230 U.S. 126 (1913).

28. Monongahela Navigation Co. v. United States, 148 U.S. 312 (1893); Adair v. United States, 208 U.S. 161 (1908); Adkins v. Children's Hospital, 261 U.S. 525 (1923); Nichols v. Coolidge, 27 U.S. 531 (1927); Untermyer v. Anderson, 276 U.S. 440 (1928); Heiner v. Donnan, 285 U.S. 312 (1932); Louisville Joint Stock Land Bank v. Radford, 295 U.S. 555 (1935).

VI

Thus the role of the Court as a policymaking institution is not simple; and it is an error to suppose that its functions can be either described or appraised by means of simple concepts drawn from democratic or moral theory. It is possible, nonetheless, to derive a few general conclusions about the Court's role as a policymaking institution.

National politics in the United States, as in other stable democracies, is dominated by relatively cohesive alliances that endure for long periods of time. One recalls the Jeffersonian alliance, the Jacksonian, the extraordinarily long-lived Republican dominance of the post-Civil War years, and the New Deal alliance shaped by Franklin Roosevelt. Each is marked by a break with past policies, a period of intense struggle, followed by consolidation, and finally decay and disintegration of the alliance.

Except for short-lived transitional periods when the old alliance is disintegrating and the new one is struggling to take control of political institutions, the Supreme Court is inevitably a part of the dominant national alliance. As an element in the political leadership of the dominant alliance, the Court of course supports the major policies of the alliance. By itself, the Court is almost powerless to affect the course of national policy. In the absence of substantial agreement within the alliance, an attempt by the Court to make national policy is likely to lead to disaster, as the Dred Scott decision and the early New Deal cases demonstrate. Conceivably, the cases of the last three decades involving the freedom of Negroes, culminating in the now famous decision on school integration, are exceptions to this generalization; I shall have more to say about them in a moment.

The Supreme Court is not, however, simply an agent of the alliance. It is an essential part of the political leadership and possesses some bases of power of its own, the most important of which is the unique legitimacy attributed to its interpretations of the Constitution. This legitimacy the Court jeopardizes if it flagrantly opposes the major policies of the dominant alliance; such a course of action, as we have seen, is one in which the Court will not normally be tempted to engage.

It follows that within the somewhat narrow limits set by the basic policy goals of the dominant alliance, the Court *can* make national policy. Its discretion, then, is not unlike that of a powerful committee chairman in Congress who cannot, generally speaking, nullify the basic policies substantially agreed on by the rest of the dominant leadership, but who can, within these limits, often determine important questions of timing, effectiveness, and subordinate policy. Thus the Court is least effective against a current lawmaking majority—and evidently least inclined to act. It is most effective when it sets the bounds of policy for officials, agencies, state governments, or even regions, a task that has come to occupy a very large part of the Court's business.[29]

Few of the Court's policy decisions can be interpreted sensibly in terms of a "majority" versus a "minority." In this respect the Court is no different from the rest of the political leadership. Generally speaking, policy at the national level is the outcome of conflict, bargaining, and agreement among minorities; the process is neither minority rule nor majority rule but what might better be called *minorities* rule, where one aggregation of minorities achieves policies opposed by another aggregation.

The main objective of presidential leadership is to build a stable and dominant aggregation of minorities with a high probability of winning the presidency and one or both houses of Congress. The main task of the Court is to confer legitimacy on the fundamental policies of the successful coalition. There are times when the coalition is unstable with respect to certain key policies; at very great risk to its legitimacy powers, the Court can intervene in such cases and may even succeed in establishing policy. Probably in such cases it can succeed only if its action conforms to and reinforces a widespread set of explicit or implicit norms held by the political leadership; norms that are not strong enough or are not distributed in such a way as to insure the existence of an effective lawmaking majority but are, nonetheless, sufficiently powerful to prevent any successful attack on the legitimacy powers of the Court. This is probably the explanation for the relatively successful work of the Court in enlarging the freedom of Negroes to vote during the past three decades and in its famous school integration decisions.[30]

Yet the Court is more than this. Considered as a political system, democracy is a set of basic procedures for arriving at decisions. The operation of these procedures presupposes the existence of certain rights, obligations, liberties and restraints; in short, certain patterns of behavior. The existence of these patterns of behavior in turn presupposes widespread agreement (particularly among the politically active and influential segments of the population) on the validity and

---

29. "Constitutional law and cases with constitutional undertones are of course still very important, with almost one-fourth of the cases in which written opinions were filed [in the two most recent terms] involving such questions. Review of administrative action ... constitutes the largest category of the Court's work, comprising one-third of the total cases decided on the merits. The remaining ... categories of litigation ... all involve largely public law questions" Frankfurter, ["The Supreme Court in the Mirror of Justice." *University of Pennsylvania Law Review* 105: 781–793, 1957], note 1, at 793.

---

30. Rice v. Elmore, 165 F.2d 387 (C.A. 4th, 1947), cert. denied 333 U.S. 875 (1948); United States v. Classic, 313 U.S. 299 (1941); Smith v. Allwright, 321 U.S. 649 (1944); Grovey v. Townsend, 295 U.S. 45 (1935); Brown v. Board of Education, 347 U.S. 483 (1954); Bolling v. Sharpe, 347 U.S. 497 (1954).

propriety of the behavior. Although its record is
by no means lacking in serious blemishes, at its
best the Court operates to confer legitimacy, not
simply on the particular and parochial policies
of the dominant political alliance, but upon the
basic patterns of behavior required for the operation of a democracy.

Democratic Justice

Ian Shapiro

Two Dimensions of Democratic Justice

Democrats are committed to rule by the people. They insist that no aristocrat, monarch, philosopher, bureaucrat, expert, or religious leader has the right, in virtue of such status, to force people to accept a particular conception of their proper common life. People should decide for themselves, via appropriate procedures of collective decision, what their collective business should be. They may reasonably be required to consult and take account of one another, and of others affected by their actions, but beyond this no one may legitimately tell them what to do. The people are sovereign; in all matters of collective life they rule over themselves.

Although this is less often commented on in the academic literature, democracy is as much about opposition to the arbitrary exercise of power as it is about collective self-government....

In a world of ideal political institutions a derivative view of the place of opposition in democratic politics might be sustainable. But in the actual world, where social orders come to be what they are in morally arbitrary ways, and where all procedures of government turn out on close inspection to be flawed, opposition must enjoy a more independent and exalted status in a persuasive account of just democratic politics....

The aspiration to avoid imposed solutions suggests that the presumption should generally be in favor of doing things through representative institutions rather than courts or other agencies, because legislatures are more democratically accountable. Even when action from above is warranted in accordance with the logic of subsidiarity, it is generally better for this action to be by elected legislatures rather than by appointed judiciaries or administrative authorities.... Notice, for now, that it is the exceptions that stand in need of justification. In this connection the argument for democratic justice exhibits an elective affinity with the approaches to constitutional adjudication that have been defended in recent years by Ruth Bader Ginsburg and Robert Burt, and it will be useful to end this statement of the general argument with some discussion of their views.

Burt conceives of a constitutional democracy as inescapably committed to two principles—majority rule and equal self-determination—that have the potential to conflict with one another. If majoritarian processes are employed to promote domination of some by others, the contradiction latent in democratic politics becomes manifest. In such circumstances democracy goes to war with itself, and an institutional mechanism is needed to resolve the conflict. This is supplied, on Burt's account, by judicial review, understood as "a coercive instrument extrinsic to the disputants" in a political struggle. Burt sees judicial review as a "logical response to an internal contradiction between majority rule and equal self-determination. It is not a deviation from that theory."[59]

---

59. Notice that this claim about necessity is agnostic with respect to whether the imperatives on which people must act are "natural" features of the human condition or "socially constructed." Whether the imperatives on which people must act are alterable—and if so, by whom and at what cost to whom—are important issues that play a role in the following discussion. But it is a common misconception to believe that questions about the alterability of the human condition depend on views about social construction. The degree to which things are alterable may not vary with the extent to which they are socially constructed at all. Many features of the natural world, ranging from the temperature of our bath water to the genetic structure of our beings, can be altered by conscious human design. As the advent of genetic engineering

If the court's legitimate role in a democracy is rooted in this logic of preventing domination through democratic process, then it follows for Burt that its activities should be limited to dealing with the consequences of the democratic contradiction. And because preventing domination is the goal, it also follows that courts should generally avoid imposing solutions of their own when democracy has wrought domination. Rather, they should declare the domination that has emerged from the democratic process unacceptable and insist that the parties try anew to find an accommodation. Thus in contrast to what many have seen as the altogether too timid approach taken by the U.S. Supreme Court in the school desegregation cases of the 1950s and after, on Burt's view the Court took the right stand. In *Brown v. Board of Education* the justices declared the doctrine of "separate but equal" to be an unconstitutional violation of the Equal Protection Clause, but they did not describe schooling conditions that would be acceptable.[60] Rather, they turned the

problem back to southern state legislatures, requiring them to fashion acceptable remedies themselves.[61] These remedies came before the Court as a result of subsequent litigation, were evaluated when they did, and were often found to be wanting.[62] But the Court avoided designing the remedy itself, and thus avoided the charge that it was usurping the legislative function.

Ginsburg, too, has made the case that when courts try to step beyond a reactive role, they undermine their legitimacy in a democracy. Although she thinks that it is sometimes necessary for the court to step "ahead" of the political process to achieve reforms that the Constitution requires, if it gets too far ahead, it can produce a backlash and provoke charges that it is overreaching its appropriate place in a democratic constitutional order.[63] She and Burt both think

indicates, those features of human life that are alterable may themselves change, so that what has to be accepted as given in one era may become subject to human modification in another. Socially constructed phenomena, by contrast, often defy all efforts at conscious human control. Markets are human constructions, yet we may be unable to regulate them so as to operate at full employment without inflation. Ethnic hatred might concededly be learned behavior, yet we may have no idea how to prevent its being reproduced in the next generation. It is a mistake to leap from the idea of social construction to that of alterability; at best, the two are contingently related.

60. By the same token, there may be circumstances in which the state lacks the relevant mix of financial and institutional resources to provide many components of a social wage needed to vindicate basic interests, but it could induce corporations to provide some of them. I think particularly here of countries like contemporary South Africa, which has almost 40 percent unemployment in many regions, chronically inadequate basic education and medical care for the majority, a col-

lapsed currency and depleted capital reserves, and a political capacity to tax that is not remotely equal to the demands it confronts. In such conditions it might be appropriate for the state to offer corporations a mix of incentives and penalties to induce them to build and run local hospitals and schools for their workers and families. Although, for reasons elaborated later in this chapter, this is a less than ideal approach to vindicating basic interests of a population, when the situation is so bad, and no feasible alternative is on the horizon, loading even these basic interests onto the employment relationship may be defensible.

61. By focusing on the imperatives that people are constrained to satisfy, I do not mean to suggest that people always value them more highly than other activities. People might resent the constraining effects of many basic interests (on themselves or on others); they might find them irksome or mundane. One could, indeed, imagine a person reasonably concluding that a life in which one can do no more than act on such imperatives is not worth living.

62. This is not to deny that how to cope with expensive addictions should figure prominently in a discussion of the collective health care provision.

63. See Lester C. Thurow, *The Future of Capitalism: How Today's Economic Forces Shape Tomorrow's World* (Morrow, 1996), pp. 26–29.

that the sort of approach adopted by Justice Blackmun in *Roe v. Wade* exemplifies this danger.[64] In contrast to the *Brown* approach, in *Roe* the Court did a good deal more than strike down a Texas abortion statute. The majority opinion laid out a detailed test to determine the conditions under which any abortion statute could be expected to pass muster. In effect, Justice Blackmun authored a federal abortion statute of his own. As Ginsburg put it, the Court "invited no dialogue with legislators. Instead, it seemed entirely to remove the ball from the legislators' court" by wiping out virtually every form of abortion regulation then in existence.[65]

On the Ginsburg-Burt view, the sweeping holding in *Roe* diminished the Court's democratic legitimacy at the same time as it polarized opinion about abortion and put paid to various schemes to liberalize abortion laws that were under way in different states. Between 1967 and 1973 statutes were passed in nineteen states liberalizing the permissible grounds for abortion. Many feminists had been dissatisfied with the pace and extent of this reform. This is why they mounted the campaign that resulted in *Roe*. Burt concedes that in 1973 it was "not clear whether the recently enacted state laws signified the beginning of a national trend toward abolishing all abortion restrictions or even whether in the so-called liberalized states, the new enactments

would significantly increase access to abortion for anyone." Nonetheless, he points out that "the abortion issue was openly, avidly, controverted in a substantial number of public forums, and unlike the regimen extant as recently as 1967, it was no longer clear who was winning the battle."[66] Following the *Brown* model, the Court might have struck down the Texas abortion statute in *Roe* and remanded the matter for further action at the state level, thereby setting limits on what legislatures might do in the matter of regulating abortion without involving the Court directly in designing that regulation. On the Ginsburg-Burt view, this would have left space for democratic resolution of the conflict, ensuring the survival of the right to abortion while at the same time preserving the legitimacy of the Court's role in a democracy.[67]

Although the tensions that arise within democratic justice differ from those that motivate Burt and Ginsburg, in three important respects their view of the appropriate role for courts in a democratic order fits comfortably within the general argument developed here. First, they articulate an appropriate institutional response to the injunction that rather than impose democracy on collective activities, the goal should be to try to structure those activities so that people will find ways to democratize things for themselves. By placing courts in a nay-saying stance of ruling out practices as unacceptable when they violate the strictures of democratic justice, courts can force legislatures and the conflicting parties they represent to seek creative democratic solutions to

---

64. On the effects of global trade on wages and employment, see Adrian Wood, *North-South Trade, Employment, and Inequality: Changing Fortunes in a Skill-Driven World* (Clarendon, 1994). For a review of literature that points to factors other than trade, principally technology, see Gary Burtless, "International trade and the rise of earnings inequality," *Journal of Economic Literature*, vol. 33 (June 1995), pp. 800–816.

65. "In fact there *is* democracy in the typical capitalist firm; it is just that investors of capital do the voting rather than workers. Converting to worker ownership means not only enfranchising the workers but also *dis*enfranchising the firm's investors." Henry Hansman, *The Ownership of Enterprise* (Harvard University Press, 1996), p. 43.

66. Candidates commonly discussed by economists include maximizing sales, capital, and managers' and own compensation subject to a profitability constraint, or maximizing the probability that profits will remain above a given threshold. For an overview, see David Kreps, *A Course in Economic Theory* (Princeton University Press, 1990), pp. 724–741.

67. Robin Archer, *Economic Democracy: The Politics of Feasible Socialism* (Clarendon Press, 1995), pp. 47–48.

their conflicts that can pass constitutional muster. Second, the Ginsburg-Burt view is attractive because it is reactive but directed; it exemplifies the creative pragmatism that motivates democratic justice. It involves accepting that there is an important—if circumscribed—role for courts in a democracy, yet it does not make the unmanageable and undemocratic administrative demands on courts that accompany more proactive views of adjudication. On this view a court might reasonably hold that a given policy should be rejected without stating (indeed, perhaps without having decided) what policy would pass muster. "This is unacceptable for reasons $a, b, c \ldots$; find a better way" is seen as an appropriate stance for a constitutional court. Finally, by recognizing the relatively greater legitimacy of legislatures and treating courts as institutional mechanisms for coping with legislative failure, the Ginsburg-Burt view takes account of the fact that no decision-making mechanism is flawless. Yet it does so in a way that is rooted in the idea that democratic procedures should be made to operate as well as possible, and when they fail, remedies should be no more intrusive on the democratic process than is necessary to repair them.

Some will object to this as too minimal a role for reviewing courts, but democrats have to concern themselves not only with courts that aspire to advance the cause of democratic justice, as they might reasonably be thought to have done in *Brown* and *Roe*, but also with courts that do not, as was the case in *Dred Scott*, the *Civil Rights Cases*, and *Lochner v. New York*.[68] Insulated from any further review, and lacking, at least in the American context, in democratic accountability, courts can put decisions of this kind

in place that may not be reversed for decades or even generations. Although it may thus be wise from the standpoint of democratic justice to embrace an activist role for a constitutional court, it is equally wise to limit courts to a circumscribed and negationist activism.

The Path to Application

My aim here has been to state the general case for a democratic conception of social justice. This I have sought to do by building on the popular view, in which considerations of democracy and justice are intimately linked, rather than conventional academic views of them as fundamentally distinct and mutually antagonistic. The account that I offer rests on the twin commitments to government and opposition in democratic theory, suggesting that there should always be opportunities for those affected by the operation of a collective practice both to participate in its governance and to oppose its results when they are so inclined. These two injunctions should reasonably be expected to have different implications in different cultures, and, within the same culture, to evolve over time and play themselves out differently in different circumstances. They are best thought of as conditioning constraints, designed to democratize social relations as they are reproduced, rather than as blueprints for social justice. . . .

---

68. For the same reason, whether the employment relationship is in the public or private sector is of no particular concern from the standpoint of democratic justice (although the strategic possibilities for advancing democratic justice may be different in public- and private-sector employment).

5 PRESIDENTIALISM VERSUS PARLIAMENTARISM

The Perils of Presidentialism
Juan Linz

Presidentialism, Multipartism, and Democracy: The Difficult Combination
Scott Mainwaring

Presidents and Assemblies
Matthew Soberg Shugart and John Carey

Minority Governments, Deadlock Situations, and the Survival of Presidential Democracies
José Antonio Cheibub

Minority Governments in Parliamentary Democracies: The Rationality of Nonwinning Cabinet Solutions
Kaare Strom

Institutional Design, Party Systems, and Governability: Differentiating the Presidential Regimes of Latin America
Joe Foweraker

Presidential Power, Legislative Organization, and Party Behavior in Brazil
Argelina Cheibub Figueiredo and Fernando Limongi

The Perils of Presidentialism

Juan Linz

... [T]he superior historical performance of parliamentary democracies is no accident. A careful comparison of parliamentarism as such with presidentialism as such leads to the conclusion that, on balance, the former is more conducive to stable democracy than the latter. This conclusion applies especially to nations with deep political cleavages and numerous political parties; for such countries, parliamentarism generally offers a better hope of preserving democracy.

Parliamentary vs. Presidential Systems

A parliamentary regime in the strict sense is one in which the only democratically legitimate institution is parliament; in such a regime, the government's authority is completely dependent upon parliamentary confidence. Although the growing personalization of party leadership in some parliamentary regimes has made prime ministers seem more and more like presidents, it remains true that barring dissolution of parliament and a call for new elections, premiers cannot appeal directly to the people over the heads of their representatives. Parliamentary systems may include presidents who are elected by direct popular vote, but they usually lack the ability to compete seriously for power with the prime minister.

In presidential systems an executive with considerable constitutional powers—generally including full control of the composition of the cabinet and administration—is directly elected by the people for a fixed term and is independent of parliamentary votes of confidence. He is not only the holder of executive power but also the symbolic head of state and can be removed between elections only by the drastic step of impeachment. In practice, as the history of the United States shows, presidential systems may be more or less dependent on the cooperation of the legislature; the balance between executive and legislative power in such systems can thus vary considerably....

Two things about presidential government stand out. The first is the president's strong claim to democratic, even plebiscitarian, legitimacy; the second is his fixed term in office....

But what is most striking is that in a presidential system, the legislators, especially when they represent cohesive, disciplined parties that offer clear ideological and political alternatives, can also claim democratic legitimacy. This claim is thrown into high relief when a majority of the legislature represents a political option opposed to the one the president represents. Under such circumstances, who has the stronger claim to speak on behalf of the people: the president or the legislative majority that opposes his policies? Since both derive their power from the votes of the people in a free competition among well-defined alternatives, a conflict is always possible and at times may erupt dramatically. There is no democratic principle on the basis of which it can be resolved, and the mechanisms the constitution might provide are likely to prove too complicated and aridly legalistic to be of much force in the eyes of the electorate. It is therefore no accident that in some such situations in the past, the armed forces were often tempted to intervene as a mediating power. One might argue that the United States has successfully rendered such conflicts "normal" and thus defused them. To explain how American political institutions and practices have achieved this result would exceed the scope of this essay, but it is worth noting that the uniquely diffuse character of American political parties—which, ironically, exasperates

Excerpted from: Juan Linz, "The Perils of Presidentialism." *Journal of Democracy* 1 (1990): 51–69. © The Johns Hopkins University Press and National Endowment for Democracy. Reprinted by permission of The Johns Hopkins University Press.

many American political scientists and leads them to call for responsible, ideologically disciplined parties—has something to do with it. Unfortunately, the American case seems to be an exception; the development of modern political parties, particularly in socially and ideologically polarized countries, generally exacerbates, rather than moderates, conflicts between the legislative and the executive.

The second outstanding feature of presidential systems—the president's relatively fixed term in office—is also not without drawbacks. It breaks the political process into discontinuous, rigidly demarcated periods, leaving no room for the continuous readjustments that events may demand. The duration of the president's mandate becomes a crucial factor in the calculations of all political actors, a fact which (as we shall see) is fraught with important consequences. . . . It is a paradox of presidential government that while it leads to the personalization of power, its legal mechanisms may also lead, in the event of a sudden midterm succession, to the rise of someone whom the ordinary electoral process would never have made the chief of state.

Paradoxes of Presidentialism

Presidential constitutions paradoxically incorporate contradictory principles and assumptions. On the one hand, such systems set out to create a strong, stable executive with enough plebiscitarian legitimation to stand fast against the array of particular interests represented in the legislature. . . . On the other hand, presidential constitutions also reflect profound suspicion of the personalization of power: memories and fears of kings and caudillos do not dissipate easily. . . .

Perhaps the best way to summarize the basic differences between presidential and parliamentary systems is to say that while parliamentarism imparts flexibility to the political process, presidentialism makes it rather rigid. Proponents of presidentialism might reply that this rigidity is an advantage, for it guards against the uncertainty and instability so characteristic of parliamentary politics. Under parliamentary government, after all, myriad actors—parties, their leaders, even rank-and-file legislators—may at any time between elections adopt basic changes, cause realignments, and, above all, make or break prime ministers. But while the need for authority and predictability would seem to favor presidentialism, there are unexpected developments—ranging from the death of the incumbent to serious errors in judgment committed under the pressure of unruly circumstances—that make presidential rule less predictable and often weaker than that of a prime minister. The latter can always seek to shore up his legitimacy and authority, either through a vote of confidence or the dissolution of parliament and the ensuing new elections. Moreover, a prime minister can be changed without necessarily creating a regime crisis.

Considerations of this sort loom especially large during periods of regime transition and consolidation, when the rigidities of a presidential constitution must seem inauspicious indeed compared to the prospect of adaptability that parliamentarism offers.

Zero-Sum Elections

. . . Presidentialism is ineluctably problematic because it operates according to the rule of "winner-take-all"—an arrangement that tends to make democratic politics a zero-sum game, with all the potential for conflict such games portend. Although parliamentary elections can produce an absolute majority for a single party, they more often give representation to a number of parties. Power-sharing and coalition-forming are fairly common, and incumbents are accordingly attentive to the demands and interests of even the smaller parties. These parties in turn retain expectations of sharing in power and, therefore, of having a stake in the system as a whole. By contrast, the conviction that he possesses independent authority and a popular mandate is likely to imbue a president with a sense of power and mission, even if the plurality that elected him is a slender one. Given such assumptions about his standing and role, he will find the inevitable opposition to his policies far more irksome and demoralizing than would a prime minister, who knows himself to be but the spokesman for a temporary governing coalition rather than the voice of the nation or the tribune of the people. . . .

The danger that zero-sum presidential elections pose is compounded by the rigidity of the president's fixed term in office. Winners and losers are sharply defined for the entire period of the presidential mandate. There is no hope for shifts in alliances, expansion of the government's base of support through national-unity or emergency grand coalitions, new elections in response to major new events, and so on. Instead, the losers must wait at least four or five years without any access to executive power and patronage. The zero-sum game in presidential regimes raises the stakes of presidential elections and inevitably exacerbates their attendant tension and polarization.

On the other hand, presidential elections do offer the indisputable advantage of allowing the people to choose their chief executive openly, directly, and for a predictable span rather than leaving that decision to the backstage maneuvering of the politicians. But this advantage can only be present if a clear mandate results. If there is no required minimum plurality and several candidates compete in a single round, the margin between the victor and the runner-up may be too thin to support any claim that a decisive plebiscite has taken place. To preclude this, electoral laws sometimes place a lower limit on the size of the winning plurality or create some mechanism for choosing among the candidates if none attains the minimum number of votes needed to win; such procedures need not

necessarily award the office to the candidate with the most votes. More common are run-off provisions that set up a confrontation between the two major candidates, with possibilities for polarization that have already been mentioned. One of the possible consequences of two-candidate races in multiparty systems is that broad coalitions are likely to be formed (whether in run-offs or in preelection maneuvering) in which extremist parties gain undue influence. If significant numbers of voters identify strongly with such parties, one or more of them can plausibly claim to represent the decisive electoral bloc in a close contest and may make demands accordingly. Unless a strong candidate of the center rallies widespread support against the extremes, a presidential election can fragment and polarize the electorate.

In countries where the preponderance of voters is centrist, agrees on the exclusion of extremists, and expects both rightist and leftist candidates to differ only within a larger, moderate consensus, the divisiveness latent in presidential competition is not a serious problem. With an overwhelmingly moderate electorate, anyone who makes alliances or takes positions that seem to incline him to the extremes is unlikely to win, as both Barry Goldwater and George McGovern discovered to their chagrin. But societies beset by grave social and economic problems, divided about recent authoritarian regimes that once enjoyed significant popular support, and in which well-disciplined extremist parties have considerable electoral appeal, do not fit the model presented by the United States. In a polarized society with a volatile electorate, no serious candidate in a single-round election can afford to ignore parties with which he would otherwise never collaborate.

A two-round election can avoid some of these problems, for the preliminary round shows the extremist parties the limits of their strength and allows the two major candidates to reckon just which alliances they must make to win. This reduces the degree of uncertainty and promotes more rational decisions on the part of both voters and candidates. In effect, the presidential system may thus reproduce something like the negotiations that "form a government" in parliamentary regimes. But the potential for polarization remains, as does the difficulty of isolating extremist factions that a significant portion of the voters and elites intensely dislike.

The Spanish Example

... Spanish politics since Franco has clearly felt the moderating influence of parliamentarism; without it, the transition to popular government and the consolidation of democratic rule would probably have taken a far different—and much rougher—course.

Let me now add a moderating note of my own. I am *not* suggesting that the polarization which often springs from presidential elections is an inevitable concomitant of presidential government. If the public consensus hovers reliably around the middle of the political spectrum and if the limited weight of the fringe parties is in evidence, no candidate will have any incentive to coalesce with the extremists. They may run for office, but they will do so in isolation and largely as a rhetorical exercise. Under these conditions of moderation and preexisting consensus, presidential campaigns are unlikely to prove dangerously divisive. The problem is that in countries caught up in the arduous experience of establishing and consolidating democracy, such happy circumstances are seldom present. They certainly do not exist when there is a polarized multiparty system including extremist parties.

The Style of Presidential Politics

... Some of presidentialism's most notable effects on the style of politics result from the characteristics of the presidential office itself. Among these characteristics are not only the great powers associated with the presidency but also the limits imposed on it—particularly those requiring cooperation with the legislative branch, a requirement that becomes especially salient when that branch is dominated by opponents of the president's party. Above all, however, there are the time constraints that a fixed term or number of possible terms imposes on the incumbent. The office of president is by nature two-dimensional and, in a sense, ambiguous: on the one hand, the president is the head of state and the representative of the entire nation; on the other hand, he stands for a clearly partisan political option. If he stands at the head of a multiparty coalition, he may even represent an option within an option as he deals with other members of the winning electoral alliance.

The president may find it difficult to combine his role as the head of what Bagehot called the "deferential" or symbolic aspect of the polity ... with his role as an effective chief executive and partisan leader fighting to promote his party and its program.... A presidential system, as opposed to a constitutional monarchy or a republic with both a premier and a head of state, does not allow such a neat differentiation of roles.

Perhaps the most important consequences of the direct relationship that exists between a president and the electorate are the sense the president may have of being the only elected representative of the whole people and the accompanying risk that he will tend to conflate his supporters with "the people" as a whole. The plebiscitarian component implicit in the president's authority is likely to make the obstacles and opposition he encounters seem particularly annoying. In his frustration he may be tempted to define his policies as reflections of the popular will and those of his opponents as the selfish designs of narrow interests. This identification of leader with people fosters a certain populism that may be a source of strength. It may also, however, bring on a refusal to acknowledge the limits of the mandate that even a majority—to say nothing of a mere plurality—can claim as democratic justification for the enactment of its agenda. The doleful potential for displays of cold indifference, disrespect, or even downright hostility toward the opposition is not to be scanted....

Unlike the rather Olympian president, the prime minister is normally a member of parliament who, even as he sits on the government bench, remains part of the larger body.... Especially uncertain in presidential regimes is the place of opposition leaders, who may not even hold public office and in any case have nothing like the quasi-official status that the leaders of the opposition enjoy in Britain, for example.

The absence in presidential regimes of a monarch or a "president of the republic" who can act symbolically as a moderating power deprives the system of flexibility and of a means of restraining power. A generally neutral figure can provide moral ballast in a crisis or act as a moderator between the premier and his opponents—who may include not only his parliamentary foes but military leaders as well. A parliamentary regime has a speaker or presiding member of parliament who can exert some restraining influence over the parliamentary antagonists, including the prime minister himself, who is after all a member of the chamber over which the speaker presides.

The Problem of Dual Legitimacy

... Ministers in parliamentary systems are situated quite differently from cabinet officers in presidential regimes. Especially in cases of coalition or minority governments, prime ministers are much closer to being on an equal footing with their fellow ministers than presidents will ever be with their cabinet appointees....

A presidential cabinet is less likely than its parliamentary counterpart to contain strong and independent-minded members. The officers of a president's cabinet hold their posts purely at the sufferance of their chief; if dismissed, they are

out of public life altogether. A premier's ministers, by contrast, are not his creatures but normally his parliamentary colleagues; they may go from the cabinet back to their seats in parliament and question the prime minister in party caucuses or during the ordinary course of parliamentary business just as freely as other members can. A president, moreover, can shield his cabinet members from criticism much more effectively than can a prime minister, whose cabinet members are regularly hauled before parliament to answer queries or even, in extreme cases, to face censure.

One need not delve into all the complexities of the relations between the executive and the legislature in various presidential regimes to see that all such systems are based on dual democratic legitimacy: no democratic principle exists to resolve disputes between the executive and the legislature about which of the two actually represents the will of the people....

Even more ominously, in the absence of any principled method of distinguishing the true bearer of democratic legitimacy, the president may use ideological formulations to discredit his foes; institutional rivalry may thus assume the character of potentially explosive social and political strife. Institutional tensions that in some societies can be peacefully settled through negotiation or legal means may in other, less happy lands seek their resolution in the streets.

The Issue of Stability

Among the oft-cited advantages of presidentialism is its provision for the stability of the executive. This feature is said to furnish a welcome contrast to the tenuousness of many parliamentary governments, with their frequent cabinet crises and changes of prime minister, especially in the multiparty democracies of Western Europe. Certainly the spectacle of political instability presented by the Third and Fourth French Republics and, more recently, by Italy and Portugal has contributed to the low esteem in which many scholars—especially in Latin America—hold parliamentarism and their consequent preference for presidential government. But such invidious comparisons overlook the large degree of stability that actually characterizes parliamentary governments. The superficial volatility they sometimes exhibit obscures the continuity of parties in power, the enduring character of coalitions, and the way that party leaders and key ministers have of weathering cabinet crises without relinquishing their posts. In addition, the instability of presidential cabinets has been ignored by students of governmental stability. It is also insufficiently noted that parliamentary systems, precisely by virtue of their surface instability, often avoid deeper crises. A prime minister who becomes embroiled in scandal or loses the allegiance of his party or majority coalition and whose continuance in office might provoke grave turmoil can be much more easily removed than a corrupt or highly unpopular president. Unless partisan alignments make the formation of a democratically legitimate cabinet impossible, parliament should eventually be able to select a new prime minister who can form a new government. In some more serious cases, new elections may be called, although they often do not resolve the problem and can even, as in the case of Weimar Germany in the 1930s, compound it.

The government crises and ministerial changes of parliamentary regimes are of course excluded by the fixed term a president enjoys, but this great stability is bought at the price of similarly great rigidity. Flexibility in the face of constantly changing situations is not presidentialism's strong suit. Replacing a president who has lost the confidence of his party or the people is an extremely difficult proposition.... What in a parliamentary system would be a government crisis can become a full-blown regime crisis in a presidential system.

The same rigidity is apparent when an incumbent dies or suffers incapacitation while in office. In the latter case, there is a temptation to conceal the president's infirmity until the end of his term. In event of the president's death, resignation, impeachment, or incapacity, the presidential constitution very often assures an automatic and immediate succession with no interregnum or power vacuum. But the institution of vice-presidential succession, which has worked so well in the United States, may not function so smoothly elsewhere....

The Time Factor

Democracy is by definition a government pro tempore, a regime in which the electorate at regular intervals can hold its governors accountable and impose a change. The limited time that is allowed to elapse between elections is probably the greatest guarantee against overweening power and the last hope for those in the minority. Its drawback, however, is that it constrains a government's ability to make good on the promises it made in order to get elected. If these promises were far-reaching, including major programs of social change, the majority may feel cheated of their realization by the limited term in office imposed on their chosen leader. On the other hand, the power of a president is at once so concentrated and so extensive that it seems unsafe not to check it by limiting the number of times any one president can be reelected. Such provisions can be frustrating, especially if the incumbent is highly ambitious; attempts to change the rule in the name of continuity have often appeared attractive.

Even if a president entertains no inordinate ambitions, his awareness of the time limits facing him and the program to which his name is tied cannot help but affect his political style....

The fixed term in office and the limit on reelection are institutions of unquestionable value in presidential constitutions, but they mean that the political system must produce a capable and popular leader every four years or so, and also that whatever "political capital" the outgoing president may have accumulated cannot endure beyond the end of his term.

All political leaders must worry about the ambitions of second-rank leaders, sometimes because of their jockeying for position in the order of succession and sometimes because of their intrigues. The fixed and definite date of succession that a presidential constitution sets can only exacerbate the incumbent's concerns on this score. Add to this the desire for continuity, and it requires no leap of logic to predict that the president will choose as his lieutenant and successor-apparent someone who is more likely to prove a yes-man than a leader in his own right.

The inevitable succession also creates a distinctive kind of tension between the ex-president and his successor. The new man may feel driven to assert his independence and distinguish himself from his predecessor, even though both might belong to the same party. The old president, for his part, having known the unique honor and sense of power that come with the office, will always find it hard to reconcile himself to being out of power for good, with no prospect of returning even if the new incumbent fails miserably. Parties and coalitions may publicly split because of such antagonisms and frustrations. They can also lead to intrigues, as when a still-prominent former president works behind the scenes to influence the next succession or to undercut the incumbent's policies or leadership of the party.

Of course similar problems can also emerge in parliamentary systems when a prominent leader finds himself out of office but eager to return. But parliamentary regimes can more easily mitigate such difficulties for a number of reasons. The acute need to preserve party unity, the deference accorded prominent party figures, and the new premier's keen awareness that he needs the help of his predecessor even if the latter does not sit on the government bench or the same side of the house—all these contribute to the maintenance of concord. Leaders of the same party

may alternate as premiers; each knows that the other may be called upon to replace him at any time and that confrontations can be costly to both, so they share power. A similar logic applies to relations between leaders of competing parties or parliamentary coalitions.

The time constraints associated with presidentialism, combined with the zero-sum character of presidential elections, are likely to render such contests more dramatic and divisive than parliamentary elections. The political realignments that in a parliamentary system may take place between elections and within the halls of the legislature must occur publicly during election campaigns in presidential systems, where they are a necessary part of the process of building a winning coalition.... A presidential regime leaves much less room for tacit consensus-building, coalition-shifting, and the making of compromises which, though prudent, are hard to defend in public....

Parliamentarism and Political Stability

This analysis of presidentialism's unpromising implications for democracy is not meant to imply that no presidential democracy can be stable; on the contrary, the world's most stable democracy—the United States of America—has a presidential constitution. Nevertheless, one cannot help tentatively concluding that in many other societies the odds that presidentialism will help preserve democracy are far less favorable.

While it is true that parliamentarism provides a more flexible and adaptable institutional context for the establishment and consolidation of democracy, it does not follow that just any sort of parliamentary regime will do. Indeed, to complete the analysis one would need to reflect upon the best type of parliamentary constitution and its specific institutional features. Among these would be a prime-ministerial office combining power with responsibility, which would in turn require strong, well-disciplined political parties. Such features—there are of course many others we lack the space to discuss—would help foster responsible decision making and stable governments and would encourage genuine party competition without causing undue political fragmentation. In addition, every country has unique aspects that one must take into account—traditions of federalism, ethnic or cultural heterogeneity, and so on. Finally, it almost goes without saying that our analysis establishes only probabilities and tendencies, not determinisms. No one can guarantee that parliamentary systems will never experience grave crisis or even breakdown.

In the final analysis, all regimes, however wisely designed, must depend for their preservation upon the support of society at large—its major forces, groups, and institutions. They rely, therefore, on a public consensus which recognizes as legitimate authority only that power which is acquired through lawful and democratic means. They depend also on the ability of their leaders to govern, to inspire trust, to respect the limits of their power, and to reach an adequate degree of consensus. Although these qualities are most needed in a presidential system, it is precisely there that they are most difficult to achieve. Heavy reliance on the personal qualities of a political leader—on the virtue of a statesman, if you will—is a risky course, for one never knows if such a man can be found to fill the presidential office. But while no presidential constitution can guarantee a Washington, a Juárez, or a Lincoln, no parliamentary regime can guarantee an Adenauer or a Churchill either. Given such unavoidable uncertainty, the aim of this essay has been merely to help recover a debate on the role of alternative democratic institutions in building stable democratic polities.

Presidentialism, Multipartism, and Democracy: The Difficult Combination

Scott Mainwaring

Choices of political institutions matter. Institutions create incentives and disincentives for political actors, shape actors' identities, establish the context in which policy-making occurs, and can help or hinder in the construction of democratic regimes. And among all of the choices regarding institutions, none is more important than the system of government: presidential, semipresidential, parliamentary, or some hybrid....

Rather than addressing general problems or strengths of presidential systems, as Linz did, or specific case studies, as several other analysts have done, this article focuses on a sizable subcategory of presidential systems: those in multiparty democracies. I argue that the combination of presidentialism and multipartism makes stable democracy difficult to sustain. Since many presidential democracies have multiparty systems, the argument has broad implications for scholarship and for the political debate about institutional choices in new democracies....

A presidential democracy has two distinguishing features.[4] First, the head of government is essentially popularly elected; this includes the U.S., where the electoral college has little autonomy with respect to the popular vote. Legislative elections and postelection negotiations do not determine executive power. Wherever the head of government is selected by the legislature, not as a second alternative where the popular vote

does not produce a clear winner, but as the fundamental process, the system is usually parliamentary[5] and never presidential. Postelection negotiations that determine which parties will govern and which will head the government are crucial in many parliamentary regimes, so they indirectly determine who will be prime minister. Such postelection negotiations are not part of the selection process of chief executives in presidential systems.

In presidential systems, the president must be the head of government. In semipresidential systems (e.g., Finland, France), a popularly-elected president is head of state but is not always the head of government. In Austria, Iceland, and Ireland, a president is elected by direct popular vote but has only minor powers and, therefore, is not the head of government. In all three countries, the system of government is parliamentary,

---

Excerpted from: Scott Mainwaring, "Presidentialism, Multipartism, and Democracy: The Difficult Combination." *Comparative Political Studies* 26(2) (July 1993): 198–228. © 1993 Sage Publications, Inc. Reprinted by permission of Sage Publications, Inc.

4. For related discussions of how presidentialism should be defined, see Linz (1994), Lijphart (1984, pp. 68–74), Riggs (1988), and Shugart and Carey (1992, p. 18–27).

5. Switzerland is an exception. The executive (which is collegial) is selected by the legislature, but the system is not parliamentary because the executive has a fixed term of office. In Bolivia, as was also the case in Chile before 1973, when no presidential candidate wins an absolute majority of the popular vote, congress elects the president. But there is a key difference between these two cases. In Chile, the congress always selected the front-runner in popular votes; it did not broker the election but rather confirmed the popular winner, so it can be considered presidential. If, however, congress plays the dominant role in selecting the president, as is the case in Bolivia, then the system is not presidential. In Bolivia, the congress gave the presidency to candidates who did not capture the most votes in 1979, 1985, and 1989. Legislative negotiations became the primary mechanism for selecting the president. Consequently, the system is not strictly presidential, but rather alternating; it is presidential when one candidate obtains an absolute majority in the popular vote, but it is a hybrid when, as has been occurring consistently, this is not the case. Because the president's term of office is fixed, the system is not parliamentary.

notwithstanding the existence of popular elections for president.[6]

The second distinguishing feature of presidential democracies is that the president is elected for a fixed time period. Most presidential democracies allow for impeachment, but this practice is rare and does not substantially affect our definition because of its extraordinary character. The president cannot be forced to resign because of a no-confidence vote by the legislature. In contrast, in a parliamentary system, the head of government is selected by the legislature and subsequently depends upon the ongoing confidence of the legislature for remaining in office; thus the time period of the chief executive's mandate is alterable.

In synthesis, following Lijphart (1984, pp. 68–74), I define presidentialism according to two dimensions: whether the chief executive is elected by the legislature and whether the term of office is fixed. . . .

Presidentialism and Stable Democracy

Stable (or continuous) democracy is defined here strictly on the basis of democratic longevity, more specifically, at least 25 years of uninterrupted democracy. . . .

Presidential systems have not fared well. Out of 31 countries that have had continuous democracy since at least 1967, only four—the debatable case of Colombia, plus Costa Rica, the U.S., and Venezuela—have presidential systems. Twenty-four stable democracies have parliamentary systems, two have semipresidential systems, and one has a hybrid. . . .

The post-1945 democracies can be divided into four categories, of which three are relevant here:

(a) democracies that, as of 1992, had enjoyed at least 25 years of uninterrupted democracy . . . ; (b) governments that at some point enjoyed at least 25 years of uninterrupted democracy, but that broke down after 1945 . . . ; (c) democratic governments that experienced breakdowns between 1945 and 1992 without making the 25-year minimum . . . ; and (d) extant democracies that have not yet met the 25 year minimum. This latter category is excluded from the present analysis because these cases cannot yet be considered stable democracies. Only 7 of 31 (22.6%) presidential democracies have endured for at least 25 consecutive years, compared with 25 of 44 parliamentary systems (56.8%), 2 of 4 hybrids (50.0%), and 2 of 3 semipresidential systems (66.7%).

The lack of stable presidential democracies could be unrelated to presidentialism, but there are reasons to believe it probably is related. Blondel and Suárez (1981), Lijphart (in press), Linz (in press), Riggs (1988), and Suárez (1982), have argued that presidentialism is less likely to promote stable democracy. I do not share all of their criticisms,[8] and most of the critics have overlooked some strengths of presidential systems (Shugart & Carey, 1992; Ceaser, 1986). Nevertheless, I agree that presidentialism is

---

6. Duverger (1980) argued that Austria, Iceland, and Ireland have semipresidential governments, but the presidents have only symbolic power in all three cases. What matters is whether these offices are largely symbolic or, conversely, whether the office holders wield considerable power.

8. Linz (1994) and Lijphart (1994) add a fourth liability: the supposedly majoritarian bent of presidentialism. I disagree with this part of their argument. The most majoritarian democracies are the Westminster style parliamentary systems with highly disciplined parties, in which the winning party controls everything for a protracted period of time, possibly despite winning well under 50% of the votes. Presidentialism is predicated upon a separation of powers, so that an opposition party or coalition can control the legislature (or one house thereof), thereby exercising some control over presidential initiatives even if it does not control the presidency. I agree with Linz and Lijphart, however, that parliamentarism is more conducive to coalition building. For a critical examination of Linz's seminal piece, see Mainwaring and Shugart (1997).

generally less favorable for democracy and that presidentialism has some distinct liabilities, three of which are highlighted in the following discussion.

Perhaps the greatest comparative liability of presidential systems is their difficulty in handling major crises. Presidential systems offer less flexibility in crisis situations because attempts to depose the president easily shake the whole system. There are no neat means of replacing a president who is enormously unpopular in the society at large and has lost most of his/her support in the legislature....

In many cases, a coup appears to be the only means of getting rid of an incompetent or unpopular president....

A second liability of presidentialism, a greater likelihood of executive/legislative deadlock, stems primarily from the separate election of the two branches of government and is exacerbated by the fixed term of office. Presidential systems are more prone to immobilism than parliamentary systems for two primary reasons. They are more apt to have executives whose program is consistently blocked by the legislature, and they are less capable of dealing with this problem when it arises. The president may be incapable of pursuing a coherent course of action because of congressional opposition, but no other actor can resolve the problem playing within democratic rules of the game.

A third problem of presidentialism stems from the direct popular election of presidents, which in itself seems desirable. The downside of direct popular elections is that political outsiders with little experience in handling congress can get elected....

Although I agree with the critics of presidentialism on these key points, none of this implies that democracy cannot be sustained by presidentialism, that presidentialism is the main explanation for the vicissitudes of democracy in certain countries, or that parliamentary government would always work better. Most presidential democracies have been in Latin America,

where in most countries, several other factors have contributed to democratic instability; in this sense, there is a possibility of overdetermination. Moreover, there is no absolutely clear correlation between the system of government and policy effectiveness. One presidential democracy (the United States) stands out as successful by most historical/comparative standards, and Costa Rica and Venezuela have strong democratic institutions with presidential systems. Many parliamentary systems have produced effective government, but some have not, with the Third and Fourth French Republics often being cited as examples. Finally, the nature of the party system and specific institutional prerogatives of the executive and legislature can either promote or undermine the viability of presidential or parliamentary democracy. There are different kinds of presidentialism and parliamentarism, and the differences between one variant and another can be crucial (Shugart & Carey, 1992); differences in the nature of the parties and party system also crucially affect how well presidential and parliamentary governments function.

Presidentialism, Multipartism, and Stable Democracy

... Among stable presidential democracies, the virtual absence of multiparty systems is striking. This observation, however, does not explain why multiparty systems are less propitious to stable presidential democracy than two-party systems. Without some logical explanation, it remains possible that this is an accident or a spurious correlation. But there are reasons to believe that the combination of presidentialism and multiparty systems makes it more difficult to achieve stable democracy.

Two-party systems, in and of themselves, are not necessarily a desideratum. They constrict the breadth of opinion represented, and they hinder the building of coalition governments, making it difficult to establish consociational forms of democracy (Lijphart 1994). As Sartori (1976, pp. 191–192) observed, two-party systems become less functional and less viable as the spread of opinion becomes greater. Nevertheless, in presidential systems a two-party format seems more favorable to stable democracy. The question is why multipartism and presidentialism make a difficult combination, why a two-party system ameliorates the problems of presidentialism, and why parliamentarism mitigates the difficulties of multipartism.

The answer to these questions, I submit, is threefold. In presidential systems, multipartism increases the likelihood of executive/legislative deadlock and immobilism. It also increases the likelihood of ideological polarization. Finally, with multipartism, presidents need to build interparty coalitions to get measures through the legislature, but interparty coalition building in presidential systems is more difficult and less stable than in parliamentary systems. . . .

Presidentialism, Multipartism, and Immobilism

Multiparty presidentialism is more likely to produce immobilizing executive/legislative deadlock than either parliamentary systems or two-party presidentialism, and presidential systems are less fitted to handle executive/legislative deadlock than parliamentary systems. Because of the separation of powers, presidential systems lack means of ensuring that the president will enjoy the support of a majority in congress. Presidents are elected independently of congress, and the winner need not come from a majority party, if one exists. In some presidential systems, candidates from small parties make successful runs for the presidency. . . .

The tendency toward executive/legislative deadlock and immobilism is particularly acute in multiparty presidential democracies, especially with highly fragmented party systems. Under these circumstances, the president is likely to

lack stable legislative support, so pushing policy measures through is apt to be more difficult. Immobilism and sharp conflict between the executive and the legislature, with potentially deleterious consequences for democratic stability and/or effective governance, often result. Protracted conflicts between the legislature and congress can lead to a decision-making paralysis (Santos, 1986). In fledgling democracies, such paralysis can have pernicious results. If, in addition to being highly fragmented, the party system is also polarized, the difficulties of governing will be compounded.

The likelihood of immobilism is lower in two-party presidential and in parliamentary systems. Having a two-party system increases the likelihood that the president will enjoy majority backing in congress, and hence decreases the probability of presidential/legislative impasse. Two-party systems are not necessarily better equipped to handle the problems created by a lack of legislative support, but they are better at avoiding this problem. . . .

Not only are multiparty presidential systems more apt to generate deadlocks, with the fixed electoral timetable and the separation of powers, presidential systems have no institutionalized means of resolving such deadlocks (Linz 1994). Because of the fixed electoral timetable, even if congress opposes a president's programs, it has no way of dismissing the president except for impeachment. Impeachment, however, is generally reserved for criminal proceedings, and legislators may have no grounds for criminally trying a president. Consequently, the opposition may believe that the only means of deposing an ineffective president is supporting a coup. The parliamentary mechanism of a no-confidence vote is not available. . . .

Two-party presidential systems also face institutional rigidity when executive/legislative deadlock occurs but, as noted earlier, presidents are more likely to have stable support in congress. In contrast to presidential systems, parliamentary systems have an institutionalized mechanism for overcoming deadlocks when they arise. A vote of no-confidence can topple the government, leading to new elections that may change the balance of power and help resolve the crisis. This provision allows for replacing, with less institutional strain, unpopular or inept executives. Frequent recourse to dismissing governments can breed instability, but this problem can be mitigated by measures such as the West German or Spanish constructive vote of no-confidence. Conversely, if a prime minister is frustrated because of the difficulty of effecting policy in the face of opposition control of the legislature, in most parliamentary systems, he/she can call new elections in an effort to achieve a majority. In either case, there are means of changing the government without threatening the regime.

Presidentialism, Multipartism, and Ideological Polarization

Two or two-and-one-half party systems are also more likely to be compatible with presidential democracy because ideological polarization is unlikely. Competition tends to be centripetal because to win a majority, the parties must win votes from the center of the political spectrum (Downs, 1957). . . . In most two-party and two-and-one-half party systems, parties with a centrist, moderate orientation dominate the electoral market. Such characteristics generally favor moderation and compromise, characteristics that in turn enhance the likelihood of stable democracy. . . .

Intense ideological divisions increase the stakes of the political game, serve as an incentive to polarization and, consequently, are less favorable to stable democracy. Such ideological divisions are unlikely in the context of a two-party system. This is one of the reasons why two-party democracies have been less prone to breakdown.

Presidentialism, Multipartism, and Party Coalitions

. . . Now I look at why presidentialism makes it difficult for multipartism to function well, focusing on problems of coalition building in presidential systems. In multiparty systems, interparty coalition building is essential for attaining a legislative majority. While the need for such coalition building exists in both presidential and parliamentary multiparty systems, three factors make building stable interparty legislative coalitions more difficult in presidential democracies than in parliamentary systems.

First, party support for the government tends to be more secure in parliamentary systems because of the way executive power is formed and dissolved. In a coalition parliamentary government, the parties forming the government choose the cabinet and the prime minister. Executive power is formed through post-election agreements among parties and is divided among several parties. The parties themselves are coresponsible for governing and are committed to supporting government policy. . . .

In presidential systems the president (not the parties) has the responsibility of putting together a cabinet. The president may make prior deals with the parties that support him or her, but these deals are not as binding as they are in a parliamentary system. Presidents are freer to dismiss ministers and to rearrange the cabinet than prime ministers in a coalition government are. . . .

Whereas in parliamentary systems, party coalitions generally take place after the election and are binding, in presidential systems, they often take place before the election and are not binding past election day. . . .

Second, in presidential systems, the commitment of individual legislators to support an agreement negotiated by the party leadership is often less secure. The extension of a cabinet portfolio does not necessarily imply party support for the president, as it does in a parliamentary system.... In contrast, in parliamentary systems, individual legislators are more or less bound to support the government unless their party decides to drop out of the governmental alliance. MPs risk bringing down a government and losing their seats in new elections if they fail to support the government (Epstein, 1964, 1967).

Finally, incentives for parties to break coalitions are stronger in presidential systems than in many parliamentary systems. In multiparty presidential systems, as new presidential elections appear on the horizon, party leaders generally feel a need to distance themselves from the president in office. By remaining a silent partner in a governing coalition, party leaders fear they will lose their own identity, share the blame for government mistakes, and not reap the benefits of its accomplishments....

References

Blondel, J., & Suarez, W. (1981). Las limitaciones institucionales del sistema presidencialista. *Criterio*, No. 1853–1854, 57–70.

Ceaser, J. C. (1986). In defense of separation of powers. In R. Goldwin & A. Kaufman (Eds.), *Separation of powers—Does it still work?* (pp. 168–193). Washington, DC: American Enterprise Institute.

Downs, A. (1957). *An economic theory of democracy.* New York: Harper.

Epstein, L. (1964). A comparative study of Canadian parties. *American Political Science Review*, 58, 46–59.

Epstein, L. (1967). *Political parties in western democracies.* New York: Praeger.

Lijphart, A. (1984). *Democracies.* New Haven, CT. Yale University Press.

Lijphart, A. (1994). Presidentialism and majoritarian democracy: Theoretical observations. In J. J. Linz & A. Valenzuela (Eds.), *Presidential or parliamentary democracy: Does it make a difference?* Baltimore: Johns Hopkins University Press.

Linz, J. J. (1994). Democracy: Presidential or parliamentary. Does it make a difference? In J. J. Linz & A. Valenzuela (Eds.), *Presidential or parliamentary democracy: Does it make a difference?* Baltimore: Johns Hopkins University Press.

Mainwaring, S., & Shugart, M. (1997). Juan Linz, presidentialism, and democracy: A critical appraisal. In A. Valenzuela (Ed.), Politics, society, and democracy: Latin America. New York: Praeger.

Riggs, F. (1988). The survival of presidentialism in America: Para-constitutional practices. *International Political Science Review*, 9, 247–278.

Santos, W. G. dos. (1986). *Sessenta e quatro: Anatomia da crise.* Sao Paulo: Vertice.

Sartori, G. (1976). *Parties and party systems: A framework for analysis.* New York: Cambridge University Press.

Shugart, M., & Carey, J. (1992). *Presidents and assemblies: Constitutional design and electoral dynamics.* New York: Cambridge University Press.

Suarez, W. (1982). El poder ejecutivo en America Latina: Su capacidad operativa bajo regimenes presidencialistas de gobierno. *Revista de Estudios Politicos*, 29, 109–144.

Presidents and Assemblies

Matthew Soberg Shugart and John Carey

Assessing the Powers of the Presidency

In this chapter we undertake a process of assessing just how powerful a president is in constitutional terms. We identify two basic dimensions of presidential power: one concerning power over legislation, the other encompassing nonlegislative powers, including authority over the cabinet and calling of early elections for congress. Additionally, because the latter powers are directly related to the question of separation of powers, we provide a comparison of presidential powers over the composition of cabinets to separation of executive from assembly. There are two main, related lessons we shall be able to draw from this exercise. First, systems that score high on presidential powers, and in particular those that are extreme on presidential legislative powers, are often those systems that have exhibited the greatest trouble with sustaining stable democracy. Second, systems that give the president considerable powers over the composition of the cabinet but also are low on separation of survival of assembly and executive powers likewise tend to be among the "troubled" cases. There are thus left two basic clusters that, we argue, are "safer" for the success of democracy: (1) those with high separation of survival of powers but low presidential legislative powers; and (2) those with low separation of survival but also low presidential authority over the cabinet. . . .

Powers of the Presidency: Legislative Powers

To assess presidential powers, it is possible to devise a simple interval scoring method on each

Excerpted from: Matthew Soberg Shugart and John Carey, *Presidents and Assemblies*. Cambridge: Cambridge University Press, 1992. © Cambridge University Press, 1992. Reprinted with the permission of Cambridge University Press.

of several aspects in which systems with elected presidencies vary. The first set of aspects entail legislative powers constitutionally granted to the president. These aspects are the veto, the partial veto, presidential authority to legislate by decree, exclusive right to initiate certain legislative proposals, budgetary initiative, and power to propose referenda. Aspects of presidential power apart from the legislative domain include cabinet formation, cabinet dismissal, lack of assembly censure, and dissolution of the assembly. The scores on each aspect of each dimension can then be summed to arrive at an overall indicator of presidential powers on the respective dimension. . . .

Powers: Legislative versus Nonlegislative

Figure 5.1 graphs the strength of the presidents across all the cases in two dimensions. Thus the very strongest presidents in both dimensions would be found in the upper right region, while presidents with no power in either dimension would be at the origin $(0, 0)$. Most of the systems commonly understood to be presidential are located on the vertical line running at 12 on the dimension of nonlegislative power. These systems are thus all identical in the extent of authority they give to the president over the government and the assembly: All have exclusive authority over the cabinet and none may dissolve the congress. These systems differ only on the dimension of presidential legislative powers, but there is a very wide range of variation on this dimension. . . .

We have divided the space of figure 5.1 into six regions, numbered counterclockwise from the upper right. Region I consists of the very powerful presidents. Presidencies in Region I have great powers in both dimensions. Region II comprises presidents with great legislative powers, but whose powers outside the legislative process are somewhat weaker. Region III is

Table 5.1
Powers of popularly elected presidents

Legislative Powers

Package Veto/Override

4 Veto with no override

3 Veto with override requiring majority greater than 2/3 (of quorum)

2 Veto with override requiring 2/3

1 Veto with override requiring absolute majority of assembly or extraordinary majority less than 2/3

0 No veto; or veto requires only simple majority override

Decree

4 Reserved powers, no rescission

2 President has temporary decree authority with few restrictions

1 Authority to enact decrees limited

0 No decree powers; or only as delegated by assembly

Budgetary Powers

4 President prepares budget; no amendment permitted

3 Assembly may reduce but not increase amount of budgetary items

2 President sets upper limit on total spending, within which assembly may amend

1 Assembly may increase expenditures only if it designates new revenues

0 Unrestricted authority of assembly to prepare or amend budget

Partial Veto/Override

4 No override

3 Override by extraordinary majority

2 Override by absolute majority of whole membership

1 Override by simple majority of quorum

0 No partial veto

Exclusive Introduction of Legislation (Reserved Policy Areas)

4 No amendment by assembly

2 Restricted amendment by assembly

1 Unrestricted amendment by assembly

0 No exclusive powers

Proposal of Referenda

4 Unrestricted

2 Restricted

0 No presidential authority to propose referenda

Nonlegislative Powers

Cabinet Formation

4 President names cabinet without need for confirmation or investiture

3 President names cabinet ministers subject to confirmation or investiture by assembly

1 President names premier, subject to investiture, who then names other ministers

0 President cannot name ministers except upon recommendation of assembly

Censure

4 Assembly may not censure and remove cabinet or ministers

2 Assembly may censure, but president may respond by dissolving assembly

1 "Constructive" vote of no confidence (assembly majority must present alternative cabinet)

0 Unrestricted censure

Cabinet Dismissal

4 President dismisses cabinet ministers at will

2 Restricted powers of dismissal

1 President may dismiss only upon acceptance by assembly of alternative minister or cabinet

0 Cabinet or ministers may be censured and removed by assembly

Dissolution of Assembly

4 Unrestricted

3 Restricted by frequency or point within term

2 Requires new presidential election

1 Restricted: only as response to censures

0 No provision

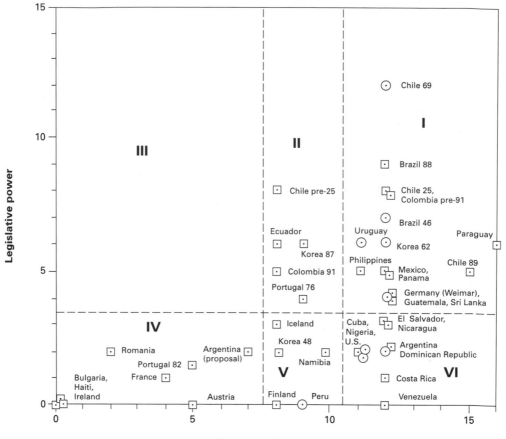

Figure 5.1
Powers of popularly elected presidents (democratic regimes that have broken down indicated by circles).

empty, reflecting the lack of any logical reason to give great legislative powers to a president whose power over the composition of governments is even weaker than those in Region II. Region IV, in the lower left of figure 5.1, contains our weakest presidents in both dimensions. Almost all of the premier-presidential regimes are located here. Region V also includes premier-presidential systems, as well as other systems with moderately powerful presidents. Finally, Region VI includes only presidential systems with relatively weak legislative powers but great powers over government formation.

If we consider the performance of the regimes in figure 5.1, we find reason to believe that the more powerful presidencies are also the more problematic. . . .

Although the sample is too small to make any claims of statistical significance, six of the ten breakdowns have occurred in the region we have suspected would be most problematic: very strong presidencies (Region I). Fully half of these cases have suffered breakdowns at some point. We thus have reason to be concerned (absent constitutional revision) about the future viability of democracy in three countries. In the 1980s, Brazil and the Philippines have adopted constitutions with powers at least as strong as in the earlier, failed constitutions. Chile has adopted a new constitution that, while weakening legislative powers compared to the earlier period, expands nonlegislative powers.

Regions II and V of figure 5.1, which contain the "confused" cases of shared presidential-parliamentary authority over cabinets, also include several cases of dubious democratic performance, although only one breakdown. . . .

We are left with two regions. One, Region IV contains three premier-presidential systems and no breakdowns.[2] The other, Region VI, contains the presidential systems with relatively weak presidential legislative powers. Of the nine cases, two (Argentina and Nigeria) have suffered breakdowns at some time. Cuba's ambiguous system . . . is also found here. We also observe that the longest-lived presidential systems—all scoring 11 or 12 on the dimension of nonlegislative power—may be found at the low end of the scale of presidential legislative powers. These cases include:

Costa Rica   United States

Dominican Republic   Venezuela

These are the four of the five longest-lived presidential democracies in the world (the other is Colombia, where presidential powers recently were reduced in both dimensions). If there really is a link, then there are reasons to be optimistic about several fledgling presidential democracies that rank low on presidential legislative powers. Regimes such as those of Argentina and El Salvador, for example, have weathered severe crises that have not been allowed to become clashes between the two elected branches of government over constitutional powers, in part because the assembly is clearly the dominant branch. . . .

Conclusions: Presidential Powers

Our examination of the dimensions of presidential power suggests the regimes with great presidential legislative powers are problematic, as are those in which authority over cabinets is shared between assembly and president. These issues need to be addressed in turn. On matters of legislation, we suggest that relatively strong assemblies should be associated with more stable and effective government relative to strong presidencies because assemblies serve as arenas for the perpetual fine-tuning of conflicts. An assembly represents the diversity of a polity far better than an executive dependent on the president's whims is likely to do. Because of the diverse forces represented in an assembly, such a body

---

2. This lack of breakdowns among the premier-presidential systems provides support for Lijphart and Rogowski's (1991) suggestion that such regimes may be especially well equipped to manage political cleavages.

has the potential for encompassing divergent viewpoints and striking compromises on them. The dual democratic legitimacies decried by critics of presidentialism—the claim that no democratic principle exists to resolve conflicts over who better can claim to represent the "will" of the electorate—are minimized to the extent that an assembly is accorded a more powerful role in legislation than is the president. Thus presidentialism with a strong congress indeed does afford a democratic principle for the regulation of interbranch conflicts; that principle is that the assembly prevails, subject to a need for compromise with the president. The relatively weaker presidents (those of Costa Rica and the United States, for example) cannot use decree legislative authority to break a "logjam" in congress, as many presidents can do with perfect legality. Thus, a fundamental conclusion is that the criticisms of presidential regimes should not be put forward as if all presidencies were created equal; rather, these criticisms apply with greatest force to strong presidents.

On the matter of authority over cabinets, again the shared control that we said typifies the president-parliamentary type goes right to the heart of the concern of many with dual democratic legitimacies. If there is no "democratic principle" that defines who fills cabinet posts, one of the most basic elements to any democracy, then conflicts of a very basic nature are likely. Are the ministers the president's ministers, or are they the assembly's? In some regimes the answer is both. In either a premier-presidential regime or a presidential regime, on the other hand, the primacy of one branch over the other is clear. Both types make for a cabinet subject (whether exclusively or primarily) to one branch or the other even when the branches are controlled by different political tendencies. This does not prevent conflict, but it is not as clearly guaranteed to generate conflict as is the president-parliamentary type. Democratic institutions are supposed to be conflict regulators, not conflict generators. Either giving great legislative powers

to the most majoritarian component (the presidency) of a regime meant to be consensual, or granting shared authority over the composition of the cabinet, is a potentially dangerous arrangement. Finally, we saw in this chapter that actual regimes, as well as a promising proposal for a directly elected "prime minister," entail varying combinations on two dimensions—separation of survival of executive and assembly, and presidential power over cabinets. In the next chapters we shall see how presidential powers interact with the means of electing the assembly and president.

Minority Governments, Deadlock Situations, and the Survival of Presidential Democracies

José Antonio Cheibub

Between 1946 and 1996, there have been 133 transitions to and from democracy in the world. Fifty-nine of these, or 45%, took place in the 23 countries of Latin America, while the remaining 74 were spread among the other 166 countries located in other areas of the world.[1]

This high level of political instability used to be explained in terms of structural variables—the degree of dependency, the level of inequality, poverty, and so on—that supposedly created conditions that were adverse to the survival of democratic regimes. More recent explanations have moved away from this focus on economic and social conditions, concentrating instead on institutional arrangements. Stimulated by the formulations first advanced by Linz (1994),[2] the breakdown of democratic regimes and the alleged "crisis of governability" of new democracies—and not only in Latin America—have been attributed to presidentialism, which, in combination with permissive electoral systems and weakly institutionalized political parties, is supposed to produce presidents whose parties do not control a majority of seats in congress, deadlocks, institutional paralysis, and ultimately the breakdown of democratic institutions.

Indeed, existing evidence shows that parliamentary democracies tend to last longer than presidential democracies and that the difference in survival rates of these two regimes is not due to the wealth of countries in which they are observed; to their economic performance; or to conditions under which they emerged, in particular the military legacy of the previous authoritarian regime.[3]

The instability of presidential democracies has been commonly accounted for by the principle of separation between executive and legislative authorities. A conventional wisdom has emerged that, first, sees the occurrence of minority governments, and the deadlock between executives and legislatures that it supposedly causes, as the predominant condition of presidential regimes. Second, because these regimes lack a constitutional principle that can be invoked to resolve conflicts between executives and legislatures, such as the vote of no confidence of parliamentary regimes, minority presidents and deadlock would provide incentives for actors to search for extraconstitutional means of resolving their differences, thus making presidential regimes prone to instability and eventual death. It is thus the separation of executive and legislative powers inherent to presidential regimes that is usually invoked to account for the fact that they die more frequently than parliamentary regimes.[4]

Excerpted from: José Antonio Cheibub, "Minority Governments, Deadlock Situations, and the Survival of Presidential Democracies." *Comparative Political Studies* 35(3) (April 2002): 384–312. © 2002 Sage Publications. Reprinted by permission of Sage Publications.

1. These numbers come from Przeworski, Alvarez, Cheibub, and Limongi (2000) and the author's update.

2. An early argument was offered in Linz (1978, pp. 71–74). See also Linz (1990a, 1990b) for further developments.

3. See Alvarez (1997) and Przeworski et al. (2000) for a comprehensive comparison of performance, political and economic, under parliamentarism and presidentialism.

4. The original formulation of this view was, of course, Linz (1978), elaborated in Linz (1994, p. 7):

Since [the president and the congress] derive their power from the vote of the people in a free competition among well-defined alternatives, a conflict is always latent and sometimes likely to erupt dramatically; there is no democratic principle to resolve it, and the mechanisms that might exist in the constitution are generally complex, highly technical, legalistic, and, therefore, of doubtful democratic legitimacy for the electorate. It is therefore no accident that in some of those situations the military intervenes as *"poder moderador."*

In this article, I examine the conditions that generate minority presidents, minority governments, and deadlock conditions in presidential regimes; and I evaluate their impact on the survival of these regimes. . . .

Minority Governments and Deadlock Situations

Minority governments are those in which the governing coalition does not control a majority of seats in the legislature or, in a bicameral system, those in which it does not control a majority of seats in at least one of the chambers. Here I am primarily interested in minority governments and not, as in much of the existing literature, in minority presidents. The latter are frequent under presidential regimes, but they are not what really matters for the operation of these regimes.[7] In much the same way as prime ministers in parliamentary systems, presidents who find themselves in a minority situation may enter into coalition to obtain the support of a majority in congress. They do so by distributing cabinet positions to parties that pledge their support to the government in congress.[8] Government, thus, is here defined by all the parties that hold cabinet positions, and the government legislative support by the sum of seats held by all the parties that are in the government. . . .

Deadlock situations are more complex to define and observe. Consider the following situation. P is the share of seats held by the government and O is the share of seats held by the

opposition. Legislation is passed by votes of at least M members of congress and, in the case of bicameral systems, bills have to be approved in both houses. Under these conditions, it is possible to distinguish the situation in which the government controls a majority of seats in congress, and hence in which congress passes bills preferred by the president, from the situation in which the government does not control a majority of seats in congress. When the latter is the case, congress approves bills that are not the ones preferred by the president. In these situations, if constitutionally allowed, the president vetoes the bill. Presidential vetoes can be overridden by at least V members of Congress, $V \geq M$. Thus, $0 < M \leq V < 100$ (see figure 5.2).

This setup defines three possible situations in terms of executive-legislative relations. One situation is defined by $P < 100 - V$ and $O \geq V$. In

8. The probability that at any given point in time a minority president (i.e., a president whose party controls less than 50% of the seats in at least one legislative house) will head a majority government is .24. However, little is known about coalition formation in presidential regimes. Part of the reason has to do with the fact that the dominant view of presidentialism implies that coalition governments are unlikely in these regimes and, when they exist, that they are precarious if not absolutely meaningless. In my opinion (Cheibub & Limongi, 2000) this view is not correct. A few analysts (e.g., Mainwaring & Shugart, 1997) have attempted to assess the partisan composition of presidential governments by measuring the legislative seats held by the parties that participated in the president's electoral coalition. They, however, recognize the limitation of this measure to indicate the size of the coalition of parties that support the president in congress, ultimately concluding that the share of seats held by the party of the president is a better measure of the president's legislative support (Mainwaring & Shugart, 1997, p. 403). To my knowledge, only very recently have some analysts focused their attention on governing coalitions in presidential regimes. See, for example, Dehesa (1997), Amorin Neto (1998), and Altman-Olin (1999).

This view has become widespread and can be found in Ackerman (2000, p. 645), González and Gillespie (1994, p. 172), Hartlyn (1994, p. 221), Huang (1997, pp. 138–139), Jones (1995a, pp. 34, 38), Linz and Stepan (1996, p. 181), Mainwaring and Scully (1995), Niño (1996, pp. 168–169), Stepan and Skach (1993), and Valenzuela (1994, p. 136), among others.

7. See Cheibub (2002) for an analysis that looks specifically at minority presidents and considers the impact of deadlock on government accountability with respect to economic outcomes.

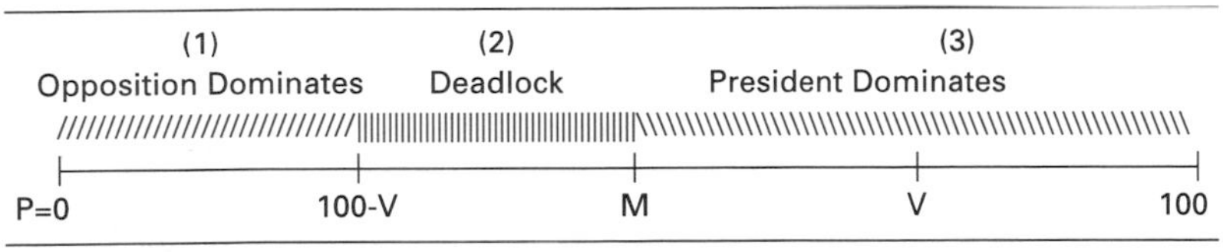

Figure 5.2
Conditions for deadlock between the president and congress when presidents have veto power and a majority of votes is required for legislative override. Note: P = share of seats held by the government coalition; M = share of members of congress necessary to approve legislation; V = share of members of congress necessary to override presidential veto.

these cases, congress passes bills preferred by the opposition and these bills are likely to become law: even if the president vetoes the bill, the opposition has the votes to override the presidential veto. In these cases, we can say that the opposition dominates. Another situation is defined by $P > M$, when congress passes bills preferred by the president, the president signs the bills, and they become law. In these cases, the president dominates. It is only when $100 - V \leq P < M$ and $M \leq O < V$ that deadlock can occur: in these cases, congress passes bills preferred by the opposition, the president vetoes these bills, and the opposition does not have enough votes to override the presidential veto. There is a stalemate between congress and the president, to which there is no automatic solution since executive and legislative have independent basis of authority. This is the situation that should make presidential regimes the most vulnerable, because both the president and the opposition would have an incentive to seek extraconstitutional solutions to the stalemate.

Empirically, thus, deadlock situations depend on the combination of institutional and political factors. On one hand, they depend on the distribution of seats in congress or, more specifically, on the share of seats held by the government. On the other hand, they depend on institutional provisions regarding the presidential veto. These provisions are whether the president has veto power, the type of congressional majority necessary to override the presidential veto, whether the system is unicameral or bicameral, and whether in bicameral systems veto override is by a vote in each chamber separately or in a joint session of both chambers....

Survival of Presidential Regimes

With the definitions of minority governments and deadlock situations in mind, it is now possible to investigate the conditions under which these situations are likely to occur in presidential regimes, the way in which they relate to each other, and the impact they are likely to have on the survival of presidential regimes. There are five main points to be noted.

The first point is that minority presidents are indeed frequent in presidential regimes....

... [O]verall, about 40% of the years of presidentialism were experienced with minority governments, higher ... in bicameral (42.54%) than in unicameral (36.46%) systems. These numbers are higher than what has been observed in (European) parliamentary systems, but not dramatically higher. As reported by Strom (1990, p. 8), studies of parliamentary governments in Europe, including his own, have found that the frequency of minority governments ranges from 30% to 37%.

Second, the occurrence of minority presidents is associated with the number of political parties, with the type of electoral system, and with the electoral cycle, as suggested by Mainwaring (1993), Jones (1995a), Shugart (1995), and others. As the descriptive patterns in table 5.2 indicate, minority presidents are more frequent when congressional elections are held under proportional representation systems, in multi-party systems (although it does not increase monotonically as the effective number of parties increases), and when presidential and legislative elections do not coincide. The occurrence of minority governments is also associated with these factors, although some of the effect is diluted by the fact that minority presidents sometimes build a majority through coalitions. . . .

Third, deadlock situations are far from being the predominant condition of presidentialism. Overall, deadlock occurs in about one third of the cases (33.52%), and it is only weakly related to the conditions that are considered to be at the root of the instability of presidential regimes: the effective number of parties, whether congressional elections are proportional or not, or whether legislative and presidential elections are concurrent. . . .

Fourth, we cannot infer anything about the survival of presidential democracies from electoral and partisan variables. The evidence that is sometimes (e.g., Mainwaring, 1993; Jones, 1995a) offered in support of the proposition that minority presidents and deadlock situations are detrimental to presidentialism is usually indirect: it is about the *conditions* that are more likely to produce a minority president, because minority presidents are assumed to produce deadlock and deadlock is assumed to have a negative effect on the survival of the regime. Thus, the type of electoral system, the number of political parties, and the electoral cycle are all found to influence the likelihood that presidents will control legislative majorities. From that, it is then inferred that these factors also affect the survival of presidential regimes. However, whereas it is indeed true, as has been seen, that these conditions affect the likelihood that presidents and their

governments will control a majority of seats in congress, it is not the case that they affect the chances of survival of presidential regimes.

Table 5.3 presents the probabilities that presidential regimes will break down as a function of electoral and partisan variables. It can be seen that neither the type of electoral system nor the relative timing of presidential and legislative elections has any impact on the survival of presidential regimes. . . .

The story with the number of political parties is somewhat more complex. It is not, contrary to Mainwaring (1993) and Jones (1995a), multipartism per se that affects the survival of presidential regimes. In presidential democracies, higher risks are associated with situations of very low pluralism, or situations conducive to moderate pluralism, which, as Sartori (1976) suggested, are the ones in which there are between two and five relevant political parties. Presidential democracies with an effective number of parties larger than five, the cases that tend to be conducive to "polarized pluralism" in Sartori's typology, have an expected life considerably higher than the presidential democracies in which the effective number of parties is fewer than five: 91 years against 25. . . .

Finally, but certainly not any less important, contrary to all expectations, minority presidents, minority governments, and deadlocks have no negative effect on the survival of presidential regimes. If arguments about the perils of presidentialism are correct, presidential democracies should face higher risks of dying when the presidency and the congress are controlled by different parties and when the conditions for deadlock between the president and the congress are present. Yet as the bottom rows in table 5.3 demonstrate this is not true. Presidential regimes are slightly more likely to die when presidential parties do not hold a majority of seats in congress. However, whatever difference there is, it disappears entirely when we allow for the fact that minority presidents sometimes form coalition governments and, hence, increase the share

Table 5.2

Frequency of minority presidents, minority governments, and deadlock situations in presidential regimes by type of legislature, effective number of political parties, electoral system, and timing of elections

	Minority presidents		Minority governments		Deadlock situations	
	%	n	%	n	%	n
All	53.35	731	40.22	726	33.52	710
Type of legislature						
Unicameral	45.85	277	36.46	277	29.67	273
Bicameral	59.93	454	42.54	449	35.96	437
Electoral system						
Majority-plurality	43.84	146	39.04	146	36.99	146
Pure proportional	54.15	554	39.42	553	32.96	540
Pure proportional + mixed	55.73	585	40.52	580	32.62	564
Effective number of parties (ENP)						
ENP ≤ 2	38.67	150	35.33	150	27.33	150
2 < ENP ≤ 3	38.08	281	33.45	281	31.49	280
3 < ENP ≤ 4	88.46	130	59.69	129	49.22	128
4 < ENP ≤ 5	63.38	71	28.17	71	28.17	71
ENP > 5	62.65	83	50.60	83	32.10	81
ENP excluding the United States and Switzerland						
ENP ≤ 2	31.13	106	26.42	106	15.09	106
2 < ENP ≤ 3	37.96	274	33.21	274	31.13	273
3 < ENP ≤ 4	88.46	130	59.69	129	49.22	128
4 < ENP ≤ 5	90.00	50	40.00	50	40.00	50
ENP > 5	98.11	53	79.24	53	50.98	51
Timing of legislative and presidential elections						
Nonconcurrent	59.68	124	45.16	124	40.32	124
Alternate	73.91	138	66.92	133	47.11	121
Nonconcurrent + alternate	67.18	262	56.42	257	43.67	245
Concurrent	45.63	469	31.34	469	28.17	465

Note: Minority presidents are the cases in which the party of the president does not control more than 50% of the seats in the legislature in a unicameral system or in at least one of the chambers in a bicameral system. Minority governments are defined similarly for the party of the president plus the parties that hold cabinet positions.

Table 5.3
Breakdown probabilities of presidential regimes by partisan, electoral, and political conditions

	Number of transitions	Number of cases	Breakdown probability
Effective number of parties (ENP)			
ENP ≤ 2	7	153	.0458
$2 < $ ENP ≤ 3	6	287	.0209
$3 < $ ENP ≤ 4	10	140	.0714
$4 < $ ENP ≤ 5	3	72	.0417
ENP > 5	1	90	.0111
Electoral system			
Majority-plurality	8	166	.0482
Proportional	22	582	.0378
Proportional + mixed	23	618	.0372
Timing of legislative and presidential elections			
Nonconcurrent	5	157	.0318
Alternate	8	146	.0548
Nonconcurrent + alternate	13	303	.0429
Concurrent	18	481	.0374
Political conditions			
Minority presidents	18	390	.0462
Majority presidents	10	341	.0293
Minority governments	17	434	.0392
Majority governments	11	292	.0377
Deadlock situations	9	238	.0378
No deadlock situations	15	472	.0318

of seats they can count on to govern. The difference between deadlock and no-deadlock situations, although in favor of the former, is rather small: Whereas 1 in every 31 presidential democracies dies when there is no deadlock, 1 in every 26 dies when there is deadlock. This difference does not seem to warrant the level of concern with deadlock that is often expressed in the comparative literature on presidentialism. . . .

To summarize, some of the commonly postulated effects of electoral and partisan factors on presidentialism can be observed empirically: the electoral system, the timing of elections, and the number of parties do affect, as expected, the legislative strength of presidents and the likelihood of minority presidents. These cases are more frequent in proportional representation systems, when presidential and legislative elections do not coincide, and when the number of parties is large. These factors also affect the occurrence of minority governments, although not as strongly. This relationship, however, does not warrant any conclusion about the survival chances of presidential democracies; neither the type of electoral system nor the timing of presidential and legislative elections has any impact on the survival of presidential regimes. The number of parties, in turn, matters for the survival of presidentialism, but not in the way and probably not for the reasons commonly postulated. What matters is not multipartism per se but whether pluralism is moderate; moderate pluralism, in turn, affects survival of presidentialism not because of its effect on the president's legislative support but most likely because of the distribution of strength among the three largest parties. Most important, none of these factors affect the likelihood of deadlock, which does not have a negative effect on the survival of presidential regimes. It seems, thus, that there must be other mechanisms operating in presidential regimes that allow them to survive under conditions that presumably would make them perish. . . .

References

Altman-Olin, David. (1999). *The politics of coalition formation and survival in multiparty presidential democracies: The case of Uruguay (1989–1999)*. Unpublished manuscript, Department of Government, University of Notre Dame, IN.

Amorin Neto, Octavio. (1998). *Of presidents, parties and ministers: Cabinet formation and legislative decision-making under separation of powers*. Unpublished doctoral dissertation, Department of Political Science, University of California, San Diego.

Cheibub, José Antonio. (2002). Presidentialism and democratic performance. In Andrew Reynolds (Ed.), *Constitutional design: Institutional design, conflict management, and democracy in the late twentieth century*. Oxford, UK: Oxford University Press.

Cheibub, José Antonio, & Limongi, Fernando. (2000, August). *Where is the difference? Parliamentary and presidential democracies reconsidered*. Paper presented at the XVIIIth World Congress of Political Science, International Political Science Association, Québec City, Canada.

Dehesa, Grace Ivana. (1997). *Goviernos de coalición en el sistema presidencial: América del Sur* [Coalition governments in presidential systems: South America]. Unpublished doctoral dissertation, European University Institute, Florence, Italy.

Jones, Mark P. (1995a). *Electoral laws and the survival of presidential democracies*. Notre Dame, IN: Notre Dame University Press.

Mainwaring, Scott. (1993). Presidentialism, multipartism, and democracy: The difficult combination. *Comparative Political Studies, 26*, 198–228.

Mainwaring, Scott, & Shugart, Matthew Soberg. (1997). Conclusion: Presidentialism and the party system. In Scott Mainwaring & Matthew Soberg Shugart (Eds.), *Presidentialism and democracy in Latin America* (pp. 394–439). Cambridge, UK: Cambridge University Press.

Sartori, Giovanni. (1976). *Parties and party systems: A framework for analysis*. Cambridge, UK: Cambridge University Press.

Shugart, Matthew Soberg. (1995). The electoral cycle and institutional sources of divided presidential government. *American Political Science Review, 89*, 327–343.

Strom, Kaare. (1990). *Minority government and majority rule*. Cambridge, UK: Cambridge University Press.

Minority Governments in Parliamentary Democracies: The Rationality of Nonwinning Cabinet Solutions

Kaare Strom

The objective of this study is to investigate the formation of minority governments in parliamentary democracies. Minority governments (or cabinets) are governments formed by parties that together control less than half of the seats in the national legislature or, operationally, the lower house of bicameral legislatures. . . .

The Incidence of Minority Governments

In order to subject minority governments to closer scrutiny, I have collected data on all recent governments in countries with a significant record of minority cabinets. . . .

The overall frequency of minority governments is 114 out of 323 governments during this period, or 35.3%, which corresponds to close to eight minority cabinets per country, or more than two per decade per country. This record can only be described as very substantial, whether in absolute or relative terms. . . . Majority party governments will almost invariably form whenever possible, that is, in any *majority situation.* In minority situations, when no majority party exists, majority coalitions and minority cabinets are the natural options. In these situations, minority solutions have been chosen 43.0% of the time. . . .

The high number of minority governments could be a misleading indicator of their commonness, if these governments tended to be of very short duration. Measured in cabinet years, minoritarian solutions account for a somewhat smaller proportion of all governments (29.1%),

Excerpted from: Kaare Strom, "Minority Governments in Parliamentary Democracies: The Rationality of Nonwinning Cabinet Solutions." *Comparative Political Studies* 17(2) (July 1984): 199–227. © 1984 Sage Publications, Inc. Reprinted by permission of Sage Publications, Inc.

yet their total tenure of more than 125 cabinet years remains very substantial. The durability advantage of majority cabinets is largely accounted for by majority party governments. In minority situations, minority governments represent 37.7% of total tenure. Thus, minority governments constitute a substantial proportion of all governments in minority situations, whether this proportion is measured in terms of the number of governments formed or their share of time in office. . . .

Explaining Minority Governments

Although the literature on minority governments is meager, it is possible to identify a conventional view of the conditions under which such governments form. Minority cabinets, it is commonly held, tend to form in unstable and conflictual political systems, whose party systems are highly fractionalized. These cabinets are suboptimal solutions, which are only resorted to when all else fails. Though causal relationships are rarely specified, minority governments are commonly associated with social and political malaise. . . .

Minority Governments and Instability

One of the propositions within the conventional explanation is that minority governments are symptoms of political instability of crisis (Friesenhahn, 1971; von Beyme, 1970). According to this view, the less stable a political system is, the more common minority governments should be. . . . The argument that minority governments reflect severe systemic crises could hardly be defended in view of the high incidence of such cabinets across a wide range of democracies. . . .

Table 5.4
Distribution of cabinet types by country

Country	Majority	Minority	Non-partisan	Total	Pct Min	Mean PB
Belgium	25	4	0	29	14	62.0
Canada	7	8	0	15	53	53.1
Denmark	3	20	0	23	87	40.1
Finland	19	11	7	37	30	54.6
France	18	12	0	30	40	51.0
Iceland	13	4	0	17	24	51.5
Ireland	10	5	0	15	33	50.5
Israel	23	2	0	25	8	62.0
Italy	26	19	0	45	42	51.8
Netherlands	15	3	0	18	17	61.6
Norway	8	10	0	18	56	47.4
Portugal	7	1	4	12	8	64.5
Spain	1	3	0	4	75	50.0
Sweden	9	10	0	19	53	47.2
United Kingdom	14	2	0	16	13	52.7
Total	198	114	11	323	35.3	53.2

Sources: Mackie and Rose (1982), Keesing's Contemporary Archives, Cook and Paxton (1975), Facts on File.
Note: Pct Min = Minority Governments as Percentage of all Governments; Mean PB = Mean Parliamentary Basis.

Minority Governments and Fractionalization

Conventionally, minority governments have also been associated with high degrees of political fragmentation and party system fractionalization (Budge and Herman, 1978). The more fractionalization the parliamentary party system, it is argued, the more difficult the formation of a winning coalition becomes, and the greater the likelihood of an undersized solution.... Table 5.5 demonstrates that the average fractionalization under which substantive minority govern ments form is *lower* than that of majority coalitions. Although the difference in fractionalization scores is by no means dramatic, it is in the opposite direction of what has been hypothesized....

Minority Governments and Polarization

Political polarization may complement or compete with fractionalization as an explanation of minority government formation. Legislatures that are polarized should experience a high incidence of minority governments, particularly under conditions of fractionalization and instability (Dodd, 1976; Powell, 1982)....

Table 5.5 reveals that polarization is related to cabinet type in a pattern almost identical to that of fractionalization. Majority party governments form in radically less polarized systems than any other cabinet type. Nonpartisan administrations are found in the most polarized, as well as the most fractionalized, systems. But there is no tendency for minority governments to form

Table 5.5
Fractionalization and polarization by cabinet type (mean values)

Cabinet type	Fractionalization (Rae's F)	Polarization	(N)
Majority Party	.575	.011	(42)
Majority Coalition	.755	.183	(156)
Minority Formal	.754	.205	(13)
Minority Substantive	.726	.145	(101)
Non-Partisan	.765	.213	(11)
All Governments	.723	.151	(323)

Sources: Mackie and Rose (1982), Powell (1982), Keesing's Archives.
Note: Polarization = Electoral support for extremist parties as proportion of parliamentary seats.

in more polarized environments than majority coalitions. On the contrary, substantive minority governments are associated with markedly lower levels of polarization than majority coalitions....

My fundamental assumption is that minority governments can be understood as results of *rational choices* made by political parties, or more specifically, by the parliamentary leaders of these organizations....

(1) Political parties are organizations that contest political elections and seek governmental office (Sartori, 1976).... For analytical purposes, I also assume that office and electoral advantage in part are valued instrumentally, and that the underlying motivation is to influence policymaking in the national assembly....

(2) The crucial point is that if policy influence is a principal objective of political parties, then government participation is not a necessary condition for payoff....

(3) The third modification of conventional coalition theory consists in the recognition that majority status is not always the *effective decision point*....

(4) Finally, political parties are not exclusively concerned with immediate objectives, but

their behavior must be understood in *temporal* terms.... Thus, decisions about cabinet formation will often take the form of a trade-off between power and electoral prospects....

How do these considerations help us make sense out of minority governments? I assume that minority governments form when the benefits of being in office are outweighed by the costs for a majority segment of the party system. I have further argued that a principal *benefit of governing* consists in the *policy influence differential* between government and opposition. The greater the opportunities for the parliamentary opposition to influence legislative policymaking, the lower the benefits of governing. The *costs of governing* refer to *anticipated electoral losses*. Government incumbency tends to result in subsequent electoral losses, and coalition governments tend to lose more than others (Powell, 1981; Strom, 1983). Moreover, coalitions typically involve policy compromises as well as projected electoral misfortunes. With these costs in mind, potential governmental parties may forego the immediate gratification of holding office. Broad coalitions should be eschewed in particular. Future office holding will figure prominently in party calculations of political prospects. A decision to remain in opposition temporarily implies no lack of interest in governing in the long run, but rather a willingness to wait for more favorable circumstances. Thus, considerations of electoral prospects will focus not only on how competitive future elections are likely to be, but also on their effect on opportunities for subsequent government participation. In fact, the impact or decisiveness of elections for cabinet formation will be a principal factor in party calculations.... The more decisive elections are, the more likely they are to deter parties from government participation....

In sum, the conditions most favorable for minority government formation are where policy can be influenced even from opposition status (low benefits of governing), and where future elections are likely to be competitive and decisive for government formation (high costs of governing). Thus, the explanatory variables are:

(1) The potential influence of the parliamentary opposition, and

(2) The decisiveness of the electoral site for government formation.

With increases in electoral decisiveness and oppositional influence, I predict that the parliamentary bases of governments will diminish, and minority governments should, under these circumstances, be more common....

Oppositional Influence

The benefits of governing depend on the opportunities for legislative influence open to opposition parties. These opportunities are in turn determined by internal parliamentary structure and procedures, as well as by the role of the legislature in the larger political system. A strong and decentralized committee structure offers much better prospects for oppositional influence than the more centralized and less deliberative mode of decision making traditionally found, such as in the British House of Commons (Lees and Shaw, 1979; Mezey, 1979). In view of the critical role of legislative committees, I have constructed an index of the potential for oppositional influence on the basis of the following dichotomized indicators:

(1) *The number of standing committees.* Committee specialization is a precondition for effective decision making. And specialization is difficult to attain without differentiation of the committee structure. In other words, a certain minimum number of standing committees is necessary for deliberation to be effective and the opposition influential. I have considered more than ten standing committees necessary for high oppositional influence. The next two indicators are also measures of specialization, and the rationale behind them parallels the one above.

(2) Whether the standing committees have *fixed areas of specialization.*

(3) Whether such areas of specialization correspond to *ministerial departments.*

(4) Whether there are any restrictions on the *number of committee assignments* per legislator. If such restrictions exist, the legislators are more likely to be specialists in the areas in which they serve. Moreover, restrictions make it more difficult for the governing parties to manipulate committee assignments to their advantage. Thus, restrictions on committee assignments should enhance oppositional influence.

(5) Whether the committee chairs are *proportionately distributed* among the parties in the legislature. The alternative is normally that the government controls all chairs, which, of course, is less desirable from the point of view of the opposition.

For the last four indicators a positive value is interpreted as a high score on the variable. The aggregate score for each country corresponds to the number of positive values; thus the range is from 0 to 5. It should be emphasized that we are concerned with structural constraints on oppositional influence, and not with the actual power

Table 5.6
Influence of opposition by country

Country	No/Com (1)	Special (2)	Corresp (3)	Membshp (4)	Chair (5)	Aggregate value
Belgium	+	+	+	−	+	4
Canada	+	+	+	−	−	3
Denmark	+	+	+	−	−	3
Finland	+	+	−	−	+	3
France	+	+	+	+	−	4
Iceland	+	+	+	+	−	4
Ireland	−	−	−	−	+	1
Israel	−	+	−	−	+	2
Italy	+	+	+	+	−	4
Netherlands	+	−	+	−	−	2
Norway	+	+	+	+	+	5
Portugal	+	+	+	−	+	4
Spain	+	+	+	−	−	3
Sweden	+	+	+	−	+	4
United Kingdom	−	+	−	−	−	1

Sources: Herman (1976) and others; see Strom (1984: 123) for details.

enjoyed by the parties out of office. This distinction is important for the direction of the causal relationship. While influential oppositions may facilitate the formation of minority governments, it is also arguable that minority governments enhance the influence of the opposition. It is much less plausible that cabinet minoritarianism would alter the committee structure of the national assembly, as measured here. Historically, there have been strong continuities in the characteristics of the legislatures under investigation. Table 5.6 presents the data on oppositional influence by country.

The Decisiveness of Elections

The second variable is the decisiveness of elections for government formation, which has been designed to tap the costs of governing. This variable consists of four theoretically derived components. These components and their indicators are as follows:

(1) *The identifiability of government options.* Unless the voters are presented with clear, preelectoral governmental choices, there can hardly be decisive elections. For each decade, countries have been scored impressionistically as low (0), medium (.5), or high (1) in preelectoral government identifiability.

(2) *Electoral volatility.* In order for elections to be decisive, there must be significant variation in the proportion of parliamentary seats captured by the various parties from election to election. As a measure of this type of competitiveness, I have chosen electoral volatility (for seats) between successive elections (Pedersen, 1979). Each government has been given the mean score for the country and decade in which it was formed.

Table 5.7
Electoral decisiveness by country (mean values)

Country	Identifiability	Volatility	Responsiveness	Proximity
Belgium	.10	.09	.60	.45
Canada	1.00	.19	.73	.87
Denmark	.76	.12	.64	.70
Finland	.00	.08	.53	.34
France	.00	.18	.47	.14
Iceland	.59	.08	.52	.63
Ireland	.87	.08	.85	.80
Israel	.14	.13	.44	.40
Italy	.12	.09	.48	.22
Netherlands	.00	.08	.46	.67
Norway	.83	.10	.70	.56
Portugal	.50	.11	.46	.33
Spain	.50	.29	1.00	.75
Sweden	1.00	.06	.52	.63
United Kingdom	1.00	.07	1.00	.72
All countries	.39	.11	.58	.48

(3) *Electoral responsiveness.* A third requirement for electoral decisiveness is that governments be formed by parties that have gained rather than lost seats at the latest election. I have scored every government formation according to the proportion of electoral gainers among its constituent parties[7]. Electoral responsiveness has then been computed as the mean responsiveness score for a given country and decade.

(4) *Proximity.* Finally, electoral decisiveness requires that governments be formed in close proximity to general elections. Proximity scores simply correspond to the proportion of all government formations taking place immediately

following a general election, again measured on a decade-to-decade basis for each country.

Electoral decisiveness is a systemic rather than governmental property. Accordingly, our measures have been computed at the systemic level. All four component variables are bounded by the values 0 and 1. Each government has then been assigned the appropriate score for its country and decade of formation. Table 5.7 presents a summary of mean electoral decisiveness scores by country.

Testing the Rationalist Explanation

The hypotheses predict that as electoral decisiveness and oppositional influence increase, the parliamentary basis of the governments formed should tend to diminish, and the likelihood of minority government formation increase. I have

---

7. Parties that exhibit no change in their proportion of seats in the most recent election have been excluded from the computations of electoral responsiveness, except when they form single-party governments. Any party gaining an absolute parliamentary majority has been counted as a winner.

Table 5.8
Parliamentary basis and numerical status by conditions of government formation

| Variable | Parliamentary basis | | | | Numerical status | |
| | Correlation Pearson's R | Regression | | | Logit | |
		Coeff	Std Err	Beta	Coeff	Std Err
Influence of opposition	−.10	−2.68**	.93	−.17	−.39**	.16
Electoral salience	−.30	−5.28**	1.05	−.30	−.95**	.18
Volatility	−.14	−39.77**	14.16	−.16	−7.56**	2.46
Responsiveness	−.22	−10.08**	4.30	−.14	−1.79**	.71

Note: Adjusted R Square (Std Regression): .147; Correct Prediction Rate (Logit): 72.8%; N = 265.
**Significant at .01 level in one-tailed tests.

tested these hypotheses by regressing the parliamentary basis of each government (including external support) on the explanatory variables. Only minority situations with partisan outcomes have been included, which is to say that majority party and nonpartisan governments have been excluded. These restrictions are essential, since it would be meaningless to attempt to predict minority government formation in situations where a majority party exists or where party politics has been suspended.

Factor analysis of the four indicators of electoral decisiveness reveals that governmental identifiability and electoral proximity load strongly on the same factor, whereas competitiveness and responsiveness do not. Evidently, electoral decisiveness is a multidimensional phenomenon, but the identifiability and proximity measures seem to capture the same dimension. The latter two indicators have therefore been combined into a single measure of *electoral salience*, since they both appear to tap the extent to which elections serve as focal events in the game of government formation[8]. Electoral salience has then been entered in the regression equation

together with the measures of volatility, responsiveness, and oppositional influence. The dependent variable (parliamentary basis) is a continuous one, with hypothetical bounds of 0 and 100. However, the qualitative difference between 49% and 51% parliamentary support is much more significant for an explanation of minority governments than the range from, for example, 55% to 75%. Hence, I have also run a logistic regression, where the governmental outcome (numerical status) is treated as a dichotomy and scored 1 for majority coalitions and formal minority governments and 0 for substantive minority governments. Table 5.8 presents the results for the equation with four independent variables.

The dependent variables have been constructed in such a way that we should expect to find consistently negative signs and significant relationships in table 5.8. And in fact the explanatory variables are related to minority government formation in the expected direction and at high levels of significance. There is also a high level of consistency between the standard regression and the logit analysis. The hypothesized relationships show up whether the governmental outcome is measured as a dichotomy (majority versus minority) or as a continuous measure of parliamentary support. And the order of significance of the various predictors is virtually

8. The measure of electoral salience has been constructed by standardizing the identifiability and proximity measures, and then, for each government, adding up the two standardized scores and dividing the sum by two.

unchanged. The predicted difference in parliamentary basis between the highest and lowest observed values on the independent variables is 10.7% for oppositional influence, 16.4% for electoral salience, 20.1% for volatility, and 10.1% for responsiveness. Clearly, electoral decisiveness is by far a stronger predictor of minority government formation than oppositional influence. Among the three dimensions of electoral decisiveness, volatility accounts for the greatest differential impact between its extreme values. However, in the normal range of variation, electoral salience has a considerably larger effect on parliamentary basis. But even volatility and responsiveness are highly significant predictors of minority government formation, each with about as much explanatory power as oppositional influence. The relatively smaller impact of oppositional influence is entirely to be expected for two reasons. Presumably the anticipation of upcoming elections may in itself be sufficient to induce parties to abstain from power, whereas a consideration of the opportunities for oppositional influence in isolation would never produce the same result. In other words, it is always better to be in government than in opposition, if the future is disregarded. Second, the explanatory power of the measure of oppositional influence may be affected by the fact that it is a somewhat crude ordinal-level variable.

The model with these four independent variables provides a respectable measure of overall fit. The standard regression model explains about 15% of the total variation in parliamentary basis. With governmental outcome dichotomized, the logit model is capable of correctly predicting 72.5% of the cases. This represents a reduction in error of approximately 18% over estimates based on the modal category.

Confronting the Competing Explanations

As a final step in the analysis of minority government formation, I have estimated models with the same two dependent variables (parliamentary basis and numerical status) and a more extensive set of predictors, representing competing explanations. Most of the additional variables have already been discussed in the analysis of the conventional explanations. The independent variables now include: electoral salience, volatility, responsiveness, oppositional influence, fractionalization, polarization, crisis duration, the number of formation attempts, constitutional investiture requirements, and the concentration of the opposition. The latter variable is a measure of the proportion of the total opposition contained in the major oppositional bloc along a left-right dimension (Dahl, 1966). Governments faced with unilateral oppositions (as in two-party systems) have an opposition concentration score of 1. If, on the other hand, the opposition is evenly divided between right and left, the score is 0.5. This measure presupposes a meaningful ordering of all relevant political parties on a left-right dimension. In the actual rankings on which the variable has been constructed, every effort has been made to maximize consistency with existing authoritative rankings. The theoretical interest in this measure stems from the conception of minority governments as governments of the political center, with bilateral oppositions. From their strategic location, they could arguably divide and rule the opposition on the extremes.

The models also include a dummy variable indicating whether there exists a constitutional provision for obligatory parliamentary investiture at the time of government formation. The reasoning here is that minority government formation is less likely if an incoming administration needs to secure a vote of confidence in its first encounter with the national assembly. Table 5.9 presents the models.

The dependent variables are the same as previously. Simple correlation coefficients with the continuous measure of parliamentary basis have been reported for illustration and in order to relate the findings to the previous bivariate

Table 5.9
Parliamentary basis and numerical status by conditions of government formation (expanded set)

Variable	Parliamentary basis				Numerical status	
	Correlation Pearson's R	Regression			Logit	
		Coeff	Std Err	Beta	Coeff	Std Err
Influence of opposition	−.09	−1.70*	.95	−.11	−.40*	.19
Electoral salience	−.29	−10.20**	1.43	−.59	−1.34**	.24
Volatility	−.16	−31.94*	13.92	−.13	−8.01**	2.79
Responsiveness	−.22	−11.22**	4.19	−.16	−2.15**	.80
Polarization	−.01	−.42**	.11	−.33	NS	
Fractionalization	−.09	NS	NS	NS	NS	
Crisis duration	−.16	NS	NS	NS	.02**	.01
Formation attempts	−.02	−.99*	.57	−.10	−.31**	.12
Opposition concentration	−.01	12.24*	6.69	.12	2.88*	1.34
Investiture	−.09	NS	NS	NS	NS	

Note: Reported coefficients are those from the reestimated equations excluding variables not significant at the .05 level. Significance levels reported for one-tailed tests. Adjusted R Square (Std Regression): .216; Correct Prediction Rate (Logit): 82.6%.
* Significant at .05 level.
** Significant at .01 level.
NS = Not significant at .05 level.

analysis of these relationships. Since many of the relationships in the model are clearly insignificant, a backward elimination procedure has been employed. Only predictors with a significant impact at the .05 level have been included in the final equations.

The introduction of these various control variables does not detract from the explanatory power of my rational choice explanation. In fact, the beta weights of both electoral salience and responsiveness have increased from the previous analysis, and all hypothesized relationships remain significant. Electoral salience is far and away the most powerful predictor of minority government formation in the logistic as well as the standard regression. Its observed range is approximately 3.1, which corresponds to a predicted difference of well over 30 percentage points in parliamentary basis. The impacts of

volatility and oppositional influence diminish somewhat when control variables are introduced. However, both relationships retain their significance, though oppositional influence only barely so, in the standard regression.

Polarization turns out to be the second strongest predictor in the standard regression, but falls to insignificance in the logit analysis. This is an interesting finding and one of the few cases of radically different results between the standard and logistic regressions. We may recall that the bivariate relationship between polarization and parliamentary basis is positive (though hardly significant) and thus contrary to conventional expectations. In the regression model high levels of polarization are in fact related to narrow parliamentary support when control variables are introduced. The conventional view is thus supported, but the results also dovetail nicely with other theoretical interpretations. High levels of polarization imply that there are large segments of the party system for which government participation is always unattractive in the short term. Polarization also means that the policy distance between parties is high and compromises accordingly costly. But the logit analysis indicates that these constraints do not produce minority governments. One interpretation of this puzzle is that polarization reduces the likelihood of oversized coalitions, but that it simultaneously induces the relevant parties to seek solutions that do not fall below the majority threshold. The size principle, then, may be particularly applicable under conditions of high polarization. Perhaps minority governments are perceived to be especially ineffective or associated with serious systemic risks under such circumstances. Such perceptions probably do exist, and they could well give responsible parliamentary leaders added incentives to seek stable and "winning" solutions. Whether minority governments are in fact less stable or effective than majority coalitions under these and other circumstances is a different question (Strom, 1983). It is also plausible that high polarization increases the value of being in office and the risks and disadvantages of opposition status.

Note that the number of formation attempts and the concentration of the opposition turn out to be significantly related in the expected directions in the multivariate analysis, despite the fact that their zero-order correlations are virtually nil. On the other hand, investiture requirements and party system fractionalization show no significant relationship to the incidence of minority governments. The unexpected tendency for minority governments to emerge from particularly *short* cabinet crises is confirmed, but only in the logit analysis. In other words, minority governments follow short crises, but radically undersized cabinets probably do not result from exceptionally brief negotiation processes.

The overall fit of the models is moderately improved with the more extensive set of inde

pendent variables. The logit model shows the more significant improvement, as the reduction in error climbs to 34%. Residual analysis reveals that the models yield the most accurate results for the Anglo-American democracies (Great Britain, Ireland, and Canada) and the Scandinavian nations, whereas Portugal and Iceland exhibit the worst fit. It is perfectly reasonable that Portuguese governments are much less likely to be minoritarian than the models would predict. Postrevolutionary Portugal probably fits my theoretical assumptions least well of all 15 polities. The regime has been too unstable for party leaders to forego voluntarily the benefits and security of holding office. Also, in a nascent democracy, risk-averse inclinations may lead politicians to eschew government solutions perceived as potentially destabilizing. On the other hand, the countries that exhibit the best fit seem to meet the theoretical assumptions of stability and oppositional security particularly well. In other words, the rationalist explanation fits best where its assumptions are most plausible.

In sum, this multivariate analysis offers substantial support for the rational choice explanation of minority government formation. However, it indicates that electoral decisiveness is more important than oppositional influence as an explanatory factor. Hence, future electoral success may be a more important consideration than immediate access to policy making when governments are formed in multiparty systems. If this is correct, then it would have profound implications for coalition theory, which has tended to ignore future electoral considerations.

Conclusions

In this analysis, I have surveyed the universe of minority governments and investigated the conditions under which they form. The analysis of minority government formation has examined macro-structural characteristics of political systems as well as the immediate processes that precede the formation of parliamentary governments. Throughout this analysis, I have sought to test two competing explanations of minority government formation. The conventional theory views minority cabinets as options of last resort under conditions of severe political stress. Accordingly, minority government formation should be associated with political instability, fractionalization, and long and difficult formation processes. My results offer little support for these propositions. In fact, in some cases the exact opposite appears to be the case. As an alternative to this conventional view, I have offered a theory that explains minority governments as rational cabinet solutions under conditions of competition rather than conflict. The data have given considerable support to this explanation.

The conventional view may not be unreasonable as a historically bounded proposition. It is not difficult to see how critical events in major countries between the world wars could give rise to negative perceptions of minority governments. Unquestionably, the fear and loathing of minority governments are results of the historical lessons of the interwar period and particularly of the experiences of the Weimar Republic. These lessons were reinforced by the fate of the Third and, subsequently, the Fourth Republic in France. However, these images do not conform to the realities of contemporary minority government formation.

Minority governments are still frequently associated with the turbulence of Southern European politics. This analysis has found them to be more common in the very different context of the Scandinavian countries. It may be just as interesting to note that the countries most influenced by the Westminster model of democracy seem to turn to minority governments rather than majority coalitions when their two-party systems fragment. My theory would predict a high likelihood of minority governments in Great Britain if the current trend toward party system fragmentation continues. In that case,

the recent evolution toward lessened centralization of government control in the House of Commons could be a critical facilitating factor (Schwarz, 1980).

Beyond factual clarification, my results should have interesting implications for our understanding of the logic of government formation in different types of party systems. Traditionally, minority governments have been portrayed as defective coalition governments. The present analysis suggests that at least *substantive* minority governments may share more characteristics with majority party governments than with majority coalitions. It may not be unreasonable to see the typical substantive minority government as an *imperfect majority party government*. These governments form as alternatives to majority coalitions in minority situations, but their mode of formation resembles that of alternative-majority two-party systems. Canada may be the country that best illustrates this practice. Formal minority governments, though few in number, appear much more akin to the conventional image of minority governments.

I also hope that this study will contribute toward an enrichment of the literature on government coalitions. Coalition theories have traditionally fared rather poorly as explanations of minority government formation. This analysis suggests the possibility of incorporating minoritarian solutions as something more than aberrations within a rational choice paradigm. I have focused on three modifications that could help coalition theory make better sense of the high frequency of undersized cabinets. The first point is that majority status need not be the effective decision point in government formation; a "winning" coalition may be neither a functional requirement nor a fundamental objective of the actors in that game. Second, even opposition status may hold certain benefits for parties interested in policy influence. And finally, coalition theories must take into account the time perspectives of the actors and the role of prospective elections as democratic constraints on political parties. It is this responsiveness to the anticipated reactions of the electorate that makes democracy special.

References

Budge, I. and V. Herman (1978) "Coalitions and government formation: an empirically relevant theory." *British J. of Pol. Sci.* 8: 459–477.

Dahl, R. A. [ed.] (1966) *Political Oppositions in Western Democracies*. New Haven: Yale University Press.

Dodd, L. C. (1976) *Coalitions in Parliamentary Government*. Princeton, NJ: Princeton University Press.

Friesenhahn, E. (1971) "Parlament and Regierung in modernen Staat," pp. 307–319 in K. Kluxen (ed.) *Parlamentarismus*. Cologne: Kiepenheuer & Witsch.

Lees, J. D. and M. Shaw [eds.] (1979) *Committees in Legislatures: A Comparative Analysis*. Durham, NC: Duke University Press.

Mezey, M. L. (1979) *Comparative Legislatures*. Durham, NC: Duke University Press.

Pedersen, M. N. (1979) "The dynamics of European party systems: changing patterns of electoral volatility." *European J. of Pol. Research* 7: 1–26.

Powell, G. B., Jr. (1982) *Contemporary Democracies*. Cambridge: Harvard University Press.

——— (1981) "Party systems as systems of representation and accountability." Presented at the annual meeting of the American Political Science Association, New York.

Schwarz, J. E. (1980) "Exploring a new role in policy making: the British House of Commons in the 1970s." *Amer. Pol. Sci. Rev.* 74: 23–37.

Strom, K. (1983) "Party goals and government performance in parliamentary democracies." Presented at the annual meeting of the American Political Science Association, Chicago.

Von Beyme, K. (1970) *Die Parlamentarischen Regierungssysteme in Europa*. Munich: R. Piper.

Institutional Design, Party Systems, and Governability: Differentiating the Presidential Regimes of Latin America

Joe Foweraker

Commonalities in Latin American Political Systems

In the broad compass of democratic political systems, the countries of Latin America comprise a distinctive sub-set, defined by a combination of presidentialism and assemblies elected on the basis of proportional representation (PR).[11] Moreover, the sub-set mainly conforms to a model of pure presidentialism, with popularly elected chief executives, the terms of both executive and assembly fixed and not contingent on mutual confidence, the government named and directed by the executive, and with at least some constitutionally granted law-making authority vested in the president.[12] But, as with most categorizations of political systems, there are possible exceptions, including Bolivia, Peru and Chile,[13] and even Ecuador, Uruguay and Guatemala.[14] But this makes no difference to the

Excerpted from: Joe Foweraker, "Institutional Design, Party Systems, and Governability: Differentiating the Presidential Regimes of Latin America." *British Journal of Political Science* 28(4) (Oct. 1998): 651–676. © 1998 Cambridge University Press. Reprinted with the permission of Cambridge University Press.

11. Arend Lijphart, "Constitutional Choices for New Democracies" in Larry Diamond and M. F. Plattner, eds, The Global Resurgence of Democracy (Baltimore and London: Johns Hopkins University Press, 1993), pp. 146–58, at p. 150; and Arend Lijphart, Electoral Systems and Party and Party Systems: A Study of Twenty-Seven Democracies, 1945–1990 (Oxford: Oxford University Press, 1994). Lijphart divides this compass into four main categories, which are presidential-plurality (United States, Philippines), parliamentary-plurality (the United Kingdom, the old Commonwealth, India and Malaysia), PR-parliamentary (Western Europe), and PR-presidential (Latin America).

12. Shugart and Carey, *Presidents and Assemblies*, p. 19.

13. Shugart and Carey allege that "where the selection of the executive involves the formation of coalitions among parties within the assembly, we cannot call the regime presidential, even if there is an initial round of voting for the executive" (Shugart and Carey, Presidents and Assemblies, p. 77). In the Bolivian case, since the president is selected by assembly bargaining, and since popular plurality winners tend to fare poorly in the process, Shugart and Carey see the system as a hybrid they call "assembly-independent." Although the Chilean system from 1925 to 1973 followed the same formal rules, in practice the assembly vote simply ratified the popular choice, and so the system remained presidential (and elections for the executive and the assembly were separated by both date and ballot structure in Chile, in ways they are not contemporarily in Bolivia). But Shugart and Carey's main doubt about the present Chilean system is the alleged power of the president to dissolve the Chamber of Deputies once in any one term (although not in the last year of the term), with no negative consequences for the executive. If this was correct, it would represent a big shift in power towards a "super-presidential" system. In fact, this provision of the 1980 Constitution was abolished under the 1989 Constitution. Although several constitutions of the sub-set allow legislative censure of ministers, doubts about Peru's categorization stem from its peculiarly potent form of censure, which makes ministers directly dependent on congress for their survival. The first Belaunde Terry administration (1963–68) was obliged to employ 178 ministers in just five years. But Linz argues that the system remains presidential, since the president remains in office for the fixed term, and can continue to appoint ministers, but cannot threaten the assembly with dissolution. See Linz, "Presidential or Parliamentary Democracy," p. 61.

14. Under the 1978 Constitution in Ecuador, ministers can be censured "for infractions committed in the execution of their official functions," which appears to imply the possibility of legal proceedings. In Uruguay, although the Constitution permits the assembly to censure and remove ministers, this can lead to its own dissolution, unless the censure motion is won by two-thirds of the vote. The assembly's power in this respect tends therefore to be one of principle not practice.

critics of PR-presidentialism, who see all these countries as beset by the same fundamental problems, leading to political instability and poor economic performance. Consequently, "the Latin American model remains a particularly unattractive option." ...

In some degree these problems are endemic to all presidential systems, since these systems embody two separate agents of the electorate, and lack of policy agreement between executive and assembly can always "cause stress in the regime."[16] Such stress tends towards gridlock (to use the language of the United States), or the kind of stalemate that subverts the legislative process.[17] Hence, these systems are not really "majoritarian," as suggested by Linz and Lijphart,[18] but, much to the contrary, often suffer the "double minority"[19] of a president elected by a plurality without majority support in the assembly. In these circumstances the assembly can always block executive initiatives, even if it cannot directly control the president, while the president remains incapable of forcing a majority in the assembly through threat of dissolution.[20]

The received wisdom on Latin American political systems tends to see presidents as dominant and assemblies as weak and subservient, with the oft-cited exceptions of Chile, Costa Rica and Uruguay.[21] The danger to the present democracies in the continent is seen either in the authoritarian residues which give extensive legislative and emergency powers to the president,[22] or in the tendency for weak parties in the assembly to delegate powers to the presidency in order to overcome stalemate and immobilism.[23] In fact, most legislation in most Latin American countries is initiated by the executive, which also tends to have both total and line-item vetoes; and presidents tend to have both decree and extensive emergency powers, including that of the state-of-siege.[24] But this need not imply that assemblies are weak in consequence, or "emasculated," still less that they willingly delegate their power to the executive.[25] On the contrary, the available evidence suggests that assemblies are powerful agents, which retain a strong ability to check the executive (in countries as different

---

In Guatemala the assembly has the power to dismiss ministers against the will of the president, if it can muster a two-thirds majority.

16. Shugart and Carey, *Presidents and Assemblies*, p. 2.

17. Stalemate was such in Brazil from 1961 to 1964, and in Chile from 1970 to 1973, that "not a single piece of ordinary legislation is passed." See Przeworski, *Sustainable Democracy*, p. 46.

18. See Linz, "Presidential or Parliamentary Democracy," and Arend Lijphart, "Democracies: Forms, Performance, and Constitutional Engineering," *European Journal of Political Research*, 25 (1994), 1–17.

19. Valenzuela, "Latin America: Presidentialism in Crisis," p. 7.

20. See Scott Mainwaring, "Presidentialism, Multipartism, and Democracy: The Difficult Combination," *Comparative Political Studies*, 26 (1993), 198–228, and Valenzuela, "Latin America: Presidentialism in Crisis."

21. Scott Mainwaring, "Presidentialism in Latin America," *Latin American Research Review*, 25 (1990), 157–179.

22. Shugart and Carey, *Presidents and Assemblies*, pp. 36–38.

23. Geddes, "Initiation of New Democratic Institutions in Eastern Europe and Latin America."

24. Mainwaring, "Presidentialism, Multipartism, and Democracy."

25. According to Geddes, the new legislatures of Eastern Europe are equally jealous of their powers, and despite the presence of strong presidencies which were established prior to or concurrently with the legislature, in all cases the legislators have tried to curtail the powers of the presidency (Geddes, "Initiation of New Democratic Institutions in Eastern Europe and Latin America," p. 29). Such observations are relevant to the notorious reluctance of recent democracies to adopt parliamentary forms, since presidentialism better answers the "legislators' desire to remain free of the party shackles that parliamentarianism would bring down on them" (Shugart, "The Inverse Relationship between Party Strength and Executive Strength").

as Brazil, Ecuador, Uruguay and Venezuela).[26] Thus, the executive often has immense difficulty in putting through an agenda, and often lacks effective means for levering a recalcitrant assembly.

It is plausible that it is this executive incapacity which tempts presidents either to seek new powers through constitutional reforms or to rule largely by decree. In this way executive-assembly stalemate can lead to decretismo, and, by extension, to the phenomenon of "delegative democracy."[27] Decretismo was typical of Colombia during the National Front years and later, with the country being under state-of-siege for 75 per cent of the time from 1958 to 1989. "Delegative democracy" has been used to characterize regimes as different as that of Menem in Argentina and (early) Fujimori in Peru. Alternatively, executive legislative deadlock can lead to military coups (Brazil 1964, Peru 1968, Chile 1973) or autogolpes[28] (Uruguay 1973, Peru 1992, and an attempted autogolpe in Guatemala 1993), and the breakdown of democracy.[29]

---

26. Mark P. Jones, *Electoral Laws and the Survival of Presidential Democracies* (Notre Dame, Ind.: University of Notre Dame Press, 1995).

27. Guillermo O'Donnell, "Delegative Democracy?" Working Paper 172, Helen Kellogg Institute, University of Notre Dame, South Bend, Ind. (1992).

28. Autogolpe refers to action by an elected president to curtail or dismantle democratic government, usually with the open collaboration or covert collusion of the military.

29. Yet this cannot be interpreted to mean that presidential regimes are necessarily more prone to breakdown than parliamentary ones. Whether it is concluded that they are so or not tends to depend on the timeframe and geographical scope of the inquiry. By focusing uniquely on "Third World" cases, Shugart and Carey are able to conclude that "just over half (52.2 percent) of the presidential regimes ... have broken down, while a higher percentage (59.1) of the parliamentary regimes have." Presidentialism is overwhelmingly a Third World phenomenon, and in this context it has fared at least as well and arguably better than parliamentarianism.

Variations in Latin American Political Systems

But it is argued that it is not presidentialism per se but "the combination of presidentialism and a fractionalized multiparty system" which is "especially inimical to stable democracy."[30] ...

Evidently, just as presidentialism is not a homogeneous regime type,[40] so PR-presidentialism is not a homogeneous category. There is considerable variation in the degrees of multipartism, party discipline, and the stability of party systems and government coalitions. At the same time, these variables will strongly affect governability by their direct and often conjoint influence on the key variable of the degree of presidential support in the assembly.[41] Most observers agree that for a PR-presidential system to govern effectively "what is really needed is a working majority" in the assembly,[42] or, at the very least, "a reasonably large congressional delegation from the president's party."[43] Without a straight majority or near majority, the president needs to build either a stable coalition majority, or shifting coalition majorities on single issues and initiatives; and a near majority will certainly facilitate such coalition formation. In this view, if PR-presidential systems break down it is not because of political polarization or "polarized pluralism,"[44] but because of the lack of a working majority. Indeed, Chile is the only

---

30. Mainwaring, "Presidentialism in Latin America," p. 168.

40. Shugart and Carey, *Presidents and Assemblies.*

41. Jones, *Electoral Laws and the Survival of Presidential Democracies*, chap. 1.

42. Mainwaring, "Presidentialism, Multipartism, and Democracy," p. 224, f. 18.

43. Scott Mainwaring and Timothy R. Scully, eds., *Building Democratic Institutions: Party Systems in Latin America* (Stanford, Calif.: Stanford University Press, 1995), p. 33.

44. Giovanni Sartori, *Parties and Party Systems: A Framework for Analysis* (Cambridge: Cambridge University Press, 1976).

case of a presidential democracy surviving for over a generation without such a majority....

... [I]t is safe to conclude that the democratic systems of Latin America can be divided between those which run plurality-concurrent executive elections, have low levels of multipartism and habitually generate presidential majorities or near-majorities in their assemblies, and those which do not.

Coalition Formation and Presidential Majorities

In large degree this conclusion does encompass the present state of our knowledge regarding institutional design and governability in the Latin American democracies. But it is only "safe" so long as the prevalence of coalition formation and coalition government is ignored, as it tends to be in the literature. In fact, even on a restrictive definition,[65] coalition governments have recurred in Bolivia, Brazil, Chile, Ecuador and Peru, and even in the mainly two-party systems of Colombia and Uruguay, while the only cases of uniformly single-party government have been Argentina, Costa Rica and Venezuela (after 1968). But, despite a number of good case studies of the process of coalition formation in Colombia,[66] Brazil[67] and Chile,[68] no systematic and comparative study of the phenomenon has yet been published. Most more casual commentary tends to refer to coalition formation as exceptional and confined to cases of extreme party fractionalization, or difficult and beset by party indiscipline and factionalism.

A recent study distinguishes 123 separate administrations in nine countries over thirty-six years, and finds sixty-nine cases of coalition government.[69] Of the sixty-six majority governments in the sample, forty-four secured their majority through coalition formation.[70] Yet the major comparative study of presidential government in Latin America, which is equally recent, in no way reflects this prevalence when addressing the question of governability.[71] On the one hand, the authors seem simply to miss this prevalence by focusing exclusively on pre-electoral coalitions (of which they find strangely few),

65. On this definition, government coalitions require both party participation in the presidential cabinet and party co-operation in the assembly.

66. Johnathon Hartlyn, *The Politics of Coalition Rule in Colombia* (New York: Cambridge University Press, 1988).

67. Lucia Hippolito, *PSD: De Raposas a Reformistas: o PSD e a Experiencia Democratica Brasileira* (Rio de Janeiro: Paz e Terra, 1985) and Sergio Henrique Abranches, "Presidencialismo de Coalizao: o Dilema Institucional Brasileiro," Dados, 31 (1988), 5–34.

68. Arturo Valenzuela, *The Breakdown of Democratic Regimes: Chile* (Baltimore, Md.: Johns Hopkins University Press, 1978).

69. Grace Ivana Dehesa, "Gobiernos de Coalicion en el Sistema Presidencial: America del Sur" (doctoral dissertation, European University Institute, Florence, 1997).

70. The cases are Argentina, Brazil, Bolivia, Chile, Colombia, Ecuador, Peru, Uruguay and Venezuela over the years 1958–94. Since Dehesa's analytical criteria for distinguishing separate administrations and for characterizing the coalition governments cannot be closely scrutinized here, these proportions should be taken as rough measures of tendency, nothing more. Argentina never has coalition government; Brazil always has coalition government; Chile and Ecuador mainly have coalition government; while Bolivia, Peru, Uruguay and Venezuela have roughly the same number of single-party and coalition governments.

71. See Mainwaring and Shugart, *Presidentialism and Democracy in Latin America.* They construct a table from twenty-two Latin American "cases" (a case comprising a country and a period, with some countries including more than one period, and with the overall period differing from country to country), which shows the mean share of assembly seats for both the president's party and the president's coalition (Table 11.1, p. 400). They included the cases of the "country" chapters in their book (Argentina, Brazil, Bolivia, Chile, Colombia, Costa Rica, Mexico, Venezuela), "plus most other Latin America cases with some recent experience of democratic elections" (p. 402)

rather than on all governing coalitions. On the other, they purport to find analytical grounds for refusing to take coalitions of any kind into account.[72] But Dehesa's data suggest that such a restrictive approach will fail to capture the real conditions of governability. Of the fifty-nine elected presidents in her sample, eighteen were elected by coalition, while seventeen went on to form post-electoral coalitions;[73] and of the thirty presidents who were initially minority presidents in the assembly, ten formed post-electoral coalitions to overcome their minority status. Interestingly … it is … the 45 per cent threshold of presidential representation in the assembly that appears to provide the incentive for coalition formation. Nine of the ten presidents forming post-electoral coalitions to overcome their minority status initially enjoyed less than 45 percent support in the assembly, which appears to confirm that this is the critical threshold below which it is difficult or impossible to mobilize ad hoc support for policy initiatives.[74]

But if interparty coalitions are highly fragile in presidential systems, as is often asserted,[75] they can be prevalent without being significant. Mainwaring and Shugart reaffirm this fragility for two main reasons. First, they argue that coalitions are basically pre-electoral and so cannot be binding after the election, going so far as to conclude that "executive power is not formed through post-electoral agreement,"[76] which is constitutionally correct, but fails to recognize the importance of post-electoral coalition-formation.

Secondly, they argue that coalitions anyway do not work because parties are so indisciplined that the support of individual deputies can never be secure. The latter stricture applies a fortiori to open-list PR systems like that of Brazil, where electoral success depends on the individual candidate's ability to attract votes, so encouraging personalism and pork-barrel politics, and a consequent lack of party loyalty. Since, in this view, coalitions are ineffective, the familiar argument about the imperfections of multiparty presidentialism still apply. Fragmented party systems tend to minimize the assembly representation of the presidential party, so impairing governability.

But party discipline may be affected not only by control of candidate selection and the list system, but by assembly rules and procedures,[77] and, in particular, by party leaders' control over key procedural resources. Mainwaring and Shugart allege, correctly, that there is insufficient

72. For instance, they exclude coalitions from their assessment of the likelihood of the president enjoying a "veto-sustaining" share of assembly seats for the dubious reason that they are only interested "in the second-worst situation imaginable in terms of partisan support: when only the president's own party remains supportive" (Mainwaring and Shugart, *Presidentialism and Democracy in Latin America*, p. 411).

73. Four of the seventeen were initially elected by coalition, and went on to expand it. Seven of the seventeen went on to form post-electoral coalitions even though they initially enjoyed a majority or near majority.

74. The structure of incentives for pre-electoral coalitions must necessarily be rather different. First, these coalitions are more frequent in multiparty systems (Chile, Brazil) than in two-party systems (Argentina, Venezuela 1972–94), with the big exception of Colombia, and the higher the number of effective parties, the stronger the tendency to coalition formation. It might also be expected that electoral rules will provide incentives or disincentives to coalition formation, but of the eighteen pre-electoral coalitions in Dehesa's sample, seven competed under plurality rules, six under majority with second-round run-off, and five under majority with congressional selection from the two or three most voted candidates. See Dehesa, Gobiernos de Coalicion en el Sistema Presidencial.

75. See Arend Lijphart, *Democracies: Patterns of Majoritarian and Consensus Government in Twenty-One Countries* (New Haven, Conn.: Yale University Press, 1984); and Mainwaring, "Presidentialism, Multipartism, and Democracy."

76. Mainwaring and Shugart, *Presidentialism and Democracy in Latin America*, p. 397.

77. Gary W. Cox and Mathew D. McCubbins, *Legislative Leviathan: Party Government in the House* (Berkeley: University of California Press, 1993).

information to draw general, comparative conclusions about the impact of these rules on party
discipline across the continent.[78] But there is
good information on and analysis of Brazil,
which Mainwaring, in his own case study, sees as
a "worst case" of indisciplined, catch-all parties,
with a robust federalism further fracturing party
coherence.[79] In his view, a fragmented party
system with highly indisciplined parties leads to
coalitional fragility and cabinet instability, and
to almost insuperable barriers to effective legislation, especially reform initiatives of any kind.
But recent research comprehensively dismantles
this construction of the legislative process in
Brazil, by demonstrating the high degree of party
discipline and legislative predictability achieved
by party leaderships in the assembly's College of
Leaders.[80] By bending the procedural rules to
their own purposes, the party leaders are able
to control legislative rhythms and outcomes, so
"party fragmentation and the fact that the president cannot count on a solid majority does
not prevent the executive's initiatives being
approved."[81]

This relatively high degree of party discipline
underpins the formation of firm and stable coalitions which are bound by ideology.[82] Indeed,

it is the fact of coalition that tends to reinforce
internal party cohesion and legislative discipline,
especially of the smaller parties. Thus, far from
being characterized by "loose and shifting coalitions," as alleged by Mainwaring, the Brazilian
assembly is clearly divided into three ideologically distinct coalitions of left, centre and right.
Consequently, party discipline in the assembly
is not so very different from that of a system of
closed lists like Venezuela's, and the rate of success of executive legislation is similar to that
found in parliamentary regimes.

Analysis of the Brazilian case cannot substitute for a fuller comparative analysis, but it suggests that Mainwaring and Shugart's failure to
pay proper attention to coalition formation may
distort their account of executive-legislative relationships in Latin America. In this account,
executive effectiveness is a function of the combination of the president's legislative powers of
decree, veto and so forth, and his so-called partisan powers, which are mainly conferred by
party support in the assembly. A lack of partisan
support, or no guarantee of an assembly majority, can be compensated by strong legislative
powers, as in the case of Brazil, where the president's powers in this regard are only inferior to
those of Yeltsin's Russia,[83] while small formal

78. Mainwaring and Shugart, *Presidentialism and Democracy in Latin America*, p. 421, fn. 26.

79. Scott Mainwaring, "Multipartism, Robust Federalism, and Presidentialism in Brazil," in Mainwaring
and Shugart, *Presidentialism and Democracy in Latin
America*, pp. 55–109.

80. Limongi and Figueiredo demonstrate that even the
least disciplined party can always expect at least 85
per cent of its members to vote with their leaders, and
calculate that 89 per cent of all voting outcomes in the
assembly conform to the predictions of party leaders.
See Fernando Limongi and Argelina C. Figueiredo,
"Partidos Politicos na Camara dos Deputados: 1989–
1994," *Dados*, 38 (1995), 497–523; and Argelina
C. Figueiredo and Fernando Limongi, "Mudanca
Constitucional, Desempenho do Legislativo e Consolidacao Institucional," *Revista Brasileira de Ciencias
Sociais*, 29 (October 1995), 175–200.

81. Figueiredo and Limongi, "Mudanca Constitucional, Desempenho do Legislativo e Consolidacao
Institucional," p. 198. Further research by Santos
reinforces these findings, and shows that the procedural
prominence of the assembly's "special committees"
bolsters the control of the legislative process by the
leaderships of the principal parties, and so facilitates
the executive agenda. See Fabiano G. M. Santos,
"Democracy and Legislative Dynamics in Brazil"
(paper presented to conference on Power Structure,
Interest Intermediation and Policy-making: Prospects
for Reforming the State in Brazil, Institute of Latin
American Studies, London, 1997).

82. Limongi and Figueiredo, "Partidos Politicos na
Camara dos Deputados."

83. Shugart and Carey, *Presidents and Assemblies*,
p. 141.

powers may be buttressed by a large and disciplined assembly majority, as was traditionally the case in Mexico. But, as we have seen, executive effectiveness in Brazil is only partly owing to presidential powers, and depends more closely on stable and disciplined coalitions in the assembly; while executive dominance in Mexico owed most to the huge accumulation of informal, metaconstitutional, powers in the presidency, which worked to dissolve any separation of powers.

Mainwaring and Shugart seek to explain why some presidential systems work better than their traditional emphasis on fragmented party systems and party indiscipline can possibly predict by recourse to the idea of presidential powers. But their rigid and dichotomous model misses the informal interplay of the two types of powers in general, and its primary expression in the process of coalition formation in particular. Consequently, they tend to overemphasize the importance of presidential powers for governability, although confessing—at least in the case of Colombia—that eventually "presidents must return to the legislature for the long-term institutionalization of reforms enacted by decree";[84] and, equally, tend to overemphasize party indiscipline and its deleterious effects on partisan powers. In sum, it is at least as plausible that it is the prevalence of coalition formation (pre- and post-electoral) that mitigates gridlock and enhances governability; and there is some evidence for this in the case-by-case distribution of presidential coalitions in recent years. . . .

Prima facie, where coalition formation has created a presidential majority, or near majority (bottom left quadrant), governability has been enhanced. For example, the Bolivian govern-

ment succeeded in implementing a difficult economic stabilization package, while the Cardoso government in Brazil (from January 1995) put through a series of radical reform measures, including a constitutional reform to allow re-election of the president himself. But where the failure to form coalitions has created minority governments (top right quadrant), instability has ensued: the suppression of democracy by autogolpe in Peru; the impeachment of the president and severe social unrest in Venezuela (despite the much vaunted discipline of its political parties); mass social protest and the forced resignation of the president in Ecuador. If nothing else, it appears that the presence or absence of majority or near majority presidential coalitions should be included in the comparative analysis of presidential democratic regimes. . . .

The present state of comparative analysis does demonstrate, beyond reasonable doubt, that the institutional variation across these regimes has significant implications for governability, understood as government stability, legislative capacity and the avoidance of gridlock. Furthermore, the five key variables in this respect all have to do, more or less directly, with electoral rules and the party system. Thus, these regimes will be more or less governable according to variations in executive electoral rules, the effective number of parties, the presidential party presence in the assembly, the degree of polarization and the conditions of coalition formation. This can be illustrated in a synoptic and simplified fashion, by dichotomizing these variables and distributing the nine South American countries which recur in all of the studies reviewed here—namely Argentina, Bolivia, Brazil, Chile, Colombia, Ecuador, Peru, Uruguay and Venezuela. . . .

On the basis of these distributions it can be suggested that the initial key to governability is a presidential party presence in the assembly which exceeds the critical threshold of 45 percent. This is determined in large degree by the effective number of parties in the system, which itself is closely conditioned by the profile of

---

84. Mainwaring and Shugart, *Presidentialism and Democracy in Latin America*, p. 52. Nor can they adequately explain how governability is to be enhanced by the kind of overweening presidential powers that facilitate "delegative democracy" and often precipitate regime break-down.

executive electoral rules. But it also appears that a high degree of polarization may promote multipartism (although the direction of causality cannot be clear), and therefore damage governability both by reducing the presidential presence in the assembly and by making it more difficult to overcome minority representation through coalition-building. Finally, favourable conditions for coalition formation can clearly compensate for the difficulties of multipartism and polarization. If this still highly hypothetical line of argument is correct, then it is possible to distinguish South America's most governable countries (Argentina, Chile, Colombia, Uruguay) from its least governable countries (Ecuador, Peru and contemporary Venezuela), with the current governability of Bolivia and Brazil remaining closely contingent on (very different) processes of coalition formation.

Presidential Power, Legislative Organization, and Party Behavior in Brazil

Argelina Cheibub Figueiredo and Fernando Limongi

Presidential regimes are considered to be prone to produce institutional deadlocks. In the generally shared view, influenced by the work of Juan Linz, presidentialism lacks a built-in mechanism to induce cooperation between the executive and legislative branches of the government.[1] Representatives and the president have different constituencies, and their mandates are independent and fixed. Hence the chances that the legislative and the executive powers will have the same agenda are small. Because the failure of the government does not affect the legislators' political survival, representatives have few incentives to support the government. Minoritarian presidents, in particular, will necessarily face congressional opposition.

Political parties are the only conceivable basis for executive-legislative cooperation. Ideally, the same disciplined party would control the presidency and a majority in the legislature. It follows that "institutional engineering" should focus on electoral formulas that reduce party fragmentation and increase party discipline.

Brazil is viewed as an extreme example of the threats to governability represented by multiparty presidential systems. Constrained by the separation of powers, Brazilian presidents must obtain political support in a congress in which party fragmentation has reached one of the highest levels ever found in the world. In addition, the open list system prevents party leaders from exerting control over candidacies and, consequently, over party members' voting decisions within the congress.[2] With this institutional framework, it is usually inferred that parties will not be disciplined and that presidents will face systematic resistance to their legislative proposals.[3]

This inference is not true. . . .

Executive Agenda and Party Behavior in the Legislature

Evidence shows that recent Brazilian presidents have had a high degree of success in enacting their legislative agendas. Post-1988 Brazilian presidents have had most of their legislative initiatives approved by the congress. This conclusion is at odds with the conventional wisdom about the Brazilian political system and presidential systems in general. Even scholars willing to acknowledge this evidence would nevertheless argue that presidents obtained approval for their agenda at a high cost by assembling majorities through bargaining individually with representatives on a case by case basis. This argument is not supported by the evidence. Analysis of roll call votes in the chamber of deputies shows that parties are disciplined and that political support for the presidential agenda comes mainly from the parties participating in the government coalition.

Excerpted from: Argelina Cheibub Figueiredo and Fernando Limongi, "Presidential Power, Legislative Organization, and Party Behavior in Brazil." *Comparative Politics* 32 (2000): 151–170. Reprinted by permission of the authors and *Comparative Politics*.

1. Juan Linz, "Presidential or Parliamentary Democracy: Does It Make a Difference?," in Juan Linz and Arturo Valenzuela, eds., *The Failure of Presidential Democracy: Comparative Perspectives* (Baltimore: The Johns Hopkins University Press, 1994), pp. 3–87; Scott Mainwaring, "Presidentialism, Multipartism, and Democracy: The Difficult Combination," *Comparative Political Studies*, 26 (1993), 198–222.

2. Barry Ames, "Electoral Rules, Constituency Pressures, and Pork Barrel: Bases of Voting in the Brazilian Congress," *Journal of Politics*, 57 (May 1995), 324–343; Barry Ames, "Electoral Strategy under Open-List Proportional Representation." *American Journal of Political Science*, 39 (May 1995), 406–433.

3. Bolivar Lamounier, "Brazil at Impasse," *Journal of Democracy*, 5 (July 1994), 72–87.

... Presidents introduced 86 percent of the bills enacted, and the overall rate of approval of executive bills, 78 percent, is high. Rejection of executive bills is rare: only twenty-four out of the 1,881 bills introduced. In contrast, legislators' proposals have much higher rejection rates, and the number of bills approved by both houses and then vetoed by the president is significant. In addition, congress approves the bills introduced by the executive much faster than it does its own proposals....

These data may not tell the whole story. Legislators can amend the bills submitted by the executive. Representatives present many amendments, and the data do not distinguish the extent to which the original proposal has been changed. But, as we show below, the representatives' amendment capacity is limited by the executive and party leaders' control over the agenda and by the executive's veto. Analysis of specific policy areas reveals that congress plays a minor "transformative role."[17]

A related objection can be raised with regard to the importance of approved bills. In the end, the approved bills may not be the really important ones. One can ask, further, whether there is an association between importance and failure to be passed, that is, whether the noncontroversial measures were passed and the controversial ones failed. Despite the obvious problem in distinguishing controversial from noncontroversial measures, it is indisputable that bills of great importance were approved. The three stabilization plans presented under different administrations—the Summer Plan, the Collor Plan, and the Real Plan—were enacted by provisional decrees, and they were approved by the legislature with minor changes.[18] If the more important measures were rejected, one should observe high rates of rejection of the provisional decrees.

However, the opposite is true. The failure of the first two plans was not necessarily due to congressional opposition. Stabilization plans can fail for other reasons than congressional opposition.

One may still object that the proposals sent to the legislature may not have represented the executive's real agenda, since presidents, anticipating the difficulties they would face in congress, might not have submitted it. This type of behavior is indeed possible, and presidents have certainly acted at times in this way, but such behavior is part of the normal working of any democratic system.

We are not arguing that the executive imposes its will on the congress. The congress is not an obstacle simply because it transforms a bill proposed by the president or because the president anticipates its legislative preferences. Under a democratic government one should expect the congress to influence policy. The real question concerns the basis of the bargaining between the president and the congress. The executive's success in winning approval of its legislative proposals in the chamber of deputies was not obtained through bargaining with individual deputies. Roll call data in the Brazilian lower house, the *Câmara dos Deputados*, show that party members tended to vote according to their leaders directives; parties were meaningful collective actors. Brazilian presidents also relied on party coalitions to win approval of their agendas. They obtained political support more or less the same way as prime ministers, by building government coalitions through the distribution of ministries to political parties and thereby securing the votes they needed in congress....

... Table 5.10 reports the average proportion of disciplined votes, that is, those votes cast in accordance with party leaders' announced directives, for the seven biggest parties (PT, PDT, PSDB, PMDB, PTB, PFL, and PPB).[20] For all

---

17. See Argelina Figueiredo and Fernando Limongi, "Instituições Políticas e Interação Executivo-Legislativo: A Agenda de Estabilização e Reformas" (Working Paper, Cebrap/Ipea, February 1998).

18. Ibid., p. 17.

20. During this period the PDS changed its name twice, to PPR and to PPB. The behavior of the members of the micro parties is not less predictable. See Limongi and Figueiredo, "Partidos Políticos," p. 520.

Table 5.10
Average proportion of disciplined votes by political party, 1989–1998

Party	% discipline	N*
PT	98.4	533
PDT	92.1	505
PSDB	90.7	538
PMDB	85.0	538
PTB	87.9	506
PFL	93.1	531
PPB	87.4	509

* Variations are due to roll calls in which the leader does not announce the party position.

parties the mean is greater than the median: that is, the distributions are concentrated on the upper tail. The PMDB presents the lowest mean discipline, while the PT is the most disciplined. But three other parties, the PFL, the PDT, and the PSDB, also have a mean discipline above 90 percent. The average floor discipline in the lower house is 90 percent; that is, for any roll call vote nine in ten representatives voted according to party leaders' recommendations. To vote with the party is the norm. In more than 90 percent of the registered cases the proportion of the disciplined vote was superior to 80 percent. In only twelve of 575 cases did the proportion of representatives voting according to party position fall below 70 percent of the floor.[21] . . .

To analyze the fate of the presidential agenda in the congress, it is necessary to know the presidential position on issues. Roll call votes are taken on the presidential agenda if the bills were introduced by the president or if the government leader stated the government's position on the issue before the voting. In these cases the president had an interest in the result of the votes and made his position on the issues known. Out of

the original 575 roll call votes 434 meet at least one of these criteria, and 165 of them were votes on amendments to the constitution that required a three-fifths quorum for approval. The general pattern, high party discipline, is not altered when the sample is restricted to the presidential agenda.

Presidents won the great majority of roll call votes. The government won 241 of the 269 roll call votes that required a simple majority, and 143 of the 165 that required a three-fifths majority. Victories were achieved through disciplined votes, and defeats due to lack of discipline were rare. . . .

Presidents may obtain partisan support on a case by case basis or by building stable coalitions. Most students of presidential systems, following Linz's original formulation, rule out the second alternative. Since presidents derive their popular mandate directly from the people, they prefer to impose their will on congress rather than attempt to form party coalitions within congress. . . .

We assumed that Brazilian presidents formed party coalition governments through the distribution of portfolios and assessed the support given by the parties in the cabinet on the floor to the presidential agenda. There are four possible situations. First, leaders of all parties holding ministerial portfolios vote in accordance with the government leader. Second, no coalition party opposes the government, but at least one leaves the vote on the issue open. Third, at least one party opposes the government. Finally, all parties within the coalition may oppose the president.

Overall, the parties composing the cabinet voted in accordance with the government leader. All party leaders indicated votes supporting the president in 77 percent of the cases. In addition, at least one party left the vote on the issue open in 11 percent of the cases. Thus, the president could count on the support of cabinet parties in 88 percent of the cases. In 11 percent of the cases the president met with the opposition of at least

---

21. The distribution is strongly skewed. Hence controlling for presence or the expected margin of victory does not alter the overall picture. Ibid., p. 523.

one party of its congressional political basis. In only four cases did all parties forming the coalition oppose the government. Therefore, cabinet parties in general supported the government. Defections occurred but were rare....

Institutional Power, Governability, and Party Support

... Why does the Brazilian executive exercise such great dominance on legislative outcomes in a multiparty system with separation of powers? Given electoral incentives and the lack of party control over candidacies, why is the voting pattern in the lower house structured by parties? How does the executive obtain political support in a system with separation of powers?

The 1988 constitution did not change either the form of government or the electoral and party legislation.[30] However, it greatly extended the legislative powers of the president. In fact, it maintained all the constitutional changes introduced by the military regarding the role of the executive in the legislative process. These institutional choices have had profound effects on the Brazilian political system and on the executive-legislative relationship....

The current level of executive dominance over legislation resembles that found in parliamentary regimes.[32] Therefore, we are observing, not an executive that simply circumvents the legislature, but rather one that controls the legislative process. Executive dominance is due primarily to the range and extension of legislative powers held by the president, which alter the nature of executive-legislative relations. The legislative powers granted to the executive by the 1988 constitution include the expansion of exclusive initiative, the right to demand urgency procedures in bringing bills up for a vote, and, most important, the power to issue provisional decrees.[33] ...

Parallel to the executive's extensive legislative power, the legislative organization is highly centralized. The speaker and party leaders exercise tight control over the legislative agenda. They are responsible for the setting of the legislative calendar. Moreover, party leaders have procedural rights that allow them to represent backbenchers (*bancadas*) and thus to control the floor. For instance, the standing orders of the lower house state that a roll call can be held whenever one is requested by a petition signed by 6 percent of the house members. To request a separate vote on an amendment, the petition has to be signed by 10 percent. A request for the consideration of a bill under urgency procedures requires the signatures of one-third of the house members or an absolute majority if the bill is to be voted on in twenty-four hours. In all these cases—requesting a roll call, considering an amendment, and requesting urgency—the party leader's signature automatically represents the will of all members of his party. Hence leaders decide procedures concerning roll calls, amendments, and urgency.

Consideration under urgency limits backbenchers' capacity to participate in the lawmaking process. As noted above, most bills are approved by this route. Under urgency procedures the bill is discharged from the committee, whether the latter has reported on the proposal or not, and then referred directly to the floor. According to house rules and practices, both the

---

30 The plebiscite held in 1993 maintained this form of government. No attempt to change electoral legislation has succeeded.

32. See George Tsebelis, "Decision Making in Political System: Veto Players in Presidentialism, Parliamentarism, Multicameralism, Multipartisms," *British Journal of Political Science,* 25 (July 1995), 304.

33. The 1988 constitution also granted the president the initiative in introducing constitutional amendments, which was absent from the 1946 constitution. It also kept changes to speed up the consideration of legislation subject to the joint deliberation of both houses through the national congress, which has specific internal rules but no permanent organizational structure.

request for and the approval of urgency procedures depend on party leaders. Moreover, the right to amend a bill considered under urgency is restricted. To be considered, an amendment needs to fulfill one of the following prerequisites: to be presented by the standing committee; to be subscribed to by 20 percent of house members (about one hundred representatives); or to be subscribed to by party leaders representing this same percentage of the representatives. In practice, only amendments supported by party leaders are considered. Thus, the rules favor party leaders, especially leaders of the larger parties. They restrict the action of the leaders of very small parties.

The extensive legislative powers held by the president and the distribution of legislative rights within the legislature in favor of party leaders explain the patterns observed in the previous section. Constitutional rules and the house's standing orders provide the executive and party leaders with the means to neutralize legislators' individualistic behavior. Members of congress may have electoral incentives to pursue their own particularistic interests, but they do not have the capacity to influence legislation to achieve them. Institutional arrangements conspire against their capacity to realize them.

Why should the leaders of the parties that belong to the presidential coalition cooperate with the executive? Why should they use their agenda powers to help the executive? Participation in the government provides parties with access to resources that individual legislators need for their political survival: policy influence and patronage. Leaders bargain with the executive; they exchange political support (votes) for access to policy influence and patronage. The executive provides party leaders with the means to punish backbenchers. The backbenchers who do not follow the party line may have their share of patronage denied.

Thus, a rather different image of the relationship among the president, party leaders, and individual legislators emerges. The image of a fragile and weak executive, blackmailed by opportunistic legislators who obtain new appointments and positions for each vote, does not hold. The executive, with the resources it controls, is in a very advantageous position. Most cabinets are formed by the formal agreement of parties, and party leaders become the main brokers in the bargaining between the executive and the legislators. Presidents do not need to bargain case by case. They are in a position to demand support for their entire legislative agenda. Once the government is formed and benefits are distributed among the members of the coalition, the president, with the help of party leaders, may threaten representatives and punish those who do not follow the party line.[35] ...

Conclusions

Representatives' behavior can not be inferred exclusively from electoral laws. Incentives to cultivate the personal vote stemming from the electoral arena may be neutralized in the legislature through the internal distribution of legislative rights. The ability of members of the congress to influence policymaking may be small. Besides access to the ballot, there are other means by which leaders can punish recalcitrant rank-and-file members.

Legislative failure is not the inevitable fate of minoritarian presidents. There are no good reasons to rule out the possibility of coalition government under presidentialism. The combination of presidentialism and a multiparty system is not necessarily a threat to governmental performance. The emphasis on electoral formulas that reduce the number of parties is not warranted. Presidents may form governments the way prime ministers do by obtaining support from a coalition of parties.

---

35. Legislators have no guarantee that their approved amendments to the budget will be implemented.

It is widely recognized that executive control over the legislative agenda is a central feature of the parliamentary system. It has been shown that the executive's predominance over legislative output, party discipline, and the working of coalitions depend upon the legislative powers concentrated in the prime minister's hands.[38] However, the legislative powers of the president have been interpreted to have different effects. They have been thought of as a means to circumvent an institution assumed to be antagonistic. In contrast, we have argued that legislative powers may provide presidents with the means to entice a part of the legislature's members into a cooperative strategy. In the end, the legislative powers of the executive may have the same effects on both systems.

This observation allows us to dispute Tsebelis' conclusion about the basic difference between parliamentary and presidential systems. According to him, control over the agenda distinguishes these two systems. "In parliamentary systems the executive (government) controls the agenda, and the legislature (parliament) accepts or rejects proposals, while in presidential systems the legislature makes the proposals and the executive (the president) signs or vetoes them."[39] In Brazil the president controls the legislative agenda. The president proposes, and the legislature accepts or rejects what he has proposed. In fact, the first alternative—acceptance—prevails, because centralized control over the agenda has profound effects on party discipline. The capacity of backbenchers to participate in the policymaking process is curtailed. Centralization denies backbenchers access to the resources they need to influence legislation. The bills and the amendments they introduce do not reach the floor. They can only vote yes or no on an agenda defined by the government. In sum, the characteristics of the decision-making process—the legislative powers of the president and the legislative organization—may be more important determinants of governability than the form of government, the characteristics of party system, or the electoral laws.

---

38. Gary Cox, *The Efficient Secret* (New York: Cambridge University Press, 1987); John Huber, *Rationalizing Parliament* (New York: Cambridge University Press, 1996).

39. Tsebelis, p. 325.

6 REPRESENTATION

Representative Government
John Stuart Mill

On Elections
Marquis de Condorcet

Liberalism against Populism
William H. Riker

Saving Democracy from Political Science
Gerry Mackie

Unlikelihood of Condorcet's Paradox in a Large Society
A. S. Tangian

Congruence between Citizens and Policymakers in Two Visions of Liberal Democracy
John D. Huber and G. Bingham Powell, Jr.

The Political Consequences of Electoral Laws
Douglas W. Rae

South Africa's Negotiated Transition: Democracy, Opposition, and the New Constitutional Order
Courtney Jung and Ian Shapiro

The Representation of Women
Anne Phillips

Representative Government

John Stuart Mill

That the Ideally Best Form of Government Is Representative Government

It has long (perhaps throughout the entire duration of British freedom) been a common saying, that if a good despot could be ensured, despotic monarchy would be the best form of government. I look upon this as a radical and most pernicious misconception of what good government is; which, until it can be got rid of, will fatally vitiate all our speculations on government.

The supposition is, that absolute power, in the hands of an eminent individual, would ensure a virtuous and intelligent performance of all the duties of government....

A good despotism means a government in which, so far as depends on the despot, there is no positive oppression by officers of state, but in which all the collective interests of the people are managed for them, all the thinking that has relation to collective interests done for them, and in which their minds are formed by, and consenting to, this abdication of their own energies. Leaving things to the Government, like leaving them to Providence, is synonymous with caring nothing about them, and accepting their results, when disagreeable, as visitations of Nature....

Such are not merely the natural tendencies, but the inherent necessities of despotic government; from which there is no outlet, unless in so far as the despotism consents not to be despotism; in so far as the supposed good despot abstains from exercising his power, and, though holding it in reserve, allows the general business of government to go on as if the people really governed themselves....

There is no difficulty in showing that the ideally best form of government is that in which the sovereignty, or supreme controlling power in the last resort, is vested in the entire aggregate of the community; every citizen not only having a voice in the exercise of that ultimate sovereignty, but being, at least occasionally, called on to take an actual part in the government, by the personal discharge of some public function, local or general....

The ideally best form of government, it is scarcely necessary to say, does not mean one which is practicable or eligible in all states of civilisation, but the one which, in the circumstances in which it is practicable and eligible, is attended with the greatest amount of beneficial consequences, immediate and prospective. A completely popular government is the only polity which can make out any claim to this character. It is pre-eminent in both the departments between which the excellence of a political constitution is divided. It is both more favourable to present good government, and promotes a better and higher form of national character, than any other polity whatsoever.

Its superiority in reference to present well-being rests upon two principles, of as universal truth and applicability as any general propositions which can be laid down respecting human affairs. The first is, that the rights and interests of every or any person are only secure from being disregarded when the person interested is himself able, and habitually disposed, to stand up for them. The second is, that the general prosperity attains a greater height, and is more widely diffused, in proportion to the amount and variety of the personal energies enlisted in promoting it.

Putting these two propositions into a shape more special to their present application; human beings are only secure from evil at the hands of others in proportion as they have the power of being, and are, self-*protecting*; and they only achieve a high degree of success in their struggle with Nature in proportion as they are

Excerpted from: John Stuart Mill, *Representative Government*. New York: E. P. Dutton, 1972.

self-*dependent*, relying on what they themselves can do, either separately or in concert, rather than on what others do for them. . . .

It is an adherent condition of human affairs that no intention, however sincere, of protecting the interests of others can make it safe or salutary to tie up their own hands. Still more obviously true is it, that by their own hands only can any positive and durable improvement of their circumstances in life be worked out. Through the joint influence of these two principles, all free communities have both been more exempt from social injustice and crime, and have attained more brilliant prosperity, than any others, or than they themselves after they lost their freedom. . . .

It must be acknowledged that the benefits of freedom, so far as they have hitherto been enjoyed, were obtained by the extension of its privileges to a part only of the community; and that a government in which they are extended impartially to all is a desideratum still unrealised. But though every approach to this has an independent value, and in many cases more than an approach could not, in the existing state of general improvement, be made, the participation of all in these benefits is the ideally perfect conception of free government. In proportion as any, no matter who, are excluded from it, the interests of the excluded are left without the guarantee accorded to the rest, and they themselves have less scope and encouragement than they might otherwise have to that exertion of their energies for the good of themselves and of the community, to which the general prosperity is always proportioned.

Thus stands the case as regards present well-being; the good management of the affairs of the existing generation. If we now pass to the influence of the form of government upon character, we shall find the superiority of popular government over every other to be, if possible, still more decided and indisputable. . . .

. . . The maximum of the invigorating effect of freedom upon the character is only obtained

when the person acted on either is, or is looking forward to becoming, a citizen as fully privileged as any other. What is still more important than even this matter of feeling is the practical discipline which the character obtains from the occasional demand made upon the citizens to exercise, for a time and in their turn, some social function. It is not sufficiently considered how little there is in most men's ordinary life to give any largeness either to their conceptions or to their sentiments. Their work is a routine; not a labour of love, but of self-interest in the most elementary form, the satisfaction of daily wants; neither the thing done, nor the process of doing it, introduces the mind to thoughts or feelings extending beyond individuals; if instructive books are within their reach, there is no stimulus to read them; and in most cases the individual has no access to any person of cultivation much superior to his own. Giving him something to do for the public, supplies, in a measure, all these deficiencies. If circumstances allow the amount of public duty assigned him to be considerable, it makes him an educated man. . . .

. . . Still more salutary is the moral part of the instruction afforded by the participation of the private citizen, if even rarely, in public functions. He is called upon, while so engaged, to weigh interests not his own; to be guided, in case of conflicting claims, by another rule than his private partialities; to apply, at every turn, principles and maxims which have for their reason of existence the common good: and he usually finds associated with him in the same work minds more familiarised than his own with these ideas and operations, whose study it will be to supply reasons to his understanding, and stimulation to his feeling for the general interest. He is made to feel himself one of the public, and whatever is for their benefit to be for his benefit. . . .

From these accumulated considerations it is evident that the only government which can fully satisfy all the exigencies of the social state is one in which the whole people participate; that any participation, even in the smallest public function, is useful; that the participation should everywhere be as great as the general degree of improvement of the community will allow; and that nothing less can be ultimately desirable than the admission of all to a share in the sovereign power of the state. But since all cannot, in a community exceeding a single small town, participate personally in any but some very minor portions of the public business, it follows that the ideal type of a perfect government must be representative.

On Elections

Marquis de Condorcet

In a free society based on equality, accurate popular choices are necessary not only for public prosperity and the safety of the state, but also to ensure the preservation of the basic principles upon which that society is grounded. . . .

The Theory of Elections

For a man who chooses alone and who wants to adhere to a strict procedure, an election is the result of a series of judgements comparing all the candidates two by two. The candidates to whom he restricts his choice are, in this case, the men he considers worthy of the place.

Similarly, an election vote is the result of those judgements which obtain a majority. In each judgement, an individual weighs up the reasons for preference between two candidates. In an election, each person's votes for or against a candidate represent these reasons, and are counted rather than weighed up. When a man compares two individuals and prefers the second to the first, and then, on comparing the second with a third, prefers the latter, it would be self-contradictory if he did not also prefer the third to the first. If, however, on making a direct comparison of the first and the third, he found reasons for preferring the first, he would then have to examine this judgement, balance the reasons behind it with those behind his other judgements (which cannot exist alongside this new one) and sacrifice the one he considers least probable.

In an election between three candidates, the three judgements which obtain majority support when the candidates are compared two by two

Excerpted from: Marquis de Condorcet, "On Elections." In *Condorcet: Foundations of Social Choice and Political Theory*. Brookfield, Vermont: Edward Elgar Publishing, 1994. Reprinted by permission.

may sometimes be inconsistent, even when the individual judgements of each voter involve no contradiction. This can easily be shown through examples and can be explained by the simple fact that the majority in favour of each of these accepted propositions is not made up of the same individuals. We must therefore reject the proposition with the smallest majority and retain the other two. Thus, whenever we are able to obtain only a fairly large probability, we must reject a proposition which is probable in itself if it excludes another which is more probable.

An election result incorporating a proposition which runs contrary to one of the majority judgements may still be very probable. In fact, this only occurs in situations where it is certain that the majority has been mistaken at least once. The probability of the result being accurate is then equal to the probability that the majority has made only one mistake regarding a certain proposition.

There is no need to point out that the contradiction which can occur between majority judgements when there are three candidates must be even more likely when there are a greater number of candidates; or that, in such cases, several of these judgements may contradict one another, meaning that the majority must necessarily have made more than one mistake. The consequences of this are the same.

The list of candidates who are put forward for election must be determined if all the members of an assembly are to give a complete vote by comparing the same candidates two by two, or to list them in order of merit, which comes to the same thing. That is, everyone must know the names of the candidates between whom the voters will be choosing.

However, it is not necessary for everyone to compare all the candidates or to form a complete list. A voter may for various reasons regard a certain number of candidates as equal to one another, either after considering their attributes or because he does not know the candidates and is therefore unable, or unwilling, to judge them....

This condition in no way restricts the voters' freedom, since it simply requires everyone to decide which candidates he wishes to choose between. The list of all those put forward in this way would then present each voter with the names of all the candidates between whom the other voters wanted the election to be conducted, and he would then have complete freedom to decide how he could share in this judgement: which candidates he wanted to rank in order of merit and which he wanted to reject entirely by placing them after all the others.

Any election method in which the votes given are incomplete will produce results which contradict the will which the majority would have had if complete votes had been collected.

The results of these incomplete votes will of course have some degree of probability of being correct, but it would be similar to that of a proposition which has been only half examined. In fact, we should support a probable proposition only when we have discovered the impossibility of incorporating new information, and as long as this impossibility lasts.

However, we would be just as far from fulfilling our aim if we forced each voter to express, not the complete vote which he actually forms, but a complete vote in an absolute sense; that is, if we forced him to establish an order of preference between all the candidates, including those he does not know. Clearly, he would then rank the latter at random and his vote could result in the election of a candidate who would not otherwise have had sufficient support. In the first case, we are neglecting judgements which should have been assessed, and in the second, we are assessing judgements which have not been given. In the first case, we are acting as if we had randomly excluded a certain number of voters, and in the second as if we were randomly giving some of them double the number of votes.

In theory, therefore an election procedure should be as follows: after having determined the list of acceptable candidates, each voter should express his complete will, whether of preference or indifference.

A table of majority judgements between the candidates taken two by two would then be formed and the result—the order of merit in which they are placed by the majority—extracted from it. If these judgements could not all exist together, then those with the smallest majority would be rejected.

This is exactly the same procedure as that followed by any individual who wants to make a considered choice by using a general, regular method which applies to all situations.

Since there is only one way of obtaining a true decision, the procedures used by a deliberative assembly should generally be as close as possible to those used when an individual examines a question for himself.

This principle can have other important applications. In this case, it allows us to develop an election method which is reasonably natural and as perfect as the nature of things permits.

Any substitute method put forward should be compared to this one in terms of the time required by an election, the degree of enlightenment of those to whom it is entrusted, the problems of outlawing the influence of intrigue, and the need both to preserve true equality between the voters and to interest them in fulfilling this function with scrupulous care and enthusiasm....

Liberalism against Populism

William H. Riker

5.A. Arrow's Theorem

... Kenneth Arrow published *Social Choice and Individual Values* in 1951. Although his theorem initially provoked some controversy among economists, its profound political significance was not immediately recognized by political scientists.[1] In the late 1960s, however, a wide variety of philosophers, economists, and political scientists began to appreciate how profoundly unsettling the theorem was and how deeply it called into question some conventionally accepted notions—not only about voting, the subject of this work, but also about the ontological validity of the concept of social welfare, a subject that, fortunately, we can leave to metaphysicians.

The essence of Arrow's theorem is that no method of amalgamating individual judgments can simultaneously satisfy some reasonable conditions of fairness on the method and a condition of logicality on the result. In a sense this theorem is a generalization of the paradox of voting (see section 1.H), for the theorem is the proposition that something like the paradox is possible in *any* fair system of amalgamating values. Thus the theorem is called the *General Possibility Theorem*.

To make the full meaning of Arrow's theorem clear, I will outline the situation and the conditions of fairness and of logicality that cannot simultaneously be satisfied.[2] The situation for amalgamation is:

1. There are *n* persons, $n \geq 2$, and *n* is finite. Difficulties comparable to the paradox of voting can arise in individuals who use several standards of judgment for choice. Our concern is, however, *social* choice, so we can ignore the Robinson Crusoe case.

2. There are three or more alternatives—that is, for the set $X = (x_1, \ldots, x_m)$, $m \geq 3$. Since transitivity or other conditions for logical choice are meaningless for fewer than three alternatives and since, indeed, simple majority decision produces a logical result on two alternatives, the conflict between fairness and logicality can only arise when $m \geq 3$.

3. Individuals are able to order the alternatives transitively: If $x \ R_i \ y$ and $y \ R_i \ z$, then $x \ R_i \ z$. If it is not assumed that individuals are able to be logical, then surely it is pointless to expect a group to produce logical results.

The conditions of fairness are:

1. *Universal admissibility of individual orderings (Condition U)*. This is the requirement that the set, D, includes all possible profiles, D, of individual orders, D_i. If each D_i is some permutation of possible orderings of X by preference and indifference, then this requirement is that individuals can choose any of the possible

1. William H. Riker, "Voting and the Summation of Preferences," *American Political Science Review*, Vol. 55 (December 1961), pp. 900–911.

2. Since many proofs are easily available to those who wish to follow up the subject, I will not reiterate the proof here. For Arrow's proof, as revised by Julian Blau, see Kenneth Arrow, *Social Choice and Individual Values*, 2nd ed. (New Haven: Yale University Press, 1963), pp. 96–100. A refined form of Arrow's proof is to be found in Amartya K. Sen, *Collective Choice and Social Welfare* (San Francisco: Holden-Day, 1970), chap. 3. See also Peter C. Fishburn, *The Theory of Social Choice* (Princeton: Princeton University Press, 1973), p. 206. Bengt Hansson, "The Existence of Group Preference Functions," *Public Choice*, Vol. 28 (Winter 1976), pp. 89–98, contains a topological proof. An informal sketch of Arrow's proof is contained in William H. Riker and Peter C. Ordeshook, *An Introduction to Positive Political Theory* (Englewood Cliffs, N.J.: Prentice-Hall, 1973), pp. 92–94.

permutations. For example, if $X = (x, y, z)$, the individual may choose any of the following 13 orderings:

1. $x\,y\,z$ 7. $x\,(y\,z)$ 10. $(x\,y)\,z$ 13. $(x\,y\,z)$
2. $y\,z\,x$ 8. $y\,(z\,x)$ 11. $(y\,z)\,x$
3. $z\,x\,y$ 9. $z\,(x\,y)$ 12. $(z\,x)\,y$
4. $x\,z\,y$
5. $z\,y\,x$
6. $y\,x\,z$ (5-1)

The justification for this requirement is straightforward. If social outcomes are to be based exclusively on individual judgments—as seems implicit in any interpretation of democratic methods—then to restrict individual persons' judgments in any way means that the social outcome is based as much on the restriction as it is on individual judgments. Any rule or command that prohibits a person from choosing some preference order is morally unacceptable (or at least unfair) from the point of view of democracy.

2. *Monotonicity.* According to this condition, if a person raises the valuation of a winning alternative, it cannot become a loser; or, if a person lowers the valuation of a losing alternative, it cannot become a winner.... Given the democratic intention that outcomes be based in some way on participation, it would be the utmost in perversity if the method of choice were to count individual judgments *negatively*, although, as I have shown, some real-world methods actually do so.

3. *Citizens' sovereignty or nonimposition.* Define a social choice as imposed if some alternative, x, is a winner for any set, D, of individual preferences. If x is always chosen, then what individuals want does not have anything to do with social choice. It might, for example, happen that x was everyone's least-liked alternative, yet an imposed choice of x would still select x. In such a situation, voters' judgments have nothing to do with the outcome and democratic participation is meaningless.

4. *Unanimity or Pareto optimality (Condition P).* This is the requirement that, if everyone prefers x to y, then the social choice function, F, does not choose y.... This is the form in which monotonicity and citizens' sovereignty enter all proofs of Arrow's theorem. There are only two ways that a result contrary to unanimity could occur. One is that the system of amalgamation is not monotonic. Suppose in D' everybody but i prefers x to y and $y\,P'_i\,x$. Then in D, i changes to $x\,P_i\,y$ so everybody has x preferred to y; but, if F is not monotonic, it may be that x does not belong to $F(\{x, y\}, D)$. The other way a violation of unanimity could occur is for F to impose y even though everybody prefers x to y. Thus the juncture of monotonicity and citizens' sovereignty implies Pareto optimality.

Many writers have interpreted the unanimity condition as purely technical—as, for example, in the discussion of the Schwartz method of completing the Condorcet rule.... But Pareto optimality takes on more force when it is recognized as the carrier of monotonicity and nonimposition, both of which have deep and obvious qualities of fairness.

5. *Independence from irrelevant alternatives (Condition I).* According to this requirement ..., a method of amalgamation, F, picks the same alternative as the social choice every time F is applied to the same profile, D. Although some writers have regarded this condition simply as a requirement of technical efficiency, it actually has as much moral content as the other fairness conditions.... From the democratic point of view, one wants to base the outcome on the voters' judgments, but doing so is clearly impossible if the method of amalgamation gives different results from identical profiles. This might occur, for example, if choices among alternatives were made by some chance device. Then it is the device, not voters' judgments in D, that determines outcomes. Even if one constructs the device so that the chance of selecting an alternative is proportional in some way to the number of people desiring it (if, for example, two-thirds of

the voters prefer x to y, then the device selects x with $p = \frac{2}{3}$), still the expectation is that, of several chance selections, the device will choose x on p selections and y on $1 - p$ selections from the same profile, in clear violation of Condition I. In ancient Greece, election by lot was a useful method for anonymity; today it would be simply a way to by-pass voters' preferences. Another kind of arbitrariness prohibited by the independence condition is utilitarian voting. Based on interpersonal comparisons of distances on scales of unknown length, utilitarian voting gives advantages to persons with finer perception and broader horizons. Furthermore, independence prohibits the arbitrariness of the Borda count....

6. *Nondictatorship (Condition D)*. This is the requirement that there be no person, i, such that, whenever $x \, P_i \, y$, the social choice is x, regardless of the opinions of other persons. Since the whole idea of democracy is to avoid such situations, the moral significance of this condition is obvious.

Finally, the condition of logicality is that the social choice is a weak order, by which is meant that the set, X, is connected and its members can be *socially* ordered by the relation, R, which is the transitive social analogue of preference and indifference combined. (This relation, as in $x \, R \, y$, means that x is chosen over or at least tied with y.) In contrast to the previous discussion, in which the method of amalgamation or choice, F, simply selected an element from X, it is now assumed that F selects repeatedly from pairs in X to produce, by means of successive selections, a social order analogous to the individual orders, D_i. And it is the failure to produce such an order that constitutes a violation of the condition of logicality.[2]

Since an individual weak order or the relation R_i is often spoken of as individual rationality, social transitivity, or R, is sometimes spoken of as collective rationality—Arrow himself so described it. And failure to produce social transitivity can also be regarded as a kind of social irrationality.

Arrow's theorem, then, is that every possible method of amalgamation or choice that satisfies the fairness conditions fails to ensure a social ordering. And if society cannot, with fair methods, be certain to order its outcome, then it is not clear that we can know what the outcomes of a fair method mean. This conclusion appears to be devastating, for it consigns democratic outcomes—and hence the democratic method—to the world of arbitrary nonsense, at least some of the time.

5.B. The Practical Relevance of Arrow's Theorem: The Frequency of Cycles

... One meaning of Arrow's theorem is that, under any system of voting or amalgamation, instances of intransitive or cyclical outcomes can occur.... Since, by definition, no one of the alternatives in a cycle can beat all the others, there is no Condorcet winner among cycled alternatives. All cycled alternatives tie with respect to their position in a social arrangement in the sense that $x \, y \, z \, x$, $y \, z \, x \, y$, and $z \, x \, y \, z$ have equal claims to being the social arrangement. Borda voting similarly produces a direct tie among cycled alternatives. Hence a social arrangement is indeterminate when a cycle exists. When the arrangement is indeterminate, the actual choice is arbitrarily made. The selection is not determined by the preference of the voters. Rather it is determined by the power of some chooser to dominate the choice or to manipulate the process to his or her advantage. Every cycle thus represents the failure of the voting process....

5.C. The Absence of Meaning

The main thrust of Arrow's theorem and all the associated literature is that there is an unresolvable tension between logicality and fairness. To guarantee an ordering or a consistent path, independent choice requires that there be some sort of concentration of power (dictators, oligarchies, or collegia of vetoers) in sharp conflict with democratic ideals. Even the weakest sort of consistency ($\beta+$ or $^*PI$) involves a conflict with unanimity, which is also an elementary condition of fairness.

These conflicts have been investigated in great detail, especially in the last decade; but no adequate resolution of the tension has been discovered, and it appears quite unlikely that any will be. The unavoidable inference is, therefore, that, so long as a society preserves democratic institutions, its members can expect that some of their social choices will be unordered or inconsistent. And when this is true, no meaningful choice can be made. If y is in fact chosen—given the mechanism of choice and the profile of individual valuations—then to say that x is best or right or more desired is probably false. But it would also be equally false to say that y is best or right or most desired. And in that sense, the choice lacks meaning. . . .

Saving Democracy from Political Science

Gerry Mackie

Although democratization is the main trend in the world today, the main intellectual trend in American political science is the view that democracy is chaotic, arbitrary, meaningless, and impossible. This trend originated with economist Kenneth Arrow's (1963) impossibility theorem, which was applied to politics by the late William Riker, political scientist at the University of Rochester. Riker's famed *Liberalism against Populism* (1982) claims that elections serve only to randomly remove officials. Define *populism* (ignore its pejorative usages) as the doctrine that political outcomes are or should be related in some way to the collective opinion or will of the free and equal citizenry. Riker, and his followers in the so-called Rochester School of political thought, are, in this special sense, *antipopulists*.

Because different voting systems may yield different outcomes from the same profile of individual voters' preferences, says Riker, "populist democracy" is *inaccurate*. The claim is made by way of examples that establish the logical possibility of such divergence. It turns out, however, that with real-world distributions of individual preference orders—individual orderings that are at least mildly correlated with one another rather than unrelated and random—the reasonable voting rules do tend to converge on the same outcomes. Next, Riker continues, given a fixed voting system, then democracy is *meaningless*: the outcome of voting is manipulable, and it is not possible to distinguish manipulated from unmanipulated outcomes because of the unknowability of private intentions underlying public actions. Riker's claim that democracy is irremediably manipulable is based on the assumption that *cycles* are ubiquitous on important issues.

Suppose that the Duckburg Troop of the Junior Woodchucks are deciding by majority voting how to spend their treasury over three alternatives, as in table 6.1. Huebert and Louis favor *A* over *B*, Huebert and Deuteronomy favor *B* over *C*, and Deuteronomy and Louis favor *C* over *A*. The collective choice *cycles* over $A > B > C > A$. It seems that there is no collective choice. Moreover, if only Huebert controlled the order of voting, he could manipulate the outcome to his first-ranked *A*, by declaring first a majority vote between *B* and *C*, and then the winner of that against *A*. Arrow's possibility theorem can be understood as a generalization of this Condorcet paradox of voting. Cycles are logically possible, but are they empirically probable? Data on real individual preference rankings show that they are distributed in a manner such that cycles are rare, and theoretical considerations predict this finding. Unfairly manipulated outcomes are possible only if cycles are a problem, and only if some political actors are unfairly granted powers not granted to others. That a mathematical model shows that those with greater formal power may have greater influence over the outcome should come as no surprise. Contrary to Riker, it does not establish that there is a problem in principle with democracy, which requires equal formal powers.

It is Riker's dramatic empirical illustrations of political disequilibrium, more than his theoretical arguments, that are responsible for the wide popularity of his antipopulist views. I have closely examined all of the well-developed empirical claims of cycling and democratic irrationality published by Riker and his followers, and I claim to show that each is mistaken, either conceptually or empirically (Mackie, forthcoming). These case studies include a cycle alleged in Congressional agricultural appropriations, agenda control in a flying club, a cycle arising from Powell's desegregation amendment in the 1956 Congress, a cycle in votes in the Senate over proposing the 17th amendment to the U.S. Constitution, a cycle in consideration of the Wilmot Proviso in 1846, a cycle over candidates

Table 6.1
Condorcet paradox of voting

	Huebert	Deuteronomy	Louis
1st	A	B	C
2nd	B	C	A
3rd	C	A	B

for the 1860 presidential election, introduction of the slavery issue in order to arbitrarily manipulate political outcomes, a cycle in consideration of the method for selecting the U.S. president at the Constitutional Convention, Lincoln's alleged "heresthetic" manipulation of the Lincoln-Douglas debates, Magnuson's alleged heresthetic manipulation of the nerve-gas issue, and further cases not from Riker's hand. If these illustrations fail, then so does the antipopulist creed.

It's not possible in the space at hand to justify my claimed findings. I present an abridged sample, however, having to do with Riker's most startling claim, that there was a cycle in the presidential election of 1860, and that choice among the candidates in that election was, in principle, arbitrary and meaningless. Riker's overarching hypothesis is that the slavery dimension of concern in antebellum American politics was suppressed by the Democratic Party manipulative elite with the Missouri Compromise of 1820. The competing Whig and Republican manipulative elite sought to revive that dimension by contriving a cycle, and succeeded spectacularly with the election of Lincoln in 1860, the story goes.

There were four major candidates in the American presidential election of 1860. They were Lincoln of the recently formed Republican Party, Douglas of the northern Democrats, Bell from a new third party, the Constitutional Unionists, and Breckinridge of the renegade southern Democrats. Lincoln received a plurality of 40 percent of the popular vote, and Riker suspects a cycle. From election data we have only voters' expression of first-ranked prefer-

ence, not what their second-, third-, and fourth-ranked preferences were. In order to conduct his analysis, Riker must infer voters' full rankings from historical considerations. He provides estimates of voters' full rankings over 15 likely of the 24 rankings possible for strong preferences over four candidates. His estimations then permit the calculation of hypothetical outcomes by alternative voting rules. The results of his exercise seem to confirm Riker's thesis that democracy is arbitrary and meaningless. Different voting rules lead to different outcomes, and by pairwise majority voting there is a cycle. Here are Riker's results:

Plurality: Lincoln > Douglas > Breckinridge > Bell

Pairwise Majority: (Douglas > Lincoln > Bell > Douglas) > Breckinridge

Borda Count: Douglas > Bell > Lincoln > Breckinridge

Approval Voting (two votes):   Bell > Lincoln > Douglas > Breckinridge

Approval Voting (three votes):   Douglas > Bell > Lincoln > Breckinridge

Riker concludes that with five methods of voting Douglas wins twice, Bell once, Lincoln once, and they are in a cycle and hence tie once. "Clearly, if my guesses are even roughly right, there was complete disequilibrium in 1860" (1982, 229).

Riker's first two rankings have to do with all those voters whom we know ranked Lincoln first. The two rankings contain 40 percent of the voting population of the entire country, so if there is a major error among them then we need go no further. Reconstructing Riker's data, he has it that about 1,794,000 voters in the free north voted for Lincoln, and he is correct enough on that. His further claim is that of those, one-fourth or about 450,000 ranked Douglas second, and three-fourths or about 1,346,000 ranked Bell second. I claim that it is the reverse, that most Lincoln voters ranked Douglas second, and few ranked Bell second.

The major controversy in the country was the extent to which slavery would be allowed in the vast territories, the so-called "free soil" question. Lincoln was most free-soil, then Douglas, then Bell, then Breckinridge (who was most pro-slavery). If the slavery dimension was of greatest concern to voters, then one would expect that Douglas would be the second choice of most Lincoln voters, not Bell. Riker does not justify his estimates, but presumably his inference that Bell was the second choice of most Lincoln voters was based on the thought that the Constitutional Unionists contained many southern members of the defunct Whig Party, and that northern former Whigs whose first choice was Lincoln would second-rank Bell from the Whiggish Constitutional Unionists rather than Douglas from their ancient enemy the Democratic Party. That did not happen, and to understand why we have to look at what the parties stood for, with special attention to the Constitutional Unionists.

The parties' platforms reflect the positions I suggest, with the exception of the Constitutional Unionists. Their brief platform is a platitudinous appeal to Constitution, Union, and Enforcement of the Laws. Because of this, and their poor showing in the election, some commentators neglect to locate them ideologically. A close reading of their platform shows, however, that their pledge of continued union is conditioned on the reestablishment of states' rights and equality between the sections as found in the original constitutional compromise. It is the original constitutional compact that commands their loyalty, not present-day misinterpretations or usurpations by the north. Outside the platform, the Constitutional Unionists believed that Congress must protect the property rights of slave-owners in the territories, the southern position on free soil. They denounced the Breckinridge Democrats for threatening secession; but did not deny the right to secede should compromise with the north fail. The southern former Whigs who were the largest faction in the organization of

the Constitutional Unionists *aspired* to attract northern former Whigs, but they largely *failed*, because, although more moderate than Breckinridge, they did not appeal to northern sentiments on free soil. The southern orientation of the Constitutional Unionists was no secret to northern voters: the party received four percent of their vote.

A look at a map of the county-level winners in the 1860 presidential elections (McPherson 1993, 128) shows that latitude is attitude. The upper north voted for Lincoln (more free soil), the lower north voted for Douglas (less free soil), the upper south voted for Bell (less slave soil), and the lower south voted for Breckinridge (more slave soil). Why would a voter in the upper north choose Lincoln? High among the reasons must be Lincoln's appeal to northern interests including his position on free soil; otherwise one of the other candidates would do. If such a voter were denied the choice of Lincoln, who would his second choice be? Why not Douglas, who is the next most adjacent on issues of northern interest? And if Douglas were not available where next would the typical upper northern voter turn? He would turn to Bell, the candidate of the upper south, of course, not to Breckinridge the candidate of the lower south. Similar reasoning would predict the ranking by the typical voter in the lower north, the upper south, and the lower south.

If voter preferences were ideologically oriented to the free soil question, then we would expect upper northern voters to rank $L > D > Bl > Br$. Aggregate data are suspect because of the mis-named "ecological fallacy." Nevertheless, such data are instructive, especially if they support a position otherwise supported by independent considerations. Aggregates at the state level show that in the upper north Lincoln was first everywhere and Douglas generally finished second. The ideological approach would predict that Bell would finish third in the northern states, but he finishes third in three and *fourth* in eight states. This is the candidate that Riker would have us believe is ranked *second* by northern Lincoln voters. In the upper north, 55 percent of voters favored Lincoln, 35 percent Douglas, eight percent Breckinridge, and two percent Bell, L > D > Br > Bl. Aggregates at the state level for the lower north, the upper south, and the lower south support the view that slavery was the primary dimension of concern.

After my first analysis of the issue, Tabarrok and Spector (1999) published an intriguing and more technically sophisticated analysis of the 1860 election. Among other things, they queried historians of the Civil War as to their views on the rankings, and 15 responded. For voters who ranked Lincoln first, the historians' median opinion was that 60% ranked Douglas second and 40% ranked Bell second. Tabarrok and Spector constructed a median historian's profile, and compared it to Riker's. The plane of possible outcomes in Tabarrok and Spector's positional-vote space, using Riker's profile, is large, and permits a large variety of rankings by way of varying the weights of a positional voting rule—from plurality to Borda count to antiplurality and everything in between. The positional vote plane using the median historian's profile is small, and "Douglas wins ... under any positional voting system which gives significant weight to second- or second- and third-ranked preferences" (278); but Lincoln wins by plurality count, which gives no weight to any preferences except for the first-ranked. Pairwise majority voting is cyclic with Riker's profile, but with the median historian's profile Douglas beats Bell by 15.1%, Bell beats Lincoln by 0.033% (three-hundredths of one percent), and Lincoln beats Breckinridge by 25.4%.

The platforms, aggregate voting data, and the opinion survey of historians support the hypothesis that Douglas and not Bell was second-ranked among most Lincoln voters. What does this revision do to Riker's demonstration that democracy is arbitrary because different voting methods result in different outcomes and that democracy is meaningless because cycles will be contrived on major issues such as the future of slavery? In the upper and lower north, Lincoln won 53% of the vote, Douglas 36%, and Bell 4%. Riker has 25% of Lincoln voters ranking Douglas second, and 75% ranking Bell second. The median historians' estimate is 60% Douglas second, and 40% Bell second. Suppose that at least 37% ranked Douglas second, and at most 63% ranked Bell second. What happens then to the arbitrarily different outcomes and the meaningless cycle? They disappear! Here are the new outcomes:

Pairwise Majority: Douglas > Lincoln > Bell > Breckinridge

Borda Count: Douglas > Lincoln > Bell > Breckinridge

Approval Voting (two votes):   Douglas > Lincoln > Bell > Breckinridge

Approval Voting (three votes):   Douglas > Bell > Lincoln > Breckinridge

Moreover, with plurality runoff, Lincoln and Douglas would go to the runoff and Douglas would win (a runoff between first-round losers Bell and Breckinridge has Bell as the winner, yielding the overall ranking D > L > Bl > Bk). All five of these voting methods select Douglas as the winner. Except for approval voting with three votes, the rules identify the same ranking: D > L > Bl > Bk.

A centrist such as Douglas should have won the 1860 election. That one didn't is due to the antidemocratic design of the electoral college, and due to the spoiler strategy of the Breckinridge faction, which perversely sought a Lincoln victory in order to justify secession. The election of Lincoln was not due to a hidden flaw in the ideal of democracy.

The Arrow theorem disclosed the logical possibility of a majority cycle, of perpetual political instability. But we observe stability rather than instability in democratic politics. Riker originally responded that cycles are common but rarely detected. Simulations show and empirical studies corroborate, however, that cycling is an empirical improbability. Riker later conceded that uncontrived cycles are quite rare, but that on major issues actors will contrive cycles by introduction of new alternatives. In order to be persuaded to abandon the concept of the public good and the idea of democracy as in some sense the expression of the people's will, most people would require that it be robustly demonstrated that the manipulation of political outcomes is frequent, harmful, and irremediable. Riker's position is that it is either theoretically impossible or empirically difficult to detect such manipulation. He is able, however, to produce spectacular anecdotes that purport to show harmful manipulation on major issues, including a demonstration that the biggest event in American history was the consequence of a contrived cycle. I have worked through each of his examples only to find that each is mistaken. Theoretical considerations about the distribution of preference orders suggest that cycles are most unlikely; empirical studies show that cycles are of no practical importance; finally, every developed and published example of a political cycle has now been challenged. Thus, I argue that after fifty years of scholarship, from the first publication of Arrow's theorem, no one has satisfactorily demonstrated the existence of a normatively troubling cycle in the real world.

The antipopulist interpretations of social choice results inspired by Riker, widely endorsed in the discipline of political science, are unsupported by evidence and must be abandoned.

References

Arrow, Kenneth J. 1963/1951. *Social Choice and Individual Values*, second edition. New Haven. Yale University Press.

Mackie, Gerry. Forthcoming. *Democracy Defended*. Cambridge: Cambridge University Press.

McPherson, James M. 1993. *Ordeal by Fire*, vol. 1, *The Coming of War*. New York: McGraw-Hill.

Riker, William H. 1982. *Liberalism Against Populism: A Confrontation between the Theory of Democracy and the Theory of Social Choice*. Prospect Heights: Waveland Press.

Tabarrok, Alexander and Lee Spector. 1999. "Would the Borda Count Have Avoided the Civil War?" *Journal of Theoretical Politics* 11: 261–288.

Unlikelihood of Condorcet's Paradox in a Large Society

A. S. Tangian

1 Introduction

1.1 Social Choice with Respect to Cardinal and Ordinal Utility

As early as in the last quarter of the 18th century, Borda, Condorcet, and Laplace mathematically investigated election by vote (see Black 1958; Young 1988; McLean and Urken 1994). Borda described cases when voting implies intuitively unacceptable results. Condorcet discovered the intransitivity of majoritarian preference, the fact known as Condorcet's paradox. Both authors developed new methods to overcome this problem with voting, which posed further problems. Laplace provided some mathematical arguments to back up Borda's model. These studies, having questioned the faithfulness of election systems, have had numerous successors and thus have given birth to a new scientific branch, the social choice theory.

Borda and Condorcet founded two different standpoints, which continue to be the two principal approaches to the problem. Borda's count is based on summing ranks of candidates in individual schedules, which are cardinal utilities. Laplace considered a model with real utilities as a logical development of Borda's model. Condorcet's count uses pairwise votes, which are ordinal data. . . .

The ordinal approach, including a majority rule, is usually considered to be 'more objective' and better substantiated than the cardinal one.

Editor's note: Tangian develops some lengthy and technical proofs to support his findings, which are not included here. For our purposes, it suffices to provide an explication of his methods and a summary of his results.

Excerpted from: A. S. Tangian, "Unlikelihood of Condorcet's Paradox in a Large Society." *Social Choice and Welfare* 17 (2000): 337–365. Reprinted by permission.

On the other hand, the intransitivity of preference discovered by Condorcet is generally inherent in all ordinal models. Thus having a rigorous methodological basis, the ordinal approach lacks the universal solvability inherent in the cardinal approach. In a general formulation, the unsolvability of the ordinal approach to social choice has been proved by Arrow (1951).

However, contrary to Condorcet's predictions, the intransitivity of social preference is seldom observed in real voting. Moreover, all democratic systems are based on different forms of voting, ignoring the unsolvability of the ordinal approach. So we have an apparent inconsistency between theory and practice.

In this paper, we analyze the cause of this inconsistency. It turns out that Condorcet's predictions are true for a quite particular combinatorial case, when an 'average voter' votes for or against certain candidates with equal probability. The related analytical studies have been done by DeMeyer and Plott (1970), May (1971), Merril and Tideman (1991), Niemi and Weisberg (1968), Garman and Kamien (1968), Gehrlein and Fishburn (1976), and Gehrlein (1983). The results of computer simulation have been reported by Campbell and Tullock (1965), Klahr (1966), Jones et al. (1995), and Van Deemen (1996).

The assumption of equal probability of voting for or against candidates means that these candidates have equal merits, a circumstance which is possible theoretically, but can hardly ever occur. Much more frequently, candidates have different merits, reflected by the vote asymmetry. We show that in such a case the probability of intransitive social preference vanishes as the number of voters increases. From this we conclude that it is very unlikely to obtain Condorcet's paradox in a real vote. . . .

. . . We prove with a probability model that group decisions based on a pairwise majority vote or on summing individual cardinal utilities (in the form of either reals, or integers, or ranks) tend to be the same as the number of individuals increases. The only exception is the case when the vote ratio for pairs of alternatives is 50%:50%. Since such an equilibrium is rather unlikely, we conclude that in most practical situations pairwise vote count and utility count are almost equivalent.

Let us explain the main idea at an intuitive level, in terms of tournaments. Imagine a chess competition with three participants A, B, and C. Due to chance, a weaker player can gain a victory over a stronger one, and the preference order on the set of players can have cycles like $A \succ B \succ C \succ A$. However, in multiple rounds, a stronger player wins more often, getting a higher total score of victories over weaker players. After a certain number of rounds, the preference order on the set of participants based on paired games will correspond to their real strength rating. (Recall that each chess professional is assigned a rating calculated with respect to his results in several tournaments.)

A pairwise vote for candidates A, B, C in a small group of voters is like a single tournament round with a risk of misrepresentation of real merits of the participants. This can result in intransitive cycles in the preference order. A vote in a large society, due to the error-vanishing effect, is similar to a multiple-round tournament where the merits of participants are revealed more accurately. If social merits of candidates are adequately reflected by the vote in an election, then the (latent) merit scale linearizes the resulting preference, as the rating scale linearizes the order of players in a multiple-round tournament.

The idea of the underlying "objective" preference being distorted in individual preferences goes back to Condorcet who has assumed probabilistic deviations from some "correct" vote. From this standpoint, the intransitivity of the majoritarian preference is no longer a paradox but rather an error to be corrected—the argument exploited by Condorcet and some other scholars.

Our approach can be explained with a reference to Black's (1958) model with single-peaked preferences. He proved the transitivity of a majority preference, having assumed an alignment of candidates such that each elector has a single-peaked preference with respect to this alignment. In our model, such an alignment is the latent social merit scale. In a large model, the deviations from this scale in individual preferences can be considered as "errors" which become negligible as the number of individuals increases.

Note that, unlike Black, we do not restrict the domain of preference profiles (combinations of individual preferences). We consider all profiles under some probabilistic assumptions (independence of voters, inequality of the mean preference probability from 0.5, that is no equilibrium of votes). Then we show that the probability of the profiles which result in an intransitive social preference vanishes as the number of voters increases. We conclude that to avoid Condorcet's paradox in a large society, there is no need to introduce any domain restriction, since the domain 'restricts itself' almost for sure in the probabilistic sense under rather weak assumptions. That is, the profiles resulting in an intransitive social preference constitute an event with vanishing probability....

In intermediate reasoning we make use of individual cardinal utilities. We assume that they do *exist* and have some probability distribution, but do not require their expressibility. This assumption is not crucial, since the question of existence of probability measures is trivial for finite models, which is our case (the number of individuals is finite, and individual utilities can be restricted to some finite grid).

Since the limit theorems of the paper are valid for arbitrary distributions, the results hold even if these distributions are not known. Here we follow the same line of reasoning as (Tanguiane 1991, 1994) while revising Arrow's paradox: We prove a property for every measure and then conclude that knowing the measure is not necessary to be sure that this property holds.

... [W]e consider a model with two alternatives. We prove that the decision obtained by voting and that obtained by summing individual cardinal utilities become the same as the number of individuals increases. The two decisions contradict each other with a significant probability only if the probability of vote for one candidate against another is equal to 0.5. This case corresponds to precisely equal social merits of the candidates which is a rare coincidence.

Then, we extend this result from a pair of alternatives to several alternatives. This gives the main statement of the paper: The social preferences based on ordinal or cardinal counts tend to become the same as the number of individuals increases. As a corollary, in a model with a large number of voters, the transitivity of the Borda preference is inherent in the preference based on pairwise vote.

... [W]e provide numerical evidence of the coincidence of results from voting and from summing individual utilities. The speed of convergence of the two methods of social decision making depends on several parameters. We classify distributions of individual cardinal utilities with respect to these parameters and interpret these classes with regard to the way of social behavior....

... [I]n most practical cases (not simultaneously vote symmetry and indifferent social response) decisions based on voting and on summing individual utilities provide close results. For a large society, reservations should be made only for the case of symmetric vote in an indifferent society.

It should be emphasized that Condorcet's paradox remains relevant for small groups. Since our model assumes the probabilistic independence of individuals, a large society means a large number of *independent* individuals. A few large coalitions with members sharing the same preference do not meet this condition. Such a model is a model with a few participants with the weight coefficients, corresponding to the size of coalitions.

Independence may be regarded as the most consistent realization of the idea of probability. Therefore, our results relate with reservations to a nonindependent probabilistic model, as demonstrating some kind of a general trend.

Besides, our results illustrate the opinion that cardinal measurements are not very important in processing ordinal data. In fact, we show that voting leads to the same results as summing cardinal utilities, implying that most essential information is already inherent in ordinal preferences.

Finally, it follows that the inaccuracy of certain election procedures should not play a decisive role in case of a large society. In particular, a majority vote will reveal the same preference as more sophisticated and "precise" methods of election that are based on cardinal utilities.

For instance, consider the presidential election in Russia for Jelzin against Sjuganow on June 16, 1996. In spite of a small vote asymmetry (34% and 32% of votes, respectively) we can expect that the social response was not indifferent (since the political programs of the candidates differed significantly). From our standpoint we can be quite sure that even a hypothetical voting system which takes into account the degree of individual preferences would give the same election result.

In conclusion we summarize the main statements of the paper.

1. Our model is not based on any domain restriction on the individual preference profiles implying the transitivity of a majority preference. We consider all profiles but show under rather weak assumptions that the probability of an intransitive collective preference is vanishing as the number of individuals increases (Condorcet has considered equiprobable collective preferences which, as one can see, is not relevant to real social choice).

2. For this purpose we assume the following

• Independence of individuals (following Condorcet, Laplace),

• Independence of ordinal and cardinal parts in individual preferences (following Borda, Laplace),

• Asymmetry of pairwise votes (Tangian).

3. In a large society, a different choice with respect to voting or summing individual utilities is statistically not significant. The solvability of a large ordinal model of social choice (transitivity of a majoritarian preference) follows from the *existence* of the dual cardinal model, not requiring its explicit knowledge.

4. In a small group, a different choice with respect to voting and summing individual utilities is statistically significant. Testing the difference requires additional information about the distribution of preference probabilities.

5. A different choice with respect to voting and summing individual utilities in caused by the following:

• a high deviation coefficient σ/μ (since $\sigma < 1$, the expectation μ must be small, that is, individuals are indifferent);

• almost symmetrical votes (p is close to $1/2$).

6. One should not worry about the imperfection of election systems based on voting:

• The risk that an intransitive preference emerges is negligible.

• Election based on voting is almost as accurate as complex systems with cardinal utilities. . . .

References

Arrow KJ (1951) *Social choice and individual values.* Wiley, New York.

Campbell CD, Tullock G (1965) A Measure of the Importance of Cyclical Majorities. *Economic Journal* 75: 853–856.

DeMeyer F, Plott Ch (1970) The Probability of a Cyclic Majority. *Econometrica* 38: 345–354.

Garman M, Kamien M (1965) The Paradox of Voting: Probability Calculations. *Behavioral Science* 10: 306–317.

Gehrlein WV (1983) Condorcet's Paradox. *Theory and Decision* 15: 161–197.

Gehrlein WV, Fishburn PC (1976) The Probability of the Paradox of Voting: A Computable Solution. *Journal of Economic Theory* 13: 14–25

Jones B, Radcliff B, Taber Ch, Timpone R (1995) Condorcet Winners and the Paradox of Voting: Probability Calculations for Weak Preference Orders. *American Political Science Review* 89: 113–144.

Klahr D (1966) A Computer Simulation of the Paradox of Voting. *American Political Science Review* 60: 384–390.

May RM (1971) Some Mathematical Remarks on the Paradox of Voting. *Behavioral Science* 16: 143–151.

McLean I, Urken AD (eds.) (1994) *Classics of Social Choice.* University of Michigan Press, Ann Arbor.

Merril, Tideman (1991) The Relative Efficiency of Approval and Condorcet Voting Procedures. *Rationality and Society* 3: 65–77.

Niemi RG, Weisberg H (1968) A Mathematical Solution for the Probability of the Paradox of Voting. *Behavioral Science* 13: 317–323.

Tanguiane AS (1991) *Aggregation and Representation of Preferences. Introduction to Mathematical Theory of Democracy.* Springer, Berlin Heidelberg New York.

Tanguiane AS (1994) Arrow's Paradox and Mathematical Theory of Democracy. *Social Choice and Welfare* 11(1): 1–82.

Young HP (1988) Condorcet's theory of voting. *American Political Science Review* 82: 1231–1244.

Congruence between Citizens and Policymakers in Two Visions of Liberal Democracy

John D. Huber and G. Bingham Powell, Jr.

Liberal democracy claims to establish connections between citizens and policymakers. The repeated processes of electoral competition and legislative bargaining are supposed to ensure that policymakers do what citizens want them to do. There are, however, at least two quite different visions of the democratic processes that can create congruence between citizen preferences and public policies.

In what we call the *Majority Control vision*, democratic elections are designed to create strong, single-party majority governments that are essentially unconstrained by other parties in the policy-making process. Policymakers are likely to do what citizens want them to do because the party that controls the government has won majority support in the election. Its announced policy comments, previous record, or both were preferred to the partisan alternative by a majority of the citizens. In the other vision, which we call the *Proportionate Influence vision*, elections are designed to produce legislatures that reflect the preferences of all citizens. After the election legislative bargaining between parties is necessary for policymaking, and the influences of the various parties in post-election bargaining processes determine the extent to which policymakers do what citizens want them to do.

In this paper, we offer a simple way to conceptualize the degree of congruence between citizens and their governments, comparing citizen self-placements on the left-right scale with the placement of the governing political parties on the same scale by expert observers. We then attempt to give explicit theoretical form to the Majority Control and Proportionate Influence visions, to link them empirically to specific types of modern democracies, and to measure their successes and failures at creating congruence. We want to know in particular how such theoretically critical features as responsible incumbent governments at the time of the election, identifiable future governments in electoral competition, proportional representation in electoral outcomes, and the formation of majority governments after the election are related to levels of congruence.

Congruence, of course, is not the only democratic virtue: some of the processes treated here as intervening may be highly valued in their own right.[1] Voters oriented to control may wish to see government formations that change in response to even small vote shifts. Voters may prefer to have very distinctive choices. Voters may prefer that policy-making be highly efficient. Permanent minorities may prefer proportionate representation and consultative legislative bargaining, especially if other processes directly impose the preferences of the majority. We therefore do not propose that congruence between citizen preferences and public policy should be the only grounds for choosing or supporting one vision over the other. We do think, however, that congruence between the preferences of citizens and the actions of policymakers constitutes a major claim and goal of liberal democracy. Thus, Dahl's "reasonable justification for democracy" posits that "a majority of citizens can induce the government to do what they most want it to do and to avoid doing what they

Excerpted from: John D. Huber and G. Bingham Powell, Jr., "Congruence between Citizens and Policymakers in Two Visions of Liberal Democracy." *World Politics*, 46 (3) (Apr., 1994), 291–326. © 1994 The Johns Hopkins University Press. Reprinted with the permission of The Johns Hopkins University Press.

1. Some of these other virtues are more fully described and elaborated in G. Bingham Powell, Jr., "Elections as Instruments of Democracy" (Manuscript, University of Rochester, 1993).

most want it not to do."[2] This is not a unique position but rather articulates more clearly than most a common assumption of those who theorize about liberal democracy. Hence, although congruence is only a part of our general interest in democratic processes, it is an important part. . . .

Alternative Visions of Democracy and Congruence

In each of the two visions of democracy examined here, there is a clear path by which both electoral and legislative processes can create congruence between the citizen median and the behavior of governments and policymakers. But the path in each vision is different and so are the areas where one may expect problems.

The Majority Control vision assumes that political power will be concentrated in the hands of identifiable governments chosen by the electorate and responsible to it. Elections involve competition between incumbent governments and challengers. Voters evaluate the past performance and future promises of each and choose the contender whose policies they expect will be closest to their preferences. That contender wins electoral and legislative majorities and comes to office committed to a set of policies favored by a citizen majority. When in office, the new government carries out those policies under the eye of the electorate, which can evict it in the next election if it fails to keep its promises.

The key stage in the Majority Control vision is clearly electoral competition: party alternatives, voter choices, and the aggregation of the two. Elections must provide voters with identifiable alternative governments; they must also produce clear control over policy-making for the party

preferred by the citizens. If these defining characteristics of majority control are achieved, then whether there is a close correspondence between voters and policymakers will depend on another feature of the election: the presence of a party or candidate located at or very near the median voter. If neither identifiable alternative government is close to the median voter, then by our definition, the majoritarian democratic process will not result in a government that is committed to "what the voters want." Responsible incumbents in office at the time of the election should be helpful: single-party majority governments that bear clear responsibility for their actions will be pressed to anticipate the citizen majority as they look to the election; voters will find it easier to evaluate the credibility of promises and to choose the party whose true position is closest to their preferences.

Scholars have offered a variety of specific models to explain how Majority Control systems can deliver policies that the citizens want. In the well-known two-party competition model proposed by Anthony Downs, the desire to win elections drives both parties toward the position of the median voter. With a single dimension of party competition, a party that fails to converge nearly to the median can always be defeated by a party that does move to the median. The strategic incentives for the parties and the rational choices of voters act together to provide victories for the party that is closest to the median.[18] If the theory of center-driven party competition were empirically true, it would provide a powerful underpinning for the claim of the Majority

---

2. Robert A. Dahl, *Democracy and Its Critics* (New Haven, Conn.: Yale University Press, 1989), 95. In a similar vein, see Hanna Pitkin, *The Concept of Representation* (Berkeley: University of California Press, 1967), 234.

18. Downs, *An Economic Theory of Democracy* (New York: Harper and Row, 1957), see also Heinz Eulau and Kenneth Prewitt, *Labyrinths of Democracy: Adaptations, Linkages, Representation and Policies in Urban Politics* (New York: Bobbs-Merril, 1973); Joseph Schlesinger, *Ambition and Politics: Political Careers in the United States* (Chicago: Rand McNally, 1966); and Joseph Schumpeter, *Capitalism, Socialism and Democracy* (New York: Harper and Row, 1942).

Control vision to create congruence. However, there is much controversy about the correspondence between Downs's theory and the empirical facts of party competition.

Since only the winning party needs to be near the citizen median to create congruence, the Majority Control vision need not depend on Downs's strategic parties. It can also encompass "mandate" versions of democracy[19] or other models in which incumbents face challengers who over time offer a large array of possible alternatives.[20] We cannot here explicate the varying assumptions of these models, but we merely note that various specific models in the broad Majority Control vision can lead to the prediction that the *winner* of the election should usually be at or near the median voter. All of these models then tend to assume that the election winner will subsequently dominate the policy-making process and implement the promised policies.

If some combination of these models proves empirically accurate, then the other (presumed) virtues of majoritarianism will be buttressed by good congruence between the preferences of the electorate and the commitments of the policy-makers. The potential problem, of course, is that various empirical studies, and also some theoretical work, show failure of competition to produce consistently a party at the median.[21]

The Proportionate Influence vision gets to a similar prediction of congruence in a very different way. The models and research associated with this vision are not directly oriented to majorities or to control, but rather are oriented to representation and bargaining. This vision is less clearly articulated in its multiple stages. At the electoral level the large literature on proportional representation stresses the fairness of having all voters' voices count in getting officials into office.[22] At the policy-making level, various analysts of accommodative or consociational democracy, most influentially Arend Lijphart, argue that minorities in deeply divided systems will want "grand coalition" arrangements that guarantee them a voice in policy-making.[23] In his model of "consensus democracy," Lijphart

19. See Anthony Birch, *Representation* (London: Macmillan, 1972); and Austin Ranney, *The Doctrine of Responsible Party Government* (Urbana: University of Illinois Press, 1962).

20. See Kollman, Miller, and Page (fn. 5); and Richard D. McKelvey and Peter C. Ordeshook, "Elections with Limited Information: A Fulfilled Expectations Model Using Contemporaneous Poll and Endorsement Data as Sources," *Journal of Economic Theory* 36 (June 1985).

21. For theoretical results, see, e.g., Alberto Alesina, "Credibility and Policy Convergence in a Two-Party System with Rational Voters," *American Economic Review* 78 (September 1988); Peter J. Coughlin, "Candidate Uncertainty and Electoral Equilibria," in James M. Enelow and Melvin J. Hinich, eds., *Advances in the Spatial Theory of Voting* (Cambridge: Cambridge University Press, 1990); Melvin J. Hinich, "Equilibrium in Spatial Voting: The Median Voter Result Is an Artifact," *Journal of Economic Theory* 16 (December 1977); Donald A. Wittman, "Candidates with Policy Preferences: A Dynamic Model," *Journal of Economic Theory* 14 (February 1977); and idem, "Spatial Strategies When Candidates Have Policy Preferences," in Enelow and Hinich. For empirical results, see, e.g., David Robertson, *A Theory of Party Competition* (London: Wiley, 1976); Ian Budge and Dennis Fairlie, *Voting and Party Competition* (London: Wiley, 1983); and Bernard Grofman, Robert Griffen, and Amihai Glazer, "Identical Geography, Different Party: A Natural Experiment on the Magnitude of Party Differences in the U.S. Senate, 1960–84," in R. J. Johnston, F. M. Shelley, and P. J. Taylor, eds. *Developments in Electoral Geography* (London: Routledge, 1990).

22. See Douglas Rae, *The Political Consequences of Electoral Laws* (New Haven: Yale University Press, 1967).

23. Lijphart, *Democracy in Plural Societies* (New Haven: Yale University Press, 1977); see also G. Lembruch, "A Non-Competitive Pattern of Conflict Management in Liberal Democracies," in Kenneth McRae, ed., *Consociational Democracy* (Toronto: McClelland and Stewart, 1974); and Jürg Steiner, "The Principles of Majority and Proportionality," *British Journal of Political Science* 1 (January 1971).

draws attention to various institutional devices less inclusive than a grand coalition that induce majorities to bargain with minorities.[24] Most of this work assumes that multiparty elections and proportional representation are highly desirable prerequisites for such negotiation.

To convert the Proportionate Influence vision into a more clearly identified model of elections connecting citizens and policymakers, we must spell out the assumptions at each of the two important stages in the process of government formation. At the election stage, the vision assumes multiple parties offering a variety of alternatives, so that all groups of citizens can find compatible parties. The parties do not—must not—converge to the center unless virtually all the voters are located very close to it.[25] At the time of the election, then, the choices of voters and the working of proportionate election laws result in a legislature with parties representing all these groups in their proportionate strength. A critical implication of this fact is that the position of the median legislator (or median party, if parties are in fact the relevant units) should be very close to that of the median voter.

The second stage of the Proportionate Influence vision concerns coalition bargaining. Since an election often creates a legislature with no single-party majority, various coalitions could form among the many parties represented. Naturally, the more diverse the electorate and, consequently, the legislature, the more possible in the abstract to build a coalition that strays from the position of the median citizen. But as in electoral competition, coalition theory predicts that in one-dimensional situations the median party will play a dominant role in government formation,[26] that is, all coalitions should include the median party, although any coalition may incorporate other parties that fall to one side or the other (or both).

Existing research does not, however, provide a clear prediction about whether the median party will dominate policy-making, even in the one-dimensional situation. Laver and Schofield and de Swann argue that the policy position of the median legislator will prevail, but Austen-Smith and Banks, in a model that integrates electoral competition and government formation, find that in equilibrium, final policy outcomes never correspond to the preferences of the median legislator.[27] More generally, in situations where a single party or coalition of parties forms a government and must maintain tight party discipline—which empirically is the case in almost all parliamentary systems—the government might be expected to make policies that correspond to its own internal median, not to the legislative median.

Thus, we have here a potential for connections—through inclusion of the median party in the coalition—without very close congruence. As in the concerns about the failure of party competition to produce at least one party at the median in the majoritarian vision, the processes that connect legislative bargaining to government policy may also lead to consistent policies off the median.

Up to this point, we have considered only the congruence between governments and citizen preferences. That is, we have assumed that

24. Arend Lijphart, *Democracies: Patterns of Majoritarian and Consensus Government in Twenty-one Countries* (New Haven: Yale University Press, 1984); see also Dahl (fn. 2), chap. 11.

25. In Lijphart's empirical analysis of "consensus" systems, the number of effective parties virtually defines one of his dimensions (fn. 24), 214.

26. For an excellent review of the coalition formation literature, see Michael Laver and Norman Schofield, *Multiparty Government: The Politics of Coalition in Europe* (Oxford: Oxford University Press, 1990), chap. 5.

27. Ibid., 111; Abram de Swaan, *Coalition Theory and Cabinet Government* (Amsterdam: Elsevier, 1973); and David Austen-Smith and Jeffrey Banks, "Elections, Coalitions, and Legislative Outcomes," *American Political Science Review* 82 (June 1988).

Table 6.2
Visions of democracy and processes that create congruence between voters and policymakers

Process stages	Majority control vision	Proportionate influence vision
Electoral competition	identifiable alternative governments, one a responsible incumbent, one or both close to the median voter	wide range of party choice; absence of explicit coalition commitments
Election outcomes	party close to median voter wins majority	proportionate legislative representation of all parties and voters
Government formation	election winner forms majority government	bargaining: government coalition includes the median legislator
Policy-making between elections	government dominates all policy-making	coalitions may change but still include median; negotiation with opposition parties may help balance government parties right or left of median party
Congruence prediction	government is the policymaker and is close to the median voter	government includes median legislator, but average weight of all policymakers will be closer to the median voter

the representation process ends with the formation of a government coalition. In practice all governments will probably be somewhat influenced by the issues raised by other parties in the legislature. . . .

Under the Majority Control vision of congruence (especially in the "mandate" formulations), one would expect that the greater the opposition influence in policy-making, the less the congruence between policymaker and citizens. In this vision, the selection of a governing party close to the citizen median should already have resulted in good congruence between final policies and the citizen majority. If all other parties have not converged to the median position, however, giving weight to the opposition after a government forms can only move the policymakers away from the median. Moreover, such influence will make it more difficult for voters to make clear retrospective judgments about government responsibility—a fact that decreases the incentives for parties to converge to the median in the first place.

In the Proportionate Influence vision, giving some weight to the opposition may pull policymakers back toward the median citizen if the

government includes the median party but extends from it to the right or left. Hence, in contrast to what we would expect in ideal Majority Control systems, giving opposition parties significant weight in policymaking may improve congruence between what citizens want and what policies result in Proportionate Influence systems; but it also may not, depending on the specific positions of the government and the other parties. . . .

Characteristics of Liberal Democratic Control Systems: Theory and Practice

The two visions of democracy are founded in experience and custom as well as in theory. [Table 6.2] suggests that we can identify features of electoral competition, electoral outcomes, and legislative bargaining that will enable us to categorize empirically the different systems according to the extent to which they follow one vision or the other. Table 6.3 presents the data necessary to accomplish this task; the data are used to categorize the systems in twelve industrial democracies for the period 1968–87. Subse-

Table 6.3
System characteristics in twelve democratic countries[a]

Country	M.C. (1) Identifiability of Future Govt.	M.C. (2) Past Govt. Status	P.I. (3) Effective No. of Parties	M.C. (4) Single Party or PEC Wins Majority	P.I. (5) Proportionality	M.C. & P.I. (6) Opposition Committee Influence
Australia	100	.44	2.5	100	87	No
Belgium	0	0	6.1	14	91	Yes
Denmark	38	0	5.4	0	97	Yes
France	38	.125	3.5	75	79	No
West Germany	100	0	2.7	100	98	Yes
Ireland	33	.33	2.6	50	95	No
Italy	0	0	3.6	0	95	Yes
Netherlands	17	0	5.1	17	95	Yes
New Zealand	100	1.0	2.0	100	80	No
Spain	100	.33	2.6	43	83	Yes
Sweden	29	.125	3.3	83	98	Yes
United Kingdom	100	.67	2.2	67	85	No

a. See text for descriptions of the measures. Data for columns 1–4 are averages from the period 1968–87. Data for column 5 are from Thomas T. Mackie and Richard Rose, *The International Almanac of Electoral History*, 3d ed. (Washington, D.C.: CQ Press, 1991), 509–10. Column 6 is based on the analysis by Strom (fn. 29, 1990), chap. 3; and Powell and Whitten (fn. 33).

quently, we will use data from 1978 to 1985 in order to test congruence.[30]

At the stage of electoral competition, the Majority Control vision stresses that the voters be able to identify future alternative governments and that responsibility for past policy-making by the incumbent government should be clear. The Proportionate Influence vision emphasizes a large number of parties offering a wide range of choices. In table 6.3 we see the countries in our study followed, in columns 1–3, by features of their electoral competition.[31] ...

---

30. It would be ideal to be able to analyze congruence for this entire twenty-year span, but since the Castles and Mair expert survey measured party positions in 1982, we have used only the 1978–85 period so that we can rely on the assumption that party positions have not changed much. There are thirty-eight governments in these twelve countries in this time period. Various readers have suggested that we extend our time period and bring in more cases, but we simply cannot locate a comparable survey of experts at another time period that asks the appropriate left-right question.

31. Some readers may be troubled by the absence of electoral laws from the analysis. Clearly the electoral law of a given political system shapes many features of electoral competition and government formation that are important to this study, including the effective number of parties, proportionality, identifiability, and the election of single-party majorities. Nonetheless, for the purposes of this study, it would be difficult—if not wrongheaded—to categorize a country as either a Majority Control or Proportionate Influence system on the basis of its electoral laws. One problem is the difficulty of developing an appropriate measure of electoral laws because each one has unique features, with important differences in aggregation rules and in districting. (For example, Spain and the Netherlands both have proportional representation [PR], but the proportionality of electoral outcomes in Spain is much lower than in the Netherlands, as shown in Table 6.3.) More important for analysis, the nature of electoral competition varies over time within systems having the same election law. In systems with single-member district pluralities, for example, if there is a minority government at the time of an election, clarity of responsibility for past policy-making will be low. In systems with PR, to take another example, there are often cases in which

Citizens, Governments, and Ideological Congruence in Majoritarian and Proportionate Influence Systems

We develop two measures, called Government Distance I and Government Distance II, of the congruence between the position of the government and the estimated position of the median voter.[38] ... Government Distance I takes the average position of all the parties in the government weighted by the size of the respective parties....

Since the number of portfolios a party receives may not be a good measure of its influence in the coalition, we developed an alternative measure, Government Distance II. This second measure assumes that the left-right position of the government coalition is dominated by the placement of the median party within it. Hence, Government Distance II is simply the left-right position of the median party within the government. Which of these two measures is more appropriate depends, of course, on whatever theory we might have about how policy-making goes on within the government. As we shall see, however, the results for both measures are quite similar.[40]

---

identifiability is high because of the formation of preelection coalitions. As our analysis focuses on election-specific characteristics of party competition, we do not use the election laws directly to classify the various political systems. However, analysis of the indirect impact of election laws on congruence under various conditions, through the features here examined, is an interesting topic for future research.

38. Since the left-right scales have discrete boundaries between the different cells, we approximate the location of the median voter using a technique described in Thomas H. Wonnacott and Ronald J. Wonnacott, *Introductory Statistics for Business and Economics*, 3d ed. (New York: John Wiley, 1984), 671.

40. The mean scores by country for Government Distance I (II) are Australia 1.35 (1.35), Belgium .74 (.74), Denmark 1.36 (1.46), France 1.96 (2.15), West Germany 1.55 (1.81), Ireland .47 (.84), Italy .92 (1.24), Netherlands .90 (.50), New Zealand .95 (.95), Sweden 1.28 (1.17), Great Britain 2.39 (2.39), and Spain 1.94 (1.94).

Comparing Congruence between Citizens and Governments in the Three Types of Systems

Table 6.5 shows the average distance scores for the three types of systems using our two different measures of the position of the government. The data show that the two measures of distance work quite similarly. It is also clear that the Majority Control and Mixed systems have governments that are on average substantially farther from the median voter than are governments in the Proportionate Influence systems: the average government in the Majority Control and the Mixed system is over 1.5 points from the median; the average government in the Proportional Influence system is about 1 point away. Even with so few cases, the difference between the mean of the Proportionate Influence systems and the mean of the Majority Control systems is statistically significant at .05 (one-tailed test).

In parentheses in table 6.5 we show the percentage of voters between the government and the median citizen. This figure depends on both the absolute distance and the distribution of

Table 6.4

Characteristics for majority control, mixed, and proportionate influence systems 1968–87 (1978–85)[a]

	System type		
	Majority control: Australia, Great Britain, New Zealand	Mixed: France, Germany, Ireland, Spain, Sweden	Proportionate influence: Belgium, Denmark, Italy, Netherlands
Electoral competition			
Identifiability	100	80	36
	(100)	(75)	(45)
Past government status	.67	.17	0
	(.80)	(.06)	(0)
Effective no. of parties	2.2	3.1	5.1
	(2.2)	(3.0)	(5.4)
Election outcomes			
Percentage of elections won by a single party or a preelection coalition	95	66	7
	(100)	(58)	(10)
Proportionality	85	92	95
	(83)	(93)	(96)
Legislative bargaining			
Percentage of committee systems that permit opposition influence	0	60	80
	(0)	(60)	(80)
Number of elections	29	29	27
	(5)	(12)	(10)

a. The top number in each cell is for the period 1968–87. The figure in parentheses is for the period 1978–85 (the period for which we analyze congruence). The top number in the "Proportionality" row is calculated using the figures in Mackie and Rose, *The International Almanac of Electoral History*, 3d ed. (Washington, D.C.: CQ Press, 1991), 510, which are calculated using only the last election reported in their study.

Table 6.5

Congruence between government and citizen left-right orientations[a]

	System type		
	Majority control	Mixed	Proportional influence
Government Distance I	1.61 (28%)	1.43 (23%)	.96 (20%)
Government Distance II	1.61 (28%)	1.55 (25%)	1.03 (20%)
N	5	16	17

a. Government Distance I measures the difference between the weighted mean left-right position of the government and the left-right position of the median voter. Government Distance II measures the difference between the left-right position of the median party in the government coalition and the left-right position of the median citizen. The numbers in parentheses give the percentage of voters between the government and the median citizen. Positions of the parties are taken from Castles and Mair (fn. 10).

voters on the left-right scale. If the voters were more dispersed in the Majority Control systems, for example, a larger distance might affect the same number of voters as does a smaller distance in the Proportionate Influence systems. However, we see the same pattern as in the absolute distances. The Majority Control systems find, on average, 28 percent of the electorate between the government and the median, whereas the figures are 23–25 percent in Mixed systems and 20 percent in the Proportionate Influence systems.

The advantage of the Proportionate Influence systems in offering greater congruence between governments and voters is somewhat theoretically unexpected. We expected that governments in the Majority Control systems would be close to the median as the direct result of party competition and voter choices (under either Downsian theory or some of the nonstrategic or partially strategic alternatives). We also expected coalition bargaining in the Proportional Influ-

ence systems might result in governments that are often farther away from the median voter. But the converse is true. The reason for the poorer performance of the Majority Control systems is basically that the two main parties in Britain and Australia are far from the median (over 2 points) during the period of our study. The closer of the two large parties does come to power, but it is still rather extreme.[41] In New Zealand the Majority Control vision seems to work better; in fact both major parties are fairly close to the median (about 1 point).

A similar problem is evident in the Mixed systems, although it is less theoretically surprising in the multiparty situations. A common pattern here is the formation of formal or informal preelection coalitions that pit right against left. These coalitions frequently fail to converge, but the one that gets a majority forms a government without bargaining with the opposition. In France, especially, both major alternative governments are very far from the median voter. In 1978 the winning conservative coalition was 2.75 from the median—the farthest in our sample. In Germany, Spain, and Sweden, too, the alternatives are rather far apart, each around 1.5 points from the median. Only in Ireland are both of the two alternatives quite close to the median.

A Regression Analysis

While the results in table 6.5 are interesting, it is troubling that we have only five cases of pure Majority Control elections. A regression analysis can help us go beyond the typology to illuminate the contribution of various properties of political systems to the degree of congruence. . . .

41. In Britain the closest parties to the median voter were the Liberals in 1979 and the Alliance in 1983, but neither of these parties won as much as a quarter of the votes, and both were heavily penalized by the election laws. The Conservatives were somewhat closer to the median than was Labour, but both large parties were rather far away.

Table 6.6
Predicting distance between the median voter and the left-right position of the government (OLS model of Government Distance I and II)

Independent Variables[a]	Dependent variable: Government Distance I			Dependent variable: Government Distance II		
	(1)	(2)	(3)	(4)	(5)	(6)
Identifiability of future government	.010	—	.009	.009	—	.0073
	(.003)		(.003)	(.003)		(.0036)
Past government status	−.52	—	−.54	−.58	—	.61
	(.40)		(.38)	(.42)		(.42)
Majority or PEC wins election	−.17	—	−.29	−.22	—	−.34
	(.30)		(.29)	(.31)		(.32)
Effective number of parties	—	−.131	−.05	—	−.14	−.08
		(.070)	(.07)		(.07)	(.08)
Proportionality of electoral outcome	—	−.047	−.041	—	−.038	−.036
		(.021)	(.020)		(.021)	(.021)
Opposition influence in committees	−.27	.44	.07	−.46	.28	−.12
	(.33)	(.33)	(.37)	(.36)	(.35)	(.40)
Intercept	.95	5.79	4.83	1.27	5.19	4.78
	(.36)	(1.80)	(1.88)	(.38)	(1.87)	(2.03)
N	38	38	38	38	38	38
Adjusted R^2	.20	.14	.26	.15	.11	.18
Standard error of the regression	.65	.68	.63	.69	.71	.68

a. The independent variables are described in the text.

Table 6.6 gives the results of six OLS regressions where the formation of a new government is the unit of analysis and the electoral and legislative characteristics described in table 6.4 are the independent variables.[42] ...

The general conclusions from the first two regressions are clear: Majority Control characteristics have mixed effects, which have the net result of moving the government away from the median voter; Proportionate Influence characteristics move the government closer to the median voter....

... [W]hen all the variables are entered into the model, the main variables from the Majority Control vision have a mixed effect with identifiability of future governments harmful to congruence; the variables from the Proportionate Influence vision are helpful to congruence.[43] The

42. Our theoretical discussion does not suggest what the appropriate functional form should be, so we examined a wide variety of functional forms and a simple linear relationship turned out to be the most appropriate for each variable.

43. Our findings regarding the Proportionate Influence variables are interesting when compared with empirical studies of budget deficits by political economists; for a recent review of this literature, see Alberto Alesina and Guido Tabellini, "Positive and Normative Theories of Public Debt and Inflation in Historical Perspectives," *European Economic Review* 36 (April 1992). Roubini

regression analysis therefore supports and clarifies the simple comparison of system types. Despite the plausibility of Downsian theory and some of the other formulations of majoritarian democracy that predict congruence, when there exist clearly identifiable future governments at election time, the elected governments tend to be far from the median voter. And despite concerns about government formation processes, as the effective number of parties and proportionality of electoral outcomes increase, congruence increases. In fact, this congruence is best when parties do not undertake preelection commitments that may lead to the formation of minority governments. To put the comparison between the two types of systems another way, on average the *failures of electoral competition* in the Majority Control (and Mixed) systems seem more serious for congruence than does the *failure of government formation* in the Proportionate Influence systems....

Citizens, Policymakers, and Ideological Congruence

Governments in parliamentary systems are not totally uninfluenced by the opposition in making policy, and the Majority Control and Proportionate Influence visions make different predictions about how the role of opposition parties should affect congruence. Consequently, an exploration of the effectiveness of the two visions

and Sachs, for example, find that systems with a high incidence of coalition and minority governments have relatively large levels of public debt; Roubini and Sachs, "Political and Economic Determinants of Budget Deficits in the Industrial Democracies," *European Economic Review* 33 (May 1989). Since the central characteristics of Proportionate Influence systems lead to coalition and minority governments, it appears that system characteristics which improve congruence between governments and citizens may also be associated with large budget deficits. We are grateful to Bill Keech for pointing this out to us.

Table 6.7
Congruence between policymakers and citizen left-right orientations[a]

	System type		
	Majority control	Mixed	Proportionate influence
Policymaker Distance I	1.17 (22%)	1.03 (18%)	.50 (10%)
Policymaker Distance II	1.17 (22%)	1.15 (20%)	.59 (12%)

a. For Policymaker Distance I and Policymaker Distance II, a party's weight is determined by whether it is a government party, a support party, or an opposition party. Policymaker Distance I uses the same measure as Government Distance I to calculate the position of the government. Policymaker Distance II uses the same measure as Government Distance II to calculate the position of the government. Further details are in the text and the appendix. The numbers in parentheses give the percentage of citizens between the Policymakers and the median citizens.

in linking policy-making and voters must look beyond the parties that formally share government responsibility....

Comparing Congruence between Citizens and Policymakers in the Three Types of Systems

Table 6.7 compares the distance between policymakers and the citizen median in the three types of systems....

... Most strikingly, congruence improves in *all* three types of systems.[48] Across all thirty-eight governments, the average distance between the median voter and the government was about 1.3; the average distance between the median voter

48. Congruence of policymakers was not greater than that of governments in every case, however. It is not a tautology. In eight of the thirty-eight cases the congruence was less for policymakers on at least one of the two measures, although the differences are usually not very large.

and the weighted policymakers was about .85. This decrease was of approximately the same magnitude for all three types of systems. This does not mean, however, that oppositions are closer to the voters than are the governments. They are not. Rather, it means that as long as we continue to weight the governments more heavily than the oppositions in our estimate of policymaking, more congruence is created by giving the oppositions *some* weight than by leaving them out of the process. . . .

Regression Analysis

Since the results from table 6.7 are interesting and somewhat unexpected, it is useful to analyze further the relationship between the system characteristics and the policymaker variables using multivariate regressions. . . .

The regression results help interpret and support the results of the simple comparison of system types. The policymaker measures show reduced distances in all types of systems. However, the Proportionate Influence systems still show a substantial advantage. Identifiability in electoral competition remains costly, although the cost is not as great in absolute terms after we upweight opposition influence on policy-making. Poor proportionality in representation remains highly costly. Single-party majority incumbents before the election seem to be helpful. Yet multiparty systems also remain somewhat helpful, as does opposition influence. The net congruence advantage is to the Proportionate Influence vision.

Concluding Comments

We have attempted to being into more precise focus two general visions of the processes that link citizens and policymakers in contemporary democracies. We should stress that the generality of our results is constrained by our research design: it may be that a different slice of time

would reveal majoritarian electoral competition in which the parties are not so extreme and proportionate influence bargaining is less centrist. Moreover, we are well aware that the "commitments" of governments and their actual policy outcomes are not necessarily the same. This difference would be especially troubling for our results if policies diverged further from promises in the Proportionate Influence systems than in the Majoritarian ones. The difficulty of identifying clear responsibility for policy in the former creates prima facie grounds for concern.

With these caveats said, the results of our analysis seem clear and consistent. In the simple comparison, contrary to our expectations from the theoretical arguments about creating congruence connections in each approach, the governments in the Proportionate Influence systems are on average significantly closer to their median voter than are governments in the Majority Control and Mixed systems. The regression analysis reassures us on this point. If voters are presented with two clear alternatives (parties or preelection coalitions), these alternatives—and resulting governments—tend to be rather distant from the median voter. If voters are presented with a wide range of choices and electoral outcomes are proportional, governments tend to be closer to the median. It is reassuring that the regression results are supportive because they allow us to take advantage of the mixture of properties in the Mixed systems, rather than relying solely on the number of pure Majority Control cases.

Our analysis of policymakers, although necessarily more speculative because of the weighting problem, is also illuminating because the results in part run counter to our initial theoretical expectations. Taking some account of opposition influence helped congruence with voters in virtually all the systems, with surprisingly large effects in the Majority Control and Mixed systems. However, the net advantage remained with the Proportionate Influence systems, which gained congruence, especially because of the strong

weighting of the opposition parties during minority government and because these systems
usually permit more opposition influence in
committees.

The results with respect to Majority Control,
and more generally with respect to high identifiability, raise an important additional question
about policy-making. We examine congruence
on a government-by-government basis, and do
not have a long enough time span to take averages of the governments over several decades.
Hence, although each government in Britain and
Australia may be quite distant from the median
voter, the *average* position over time might be
much closer to the center. Of course, the long
predominance of such governments as the Conservatives in Britain from 1979 to the present
(or the conservative coalition in France from
1958 to 1981) may imply that this oscillation
does not redress the balance very quickly (or
at all).

The appropriate time frame for congruence is
an important issue for future research. The relationships between congruence and other features
of democratic government frequently proposed
as desirable (stability, efficiency, responsibility)
remain another rich area for exploration. The
consideration of these questions reminds us
again of the challenging empirical, theoretical,
and normative issues associated with the study of
congruence. For this reason, we see the current
results as a contribution, not a conclusion, to
our understanding of the fascinating problem of
the electoral connection between citizens and
policymakers. . . .

The Political Consequences of Electoral Laws

Douglas W. Rae

Variations of Degree

The degree to which seat allocations diverge from the condition of perfect proportionality is a function of two electoral law variables: (1) electoral formulae, and (2) district magnitudes. As a rule, P.R. formulae and high district magnitudes produce more nearly proportional results, while "first-past-the-post" formulae and low district magnitudes produce the greatest disproportionality (i.e. the greatest advantage for large parties over small ones). Let me consider the two electoral law variables individually, beginning with the electoral formulae.

Electoral formulae diverge from proportionality along two institutional dimensions. First, proportional representation formulae produce smaller deviations from proportionality than "first-past-the-post" formulae, whether the latter are based on pluralities or majorities.[9] Second, highest averages P.R. formulae diverge farther from proportionality than largest remainder P.R. formulae.[10] The first difference—between P.R. and "first-past-the-post" formulae—is by far the greater of the two.

It follows that P.R. formulae are likely to minimize (but not to eradicate) the general bias of electoral formulae in favor of strong parties. P.R. formulae give a smaller advantage to the strong elective parties and exact a smaller price from weak ones.[11] They give a smaller bonus to the strongest single elective party.[12] And, naturally enough, they are less apt to deny representation to elective parties.[13]

The proportionality of seat allocation also varies with the number of seats assigned to electoral districts—district magnitudes. Where many seats are allocated in each electoral district, the outcome is likely to approximate proportionality.[14] But where fewer seats are allocated in each district, outcomes are likely to diverge more sharply from proportionality.[15] This relationship is, however, curvilinear: as district magnitudes increase, disproportionality decreases at a decreasing rate.[16] Another way to put the same thing is: as district magnitude increases, the proportionality of outcome increases at a decreasing rate.[17] One need not be surprised that the bonus obtained by the strongest party declines as district magnitude rises.[18]

Since plurality formulae are always associated with a single-member district, it is hard to distinguish the disproportionality of these formulae from that of the single-member district's low magnitude. Indeed the distinction has no empirical meaning, except in the Australian case, where a majority formula is associated with a single-member district.

Given that the defractionalization pattern, which works in favor of fewer, stronger legislative parties, is a general fact of electoral life, it is also evident that specific institutions produce variations of degree within the pattern. Political ingenuity can render the defractionalizing pattern stronger or weaker through the manipulation of the institutional variables: electoral formulae and district magnitudes.

Suppose one wanted to design an electoral law that would maximize the defractionalizing

Excerpted from: Douglas W. Rae, *The Political Consequences of Electoral Laws*, revised edition. New Haven: Yale University Press, 1971. Reprinted by permission.

9. Differential Proposition Four.
10. Differential Proposition Nine.
11. Differential Proposition One.
12. Differential Proposition Two.

13. Differential Proposition Five.
14. Differential Proposition Ten.
15. Differential Proposition Ten.
16. Differential Proposition Eleven.
17. Differential Proposition Eleven.
18. Differential Proposition Thirteen.

pattern, producing strong advantages for strong parties, strong penalties for weak ones, and often "manufacturing" legislative majorities. The findings of this study suggest that the *single-member district* is the only necessary instrument. With these very low district magnitudes, the advantage of strong parties will be maximized, no matter what formula is used. Plurality and majority formulae will behave in the same way, defractionalizing legislative party systems by favoring fewer stronger parties. For that matter, even P.R. formulae would have the same effect in single-member districts. Because only one party can win in each district, the strong parties benefit at the expense of the weak ones, and legislative party systems are composed of fewer, stronger parties.[19]

Suppose, on the other hand, that one were worried about proportionality, and wished therefore to minimize defractionalization, giving each party its electoral due—no more and no less. Given these objectives, he should insist on a *P.R. formula*, preferably based on the *largest remainder procedure*, linked with *high district magnitudes* (i.e. many seats per district). It would probably not be worthwhile to expand the districts beyond ten or twenty seats, since the added proportionality seems to decline rapidly beyond that level. But with very low district magnitudes (i.e. less than six seats per district), even the largest remainder P.R. formula would produce a very substantial defractionalizing effect.

Distal Consequences of Electoral Laws

Do the short-run effects we have been discussing have long-run consequences for party systems? What are they? These questions can be answered only with considerable caution, since party sys-

tems are influenced by many variables—social, economic, legal, and political. Proximal effect of electoral law upon the legislative representation of parties is to be counted only one of many determining forces. And it is, secondly, impossible to sort out all the contributing factors, or to assign even approximate weights to them. Worse yet, electoral laws are themselves shaped by party systems.

In the face of these difficulties, one can only suggest limited connections. I have chosen to formulate my commentary in response to the question: "Where electoral laws do in fact make a long-run difference, which specific properties of electoral laws are apt to produce what differences?" By choosing to work within the assumption that electoral laws do exert long-run effects, yet without demonstrating this assumption's validity, I have settled for a very limited level of analysis. But to do more would require not one, but twenty or more, developmental studies, each devoted to a single country. The limited suggestions offered here may provide some guidelines for research of that kind, and may have at least tentative significance in their own right.

Party systems vary over a continuum, from non-fractionalization in one-party systems to extreme fractionalization in systems where a great many parties compete on about equal terms. Among the party systems analyzed in this study, the actual range of variation lies between two less distant points: U.S.-style, two-party competition and Israeli-type multi-partism. Every party system, at any one point in time, may be assigned a place on this continuum, although (and this is important) individual systems may move along these scales, toward or away from the empirical extreme of two-party competition.

How do electoral systems influence the movement of systems on the fractionalization continuum? I wish to suggest that the pattern of proximal defractionalization described above is the source of whatever influence electoral laws have on the fractionalization of party systems.

---

19. This assertion must be modified where parties which are weak on a national scale enjoy pockets of local support, enabling them to profit from the single-member district in those areas.

Where the pattern is strong—large parties are greatly advantaged—the electoral system exerts pressure on the system for two-party competition. But where the pattern is weak—large parties are only slightly advantaged—a weaker, often negligible, pressure is exerted in that direction. The defractionalizing pattern is a restraint on the fractionalization of party systems, and the effective pressure exerted by electoral laws varies with the intensity of the defractionalizing pattern itself. Multi-partism is most likely where electoral laws produce a weak defractionalizing pattern, and two-party competition most likely where the electoral laws produce a strong defractionalizing effect.

Now, according to my earlier comments, the defractionalizing pattern is complex. It entails at least five related subpatterns: (1) the advantage of large parties over small ones in the division of legislative seats; (2) the awarding of a "bonus" in seats to the strongest party; (3) the exclusion of small parties from the legislative arena; (4) the overall defractionalization of legislative party systems; and (5) the fairly frequent creation of "manufactured majorities" in legislative party systems. These are the subpatterns present in all electoral systems, but stronger in some than others, which constitute the defractionalizing process that seems so important. The question thus becomes, "What electoral law variables produce this syndrome?"

The answer to this question was foretold in the examination of proximal effects. Here let me recapitulate the effects of these institutions, with attention to the contribution they make to the shaping of party systems over time. Logically, the sequence of inferences is: (a) electoral law variables to intensity of the defractionalizing pattern, and, with less confidence, (b) the intensity of the defractionalizing pattern to the long-run fractionalization of the party system.[20]

What electoral law provisions intensify the defractionalizing pattern and therefore seem likely to exert pressure toward two-party competition? The answer is simple: the single-member district, or, failing that, small multi-member districts. In a single-member district, almost any formula[21]—the plurality is most common—is likely to advantage the strong parties and, in general, to establish the defractionalizing pattern. This much is confirmed by the analysis of proximal effects. But what about the long-range effects? The findings of the study show a fairly consistent association between single-member plurality formulae and two-party systems.[22]

A causal interpretation of this association falls upon several exceptions, the clearest of which are Canadian and Austrian. Nevertheless, the combination of the proximal defracationalizing pattern and the distal association with two-party competition suggests that the single-member district is likely to contribute to the development and sustenance of two-party systems. Other factors, such as regional minorities, may reverse this condition, as is the case in Canada. But, insofar as the electoral law exerts a controlling pressure, the single-member district is likely to press the system toward two-party competition.

And what arrangements are most likely to press party systems toward multi-partism, because they exert a very weak defractionalizing effect? These would be the institutions that optimize the proportionality of outcomes: largest remainder P.R. formulae, operating in high magnitude electoral districts. Because the outcomes are more nearly proportional under these provisions, the defractionalizing process is weakened. Is there an association between these arrangements and multi-partism? The study's findings show that there is:

---

20. A third inference is from the degree to which an electoral system is presently fractionalized to the kind of electoral laws adopted for future elections.

---

21. The French double ballot may be an exception, although limited evidence suggests that it is not.

22. Differential Proposition Three and Similarity Proposition Seven.

1. In general, P.R. formulae are associated with more fractionalized elective and parliamentary party systems.[23]

2. Among P.R. formula electoral laws, those using the largest-remainder procedure are associated with greater fractionalization, both elective and parliamentary, than are those using highest-average procedures.[24]

3. High district magnitudes are associated with greater fractionalization in both elective and parliamentary systems.[25]

The distal association between these institutions and high fractionalization, even when seen beside the weakness of the proximal defractionalizing pattern which they produce, does not suggest a simple *causal* relationship. It does, however, imply that insofar as the electoral law exerts a controlling pressure, these provisions are apt to press systems toward multi-partism and away from two-party competition.

These conclusions suggest that the statesman who must choose between electoral laws confronts a dilemma. On the one hand, he may opt for highly proportional election outcomes, in which case he is likely to encourage the fractionalization of party systems over time. Or, on the other hand, he may opt to encourage the development and maintenance of two parties, or less fractionalized multi-party competition, with the price being less proportional outcomes. These alternatives may not be inevitable, but the findings reported here make them seem probable: if proportionality, then multi-partism; but if two-party competition, then also a disproportional outcome.[26] ...

---

23. Differential Proposition Six.

24. Differential Proposition Nine.

25. Differential Proposition Twelve.

26. The time-sequence data for the twenty-year period I have studied do not produce clinching evidence for these speculations: except for West Germany, there is no system which changes drastically in its degree of fractionalization. But that is not altogether surprising,

Election Outcomes and Government Stability

It is generally supposed that election outcomes—allocations of seats among parties—quite directly determine which party or coalition will control a parliamentary government. So, for example, one of our most sophisticated accounts holds out these conditions for representative democracy: "A single party (or coalition of parties) is chosen by popular election to run the governing apparatus," and "Any party (or coalition of parties) receiving the support of a majority of those voting is entitled to take over the powers of government until the next election."[16] It is revealing that these requirements, most obviously the second, lead to logical contradictions and must therefore be violated by any empirical system of parliamentary politics. Since this logical difficulty carries our attention toward an important empirical question, let me begin by examining it briefly.

During a campaign, we have n_e parties. Before the electorate decides, one can imagine that any of $2^{n_e} - 1$ parties or coalitions might command majorities and form a government. Thus,

---

since all of the systems, save Germany and Israel, had been in operation for many decades before the period covered by this study. Historical analyses of the individual systems would be of interest. I must conclude that association, but not sequential data, support my speculations.

16. Anthony Downs, *An Economic Theory of Democracy* (New York: Harper & Row, 1957) pp. 23–24. A related but less clearcut difficulty arises in Robert Dahl's notion of polyarchy, when it is required that alternatives with more votes replace alternatives with fewer. See *A Preface to Democratic Theory* (Chicago: University of Chicago Press, 1956), Chap. 3. In both cases, the problem arises, I think, because the authors are thinking primarily about two-party systems and only secondarily about multiparty systems. In Dahl's analysis the requirement is stated as an ideal, but in Downs's it is treated (incorrectly) as a feature which "in practice" distinguishes democracy from other forms.

with three electoral parties one can imagine $2^3 - 1 = 7$ conceivable governments (e.g. A, B, C, AB, AC, BC, ABC.) According to "common sense" and Downs's stipulations, the election outcome should reduce this set of possibilities to one, *the* party or coalition which commands a majority. But if more than one party wins representation, this cannot be literally true. If np parties win representation, the election outcome must leave open the possibility of exactly 2^{np-1} distinct majority governments. The effect of an election outcome is thus to reduce the set of potential majority governments without "picking" a single government. If, for example, three parties win representation, then exactly $2^{3-1} = 4$ possible governments must remain *no matter how seats are divided among these parties*. And this implies that both of Downs's requirements are unrealizable: the election itself cannot pick *a* party or coalition to govern, and *some* parties or coalitions holding majorities must inevitably be denied control of government (e.g. $2^{np-1} = 1$). This very formal difficulty is not without its relevance to experience.

If a single party wins a majority of its own, the difficulty is merely technical. Say that A holds a majority over B and C. It is still true that the election permits four possible governments (A, AB, AC, ABC) but there are compelling reasons to presume that one will be chosen (A). In this event, we need only add the stipulation that potential governments with inessential members (AB, AC, ABC, in our example) may be ignored. One might suppose that the problem could thus be reduced to a linguistic quibble were it not for the fact that about two-thirds of all parliamentary elections fail to produce single-party majorities (of 107 elections analyzed in the original study, only 8 produced natural majorities, 25 produced manufactured majorities, and the remaining 74 produced neither). Thus a more typical case occurs when no single party holds a majority and one is left without an obvious choice of government. Thus, if A, B, and C each have less than half the seats in a parliament, then

the possible governments include AB, AC, BC, and ABC. This is a more than technical violation of Downs's requirement, for it leaves an open set of potential governments (and, significantly, a choice of potential alternatives to any government that forms).

A useful example is offered by the 1963 election of the Icelandic parliament (the *Althingi*). The Independence Party obtained 24 seats, the Progressives 19, the Communists 8, and the Social Democrats 7. With four electoral parties, one might have imagined $2^4 - 1 = 15$ possible governments, and (since no party was denied representation) the outcome simply restricts this to a subset of $2^{4-1} = 8$ groupings that command majorities and could conceivably form governments. To each of these, there naturally corresponds a potential set of opposition parties:

	Possible Government	Possible Opposition
1.	Ind, Prog, Com, SD	nil
2.	Ind, Prog, Com	SD
3.	Ind, Prog, SD	Com
4.	Prog, Com, SD	Ind
5.	Ind, Com, SD	Prog
6.	Ind, SD	Prog, Com
7.	Ind, Prog	SD, Com
8.	Ind, Com	Prog, SD

The election itself comes to a very partial arbitration of the question "Who governs?" Only seven of the fifteen otherwise conceivable governments have been eliminated, leaving eight possibilities. Each party is a member of at least five such possible governments, and no party belongs to all eight. The effective choice must therefore rest with party leaders as they are influenced by conflicts and compatibilities of program, ideology, or personality in the formation of coalitions. It is a choice *bounded* but left undecided by the election outcome. As it happens, government 6 (Independence–Social Democrat) was formed in 1963, but roughly similar outcomes have since World War II, also led to the formation of governments 3, 4, and 7.[17] Unless the process of government formation is understood by the electorate, this surely raises important difficulties for theories of electoral representation, for it is impossible to see how the citizen could draw useful associations between his voting decision and the eventual choice of a government.[18]

Parliaments that are fractionalized enough to produce these uncertainties[19] would seem especially prone to government instability, for at least two reasons. First, their numerical structures offer *wide opportunity for the destruction of governments*. With more than one party-elite in a government, it is possible to reach a vote of no confidence even without a breach of party discipline. And, as the number of essential partners increases, one might expect an actuarial increase in the frequency with which a particular decision alienates a member party, bringing a new election or a change of governments without one. Moreover, since only one of 2^{n_p-1} possible governments has been formed, it seems probable that member parties could, at some point, identify alternative partners with whom a more attractive government could be formed. These reasons are very roughly analogous to the structural relations outlined for partisan insurgency earlier, although their interconnections are less clear. A second reason points toward the likelihood that highly fractionalized parliaments are indices of intense political conflict. If this is

so, then there will be a convergence of strong motives and wide opportunities for changes of government in such systems.

Unhappily, none of these conjectures can be mistaken for a theory. And, although coalition behavior has been the object of intensive study in recent years, research on the specific question of stability remains inconclusive. We do, however, have a useful exploration of several common-sense hypotheses in a recent study by Michael Taylor and V. M. Herman.[20] These authors considered 196 governments in 19 countries (those studied here, minus the U.S. and Switzerland, plus Japan) from the end of World War II up to 1969. They define "government stability" in calendar days elapsed without a change of prime minister or party support.[21] Their study is an effort to treat variation in stability as a function of the parliamentary party system variables discussed here. The most straightforward of their results are these.

Independent Variable	Product-Moment Correlation with Government Stability
(1) Number of parliamentary parties (n_p)	−.39
(2) Fractionalization of parliamentary parties (F_p)	−.448
(3) Number of parties in government	−.307
(4) Proportion of seats held by anti-system parties	−.450

These results tend to confirm the intuitive expectations sketched out above, but they do not include the most plausible explanation turned

---

17. Nils Andrain.

18. See Downs, pp. 142–63 for a discussion of these difficulties. In Thomas Casstevens, "An Axiom About Voting," *American Political Science Review*, 62 (1968), 205–07, an attempt is made to show that (on a simplistic assumption about "winning" and a vitiating assumption about the probabilities of parties doing so) the voter should always just vote for his most preferred party.

19. If parliamentary fractionalization reaches .5, there may be no single-party solution, and if it reaches .75, there cannot possibly be such a solution.

---

20. "Party Systems and Government Stability," *American Political Science Review*, 65 (1971), 28–37.

21. In this, they follow an earlier study, Jean Blondel, "Party Systems and Patterns of Government in Western Democracies," *Canadian Journal of Political Science*, 1 (1968), 180–203.

up by the Taylor-Herman study. It is interesting that their effort to include ideological distances in the notion of fractionalization actually weakened its relationship to instability (to $-.417$.) But the related distinction between anti-system and pro-system parties nevertheless proved highly interesting (variable 4 above.) Their best explanation turns on the joint effect of "proportion anti-system" and the fractionalization of seats among the remaining parties. Using these two variables in a multiple regression estimate they find a fit of $R = .496$. Ironically, the estimate is improved slightly ($R = .506$) if right-wing anti-system seats are dropped, leaving only communist seats in the proportion anti-system. The apparent explanation for this account is that, if anti-system parties always refuse to support governments, the proportion of available votes required is increased (being $r/2(r - a)$ where r is the parliament's size and a is the size of the anti-system contingent). The effective decision rule for sustaining governments thus grows more restrictive with increases in anti-system representation (or communists) and is less easily met as remaining seats grow more fractionalized. This seems, at any rate, the most plausible conjecture.

Although this section is less developed analytically than its predecessor, its *tendence* is similar—to suggest complexity of interconnection. I will not attempt to draw all of these connections together here, but finish with the conjecture that this analysis concerns itself with only a few fragments of the immeasurably *more* complex pattern by which ruling groups, as they are sustained and replaced over time, leave their marks on publics and the policies by which they are governed.

South Africa's Negotiated Transition: Democracy, Opposition, and the New Constitutional Order

Courtney Jung and Ian Shapiro

In 1965, Robert Dahl remarked that "of the three great milestones in the development of democratic institutions—the right to participate in governmental decisions by casting a vote, the right to be represented, and the right of an organized opposition to appeal for votes against the government in elections and in parliament—the last is, in a highly developed form, so wholly modern that there are people now living who were born before it had appeared in most of Western Europe."[7] He might perhaps have added that opposition is also the milestone that has been least studied by contemporary political scientists. . . .

Although the notion of a loyal opposition finds its origins in monarchical rather than democratic politics, democratic systems rely on institutionalized oppositions, and it is doubtful that any regime could long survive as minimally democratic without them.[10]

This is true for at least three related reasons. The first is functional, having to do with the peaceful turnover of power by governments that lose elections. . . . If democratic politics is seen as requiring at a minimum that there be turnover of power among elites, then there must be sites for counterelites to form and campaign as potential alternative governments. Such opposition requires the permissive freedoms of speech and association as well as the presence of institutions and practices that make it possible for counterelites to organize and inform themselves so as to be able to contest for power. . . . If the opposition is not thus perceived, then the possibility of turnover is diminished and crises for the government are correspondingly more likely to become crises for the democratic regime.

This suggests a second reason why opposition institutions matter: for the legitimacy of the democratic political order. Providing the institutional space for opposition is essential for ensuring that discontent and dissatisfaction can be directed at particular governments rather than at the democratic regime itself . . . Unless there are such institutional outlets for dissent within the regime's institutions, those who are discontented with the status quo may not even distinguish the government from the regime, undermining the possibility of the ebb and flow of competitive party politics that democracies require. . . .

Last, institutional arrangements that facilitate loyal opposition perform important public-interest functions in democracies. They are necessary to ensure the presence of healthy political debate. They encourage competition over ideas among elites and counterelites, and this leads to demands for reason giving and coherence in public debate. Moreover, opposition institutions empower groups and individuals who have an interest in asking awkward questions, shining light in dark places, and exposing abuses of power. Without an organized political opposition that has rights to information and other resources, governing in secret becomes all too tempting for the administration of the day. Governments always have incentives to camouflage mistakes or controversial decisions that might otherwise threaten their popularity and to misuse the perquisites of office. Unless their members know that they can be called to public account for their actions, the temptation to act

Excerpted from: Courtney Jung and Ian Shapiro, "South Africa's Negotiated Transition: Democracy, Opposition, and the New Constitutional Order." *Politics and Society* 23(3): 269–308. © 1995 Sage Publications, Inc. Reprinted by permission of Sage Publications, Inc.

7. Robert A. Dahl, *Political Opposition in Western Democracies* (New Haven: Yale University Press, 1965), p. xiii.

10. Barrington Moore, Jr., *Liberal Prospects under Soviet Socialism: A Comparative Historical Perspective* (New York: Averell Harriman Institute, 1989), pp. 8, 25. . . .

on these incentives will in many cases prove irresistible.

II. The Opposition/Nonopposition Continuum

Although the principal alternative to democratic systems that institutionalize opposition may be authoritarian systems that repress it, many systems of government are designed to channel dissent and opposition away from national political institutions and otherwise to diffuse it. Such systems are usually defended on the grounds that disagreements in the society in question are so potentially explosive that anything else will result in the war of all against all. Many orthodox prescriptions for "divided" societies—those in which unbridgeable divisions among the population are thought to preclude pluralist politics—take this form. Perhaps the best known of these is Lijphart's consociational model of minority vetoes and enforced coalitions, which might be thought of as occupying a position at the far end of a continuum from the opposition model just sketched.[13]

Consociational models of democracy emphasize participation and representation to the virtual exclusion of opposition. Their organizing principles are proportionality in the electoral system, an institutional structure that forces power sharing and a system of mutual vetoes among "a cartel of elites,"[14] and a predisposition toward robust federalism to insulate territorially based minorities from the power of whoever controls national political institutions. Advocates of consociational democracy contend that particularly when societies are deeply di-

vided along ethnic lines, if democracy can be realized at all it will be only if the effects of majority rule are mitigated by institutional devices of this sort. The assumption is that ethnic divisions so completely overdetermine other conflicts, and that they are so intense and enduring (if not primordial), that the only viable institutional recipe is one that is designed to minimize political competition and keep the groups from getting at one anothers' throats.

Consociational systems undermine the functional, legitimacy-generating, and public-interest roles of opposition discussed in section I. With regard to the first, consociational systems are not designed to foster alternation of major parties in power. Instead, they permit the same combination of elites to entrench themselves at the peaks of spoils and patronage hierarchies more or less continuously. The democratic benefits that can accrue from "tossing the rascals out" are therefore unavailable. On the legitimacy front, because consociational arrangements ensure that every major political player is part of the government, there is little basis for the disaffected to differentiate the government from the regime. It is hard for an ethos of loyal opposition to develop when there is no institutional outlet.[15] Those who are not in government are removed from politics altogether, making it more likely that they will turn to extra-institutional politics if they can. With regard to the public-interest role of opposition politics, consociational systems do not give powerful parliamentary players incentives to keep government honest by shining light in dark corners. Because consociational systems require high levels of consensus among governing

---

13. See Arend Lijphart, *Democracy in Plural Societies* (New Haven: Yale University Press, 1977), and *Power-Sharing in South Africa* (Berkeley: University of California Institute of International Studies, 1985).

14. Arend Lijphart, "Consociational Democracy," *World Politics* 4, no. 2 (January 1969), pp. 213–215, 222.

15. This insight is at the core of Horowitz's critique of consociational systems: that the very circumstances in which they are most needed—when there are powerful divisions in the society—are the circumstances when they are also least likely to be effective; see Donald L. Horowitz, *A Democratic South Africa? Constitutional Engineering in a Divided Society* (Berkeley: University of California Press, 1991), pp. 142–143.

elites, the only way for anyone in the governing elite to get her way on issues that matter intensely to her is to give other powerful players what they want on issues that matter intensely to them. Therefore, mutual vetoes can be expected to lead to mutual logrolling, rather than to political confrontations among elites, and to promote insider clubism. By the same token, logrolling minimizes the likelihood that government elites will be called to account by members of potential alternative governments. In short, consociational systems, based on the politics of elite coalitions, maximize both representation and participation in government, but at the price of almost complete abandonment of a viable opposition politics.

The position of a regime along the opposition/nonopposition continuum depends on the electoral system and on the divisions of power within the legislature and between the legislature and the executive. First-past-the-post electoral systems based on single-member districts are likely to produce two-party systems and, as a result, strong parliamentary oppositions.[16] These oppositions may or may not have the potential to become alternative governments (depending on their potential grass roots support). Nonetheless, they will have an interest in becoming magnets for antigovernment sentiment, which should give them incentives to perform at least some of the conventional functions of loyal oppositions: organizing and channeling dissent, disseminating information, and exposing government corruption. Thus although two-party–dominated plurality systems have high barriers to entry and are comparatively unrepresentative, they produce significant institutionalized opposition.

Things will be less predictable in multiparty systems dependent on coalition governments. Given the well-documented propensity of proportional representation to produce party frac-

tionalization, particularly when constituencies are large and thresholds are low,[17] unconstrained proportional representation makes parliamentary structure unpredictable. In certain circumstances it may produce strong opposition coalitions and alternation in government, as is sometimes the case in Israel and The Netherlands. In other circumstances, such as Austria and Switzerland, the major parties will often govern in coalition. Given the unpredictability of unconstrained proportional representation versus the predictability of first-past-the-post plurality systems in generating two-party politics, one would not choose the former over the latter if the goal was to produce oppositional rather than consociational parliamentary politics.

Whether a system is presidential or parliamentary also affects the prospects for institutionalized opposition. Parliamentary systems link the fortunes of the executive to those of the majority party in parliament, so that institutionalized opposition is apt to be centered in the legislature. In presidential systems, significant opposition may occur between the executive and the legislature, depending on the powers of the presidency (e.g., whether they include the power to appoint a cabinet or to conduct some affairs unilaterally) and the interactions between the electoral rules for parliament and presidency. An electoral system that produces a government consisting of all the powerful players in the legislature is likely to weaken the presidency, reducing the president, in the limiting case, to a figurehead. If the president's party is a minority

---

16. Douglas W. Rae, *The Political Consequences of Electoral Laws* (New Haven: Yale University Press, 1967).

17. Arend Lijphart, *Electoral Systems and Party Systems* (Oxford: Oxford University Press, 1994). Rae suggests that with proportional representation, small and medium-sized constituencies and higher thresholds combine to limit fractionalization and give parties incentives to form blocs, whether in government or opposition. In effect the constraints make multiparty systems operate more like two-party systems: see Douglas W. Rae "Using District Magnitude to Regulate Political Party Competition," *Journal of Economic Perspectives* 9, no. 1 (winter 1995), pp. 65–75.

in the legislature, as is often the case in Brazil for instance, he has to seek support from the majority (opposition) party to avoid governmental paralysis. This type of system tends closely to approximate a power-sharing type of arrangement. If, however, the constitution confers substantial autonomous power on the president, as it does in the United States, the president may be an institutional figure to be reckoned with even if his party is a minority in the legislature. For presidential systems to be relatively close to the opposition end of the continuum in virtue of their presidentialism, then, either presidents must be institutionally powerful or there must be significant minority parties in the legislature with which they can ally themselves. As the latter is less predictably so in proportional representation systems, it is less predictably the case in presidential proportional representation systems. Perhaps for this reason, observers have noticed a coincidence of presidential proportional representation systems and power-sharing governments.[18] ...

18. Scott Mainwaring, "Presidentialism, Multiparty Systems, and Democracy: The Difficult Equation," *Comparative Political Studies* 26, no. 2 (1993), pp. 198–230; Arend Lijphart, "Democratization and Constitutional Choices in Czechoslovakia, Hungary, and Poland, 1989–1991," *Journal of Theoretical Politics* 4, no. 2 (1993), p. 209.

The Representation of Women

Anne Phillips

In the countries that lay claim to the title of democracy, women have enjoyed many decades of formal equality, sharing with men the right to vote, to stand in elections, to compete for any office (political—not yet religious) in the land. Their participation in voting is now much the same as men's. Yet almost regardless of the date at which women won their rights (ranging from 1902 in Australia, 1919 in West Germany, 1920 in the USA, 1928 in the UK, to the much delayed 1971 in Switzerland), there has been a marked consistency in the figures for female participation in national and local politics. With the major recent exception of the Nordic countries (to which I shall return), women figure in national politics at something between 2 and 10 per cent; in Britain and the USA, women have found it notoriously hard to break the 5 per cent barrier.

Figures for local politics are only marginally more promising. By 1983, women representatives had captured 13 per cent of the seats on West German local councils; 14 per cent on the French conseils municipaux; 14.4 per cent on county councils in England and Wales; 11.1 per cent on regional councils in Scotland; and 7.9 per cent on district councils in Northern Ireland (Lovenduski 1986). By 1985, women made up 14 per cent of the membership of municipal and township governing boards in the United States, but had been elected to mayor in only four of the hundred largest cities (Randall 1987:105). The percentages are nothing to write home about, and women's relatively higher profile in local politics only confirms what is frequently observed: that the numbers rise where the power of the office is less. We all know there are more men than women in politics, but the details still come

Excerpted from: Anne Phillips, *Engendering Democracy*. Cambridge: Polity Press, 1991. Reprinted by permission.

as a shock: only forty-three women out of 650 members of the British parliament? Only twenty-eight women out of 435 members of the US House of Representatives? What kind of democracy is this?

Liberal democracy makes its neat equations between democracy and representation, democracy and universal suffrage, but asks us to consider as irrelevant the composition of our elected assemblies. The resulting pattern has been firmly skewed in the direction of white middle-class men, with the under-representation of women only the starkest (because they are half the population) among a range of excluded groups. The campaign for women's right to vote was always linked to a parallel campaign for women's right to be elected. Success in the first has not brought much joy in the second....

The under-representation of women within conventional politics is nonetheless crucial in thinking about democracy and gender. The general critique of liberal democracy leaves a teasing vacuum on what could serve as alternatives, while the questions raised over the two most common alternatives suggest that neither can be simply adopted in its place. We can perhaps move on to more substantial ground if we examine more closely the weaknesses (and possibly strengths) of current liberal democratic practice. What does the under-representation of women add to the understanding of democracy? It shows that there is a problem undoubtedly, but is the problem then in the theory or application? Setting aside for the moment what may be more fundamental problems with liberal/representative democracy, can we anticipate a trend towards sexual parity? Is there a theoretical problem with the "representation of women," an incongruity between this and the assumptions of liberal democracy?... [D]oes feminism provide us with a novel angle on these issues, a different way of conceiving either possibilities or limits? There are two major aspects of this, which I shall discuss in separate sections. What are the theoretical issues implied in the notion of representation? What are the chances of electing more women?

"Mirror" Representation

Confront people with the damning evidence on the number of women elected and they tend to divide into those who think this matters and those who say it does not. Much of the disagreement reflects the complacency, not to say dishonesty, of those who enjoy a monopoly of power, but there are more intriguing issues at stake. As with many feminist demands, the case for greater parity in politics has been made in three ways (Hernes 1987). Part of it relies on a notion of basic justice, and fits within a broad sweep of arguments that challenges sexual segregation wherever it occurs. Just as it is unjust that women should be cooks but not engineers, typists but not directors, so it is unjust that they should be excluded from the central activities in the political realm; indeed, given the overarching significance of politics, it is even more unfair that women should be kept out of this. But for the hundred years and more that access to political power has been an issue, women's organizations have combined the case for justice with at least one additional point. Sometimes the argument is that women would bring to politics a different set of values, experiences and expertise: that women would enrich our political life, usually in the direction of a more caring, compassionate society. A more radical version is that men and women are in conflict and that it is nonsense to see women as represented by men.

The case for justice says nothing about what women will do if they get into politics, while the two further arguments imply that the content of politics will change. All unite in seeing a sexual disproportion between electors and elected as evidence that something is wrong. The striking homogeneity of our existing representatives is proof enough of this, since if there were no sub-

stantial differences between men and women, or between black people and white, then those elected would undoubtedly be a more random sample from those who elect. Consistent underrepresentation of any social category already establishes that there is a problem. Such a marked variance from the population as a whole could never be an accidental result. Leaving aside as mere prejudice the notion that women are "naturally" indifferent to politics, there must be something that prevents their involvement. The argument from justice then calls on us to eliminate or moderate whatever obstacles we find to women's participation, while the arguments from women's different values or different interests go one stage further. The sexual differentiation in conditions and experience has produced a specifically woman's point of view, which is either complementary or antagonistic to the man's. Any system of representation which consistently excludes the voices of women is not just unfair; it does not begin to count as representation.

All three arguments are at odds with what has become the orthodoxy, for while there are a number of competing versions on offer, the idea that representatives should in some way "mirror" those they represent is probably the most contested. . . .

The dominant practice in most contemporary democracies is a muddled combination of both accountability and autonomy. Our representatives are said to represent our views (political parties present us with alternative policies, and we make a choice between them), but only in the vaguest of ways (election manifestos offer bland generalities, and those elected then fill in the details themselves). Those elected are seen as carrying some responsibility for their area, but are not permitted to take this too far, for they are ultimately bound by party lines. On any of the major social or demographic characteristics (age, sex, race, class) they do not represent us at all. Taking the example of British Members of Parliament: lawyers make up the largest single occupational group; women have only just pushed beyond five percent of the total; and the proportion of the population that is nonwhite is currently "represented" by a mere handful of MPs, whose election in 1987 marked the first substantial breach in the white monopoly....

Representative democracy cannot produce a perfect reflection of society: the only guarantee of that would be all the citizens meeting together in national assembly. Within the limits of representation, it is hard to see how to get agreement on the categories to be covered. Even where such agreement becomes possible, proportionality inevitably reduces local autonomy, for it must involve some form of national party directive over the kind of candidates each constituency should choose. But arguments that rely on the impossibility of one extreme in order to justify its opposite are always suspect, and as long as those who speak for us are drawn from such an *un*representative sample, then democracy will remain profoundly flawed. The obstacles that deny certain people the chance of election are as undemocratic in their way as the laws that once excluded them from the right to vote. And moving on to the more positive point, different experiences do create different values, priorities, interests; while we may all be capable of that imaginative leap that takes us beyond our own situation, history indicates that we do this very partially, if at all. Those who regard the current situation with complacency are not too far in spirit from the nineteenth-century apologists of male suffrage, who claimed that a man spoke for himself and "his" woman, and thus that the woman had no need for a separate voice. Where there are different interests and different experiences, it is either naive or dishonest to say that one group can speak for us all....

It is easy enough to show that women are under-represented in politics, and not too much more difficult to make the case that women are oppressed. On both counts something should surely be done. The disproportion between those elected and those who elect is too astounding to

be attributed to accident, while the fact that it serves those who are already advantaged is too striking for any democrat to ignore. The difficulties arise in the next stage, for within the framework of representative democracy, it is political parties that have provided the vehicle for representation, and in its more substantial sense, the representation of women does not fit. "Women" are not homogeneous and do not speak with a single voice....

... Those who resist an increase in women's representation no doubt harbour similar fears, anticipating that the women elected will alter the game. I hope there will be changes, but in the interests of democratic accountability these have to take place in the open, through the decision-making processes of each party and the publicity of electoral campaigns. We cannot jump too easily into the notion that there is an interest of women; and short of women's constituencies or women's elections, there is no clear mechanism for their representation.

The relative autonomy of politics

Let me now turn the argument the other way. I have said that the case for more women representatives rests partly on a notion of equality in participation and partly on a notion of reflection, and that neither in principle nor in practice can this guarantee that women are then represented *as women*. We can anticipate that more women elected will shift the context and priorities of public policy, but cannot say this is necessarily so, nor indeed presume that their choices would win general acclaim. The problem may be even more acute. If feminists are right in the critiques they have developed of liberal democracy, then the nature of the public/private divide may make even equal numbers an impossible dream. If the constraints on women's political activity are set by their economic and social position, then the idea that you could have a parliament made up equally of men and women, without *also* having substantial changes in social relations, is nonsensical. The absurdity lies not in thinking that women would prove no different from men, but in imagining that they could ever get into such positions of power until after the changes were made. A democracy may require the policies on equality before the equality of representation—and yet without the second what hope is there of the first? . . .

Explanations for women's relative invisibility in politics tend to be multi-causal—which is probably why I used to find them tedious, for they lack the drama of the singular cause. Women have been socialized into regarding politics as an alien affair; women are constrained by their responsibilities as mothers, and indeed their general role as carers for the young, sick and old, all of which make the commitments of full-time politics an almost impossible choice; women are under-represented in the jobs that most favour political careers; women are discouraged by the attentions of a hostile media; women are actively excluded by the male selectorates who guard the gateways to political life (Randall 1987). Within the general tendency to give due weight to each of these factors, there are still important variations in emphasis. Some writers have focused more on what stops women coming forward, and others on the male barriers when they nonetheless do (Lovenduski and Hills 1981 is an example of the latter). And some writers focus attention on political conditions, while others identify the social and economic obstacles to change.

In the more "political" category are the arguments about proportional representation, which have been most associated in the British context (they are less of an issue elsewhere) with the work of Elizabeth Vallance (1979) and more recently Pippa Norris (1985). Single-member constituencies with a first-past-the-post system for selecting the winner are said to stack the cards in favour of the male, for in our sex-divided patriarchal societies, the man is the norm, the woman peculiar. . . .

. . . [I]n a multi-member constituency the selectorate might take the risk and indeed,

when they are choosing not one but three or five candidates, it begins to look odd if they are all of them the same. In particular, where elections are organized through party lists there is considerably more scope for dictating sexual composition. It becomes possible to set a minimum quota for each sex in the winnable positions, or, even more ambitiously, to put men and women in alternate order on the list and produce parity in the final results. The evidence from Europe is not decisive but certainly suggestive. Those countries which rely on the single-member, first-past-the-post system have found it hardest to advance on the 5 per cent token representation. Most of those with a system of multi-member constituencies and party lists edge towards a 10 per cent representation of women. All those that stand out as spectacularly progressive employ proportional representation with party lists (Norris 1985; Lovenduski 1986; Haavio-Mannila et al. 1985).

General arguments for and against proportional representation establish the difficulties in saying what is most democratic. The single transferable vote system allows voters to indicate a hierarchy of preferences, and protects us against a situation in which party A wins with a minority of votes, when parties B and C are between them the first and second preferences of the majority. The implication, however, is that the party that ends up with most seats could be one that has fewer first preference votes—and if people really wanted their first choice, but only marginally preferred their second to their third, this could be a compromise that leaves the majority unhappy. The multi-member constituency can iron out some of the inequalities in first-past-the-post systems, but the smaller parties within each constituency may still end up with no members in parliament even if their support through the nation turned out quite impressive. The additional or mixed member system tries to deal with this by leaving some (usually half) seats selected on the first-past-the-post system, but distributing the remainder in proportion to the parties' share of the national vote. The problem here is that if the way we vote in our constituencies is still premised on our perception of which parties have the most chance in our area (we don't simply vote for what we most want, but for what we prefer given what we think others will do) then the figures for national voting cannot be presumed to reflect genuine preference. And, as opponents of any of these systems will argue, proportional representation can give undue influence to the small party that then holds the balance of power. Getting a "fair" reflection of parties in parliament does not guarantee fair reflection in government.

In terms of the "mirror" effect of reflecting the population, however, some form of proportional representation wins hands down over first-past-the-post systems (and when the New Zealand Commission on Electoral Reform recommended the abolition of Maori seats, it was with the proviso that the country should switch to a mixed member proportional system, thereby increasing Maori chances of election). In her study of "Women's legislative participation in Western Europe" (1985) Pippa Norris compares twenty-four liberal democracies, including eighteen in Western Europe, to assess the correlation between the numbers of women elected and institutional, cultural and socioeconomic conditions. The institutional differences refer to the electoral system: whether the country operates a party list proportional system or some version of majoritarianism, including first-past-the-post, alternative vote and single transferable vote systems. Cultural differences were defined by the strength of Catholicism versus Protestantism (the former seen as more traditionalist for women), and with the help of data contributed by nine countries in the European Community in a survey on attitudes to sexual equality in politics. Socio-economic differences were roughly identified by the proportions of women in the labour force, their proportions in higher education and their proportions in the professions.

As in any cross-national survey, the measures are a bit rough and ready, but the results proved striking enough. Differences in electoral systems emerged as by far the most significant in relation to the election of women, followed at some distance by positions on the index of political egalitarianism. The dominant religion proved insignificant, as did socio-economic conditions. Among the notable individual examples, Switzerland is particularly convincing. Women were not granted full equal rights till 1971, and the society is so traditional in its views that as late as 1982 male citizens were still voting in one canton to deny women the vote in local elections. Swiss women nonetheless weigh in at over 10 per cent in the Nationalrat—under a system of proportional representation (Norris 1985:99).

Ten per cent is no great cause for rejoicing, and the fact that a particular electoral system can marginally enhance women's participation does not take us very far down the road. Looking beyond the clear evidence that proportional representation offers more favourable conditions for women to be elected, what dictates when real parity will be won? Is it a matter of women's political mobilization, both inside and outside of party politics, which can make sexual equality a question of public concern? Does it depend in any way on shifts in economic and social arrangements: an equalization in male and female rates of participation in the labour market? a desegregation in the jobs that men and women typically do? Is the heart of the matter the conditions under which children are cared for and reared, so that as long as this remains the private responsibility of invisible women, there is limited time for them to invade men's political sphere? Coming as I do from a tradition that has viewed political equalities as a reflex, however complicated and over-determined, of social and economic equalities, I thought for many years that a social revolution was the only real answer. As long as women are positioned as the dependants of men—a positioning which seems to rest on such an interlocking of social, economic and cultural forces that it is hard to know where to begin—it had seemed inconceivable to me that men and women could take equal parts in the political realm. Add on to this the more specifically feminist analysis of the relationship between public and private, which sees the determined amnesia over the domestic domain as central to liberal democracy, and the facts required no further explanation. What else could one possibly expect? What has shifted me towards the more political end of the spectrum—to the belief, that is, that greater political equality is possible even pending fundamental social transformation—is the recent experience of the Nordic countries.

Women in Nordic Countries

Up till the 1960s there was not much to choose between any of the countries in Western or Northern Europe: a somewhat more damning obstructionism in first-past-the-post systems; a more conservative tendency where the church held its sway; generally just the deafening dominance of men. By 1984, however, women had taken 15 per cent of the parliamentary seats in Iceland, 26 per cent in Norway and Denmark, 28 per cent in Sweden and 31 per cent in Finland (Lovenduski 1986:152). In 1985, Norway took the world record. Women made up 34.4 per cent of the Storting (the national assembly), held eight out of eighteen cabinet posts, contributed 40.5 per cent of the membership of county councils and contributed 31.1 per cent of the membership of municipal councils. The relatively poor performance of women in Iceland further confirms the role played by electoral systems, for while Iceland shares with other Nordic countries the practice of proportional representation, the small number of constituencies combines with a large number of parties to mean that few parties can anticipate winning more than two seats in any one constituency. As in so many countries, women are typically nominated to the "ornamental" positions on a party's list, with the first two places secured to men. Their position is thus more comparable to that in first-past-the-post systems (Skard and Haavio-Mannila 1985b).

Taking these countries as a whole, what is striking is that, despite significant economic differences with countries in Western Europe, the pattern of women's employment and the presumption of women's primary responsibilities for children are not so many miles away from the European norm....

... The social position of women is still informed by the statistically anachronistic but nonetheless powerful assumption that men occupy the world of work and women the world of the home.

The contrasts seem puzzling indeed. In 1988 I attended a forum that brought together feminists from Western and Northern Europe, centring much of its discussion around the impact of quota systems in increasing the political profile of women. The women from West Germany were still digesting the causes and consequences of the recent conference decision of the German Social Democratic Party (SPD), which just that year had committed itself to a minimum of 25 per cent women among its Bundestag members at the next election, progressing to a minimum of 40 per cent in the course of the next ten years. Feminists from Britain could hardly begin to conceive the conditions under which comparable decisions might be reached in Britain. By contrast, those from Norway or Sweden had experienced quota systems for so long that they could barely remember when they won this battle—or indeed if it was a battle at all!

The pattern, in fact, was as follows. In the 1970s a number of Scandinavian parties adopted the principle of at least 40 percent female representation at all levels of elected delegation within the party itself. This was adopted by the Swedish Liberal Party and the Swedish Communist Party in 1972, by the Norwegian Liberal Party in 1974 and the Norwegian Socialist Left Party in 1975, and by the Danish Socialist People's Party in 1977 (Skard and Haavio-Mannila 1985a). In the 1980s there was a push to extend this to the level of female representation in national parliaments. In 1980, parties in both Norway and Sweden proposed legislation that would commit *all* political parties to a minimum of 40 per cent women on their electoral lists; failing the success of this bid, various parties introduced the practice unilaterally (Skard and Haavio-Mannila 1985b). In 1983, for example, the Norwegian Labour Party introduced a 40 per cent quota for candidates in local and national elections and, as the largest party after the 1985 elections, contributed significantly to the lead that Norway then assumed. Among the parties that remain ideologically opposed to the principle of a quota system, there has also been substantial movement: the Norwegian Conservative Party espouses "competence" in opposition to formal quotas, but women nonetheless make up 30 per cent of its current national representation (Skjeie 1988). Again this seems to confirm the importance of specifically political factors. Once a few parties have put their toes in the water, the exigencies of competition require that the others do not lag too far behind.

The initial moves towards increasing women's representation pre-dated—or at the latest coincided with—the emergence of the contemporary women's movement; indeed, with the exception of Denmark and to a lesser extent Iceland, the Nordic countries were rather slow to develop the characteristically counter-cultural politics of second wave feminism. This itself is rather daunting in its implications. Through most of Europe, the women's movement showed little enthusiasm for the conventionalities of representative democracy, and it was not till quite late in the 1970s that feminists began to look to existing political parties as an important arena for change. Many parties had their own women's organizations, often dating from the late nineteenth century when women members were mobilized to perform various supportive or fund-raising activities. At key periods, these women's sections had worked hard to raise feminist issues, but this early history was lost to most of the activists in the new women's movement; outside of the Nordic countries, connections were rarely made.

Yet in Sweden, Norway and Finland, it was the women's sections in the social democratic parties that began to make the running, and in a chronology that has no parallel in the rest of Europe, it is the 1950s that are described as the "decade of the build-up" and the 1960s as the "explosive decade" (Eduards et al. 1985:136)....

The remarkable levels of female participation in these countries can I think be explained by a combination of three factors. The first is the enabling condition of their systems of proportional representation, which opens up but does not guarantee more space. The second is the strength of women's organizations within the traditional social democratic parties, and the political choices made by feminists who have attached greater significance to conventional power. The third is the differences between liberal and social democracy, which hinge around a different relationship between public and private spheres; women's position has been made a more explicit public concern. Each of these begs questions about what explains them in turn, but they combine to highlight the importance of *politics*, and the scope for specifically political change.

This does not mean the road is now clear. We can draw some reassurance from the effects of example and competition and anticipate that the process will speed up once the first stages are won. But repeating the experience of one country in another is not easy, and when Pippa Norris identified the importance of proportional representation she found herself correspondingly depressed. "Given the many institutional barriers to political equality, including a resistance to the implementation of electoral reform in majoritarian systems, it seems unlikely that cross-national differences in the political position of women will diminish in the near future" (1985:100). All the trends seem to suggest a continuing growth in female participation in wage employment, higher education and the professions. By early 1989, even the Conservative Government in Britain had woken up to the anticipated shortages of skilled labour and burst forth in a series of unlikely pronouncements on the desirability of increasing the proportion of women in higher education, of establishing work-place nurseries (not of course financed by the state), and encouraging more women to work. But if the entry of women into higher education and paid employment has limited impact on their numbers in elected office (as the example of the United States reveals all too clearly), none of these changes can be expected to make much difference. It is crass materialism to say that what is "only" political is therefore more open to change. On the other hand, if it *is* a matter of politics we do at least know where to begin.

With all its limitations, representative democracy is not necessarily inimical to the election of women, and indeed gender may now prove less intransigent than class. I do not hold out great hopes for my own country, but find it entirely plausible that liberal and, more specifically, social democracies will witness a growing proportion of women in politics, even pending that social revolution I once thought a necessary condition. But those elected will be peculiarly skewed to a certain kind of woman who, like the generations of men who went before her, will be a well-educated professional, and devoted to politics full time. Even in the Nordic countries, the marked shifts of recent years do not guarantee access for all women, any more than previous patterns of elected and corporate representation guaranteed access for all men. The women elected to parliament may be thoroughly "unrepresentative" in terms of their class, their income, the number and age of their children, or whether they previously worked full or parttime. The fact that gender quotas are increasingly accepted is no doubt a reflection of this: with women distributed (however unevenly) across the range of occupations and professions, they can be incorporated into our representative assemblies without disturbing the conventions of competence and leadership, and without disrupting the dominance of class. However distant

the prospect of a gender quota may seem to feminists in Britain or the United States, it is at least conceivable. No one even talks of a formal quota for class.

Representative democracy may prove itself more amenable than I once thought to the election of women, but it has trouble with their "representation." Grounded as it is in a tradition that rests on the abstract individual, liberal/representative democracy has to define politics as the realm of public rationality in which we contest opposing ideas. The least democratic versions of this will leave the bulk of issues to be settled by those elected, and the electorate as a whole will be permitted to make its occasional foray into the voting booth only to indicate a preference over who these people should be. More radical versions will try to commit the representatives to an explicitly delineated set of policies and ideas, so that we will not only be able to "punish" those who disappoint us by not voting for them the next time round, but can more positively influence the decisions they make. Here the emphasis will be on party congresses, definite commitments, explicit proposals, a heightened profile for ideas.

The representation of women *as women* potentially founders on both the difficulties of defining the shared interests of women and the difficulties of establishing mechanisms through which these interests are voiced. It has been noted that women politicians are often reluctant to see themselves as representing women. While we may regret this refusal of feminist concerns, we cannot jump straight to the opposite camp. Feminism should not give unwitting support to a version of democracy that rests too exclusively on trust, as if merely by virtue of their sex women can presume a mandate to speak for us all. The representation of women as women does not fit within the framework of representative democracy, and while this may count as ammunition in the battle for democracy of a different kind, it should not be glossed over in discussions of change.

References

Bashevkin, Sylvia (ed.) 1985: *Women and Politics in Western Europe*. London: Frank Cass.

Eduards, Maud, Halsaa, Beatrice and Skjeie, Hege 1985: Equality: how equal? In Haavio-Mannila et al. 1985.

Graubard, Stephen R. (ed.) 1986: *Norden: The Passion For Equality*. Norwegian University Press.

Haavio-Mannila, Elina, Dahlerup, Drude, Eduards, Maud et al. 1985: *Unfinished Democracy: Women in Nordic Politics*. Pergamon.

Hernes, Helga Maria 1987: *Welfare State and Woman Power: Essays in State Feminism*. Norwegian University Press.

Lovenduski, Joni 1986: *Women and European Politics: Contemporary Feminism and Public Policy*. Wheatsheaf.

Lovenduski, Joni and Hills, Jill (eds.) 1981: *The Politics of the Second Electorate: Women and Public Participation*. Routledge and Kegan Paul.

Norris, Pippa 1985: Women's legislative participation in Western Europe. In Bashevkin 1985.

Randall, Vicky 1987: *Women and Politics*, 2nd edn. Macmillan.

Skard, Torild and Haavio-Mannila, Elina 1985a: Mobilization of women at elections. In Haavio-Mannila et al. 1985.

——— 1985b: Women in parliament. In Haavio-Mannila et al. 1985.

——— 1986: Equality between the sexes: myth or reality. In Graubard 1986.

Skjeie, Hege 1988: *The Feminization of Power: Norway's Political Experiment (1986–)*. Institute for Social Research, Norway.

Vallance, Elizabeth 1979: *Women in the House*. Athlone.

7 INTEREST GROUPS

The Governmental Process: Political Interests and Public Opinion
David B. Truman

The Logic of Collective Action: Public Goods and the Theory of Groups
Mancur Olson

Neo-Pluralism: A Class Analysis of Pluralism I and Pluralism II
John F. Manley

The Theory of Economic Regulation
George J. Stigler

Interest Intermediation and Regime Governability in Contemporary Western Europe and North America
Philippe C. Schmitter

Inside Campaign Finance: Myths and Realities
Frank J. Sorauf

The Governmental Process: Political Interests and Public Opinion

David B. Truman

Men, wherever they are observed, are creatures participating in those established patterns of interaction that we call groups. Excepting perhaps the most casual and transitory, these continuing interactions, like all such interpersonal relationships, involve power. This power is exhibited in two closely interdependent ways. In the first place, the group exerts power over its members; an individual's group affiliations largely determine his attitudes, values, and the frames of reference in terms of which he interprets his experiences. For a measure of conformity to the norms of the group is the price of acceptance within it. Such power is exerted not only by an individual's present group relationships; it also may derive from past affiliations such as the childhood family as well as from groups to which the individual aspires to belong and whose characteristic shared attitudes he also holds. In the second place, the group, if it is or becomes an interest group, which any group in a society may be, exerts power over other groups in the society when it successfully imposes claims upon them.

Many interest groups, probably an increasing proportion in the United States, are politicized. That is, either from the outset or from time to time in the course of their development they make their claims through or upon the institutions of government. Both the forms and functions of government in turn are a reflection of the activities and claims of such groups. The constitution-writing proclivities of Americans clearly reveal the influence of demands from such sources, and the statutory creation of new functions reflects their continuing operation. Many of these forms and functions have received such widespread acceptance from the start or

Excerpted from: David B. Truman, *The Governmental Process: Political Interests and Public Opinion*. Westport, Conn.: Greenwood Press, 1951.

in the course of time that they appear to be independent of the overt activities of organized interest groups. The judiciary is such a form. The building of city streets and the control of vehicular traffic are examples of such a function. However, if the judiciary or a segment of it operates in a fashion sharply contrary to the expectations of an appreciable portion of the community or if its role is strongly attacked, the group basis of its structure and powers is likely to become apparent. Similarly, if street construction greatly increases tax rates or if the control of traffic unnecessarily inconveniences either pedestrians or motorists, the exposure of these functions to the demands of competing interests will not be obscure. Interests that are widely held in the society may be reflected in government without their being organized in groups. They are what we have called potential groups. If the claims implied by the interests of these potential groups are quickly and adequately represented, interaction among those people who share the underlying interests or attitudes is unnecessary. But the interest base of accepted governmental forms and functions and their potential involvement in overt group activities are ever present even when not patently operative.

The institutions of government are centers of interest-based power; their connections with interest groups may be latent or overt and their activities range in political character from the routinized and widely accepted to the unstable and highly controversial. In order to make claims, political interest groups will seek access to the key points of decision within these institutions. Such points are scattered throughout the structure, including not only the formally established branches of government but also the political parties in their various forms and the relationships between governmental units and other interest groups.

The extent to which a group achieves effective access to the institutions of government is the resultant of a complex of interdependent factors. For the sake of simplicity these may be classified in three somewhat overlapping categories: (1) factors relating to a group's strategic position in the society; (2) factors associated with the internal characteristics of the group; and (3) factors peculiar to the governmental institutions themselves. In the first category are: the group's status or prestige in the society, affecting the ease with which it commands deference from those outside its bounds; the standing it and its activities have when measured against the widely held but largely unorganized interests or "rules of the game;" the extent to which government officials are formally or informally "members" of the group; and the usefulness of the group as a source of technical and political knowledge. The second category includes: the degree and appropriateness of the group's organization; the degree of cohesion it can achieve in a given situation, especially in the light of competing group demands upon its membership; the skills of the leadership; and the group's resources in numbers and money. In the third category, are: the operating structure of the government institutions, since such established features involve relatively fixed advantages and handicaps; and the effects of the group life of particular units or branches of the government.

The product of effective access, of the claims of organized and unorganized interests that achieve access with varying degrees of effectiveness, is a governmental decision. Note that these interests that achieve effective access and guide decisions need not be "selfish," are not necessarily solidly unified, and may not be represented by organized groups. Governmental decisions are the resultant of effective access by various interests, of which organized groups may be only a segment. These decisions may be more or less stable depending on the strength of supporting interests and on the severity of disturbances in the society which affect that strength.

A characteristic feature of the governmental system in the United States is that it contains a multiplicity of points of access. The federal system establishes decentralized and more or less independent centers of power, vantage points from which to secure privileged access to the national government. Both a sign and a cause of the strength of the constituent units in the federal scheme is the peculiar character of our party system, which has strengthened parochial relationships, especially those of national legislators. National parties, and to a lesser degree those in the States, tend to be poorly cohesive leagues of locally based organizations rather than unified and inclusive structures. Staggered terms for executive officials and various types of legislators accentuate differences in the effective electorates that participate in choosing these officers. Each of these different, often opposite, localized patterns (constituencies) is a channel of independent access to the larger party aggregation and to the formal government. Thus, especially at the national level, the party is an electing-device and only in limited measure an integrated means of policy determination. Within the Congress, furthermore, controls are diffused among committee chairmen and other leaders in both chambers. The variety of these points of access is further supported by relationships stemming from the constitutional doctrine of the separation of powers, from related checks and balances, and at the State and local level from the common practice of choosing an array of executive officials by popular election. At the Federal level the formal simplicity of the executive branch has been complicated by a Supreme Court decision that has placed a number of administrative agencies beyond the removal power of the president. The position of these units, however, differs only in degree from that of many that are constitutionally within the executive branch. In consequence of alternative lines of access available through the legislature and the executive and of divided channels for the control of administrative policy, many nominally executive agencies are at various times virtually independent of the chief executive.

Although some of these lines of access may operate in series, they are not arranged in a stable and integrated hierarchy. Depending upon the whole political context in a given period and upon the relative strength of contending interests, one or another of the centers of power in the formal government or in the parties may become the apex of a hierarchy of controls. Only the highly routinized governmental activities show any stability in this respect, and these may as easily be subordinated to elements in the legislature as to the chief executive. Within limits, therefore, organized interest groups, gravitating toward responsive points of decision, may play one segment of the structure against another as circumstances and strategic considerations permit. The total pattern of government over a period of time thus presents a protean complex of crisscrossing relationships that change in strength and direction with alterations in the power and standing of interests, organized and unorganized.

There are two elements in this conception of the political process in the United States that are of crucial significance and that require special emphasis. These are, first, the notion of multiple or overlapping membership and, second, the function of unorganized interests, or potential interest groups.

The idea of overlapping membership stems from the conception of a group as a standardized pattern of interactions rather than as a collection of human units. Although the former may appear to be a rather misty abstraction, it is actually far closer to complex reality than the latter notion. The view of a group as an aggregation of individuals abstracts from the observable fact that in any society, and especially a complex one, no single group affiliation accounts for all of the attitudes or interests of any individual except a fanatic or a compulsive neurotic. No tolerably normal person is totally absorbed in any group in which he participates. The diversity of an individual's activities and his attendant interests involve him in a variety of actual and potential groups. Moreover, the fact that the genetic experiences of no two individuals are identical and the consequent fact that the spectra of their attitudes are in varying degrees dissimilar means that the members of a single group will perceive the group's claims in terms of a diversity of frames of reference. Such heterogeneity may be of little significance until such time as these multiple memberships conflict. Then the cohesion and influence of the affected group depend upon the incorporation or accommodation of the conflicting loyalties of any significant segment of the group, an accommodation that may result in altering the original claims. Thus the leaders of a Parent-Teacher Association must take some account of the fact that their proposals must be acceptable to members who also belong to the local taxpayers' league, to the local chamber of commerce, and to the Catholic Church.

The notion of overlapping membership bears directly upon the problems allegedly created by the appearance of a multiplicity of interest groups. Yet the fact of such overlapping is frequently overlooked or neglected in discussions of the political role of groups. James Madison, whose brilliant analysis in the tenth essay in *The Federalist* we have frequently quoted, relied primarily upon diversity of groups and difficulty of communication to protect the new government from the tyranny of a factious majority. He barely touched on the notion of multiple membership when he observed, almost parenthetically: "Besides other impediments, it may be remarked that, where there is a consciousness of unjust or dishonorable purposes, communication is always checked by distrust in proportion to the number whose concurrence is necessary." John C. Calhoun's idea of the concurrent majority, developed in his posthumously published work, *A Disquisition on Government* (1851), assumed the unified, monolithic character of the groups whose liberties he was so anxious to protect.

When his present-day followers unearth his doctrines, moreover, they usually make the same assumption, although implicitly.[4] Others, seeking a satisfactory means of accounting for the continued existence of the political system, sometimes assume that it is the nonparticipant citizens, aroused to unwonted activity, who act as a kind of counterbalance to the solid masses that constitute organized interest groups.[5] Although this phenomenon may occur in times of crisis, reliance upon it reckons insufficiently with the established observation that citizens who are nonparticipant in one aspect of the governmental process, such as voting, rarely show much concern for any phase of political activity. Multiple membership is more important as a restraint upon the activities of organized groups than the rarely aroused protests of chronic nonparticipants.

Organized interest groups are never solid and monolithic, though the consequences of their overlapping memberships may be handled with sufficient skill to give the organizations a maximum of cohesion. It is the competing claims of other groups *within* a given interest group that threaten its cohesion and force it to reconcile its claims with those of other groups active on the political scene. The claims within the American Medical Association of specialists and teaching doctors who support group practice, compulsory health insurance, and preventive medicine offer an illustration. The presence within the American Legion of public-housing enthusiasts and labor unionists as well as private homebuilders and labor opponents provides another example. Potential conflicts within the Farm Bureau between farmers who must buy supplementary feed and those who produce excess feed grains for the market, between soybean growers and dairymen,

4. Cf. John Fischer: "Unwritten Rules of American Politics," *Harper's Magazine* (November, 1948), pp. 27–36.

5. Cf. Herring: *The Politics of Democracy*, [New York: W. W. Norton, 1940,] p. 32.

even between traditional Republicans and loyal Democrats, create serious political problems for the interest group. Instances of the way in which such cleavages impose restraints upon an organized group's activities are infinitely numerous, almost as numerous as cases of multiple membership. Given the problems of cohesion and internal group politics that result from overlapping membership, the emergence of a multiplicity of interest groups in itself contains no dangers for the political system, especially since such overlapping affects not only private but also governmental "members" of the organized group.

But multiple membership in organized groups is not sufficiently extensive to obviate the possibility of irreconcilable conflict. There is little overlapping in the memberships of the National Association of Manufacturers and the United Steelworkers of America, or of the American Farm Bureau Federation and the United Automobile Workers. Overlapping membership among relatively cohesive organized interest groups provides an insufficient basis upon which to account for the relative stability of an operating political system. That system is a fact. An adequate conception of the group process must reckon with it. To paraphrase the famous words of John Marshall, we must never forget that it is a going polity we are explaining.

We cannot account for an established American political system without the second crucial element in our conception of the political process, the concept of the unorganized interest, or potential interest group. Despite the tremendous number of interest groups existing in the United States, not all interests are organized. If we recall the definition of an interest as a shared attitude, it becomes obvious that continuing interaction resulting in claims upon other groups does not take place on the basis of all such attitudes. One of the commonest interest group forms, the association, emerges out of severe or prolonged disturbances in the expected relationships of individuals in similar institutionalized groups. An association continues to function as long as it succeeds in ordering these disturbed relationships, as a labor union orders the relationships between management and workers. Not all such expected relationships are simultaneously or in a given short period sufficiently disturbed to produce organization. Therefore only a portion of the interests or attitudes involved in such expectations are represented by organized groups. Similarly, many organized groups—families, businesses, or churches, for example—do not operate continuously as interest groups or as political interest groups.

Any mutual interest, however, any shared attitude, is a potential group. A disturbance in established relationships and expectations anywhere in the society may produce new patterns of interaction aimed at restricting or eliminating the disturbance. Sometimes it may be this possibility of organization that alone gives the potential group a minimum of influence in the political process. Thus Key notes that the Delta planters in Mississippi "must speak for their Negroes in such programs as health and education," although the latter are virtually unorganized and are denied the means of active political participation.[6] It is in this sense that Bentley speaks of a difference in degree between the politics of despotism and that of other "forms" of government. He notes that there is "a process of representation in despotisms which is inevitable in all democracies, and which may be distinguished by quantities and by elaboration of technique, but not in any deeper 'qualititative' way." He speaks of the despot as "representative of his own class, and to a smaller, but none the less real, extent of the ruled class as well."[7] Obstacles to the development of organized groups from potential ones may be presented by inertia or by the activities of opposed groups, but the possi-

bility that severe disturbances will be created if these submerged, potential interests should organize necessitates some recognition of the existence of these interests and gives them at least a minimum of influence.

More important for present purposes than the potential groups representing separate minority elements are those interests or expectations that are so widely held in the society and are so reflected in the behavior of almost all citizens that they are, so to speak, taken for granted. Such "majority" interests are significant not only because they may become the basis for organized interest groups but also because the "membership" of such potential groups overlaps extensively the memberships of the various organized interest groups.[8] The resolution of conflicts between the claims of such unorganized interests and those of organized interest groups must grant recognition to the former not only because affected individuals may feel strongly attached to them but even more certainly because these interests are widely shared and are a part of many established patterns of behavior the disturbance of which would be difficult and painful. They are likely to be highly valued.

These widely held but unorganized interests are what we have previously called the "rules of the game." Others have described these attitudes in such terms as "systems of belief," as a "general ideological consensus," and as "a broad body of attitudes and understandings regarding the nature and limits of authority."[9] Each of

6. Key: *Southern Politics*, [New York: Vintage Books, 1949,] pp. 235 and *passim*.

7. Bentley: *The Process of Government*, [Chicago: The University of Chicago Press, 1908,] pp. 314–315. Copyright 1908 by and used with the permission of Arthur F. Bentley.

8. See the suggestive discussion of this general subject in Robert Bierstedt: "The Sociology of Majorities," *American Sociological Review*, Vol. 13, no. 6 (December, 1948), pp. 700–710.

9. Kluckhohn: *Mirror for Man*, [New York: Whittlesey House, 1949,] pp. 248 and *passim*; Sebastian de Grazia: *The Political Community: A Study of Anomie* (Chicago: University of Chicago Press, 1948), pp. ix, 80, and *passim*; Almond: *The American People and Foreign Policy*, [New York: Harcourt, Brace, 1950,] p. 158; Charles E. Merriam: *Systematic Politics* (Chicago: University of Chicago Press, 1945), p. 213.

these interests (attitudes) may be wide or narrow, general or detailed. For the mass of the population they may be loose and ambiguous, though more precise and articulated at the leadership level. In any case the "rules of the game" are interests the serious disturbance of which will result in organized interaction and the assertion of fairly explicit claims for conformity. In the American system the "rules" would include the value generally attached to the dignity of the individual human being, loosely expressed in terms of "fair dealing" or more explicitly verbalized in formulations such as the Bill of Rights. They would embrace ... "the democratic mold," that is, the approval of forms for broad mass participation in the designation of leaders and in the selection of policies in all social groups and institutions. They would also comprehend certain semi-egalitarian notions of material welfare. This is an illustrative, not an exhaustive, list of such interests.

The widely held, unorganized interests are reflected in the major institutions of the society, including the political. The political structure of the United States, as we have seen, has adopted characteristic legislative, executive, and judicial forms through the efforts of organized interest groups. Once these forms have been accepted and have been largely routinized, the supporting organized interest groups cease to operate as such and revert to the potential stage. As embodied in these institutional forms and in accepted verbal formulations, such as those of legal and constitutional theory, the interests of these potential groups are established expectations concerning not only *what* the governmental institutions shall do, but more particularly *how* they shall operate. To the extent that these established processes remain noncontroversial, they may appear to have no foundation in interests. Nevertheless, the widespread expectations will receive tacit or explicit deference from most organized interest groups in consequence of the overlapping of their memberships with these potential groups.[10] Violation of the "rules of the

game" normally will weaken a group's cohesion, reduce its status in the community, and expose it to the claims of other groups. The latter may be competing organized groups that more adequately incorporate the "rules," or they may be groups organized on the basis of these broad interests and in response to the violations.

The pervasive and generally accepted character of these unorganized interests, or "rules," is such that they are acquired by most individuals in their early experiences in the family, in the public schools (probably less effectively in the private and parochial schools), and in similar institutionalized groups that are also expected to conform in some measure to the "democratic mold." The "rules" are likely to be reinforced by later events. Persons who aspire to, or occupy, public office of whatever sort are particularly likely to identify with these expected behaviors as part of their desired or existing roles. With varying degrees of effectiveness the group life of government agencies—legislative, executive, and judicial—reinforces the claims of these unorganized interests, which overlap those of the official group itself and those of "outside" political interest groups. Marked and prolonged deviation from these expected behaviors by public officials, who are expected to represent what Bentley calls the "'absent' or quiescent group interests," will normally produce restrictive action by other governmental functionaries, by existing organized interest groups, by ones newly organized in consequence of the deviations, or by all three.

It is thus multiple memberships in potential groups based on widely held and accepted interests that serve as a balance wheel in a going political system like that of the United States. To some people this observation may appear to be a truism and to others a somewhat mystical notion. It is neither. In the first place, neglect of this function of multiple memberships in most dis-

---

10. Cf. Bentley: *The Process of Government*, p. 397, and MacIver: *The Web of Government*, [New York: Macmillan, 1947,] p. 79.

cussions of organized interest groups indicates that the observation is not altogether commonplace. Secondly, the statement has no mystical quality; the effective operation of these widely held interests is to be inferred directly from verbal and other behavior in the political sphere. Without the notion of multiple memberships in potential groups it is literally impossible to account for the existence of a viable polity such as that in the United States or to develop a coherent conception of the political process. The strength of these widely held but largely unorganized interests explains the vigor with which propagandists for organized groups attempt to change other attitudes by invoking such interests.[11] Their importance is further evidenced in the recognized function of the means of mass communication, notably the press, in reinforcing widely accepted norms of "public morality."[12]

The role of the widespread unorganized interests and potential groups does not imply that such interests are always and everywhere dominant. Nor does it mean that the slightest action in violation of any of them inevitably and instantly produces a restrictive response from another source. These interests are not unambiguous, as the long history of litigation concerning freedom of speech will demonstrate. Subjectively they are not all equally fundamental. Thus since the "rules" are interests competing with those of various organized groups, they are in any given set of circumstances more or less subject to attenuation through such psychological mechanisms as rationalization. Moreover, the means of communication, whether by word of mouth or through the mass media, may not

adequately make known particular deviations from the behavior indicated by these broad interests.

In a relatively vigorous political system, however, these unorganized interests are dominant with sufficient frequency in the behavior of enough important segments of the society so that, despite ambiguity and other restrictions, both the activity and the methods of organized interest groups are kept within broad limits. This interpretation is not far from Lasswell's view of the state as a relational system defined by a certain frequency of subjective events.[13] According to his definition, "the state ... is a time-space manifold of similar subjective events.... That subjective event which is the unique mark of the state is the recognition that one belongs to a community with a system of paramount claims and expectations."[14] All citizens of the state as thus conceived need not experience this "event" continuously or with equal intensity. Nor need the attitudes of all citizens be favorable toward these "claims and expectations." But the existence of the state, of the polity, depends on widespread, frequent recognition of and conformity to the claims of these unorganized interests and on activity condemning marked deviations from them. "All this," says Lasswell, "is frequently expressed as the 'sense of justice'...."[15]

Thus it is only as the effects of overlapping memberships and the functions of unorganized interests and potential groups are included in the equation that it is accurate to speak of governmental activity as the product or resultant of interest group activity. As Bentley has put it:

There are limits to the technique of the struggle, this involving also limits to the group demands, all of which is solely a matter of empirical observation.... Or, in other words, when the struggle proceeds too

11. Cf. Lazarsfeld *et al.: The People's Choice*, [New York: Columbia Univ. Press, 1948,] preface to 2d edition, pp. xxi–xxii.

12. Cf. Paul F. Lazarsfeld and Robert K. Merton: "Mass Communication, Popular Taste and Organized Social Act," in Lyman Bryson (ed.): *The Communication of Ideas* (New York: Harper and Brothers, 1948), pp. 102 ff.

13. Lasswell: *Psychopathology and Politics*, [Chicago: University of Chicago Press, 1934,] pp. 240–261.

14. Ibid., p. 245.

15. Ibid., p. 246.

harshly at any point there will become insistent in the society a group more powerful than either of those involved which tends to suppress the extreme and annoying methods of the groups in the primary struggle. It is within the embrace of these great lines of activity that the smaller struggles proceed, and the very word struggle has meaning only with reference to its limitations.[16]

To assert that the organization and activity of powerful interest groups constitutes a threat to representative government without measuring their relation to and effects upon the widespread potential groups is to generalize from insufficient data and upon an incomplete conception of the political process. Such an analysis would be as faulty as one that, ignoring differences in national systems, predicted identical responses to a given technological change in the United States, Japan, and the Soviet Union. . . .

---

16. Bentley: *The Process of Government*, p. 372. Copyright 1908 by and used with the permission of Arthur F. Bentley.

The Logic of Collective Action: Public Goods and the Theory of Groups

Mancur Olson

A Theory of Groups and Organizations

A. The Purpose of Organization

Since most (though by no means all) of the action taken by or no behalf of groups of individuals is taken through organizations, it will be helpful to consider organizations in a general or theoretical way.[1] The logical place to begin any systematic study of organizations is with their purpose. But there are all types and shapes and sizes of organizations, even of economic organi-

zations, and there is then some question whether there is any single purpose that would be characteristic of organizations generally. One purpose that is nonetheless characteristic of most organizations, and surely of practically all organizations with an important economic aspect, is the furtherance of the interests of their members. . . .

The kinds of organizations that are the focus of this study are *expected* to further the interests of their members.[6] Labor unions are expected to strive for higher wages and better working conditions for their members; farm organizations are expected to strive for favorable legislation for their members; cartels are expected to strive for higher prices for participating firms; the corporation is expected to further the interests

1. Economists have for the most part neglected to develop theories of organizations, but there are a few works from an economic point of view on the subject. See, for example, three papers by Jacob Marschak, "Elements for a Theory of Teams," *Management Science*, I (January 1955), 127–137, "Towards an Economic Theory of Organization and Information," in *Decision Processes*, ed. R. M. Thrall, C. H. Combs, and R. L. Davis (New York: John Wiley, 1954), pp. 187–220, and "Efficient and Viable Organization Forms," in *Modern Organization Theory*, ed. Mason Haire (New York: John Wiley, 1959), pp. 307–320; two papers by R. Radner, "Application of Linear Programming to Team Decision Problems," *Management Science*, V (January 1959), 143–150, and "Team Decision Problems," *Annals of Mathematical Statistics*, XXXIII (September 1962), 857–881; C. B. McGuire, "Some Team Models of a Sales Organization," *Management Science*, VII (January 1961), 101–130; Oskar Morgenstern, *Prolegomena to a Theory of Organization* (Santa Monica, Calif.: RAND Research Memorandum 734, 1951); James G. March and Herbert A. Simon, *Organizations* (New York: John Wiley, 1958); Kenneth Boulding, *The Organizational Revolution* (New York: Harper, 1953).

6. Philanthropic and religious organizations are not necessarily expected to serve only the interests of their members; such organizations have other purposes that are considered more important, however much their members "need" to belong, or are improved or helped by belonging. But the complexity of such organizations need not be debated at length here, because this study will focus on organizations with a significant economic aspect. The emphasis here will have something in common with what Max Weber called the "associative group"; he called a group associative if "the orientation of social action with it rests on a rationally motivated agreement." Weber contrasted his "associative group" with the "communal group" which was centered on personal affection, erotic relationships, etc., like the family. (See Weber, [*Theory of Social and Economic Organization*, translated by Talcott Parsons and A. M. Henderson. New York: Oxford University Press, 1947,] pp. 136–139, and Grace Coyle, *Social Process in Organized Groups*, New York: Richard Smith, Inc., 1930, pp. 7–9.) The logic of the theory developed here can be extended to cover communal, religious, and philanthropic organizations, but the theory is not particularly useful in studying such groups. . . .

of its stockholders;[7] and the state is expected to further the common interests of its citizens (though in this nationalistic age the state often has interests and ambitions apart from those of its citizens).

Notice that the interests that all of these diverse types of organizations are expected to further are for the most part *common interests*: the union members' common interest in higher wages, the farmers' common interest in favorable legislation, the cartel members' common interest in higher prices, the stockholders' common interest in higher dividends and stock prices, the citizens' common interest in good government. It is not an accident that the diverse types of organizations listed are all supposed to work primarily for the *common* interests of their members. Purely personal or individual interests can be advanced, and usually advanced most efficiently, by individual, unorganized action. There is obviously no purpose in having an organization when individual, unorganized action can serve the interests of the individual as well as or better than an organization; there would, for example, be no point in forming an organization simply to play solitaire. But when a number of individuals have a common or collective interest—when they share a single purpose or objective—individual, unorganized action (as we shall soon see) will either not be able to advance that common interest at all, or will not be able to advance that interest adequately. Organizations can therefore perform a function when there are common or group interests, and though organizations often also serve purely personal, individual interests, their characteristic and primary function is to advance the common interests of groups of individuals. . . .

Just as those who belong to an organization or a group can be presumed to have a common interest,[11] so they obviously also have purely individual interests, different from those of the others in the organization or group. All of the members of a labor union, for example, have a common interest in higher wages, but at the same time each worker has a unique interest in his personal income, which depends not only on the rate of wages but also on the length of time that he works.

B. Public Goods and Large Groups

The combination of individual interests and common interests in an organization suggests an analogy with a competitive market. The firms in a perfectly competitive industry, for example, have a common interest in a higher price for the industry's product. Since a uniform price must prevail in such a market, a firm cannot expect a higher price for itself unless all of the other firms in the industry also have this higher price. But a

---

7. That is, its members. This study does not follow the terminological usage of those organization theorists who describe employees as "members" of the organization for which they work. Here it is more convenient to follow the language of everyday usage instead, and to distinguish the members of, say, a union from the employees of that union. Similarly, the members of the union will be considered employees of the corporation for which they work, whereas the members of the corporation are the common stockholders.

11. Any organization or group will of course usually be divided into subgroups or factions that are opposed to one another. This fact does not weaken the assumption made here that organizations exist to serve the common interests of members, for the assumption does not imply that intragroup conflict is neglected. The opposing groups within an organization ordinarily have some interest in common (if not, why would they maintain the organization?), and the members of any subgroup or faction also have a separate common interest of their own. They will indeed often have a common purpose in defeating some other subgroup or faction. The approach used here does not neglect the conflict within groups and organizations, then, because it considers each organization as a unit only to the extent that it does in fact attempt to serve a common interest, and considers the various subgroups as the relevant units with common interests to analyze the factional strife.

firm in a competitive market also has an interest in selling as much as it can, until the cost of producing another unit exceeds the price of that unit. In this there is no common interest; each firm's interest is directly opposed to that of every other firm, for the more other firms sell, the lower the price and income for any given firm. In short, while all firms have a common interest in a higher price, they have antagonistic interests where output is concerned. This can be illustrated with a simple supply-and-demand model. For the sake of a simple argument, assume that a perfectly competitive industry is momentarily in a disequilibrium position, with price exceeding marginal cost for all firms at their present output. Suppose, too, that all of the adjustments will be made by the firms already in the industry rather than by new entrants, and that the industry is on an inelastic portion of its demand curve. Since price exceeds marginal cost for all firms, output will increase. But as all firms increase production, the price falls; indeed, since the industry demand curve is by assumption inelastic, the total revenue of the industry will decline. Apparently each firm finds that with price exceeding marginal cost, it pays to increase its output, but the result is that each firm gets a smaller profit. Some economists in an earlier day may have questioned this result,[12] but the fact that profit-maximizing firms in a perfectly competitive industry can act contrary to their interests as a group is now widely understood and accepted.[13] A group of profit-maximizing firms can act to reduce their aggregate profits because in perfect competition each firm is, by definition, so small that it can ignore the effect of its output on price. Each firm finds it to its advantage to

increase output to the point where marginal cost equals price and to ignore the effects of its extra output on the position of the industry. It is true that the net result is that all firms are worse off, but this does not mean that every firm has not maximized its profits. If a firm, foreseeing the fall in price resulting from the increase in industry output, were to restrict its own output, it would lose more than ever, for its price would fall quite as much in any case and it would have a smaller output as well. A firm in a perfectly competitive market gets only a small part of the benefit (or a small share of the industry's extra revenue) resulting from a reduction in that firm's output.

For these reasons it is now generally understood that if the firms in an industry are maximizing profits, the profits for the industry as a whole will be less than they might otherwise be.[14] And almost everyone would agree that this theoretical conclusion fits the facts for markets characterized by pure competition. The important point is that this is true because, though all the firms have a common interest in a higher price for the industry's product, it is in the interest of each firm that the other firms pay the cost—in terms of the necessary reduction in output—needed to obtain a higher price.

About the only thing that keeps prices from falling in accordance with the process just described in perfectly competitive markets is outside intervention. Government price supports, tariffs, cartel agreements, and the like may keep the firms in a competitive market from acting contrary to their interests. Such aid or intervention is quite common. It is then important to ask how it comes about. How does a competitive industry obtain government assistance in maintaining the price of its product? . . .

---

12. See J. M. Clark, *The Economics of Overhead Costs* (Chicago: University of Chicago Press, 1923), p. 417, and Frank H. Knight, *Risk, Uncertainty and Profit* (Boston: Houghton Mifflin, 1921), p. 193.

13. Edward H. Chamberlin, *Monopolistic Competition*, 6th ed. (Cambridge, Mass.: Harvard University Press, 1950), p. 4.

14. For a fuller discussion of this question see Mancur Olson, Jr., and David McFarland, "The Restoration of Pure Monopoly and the Concept of the Industry," *Quarterly Journal of Economics*, LXXVI (November 1962), 613–631.

There is a striking parallel between the problem the perfectly competitive industry faces as it strives to obtain government assistance, and the problem it faces in the marketplace when the firms increase output and bring about a fall in price. *Just as it was not rational for a particular producer to restrict his output in order that there might be a higher price for the product of his industry, so it would not be rational for him to sacrifice his time and money to support a lobbying organization to obtain government assistance for the industry. In neither case would it be in the interest of the individual producer to assume any of the costs himself. A lobbying organization, or indeed a labor union or any other organization, working in the interest of a large group of firms or workers in some industry, would get no assistance from the rational, self-interested individuals in that industry.* This would be true even if everyone in the industry were absolutely convinced that the proposed program was in their interest (though in fact some might think otherwise and make the organization's task yet more difficult)....

Some critics may argue that the rational person will, indeed, support a large organization, like a lobbying organization, that works in his interest, because he knows that if he does not, others will not do so either, and then the organization will fail, and he will be without the benefit that the organization could have provided. This argument shows the need for the analogy with the perfectly competitive market. For it would be quite as reasonable to argue that prices will never fall below the levels a monopoly would have charged in a perfectly competitive market, because if one firm increased its output, other firms would also, and the price would fall; but each firm could foresee this, so it would not start a chain of price-destroying increases in output. In fact, it does not work out this way in a competitive market; nor in a large organization. When the number of firms involved is large, no one will notice the effect on price if one firm increases its output, and so no one will change

his plans because of it. Similarly, in a large organization, the loss of one dues payer will not noticeably increase the burden for any other one dues payer, and so a rational person would not believe that if he were to withdraw from an organization he would drive others to do so....

However similar the purposes may be, critics may object that attitudes in organizations are not at all like those in markets. In organizations, an emotional or ideological element is often also involved. Does this make the argument offered here practically irrelevant?

A most important type of organization—the national state—will serve to test this objection. Patriotism is probably the strongest non-economic motive for organizational allegiance in modern times. This age is sometimes called the age of nationalism. Many nations draw additional strength and unity from some powerful ideology, such as democracy or communism, as well as from a common religion, language, or cultural inheritance. The state not only has many such powerful sources of support; it also is very important economically. Almost any government is economically beneficial to its citizens, in that the law and order it provides is a prerequisite of all civilized economic activity. But despite the force of patriotism, the appeal of the national ideology, the bond of a common culture, and the indispensability of the system of law and order, no major state in modern history has been able to support itself through voluntary dues or contributions. Philanthropic contributions are not even a significant source of revenue for most countries. Taxes, *compulsory* payments by definition, are needed. Indeed, as the old saying indicates, their necessity is as certain as death itself.

If the state, with all of the emotional resources at its command, cannot finance its most basic and vital activities without resort to compulsion, it would seem that large private organizations might also have difficulty in getting the individuals in the groups whose interests they attempt to advance to make the necessary contributions voluntarily.[19]

The reason the state cannot survive on voluntary dues or payments, but must rely on taxation, is that the most fundamental services a nation-state provides are, in one important respect, like the higher price in a competitive market: they must be available to everyone if they are available to anyone. The basic and most elementary goods or services provided by government, like defense and police protection, and the system of law and order generally, are such that they go to everyone or practically everyone in the nation. It would obviously not be feasible, if indeed it were possible, to deny the protection provided by the military services, the police, and the courts to those who did not voluntarily pay their share of the costs of government, and tax-

ation is accordingly necessary. The common or collective benefits provided by governments are usually called "public goods" by economists, and the concept of public goods is one of the oldest and most important ideas in the study of public finance. A common, collective, or public good is here defined as any good such that, if any person X_i in a group $X_1, \ldots, X_i, \ldots, X_n$ consumes it, cannot feasibly be withheld from the others in that group.[21] In other words, those

---

19. Sociologists as well as economists have observed that ideological motives alone are not sufficient to bring forth the continuing effort of large masses of people. Max Weber provides a notable example:

"All economic activity in a market economy is undertaken and carried through by individuals for their own ideal or material interests. This is naturally just as true when economic activity is oriented to the patterns of order of corporate groups ...

"Even if an economic system were organized on a socialistic basis, there would be no fundamental difference in this respect.... The structure of interests and the relevant situation might change; there would be other means of pursuing interests, but this fundamental factor would remain just as relevant as before. It is of course true that economic action which is oriented on purely ideological grounds to the interest of others does exist. But it is even more certain that the mass of men do not act in this way, and it is an induction from experience that they cannot do so and never will....

"In a market economy the interest in the maximization of income is necessarily the driving force of all economic activity." (Weber, pp. 319–320.)

Talcott Parsons and Neil Smelser go even further in postulating that "performance" throughout society is proportional to the "rewards" and "sanctions" involved. See their *Economy and Society* (Glencoe, Ill.: Free Press, 1954), pp. 50–69.

21. This simple definition focuses upon two points that are important in the present context. The first point is that most collective goods can only be defined with respect to some specific group. One collective good goes to one group of people, another collective good to another group; one may benefit the whole world, another only two specific people. Moreover, some goods are collective goods to those in one group and at the same time private goods to those in another, because some individuals can be kept from consuming them and others can't. Take for example the parade that is a collective good to all those who live in tall buildings overlooking the parade route, but which appears to be a private good to those who can see it only by buying tickets for a seat in the stands along the way. The second point is that once the relevant group has been defined, the definition used here, like Musgrave's, distinguishes collective good in terms of infeasibility of excluding potential consumers of the good. This approach is used because collective goods produced by organizations of all kinds seem to be such that exclusion is normally not feasible. To be sure, for some collective goods it is physically possible to practice exclusion. But, as Head has shown, it is not necessary that exclusion be technically impossible; it is only necessary that it be infeasible or uneconomic. Head has also shown most clearly that nonexcludability is only one of two basic elements in the traditional understanding of public goods. The other, he points out, is "jointness of supply." A good has "jointness" if making it available to one individual means that it can be easily or freely supplied to others as well. The polar case of jointness would be Samuelson's pure public good, which is a good such that additional consumption of it by one individual does not diminish the amount available to others. By the definition used here, jointness is not a necessary attribute of a public good.

who do not purchase or pay for any of the public or collective good cannot be excluded or kept from sharing in the consumption of the good, as they can where noncollective goods are concerned.

Students of public finance have, however, neglected the fact that *the achievement of any common goal or the satisfaction of any common interest means that a public or collective good has been provided for that group.*[22] The very fact that a goal or purpose is *common* to a group means

that no one in the group is excluded from the benefit or satisfaction brought about by its achievement. As the opening paragraphs of this chapter indicated, almost all groups and organizations have the purpose of serving the common interests of their members.... It is of the essence of an organization that it provides an inseparable, generalized benefit. It follows that the provision of public or collective goods is the fundamental function of organizations generally. A state is first of all an organization that provides public goods for its members, the citizens; and other types of organizations similarly provide collective goods for their members.

And just as a state cannot support itself by voluntary contributions, or by selling its basic services on the market, neither can other large organizations support themselves without providing some sanction, or some attraction distinct from the public good itself, that will lead individuals to help bear the burdens of maintaining the organization. The individual member of the typical large organization is in a position analogous to that of the firm in a perfectly competitive market, or the taxpayer in the state: his own efforts will not have a noticeable effect on the situation of his organization, and he can enjoy any improvements brought about by others whether or not he has worked in support of his organization....

Nontechnical Summary of Section D

... [C]ertain small groups can provide themselves with collective goods without relying on coercion or any positive inducements apart from the collective good itself.[53] This is because in

---

As later parts of this chapter will show, at least one type of collective good considered here exhibits no jointness whatever, and few if any would have the degree of jointness needed to qualify as pure public goods. Nonetheless, most of the collective goods to be studied here do display a large measure of jointness. On the definition and importance of public goods, see John G. Head, "Public Goods and Public Policy," *Public Finance*, vol. XVII, no. 3 (1962), 197–219; Richard Musgrave, *The Theory of Public Finance* (New York: McGraw-Hill, 1959); Paul A. Samuelson, "The Pure Theory of Public Expenditure," "Diagrammatic Exposition of A Theory of Public Expenditure," and "Aspects of Public Expenditure Theories," in *Review of Economics and Statistics*, XXXVI (November 1954), 387–390, XXXVII (November 1955), 350–356, and XL (November 1958), 332–338. For somewhat different opinions about the usefulness of the concept of public goods, see Julius Margolis, "A Comment on the Pure Theory of Public Expenditure," *Review of Economics and Statistics*, XXXVII (November 1955), 347–349, and Gerhard Colm, "Theory of Public Expenditures," *Annals of the American Academy of Political and Social Science*, CLXXXIII (January 1936), 1–11.

22. There is no necessity that a public good to one group in a society is necessarily in the interest of the society as a whole. Just as a tariff could be a public good to the industry that sought it, so the removal of the tariff could be a public good to those who consumed the industry's product. This is equally true when the public-good concept is applied only to governments; for a military expenditure, or a tariff, or an immigration restriction that is a public good to one country could be a "public bad" to another country, and harmful to world society as a whole.

---

53. I am indebted to Professor John Rawls of the Department of Philosophy at Harvard University for reminding me of the fact that the philosopher David Hume sensed that small groups could achieve common purposes but large groups could not. Hume's argument is however somewhat different from my own. In *A Treatise of Human Nature*, Everyman edition (London: J. M. Dent, 1952), II, 239, Hume wrote: "There is no quality in human nature which causes more fatal errors

some small groups each of the members, or at least one of them, will find that his personal gain from having the collective good exceeds the total cost of providing some amount of that collective good; there are members who would be better off if the collective good were provided, even if they had to pay the entire cost of providing it themselves, than they would be if it were not provided. In such situations there is a presumption that the collective good will be provided. Such a situation will exist only when the benefit to the group from having the collective good exceeds the total cost by more than it exceeds the gain to one or more individuals in the group. Thus, in a very small group, where each member gets a substantial proportion of the total gain simply because there are few others in the group, a col-

lective good can often be provided by the voluntary, self-interested action of the members of the group. In smaller groups marked by considerable degrees of inequality—that is, in groups of members of unequal "size" or extent of interest in the collective good—there is the greatest likelihood that a collective good will be provided; for the greater the interest in the collective good of any single member, the greater the likelihood that that member will get such a significant proportion of the total benefit from the collective good that he will gain from seeing that the good is provided, even if he has to pay all of the cost himself. . . .

The "By-Product" and "Special Interest" Theories

A. The "By-Product" Theory of Large Pressure Groups

If the individuals in a large group have no incentive to organize a lobby to obtain a collective benefit, how can the fact that some large groups are organized be explained? Though many groups with common interests, like the consumers, the white-collar workers, and the migrant agricultural workers, are not organized,[1] other large groups, like the union laborers, the farmers, and the doctors have at least some degree of organization. The fact that there are many groups which, despite their needs, are not organized would seem to contradict the "group theory" of the analytical pluralists; but on the other hand the fact that other large groups have been organized would seem to contradict the theory of "latent groups" offered in this study.

---

in our conduct, than that which leads us to prefer whatever is present to the distant and remote, and makes us desire objects more according to their situation than their intrinsic value. Two neighbours may agree to drain a meadow, which they possess in common: because it is easy for them to know each other's mind; and each must perceive, that the immediate consequence of his failing in his part, is the abandoning of the whole project. But it is very difficult, and indeed impossible, that a thousand persons should agree in any such action; it being difficult for them to concert so complicated a design, and still more difficult for them to execute it; while each seeks a pretext to free himself of the trouble and expense, and would lay the whole burden on others. Political society easily remedies both these inconveniences. Magistrates find an immediate interest in the interest of any considerable part of their subjects. They need consult nobody but themselves to form any scheme for promoting that interest. And as the failure of any one piece in the execution is connected, though not immediately, with the failure of the whole, they prevent that failure, because they find no interest in it, either immediate or remote. Thus, bridges are built, harbours opened, ramparts raised, canals formed, fleets equipped, and armies disciplined, everywhere, by the care of government, which, though composed of men subject to all human infirmities, becomes, by one of the finest and most subtle inventions imaginable, a composition which is in some measure exempted from all these infirmities."

1. "When lists of these organizations are examined, the fact that strikes the student most forcibly is that *the system is very small*. The range of organized, identifiable, known groups is amazingly narrow; there is nothing remotely universal about it." E. E. Schattschneider, *The Semi-Sovereign People* (New York: Holt, Rinehart & Winston, 1960), p. 30.

But the large economic groups that are organized do have one common characteristic which distinguishes them from those large economic groups that are not....

The common characteristic which distinguishes all of the large economic groups with significant lobbying organizations is that these groups are also organized for some *other* purpose. The large and powerful economic lobbies are in fact the by-products of organizations that obtain their strength and support because they perform some function in addition to lobbying for collective goods.

The lobbies of the large economic groups are the by-products of organizations that have the capacity to "mobilize" a latent group with "selective incentives." The only organizations that have the "selective incentives" available are those that (1) have the authority and capacity to be coercive, or (2) have a source of positive inducements that they can offer the individuals in a latent group.

A purely political organization—an organization that has no function apart from its lobbying function—obviously cannot legally coerce individuals into becoming members. A political party, or any purely political organization, with a captive or compulsory membership would be quite unusual in a democratic political system. But if for some nonpolitical reason, if because of some other function it performs, an organization has a justification for having a compulsory membership, or if through this other function it has obtained the power needed to make membership in it compulsory, that organization may then be able to get the resources needed to support a lobby. The lobby is then a by-product of whatever function this organization performs that enables it to have a captive membership.

An organization that did nothing except lobby to obtain a collective good for some large group would not have a source of rewards or positive selective incentives it could offer potential members. Only an organization that also sold private or noncollective products, or provided social or recreational benefits to individual members, would have a source of these positive inducements.[2] Only such an organization could make a joint offering or "tied sale" of a collective and a noncollective good that could stimulate a rational individual in a large group to bear part of the cost of obtaining a collective good.[3] There are

---

2. An economic organization in a perfectly competitive market in equilibrium, which had no special competitive advantage that could bring it a large amount of "rent," would have no "profits" or other spare resources it could use as selective incentives for a lobby. Nonetheless there are many organizations that do have spare returns they can use for selective incentives. First, markets with some degree of monopoly power are far more common than perfectly competitive markets. Second, there are sometimes important complementaries between the economic and political activities of an organization. The political branch of the organization can win lower taxes or other favorable government policies for the economic branch, and the good name won by the political branch may also help the economic branch. For somewhat similar reasons, a social organization may also be a source of a surplus that can be used for selective incentives.

An organization that is not only political, but economic or social as well, and has a surplus that provides selective incentives, may be able to retain its membership and political power, it certain cases, even if its leadership manages to use some of the political or economic power of the organization for objectives other than those desired by the membership, since the members of the organization will have an incentive to continue belonging even if they disagree with the organization's policy. This may help explain why many lobbying organizations take positions that must be uncongenial to their membership, and why organizations with leaders who corruptly advance their own interests at the expense of the organization continue to survive.

3. The worth of the noncollective or private benefit would have to exceed its cost by an amount greater than the dues to the lobbying branch of the organization, or the joint offering would not be sufficient to attract members to the organization. Note that ... selective incentives were defined to be values larger in absolute magnitude than an individual's share of the costs of the collective good.

for this reason many organizations that have both lobbying functions and economic functions, or lobbying functions and social functions, or even all three of these types of functions at once.[4] Therefore, in addition to the large group lobbies that depend on coercion, there are those that are associated with organizations that provide noncollective or private benefits which can be offered to any potential supporter who will bear his share of the cost of the lobbying for the collective good.

The by-product theory of pressure groups need apply only to the large or latent group. It *need not* apply to the privileged or intermediate groups, because these smaller groups can often provide a lobby, or any other collective benefit, without any *selective* incentives.... It applies to latent groups because the individual in a latent group has no incentive voluntarily to sacrifice his time or money to help an organization obtain a collective good; he alone cannot be decisive in determining whether or not this collective good will be obtained, but if it is obtained because of the efforts of others he will inevitably be able to enjoy it in any case. Thus he would support the organization with a lobby working for collective goods only if (1) he is coerced into paying dues to the lobbying organization, or (2) he has to support this group in order to obtain some other noncollective benefit. Only if one or both of these conditions hold will the potential political power of a latent group be mobilized....

---

4. An organization that lobbied to provide a collective good for a large group might even obtain its selective incentives by lobbying also for noncollective "political" goods, like individual exceptions to (or advantageous interpretations of) a general rule or law, or for patronage for particular individuals, etc. The point is not that the organization must necessarily also be economic or social as well as political (though that is usually the case); it is rather that, if the organization does not have the capacity to coerce potential members, it must offer some noncollective, i.e., selective, benefit to potential members.

Neo-Pluralism: A Class Analysis of Pluralism I and Pluralism II

John F. Manley

To anyone interested in understanding political power in the United States, social scientists offer three main general theories: pluralism, the most widely accepted theory; pluralism's old antagonist, elitism, the next most widely accepted theory; and class or structural analysis, whose *locus classicus* is Karl Marx's *Capital*, which is generally not accepted at all.[1]

Pluralism, elitism, and class analysis have divided students of power for decades, but there is little doubt that pluralism is the dominant theory or paradigm of power among American social scientists. Although research regularly turns up evidence supporting the other two theories (Higley and Moore, 1981, p. 595), it is no empty boast for pluralists to claim a generally favorable response to their critique of elitism and class analysis (Polsby, 1980, p. 141).[2]

In the past several years, however, political and economic developments in the United States have placed the pluralist paradigm under a good deal of strain. Even inside the pluralist school,

serious doubts have arisen about the theory's ability to explain the American system. Strong doubts have arisen, too, about the relationship between pluralism and such central issues of democratic theory as equality, distributive justice, and peaceful social change. If Kuhn (1962, p. 52) is right that scientific understanding advances when old paradigms are supplanted by new theories that are thought to be better able to account for strategically important facts, it may be time to begin the search for a theory that is better than pluralism at explaining class and group power in the United States. So, at any rate, is the suggestion of this article.

At one time, pluralism was a reasonably coherent theory whose claims appeared to many

Excerpted from: John F. Manley, "Neo-Pluralism: A Class Analysis of Pluralism I and Pluralism II." *American Political Science Review* 77, no. 2 (1983): 368–383. © American Political Science Association. Reprinted with the permission of the American Political Science Association and Cambridge University Press.

1. In using the term structural analysis I do not want to get embroiled in contemporary controversies among Marxists over structuralism, instrumentalism, and the like. By structural analysis I mean to conjure nothing more than Marx's emphasis on the structure of classes stemming from the division of society into those who own and control the basic means of production, and those who do not. Marxism is a theory that puts class structure at the center of its analysis. Nothing more than this perspective is suggested here. I would like to thank the following people for comments on an earlier version of this article: Kennette Benedict, Sue Bessmer, Heinz Eulau, Ken Dolbeare, Nancy Hartsock, Henry Levin, Rick Olquin, Ben Page, and Don Share.

2. Assessing the pluralist paradigm is complicated by the fact that the three theories of power are by no means neatly distinguished in the literature. In Polsby's hands, for example, pluralism rejects five central propositions of the "stratificationist literature" which embrace propositions from both elite and class analysis: the upper class rules local community life; political and civic leaders are subordinate to the upper class; a single "power elite" rules locally; this elite rules in its own interest; and social conflict takes place between the upper and lower classes (Polsby, 1980, pp. 8–13). Additional complications are that much leading work on elite theory has been done not on local communities where pluralist research has often been concentrated, but on the national power structure. And although some elitists are fairly comfortable with class analysis (Domhoff, 1978, p. 140), such a leading figure as C. Wright Mills takes pains to reject it (Mills, 1959, p. 277)

Porous boundaries among the three theories, coupled with internal variations among those who may be identified with one of the three camps, make comparisons difficult (Nicholls, 1974). But if these theories are to be useful in understanding the realities of power, it seems necessary to identify some propositions on which pluralists tend to agree, and to critique these propositions from opposing perspectives.

political scientists to be solidly supported by empirical research. Pluralism—what we shall call pluralism I—asserts that the American power structure is made up of many competing elites, not just one. Different elites with low elite overlap operate in different issue areas. Political and economic power are by no means evenly distributed among the population, but inequality is "noncumulative," i.e., most people have some power resources, and no single asset (such as money) confers excessive power.

Pluralism I also sees the political system as reasonably open to multiple interests if these interests feel strongly enough about an issue to mobilize pressure. The power system is, to be sure, untidy, but the pulling and hauling of diverse groups promotes "polyarchy." "Polyarchy" is Robert Dahl's and Charles Lindblom's term for systems run according to putative democratic rules of the game (Dahl & Lindblom, 1976, p. 277.)[3]

When, in 1967, Dahl published the first edition of his textbook, *Pluralist Democracy in the United States*, he identified multiple centers of power and limited popular sovereignty as the two basic axioms of American pluralism. He claimed, moreover, certain advantages for such a system: 1) power was tamed and coercion minimized; 2) the consent of all citizens was promoted (in the long run); and 3) the system fostered the peaceful settlement of conflicts to the mutual benefit of most if not all the contending parties (Dahl, 1967, p. 24). Pluralism was thus offered as a theory of power in America and as justification as well.

In addition to the above ideas, pluralists prided themselves on hard, realistic analyses of politics. Even though the basic theory tended

to buttress the system, many pluralists were scrupulous in noting the system's flaws and deficiencies. Indeed, the contradiction between the theory's tendency to support the system and the system's increasingly disturbing performance has generated questions about the paradigm. Pluralism may be partial to the system, but pluralists are not necessarily blind. Ironically, some of the most thoughtful pluralists are currently among the most severe critics of the workings of American polyarchy.

If, as Marxists and non-Marxists agree, it is important for system maintenance to have a coherent theory that explains and justifies the system, it is cause for reflection that in recent years the theory of pluralism appears no more healthy than the system itself. Beginning with Vietnam, the American political economy has frequently resembled anarchy more than polyarchy. Such debilitating developments as the war, Watergate, persistent inflation and unemployment, the forced retrenchment of the so-called welfare state, and the deepening of gross inequalities have moved such leading pluralists as Dahl and Lindblom so far to the "left" that scholars now talk of something called "neo" or "postpluralism." That pluralism stands in need of revision causes no surprise. No theory as closely tied to the system as pluralism could be unaffected by that system's performance. But it must be asked, how far "left" can pluralism go without exposing the need for a new, nonpluralist theory that may better fit the realities of political and economic power in the United States?

As measured by pluralism's own values, not just Marx's, the performance of the American political economy has been so poor that the theory of pluralism, in an effort to adapt, has been thrown into confusion. The two men who probably did more than anyone else in the past 30 years to modernize the theory of pluralism, Dahl and Lindblom, have been so disturbed by the system's performance that they have issued radical-sounding calls for major structural reforms and redistribution of wealth and income,

---

3. From here on, polyarchy will not be placed in quotation marks, but this does not mean that I accept it as an accurate description of the American system. Polyarchy is a term that contains descriptive and evaluative meanings that are, at best, highly problematic when applied to American political economy.

and have even questioned the capitalist system itself. The problem, from the theoretical point of view, is that these changes in pluralism—which are so extensive that one may now distinguish between pluralism I and pluralism II—clash with previously received wisdom about the nature and legitimacy of power in America. As a result, pluralism II now calls into serious question much of what generations of American political scientists have taught and believed is true about pluralist democracy in the United States. . . .

Pluralism has traditionally downplayed class, but there is a related and equally important difference between pluralism and class analysis. These theories have historically been caught up in the battle between socialism and capitalism that has raged since the mid-nineteenth century. Social scientists, however much they may claim value-neutrality in their work, can hardly deny the political implications of a position that denies either the existence or importance of social classes. If classes in capitalist society are so fragmented that the concept of class is of doubtful analytical utility, then the Marxian analysis and critique of capitalism are seriously undermined. If, on the other hand, class is found to be of prime significance, the work of Marx, and the corresponding socialist critique of capitalism, take on added force. As a theory of how society works, pluralism may claim that all it does is report, not evaluate, the facts. In sharp contrast, class analysis openly deplores the facts it considers of paramount importance to understanding capitalist society. Whatever one's position on the possibility of value-free social research, however, there is no doubt that until recently, pluralism, in sharp contrast with class analysis, rarely raised questions about the legitimacy of capitalism. . . .

To be sure, neither Dahl nor Lindblom is unmindful of the potential strains between socialism and pluralist democracy, but their mature theory seems to take pluralism far toward a reconciliation with Marxist class analysis. It may, therefore, come as something of a shock to realize that Dahl and Lindblom appear simultaneously to uphold most of the essential elements of pluralism I. Pluralism II now tries to hold in balance severe criticisms of the system's performance, the need for major structural reforms, support for redistribution of wealth and income, and more government ownership of private enterprise, at the same time that it supports social pluralism as necessary for democracy, denies the special importance of class, reconfirms the inevitability and value of incremental change, and sees incrementalism as a way of achieving major structural reforms. The problem, from the theoretical point of view, is that pluralism II still defends many features of the system that perpetuate the social results it now deplores. Obviously, pluralism is not proved false merely because the system does not attain the goals held by Dahl and Lindblom. But there is no doubt that the system's failure to live up to their expectations has induced them to make major alterations in the theory.

Dahl and Lindblom decry the "incapacities" and even the "perversities" of American polyarchy because, even after years of opportunity, it failed to live up to their expectations of progress on economic and social equality. They charge that the politico-economic system "remains both sluggish and feckless in advancing on problems on which it has the advantage of decades of experience in policy making: poverty and maldistribution of income and wealth, racial inequality, health care, public education, inflation and unemployment, and industrial relations, for example" (Dahl & Lindblom, 1976, p. xxi).

But unless one assumes that capitalist polyarchy in time will advance equality to a significant extent, there is no reason for surprise (or lamentation) at its failure to do so. Class analysis and, to a lesser extent, elitism see the maintenance of inequality under capitalism not as a failure of polyarchy—not an incapacity or even a perversity—but as the whole point. Only liberal reformers lament polyarchy's failure to promote equality. Conservatives oppose most such efforts, whereas those on the left see government as part of a larger problem, the political economy of capitalism.

Herein may lie part of the key to understanding why pluralism II is not as radical a departure from pluralism I as it might at first appear. The critical quotes from Dahl and Lindblom, all of which express part of what they believe, are held in tandem with a logically incompatible set of ideas. Only out of complete context is pluralism II consistent with such radical ideas as major structural reform, redistribution of wealth and income, and substantive equality. Grave shortcomings of polyarchy are noted, to be sure. Once-sacred cows, including free enterprise, are seriously questioned. But pluralism still holds that the system's gaps and omissions and downright failures can be corrected without specifying how much structural change or redistribution of wealth and income are needed. The system needs major structural reform, to be sure, but, as we shall see, major structural reform does not mean basic alterations in class structure or class power. Despite an appeal by Dahl and Lindblom for "Marxist humanists" to join pluralists in a united front behind the integrity of autonomous groups, pluralism remains profoundly at odds with class analysis. Endorsement of such socialistic-sounding proposals as redistribution of wealth and income seems to close the gap, but this is illusory. A closer look indicates that the theories are, on balance, far apart on most essential questions. Pluralism and class analysis, it appears, cannot be logically integrated without great distortion in the substantive integrity of both theories.

To explore this theme it will be useful to examine first the issue of social vs. private ownership and control of property. Class analysis and pluralism are then shown to clash, as always, over the question of equality. Pluralist political theory and a capitalist economy, it is argued, are more consistent with social inequality than equality. When coupled with the contradiction between pluralism's attachment to incremental change and the call for major structural reforms, this contradiction exposes the incompatibilities that still divide the two theories. In the final analysis, I argue, Dahl and Lindblom try to resolve the contradictions of pluralist theory by supporting increased incremental changes in a system with essential structural inequalities— inequalities that they themselves increasingly realize. . . .

Class analysis sees capitalism as a political economy objectively rooted in unequal power based on the unequal private ownership and control of the necessary means of social production. Changes in capitalism must perforce raise questions of class conflict, not mere public opinion formation. By failing to take such considerations fully into account, Dahl and Lindblom have from the class perspective only weakly anchored their critical analysis of capitalism. As a necessary consequence, their call for reforms is likewise only loosely based, theoretically speaking.

The Pluralist Theory of Equality

Historically, pluralism and class analysis have clashed head-on over the issue of equality. Both theories endorse equality and present themselves as ways of attaining it, but this is possible only because they have meant radically different things by the term. Pluralist democracy, furthermore, pits equality as a value against a second great democratic value, liberty, and tends to see the two as trade-offs. In the nineteenth century, as Lindblom (1977, p. 163) notes, "Marx and the socialists became the spokesmen for equality, liberals the spokesmen for liberty." Since then, as he also notes, the value of equality has been subordinated to liberty in liberal democratic theory.

Marx and later socialists deny the contradiction between equality and liberty. True liberty is impossible without equality; to be truly free, individuals in society must be roughly equal in the means necessary to exercise freedom. Far from being opposed to liberty, equality is its necessary condition.

For Dahl (1982, p. 108) "Democracy is and has always been closely associated in practice with private ownership of the means of production." By democracy, of course, Dahl means liberal or bourgeois democracy, not democracy in the socialist sense. But the close connection between capitalism and liberal democracy raises the knotty issue of substantive equality vs. equality of opportunity. If the means of production are privately and unequally owned under capitalism, capitalism seems to be based on substantive economic inequality, from which flows, as Dahl admits, a certain level of political inequality. The only form of equality that is logically compatible with substantive inequality is equality of opportunity which, as Scharr (1967) and others have argued, is really the equal opportunity to become unequal. From Thomas Jefferson's defense of the natural aristocracy of talent, through social Darwinism's defense of the survival of the fittest, to present-day exaltations of individualism and competition, liberal democracy has consistently defended equal opportunity and the inequalities in the distribution of rewards that flow naturally from it. The question this raises is, of course: Can pluralist or liberal democracy be reconciled with class or socialist democracy if the two theories conflict so profoundly over the priority and meaning of equality?

The decisive shift of pluralism II is toward substantive equality and away from equal opportunity as the preferred democratic ideal. Having called for the redistribution of wealth and income, Dahl and Lindblom (1976) logically break the historical connection between capitalism and liberal democracy. They also partially correct pluralism's tendency to separate political and economic equality by noting that, "We cannot move closer to greater equality in access to political resources without greater equality in the distribution of, among other things, wealth and income" (p. xxxii). Dahl (1982, p. 117), writing

separately a few years later, concludes that the "distribution of advantages and disadvantages is often arbitrary, capricious, unmerited, and unjust, and in virtually all advanced countries no longer tolerable." It is so intolerable, in fact, that he has kind words to say for central government tax and transfer payments to reduce inequality, as long as individuals are free to spend as they choose.

There are, however, three major defects in pluralism's treatment of equality. First, pluralism has no clear criteria or standard for assessing what is just or unjust about the distribution of values in society. Second, pluralism treats public opinion as the explanation of inequality in the United States and as the vehicle for future egalitarian changes. Third, not all groups in the pluralist United States are equal, as pluralism grants in the privileged-position-of-business argument, but the special place of business has not yet been fully integrated into a theory rooted in multiple, independent, and autonomous groups as the necessary building blocks of pluralist democracy.

Just and Unjust Distribution

Pluralism's discussion of equality is curiously indeterminate because pluralism lacks a clear principle or theory for assessing just and unjust distributions of wealth, income, and property. It lacks a theory of value. Consider the issue of political equality. Because political equality is obviously undermined to some degree by economic inequality, pluralism's call for redistribution makes good logical sense. But in the past, pluralism has not set equality of conditions as its goal. Without an underlying theory of value, it is impossible to assess clearly and logically why a particular distribution is just or unjust. "Inequalities in distribution are, of course, not inherently unjust" (Dahl & Lindblom, 1976, p. xxxi). In other words, inequality is not in principle bad; ceteris paribus, some inequality is in principle just. Inequality, then, is not a matter of principle but of pragmatics: the degree of inequality exceeds any principle of distributive justice Dahl and Lindblom find acceptable. They therefore deplore the gross level of inequality and call for (unspecified) egalitarian changes.

When Dahl and Lindblom endorse the redistribution of wealth and income, they endorse substantive equality, not mere equality of opportunity. When they endorse structural reforms, the suggestion is made that structural reforms should be made to promote substantive equality. But when they simultaneously argue that inequality is not unjust per se and do not confront the key issue of degrees of inequality, they cloud the case for equality. The flip side of the question of how much equality pluralism supports is how much inequality it is willing to tolerate. In Dahl's case the argument for redistribution and equality leads to a box canyon of an indefinite number of principles that might be used to allocate incomes, no one of which is clearly or theoretically superior to the others (Dahl, 1982, pp. 135–137). Economics, to which Dahl turns for help, lacks a theory of value that can address just and unjust distributions (1982, p. 134). The marginal theory of value does not traffic in such philosophical issues and hence is of no help. Unless and until pluralism addresses the question of how much equality is just or unjust, the critical question of degree goes begging. Calls for more equality, however attractive they may sound politically, remain unsupported theoretically....

A related problem with pluralism's treatment of equality is the theory's tendency, still, to separate political equality from economic equality, a separation which, for class analysis, makes little sense. Pluralism is quite clear that economic inequality frequently undermines political equality, but in Dahl's work, for all the apparent support for redistribution, the theory actually shies away from making an unequivocal endorsement. In his essay on liberal democracy, Dahl (1979a, pp. 65–66) rejects direct redistribution on grounds that it would require a major histor-

ical commitment to distributive justice, and such major changes are unlikely in the American system where intense minorities are powerful. These pragmatic objections, however valid, should not be allowed to mask the logical dilemma: if, as pluralism now grants, economic resources are often directly convertible into political resources, it seems to follow that political equality requires the redistribution of economic resources. Dahl, however, refuses to go this far. He prefers regulating the political effects of economic inequalities, a position that, at best, deals only indirectly with the problem. Regulating the political effects of economic inequality (e.g., by controlling campaign contributions) may promote equality indirectly, but it seems a major concession and a move away from pluralism II's seeming acceptance of greater substantive equality as a social goal.

How does class analysis approach equality under capitalist social relations? Such questions raise a host of complex issues that cannot be discussed here, but the starting point of any comparison would have to be Marx's audacious claim in volume 3 of *Capital* that he had uncovered the innermost secret, the hidden basis of the entire social structure of capitalism, and with it the political form of the capitalist state. What was the key that could unlock so much knowledge? It was the relationship between capitalists and workers "in which unpaid surplus labour is pumped out of direct producers, [and which] determines the relationship of rulers and ruled, as it grows directly out of production itself and, in turn, reacts upon it as a determining element" (Marx, 1967, III, p. 791).

Marx was quick to recognize that although he saw the surplus-labor relationship as the key to understanding capitalism, the same economic base could give rise to infinite variation depending on innumerable different empirical circumstances, natural environment, and racial relations, among other determinants. But the important point for this discussion is that Marx's claim points up a key difference between pluralism and class analysis: class analysis proceeds from an explicit theory of value; pluralism does not.

Marx anchors *Capital* in a theory of value for a very good reason. Without a theory of value, he was at a loss to present a principled attack on capitalism. He might personally deplore inequality, but he needed a theory of value to establish socialism as *qualitatively* superior to capitalism. His answer was the labor theory of value and, for all the debate that has surrounded that theory of value, at least he had one....

... However flawed Marx's labor theory may be, future comparisons of pluralism and class analysis await the former's attention to a theory of value that can address the question of just and unjust distribution. Until that theory is offered, the two theories cannot join clearly on the most fundamental question of all: why, if everywhere men and women are born equal, are the many everywhere regularly chained in submission to the few?

Public Opinion

A second problem with the pluralist treatment of equality is that, again, the problem is laid at the doorstep of the American people. Speaking of their call for a "fairer" share of income and wealth: "Until more Americans accept this view and act on it, the United States will not be the progressive society we wrongly assumed it to be at the time we wrote. Polyarchy may continue to exist at the present level, but democracy will still remain a long way off" (Dahl & Lindblom, 1976, p. xxxii). Both Dahl and Lindblom repeat these arguments in their post-1976 work.

There are dangers in conceptualizing the problem in terms of public opinion. One danger is that one of the best known surveys on equality in America shows that the mass of the American people has been more supportive of economic equality than the elites (McClosky, 1964, p. 369). But public opinion is notoriously volatile, and this is not the main point. Far more significant, from the class perspective, is the unreality of relying on public opinion to advance equality. These are matters that, under capitalism, are systematically excluded from the American political arena. It is hardly the American people's fault that wealth and income are highly concentrated. Nor will public opinion necessarily bring about more equality. In a capitalist setting economic equality is not even a virtue, let alone a matter to be decided by public debate. The realization of equality requires fundamental changes in the system that makes inequality a virtue, a system strengthened, perhaps inadvertently, by theories of distributive justice which, in the name of equality, justify its opposite.

The Imperfect Balance of Group Power

If the level of equality is viewed as a structural feature of the political economy and not a matter of public opinion, what is the relationship between equality and another feature of the American system, the existence of groups? According to Dahl and Lindblom, social pluralism, defined as a diversity of autonomous social organizations, is a necessary condition of polyarchy. But pluralism sees two nagging flaws in polyarchy. First, not all groups are equal; not everyone organizes at the same rate, and power resources are not evenly distributed. Specifically, the better-off participate more. "As a consequence, government decisions reflect and reinforce a structure of inequalities" (Dahl & Lindblom, 1976, p. xxxvi). This pluralism acknowledges.

A related inegalitarian feature of polyarchy is the privileged position of business. Business is not just another interest group. True, it plays a powerful interest-group role. But it also tran scends such a limited role. As Dahl and Lindblom describe it, the American political economy is co-directed unequally by business and government, and in that order. Great public decisions are left to the market; government's job is to induce (not command) business to perform its functions. Pluralist theories that stress balance and countervailing power among interest groups, and fail to take into account the unique advantages enjoyed by business, are thereby impeached by Dahl and Lindblom.

Having thus arrived roughly at where Marx began, Dahl and Lindblom nevertheless continue to endorse the theory and practice of pluralism. Indeed, they even detect a lessening of antipathy toward pluralism among European "Marxist humanists" and suggest an emerging consensus on the need for autonomous groups as a bridge between the two opposing theoretical camps. As Dahl and Lindblom see it, the rigidly antipluralist Marxism of Stalin is on the way out, so the door is open to a reconciliation between pluralism and "Marxist humanism."

"But what about equality?" the skeptic may well ask. If even pluralists agree that business occupies a superior position in capitalism, if pluralists recognize that differential group power may act as an obstacle to democratization, and if pluralist politics tends to reflect and reinforce the advantages of the better-off, business-oriented groups may so impede equality that some centralizing, democratic, public force may be necessary to advance the egalitarian cause.

Dahl and Lindblom admit this possibility, but reject it. In fact, they offer no solution to the tension between unequal social pluralism and democratic equality, but they are clear about defending groups, and while rejecting one form of Marxism, they extend an olive branch to another. In their words, "Whatever the best solution to this problem (of equality) may be, for Americans, at least, it is not to be found, in our view, in destroying organizational autonomy and replacing autonomy with centralization, command, hierarchy, bureaucracy, and domination by an enlightened elite" (Dahl & Lindblom, 1976, p. xxxvi).

Portraying the alternative to social pluralism as "domination by an enlightened elite" may not exhaust the possibilities, but it is less important here to debate the point than to note that pluralism II is as ideologically committed to social pluralism as was pluralism I. Pluralism puts considerable emphasis on the social and economic inequalities that undermine political equality. It now recognizes the unique position of one elite, business, in the American political economy. But, as E. E. Schattschneider put it years ago, the "flaw in the pluralist heaven is that the heavenly chorus sings with a strong upper-class accent" (Schattschneider, 1960, p. 35). One has to ask whether or not Dahl and Lindblom have faced up to the contradictions they increasingly perceive among social pluralism, equality, and polyarchy. Their faith in the superiority of social pluralism and polyarchy over currently available alternatives remains strong, but the special place accorded business has not yet been squared with a theory emphasizing a multiplicity of groups as a precondition of pluralist democracy.

The central question, of course, is *can* the privileged position of business be squared with pluralist democracy? Lindblom suggests it can't. Dahl's answer is less clear....

... [I]f it is true that pluralism has always recognized that not all groups are equal, it is also true that pluralism seems to require the assumption of at least some rough equality among groups for a system to be a polyarchy. Unless power is decentralized among many groups, pluralism is falsified, and some form of elite theory or class analysis better fits the empirical facts. The balance may be imperfect, but it is hard to see how pluralism can dispense with the notion of some sort of balance, some sort of rough parity or countervailing power, without sliding over into elite or class explanations of power. So far pluralism has not specified the parameters or levels of power distribution necessary for a system to be judged a pluralist democracy. But if business is as privileged and as powerful as pluralism now says, vexing questions are raised about the democratic character of capitalist regimes. Class analysis, of course, asserts that the power of business in a capitalist system makes liberal democracy a contradiction in terms. On this point, as on so many others, the two theories stand so far apart that they are best seen as implacable opponents than as potential partners for a merger.

Structural Reform

One area of agreement between pluralism II and class analysis is the dismal performance of the American political economy in the past few decades. Both theories support major "structural" changes. But on close inspection, they mean very different things by structural reform. In fact, pluralism's call for structural reform is so conditional and narrowly defined that the two theories remain fundamentally divided over this question.

"Structural reform" is, of course, an idea closely associated with social democratic critiques of capitalism. The basic idea is that transformational changes can be made in capitalism to reduce or eliminate such serious capitalist "perversities" as inequality. The endorsement of structural reform apparently brings pluralism and class analysis, capitalism and socialism, closer together.

But here Dahl and Lindblom take a step that radically alters their course and demonstrates the continuing split between the two theories. It occurs when they question a feature of polyarchy with which they are prominently associated: incrementalism. . . .

Far from abandoning incrementalism, however, Dahl and Lindblom, in their joint work and in subsequent individual publications, argue pragmatically that to propose nonincremental changes in a society only capable of incremental change is virtually a waste of time (Dahl, 1982, pp. 120–126; Lindblom, 1977, ch. 19). No one knows, they assert, how to design a political system regularly capable of more than incremental change. . . . With the removal of some veto powers, they promise, incremental change

will work its effects on various problems confronting American society.

From the reaffirmation of incrementalism, which by definition ensures at best slow changes in the status quo, one might expect Dahl and Lindblom to caution against major reforms, but they do not. They believe major structural reforms follow from their analysis: "It follows from all we have said that we believe that major structural reforms are required in the American political-economic system" (Dahl & Lindblom, 1976, p. xli).

It might be asked, however, that if incrementalism is a rational aid to change, if incrementalism assures progress (albeit slow) on social problems, and if in any event nonincremental change occurs so rarely, why the call for required structural reforms in the American politico-economic system? As defenders of incrementalism and incremental change, do Dahl and Lindblom mean by structural reform what most people mean? Does structural reform mean the replacement of capitalism by a dominantly socialist political economy? Or is structural reform another name for incremental change— souped-up incremental change, but nonetheless incremental?

The fact is that pluralism II's support for government ownership and control is softened by several caveats: the issue of control precedes the issue of ownership, so if other control mechanisms can be found, they may supersede government; government ownership is declared to be definitely not a sufficient means to public control; in many cases it is probably not even a necessary means; and in some cases it may be a hindrance. . . .

I think it is fair to conclude that Dahl and Lindblom's endorsement of government ownership as a means of public control is, at most, limited.

More broadly, the case for major structural reforms concentrates on defects in the existing decision-making and policymaking institutions of society, *not* class structure. Perhaps most surprising of all, when Dahl and Lindblom face the question of how such reforms are to be brought about, they answer—by the institutions themselves. . . .

. . . Dahl and Lindblom are aware that their position leaves them open to the charge that they suffer from a "residual naive optimism of liberalism." But social institutions, they reply, do change. Reforms do occur. And what is the best and most common method by which these necessary changes occur? Incrementalism.

Pluralism II resoundingly affirms incrementalism as the preferred method of achieving major structural reforms in polyarchy. How does pluralism II arrive at this conclusion? It detects in incrementalism a hitherto overlooked capacity to undermine the status quo. By increasing the pace of incremental change, small accretions, far from being ways of ensuring modest changes in the status quo, will transform the system. . . .

It is certainly arguable how much structural reform can be smuggled into the American system through incremental methods, but further complications arise from a related contention. Although affirming the need for major structural reform, Dahl and Lindblom oppose any changes in the "general values" for which the American system stands. Changes in general values are neither necessary nor desirable. Structural reforms, then, are limited to those features of the system that inhibit changes in "proximate goals," not general values.

When Dahl and Lindblom discuss general values, they seem to be referring to such abstract values as freedom, democracy, political equality, and majority rule. These values are sacrosanct (though not absolute). The biases of American institutions against changes in these values should be maintained. Faster incremental change is therefore restricted to "proximate goals." Here they endorse not only the removal of barriers against change, but their replacement by biases toward change. . . .

. . . [U]nless pluralism faces squarely how much change in the private enterprise system

or in the distribution of wealth is necessary to achieve such values as freedom and equality, the basic questions go begging. In contrast, class theory asserts a *contradiction* between Lindblom's grand issues and the general values for which pluralism and class analysis both stand. The pluralist position is much less clear. Pluralism now admits some connection between grand issues and general values, but is fuzzy about the crucial question of whether or not there is a contradiction, and how much change in the grand issues (e.g., private enterprise) is needed to promote the grand values (e.g., political equality). Class or structural analysis insists that the grand values *cannot* be attained within the confines of capitalism; pluralism either takes no such clear-cut stand or affirms the opposite. This crucial difference, when added to class theory's insistence on nonincremental changes in class structure, and pluralism's clear preference for incremental changes not in class structure but in social institutions, clarify crucial differences between the two theories.

Clearly pluralism and class analysis mean very different things by the term "structural reform." Marxist class theory and even social democratic theories use the term to apply to changes in capitalism and the class structure embedded in capitalist social relations. In sharp contrast, recent pluralist theory does not address the question of class structure in contemplating structural reform. Indeed, pluralism contends that structural reforms may emanate from the market system that structural analysis means to transform. In assessing pluralism's call for structural reform, therefore, it is crucial to note the singular interpretation given the term. When pluralists propose structural reforms they are not talking about egalitarian changes in the class structure of American capitalist society. They are not talking about "phasing out" the capitalist class through redistributive taxes, controls on inheritance, or a levelling of work hierarchies and rewards. Major structural reform for Dahl and Lindblom means changes in the existing decision-making institutions of society; moreover such changes are to be brought about slowly through incrementalism. It is hard to see how class analysis and pluralism can be brought closer together unless and until they agree that such "grand issues" as the private enterprise system itself, and the class structure that goes with it, should not only be placed on the political agenda but resolved in such a way that non-incremental progress is made toward true substantive equality....

... In pluralist theory, classes have merely a nominal existence compared to groups; in class analysis, groups are seen and analyzed as fractions or sub-parts or classes. Until some reconciliation of this conflict is offered, it is hard to see how class analysis and pluralism can be joined along the lines attempted by Dahl and Lindblom.

Summary and Conclusion

Pluralism II updates pluralist theory in light of such incapacities and perversities as Vietnam, Watergate, and persistent economic and political inequality. Despite an opening to the left, however, pluralism II remains a theory that is logically more compatible with, and supportive of, a capitalist political economy than a socialist one.

Class analysis and pluralism are profoundly split over equality (Dahl, 1979b; Green, 1979). Pluralism now pays attention to the problem of economic and political inequality, but it falls short of endorsing full substantive equality as a social goal. As Bell has noted, the claim for equality of result is a socialist ethic, as equality of opportunity is the liberal ethic (Bell, 1972, p. 48). Marxian socialism points toward substantive equality because it is rooted in a theory of value that stresses the collective involvement of all members of society in producing social goods. Pluralism lacks a clear theory of value, but its historic attachment to equality of opportunity seems to ensure the acceptance of more social

inequality than is tolerable in class theory. This seems true, moreover, even if pluralism accepts Rawls's theory of distributive justice as its own. It bears repeating that the difference principle defends inequalities as just as long as they make everyone better off; it is not a straightforward argument for substantive equality.

Pluralism I and II, then, despite the call (at least by Lindblom) for redistribution, seem more compatible with equality of opportunity than equality of results. Equal opportunity to compete in a race that necessarily results in a small number of winners and a large number of losers is Orwellian newspeak. It defends inequality in the name of equality (Scharr, 1967, p. 234), and helps induce mass acquiescence in the perpetuation of an unequal social order. To the extent that pluralism does the same, it belies the espousal of substantive equality through the redistribution of wealth and income.

In the structural view, inequality under capitalism is not a by-product of the system that is amenable to polyarchal corrections. It is a structural imperative. It is one of the things that makes capitalism capitalism and distinguishes it from socialism. From the class perspective, inequality is as likely to be significantly reduced or eliminated under capitalism as the meek are to inherit the earth. The fundamental reason this is so is the essential, structural relationship between capital and labor in a capitalist society: they are, by definition, unequal....

It might be judged excessive to contend that pluralism is in danger of imploding from internal contradictions, but in light of the difficulties raised above, it might not be excessive to suggest that pluralist theory is in need of some clarification.

A class or structural analysis of American political economy seems more consistent with the fact of gross inequality in wealth, income, and power under capitalism. Capitalism makes a fetish of commodities, not equality. Indeed, it presumes unequal natural talents and abilities and rewards, and justifies them under the theory of equal opportunity. Pluralist theories would be more consistent if they dropped the untenable adherence to substantive equality and faced up to the reality of inequality in the system of which the theory of pluralism is an integral part. Class analysis not only conforms better to many of the empirical realities of American political economy, which saves it from wounded surprise over the system's performance, but it clearly and consistently adheres to egalitarian standards that flow from its analysis of the class structure of capitalism. If American social science means to explain better, let alone help change the American political economy, the pluralist-elitist debate might well be redirected in favor of explorations in class analysis.

References

Bell, D. Meritocracy and equality. *The Public Interest*, 1972, *29*, 29–68.

Dahl, R. A. *Pluralist democracy in the United States.* Chicago: Rand McNally, 1967.

Dahl, R. A., & Lindblom, C. E. *Politics, economics, and welfare.* Chicago: University of Chicago Press, 1976.

Dahl, R. A. Liberal democracy in the United States. In W. S. Livingston (Ed.), *A prospect for liberal democracy.* Austin: University of Texas Press, 1979a, 57–72.

Dahl, R. A. What is political equality? *Dissent*, 1979b, *26*, 363–368.

Dahl, R. A. *Dilemmas of pluralist democracy.* New Haven, Conn: Yale University Press, 1982.

Domhoff, G. W. *Who really rules?* Santa Monica, Calif.: Goodyear Publishing, 1978.

Green, P. What is political equality. *Dissent*, 1979, *26*, 351–368.

Higley, J., & Moore, G. Elite integration in the United States and Australia. *American Political Science Review*, 1981, *75*, 581–597.

Kuhn, T. *The structure of scientific revolutions.* Chicago: University of Chicago Press, 1962.

Lindblom, C. E. *Politics and markets.* New York: Basic Books, 1977.

Marx, K. *Capital* (Vols. 1, 3). New York: International Publishers, 1967.

McClosky, H. Consensus and ideology in American politics. *American Political Science Review*, 1964, *58*, 361–382.

Mills, C. W. *The power elite.* New York: Oxford University Press, 1959.

Nicholls, D. *Three varieties of pluralism.* New York: St. Martin's Press, 1974.

Polsby, N. W. *Community power and political theory.* New Haven, Conn.: Yale University Press, 1980.

Scharr, J. Equality of opportunity and beyond. In J. R. Pennock & J. W. Chapman (Eds.), *Equality.* New York: Atherton Press, 1967.

Schattschneider, E. E. *The semi-sovereign people.* New York: Holt, Rinehart and Winston, 1960.

The Theory of Economic Regulation

George J. Stigler

The state—the machinery and power of the state—is a potential resource or threat to every industry in the society. With its power to prohibit or compel, to take or give money, the state can and does selectively help or hurt a vast number of industries. That political juggernaut, the petroleum industry, is an immense consumer of political benefits, and simultaneously the underwriters of marine insurance have their more modest repast. The central tasks of the theory of economic regulation are to explain who will receive the benefits or burdens of regulation, what form regulation will take, and the effects of regulation upon the allocation of resources.

Regulation may be actively sought by an industry, or it may be thrust upon it. A central thesis of this paper is that, as a rule, regulation is acquired by the industry and is designed and operated primarily for its benefit. There are regulations whose net effects upon the regulated industry are undeniably onerous; a simple example is the differentially heavy taxation of the industry's product (whiskey, playing cards). These onerous regulations, however, are exceptional and can be explained by the same theory that explains beneficial (we may call it "acquired") regulation....

... We assume that political systems are rationally devised and rationally employed, which is to say that they are appropriate instruments for the fulfillment of desires of members of the society. This is not to say that the state will serve any persons's concept of the public interest: indeed the problem of regulation is the problem of discovering when and why an industry (or other group of likeminded people) is able to use the state for its purposes, or is singled out by the state to be used for alien purposes.

Excerpted from: George J. Stigler, *The Citizen and the State: Essays on Regulation.* Chicago: University of Chicago Press, 1975. Reprinted by permission.

What Benefits Can a State Provide to an Industry?

The state has one basic resource which in pure principle is not shared with even the mightiest of its citizens: the power to coerce. The state can seize money by the only method which is permitted by the laws of a civilized society, by taxation. The state can ordain the physical movements of resources and the economic decisions of households and firms without their consent. These powers provide the possibilities for the utilization of the state by an industry to increase its profitability. The main policies which an industry (or occupation) may seek of the state are four.

The most obvious contribution that a group may seek of the government is a direct subsidy of money. The domestic airlines received "air mail" subsidies (even if they did not carry mail) of $1.5 billion through 1968. The merchant marine has received construction and operation subsidies reaching almost $3 billion since World War II. The education industry has long shown a masterful skill in obtaining public funds: for example, universities and colleges have received federal funds exceeding $3 billion annually in recent years, as well as subsidized loans for dormitories and other construction. The veterans of wars have often received direct cash bonuses....

The second major public resource commonly sought by an industry is control over entry by new rivals. There is considerable, not to say excessive, discussion in economic literature of the rise of peculiar price policies (limit prices), vertical integration, and similar devices to retard the rate of entry of new firms into oligopolistic industries. Such devices are vastly less efficacious (economical) than the certificate of convenience and necessity (which includes, of course, the import and production quotas of the oil and tobacco industries)....

We propose the general hypothesis: every industry or occupation that has enough political power to utilize the state will seek to control entry. In addition, the regulatory policy will often be so fashioned as to retard the rate of growth of new firms. For example, no new savings and loan company may pay a dividend rate higher than that prevailing in the community in its endeavors to attract deposits.[2] The power to limit the selling expenses of mutual funds, which is soon to be conferred upon the Securities and Exchange Commission, will serve to limit the growth of small mutual funds and hence reduce the sales costs of large funds....

A third general set of powers of the state which will be sought by the industry are those which affect substitutes and complements. Crudely put, the butter producers wish to suppress margarine and encourage the production of bread. The airline industry actively supports the federal subsidies to airports; the building trade unions have opposed labor-saving materials through building codes....

The fourth class of public policies sought by an industry is directed to price-fixing. Even the industry that has achieved entry control will often want price controls administered by a body with coercive powers. If the number of firms in the regulated industry is even moderately large, price discrimination will be difficult to maintain in the absence of public support. The prohibition of interest on demand deposits, which is probably effective in preventing interest payments to most non-business depositors, is a case in point. Where there are no diseconomies of large scale for the individual firm (e.g., a motor trucking firm can add trucks under a given license as common carrier), price control is essential to achieve more than competitive rates of return.

Limitations upon Political Benefits

These various political boons are not obtained by the industry in a pure profit-maximizing form. The political process erects certain limita-

tions upon the exercise of cartel policies by an industry. These limitations are of three sorts.

First, the distribution of control of the industry among the firms in the industry is changed. In an unregulated industry each firm's influence upon price and output is proportional to its share of industry output (at least in a simple arithmetic sense of direct capacity to change output). The political decisions take account also of the political strength of the various firms, so small firms have a larger influence than they would possess in an unregulated industry....

Second, the procedural safeguards required of public processes are costly. The delays which are dictated by both law and bureaucratic thoughts of self-survival can be large....

Finally, the political process automatically admits powerful outsiders to the industry's councils. It is well known that the allocation of television channels among communities does not maximize industry revenue but reflects pressures to serve many smaller communities. The abandonment of an unprofitable rail line is an even more notorious area of outsider participation.

These limitations are predictable, and they must all enter into the calculus of the profitability of regulation of an industry....

The Costs of Obtaining Legislation

When an industry receives a grant of power from the state, the benefit to the industry will fall short of the damage to the rest of the community. Even if there were no deadweight losses from acquired regulation, however, one might expect a democratic society to reject such industry requests unless the industry controlled a majority of the votes.[6] ... To explain why many industries

---

2. The Federal Home Loan Bank is the regulatory body. It also controls the amount of advertising and other areas of competition.

---

6. If the deadweight loss (of consumer and producer surplus) is taken into account, even if the oil industry were in the majority it would not obtain the legislation if there were available some method of compensation (such as sale of votes) by which the larger damage of the minority could be expressed effectively against the lesser gains of the majority.

are able to employ the political machinery to their own ends, we must examine the nature of the political process in a democracy.

A consumer chooses between rail and air travel, for example, by voting with his pocketbook: he patronizes on a given day that mode of transportation he prefers. A similar form of economic voting occurs with decisions on where to work or where to invest one's capital. The market accumulates these economic votes, predicts their future course, and invests accordingly.

Because the political decision is coercive, the decision process is fundamentally different from that of the market. If the public is asked to make a decision between two transportation media comparable to the individual's decision on how to travel—say, whether airlines or railroads should receive a federal subsidy—the decision must be abided by everyone, travelers and non-travelers, travelers this year and travelers next year. This compelled universality of political decisions makes for two differences between democratic political decision processes and market processes.

1. The decisions must be made simultaneously by a large number of persons (or their representatives): the political process demands simultaneity of decision. . . .

The condition of simultaneity imposes a major burden upon the political decision process. It makes voting on specific issues prohibitively expensive. . . . To cope with this condition of simultaneity, the voters must employ representatives with wide discretion and must eschew direct expressions of marginal changes in preferences. This characteristic also implies that the political decision does not predict voter desires and make preparations to fulfill them in advance of their realization.

2. The democratic decision process must involve "all" the community, not simply those who are directly concerned with a decision. In a private market, the non-traveler never votes on rail versus plane travel, while the huge shipper casts many votes each day. The political decision

process cannot exclude the uninterested voter: the abuses of any exclusion except self-exclusion are obvious. Hence, the political process does not allow participation in proportion to interest and knowledge. . . .

These characteristics of the political process can be modified by having numerous levels of government . . . and by selective use of direct decision. The chief method of coping with the characteristics, however, is to employ more or less full-time representatives organized in (disciplined by) firms which are called political parties or machines.

The representative and his party are rewarded for their discovery and fulfillment of the political desires of their constituency by success in election and the perquisites of office. If the representative could confidently await reelection whenever he voted against an economic policy that injured the society, he would assuredly do so. Unfortunately virtue does not always command so high a price. If the representative denies ten large industries their special subsidies of money or governmental power, they will dedicate themselves to the election of a more complaisant successor: the stakes are that important. This does not mean that every large industry can get what it wants or all that it wants: it does mean that the representative and his party must find a coalition of voter interests more durable than the anti-industry side of every industry policy proposal. A representative cannot win or keep office with the support of the sum of those who are opposed to: oil import quotas, farm subsidies, airport subsidies, hospital subsidies, unnecessary navy shipyards, an inequitable public housing program, and rural electrification subsidies.

The political decision process has as its dominant characteristic infrequent, universal (in principle) participation, as we have noted: political decisions must be infrequent and they must be global. The voter's expenditure to learn the merits of individual policy proposals and to express his preferences (by individual and group representation as well as by voting) are determined by expected costs and returns, just as they are in the private marketplace. The costs of comprehensive information are higher in the political arena because information must be sought on many issues of little or no direct concern to the individual, and accordingly he will know little about most matters before the legislature. The expressions of preferences in voting will be less precise than the expressions of preferences in the marketplace because many uninformed people will be voting and affecting the decision.[7]

The channels of political decision-making can thus be described as gross or filtered or noisy. If everyone has a negligible preference for policy A over B, the preference will not be discovered or acted upon. If voter group X wants a policy that injures non-X by a small amount, it will not pay non-X to discover this and act against the policy. The system is calculated to implement all strongly felt preferences of majorities and many strongly felt preferences of minorities but to disregard the lesser preferences of majorities and minorities. The filtering of grossness will be reduced by any reduction in the cost to the citizen of acquiring information and expressing desires and by any increase in the probability that his vote will influence policy.

The industry which seeks political power must go to the appropriate seller, the political party. The political party has costs of operation, costs of maintaining an organization and competing in elections. These costs of the political process are viewed excessively narrowly in the literature on the financing of elections: elections are to the political process what merchandising is to the

process of producing a commodity, only an essential final step. The party maintains its organization and electoral appeal by the performance of costly services to the voter at all times, not just before elections. Part of the costs of services and organization are borne by putting a part of the party's workers on the public payroll. An opposition party, however, is usually essential insurance for the voters to discipline the party in power, and the opposition party's costs are not fully met by public funds.

The industry which seeks regulation must be prepared to pay with the two things a party needs: votes and resources. The resources may be provided by campaign contributions, contributed services (the businessman heads a fundraising committee), and more indirect methods such as the employment of party workers. The votes in support of the measure are rallied, and the votes in opposition are dispersed, by expensive programs to educate (or uneducate) members of the industry and of other concerned industries.

These costs of legislation probably increase with the size of the industry seeking the legislation. Larger industries seek programs which cost the society more and arouse more opposition from substantially affected groups. The tasks of persuasion, both within and without the industry, also increase with its size. The fixed size of the political "market," however, probably makes the cost of obtaining legislation increase less rapidly than industry size. The smallest industries are therefore effectively precluded from the political process unless they have some special advantage such as geographical concentration in a sparsely settled political subdivision. . . .

Conclusion

The idealistic view of public regulation is deeply imbedded in professional economic thought. So many economists, for example, have denounced the ICC for its pro-railroad policies that this has become a cliché of the literature. This criticism

---

7. There is an organizational problem in any decision in which more than one vote is cast. If because of economies of scale it requires a thousand customers to buy a product before it can be produced, this thousand votes has to be assembled by some entrepreneur. Unlike the political scene, however, there is no need to obtain the consent of the remainder of the community, because they will bear no part of the cost.

seems to me exactly as appropriate as a criticism of the Great Atlantic and Pacific Tea Company for selling groceries, or as a criticism of a politician for currying popular support. The fundamental vice of such criticism is that it misdirects attention: it suggests that the way to get an ICC which is not subservient to the carriers is to preach to the commissioners or to the people who appoint the commissioners. The only way to get a different commission would be to change the political support for the Commission, and reward commissioners on a basis unrelated to their services to the carriers.

Until the basic logic of political life is developed, reformers will be ill-equipped to use the state for their reforms, and victims of the pervasive use of the state's support of special groups will be helpless to protect themselves. Economists should quickly establish the license to practice on the rational theory of political behavior....

Interest Intermediation and Regime Governability in Contemporary Western Europe and North America

Philippe C. Schmitter

Virtually all efforts to understand the generic nature of contemporary political behavior and its policy products rely on the notion that the promotion and protection of self-regarding objectives "rightly and rationally understood" provide the motive force, and the capacity to prevail over the interest efforts of others provides the explanation for likely outcomes. The emergence and triumph of capitalism and industrialization have provided not only a differentiated set of categories for identifying and a suitable means for calculating those interest(s); they have also ensured through interdependence and competition that one must indeed consider self-regarding objectives or suffer dire consequences.

The purpose of this chapter is not to lament the replacement or effacement of more "noble" motives in political life. Nor is it to measure the extent to which selfish, vested behavior is, in fact, characteristic of the politics of advanced industrial/capitalist societies.[1] Rather, it assumes the predominance of such motivation and seeks to explore (and tentatively to test) the consequences that the emergence of different modes of formalized interest intermediation have had on the governability of contemporary Western European and North American polities....

The neotraditional science of politics may recognize and even exalt the pursuit of interests but concludes that the very logic of industrialization will produce such a multiplicity of dynamic, ephemeral, overlapping and countervailing efforts to protect and promote self-regarding objectives that the resultant "pluralist" system will be both self-equilibrating and self-legitimating. All with interests will get a democratic chance to play in the game; none, however, will be capable of controlling its course or rigging its outcome. From this perpective, the danger of ungovernability and/or instability arises from outside the game of interest politics—from passionate, irrational subversives who refuse to play according to the established rules, who insist on turning the game toward more exalted goals, and who force the otherwise benevolent umpire to use coercion in order to ensure the continued governability of the system.

The currently fashionable perspective of the "policy sciences" suggests yet another explanation for (un)governability or (in)stability. Again, the pursuit of ignoble, vested interests is acknowledged as providing the predominant motive for political action, but in contrast to the optimism of pluralists, the "policy scientists" see a real danger in such unbridled selfishness. Too much of it by too wary and too well-organized actors leads to "overload," to an excess of demands on public authorities beyond their capacity for satisfying such claims. As the governing systems of advanced industrial/capitalist societies decline in efficiency, efficacy, and legitimacy under such an imbalance, more and more dissatisfied interests find they must make more and more noise and engage in more and more unconventional behavior to gain effective access—and this leads only to more and more overload and ungovernability.

This chapter contends in particular with the latter, "overload school." In the process it will advance arguments (and marshal some data) to demonstrate that the pursuit of lowly self-

Excerpted from: Philippe C. Schmitter, "Interest Intermediation and Regime Governability in Contemporary Western Europe and North America." In *Organising Interests in Western Europe*, edited by Suzanne Berger. Cambridge: Cambridge University Press, 1983. Reprinted by permission.

1. For an excellent, if rather nostalgic and petulant, critique of modern political science for having replaced the more exalted vision of affective "community" with a prosaic, limited vision of instrumental "partnership," see Clarke E. Cochran, "The Politics of Interest: Philosophy and the Limitations of a Science of Politics," *American Journal of Political Science* 25(4) (1973): 745–66.

regarding interests can have high-level consequences for the governability of advanced industrial/capitalist polities. Arguments are also proffered that pluralism is *not* the likely form that interest intermediation will take in these polities, and moreover that where it has been most prevalent it has had an effect on governability contrary to that presumed by its leading theorists and ideologues.

The "Mode" of Interest Intermediation and the Problem of Governability

The principal orienting hypothesis of this chapter is simple: *The relative governability of contemporary, highly industrialized, advanced capitalist polities is less a function of aggregate overload, of "imbalance" between the sum total of societal demands and state capabilities, than of the discrete processes that identify, package, promote, and implement potential interest claims and commands.* In an aggregate sense, there has always been more of a demand for imperative coordination and authoritative allocation than the state was capable of supplying, and the "gap" was (and still is) filled by physical repression and symbolic manipulation. . . .

What have changed extensively and irreversibly are the processes of political intermediation by which the potential volume of societal demands is captured and focused and through which the eventual pattern of public policies is evaluated and sifted. To an extent this has been recognized in the literature on ungovernability and overload, but the emphasis has always been placed on the party, legislative, and cabinet nexus. . . .

My . . . hunch . . . is that although those who have emphasized the confusion and decline in party and parliament focus correctly on the distinctly *political* processes of intermediation, they have mistaken the symptoms for the disease. The key to understanding the various crises of governability lies in the dimly lit arena of func-

tional interest intermediation through highly formalized and specialized organizations in direct relation with the bureaucratic apparatus of the modern state. The collapse of new social contracts; the burgeoning demand for guaranteed and privileged access; the clash of representative jurisdictions; the quest for authenticity and participation at all levels of authority, private as well as public; the mobilization and militancy of previously quiescent groups such as civil servants and public dependents; the clamor for and revolt against raising state expenditures and governmental regulation; the increasing sensitivity to relative deprivation and inequalities within as well as between social classes; the explosion of subnational ethnicity; the sudden emergence of single-issue movements, not to mention the principal defining characteristics of (un)governability (to be discussed *infra*): (1) the tendency to resort to unprecedented, extralegal means of political expression; (2) the dwindling of elite cohesion and hegemony; and (3) the diminished capacity of the state to secure resources and implement policies—most, if not all, of these find their expression in and irresolution through the structures of specialized intermediation for class, sectoral, professional, regional, ethnic, sexual, and generational interests. It is not parties and elections that bring most of these problems, dilemmas, or contradictions to the agenda of the state, although they may be indirectly affected by them. Individual partisan allegiance and the territorial clustering of notables, those two pillars of the liberal democratic, civic-cultured, bourgeois-dominant political order, have been gradually but firmly overtaken by the third, heretofore less prominent, aspect of that mode of domination: the implacable pursuit of self-interest, rightly and rationally understood, through specialized, functionally differentiated organizations. . . .

Now we are in a position to make our second hunch more explicit. The key to differing degrees of governability lies less in the "objective" magnitudes of macroeconomic performance, social cleavages, and class relations than in the way differentiated interests are "intermediated" between civil society and the state. Our discussion has suggested the specific empirical dimensions relevant to the explanation of differences in outcome: representational coverage, membership density, and corporatist structure. *Polities in which interests are processed through formal associations that cover the widest variety of potential interests with national networks of representation, that have the highest proportion of those potentially affected as members, and whose pattern of interaction with the state is monopolistic, specialized, hierarchical, and mutually collusive should be more orderly, stable, and effective,* at least in the short run, given the conditions of contemporary governance. Put a different way, those countries previously "fortunate" enough to have developed a pluralist mode of interest intermediation with its multiple, overlapping, spontaneously formed, voluntaristically supported, easily abandoned, and politically autonomous associations, are likely to find it a serious impediment to governability in the postliberal, advanced, capitalist state....

The use of the concept of "corporatism" by other authors ... and the even more varied uses to which it has been put elsewhere[8] makes it

necessary to spell out the definition used here and its operational limitations. First and foremost, "societal corporatism" does not refer to any historically specific ideology, world view, political culture, or even any set of collective aspirations.[9] ... Societal corporatism as used here is located in the realm of institutional behavior, not that of individual values or collective aspirations.

Second, it refers to a mode of arranging the political process, indeed, structuring part of the political process. It is not a way of organizing all of society or running the economy. Societal corporatism is "compatible" with a wide range of social institutions and is not an "alternative" to capitalist exploitation but, at least in some countries, an integral part of it.

The part of the political process to which societal corporatism refers I have called "interest intermediation." It encompasses both the means through which interests are transferred from, aggregated over, and articulated for members to collective decision-making bodies, public or private (*representation*), and the ways in which interests are taught to, transmitted to, and imposed on members by associations (*social control*). The concept "intermediation" is also meant to convey the likelihood that interests may be generated from within formal associations themselves, independent of member preferences and authoritative commands....

Governability, or better, its inverse, ungovernability, would seem, from the literature on Western Europe and North America, to be composed of three general properties:[18] (1) *un-*

---

8. The literature on corporatism in advanced industrial/capitalist societies has grown enormously in recent years. A compilation of most of the more important theoretical pieces will be appearing shortly in P. Schmitter and G. Lehmbruch (eds.), *Trends Toward Corporatist Intermediation* (London: Sage Publications). For a critical summary of this literature and its dissection into divergent "schools," see Leo Panitch, "Recent Theorizations of Corporatism: Reflections on a Growth Industry," paper presented at ISA World Congress, Panel on Interest Intermediation and Corporatism, Uppsala, August 14–9, 1978, and Kevin Bonnett, "Corporatist Developments in Advanced Capitalist Society: Competing Theoretical Perspectives," paper presented at the SSRC (Great Britain) Conference on Institutionalisation, University of Sussex, September 8–11, 1978.

---

9. For a brief discussion of the extraordinary ideological diversity of those who have historically and contemporarily advocated something called or resembling corporatism, see P. Schmitter, "Still the Century of Corporatism?" [*Review of Politics* 36(1) (1974): 85–131,] pp. 87–9.

18. Actually, the American literature either tends to stress or is criticized for ignoring yet a fourth dimension: *unlawfulness* or efforts by high-level corporate

ruliness or citizen-initiated efforts to influence public choices in violent, illegal, or unprecedented ways; (2) *unstableness* or the failure of efforts by elite political actors to retain their positions of dominance or to reproduce preexisting coalitional arrangements; (3) *ineffectiveness* or the decline in the capacity of public executives or administrators to secure compliance with or to attain desired collective goals through the imperative coordinations or authoritative allocations of the state.....

Interest Promotion and Partisan Mobilization as Possible Causes of (Un)governability

Having identified ... three dimensions of (un)governability ... we can now turn to interest intermediation for a possible rival explanation. Two aspects of the pursuit of self-regarding goals have attracted our attention. One is quantitative: Are the polities of Western Europe and North America less ruly, stable, and effective simply because everyone is finally getting organized? The other is qualitative: Does the form that intermediation has taken historically determine the relative governability of these polities today? The first we have measured by the density of membership in working-class associations; the latter by a rank-ordered indicator of corporatist features in national labor peak associations.

The statistical measures (Spearman's rank-order coefficients) ... provide a rather clear answer to both the general question of the importance of interest intermediation for regime governability and the more specific question of which aspect of the pursuit of interests— quantity or quality—is more relevant to understanding macrolevel ruliness, stableness, and effectiveness. The coordinal relationship between the indicator of societal corporatism and that of citizen unruliness (-0.73) is the most significant we have yet observed. The fit is so close that relatively few deviant cases arise to challenge our finding.... The correlation with fiscal ineffectiveness (-0.63) is also highly significant. Again, we find it impossible to predict the rank ordering of governmental unstableness. Perhaps this is yet another indication that it is simply not part of the contemporary governability–ungovernability syndrome or that, if it is, our operationalization is defective. Density of membership was not impressively related to any of the three dimensions. What seems to count is not *whether* everyone is getting organized for the pursuit of specialized class and sectoral self-interest but *how* they are doing so.

One is tempted to exclaim "Eureka!" at this point and rest the analysis. Given the likely measurement error and the crudeness of the statistical instrument, it is doubtful that any rank-order correlation between independent variables could top 0.73 without being a tautological or spurious measure of the same underlying phenomenon. We might, therefore, conclude with the counterintuitive finding that (*pace* Madison) corporatism, not pluralism, is the best formula "to break and control the violence of faction" in the post-liberal, advanced-capitalist polity. Rather than proliferating the "number of citizens" and the "sphere of interests," the modern conservative ruler concerned with governability would diminish their number, encourage their centralization and concentration of authority, grant them privileged monopolistic access, and, above all, extend the sphere of governance by licensing or devolving upon them powers to take decisions binding on their members and even on nonmembers. In this way, "responsible," private governments can collaborate in controlling citizen-initiated protest and in ensuring proper fiscal discipline and management. The direct burden on the state is lightened, and the resulting policy

---

power holders, public or private, to escape legal and constitutional constraints in their pursuit of advantage and survival. Euro-centric treatments may occasionally mention leadership incompetence, but rarely dishonesty or illegality as part of the ungovernability syndrome.

outputs are made a good deal less visible. On the other side, the relative autonomy of these associations is respected, so that periodic withdrawals from collusion with those in power is tolerated when the disparity between ruling imperatives, organizational goals, and member interests becomes too great and threatens to provoke direct action by the grass roots or to spill over into the electoral arena. Interest associations, and not just political parties, can take a *cure d'opposition*.[23]

Ruling elites in many of the more troubled Western European and North American polities seem to have arrived at the same conclusion as we have in this chapter: In advanced capitalist, highly industrialized societies, there is a strong positive relationship between a societal corporatist mode of interest intermediation and relative governability (or at least citizen ruliness and fiscal effectiveness)....

Much of the resistance to corporatization comes from existing interest associations that prize their organizational autonomy and defend their traditionally pluralistic ways of operating. In fact, previous efforts in imposing a solution from above were accompanied by the severe repression of such associations, especially those representing the working class, and the establishment of a wide range of other authoritarian practices—*vide* Fascist Italy or Franco Spain. Where, however, this mode of interest intermediation evolved gradually and voluntarily within a liberal democratic regime, it depended on concordant and supportive changes in a second realm of formal intermediation between civil society and the state—partisan mobilization.

The most obvious supportive change in the party system was the emergence and eventual participation in power of reformist Social Democratic or Labour parties.[25] Although they did not often stress corporatism at the ideological level—if only because their Catholic or conservative opponents had often preempted the idea—their own internal organizational relationship with the trade-union movement certainly resembled it, and their acceptance of a "responsible" promotion of working-class interests within the framework of capitalism definitely was a prerequisite for its eventual success....

... [A]nother dimension of partisan mobilization may be of even greater importance than Social Democratic predominance.... [O]ne can roughly estimate the predictability of individual voting preferences from knowledge of that individual's occupation, religion, and regional location. The aggregate predictive capacity of these three potential cleavage dimensions varies enormously.... [B]ut what seems to be most significantly associated with "governable" macro-outcomes is the predictability produced by some combination of all three—the extent to which the voter's individual partisan choice is firmly "locked into" the basic elements of differentiation in the society, regardless of which of those elements is performing the task.

These additional findings strengthen considerably the credibility of our earlier hypothesis that the relative governability of Western European and North American polities is more affected by the qualitative nature of their systems of intermediation than by the quantitative magnitude of the economic and social problems they face. The mode of organization of and control over function- and issue-specific interests emerges as most significant, but its role is contingent on two major coordinant developments in the mode of

---

23. The instability of such corporatist arrangements is stressed in Birgitta Nedelmann and Kurt G. Meier, "Theories of Contemporary Corporatism: Static or Dynamic," *Comparative Political Studies* 10(1) (April 1975): 39–60. Also, the article by Gerhard Lehmbruch in the same special issue entitled "Liberal Corporatism and Party Government," pp. 91–126, deals with voluntary, tactical *cures d'opposition* taken by corporatist actors.

---

25. Leo Panitch is largely responsible for my seeing the "Social Democratic connection." "The Development of Corporatism in Liberal Democracies," *Comparative Political Studies* 10(1) (1977): 61–90.

partisan articulation: its relative domination by Social Democratic-type parties and its predictable rootedness in the cleavage structure of the society. It is, of course, not clear from these cross-sectionally associated outcomes whether, as Stein Rokkan has suggested, the functional "second tier" of corporatist intermediation was created out of an elite *reaction against* the emergence of Social Democracy in the "primary tier" of territorial representation,[26] or whether it emerged as a direct *product* of the efforts of Social Democrats at integrating themselves within the structures of the capitalist economy and liberal polity.[27] ...

Societal corporatism and the "locking in" of voter preferences to the cleavage structure do not appear to be parts of a tightly related historical process. It could be argued that they represent independent efforts to organize networks of intermediation between civil society and the state—the one focusing on functional, especially occupational and sectoral interests; the other appealing more to territorial, religious, and cultural interests, with class as the crucial area for their competition and/or cooperation. When, however, they combine through highly predictable patterns of party identification and highly specialized patterns of monopolistic representation and social control, the relative ruliness and effectiveness of the outcome is impressive. This speculative finding seems diametrically contrary to pluralist orthodoxy, which identifies "political stability" (the lexical forerunner of "governability") with moderate, broadly aggregative, sociologically diverse, and weakly structured political parties, and with voluntaristic, multiple, overlapping, and autonomous interest associations. From our data manipulations, this emerges almost as a formula for trouble in the highly industrialized, advanced-capitalist, post-

liberal polities of Western Europe and North America.

Instead of a Conclusion

The foregoing empirically grounded conclusions about the relevance of intermediation processes, especially societal corporatism, for contemporary governability seem compelling. They may even lead some to the comforting thought that the problems, dilemmas, and contradictions of the status quo do not have to be resolved. It might seem that ruling elites have only to tinker with their systems of partisan and interest intermediation to dissipate their current troubles. If this should be the lesson they draw (and there is considerable evidence many have), they are destined to be disappointed. Not only are such institutional networks the product of very lengthy and complex historical forces but they are also subject to strong emergent organizational properties that guide their development and insulate them from ameliorative meddlings from above. Previous attempts at molding interest and partisan intermediation systems to "fit" the needs of the mode of political domination and the exigencies of economic exploitation have had to involve much more than mere tinkering. Even where societies have protractedly suffered through the repression necessary to impose such comprehensive state corporatist "solutions," dominant classes have only managed to buy time and accumulate tensions, as in contemporary Spain and Portugal.

However compelling, the conclusions reached in this chapter are time contingent. They refer to a rather narrow period, roughly the 1960s through the early 1970s. ...

Those polities that did acquire highly centralized, monopolistic interest associations and well-structured, "pillared" political parties and which, therefore, were better able to negotiate voluntaristically and to enforce effectively a series of collaborative policy arrangements and

---

26. *Citizens, Elections, Parties* (New York: David McKay, 1970), pp. 40–3.

27. Something like this seems to be implied by Leo Panitch, op. cit.

crisis-induced pacts are, indeed, beginning to show strains. That delicate combination of ruling imperatives, organizational goals, and member interests that lies at the heart of the corporatist effort has been called increasingly into question. The decline of public, that is, system-wide, deliberative processes, the segmentation of policy into discrete functional compartments, and the inequity produced by mutually supportive deals among organizationally privileged minorities have led to a revived concern with "the public interest." The legitimacy of leaders protected within highly oligarchic and professionalized interest associations from direct contact with and accountability to members has diminished, as has the willingness of members to comply with the constraints of private governments. The overaggregation of interests through peak associations has left un- or underrepresented certain emergent, more specialized groups, just as their close collusion with power has made the exclusion of diffuse, dispersed, underorganized categories more obvious and less bearable. The demand for personal authenticity and democratic participation on the part of individuals has grown at the expense of mere role satisfaction and vicariously obtained advantage. New "style and quality" issues have emerged, cutting across established functional hierarchies and resulting in numerous single-issue movements and spontaneous protest actions. Awareness that inflation is the real hiding hand equilibrating outcomes and invisibly determining the distribution of benefits has upset many a carefully negotiated social contract or sectoral arrangement. All this points to an uncertain future for today's "corporatist successes."

The sources of contradiction/dilemma inherent in this scheme are multiple and of unequal importance. Generically, they can be reduced to four types, depending on (1) whether the institutional locus of emerging difficulty comes from within the universe of interest associations or from other organizations, such as political parties and social movements, and (2) whether

the substantive issues at stake involve an exacerbation or rupture within existing problem content, or a shift in the definition of actor interest to some new domain of concern....

For most convinced liberals or pluralists, the principal difficulty of societal corporatism lies in the internal political process of interest associations. Their stress on professionalized representation by experts, long-term calculations of interest, high-level aggregation of demands, and official recognition of status, on the one hand, and their practices of oligarchic co-optation, centralized organization, bureaucratized exchanges, and interdependence with public authority, on the other, make these associations vulnerable to member dissatisfaction. The most common type of challenge, according to this perspective, comes from "rank-and-file revolts": wildcat strikes, internal factionalism, organizational splits, "voting with one's feet," ideological gambits, accusations of traitorous behavior, and so on—all in the name of authenticity in representation and democracy in procedure.

Without denying this latent threat or the occasional presence of some of these phenomena in even the most established and accomplished of societal corporatist arrangements, such revolts are not, in my view, capable of countermanding the trend. They may cause collaborative associations to take a *cure d'opposition* by withdrawing from corporatist practices for a period of time; they may even compel some associations to engage in imprudent tactics of confrontation and intransigence—especially where the revolt is backed by accountability to some extra-associational political process, such as *Mitbestimmung* or *élections sociales*—but normally these revolts are easy to encapsulate or even exploit for corporatist ends. It is not just that association leaders have at their disposition that arsenal of incumbency resources that Michels and his successors have so extensively documented but that this pluralist view ignores the extent to which the modern interest association has become more and more a service agency and less and less a focus of political aspiration or personal identity. The member pays a fee for services performed (and increasingly does so involuntarily) and demands in return some measure of efficiency and effectiveness in their performance. To the extent that he or she aspires to fellowship, authenticity, participation, self-expression, and so forth, the political party or social movement offers a much more attractive outlet for such passions and moral imperatives.

It is this tendency for the contradictions of corporatism to spill over into wider arenas of public choice and forms of political mobilization—while remaining basically within the nexus of class, sectoral, and professional interests—that is stressed by Marxist critics of the trend. Because societal corporatism is but a superstructural rearrangement of institutions that cannot dissolve the class-based, structural contradictions of capitalism (not to mention accomplish the lesser task of resolving sectoral clashes and professional disputes), they argue it must ultimately fail. It may succeed in the short run in making ad hoc adjustments and generating crisis-induced palliatives, but these are bound to accumulate, to produce further policy irrationalities, and to establish greater rigidities in the system. These may even contribute to the system's demise. Although the proponents of this view of corporatism often point to the same "rank-and-file" events as the pluralists, they stress the extent to which these go beyond the limited agenda of specialized interests, personal moral sentiments, and/or formal democratic aspirations, and serve to mobilize a broad class consciousness and activity across a wider variety of intermediary institutions: political parties, social movements, intellectual currents, and so forth.

Although this approach to the contradictions of corporatism is more sensitive to the changing nature of modern interest associations, it frequently overestimates the evidence for class mobilization and underestimates the barriers to it, thus indulging in a great deal of *ex ante* wishful

thinking and *ex post* retractions. If the institutions and practices of societal corporatism, by and large forged during the post-World War II boom years, manage to survive the present general crisis of capitalism (and even to do so at less cost to subordinate classes in terms of job security, real wages, and social benefits), then some revision of the class-mobilization scenario of its demise will definitely be in order.

A third source of contradiction and type of response suggests that corporatism will be threatened by the emergence of new substantive interests or by a shift in the salience of older, previously subordinate, interests. These should provide the basis for a new wave of aggressive associability that will seek access to the established corporatist arrangement. According to this perspective, societal corporatism has succeeded so far largely because it has been partial. It has involved primarily or exclusively those interests generated by the economic division of labor in society—classes, sectors, and professions for short. This has permitted these better-organized, collaborative actors to pass on the costs of their mutually self-serving agreements to the un- or underorganized. If the latter interests, for example, tenants, renters, pensioners, pedestrians, taxpayers, foreigners, workers, automobile drivers, students, sufferers from pollution, payers of insurance premiums, television watchers, welfare recipients, hospital patients, all "policy takers" (to use an appropriate phrase from Claus Offe's chapter) were to create singular, monopolistic, hierarchically structured, officially sanctioned associations, previous externalities would become internalized within the system of organized interest politics and make decisions vastly more difficult. Also, some of the new or more recently salient criteria of differentiation/exploitation—ethnic identity, regional location, religion, sex, age, language, and so on—might cut across existing functional categories or, where they did not, infuse them with renewed passion or ideological fervor. Either shift could seriously jeopardize the stable organizational base, the long-term interest definition, and the predictable contractual capacity of corporatist intermediaries.

The problem with this scenario is that in order for dispersed "entitled" interests, oriented almost exclusively around the provision of public goods, to obtain sufficient resources and access, they must depend on the sponsorship and connivance of public authorities. Their corporatization is less likely to be "societal" than "state" in inspiration, and this raises the question of *why* those in formal power would take such an initiative or *whether* they would be permitted to do so by vested established interests already sharing the benefits of privileged access. In the event that the source of new interest or salience lies in the "cultural division of labor,"[29] the resultant need to mobilize identities around broad ideological goals should make corporatization insufficient. Mere specialized participation in a complex set of policy compromises and services is no adequate substitute for having one's own state or dominating the whole political process.

This brings us to the fourth type of contradiction in which those new status, style, and identity issues cannot be contained within the bounds of "mere" interest intermediation and spill over into other forms of collective political activity. These range from public interest lobbies to spontaneous protests, "green" parties, and successionist movements. Their broader goals, greater intensities, unconventional tactics, and crosscutting differentiations would both weaken existing corporatist associations and shift the attention of the entire political process away from the issues and tactics the latter are most capable of handling. Whether this would be sufficient to dissolve existing corporatist arrangements or to arrest further movement in that direction depends ultimately on if the emergent cultural identities, status sensitivities, situs calculations,

territorial loyalties, and/or qualitative demands prove to be permanent. Are they capable of displacing over a protracted period the "functional" cleavages inherent in capitalist property relations and the industrial division of labor? Some may turn out to be ephemeral, especially in conditions of renewed scarcity. Others may be successfully accommodated through symbolic concessions, territorial readjustments, partisan restructuring, and so forth. If so, the apparent shifts in content, despite their raucousness and occasional attention-gathering capability, are not likely to be successful in countervailing the trend toward societal corporatism. At most, they might delay its emergence for a while, or keep it confined to a narrower range of policy arenas.[30]

All the sources of contradiction discussed briefly here originate within civil society, that is, in the economic, social, and cultural division of labor. An alternative possibility, not usually entertained by students of corporatism, is that problems might arise from within the political order itself, which could limit the spread or encourage the dissolution of such arrangements. Instead of just facilitating the management of the state, they could eventually threaten the status and resources of public authorities and party politicians and introduce additional rigidities and irrationalities into public policy making. State bureaucrats might find that devolution of authority to corporatist intermediaries deprives them of their unique status and of important instruments for resolving broader public issues and intersectoral conflicts. Professional politicians are likely to resist the progressive short-circuiting of party channels, territorial

29. Michael Hechter, "Group Formation and the Cultural Divisions of Labor," *American Journal of Sociology* [84(2) (1978): 293–318].

30. Cf. a recent essay by Robert Salisbury, where the continued strength of constituency is regarded as a fundamental element inhibiting the emergence of societal corporatism in the United States—along with other factors. "On Centrifugal Tendencies in Interest Systems: The Case of the United States," paper presented at the ISA World Congress, Panel on Interest Intermediation and Corporatism, Uppsala, August 14–9, 1978.

constituencies, and legislative processes. To the extent these dilemmas become important, the result is less likely to be renewed militancy, ideological mobilization, or new collective struggles than a legalistic reform effort to preserve the "sanctity" and "distinctiveness" of state/public institutions and to regulate the activities and resources of interest associations.[31]

All these potential sources of difficulty for the future of societal corporatism, and for the relative governability that has accompanied it, can be discerned, to differing degrees, in the contemporary politics of advanced industrial/capitalist societies. Corporatism's very success at keeping political life ruly and effective has been purchased at the price of organizational sclerosis, rigidification of differentials, perpetuation of inequalities, and, most of all, disregard for the individualistic norms of citizen participation and accountability characteristic of a liberal democratic order. How long this form of corporatism can continue in its pragmatic manner to produce such negative behavioral effects and to ignore such fundamental normative aspirations, without resort to coercion, is questionable. Just as it has proved hard to "tone down" established pluralist structures unsuccessful in dealing with existing problems, so it may be difficult to "tune up" previously successful corporatist ones to meet emerging issues.

---

31. Here the recent discussion of a *Verbändegesetz* in Western Germany is a case in point....

Inside Campaign Finance: Myths and Realities

Frank J. Sorauf

The question of motive haunts every campaign finance system relying on voluntary contributions. *Why* do they give? When a disclosure system discloses as much as the American one does about a visible set of organized givers representing society's major interests, the question rises to a salience that campaign finance rarely achieves. The answer to it is beyond dispute; they give to influence governmental decisions. The hard questions come next: the nature of the influence the contributors seek, the ways they go about seeking it, and the extent to which they achieve it.

The debate over the purchase of legislatures is not about generic contributors. It is about PAC contributors, whether they appear explicitly or are merely implied in such phrases as "the best Congress money can buy." Their splendid visibility as the organizations of the "special interests" links them and their contributions to the ongoing, century-long debates over the three-way alliance of money, organization, and interest in American politics. Now that PACs increasingly give to secure legislative access, a strategy in which their ties both to incumbents and to lobbyists are closer, they underscore all of the old concerns. We no longer talk of PAC attempts to penetrate electoral politics but of their part in the traditional struggle of interests in American legislatures. Almost imperceptibly, but fundamentally, the debate has shifted from influence in election outcomes to influence over legislative outcomes.

Thanks to the reporting and publicity the FECA forced on candidates, PACs, and parties, the FEC oversees the largest data archive on any system of campaign finance anywhere in the world. Its

data are easily accessible, and the "law of available data" has led to a flowering of research on them, both by the scholarly community and by journalists and public-interest organizations. Their industriousness has produced works of many genres, but one of the most common—a veritable industry in itself—is the exploration of the PAC-Congress nexus. The variants on the theme, too, are recognizable: the largest PAC contributors to congressional candidates over a cycle or a decade, the major recipients of PAC money in the Congress, the contributions from PACs of one industry to the members of one committee or to supporters of a particular bill or cause, the mounting flow of PAC money from one sector of the economy as its interests are threatened or challenged. Often the investigations have a current stimulus; they are the campaign finance angle on the broader story, say, of the savings-and-loan crisis, the rewriting of the federal tax code, or the attempt to pass the Brady bill's restrictions on the sale of handguns.

Such reports share one limiting defect: they establish correlation, not cause. Yes, PACs do largely give money to candidates who will vote the way they want them to; it would be surprising if that were not the case. Contributors contribute to like-minded candidates, just as voters vote for like-minded candidates. That relationship is easy to document, but the harder question remains: do PACs contribute to candidates because they know how they will vote, or do legislators conform to the wishes of PACs that gave money to their campaigns? Does the money follow the votes, or do the votes follow the money? It is a problem in simultaneous cause, cause that seems to move both ways between one act and another. Any analysis of campaign finance is repeatedly bedeviled by such problems....

Academic scholars, for their part, attack the same questions in more systematic ways. They cannot, however, escape the need to establish

Excerpted from: Frank J. Sorauf, *Inside Campaign Finance: Myths and Realities.* New Haven: Yale University Press, 1992. © Yale University Press. Reprinted by permission.

correlations and to infer cause from them, nor can they escape the problem of simultaneity in doing so. Using larger bodies of data—large numbers of roll-call votes, for instance—and more sophisticated measures of correlation, they generally find little if any relationship between the money and the votes....

How does one explain the gap between popular knowledge and academic conclusion? In part it results from the usual popular overestimation of PAC will and capacity. PACs themselves are more realistic about their bargaining position with incumbents than is the general public. They say over and over that they want to support like-minded men and women in public office and that they seek only "access" to legislators, an opportunity to persuade or make a case. Organizationally they are not adapted to greater political ambitions than that, and they have come slowly to realize it....

Such conclusions run counter to the conventional wisdom, and like most academic writing on campaign finance, they fail to disturb or dislodge it. The supporters of the conventional wisdom are tireless, and they have a platform. They also have telling testimony from members of Congress that PACs do indeed change votes—always the votes of other members—with their contributions....

The common sense of the word *access* also makes the case for the conventional wisdom. If access is indeed the goal of PAC contributions, will PACs settle merely for the "opportunity to persuade"? Won't they expect success in a certain number of instances? Will they be satisfied with an invitation to the gaming table if they lose every spin of the wheel? Moreover, the nature of influence in a legislative body involves much more than final roll-call votes. PACs exert influence at other points in the legislative process—in initiatives not taken, in committee amendments, or in special rules affecting floor consideration. Some academic political scientists, one should add, have long shared reservations about an exclusive reliance on roll calls....

Political scientists Richard Hall and Frank Wayman begin the report of their research on PAC money and House committees by reconstructing the logic of what PACs seek with their contributions.... Hall and Wayman focus ... on three House committees and three different issues before them—and on the effects of PAC contributions to members of the committees. Instead of using votes in committee as the dependent variable, Hall and Wayman construct a measure of various kinds of participation in the business of committees (such as speaking in committee or offering amendments during markup). In each of the three cases they found that PAC contributions had a moderate but significant degree of influence, explaining more than 55 percent of the variance in participation by individual members. PAC money, therefore, mobilized already like-thinking members to more active support of the PACs' interests in committee....

... Regardless of why the PACs give, they seem to get heightened activity and support from their congressional sympathizers. We are left, however, to speculate about the ultimate results of such support and activity on congressional decisions.

A consensus about PAC influence is emerging among scholars of campaign finance. It is founded on two central conclusions. First, the influence of PAC contributions tends to be strongest on the narrower, less visible issues before the Congress. Members have long called them "free votes," free in that they are liberated from the usually dominant influences of party, district, leadership, and mass opinion. These are the votes available for less influential constituencies (such as contributors) or even for classic legislative log-rolling or horse-trading. Second, the influence of contributions can be directed at all the points of access and influence in the legislative process in the Congress. The kinds of policy refinements and strategic maneuvers crafted in committee may be important for specific interests even though they do not involve great issues of policy. The same can be said of many appointments to the courts and to executive agencies. Contributors do not necessarily seek, or even expect, to score impressive policy victories measured by final roll-call votes. In the world of reduced expectations in which PACs are forced to live, the smaller accomplishments have to suffice.

The Hall and Wayman findings narrow the gulf between the academy and conventional wisdom, but the gulf remains. In part it results from major disagreements about evidence and authority, about the credibility of participants and observers in the Congress versus the data-based analyses of scholars, and about fundamental questions of what evidence it takes to come to conclusions. In essence, the gulf reflects different wills to believe. Some scholarship, to be sure, but even more journalistic analysis, begins with deeply set convictions, rooted in the Progressive worldview, about the impact of money on public officials. The line between dispositions to believe and foregone conclusions is very thin.

Most durable are the differences across the gulf on analytical issues. One concerns the credibility of the testimony of participants, and even the weight their words carry vis-à-vis the detailed data of the scholars. . . .

. . . The danger of granting authority status to participants—contributors or recipients—is that authority is conferred even on clearly self-serving conclusions merely because the authority's message is useful or congenial.

Beneath the controversies over the conventional wisdoms, there are also great differences over who carries the burden of proof. Scholars will not readily consent to demands that they accept responsibility for proving or disproving an assertion they do not make: the one about PACs' buying influence over the making of policy. Nor will they concede that any assertion is valid until it is disproven. Ultimately, however, the debate comes down to the kinds and weight of evidence that will establish the tie between

money and votes or other activity in the Congress. One of the greatest strengths of any conventional wisdom is that by definition it is validated by the sheer number of people who subscribe to it. Such validation does not yield easily to the desiccated numbers and equations of empirical social science.

The conventional wisdom is vulnerable also for its assumption that PACs dominate the exchange between contributor and candidate—an analytical predisposition that comes out of the late 1970s. But we now have abundant evidence that the exchange is bilateral rather than unilateral, that candidates have leverage in it, and that the incumbents among them increased that leverage in the 1980s as their reelection rates soared. As PACs have shifted more and more to the support of incumbents, and to the search for access to them, their freedom of action has diminished. Whereas incumbents have organized with increasing effectiveness, PACs have not. Nor have they maintained their ability to enforce expectations. PAC sanctions depend on the value of withdrawn contributions, and since PACs have continued to disperse their contributions widely, the average PAC contribution amounts to well less than one-half of 1 percent of the average House incumbent's receipts in an electoral cycle. Even a major contribution of $5,000 or more accounts for only a few percent of the average candidate's receipts. Consequently, the PAC position in the 1990s is not what it was in the 1970s.

Finally, the countervailing controls of American pluralism constrain even the most determined PACs. Organizations of interests have greatly proliferated since the 1970s. The larger the number of groups (that is, PACs), the greater the offsetting and limiting effect on the political claims of any one of them. The greater the number of PACs making contributions to a specific member of Congress, the greater the likelihood that the claims of one on his or her loyalties will be opposed by the claims of another. . . .

A caveat to that conclusion is, however, in order. The mechanism of offsetting, countervailing group activity probably best fits policy disputes over the larger issues that are part of broader ideological positions—over issues such as medicaid funding or hazardous waste disposal. The model works less well when the dispute is single-sided, where the activity of one set of interests does not jolt another set of interests, perhaps those of consumers, into action. The nonresponding interests may be too general, too invisible, or of too low a priority to warrant political action. So, the hypothesis of countervailing interests meshes well with the conclusion that PACs have their greatest impact on the less visible politics of narrow and particularistic interests in which the conflicts, and thus the controls, of pluralism are not joined. . . .

That an increasingly national "contributor constituency" has entered American electoral politics seems beyond contest. Electoral politics remain local because the constituencies are geographically defined with only one representative and two senators per constituency and because the American political parties have been decentralized and local. Now PACs and other representatives of national interests find a small but measurable additional edge in electoral politics. They increasingly ally themselves with the lobbying of the interests they share, and it becomes increasingly difficult to say whether their victories come through contributing or lobbying. It is far easier to say simply that contributions have become one more limited means among many in the pursuit of policy goals—and one more piece of evidence that the localism of American electoral politics is increasingly anomalous. Campaign finance serves as a shaper of national politics as well as one of its consequences . . .

. . . It is precisely on the maldistribution of campaign money, especially the paucity of it in the hands of challengers, that the second great argument of the post-1974 regime centers. After the alleged buying of the Congress, it is the alleged buying of the elections to the Congress that most worries Americans. Many of them are convinced that incumbents are winning reelection at such stunning rates precisely because the incumbents have too much money and their challengers have too little.

The facts are undeniable. Challenger financing has deteriorated in the 1980s by all measures. . . .

. . . General-election challengers found it increasingly difficult to raise money from PACs; PACs gave them 25.8 percent of their contributions to House candidates in 1980, but only 6.7 percent in 1990. House challengers, in fact, became increasingly dependent on their own resources. . . .

For mass opinion and its shapers, such data lead to an easy conclusion. Incumbents win so often because they outspend their opponents so greatly, and challengers fail to win because they lack the resources with which to mount a winning campaign. For the scholarly community the conclusion does not come as easily, for once again they see a problem in simultaneous cause. Do candidates win because they spend more money, or do they get more money, and spend it, because they are likely to win? The structure of the causal problem is much like the problem of simultaneous cause in PAC contributions and policy outcomes in the Congress: Is the financial contribution made because of expectations about the recipient's victory some months hence, or does the contribution actually buy the campaigning that shapes the election outcome? That is, do underfunded candidates fail because contributors think their fate is sealed months before election day?

The other side of the argument is equally straightforward: challengers lose because they cannot spend enough. It is a fact not only that challengers in the aggregate fail to raise and spend the sums incumbents do, but also that the challengers who spend the most collectively win the greater share of the two-party vote. The percentage of challengers' general-election vote rises

Table 7.1

Relationship between challenger spending and challenger vote share: 1984–1988*

Challenger: Incumbent spending ratios	Median general election vote (%)		
	1984	1986	1988
Up to 1:3	28	27	27
1:3 to 1:2	36	35	37
1:2 to 1:1	43	41	40
1:1 to 2:1	45	38	43
More than 2:1	46	41	39
Challenger total spending ranges	1984	1986	1988
Up to $5,000	24	23	24
$5,000 to $25,000	27	26	26
$25,000 to $75,000	32	30	29
$75,000 to $250,000	38	35	36
More than $250,000	45	43	42

*Includes only major-party, general-election House challengers running against an incumbent in the general election.
Source: Federal Election Commission.

as they narrow the incumbent-challenger spending ratio or as they increase their dollar spending in the campaign (table 7.1).

Before one leaps to the conclusion that incumbents win and challengers lose because of the state of their campaign resources, there are contrary bits of data to reckon with. House incumbents won reelection at rates well above 90 percent long before they established their present funding superiority; the cumulative reelection percentage of House incumbents from 1950 through 1970 was 91.8 percent.[16] Furthermore, the general political strength of incumbents can

easily be traced, not to their campaign treasuries, but to all of the advantages of office they enjoy. The postal frank, their easy access to the media, their district offices, and their staffs for "servicing" constituents all have grown in recent decades, at least partly to buttress their reelection chances.[17] Less obviously, perhaps, the growing difference between the receipts and the expenditures of incumbents—their larger sums of cash on hand—suggests that contributors give to them not to help them win but because they are going to win, a conviction that accounts for the PACs' having reduced their support of challengers. But all of these clues aside, the major attack on this problem in simultaneity has come in the scholarly work of Gary Jacobson.

The problem is easily defined. The percentage of the vote the challengers get is related to the sums they spend; the greater the dollars, the greater the votes. Money and votes are reciprocally related, however, because challengers raise money on expectations about their ability to get votes. So, how to show that the spending of challengers actually does affect the size of the vote they get? One way is through the same two-stage least-squares procedures Janet Grenzke used to stipulate the direction of cause in the similar problem of the correlation between PAC contributions and the roll-call votes of their recipients in Congress. A second is to use poll data to relate incremental changes in spending to incremental changes in probable vote stage by stage during the campaign. Both avenues brought Jacobson to the conclusion that challenger spending did indeed lead to increases in challenger votes.[18]

16. That is, 4064 of 4428 incumbents seeking reelection were successful. Data from Norman J. Ornstein, Thomas E. Mann, and Michael J. Malbin, *Vital Statistics on Congress, 1989–1990* (Washington: Congressional Quarterly, 1990), p. 56.

17. Generally on the use of congressional perquisites for developing constituent support, see Morris A. Fiorina, *Congress: Keystone of the Washington Establishment* (New Haven: Yale University Press, 1977).

18. Gary C. Jacobson, *Money in Congressional Elections* (New Haven: Yale University Press, 1980). See also Jacobson's restatement and reconsideration in "Money and Votes Reconsidered: Congressional Elections, 1972–1982," *Public Choice* 47 (1985), pp. 7–62.

The dynamic that relates challenger money to challenger votes can then be outlined. Spending money in the campaign buys visibility and greater "likely support" for challengers, which also means that spending results in the rising expectations that enables them to raise even more money.... The problem, therefore, is that although money *would* help them greatly, challengers have increasing trouble in raising it in the first place.

The importance of campaign funds for challengers, moreover, was highlighted by Jacobson's conclusion that incumbent spending produced no increase in the incumbent's share of the vote. In fact, the more incumbents spent, the worse they did—not because their spending lost them votes, but because they had to spend more when challengers began to encroach on their electoral margins. Other scholars have challenged that finding about incumbent spending, and the debate is yet to be resolved.[20] Nonetheless, few would argue that the effect of incumbent spending matches that of challenger spending; it seems likely, at least, that one increment of challenger spending, an extra $25,000 perhaps, has more effect on voter awareness than does the same increment in incumbent spending. If the challenger is spending at lower levels than is the incumbent, challenger spending will also be more efficacious per increment because of the decreasing marginal utility—the smaller successive impact on the vote of each increment—of campaign spending.

Incumbents continue to outspend and then to outpoll their challengers, but to conclude that incumbents "buy" reelection or that spending leads to the margin of victory misstates the problem somewhat. Incumbents build support in their constituencies largely by virtue of the perquisites of office and by reason of the visibility and name recognition they routinely achieve. Ultimately the greatest advantage the incumbents have is not their campaign money, it is the expectation early in the election cycle that they can and will win reelection. It is that expectation that makes it so difficult for challengers to raise the money by which they might effectively overcome the incumbents' advantage in the campaign and election.

For Americans who value competitiveness in elections, the issue is of the greatest magnitude. It is simply that the campaign finance system offers challengers no weapons with which to overcome the advantages of incumbency. The challengers lack money because the incumbents' reelection prospects are so strong as to discourage both the emergence of appealing challengers and the willingness of potential contributors to invest in electoral politics. The solution to the problem, therefore, rests either in reducing the advantages of incumbency or in getting money to challengers in time to entice both strong candidates and more contributors. The post-74 regime faces no greater challenge.

Artful Dodging and Skillful Avoiding

The conventional wisdom is right at last: the regulatory vessel is in fact leaking. Important activity and individuals escape its requirements for reporting, and money flows outside of its controls in swelling torrents. One need only tick off the specifics: bundling, soft money, brokers, independent spending, fund-raisers netting six-figure totals in America's urban centers. However one may wish to describe the structural flaws—as "leaks" or "loopholes"—the integrity

For another review of the theoretical problem and additional poll data, see Jacobson, "The Effects of Campaign Spending in House Elections: New Evidence for Old Arguments," *American Journal of Political Science* 34 (May 1990), pp. 334–362.

20. Contra the Jacobson conclusion, see Donald P. Green and Jonathan S. Krasno, "Salvation for the Spendthrift Incumbent: Reestimating the Effects of Campaign Spending in House Elections," *American Journal of Political Science* 32 (November 1988), pp. 884–907.

of the post-1974 regulatory structure is at grave risk.

The assault on the structure of regulation, the statutorily defined campaign finance system, comes in various ways. There are, first, the actors and the activity in violation of explicit statutory limits. The individuals exceeding the $25,000 annual limit on contributions are the most widely publicized case; ambitious investigators now vie to find new miscreants in the computer records of the FEC. Second, there are the invisible brokers and transactions that remain only partially within the governance of the system; the money they raise, and its origins, are reported, but neither their role nor the aggregate sums they organize are. Similar are the formal bundlers, many of whom press the limits of permissible control over contributions. Third, there are the sums raised and spent outside of the limits of the system. Soft money (previously discussed) and independent spending provide the major examples. The 1974 amendments to the FECA set strict limits on the sums of money that groups or citizens could spend independently in a campaign—that is, without the control or even the knowledge of any candidate. Like everything else in the FECA those provisions have a history. Spending by groups other than the candidates had been the stock device for dodging earlier attempts to control spending and insure full

reporting of all contributions. The Supreme Court, however, struck down those limits in *Buckley* v. *Valeo*, leaving only the requirement that independent expenditures be reported to the FEC. . . .

The post-1974 beginnings of independent spending are obscure. Record keeping at the FEC was in its infancy in 1976, and its data on independent spending in that cycle are incomplete; the best guess is that about $2 million was spent independently, with all but $400,000 spent in the presidential campaign. Another $300,000 or so was spent in the 1978 congressional elections, and then came the eye-grabbing jump to a total of $16.1 million in 1980 (table 7.2). . . .

Even at their zenith, independent expenditures on congressional elections never accounted for major sums. The record $9.4 million in 1986 was only 2 percent of the cash expenditures ($450.3 million) by all candidates in that year's campaigns. Moreover, the effective sums were greatly exaggerated. The splashiest spenders in the 1980s—NCPAC and an assortment of PACs supporting Republican presidential candidates— were PACs without parent organizations, "nonconnected PACs" in the parlance of the FEC. They raised their money in costly direct-mail solicitations; and with no parent to pay overhead, not to mention fund-raising expenses (postage, printing, computerized mailing lists), they had to

Table 7.2

Independent spending in presidential and congressional elections: 1980–1988

Year	Presidential			Congressional		
	Total $	% against	% rep	Total $	% against	% rep
1980	$13.75 m	5.9%	96.6%	$2.34 m	58.9%	83.9%
1982	$ .19 m	.8%	50.2%	$7.10 m	72.5%	75.9%
1984	$17.47 m	4.8%	93.4%	$5.95 m	44.3%	49.7%
1986	$ .84 m	5.4%	88.9%	$9.36 m	14.2%	58.9%
1988	$14.13 m	24.8%	94.9%	$7.21 m	16.5%	64.1%
1990	$ .50 m	35.1%	98.0%	$1.77 m	15.7%	48.6%

Source: Federal Election Commission.

absorb all of these costs out of the money they raised. Estimates vary, but shrewd and careful reports found that only 5 to 20 percent of their receipts went into campaign activity as it is usually understood—into television or newspaper ads or campaign brochures or mailings.

... Independent spending created intra-organizational problems for the PACs that tried it; some of their donors either did not approve of it generally, or they were outraged at the PACs' choice of targets. It also raised the wrath of incumbents, especially when it was spending in favor of challengers, and they quickly learned to ignite voter backlash to it. Indeed, candidates complained even when the spending favored them; none of them wanted any part of what the public sees as their campaigns to be beyond their control.

Those explorations by mainline PACs opened up another issue that had festered for some years: the meaning of independence. How, for instance, could a large PAC making contributions to congressional candidates and discussing their campaigns with them also make independent expenditures in which there was no cooperation or contact with the candidate? Or what of an independently financed media campaign supporting candidate J when the commercials are designed and placed by the same media consultants working for candidate J's campaign? And how are voters to know who is responsible for independent expenditures on television when the credit line is invisible to most viewers? Independence comes down in the end to very small but very important details. ...

Independent expenditures happen to exploit a gap in the regulatory system created by the Supreme Court's application of the First Amendment to it. Soft money, however, flows in presidential campaigns as a result of an intended exclusion from the system and the constitutional status of American federalism. Most of the bundling and high-stakes brokering result from the failure of the authors of the FECA, whether out of faintheartedness or lack of foresight, to place

intermediaries securely within the regulatory structure. So, the natures of the leaks differ; they are far too varied in both origin and purpose to bear the single pejorative label of loophole. Calling them loopholes blurs moral and ethical distinctions in a subject in which moral and ethical judgments abound.

Such judgments are the first reason for concern about the integrity of the regulatory structure. Its impairments invite and receive public denunciation of campaigns, campaigners, and campaign finance. Americans do not take kindly to avoidance, no matter how legal or even ethical, of systems of regulation; avoidance carries the stigma of self-servingness compounded by excessive cleverness. Independent spenders may be exercising a First Amendment right in the most open and direct way, but they are not treated much more charitably than the trimmers and shavers who bundle ever more creatively to escape the statutory limits on the size of contributions. In short, breaches in the integrity of the structure give rise to blanket judgments untempered or ungraded by any fine distinctions among the kinds of breaches.

The problems, however, extend beyond those of public judgment. The breaches create massive administrative problems, especially in reporting. Again, independent spending is a splendid case in point. The only other spending in the campaign permitted by the FECA is that by the candidates and the party committees, both of which must register with the FEC and make periodic reports to it. Their officials become institutionalized reporters and trained compliers, most of them also aided by accountants, lawyers, and computer software. ...

On this and other matters of administration and enforcement, the FEC suffers from an uncertain authority. The placement of exchanges and flows of money on the peripheries of the regulatory system means, in effect, that they sit also on the peripheries of the FEC's authority. One need only cite the great controversies, including the intervention of the federal district court for the

District of Columbia, over the FEC's handling of the soft-money controversy. It has been almost equally vexed by the bundling inventions of the National Republican Senatorial Committee. Underfunded by the Congress and kept on a short leash for 15 years, the FEC has never been able to establish its independence as a regulator; its even division between three Democrats and three Republicans has additionally made it difficult for the Commission to deal with problems that are inevitably partisan. These leaks in the regulatory system have only further embarrassed it and given its sterner critics more reason for criticism.[23]

Administrative problems are closely related to mechanisms of responsibility. The major institutionalized actors—PACs, parties, and candidates—respond to various systems of control or responsibility: voters, members, parent organizations, representative bodies, public officials, or mass opinion, as the case may be. On the other hand, brokers such as Charles Keating or a well-heeled individual contributor make no reports to the FEC, and no other institutions or responsible bodies stand behind them. With no visibility and no long-term interest in the political system, the brokers may have no political reputation at stake; often, too, they offer no target at which the wrath of voters can be directed. The political controls of reputation and the ballot box are imperfect at best, but they do work more effectively on visible, committed political actors with continuing stakes in politics.

When the integrity of the regulatory system suffers, so too do the morale and the law-abidingness of those clearly within the regulatory perimeters. Compliance with both the letter and the spirit of a regulatory structure cannot easily survive the impression that the structure catches only some of the players while others go free. The belief that "I've been playing by the rules while those guys have been getting away with murder" has a corrosive effect on compliance. And compliance is that act of self-enforcement on which all legitimate and effective systems of regulation depend.

It almost goes without saying that breaches in the regulatory system sabotage the achievement of the initial purpose of the regulation. If the purpose was to limit PAC contributions to $5,000 per candidate per election, any modus operandi that permits groups of potential PAC contributors to give their cash instead as individuals defeats both the limit and the congressional intent that their money be identified with the interest that recruited it.

Are Campaigns Too Expensive?

Each round of debates over congressional campaign finance is, in the words of Yogi Berra, déjà vu all over again. Putting a cap on campaign expenditures was high on the agenda of reform in 1974, and it still is. The Supreme Court struck down the FECA's limits on all spending in *Buckley,* and reformers have been trying to find a way of restoring them ever since. So strongly convinced are the American people that campaigns cost too much, so firmly placed on the agenda of reform is the issue, that it flourishes in the 1990s despite the stability of expenditures in congressional campaigns. Not only does the issue persist, but its rhetoric about skyrocketing and escalating expenditures remains impervious to any new realities.

It is virtually a truism that the case for spending limits rests on the premise that the costs of campaigning are too great. It is far less easy, though, to establish that they are in fact too great. For many American adults the standards for making such a judgment are implicit; the spending is just "too much"—too much perhaps by standards of middle-class personal finance, too much because of the imagined rate of runaway increase in them. Or too much perhaps

23. See, for example, Brooks Jackson, *Broken Promise: Why the Federal Election Commission Failed* (New York: Priority Press, 1990).

in terms of value, in terms of the worth of the product or service the money produces. The campaigns, or the parts of them they happen to notice, are simply not worth those sums, just as $40 is not too much for a good steak dinner but is an outrageous price for a bad one.

The many cries of "too much" reflect negative judgments about politics and the entire public sector. Those judgments similarly govern public opinion about the salaries of public officials. Inherent in them is a double standard, one code of behavior for the private sector and another for the public sector. Political scientists are fond of making the public-private comparison in campaign finance with data on advertising expenditures, for advertising campaigns are, like campaigns for public office, an exercise in information and persuasion. Americans are shocked by total expenditures of $445.2 million in the congressional campaigns of 1990, but in that same year Sears Roebuck, the giant merchandiser, had an advertising budget in excess of $1.4 billion.

The case against present spending levels is much stronger on pragmatic or consequential grounds. These arguments are, however, not about spending per se but about the need to raise the money in order to spend it. They go this way:

• Present levels of spending are too high because in order to raise the funds to spend, elected public officials must take too much time and energy from their public responsibilities. It is now almost a commonplace that a U.S. senator must raise $12,000 a week for six years in order to amass the $3.5 to $4 million for a typical Senate campaign.

• Furthermore, the pressures to raise those sums for a Senate race, or close to half a million for a House campaign, drive candidates to seek money in large sums at a time when contribution limits are shrinking because of inflation. Initially, candidates replaced small individual contributors with large PAC contributions, and now even the usual PAC contribution is small compared to

the take at a brokered fundraiser in Los Angeles. A senator can make a flying trip to a distant spot for a quick reception and return to Washington with $50,000 or $100,000 in campaign resources. Spending levels, that is, affect how money is raised, where it is raised, and with whose help it is raised.

• The ability to raise funds becomes a substantial qualification for candidates. Candidates of knowledge, experience, and even wisdom may lack the skills or the stomach for begging funds from people they scarcely know; the need to do it may discourage them from seeking office. Worse than such a shrinking of the pool of talent is the possibility that the consequence will be to recruit and elect candidates whose skills in raising money and conducting a campaign are their chief or even their only major attributes.

The problem with elevated spending levels seems to be that one needs to raise the money in the first place. . . .

Leaving aside the strength of popular and reformist feelings on the point, there is a basic conceptual problem here. Not one, but two issues are entwined: the need for the money and the costs to the system of raising it. It is easier to justify the spending levels than the effort that has to go into raising the cash in the first place. So, we are raising too much money and yet not really spending enough in the campaigns for Congress. . . . Even the experts and activists find it difficult to reach a judgment about American campaign finance. The mass public necessarily comes to its understandings about it without any profound knowledge, often without even basic information. Citizens are compelled to watch the shadows projected on the vast wall in front of them. They take their conclusions and judgments as they see them in the dance of distorted images. Of necessity, their judgments are the judgments of those who project the images.

In the opinions on all of the major concerns about the post-1974 system, the consonances and dissonances are consistent. Whether it is the PAC-

Congress connection, the impact of money on the winning of elections, or the judgments about spending levels, mass opinion and image-making opinion are in agreement. Their consensus, moreover, diverges in all three instances from much of scholarly and other expert opinion.[27] ... It is hardly a novel outcome, for expert opinion is often at odds with mass opinion over the analysis of public problems and policy solutions. It is, in fact, one of the oldest and most troubling dilemmas in the governance of mass, popular democracies.

The successes and failures of the post-1974 regime present the dilemma in a heightened form. Mass opinion about campaign finance increasingly feeds a cynicism about, even a rejection of, basic democratic processes. Any threat to mass involvement in or acceptance of electoral politics threatens the essence of representative government. The resulting conflict of equities could not be more disturbing. Is one to adopt policies that address the real problems of the system, as the informed best understand them, or ought one to devise change that will lay to rest the fears and anger of a disaffected public? Can we indeed win back disaffected citizens and solve real public problems at the same time? It is the hardest of the policy questions, this intersection of image and reality, of mass politics and expert prescription—especially when the divergence is not only over ultimate policy goals, but over the reality of the problem itself.

Whether by accident or prescience, the justices of the U.S. Supreme Court recognized the dilemma in the majority opinion in *Buckley* v. *Valeo*. Congress could act to limit the constitutionally protected flow of campaign money only in the case of "corruption or the appearance of corruption," either in the instance of certifiable corruption by some unspecified standards, or in the instance of some widespread belief that institutions were being corrupted. So, Congress might apparently act on the basis of one reality or the other, on the basis of the image behind the viewer or the image projected on the wall. Is it to make no difference if one reality could meet standards of truth or validity and the other could not? The answer, in the world of democratic politics, depends on crafting reforms that serve both reality and its appearances.

---

27. I want to be clear that in referring to scholarly opinion I am talking about more than my judgments. I have cited examples of scholarly opinion about the first two issues; as for the question of spending levels, see, inter alia, Larry J. Sabato, *Paying for Elections: The Campaign Finance Thicket* (New York: Priority Press, 1989), especially chapters 2 and 3.

8 DEMOCRACY'S EFFECTS

The Economics and Politics of Growth
Karl de Schweinitz, Jr.

Rent Seeking and Redistribution under Democracy versus Dictatorship
Ronald Wintrobe

Dictatorship, Democracy, and Development
Mancur Olson

Freedom Favors Development
Amartya Sen

Political Regimes and Economic Growth
Adam Przeworski, Michael E. Alvarez, José Antonio Cheibub, and Fernando Limongi

Democracy in America
Alexis de Tocqueville

Does Democracy Engender Justice?
John E. Roemer

Facing up to the American Dream: Race, Class, and the Soul of the Nation
Jennifer L. Hochschild

Beyond Tocqueville, Myrdal, and Hartz: The Multiple Traditions in America
Rogers M. Smith

The Economics and Politics of Growth

Karl de Schweinitz, Jr.

Economic growth may be defined as the process which gives rise to an increase in per capita, or average, income....

... The concern here is with the political consequences of the economic transition from one stage to another, rather than with the measurement of economic welfare....

The proximate requirements for economic growth may be stated quite briefly: increased employment of resources per capita and/or increased efficiency in the employment of existing resources....

Whether growth is achieved through the increased use of inputs per capita or through increased efficiency, one process stands out as being crucially important—investment. Investment may be defined as an addition to plant and equipment and/or inventories. It involves the production of that type of output which expands the capacity of an economy. Obviously, when an economy grows through the accumulation (the increase) of capital, investment is taking place. Perhaps less obviously, investment also is basic to growth through an increase of the other resources—land and labor....

The Rationale of Investment and the Nature of Entrepreneurial Activity

The paramount importance of investment in economic growth necessitates further inquiry about its rationale and the conditions which make it possible. Who invests and why? What is the nature of the decision-making process which induces some individuals to commit resources to the expansion of future output? Do all invest-

Excerpted from: Karl de Schweinitz, Jr., *Industrialization and Democracy: Economic Necessities and Political Possibilities*. Glencoe, Ill.: The Free Press.

ment decisions involve uncertainty? How are the benefits of investment distributed?

In attempting to answer these questions it will be convenient to distinguish between private and public motives for investment. Assuming that a private individual maximizes profit, he will invest if he anticipates that his income will increase at least as much as the added costs he incurs....

The public motivation for investment is similar, but with this difference: a public authority, in calculating the feasibility of an investment project, balances social income against social costs and will carry out the project only if he expects a greater return *to society* from resources in the contemplated project than in alternative uses. Where the private investor is maximizing values derived from his own utility function, the public investor is maximizing values derived from a social welfare function.[2] ...

Though private and public investment are motivated by different rationales, they both focus on the expansion of future output and, therefore, have characteristics in common. First of all, to greater or less extent the decision to invest is made in the face of uncertainty....

One may infer from its inherent uncertainty that investment requires a person with rather

---

2. The question of investment criteria is a good deal more complex than indicated in the text. Of all the phases of economics, capital theory is perhaps the most difficult and obscure because of ineluctable theoretical problems involved in the treatment of time. Those who are interested in these problems in the context of economic development may find the following references useful: A. E. Kahn, "Investment Criteria in Development," *Quarterly Journal of Economics*, LXV, February, 1951, pp. 38–61; W. Galenson and H. Leibenstein, "Investment Criteria, Productivity, and Economic Development," *idem*, LXIX, August, 1955, pp. 343–370; R. C. Blitz, "Capital Longevity and Economic Development," *American Economic Review*, XLVIII, June, 1958, pp. 313–329.

uncommon, if not unique, characteristics. He must have the capacity to calculate his chances of success on the basis of signals that the existing economic environment flashes to him. He must have the ability to obtain and organize the resources for constructing additional or new plant and equipment. Above all, he must have confidence that the future will validate his present choice of action, which is to say that he believes that he can manipulate the environment to achieve the ends he has set for himself. We enumerate these characteristics because they suggest that entrepreneurial talents will not be widespread in any society and will be particularly limited in a subsistence society.[4] For the latter tends to obviate problems of uncertainty by adhering to customary or traditional patterns of performance. The typical individual in a subsistence economy then will not be accustomed to change, and still less to the notion that he can influence the shape of the environment by his actions.

The inference that entrepreneurs are a minority group is further supported by a second characteristic that private and public investment have in common, namely their dependence on the withdrawing of resources from present consumption. The restriction of consumption, that is saving, raises issues which are particularly germane to our analysis, for they relate to problems of conflicts in preferences. In a subsistence economy, the members of the community will necessarily try to consume all output produced. No matter how they may feel about the virtues of allocating resources to investment, they have no choice, given the immediacy of the struggle for existence, but to maximize present consumption. In short, their propensity to consume approaches

unity. Yet growth requires that resources be released from present consumption for allocation to investment.

How can this impasse be surmounted? In general there are two answers to the question. One, income can be distributed in such a way that a disproportionate share is placed at the disposal of those who will be willing to refrain from consuming it. This method, of course, involves the generation of saving through an unequal distribution of income. Two, government may impose taxes on households which reduce the level of disposable income available for consumption. Neither with the one alternative nor the other does the mass of individuals make an unencumbered choice between consumption and saving. In both cases they are forced to save, in the one through the medium of capitalists, in the other through the medium of government officials.

Let us restate the problem now in terms that will bring out the essential preference conflict involved in growth at low levels of income. In a subsistence economy, the time preference of the overwhelming majority of the population will be so high that no monetary reward, however great, can induce them to forego present consumption. If growth is to take place, some members of the community with a low enough time preference to allow them to calculate the advantages of future versus present output must gain title to resources. In short, the preferences of a minority must take precedence over those of a majority....

Economic Obstacles to the Industrial Transformation

With these notions about investment before us, we come now to the crucial issue of economic growth. We know that a subsistence economy hardly invests more than the amount necessary to maintain the value of its meager capital stock, reflecting a set of social institutions which maximize traditional and customary values. We also

---

4. See Clark Kerr, John T. Dunlop, Frederick H. Harbison, and Charles A. Myers, *Industrialism and Industrial Man*, Cambridge, Mass., 1960 for an analysis of the role of entrepreneurial or industrializing elites in economic development, especially as it affects the relationships between labor and management.

know that high-income economies invest a high proportion of their national income and have acquired the kinds of institutions and attitudes which more or less automatically sustain the saving and investment processes essential to growth. How, then, in the words of Professor Lewis, does an economy change from a situation in which it is investing less than 5 percent of its national income to one in which it is investing more than 12 percent?[7] ...

... [T]he capital-output concept is a useful means for suggesting the dimensions of the tasks confronting an economy which intends to rise above the subsistence status. What is at issue here is the amount of investment that is required on the average to produce a unit of output. The lower the capital-output ratio the more rapidly a given amount of investment will give rise to increased output.[10] ...

... [I]t would appear to be a reasonable hypothesis that when a subsistence economy enters upon a stage of development in which its rate of net investment rises to a permanently higher level, marginal capital-output ratios at first rise and then subsequently fall. The reasons for suggesting this hypothesis are as follows. Technical capital coefficients tend to be highest in the transportation, communication, and utility sectors of an economy and lowest in manufacturing. This is to say, it takes a greater amount of capital to produce one unit of transportation than it does to produce one unit of manufactured goods. When, however, an economy first starts to grow

it may allocate to transportation and the other utilities a disproportionate share of its investment. This is done in order to construct the social overhead capital which provides manufacturing concerns with the means for marketing output and employing inputs. Accordingly, one would expect capital-output ratios to rise during this period of utility construction. Subsequently when this sector of the economy does not require a disproportionate share of the community's investment, the output of sectors with lower capital-output ratios may experience a relatively greater expansion, thus leading to a decline in the overall capital-output ratio. Furthermore, during the early stage of growth when the labor force has not yet acquired the habits of industrial discipline, a given stock of capital will not yield its maximum output because of absenteeism, excessive turnover, and because of improper and inadequate capital maintenance. These problems will be resolved as the industrial labor force comes of age, leading to labor's more efficient utilization of the existing capital stock.

If this hypothesis is correct, it suggests that "the take-off" is characterized not only by a proportionate rise in net investment, but by a period in which there is a longer than "normal" wait for the appearance of the increased output contingent upon investment. Consider what this means in more concrete terms. During the take-off, or what conventionally is called an industrial revolution, railways, canals, roads, harbors, steel plants, and other facilities essential to an interdependent industrial economy are being constructed. The limit to the development of the economy is the availability of saving rather than the existence of investment opportunities.

Indeed, so great is the pressure on resources for the construction of industrial and social capital that not all demands can be satisfied simultaneously. Something has to give. In the face of capital scarcities some projects will be postponed, or, if undertaken, constructed with materials that economize capital. Thus it may be the case, for example, that urban housing is not

7. W. Arthur Lewis, "Economic Development with Unlimited Supplies of Labor," *The Manchester School*, XXII, May, 1954, pp. 139–191.

10. In part the rapid growth of output in the Soviet Union is attributable to the emphasis planners have placed on activities characterized by low capital-output ratios at the expense of activities characterized by high capital-output ratios. Thus the industrial and manufacturing sectors of the Soviet economy have been given greater weight than the housing and transportation sectors, which typically absorb a large volume of resources before yielding increments to output.

expanded at a fast enough rate to take care of the influx of workers from the rural sector of the economy leading to overcrowded conditions in cities. Or perhaps additional housing is constructed from flimsy, nondurable materials which deteriorate rapidly. Urban communities may neglect their health and recreational services. Factories may be constructed with inadequate safety devices.

While the economy is cutting corners on some kinds of investment and refraining from other kinds, the investment being undertaken yields its return slowly. . . .

The Population Barrier to Growth

. . . The most commonly discussed barrier to growth, the surmounting of which seems to require the expenditure of a concentrated dose of social energy, is the possible population explosion it induces. In a subsistence economy birth rates and mortality rates are both relatively high. If with the onset of economic growth mortality rates decline before birth rates, then the rate of population growth will increase. If it increases rapidly enough, it may abort per capita income increases and, indeed, may even lower per capita income. The reasons why output growth and population growth may be functionally related are well known. The increased production of subsistence goods such as grain may lower mortality rates by improving diets and increasing resistance to disease. The draining of swamps and the use of DDT reduce the incidence of malaria and yellow fever. Increased educational opportunity facilitates the spread of higher standards of public health and hygiene. While the expansion of the output of consumers' goods and/or investment goods may decrease the mortality rate, the birth rate, at least for a time, remains insensitive to these changes. Only when households come to recognize family limitation as a desirable goal and have the knowledge for and means of doing so will birth rates fall. Since this

view represents a fundamental change and reorientation of values, economic growth can be expected to induce it, if ever it does, only after the passage of a considerable length of time. In the meantime, mortality rates decline and population explodes.

The Welfare Problem during the Industrial Revolution

The take-off, then, raises a formidable standard of living, or what for shorthand purposes we shall call a welfare problem. . . . The take-off stage is characterized by forces which tend to prevent marked improvement in the standard of living of the masses of people. . . .

Given the utilitarian idea of welfare, there are three factors affecting it which we consider particularly relevant to our analysis, two relating to supply conditions and one to demand conditions. Consider first the level of income and employment. If a subsistence economy fully employed available resources including labor and produced enough only to provide the members of society with a minimal standard of living, then a rise in the rate of net investment would imply a decrease in the output of consumers' goods and a decline in short-run welfare.[13] . . . The assumption of full employment, however, does not appear to be especially valid in the conditions of a subsistence economy. First of all, there is likely to be a surfeit of population with many workers unable to find full-time employment under the

---

13. This proposition is correct if welfare is measured solely in terms of the current output of consumer goods. If, however, welfare is measured in terms of the pattern of consumption over time, then it may not be valid. For it is conceivable that people might be willing to have their subsistence reduced now, if they thought it would lead to the expansion of consumable output tomorrow. In addition to the difficulties mentioned in the text previously, problems of this sort involving time preferences and intertemporal comparisons make the concept of welfare in economics all the more elusive.

existing organization of production. Second, many workers who are ostensibly employed may not be contributing much, if anything, to output.... Unemployed labor, whether overt or covert in inefficient employments, permits the expansion of investment without an absolute decrease in the output of consumption goods.... The proportionate rise of net investment, therefore, comes out of an increasing rather than a given income.

While the conditions of aggregate investment during the industrial revolution do not preclude increases of welfare, the allocation of investment—the second supply factor—raises some problems for which there is no easy solution. As indicated previously, capital scarcities during the period will compel the cutting back or holding back of certain types of investment projects....

In raising this question we have introduced the third factor affecting welfare, namely the subjective element of demand, preferences, and expectations.... A number of things may happen to people's expectations during the period of the industrial revolution. As workers move into the industrial community, their image of reality more adequately reflects conditions as they are and they become aware of the shortcomings of their new environment in concrete terms. Prior to moving, rumors of high wages may have subordinated rumors about crowded housing facilities. After moving, high wages become a particular bundle of goods and services that urban society affords the workers. If the welfare component of this bundle of goods and services during the industrial revolution is constrained by investment priorities necessitated by growth, then the expectations formed at one remove from the industrial-urban environment are likely to be frustrated.

This might not be a matter of great moment if it were safe to assume that expectations of people were quickly and easily adjusted to circumstances as they found them. When housing turned out to be worse than expected, if people simply devalued the housing component in their utility function, there might be no difficulty. But this is most unlikely. Indeed, expectations may be raised under the influence of new preferences and demands acquired in the industrial-urban community. We are referring to the impact of the so-called demonstration effect. As first formulated by Duesenberry, the demonstration effect related to the propensity of people when confronted by a decline in disposable income to try to maintain the highest standard of living they had attained in the past.[16] Here it refers to the tendency of people to acquire higher consumption aspirations when they come in contact with a standard of living higher than that to which they have been accustomed. The urban-industrial community is an active disseminator of the demonstration effect. If people live in squalid and cramped gerrybuilt houses, they can observe others who live in sumptuous quarters. If they cannot pay the price of admission to the theater or other forms of urban entertainment, they at least know something about the entertainment that is available. To put it another way, in the urban community the inequality of wealth and income is more visible than in the rural community and therefore acts as a greater stimulant in the formation of new preferences among the less privileged members of society.

The welfare problem of the industrial revolution may be contrasted to the problems which J. K. Galbraith sees afflicting the Affluent Society. In the latter the basic wants have been more or less satisfied and production is geared to the satisfaction of wants of less urgency....

On the other hand, the opposite problem holds for the economy entering upon the early stages of development. Wants increase faster than the output of consumer goods, for while the structural capital of an industrial economy is being built, the wants of the community grow with-

---

16. James S. Duesenberry, *Income, Saving and the Theory of Consumer Behavior*, Cambridge, Mass., 1949.

out the special effort and blandishments of the advertisers. So basic are they that when people become aware of higher standards in their satisfaction, they can quickly revise their preferences and acquire greater expectations....

The Individual and Collectivist Response to the Welfare Problem

Another aspect of the "hump" implicit in our discussion of the welfare problem during the industrial revolution suggests an important link between economic growth and the problems of the political system. If wants expand more rapidly than the output of consumers' goods, it is reasonable to expect that the people whose expectations are frustrated and who do not receive what they think they are entitled to will attempt to do something about it.... Generally, one may distinguish two quite different responses. One, individuals might accept the economic order as they see it with the goals it represents and the drives it maximizes and try to acquire the perquisites of the privileged members of society by their own individual efforts. If entrepreneurship is the route to wealth, so be it. Alternatively, individuals might band together in organizations in order to improve their status in society. Working through trade unions, they might try to raise wage rates and influence other conditions of labor through the exercise of their collective strength. Similarly, they might engage in political activity to achieve a change in the institutional environment favorable to their interests, e.g., minimum wage legislation.

... Entrepreneurship requires a rare combination of qualities, the capacity to evaluate the uncertainties of the future, a belief in one's ability to manipulate and control the environment, and command of scarce capital resources. These qualities only fall to a minority. The majority, therefore, may react to the frustrations of the industrial revolution by turning to some kind of collective action....

The Political Problem of the Industrial Revolution

We are now at a point in our analysis where we can state the essence of the political problem raised by the process of economic growth. Whatever the specific institutional factors which trigger it, a small group of men assume responsibility for the investment projects which mark out the path of the economy's development. While this group has first claim to the increased output generated in the early stages of growth, a far larger number of people is thrust into circumstances where their wants start to run ahead of the capacity of the economy to satisfy them. The resulting discontent and dissidence may manifest itself in disorders—riots, strikes, mob demonstrations—which threaten the political stability of the society. Governmental leaders, therefore, as a necessary part of maintaining the prerogatives of office and political power, must deal with these disorders and attempt to maintain social order in the community. But in performing this task there is one thing they cannot do, if they are concerned with facilitating the continued growth of the economy: they cannot try to solve the political problem by acceding to the demands of the masses of workers and granting them rights commensurate with the rights of the privileged members of society. For growth at the early critical stage of the take-off is a discriminatory process which favors the few who are able to take the steps necessary to raise the rate of net investment. If the political system chooses to support the consumption goals of the many against the growth goals of the few, then growth, if not aborted, will surely be slowed down.

Suppose, for example, that trade unions are able to organize effectively as rapidly as workers move into the urban-industrial sector of the economy and therefore can bring pressure on entrepreneurs for increased wages. Profit rates will fall diminishing the volume of retained earnings which at early stages of development very likely are the most important source of saving. Or, perhaps more significantly, suppose trade unions are able to impose on entrepreneurs rules and regulations with respect to the employment of workers which inhibit the ability of the former to experiment with different uses of capital. Growth through increased efficiency in the utilization of resources might then be so far restricted. Again, consider a political branch of a labor movement which is well organized to pressure government into granting workers the many benefits of the welfare state. The resulting old age, health, and unemployment measures may divert resources away from the construction of the utilities essential for subsequent growth through their effect on the distribution of income. If taxes on entrepreneurs rise to finance these programs the funds available for the accumulation of real capital will be decreased.

Granted that the aspirations and demands of dissident workers must somehow be contained or repressed in order to preserve the conditions for further growth, how can governmental authorities be sure that the measures they take do not also kill off the democratic potential to which the organized activities of workers give rise? The subsistence economy, we have argued, cannot sustain a democratic political society and one of the things which must happen to foster development towards democracy is the dissemination of the idea that individual action does matter and that individuals can influence the state of the community through participation in political life. The dissidence and discontent of the early stages of the industrial revolution are among the influences which may lead individuals to acquire democratic attitudes. Irritated by the circumstances in which they find themselves and no longer able to believe in the immutability of an environment which is visibly changing, workers may be induced to remedy their own condition rather than accept the writ of tradition and authority. The answer to the question raised at the beginning of this paragraph, of course, is that

governmental leaders at early stages of development are not themselves particularly interested in fostering the democratic potential of workers. They are not trying to create a democratic society. Rather they are trying to maximize their tenure of power by taking the steps necessary to retain office. The question then can be rephrased: How can nondemocratic governmental leaders cope with the tensions of the industrial labor force in such a way as to allow economic growth to continue to take place without destroying the democratic tendencies which growth may contain? We will seek the answer to this paradoxical question in the experience of the industrialization of the western world. First, however, we must pose a hypothesis about growth and democracy which relates the emergence of the latter to the point or period in history when the former takes place. . . .

Rent Seeking and Redistribution under Democracy versus Dictatorship

Ronald Wintrobe

1 Introduction

The idea that "too much" democracy is bad for economic development has resurfaced again in recent years. In the economic literature, the main reason advanced is that democracy is "plagued" by redistributional impulses. Perhaps the most famous work to advance this theme is Mancur Olson's (1982) *The Rise and Decline of Nations*, in which interest groups are reclassified as "distributional coalitions" that pursue their own selfish interests at the expense of overall economic efficiency. The older and more established the democracy, the larger the number of distributional coalitions that have a chance to form and the more the economic landscape is "rent" with inefficient laws, regulations, and other practices that hinder growth. In a similar vein, the vast literature on rent-seeking, originated by Tullock (1967), Krueger (1974), and Posner (1975), identified rent-seeking and its associated social costs with democratic government and thus made it possible, by a strange twist of logic in which democracy is identified with the proliferation of economic monopolies, for monopoly to be elevated to the status of a serious problem.

Although critical of democratic processes, none of the above-named authors has embraced the notion that authoritarianism can facilitate economic development, and indeed, Mancur Olson in particular has forcefully argued the opposite (Olson, 1993). However, the closely related idea that insulating economic policy from democratic processes—"a little bit"[1] of dictatorship—can be good for economic develop-ment has gained currency, especially in political science and among theorists of development from both economics and political science who specifically point to the capacity of authoritarian states to resist distributional pressures as the key to successful development. The most influential contemporary exponent of this view seems to be Stephen Haggard (1990), although the argument is much older....

This essay considers the popular idea that democratic governments inhibit growth because of excess redistributory activity or rent-seeking. I ask the question: on theoretical grounds, which type of regime can be expected to engage in more redistribution—democracy or dictatorship?

2 Dictatorship, Democracy, and Redistribution

... Although I do not present a formal proof, I develop and defend a simple proposition: *Dictatorships tend to redistribute income more than democracies do*. If the analysis is correct, it obviously casts doubt on the proposition that democracies are less efficient than dictatorships because they are more capable of resisting demands for redistribution....

... [T]he argument proceeds essentially by taking existing models of the level of redistribution under democracy and then showing that, in a well-defined sense, the amount of redistribution in the model of dictatorship is larger than this. Specifically, suppose that, under the benchmark free-market case, the distribution of income is given by $x_1, \ldots, x_n$. Now suppose we assume a normal (not necessarily minimal) democratic government and ask what happens to this distribution. Of course, what happens depends on the model of democracy used, and there is at present

Excerpted from: Ronald Wintrobe, "Rent Seeking and Redistribution under Democracy versus Dictatorship." In *Understanding Democracy: Economic and Political Perspectives*. Ed. Albert Breton, Gianluigi Galeotti, Pierre Salmon, and Ronald Wintrobe. Cambridge: Cambridge University Press, 1997. Reprinted with the permission of Cambridge University Press.

1. The case for massive dictatorship, for instance that communism is better able to promote economic growth than capitalism, is no longer fashionable.

no common agreement on the effect of democratic government on the distribution of income. In the standard, median-voter model, there is no solution to this problem, because, under majority rule, no majority coalition is dominant and the outcome simply cycles among the alternatives available. There are, however, other models that do obtain determinant results: Meltzer and Richard's (1981) model, in which income is redistributed from the mean to the median (in terms of income) voter; Becker's (1983) model of interest group pressure; and the probabilistic voting model of Coughlin (1986) and others. We will consider all three of these models. Each of them can be thought of as producing a vector of incomes $y_1, \ldots, y_n$.

The next step is to impose a dictatorship and see what happens to the distribution of income. Call the resulting distribution of income $z_1, \ldots, z_n$. Our central proposition is that the distribution of income under dictatorship $z_1, \ldots, z_n$ is "further away" from the benchmark free-market cases $x_1, \ldots, x_n$ than the distribution of income under any of the three models of democracy $y_1, \ldots, y_n$. Alternatively, and more formally, the proposition is that dictatorship is characterized by more redistributive "activity," that is,

$$\sum_{i=1}^{n} (z_i - x_i)^2 > \sum_{i=1}^{n} (y_i - x_i)^2 \qquad (1)$$

Why would this be so? Before proceeding to a more formal analysis, let us consider a couple of reasons why we should expect this result. The first has to do with the origins of dictatorship. As discussed elsewhere, the simplest explanation for the rise of dictatorship is that in societies with polarized preferences, or low trust between the citizens and the parties, or where there is no willingness to compromise, there are really only two possibilities: Either the party that gains office in democratic voting tries to implement its preferred position, in which case large social conflict will ensue, or the society will be simply paralyzed by inaction. The "allure" of dictatorship under these circumstances is obvious; either the left or the right, if it takes power by force, will be able to eliminate its opposition through repression and in this way be able to implement its program. Either alternative implies a massive redistribution of income compared to that typical under democracy.

A second explanation of the redistributive tendencies of dictatorship is implicit in Przeworski's (1991) analysis of "self-enforcing" democracy. Przeworski suggests that for democracy to be stable, it must be self-enforcing, and for that to be true, the competitive political process cannot result in outcomes highly adverse to any major group's interest. If it did, it would benefit that group to subvert democracy rather than support it. The dictator faces no such constraint.

A third line of thought concerns the rent-seeking process. To elaborate the process, we first have to discuss a serious flaw in the standard model of rent-seeking. Explaining this flaw will illustrate some of the ways in which the distribution of rents differs between democracies and dictatorships. In the standard model, citizens and interest groups compete for rents through "wasteful" activities such as lobbying, hiring lawyers, and so on. Thus in the case of a $10,000 "prize," with 10 groups competing, each of which has an equal chance of getting the rent, the expected value of the rent to each competitor is $1,000. If the competitors are risk neutral, each of them will waste up to $1,000 attempting to obtain the prize. The problem with this model is that the process is irrational *from the point of view of politicians*. They give out a monopoly rent worth $10,000 and receive nothing in return. A rational politician would organize the process differently. For example, she would suggest to the competitors that they should offer cash payments instead of wasting the time of politicians through their lobbying activities. (It is essential to the model that it makes no difference which of the competitors gets the prize; hence the lobbying activity is pure waste to the politicians as well as to society.) But if bribes instead of lobbying are used, the $10,000 that is received in bribes by the politicians is not waste, but a pure transfer to politicians from interest groups, which represents no *social* waste or deadweight loss at all.

To see some other ways in which the rent-seeking process can be organized consider what typically happens under dictatorship. Dictators, at least of the more "successful" (i.e., relatively long-lived) variety, often know how to organize things so that they get a substantial return out of the process of rent-seeking. Indeed, under many regimes the distribution of rents reached legendary proportions....

In ... these systems, resources are not wasted bidding for the rents of the public sector. Rents are given out, and the dictator receives political support or money payments or other things ... in return. In other words, there is *no waste*, in the economic sense. One explanation for the difference in the way rents are distributed under dictatorship versus under democracy is that dictators typically impose restrictions on entry into competition for the rents given out by the state. Sometimes the rents are reserved for specific groups....

In part, the reason for this is obvious: If free competition for rents is allowed, and support depends on receiving net benefits from the state, then, because rent-seeking results in net *losses*, dictators would lose support by distributing rents through an openly competitive process!

How does democracy differ? Restrictions on entry into bidding processes for rights and privileges, goods, and services distributed by the state, which are characteristic of authoritarian governments, are clearly inconsistent with the very notion of democracy. A typical democracy will impose conditions like the following in any process of allocating public resources:

(1) No restrictions are imposed on who can bid, except of a technical nature.

(2) The winning bid should be selected on the basis of criteria involving net benefit to the public such as the worth of the project, costs, etc., and not on the political connections, race, ethnicity, status, and so on of the bidders.

(3) The process of bidding should be as open as possible and be open to review by an independent judiciary.

The inefficiency of democracy, according to the rent-seeking model, is now exposed. All of these conditions imply that more resources will be wasted under the bidding process in democracy. In short, *democracy is a much more wasteful system than dictatorship.*

The problem with the theory is that losses from pure rent-seeking implies that there are gains from trade between politicians and rent seekers. To the extent that trade between these groups takes place (through bribery, corruption, extortion, etc.), the waste in the process will be eliminated. Consequently, if transaction costs between these groups are low, the equilibrium will not be as described in the rent-seeking model, but instead will be the "corruption" equilibrium with no waste but with a defrauded public. On the other hand, suppose that these transactions are prevented, because the rules against influence peddling, bribery, and extortion (the existence of which are characteristic of democracy everywhere) are well-enforced by alert and powerful independent authorities. This gives a second possible equilibrium, in which fair competition among bidders is enforced. If this bidding results in rents being distributed to those who bid the lowest or who offer the public the most in the way of benefits, then this process produces something useful. The natural name to give this equilibrium is "strong democracy."

The rent-seeking model rules out this outcome by assuming that it makes no difference who wins the contest and that no social benefits result from the bidding process. Combining these assumptions with the assumption that the rules against corruption and the enforcement of them are so powerful that corruption is eliminated gives a third possible equilibrium: waste. A more appropriate name for this equilibrium is "irrational" because it implies that political institutions are fundamentally irrational in design: They are there to ensure the persistence of waste....

At this point, the reader may be tempted to ask, What difference does it make? Suppose that the losses from rent-seeking are not genuine waste in the economic sense, but "merely" unauthorized (in effect, fraudulent) transfers to politicians and bureaucrats. It is true that these are not waste in the sense of economic theory, but they are certainly not what the cost–benefit analysis promised! If the proper equilibrium involves corruption, not rent-seeking, isn't that bad enough?

One reason for insisting on the distinction between corruption and rent-seeking is that the solutions to these two problems can be vastly different. In particular, it is easy to imagine that a "little bit of authoritarianism" might possibly reduce rent-seeking (which after all is a form of political competition). It is much more difficult to believe that autocracy is the solution to corruption. Under autocracy, there are fewer or no constraints on the practice of rent distribution by independent courts or an inquisitory free press; political dictatorships have a significantly larger capacity to organize the distribution of rents in order to maximize their own "take" in the case of bribes or to generate the most political support. Moreover, the dictator is capable of sanctioning nonrepayment directly, solving the enforcement problem that is inherent in rent-seeking trades in a way that no democracy is capable of. In addition, as I have suggested elsewhere, the dictator lacks the alternative ways of creating trust or support characteristic of democracy. The distribution of rents in exchange for loyalty is therefore her major avenue for developing political support or trust.

This reasoning relies on the capacity of dictators to *repress* the political or economic rights of its citizenry as the key to its redistributive tendency. And indeed, the most common defi-

nition of dictatorship in the literature of political science essentially distinguishes dictatorship from democracy on this ground. In this third line of analysis we will hold to this definition but pursue the analysis in a bit more depth by looking at models of redistribution under democracy....

The simplest model of political redistribution under democracy is probably Becker's (1983) model of competition among interest groups. Most of the analysis is conducted with just two homogeneous groups, s and t, who engage in political activity in order to raise the incomes of their members. Both groups produce political "pressure," and in equilibrium, group s receives a subsidy financed by taxes on group t. The size of the tax and subsidy is determined by deadweight losses (which rise as the tax or subsidy rises) and by the fact that the "loser" in the political game (the taxed group t) need not passively accept his losses but can limit them through lobbying, threats, disobedience, migration, and other kinds of political pressure. However, no model of the political system is presented; rather, the analysis is explicitly intended to apply to many different kinds of political systems including dictatorship (Becker, 1983, p. 375).

Suppose, however, that the equilibrium described by Becker corresponds to that under democracy. How would it change if this democracy were taken over by a dictatorship? There are two main forces that would affect the outcome. The first is that the dictator has the power to repress opposition to his policies; the second is that the dictator is more insecure about his political support, because, as discussed in the previous section, among other things, the overt proffering of support from those over which he has power is necessarily less reliable than offers of support to a democratic politician. If the preferences and constellation of power relations between the two groups is unchanged (the analysis would be unchanged if many groups were assumed), the most reasonable assumption to make is that the dictator achieves power with the support of the subsidized group. The dictator, however, has the power, which was unavailable to a democratic politician, to directly repress pressure by the taxed group by banning their political organizations, refusing to permit their views to appear in the media, refusing to allow them to meet or organize, and jailing, torturing, or even executing their leaders. Moreover, the dictator either maximizes power or consumption, subject to the power constraint. In either case, repressing the opposition is obviously beneficial to him. In terms of Becker's analysis, the effect of political repression is the same as if the taxed group experienced a reduction in its capacity to produce pressure, as described in Becker's Proposition 1. The result is an increase in the size of the subsidy to group s and an increase in the tax on group t, that is, more redistribution than in the democratic case.

This conclusion seems straightforward and obvious enough and is derived solely on the assumption that the dictator has an interest in power and possesses an instrument—the capacity for political repression—that is unavailable to a democratic politician. If, in addition, we were to consider the second characteristic of dictatorship discussed above—namely, his insecurity—this would only reinforce the conclusion just obtained. The dictator will want to increase the size of the subsidy to the winners of the political game in order to guarantee their loyalty. To put it differently, repressing the opposition would appear to raise the probability of the dictator's survival in office, as would the distribution of extra rents to keep her supporters loyal. Again, therefore, more redistribution (larger taxes on the losers and bigger subsidies to the winners) is to be expected.

A second, widely used model of redistribution is that developed by Meltzer and Richard (1981). In that model, the decisive voter in a democracy is the median voter, and so long as her income is less than the mean income, there is redistribution from the (more productive) rich to the (less pro-

ductive) poor and middle-income voters. In one sense, the model is already a model of dictatorship because the tax rate is chosen by a "decisive voter" who, under democracy, is taken to be the median voter. The tax rate in turn determines the level of redistribution. If, on the other hand, the decisive voter was poor, he would choose a higher tax rate, resulting in more redistribution; but if rich he would choose a lower one, resulting in less redistribution.

However, the model simply does not allow for any mechanism by which redistribution can be effected from the poor. Thus none of the strategies discussed in Stigler's (1970) famous paper on Director's law, which alleged that redistribution in a democracy was typically from both the rich and the poor to the middle classes, and included such practices as tax exemptions, minimum-wage laws, farm policy, regulation, licensing practices, and so on, can be introduced into the model, in which redistribution is financed by a single tax rate that applies equally to everyone. Nor can any of the practices used by dictators who have drastically redistributed from the poor to the rich ... be discussed within this model. So the model is not very useful for our purposes. However, given these qualifications, a genuine dictatorship could be introduced into the model by empowering the "decisive voter" with the capacity to repress opposition. In that case, provided only that this permits higher taxation than is possible under democracy at any given level of productivity, the dictator in the model would presumably repress the rich, leading, again, to more redistribution, in this case from the rich to the poor and middle-income members of society.

The third widely used model of income redistribution under democratic governments is the probabilistic voting model. In simplified form (Mueller, 1989), there are two candidates, each of which maximizes expected votes. Let P_{1i} equal the probability that voter i will vote for Party 1, and consider a pure redistribution problem in which the government is faced simply with the problem of distributing $X among the n voters. Each party's "platform" is then simply a proposed allocation of the $X among the n voters. So each party maximizes

$$\left[\sum_i P_{1i} = \sum_i f_i(U_i(x_{1i}) - U_i(x_{2i}))\right]$$
$$+ \lambda\left[X - \sum_i x_{1i}\right] \tag{2}$$

Because Party 2 maximizes its expected vote total as well, the two parties propose a common platform, the equilibrium condition for which is

$$f_i' U_i' = f_j' U_j' \tag{3}$$

so in democratic equilibrium, each party maximizes a weighted sum of voters' utilities, where a voter's "weight" (and therefore the sum allocated to that voter) is proportional to her "responsiveness" (f_i) to an increase in $U_{1i} - U_{2i}$. In a sense, then, the more "disloyal" the voter to either party, the more that voter will receive as the result of democratic political competition.

This conclusion makes sense if voters are sensitive or responsive to changes in the utilities promised by the parties for nonpolicy reasons, that is, if a voter is a Democrat because his parents were Democrats, and he doesn't care about the policies of the Democratic party but cares about pleasing his parents. Voters like that can be "exploited" by politicians by actually giving them less than they would get if they were less loyal to the Democratic party. However, if the reason a Democratic voter will not easily switch to the Republican side is because the voter is relying on the reputation of the Democratic party to take care of him and others like him by giving him a disproportionate share of the spoils, then the party that attempts this strategy of exploitation will lose its reputation. Indeed, voters who would be tempted to be loyal to a particular party will anticipate that the parties will take advantage of them in this way, that

is, they will realize that loyalty does not pay and will refuse to extend it. So the political strategy unravels. . . .

Coughlin et al. (1990) develop a model of interest group influence on democratic government that solves this problem in a different way. In the model each member of an interest group has a (nonpolicy) bias b_{ij}. If $b_{ij} > 0$, this implies a positive bias in favor of the government. The b_{ij} are not known to the government or the opposition, but are represented by a random variable distributed uniformly over the interval (ℓ_i, r_i) with density a_i. Candidates are assumed to know the distribution of bias terms, but not their individual values. So although they cannot know with certainty how a given individual will vote, they can predict that they will pick up a greater fraction of an interest group's vote, the greater the difference in the utility their platform promises the representative interest group member over that of their opponent. In our terms, this gives candidates an incentive to distribute rents to interest groups. Now f_i' can be interpreted as the probability of winning the vote of a member of interest group i. The greater the density of the distribution a_i the larger f_i' is and the more that interest group will receive from both the government and opposition in equilibrium.

Consequently, interest group influence is negatively related to the dispersion of the bias terms, that is, to the degree of uncertainty on the part of politicians about the preferences of the members of the interest group. In equilibrium, democratic politicians act as if they maximized a weighted sum of voters' utilities, where the weights are positively related to interest group influence, that is, negatively related to the dispersion of the bias terms.

Now suppose that a dictator takes over this democratic polity, as before. The dictator can be presumed to face some opposition and to be able to win support from interest groups to the extent that he can "credibly" promise more than the opposition. Assume that the distribution of the bias terms is unchanged, as before. The dictator is unlike a democratic politician in two main respects: (1) He has the power to repress opposition to his policies; and (2) he does not and is not driven by competition to maximize expected "votes" (support). Is there a way that the dictator can improve on the democratic equilibrium; that is, is there a way that funds can be reallocated among the citizens in such a way as to increase the dictator's power? It seems clear that he can, although a precise description of the optimal strategy is difficult. From his point of view, there are two dimensions along which the voters can be ordered: in terms of the size of their f', and in terms of the size of their b_{ij}. Thus imagine that the dictator is sitting at a table, and in front of him he has a list of the interest groups under his control, to each of which is attached estimates of that group's f_i' and b_{ij} (prepared by a consulting firm). The dictator wants to order these groups for the purpose of deciding whom to repress, and to whom to distribute rents so as to buy their loyalty. The problem he faces is that the ordering produced by the f' is not the same as the ordering produced by the b_{ij}. For example, some of those groups with low f' support the dictator (high, positive b_{ij}) whereas others favor the opposition (negative b_{ij}).

However, some decisions are easy to make. Those who rank low on the f' scale and who are opposed to his policies (negative bias) are obvious candidates for repression. They oppose him, and they cannot easily be turned around with the kind of rents he is prepared to distribute (low f'). So long as repression is not too expensive, the dictator can gain power by silencing these people. This also makes it easy to subject them to taxation and regulation. These funds can then be redistributed in the form of rents to those whose loyalty can be purchased more easily or assuredly, namely, those with high f'. They *can* be bought, and it is better to make sure they remain so by giving them more than they received under democracy. Through these gifts, the dictator again accumulates more power. Finally,

those groups with low f' and positive bias will not be repressed (they support him, on the average) but need not be showered with gifts, because a low f' implies that the expected increase in loyalty from so doing is not large.

Of course, other factors besides those considered in this simple model might be relevant in determining the dictator's optimal choices, such as the nature of the regime's ideology or the degree of ideological "connectedness" among different groups.[7] If we ignore these and assume only two groups, the "winners" (high f') and "losers" (low f' and negative bias) in the analysis above, then it is clear that the benefits and burdens of the public sector will be distributed more unequally among these groups under dictatorship than democracy. Thus, letting a_i represent the weights on the utilities of different groups in the dictator's social welfare function, or in the social welfare function implicitly maximized in the probabilistic voting model of democracy, and specifying group 1 (high f') as the taxed group, the analysis implies

$$a_1^z < a_1^y \tag{4}$$

and if group 2 is the favored group (low f' and negative bias),

$$a_2^z > a_2^y \tag{5}$$

Proposition (1) above—that dictatorships tend to redistribute more than democracies—follows directly.

3 Redistribution in Capitalist Authoritarian States

So far in this paper I have argued that one popular explanation for the success of many devel-

---

7. Axelrod (1984, ch. 4) finds "minimum connected winning coalition" to be superior to the minimum winning coalition concept in explaining coalition formation in democratic politics.

oping countries with authoritarian political systems such as South Korea or Singapore—namely, that the authoritarian governments there redistribute less or are less subject to inefficiencies caused by rent-seeking than democracies—is misguided. I have tried to show, on the contrary, that *all* dictators can be expected to redistribute more than democracies do. As far as the facts are concerned, I know of no systematic evidence on this question, but it is well known that there is massive redistribution in totalitarian dictatorships and that most left-wing dictatorships tend to be redistributive in nature. It might appear more controversial to contend that the analysis applies also to "capitalist authoritarian" dictatorships, but I have no hesitation in suggesting that it applies to these countries as well. The point has been missed, in my view, because of the "fallacy of the free market," that is, the common assumption in this literature that markets operate costlessly, so that to have free markets, it is only necessary for the government to get out of the way. Once the central point of the efficiency wage literature is grasped, that power relationships are central to competitive market behavior, then it is clear that how markets work depends on how property rights are specified and enforced....

Although I do not have the space here to provide proper details, perhaps enough has been said to suggest that the economic success of "capitalist authoritarian" governments is not difficult to explain. It is not because they do not redistribute income, but because they *do* redistribute income—in particular, by adopting measures that transfer rights over the control of labor from labor to capital. Dictators whose support is based on capital (either domestic or international) have an obvious reason to be future oriented, because the future returns to capital are capitalized into its price, and an increased prospect of economic growth that raises those returns increases the wealth of capital owners in the present. Moreover, to the extent that these regimes successfully discipline labor, and attract capital investment, the marginal product of labor is raised, possibly bringing long-run increases in real wages as well [though as of 1990, real wages in Chile, for example, were not much above their 1970 levels (Bresser-Pereira, et al. 1993)]. This is not a complete explanation of the economic success of these countries, because many other elements (especially their export orientation) obviously enter the picture as well. But, insofar as the rent-seeking and redistributive elements of policy are concerned, this explanation strikes me as superior to the idea that their success is due to an absence of redistribution.

References

Becker, G. 1983. A theory of competition among pressure groups for political influence, *Quarterly Journal of Economics*, 98, 371–400.

Bresser Pereira, L. C., J. M. Maravall, and A. Przeworski. 1993. *Economic Reform in New Democracies: A Social Democratic Approach*, Cambridge University Press, Cambridge.

Coughlin, P. 1986. Elections and income redistribution, *Public Choice*, 50, 27–99.

Coughlin, P., D. Mueller, and P. Murrell. 1990. Electoral politics, interest groups and the size of government, *Economic Inquiry*, 28, 682–705.

Haggard, S. 1990. *Pathways from the Periphery: The Politics of Growth in the Newly Industrializing Countries*, Cornell University Press, Ithaca, N.Y.

Krueger, A. O. 1974. The political economy of the rent-seeking society, *American Economic Review*, 64, 291–303.

Meltzer, A. H., and S. F. Richard. 1981. A rational theory of the size of government, *Journal of Political Economy*, 89, 914–927.

Mueller, D. 1989. *Public Choice II*, Cambridge University Press, New York.

Olson, M. 1982. *The Rise and Decline of Nations*, Yale University Press, New Haven, Conn.

———. 1993. Dictatorship, democracy and development, *American Political Science Review*, 87, 567–575.

Posner, R. A. 1975. The social costs of monopoly and regulation, *Journal of Political Economy*, 83, 807–827.

Przeworski, A. 1991. *Democracy and the Market: Political and Economic Reforms in Eastern Europe and Latin America*, Cambridge University Press, New York.

Stigler, G. 1970. Director's law of public income redistribution, *Journal of Law and Economics*, 13, 1–10.

Tullock, G. 1967. The welfare cost of tariffs, monopolies, and theft, *Western Economic Journal*, 5, 224–232.

Dictatorship, Democracy, and Development

Mancur Olson

In my student days, in reading Edward Banfield's (1958) account of the beliefs of the people in a poor village in Southern Italy, I came upon a remarkable statement by a village monarchist. He said, "Monarchy is the best kind of government because the King is then owner of the country. Like the owner of a house, when the wiring is wrong, he fixes it" (p. 26). The villager's argument jarred against my democratic convictions. I could not deny that the owner of a country would have an incentive to make his property productive. Could the germ of truth in the monarchist's argument be reconciled with the case for democracy?

It is only in recent years that I have arrived at an answer to this question. It turns out that for a satisfactory answer one needs a new theory of dictatorship and democracy and of how each of these types of government affects economic development. Once this new theory is understood, one can begin to see how autocracies and democracies first emerge. I shall set out this conception in a brief and informal way and use it to explain some of the most conspicuous features of historical experience.

The starting point for the theory is that no society can work satisfactorily if it does not have a peaceful order and usually other public goods as well. Obviously, anarchic violence cannot be rational for a society: the victims of violence and theft lose not only what is taken from them but also the incentive to produce any goods that would be taken by others. There is accordingly little or no production in the absence of a peaceful order. Thus there are colossal gains

from providing domestic tranquility and other basic public goods. These gains can be shared in ways that leave everyone in a society better off....

Excerpted from: Mancur Olson, "Dictatorship, Democracy, and Development." *American Political Science Review* 87(3) (Sep. 1993): 567–576. © 1993 American Political Science Association. Reprinted with the permission of the American Political Science Association and Cambridge University Press.

The First Blessing of the Invisible Hand

Why, then, have most populous societies throughout history normally avoided anarchy? An answer came to me by chance when reading about a Chinese warlord (see Sheridan 1966). In the 1920s, China was in large part under the control of various warlords. They were men who led some armed band with which they conquered some territory and who then appointed themselves lords of that territory. They taxed the population heavily and pocketed much of the proceeds. The warlord Feng Yu-hsiang was noted for the exceptional extent to which he used his army for suppressing bandits and for his defeat of the relatively substantial army of the *roving bandit*, White Wolf. Apparently most people in Feng's domain found him much preferable to the roving bandits.

At first, this seems puzzling: Why should warlords, who were *stationary bandits* continuously stealing from a given group of victims, be preferred, by those victims, to roving bandits who soon departed? The warlords had no claim to legitimacy and their thefts were distinguished from those of roving bandits only because they took the form of continuing taxation rather than occasional plunder.

In fact, if a roving bandit rationally settles down and takes his theft in the form of regular taxation and at the same time maintains a monopoly on theft in his domain, then those from whom he exacts taxes will have an incentive to produce. The rational stationary bandit will take only a *part* of income in taxes, because he will be able to exact a larger total amount of income from his subjects if he leaves them with an incentive to generate income that he can tax.

If the stationary bandit successfully monopolizes the theft in his domain, then his victims do not need to worry about theft by others. If he steals only through regular taxation, then his subjects know that they can keep whatever proportion of their output is left after they have paid their taxes. Since all of the settled bandit's victims are for him a source of tax payments, he also has an incentive to prohibit the murder or maiming of his subjects. With the rational monopolization of theft—in contrast to uncoordinated competitive theft—the victims of the theft can expect to retain whatever capital they accumulate out of after-tax income and therefore also have an incentive to save and to invest, thereby increasing future income and tax receipts. The monopolization of theft and the protection of the tax-generating subjects thereby eliminates anarchy. Since the warlord takes a part of total production in the form of tax theft, it will also pay him to provide other public goods whenever the provision of these goods increases taxable income sufficiently.

In a world of roving banditry there is little or no incentive for anyone to produce or accumulate anything that may be stolen and, thus, little for bandits to steal. Bandit rationality, accordingly, induces the bandit leader to seize a given domain, to make himself the ruler of that domain, and to provide a peaceful order and other public goods for its inhabitants, thereby obtaining more in tax theft than he could have obtained from migratory plunder. Thus we have "the first blessing of the invisible hand": the rational, self-interested leader of a band of roving bandits is led, as though by an invisible hand, to settle down, wear a crown, and replace anarchy with government. The gigantic increase in output that normally arises from the provision of a peaceful order and other public goods gives the stationary bandit a far larger take than he could obtain without providing government.

Thus government for groups larger than tribes normally arises, not because of social contracts or voluntary transactions of any kind, but rather because of rational self-interest among those who can organize the greatest capacity for violence. These violent entrepreneurs naturally do not call themselves bandits but, on the contrary, give themselves and their descendants exalted titles. They sometimes even claim to rule by divine right. Since history is written by the winners, the origins of ruling dynasties are, of course, conventionally explained in terms of lofty motives rather than by self-interest. Autocrats of all kinds usually claim that their subjects want them to rule and thereby nourish the unhistorical assumption that government arose out of some kind of voluntary choice. . . .

Any individual who has autocratic control over a country will provide public goods to that country because he has an "encompassing interest" in it.[5] The extent of the encompassing interest of an office-holder, political party, interest group, monarch, or any other partial or total "owner" of a society varies with the size of the stake in the society. The larger or more encompassing the stake an organization or individual has in a society, the greater the incentive the organization or individual has to take action to provide public goods for the society. If an autocrat received one-third of any increase in the income of his domain in increased tax collections, he would then get one-third of the benefits of the public goods he provided. He would then have an incentive to provide public goods up to the point where the national income rose by the reciprocal of one-third, or three, from his last unit of public good expenditure. Though the society's

---

5. For the definition of an encompassing interest and evidence of its importance, see Olson 1982. The logical structure of the theory that encompassing interests will be concerned with the outcome for society whereas narrow groups will not is identical with the logic that shows that small groups can engage in voluntary collective action when large groups cannot.

income and welfare would obviously be greater from a larger expenditure on public goods, the gain to society from the public goods that a rational self-interested autocrat provides are nonetheless often colossal. Consider, for example, the gains from replacing a violent anarchy with a minimal degree of public order.

From history, we know that the encompassing interest of the tax-collecting autocrat permits a considerable development of civilization. From not long after the first development of settled agriculture until, say, about the time of the French Revolution, the overwhelming majority of mankind was subject to autocracy and tax theft. History until relatively recent times has been mostly a story of the gradual progress of civilization under stationary bandits interrupted by occasional episodes of roving banditry. From about the time that Sargon's conquests created the empire of Akkad until, say, the time of Louis XVI and Voltaire, there was an impressive development of civilization that occurred in large part under stationary banditry.[6]

The Grasping Hand

We can now begin to reconcile the village monarchist's insight and the foregoing argument with the case for democracy. Though the village monarchist was right in saying that the absolute ruler has as much incentive to fix what needs repair as the owner of a house, his analogy is nonetheless profoundly misleading. The autocrat is not in a position analogous to the owner of a single house or even to the owner of all housing,

but rather to the owner of *all* wealth, both tangible and human, in a country. The autocrat does indeed have an incentive to maintain and increase the productivity of everything and everyone in his domain, and his subjects will gain from this. But he also has an incentive to charge a *monopoly* rent and to levy this monopoly charge on *everything*, including human labor.

In other words, the autocratic ruler has an incentive to extract the maximum possible surplus from the whole society and to use it for his own purposes. Exactly the *same* rational self-interest that makes a roving bandit settle down and provide government for his subjects also makes him extract the maximum possible amount from the society for himself. He will use his monopoly of coercive power to obtain the maximum take in taxes and other exactions....

Although the forms that stationary banditry has taken over the course of history are diverse, the essence of the matter can be seen by assuming that the autocrat gets all of his receipts in the form of explicit taxation. The rational autocrat will devote some of the resources he obtains through taxation to public goods but will impose far higher tax rates than are needed to pay for the public goods since he also uses tax collections to maximize his net surplus. The higher the level of provision of public goods, given the tax rate, the higher the society's income and the yield from this tax rate. At the same time, the higher the tax rate, given the level of public-good provision, the lower the income of society, since taxes distort incentives....

Though the subjects of the autocrat are better off than they would be under anarchy, they must endure taxes or other impositions so high that, if they were increased further, income would fall by so much that even the autocrat, who absorbs only a portion of the fall in income in the form of lower tax collections, would be worse off.

There is no lack of historical examples in which autocrats for their own political and military purposes collected as much revenue as they possibly could....

6. Many of the more remarkable advances in civilization even in historic times took place in somewhat democratic or nondictatorial societies such as ancient Athens, the Roman Republic, the North Italian city-states, the Netherlands in the seventeenth century, and (at least after 1689) Great Britain. The explanation for the disproportionate representation of nonautocratic jurisdictions in human progress is presented later in the article.

The Reach of Dictatorships and Democracies Compared

How would government by a rational self-interested autocrat compare with a democracy? Democracies vary so much that no one conclusion can cover all cases. Nonetheless, many practical insights can be obtained by thinking first about one of the simplest democratic situations. This is a situation in which there are two candidates for a presidency or two well-disciplined parties seeking to form the government. This simplifying assumption will be favorable to democratic performance, for it gives the democracy an "encompassing" interest rather like the one that motivates the stationary bandit to provide some public goods. I shall make the opposite assumption later. But throughout, I shall avoid giving democracy an unfair advantage by assuming better motivation. I shall impartially assume that the democratic political leaders are just as self interested as the stationary bandit and will use any expedient to obtain majority support.

Observation of two-party democracies tells us that incumbents like to run on a "you-never-had-it-so-good" record. An incumbent obviously would not leave himself with such a record if, like the self-interested autocrat, he took for himself the largest possible net surplus from the society. But we are too favorable to democracy if we assume that the incumbent party or president will maximize his chances of reelection simply by making the electorate as a whole as well-off as possible.

A candidate needs only a majority to win, and he might be able to "buy" a majority by transferring income from the population at large to a prospective majority. The taxes needed for this transfer would impair incentives and reduce society's output just as an autocrat's redistribution to himself does. Would this competition to buy votes generate as much distortion of incentives through taxation as a rational autocracy

does? That is, would a vote-buying democratic leader, like the rational autocrat, have an incentive to push tax rates to the revenue-maximizing level?

No. Though both the majority and the autocrat have an encompassing interest in the society because they control tax collections, the majority in addition earns a significant share of the market income of the society, and this gives it a more encompassing interest in the productivity of the society. The majority's interest in its market earnings induces it to redistribute less to itself than an autocrat redistributes to himself. This is evident from considering an option that a democratic majority would have if it were at the revenue-maximizing tax rate. At the revenue-maximizing tax rate, a minuscule change in the tax rates will not alter tax collections. A minuscule *increase* in the tax rate will reduce the national income by enough so that even though a larger percentage of income is taken in taxes, the amount collected remains unchanged, and a tiny *reduction* in the tax rate will increase the national income so much that even though a smaller percentage is taken in taxes, receipts are unchanged. This is the optimal tax rate for the autocrat because changes in the national income affect his income only by changing tax collections.

But a majority at the revenue-maximizing tax rate is bound to increase its income from a *reduction* in tax rates: when the national income goes up, it not only, like the autocrat, collects taxes on a larger national income but also earns more income in the market. So the optimal tax rate for it is bound to be lower than the autocrat's....

More generally, it pays a ruling interest (whether an autocrat, a majority, or any other) to stop redistributing income to itself when the national income falls by the reciprocal of the share of the national income it receives. If the revenue-maximizing tax rate were one-half, an autocrat would stop increasing taxes when the national income fell by two dollars from his last dollar of tax collection. A majority that, say, earned three-fifths of the national income in the market and found it optimal to take one-fifth of the national income to transfer to itself would necessarily be reducing the national income by five-fourths, or $1.25, from the last dollar that it redistributed to itself. Thus the more encompassing an interest—the larger the share of the national income it receives taking all sources together—the less the social losses from its redistributions to itself. Conversely, the narrower the interest, the less it will take account of the social costs of redistributions to itself.

This last consideration makes it clear why the assumption that the democracy is governed by an encompassing interest can lead to much-too-optimistic predictions about many real-world democracies. The small parties that often emerge under proportional representation, for example, may encompass only a tiny percentage of a society and therefore may have little or no incentive to consider the social cost of the steps they take on behalf of their narrow constituencies. The special interest groups that are the main determinant of what government policies prevail in the particular areas of interest to those interest groups have almost no incentive to consider the social costs of the redistributions they obtain. . . .

It would therefore be wrong to conclude that democracies will necessarily redistribute less than dictatorships. Their redistributions will, however, be shared, often quite unequally, by the citizenry. Democratic political competition, even when it works very badly, does not give the leader of the government the incentive that an autocrat has to extract the maximum attainable social surplus from the society to achieve his personal objectives.

Long Live the King

We know that an economy will generate its maximum income only if there is a high rate of investment and that much of the return on long-term investments is received long after the investment is made. This means that an autocrat who is taking a long view will try to convince his subjects that their assets will be permanently protected not only from theft by others but also from expropriation by the autocrat himself. If his subjects fear expropriation, they will invest less, and in the long run his tax collections will be reduced. To reach the maximum income attainable at a given tax rate, a society will also need to enforce contracts, such as contracts for long-term loans, impartially; but the full gains are again reaped only in the long run. To obtain the full advantage from long-run contracts a country also needs a stable currency. A stationary bandit will therefore reap the maximum harvest in taxes—and his subjects will get the largest gain from his encompassing interest in the productivity of his domain—only if he is taking an indefinitely long view and only if his subjects have total confidence that their "rights" to private property and to impartial contract enforcement will be permanently respected and that the coin or currency will retain its full value.

Now suppose that an autocrat is only concerned about getting through the next year. He will then gain by expropriating any convenient capital asset whose *tax yield* over the year is less than its *total* value. He will also gain from forgetting about the enforcement of long-term contracts, from repudiating his debts, and from coining or printing new money that he can spend even though this ultimately brings inflation. At the limit, when an autocrat has no reason to consider the future output of the society at all, his incentives are those of a roving bandit and that is what he becomes.[10]

---

10. When war erodes confidence about what the boundaries of an autocrat's domain will be, an autocrat's time horizon with respect to his possession of any given territory shortens—even if he believes that he will remain in control of some territory somewhere. In the limit, complete uncertainty about what territory an autocrat will control implies roving banditry. The advantages of stationary banditry over roving banditry are obviously greatest when there are natural and militarily defensible frontiers. Interestingly, the earliest

To be sure, the rational autocrat will have an incentive, because of his interest in increasing the investment and trade of his subjects, to promise that he will never confiscate wealth or repudiate assets. But the promise of an autocrat is not enforceable by an independent judiciary or any other independent source of power, because autocratic power by definition implies that there cannot be any judges or other sources of power in the society that the autocrat cannot overrule. Because of this and the obvious possibility that any dictator could, because of an insecure hold on power or the absence of an heir, take a short-term view, the promises of an autocrat are never completely credible. Thus the model of the rational self-interested autocrat I have offered is, in fact, somewhat too sanguine about economic performance under such autocrats because it implicitly assumed that they have (and that their subjects believe that they have) an indefinitely long planning horizon.

Many autocrats, at least at times, have had short time horizons: the examples of confiscations, repudiated loans, debased coinages, and inflated currencies perpetrated by monarchs and dictators over the course of history are almost beyond counting. . . .

Democracy, Individual Rights, and Economic Development

We have seen that whenever a dictator has a sufficiently short time horizon, it is in his interest

---

states in history emerged mainly in what one anthropologist calls "environmentally circumscribed" areas, that is, areas of arable land surrounded by deserts, mountains, or coasts (see Carneiro 1970). The environmental circumscription not only provides militarily viable frontiers but also limits the opportunity for defeated tribes to flee to other areas in which they could support themselves (as Carneiro points out). This in turn means that the consensual democracy characteristic of the earliest stages of social evolution is, in these geographical conditions, replaced by autocratic states earlier than in other conditions.

to confiscate the property of his subjects, to abrogate any contracts he has signed in borrowing money from them, and generally to ignore the long-run economic consequences of his choices. Even the ever-present possibility that an autocracy will come to be led by someone with a short time horizon always reduces confidence in investments and in the enforcement of long-run contracts. What do the individuals in an economy need if they are to have the maximum confidence that any property they accumulate will be respected and that any contracts they sign will be impartially enforced?

They need a secure government that respects individual rights. But individual rights are normally an artifact of a special set of governmental institutions. There is no private property without government! In a world of roving bandits some individuals may have possessions, but no one has a claim to private property that is enforced by the society. There is typically no reliable contract enforcement unless there is an impartial court system that can call upon the coercive power of the state to require individuals to honor the contracts they have made.

But individuals need their property and their contract rights protected from violation not only by other individuals in the private sector but also by the entity that has the greatest power in the society, namely, the government itself. An economy will be able to reap all potential gains from investment and from long-term transactions only if it has a government that is believed to be both strong enough to last and inhibited from violating individual rights to property and rights to contract enforcement. What does a society need in order to have a government that satisfies both of these conditions?

Interestingly, the conditions that are needed to have the individual rights needed for maximum economic development are exactly the same conditions that are needed to have a *lasting* democracy. Obviously, a democracy is not viable if individuals, including the leading rivals of the administration in power, lack the rights to free speech and to security for their property and contracts or if the rule of law is not followed even when it calls for the current administration to leave office. Thus the *same* court system, independent judiciary, and respect for law and individual rights that are needed for a lasting democracy are also required for security of property and contract rights.

As the foregoing reasoning suggests, the only societies where individual rights to property and contract are confidently expected to last across generations are the securely democratic societies. In an autocracy, the autocrat will often have a short time horizon, and the absence of any independent power to assure an orderly legal succession means that there is always substantial uncertainty about what will happen when the current autocrat is gone. History provides not even a single example of a long and uninterrupted sequence of absolute rulers who continuously respected the property and contract-enforcement rights of their subjects. Admittedly, the terms, tenures, and time horizons of democratic political leaders are perhaps even shorter than those of the typical autocrat, and democracies lose a good deal of efficiency because of this. But in the secure democracy with predictable succession of power under the rule of law, the adjudication and enforcement of individual rights is not similarly short-sighted. Many individuals in the secure democracies confidently make even very-long-term contracts, establish trusts for great-grandchildren, and create foundations that they expect will last indefinitely and thereby reveal that they expect their legal rights to be secure for the indefinite future.

... Though experience shows that relatively poor countries can grow extraordinarily rapidly when they have a strong dictator who happens to have unusually good economic policies, such growth lasts only for the ruling span of one or two dictators. It is no accident that the countries that have reached the highest level of economic development and have enjoyed good economic performance across generations are all stable democracies. Democracies have also been about twice as likely to win wars as have dictatorships (Lake 1992). ...

The Different Sources of Progress in Autocracies and Democracies

. . .

The use of the same motivational assumption and the same theory to treat both autocracy and democracy ... illuminates the main difference in the sources of economic growth and the obstacles to progress under autocracy and under democracy. In an autocracy, the source of order and other public goods and likewise the source of the social progress that these public goods make possible is the encompassing interest of the autocrat. The main obstacle to long-run progress in autocracies is that individual rights even to such relatively unpolitical or economic matters as property and contracts can never be secure, at least over the long run.

Although democracies can also obtain great advantages from encompassing offices and political parties, this is by no means always understood (Olson 1982, 1986); nor are the awesome difficulties in keeping narrow special interests from dominating economic policymaking in the long-stable democracy. On the other hand, democracies have the great advantage of preventing significant extraction of social surplus by their leaders. They also have the extraordinary virtue that the same emphasis on individual rights that is necessary to lasting democracy is also necessary for secure rights to both property and the enforcement of contracts. The moral appeal of democracy is now almost universally appreciated, but its economic advantages are scarcely understood.

References

Banfield, Edward. 1958. *The Moral Basis of a Backward Society*. Glencoe, IL: Free Press.

Lake, David A. 1992. "Powerful Pacifists: Democratic States and War." *American Political Science Review* 86: 24–37.

Olson, Mancur. 1982. *The Rise and Decline of Nations.* New Haven: Yale University Press.

Olson, Mancur. 1986. "A Theory of the Incentives Facing Political Organizations: Neo-corporatism and the Hegemonic State." *International Political Science Review* 7: 165–89.

Sheridan, James E. 1966. *Chinese Warlord. The Career of Feng Yu-hsiang.* Stanford: Stanford University Press.

Freedom Favors Development

Amartya Sen

... It is true that some relatively authoritarian states (such as Lee's Singapore, South Korea under military rule and, more recently, China) have had faster rates of economic growth than some less authoritarian states (such as India, Costa Rica and Jamaica). But the overall picture is much more complex that such isolated observations might suggest.

Systematic statistical studies give little support to the view of a general conflict between civil rights and economic performance.... The general thesis in praise of the tough state suffers not only from casual empiricism based on a few selected examples, but also from a lack of conceptual discrimination. Political and civil rights come in various types, and authoritarian intrusions take many forms. It would be a mistake, for example, to equate North Korea with South Korea in the infringement of political rights, even though both have violated many such rights....

It is also necessary to examine more rigorously the causal process that is supposed to underlie these generalizations about the impact of authoritarianism on prosperity. The processes that led to the economic success of, say, South Korea are now reasonably well understood. A variety of factors played a part, including the use of international markets, an openness to competition, a high level of literacy, successful land reforms and the provision of selective incentives to encourage growth and exports. There is nothing to indicate that these economic and social policies were inconsistent with greater democracy, that they had to be sustained by the elements of authoritarianism actually present in South Korea.

Excerpted from: Amartya Sen, "Freedom Favors Development." *New Perspectives Quarterly* 13, no. 4 (1996). © Center for the Study of Democratic Institutions. Reprinted by permission.

The fundamental importance of political rights is not refuted by some allegedly negative effect of these rights on economic performance. In fact, the instrumental connections may even give a very positive role to political rights in the context of deprivations of a drastic and elementary kind: whether, and how, a government responds to intense needs and sufferings may well depend on how much pressure is put on it, and whether or not pressure is put on it will depend on the exercise of political rights such as voting, criticizing and protesting.

Consider the matter of famine. I have tried to argue elsewhere that the avoidance of such economic disasters as famines is made much easier by the existence, and the exercise, of various liberties and political rights, including the liberty of free expression. Indeed, one of the remarkable facts in the terrible history of famine is that no substantial famine has ever occurred in a country with a democratic form of government and a relatively free press....

Is this historical association between the absence of famine and the presence of political freedom a causal one, or is it simply an accidental connection? The possibility that the connection between democratic political rights and the absence of famine is a "bogus correlation" may seem plausible when one considers the fact that democratic countries are typically rather rich, and thus immune to famine for other reasons. But the absence of famine holds even for those democratic countries that happen to be poor, such as India, Botswana and Zimbabwe.

There is also what we might call "intertemporal evidence," which we observe when a country undergoes a transition to democracy. Thus India continued to have famines right up to the time of independence in 1947.... Since independence, however, and the installation of a multiparty democratic system, there has been no substantial famine, even though severe crop failures and food scarcities have occurred often enough (in 1968, 1973, 1979 and 1987).

Why might we expect a general connection between democracy and the nonoccurrence of famines? The answer is not hard to find. Famines kill millions of people in different countries in the world, but they do not kill the rulers. The kings and the presidents, the bureaucrats and the bosses, the military leaders and the commanders never starve. And if there are no elections, no opposition parties, no forums for uncensored public criticism, then those in authority do not have to suffer the political consequences of their failure to prevent famine. Democracy, by contrast, would spread the penalty of famine to the ruling groups and the political leadership.

There is, moreover, the issue of information. A free press, and more generally the practice of democracy, contributes greatly to bringing out the information that can have an enormous impact on policies for famine prevention, such as facts about the early effects of droughts and floods, and about the nature and the results of unemployment. The most elementary source of basic information about a threatening famine is the news media, especially when there are incentives, which a democratic system provides, for revealing facts that may be embarrassing to the government, facts that an undemocratic regime would tend to censor. Indeed, I would argue that a free press and an active political opposition constitute the best "early warning system" that a country threatened by famine can possess....

The connection between political rights and economic needs can be illustrated in the specific context of famine prevention by considering the massive Chinese famines of 1958–61....

The so-called "Great Leap Forward," initiated in the late 1950s, was a massive failure, but the Chinese government refused to admit it and continued dogmatically to pursue much the same disastrous policies for three more years. It is hard to imagine that this could have happened in a country that goes to the polls regularly and has an independent press. During that

terrible calamity, the government faced no pressure from newspapers, which were controlled, or from opposition parties, which were not allowed to exist....

These issues remain relevant in China today. Since the economic reforms of 1979, official Chinese policies have been based on the acknowledgment of the importance of economic incentives without a similar acknowledgment of the importance of political incentives. When things go reasonably well, the disciplinary role of democracy might not be greatly missed; but when big policy mistakes are made, this lacuna can be quite disastrous. The significance of the democracy movements in contemporary China has to be judged in this light....

Another set of examples comes from sub-Saharan Africa, which has been plagued by persistent famine since the early 1970s. There are many factors underlying the susceptibility of this region to famine, from the ecological impact of climatic deterioration—making crops more uncertain—to the negative effects of persistent wars and skirmishes. But the typically authoritarian nature of many of the sub-Saharan African polities also has something to do with the frequency of famine.

One must not deny that there were African governments, even in one-party states, that were deeply concerned about averting disasters and famine. Examples of this range from the tiny country of Cape Verde to the politically experimental nation of Tanzania. But quite often the absence of opposition and the suppression of free newspapers gave the respective governments an immunity from social criticism and political pressure that translated into thoroughly insensitive and callous policies....

In making such arguments, of course, there is the danger of exaggerating the effectiveness of democracy. Political rights and liberties are permissive advantages, and their effectiveness depends on how they are exercised. Democracies have been particularly successful in preventing disasters that are easy to understand, in which sympathy can take an especially immediate form. Many other problems are not quite so accessible. Thus India's success in eradicating famine is not matched by a similar success in eliminating non-extreme hunger, or in curing persistent illiteracy, or in relieving inequalities in gender relations. While the plight of famine victims is easy to politicize, these other deprivations call for deeper analysis, and for greater and more effective use of mass communication and political participation—in sum, for a further practice of democracy.

A similar observation may be made about various failings in more mature democracies as well. For example, the extraordinary deprivations in health care, education and social environment of African Americans in the US make their mortality rates exceptionally high....

But, again, the remedy of these failures in the practice of democracy turns, to a great extent, on the fuller use of political and civil rights, including more public discussion, more accessible information and more concrete proposals....

Political rights are important not only for the fulfillment of needs, they are crucial also for the formulation of needs. And this idea relates, in the end, to the respect that we owe each other as fellow human beings....

... The importance of political rights for the understanding of economic needs turns ultimately on seeing human beings as people with rights to exercise, not as parts of a "stock" or a "population" that passively exists and must be looked after. What matters, finally, is how we see each other.

Political Regimes and Economic Growth

Adam Przeworski, Michael E. Alvarez, José Antonio Cheibub, and Fernando Limongi

Introduction

With the birth of new nations in Asia and Africa, the fear that democracy would undermine economic growth began to be voiced in the United States. The first statements to that effect were perhaps those by Walter Galenson and by Karl de Schweinitz, who argued, both in 1959, that in poor countries democracy unleashes pressures for immediate consumption, which occurs at the cost of investment, hence of growth. Galenson mentioned both the role of unions and that of governments. He thought that unions "must ordinarily appeal to the worker on an all-out consumptionist platform. No matter how much 'responsibility' the union leader exhibits in his understanding of the limited consumption possibilities existing at the outset of industrialization, he cannot afford to moderate his demands." As for governments, he observed that "the more democratic a government is, ... the greater the diversion of resources from investment to consumption." According to de Schweinitz (1959: 388), if trade unions and labor parties "are successful in securing a larger share of the national income and limiting the freedom for action of entrepreneurs, they may have the effect of restricting investment surplus so much that the rate of economic growth is inhibited." That argument enjoyed widespread acceptance under the influence of Huntington, who claimed that "the interest of the voters generally leads parties to give the expansion of personal consumption a higher priority via-à-vis investment than it would re-

ceive in a non-democratic system" (Huntington and Domiguez 1975: 60; Huntington 1968).

Democracy was thus seen as inimical to economic development. Moreover, via a rather dubious inference, proponents of that view concluded that dictatorships were therefore better able to force savings and launch economic growth. To cite a more recent statement: "Economic development is a process for which huge investments in personnel and material are required. Such investment programs imply cuts in current consumption that would be painful at the low levels of living that exist in almost all developing societies. Governments must resort to strong measures and they enforce them with an iron hand in order to marshal the surpluses needed for investment. If such measures were put to a popular vote, they would surely be defeated. No political party can hope to win a democratic election on a platform of current sacrifices for a *bright future*" (Rao 1984: 75).[1]

The reasoning bears reconstruction. First, that argument assumes that poor people have a higher propensity to consume.[2] This is why democracy may be compatible with growth at high but not at low levels of income. Second, the

Excerpted from: Adam Przeworski, Michael E. Alvarez, José Antonio Cheibub, and Fernando Limongi, *Democracy and Development: Political Institutions and Well-Being in the World, 1950–1990*. Cambridge: Cambridge University Press, 2000. © Adam Przeworski, Michael E. Alvarez, José Antonio Cheibub, and Fernando Limongi, 2000. Reprinted with the permission of Cambridge University Press.

---

1. At least Huntington and his collaborators wrote during a period when many dictatorships, "authoritarian" and "totalitarian," did grow rapidly. But Rao's assertion was made in 1984, after the failure of several Latin American authoritarian regimes and Eastern European communist regimes was already apparent.

2. Pasinetti (1961) claimed that the propensity to consume is higher for workers than for capitalists, and Kaldor (1956) believed that it is higher for wages than for profits, whereas the scholars discussed here seem to assume that in general the marginal propensity to consume declines with income. Barro and Sala-i-Martin (1995: 77–79) show that in the optimal growth model the savings rate decreases as a result of the substitution effect and increases in income as a consequence of the income effect, the net effect being ambivalent.

underlying model of growth attributes it to the increase in the stock of physical capital. Finally, democracy is always responsive to pressures for immediate consumption. The chain of reasoning is thus the following: (1) Poor people want to consume immediately. (2) When workers are able to organize, they drive wages up, reduce profits, and reduce investment (by lowering either the rate of return or the volume of profit or both). (3) When people are allowed to vote, governments tend to distribute income away from investment (either they tax and transfer or they undertake less public investment). (4) Lowering investment slows down growth. Note, as well, that this reasoning implies that the impact of mean-preserving inequality on growth is ambivalent: In the Kaldor-Pasinetti models, inequality promotes growth, as it increases the incomes of those who save more, but in the median-voter models it slows down growth to the extent to which the political system responds to demands for redistribution.

Arguments in favor of democracy are not equally sharp, but they all focus in one form or another on allocative efficiency: Democracies can better allocate the available resources to productive uses. One view is that because authoritarian rulers are not accountable to electorates, they have no incentive to maximize total output, but only their own rents. As a result, democracies better protect property rights, thus allowing a longer-term perspective to investors. There is also a vague sense that by permitting a free flow of information, democracies somehow improve the quality of economic decisions.

According to the first view, the state is always ready to prey on the society (North 1990), and only democratic institutions can constrain it to act in a more general interest. Hence, dictatorships, of any stripe, are sources of inefficiency. Barro (1990), Findlay (1990), Olson (1991), and Przeworski (1990) have constructed models that differ in detail but generate the same conclusion. These models assume that some level of government intervention in the economy is optimal for

growth. Then they all show that, depending on the details of each model, dictatorships of various stripes can be expected to undersupply or oversupply government activities. One interesting variant of this approach is by Robinson (1995), who thinks that dictators are afraid, at least under some conditions, that development would give rise to political forces that would overturn them, and thus they deliberately abstain from developmentalist policies.

Perhaps the best-known informational argument is based on the Drèze and Sen (1989) observation that no democracy ever experienced a famine, which they attribute to the alarm role of the press and the opposition. Thus, Sen (1994a: 34) observes that "a free press and an active political opposition constitute the best 'early warning system' that a country threatened by famine can possess." He also cites an unlikely source, Mao, reflecting on the great Chinese famine of 1962, to the effect that "without democracy, you have no understanding of what is happening down below." Yet it is not apparent whether this is an argument strictly about avoiding disasters or about average performance.[3]

This summary makes no pretense to being exhaustive. All we want to highlight is that the arguments in favor of dictatorship and those in favor of democracy are not necessarily incompatible. The arguments against democracy claim that it hinders growth by reducing investment; the arguments in its favor maintain that it fosters growth by promoting allocative efficiency. Both may be true: The rate at which productive factors grow may be higher under dictatorship, but

---

3. Sah and Stiglitz (1988) compared the quality of the decisions whether or not to undertake a series of economic projects made under different decision rules. Their conclusions are ambivalent: Although majority rule is conducive to good decisions under many conditions, decisions by smaller groups are better when the costs of information are high, whereas decisions by larger groups are superior when the chances of adopting a bad project are high.

the use of resources may be more efficient under democracy. And because these mechanisms work in opposite directions, the net effect may be that there is no difference between the two regimes in the average rates of growth they generate. The patterns of growth may differ, but the average rates of growth may still be the same.

Rates of growth may thus differ between regimes either because the productive inputs increase at different rates or because they are used with different efficiencies....

Political Regimes and Economic Growth

The observed rate of growth of total income ($YG = \dot{Y}/Y$) is higher under dictatorships, 4.42, than under democracies, 3.95, implying that income doubles in 15.8 years under dictatorship and in 17.7 years under democracy. Yet we already know that one should not draw inferences from the observed values.

To identify the effect of regimes, we need to distinguish the effects of the conditions under which these regimes were observed from the effect of regimes. We present first the results concerning the effect of regimes on the growth of productive inputs, then those concerning the efficiency with which these inputs are used under each regime, and, finally, the conclusions about the overall effect of regimes on the growth of total income.

Do productive inputs grow at the same rate under the two regimes? The claim that democracy undermines investment, whether in general or only in poor countries, finds no support in the evidence. The observed average share of investment in gross domestic product (GDP), $INV = I/Y$, was in fact much higher in democracies, 20.90 percent, than in dictatorships, 14.25 percent. But because investment shares increase with per capita income, and because, as we already know, dictatorships have generally existed in poorer countries, this could be just an effect of income. Indeed, controlling for income, as well

as for a number of other variables in a selection model, shows that regimes have no overall effect on investment.[6] ...

... [E]ven if pressures for immediate consumption are higher in poor countries, democracies do not transform them into lower rates of investment than do dictatorships. Poor countries simply invest little regardless of their regime....

In turn, the rate of growth of the labor force ($LFG = \dot{L}/L$) is higher under dictatorships.... The observed values are 2.27 percent per annum under dictatorships and 1.61 under democracies....

Because the labor force grows at a slower rate in wealthier countries, one might suspect again that this difference is due to the distribution of regimes by income. Some of it is, but not enough to eradicate the effect of regimes. Even when the regimes are matched for their income, their colonial heritage, and the frequencies of Catholics, Protestants, and Moslems, even if they are matched for demand (2SLS), or for the lagged rate of population growth (HATANAKA estimator), or for country-specific effects (PANEL estimator), as well as for the factors affecting selection, and, in a smaller sample, for the labor-force participation of women (LFPW), the labor force grows faster under dictatorships....

To examine the effect of regimes on the efficiency with which resources are used in production, we need to compare the coefficients of the respective production functions. The constant measures total factor productivity, and the coef-

---

6. The variables in the investment equation include lagged investment share (given that investment decisions made one year take time to realize, INVLAG), lagged per capita income (an instrument for expected domestic demand, LEVLAG), the average rate of growth in the world (a measure of world demand, WORLD), and the relative price of investment goods (PINV). Alternatively, we estimate a 2SLS model with the predicted growth rate as an instrument for the current demand. For a review of econometric models of investment, see Rama (1993).

ficients on capital and labor represent the elasticities of output with regard to these factors.

... The elasticity with regard to capital is slightly higher in dictatorships, but elasticity with regard to labor is higher in democracies. Hence, one is led to conclude that democracies benefit more from technical progress and use labor more effectively, but dictatorships more efficiently employ the physical capital stock....

What, then, is the overall effect of regimes on growth? Assuming that the two regimes exist under the same conditions reduces the difference between the expected growth rates almost to zero....

Because the labor force grows faster under dictatorship even when the two regimes are matched for exogenous conditions, lines with "LFG endogenous" in table 8.1 take the rate of growth of the labor force at the mean values observed for each regime. These results are somewhat more favorable to dictatorships. But the difference between regimes is still minuscule. Hence, there is no reason to think that the regime type affects the rate of growth of total income.

Another way to test the effect of regimes is to focus on the countries that experienced regime changes. Here again, however, one should proceed prudently. Countries in which regimes are unstable may be different from those that have had single regimes persisting during the entire period. Yet the observed average rate of growth was the same in those countries that did not experience any regime transitions and in those that underwent one or more regime changes: The rate of growth for the former was 4.23 percent ($N = 2,813$), and for the latter 4.25 ($N = 1,313$). Stable dictatorships grew at the rate of 4.38 percent ($N = 1,709$), whereas dictatorships in the countries that also experienced democracy grew at the rate of 4.51 ($N = 772$). Stable democracies grew at the rate of 3.98 percent ($N = 1,104$), and democracies that rose from or gave way to dictatorships grew at 3.88 percent ($N = 541$). Hence, there is no reason to think that growth

in the countries where regimes were stable was different from that in countries where regimes changed.[12]

With this reassurance, we can compare the rates of growth of democracies preceding dictatorships with those of democracies following dictatorchips, and vice versa. The average rate of growth during all the years of democracies preceding dictatorships was 4.49 percent ($N = 290$), and for dictatorships following democracies, 4.37 ($N = 425$). Hence, transitions from democracy to dictatorship did not affect the rate of growth. Growth during all the years of dictatorships preceding democracies was higher, at the average of 4.74 percent ($N = 607$), than the average of 3.64 percent ($N = 371$) during all the democratic years that followed. But because recovery from the crises accompanying transitions to democracy is slow, and the observations are right-hand censored, the conclusion that transitions to democracy slow down growth would be erroneous. Just note that many of the democratic observations followed transitions from either bureaucratic-authoritarian or communist dictatorships during the 1980s, including the very end of the decade. Because those democracies did not have time to recover by 1990, they weigh down the democratic average.

In sum, neither the selection-corrected values for the entire sample nor the paths of growth associated with regime transitions give any support to the claim that regime types affect the rate of growth of total income. Selection-corrected average rates of growth are the same for the two regimes. And there is no reason to think that steady-state rates of growth would be different under the two regimes when countries experience regime transitions.

The first conclusion, therefore, must be that political regimes have no impact on the rate of growth of total income. The arguments about

---

12. For a more extensive discussion of the effect of regime stability on growth, see Chapter 5 [of *Democracy and Development*].

Table 8.1
Selection-corrected estimators of the rate of growth of income (YG)

| Estimator | Regime means | | Regime effect | |
	Dictatorships ($N = 2{,}396$)	Democracies ($N = 1{,}595$)	Constant ($N = 3{,}991$)	Individual
Biased	4.43	3.92	−0.0227	0.0006
	(6.94)	(4.82)	(0.1252)	(0.4908)
Unconstrained OLS	4.30	4.24		
	(5.02)	(4.48)		
Constrained OLS (LFG exogenous)	4.22	4.37		
	(5.17)	(4.60)		
Constrained OLS (LFG endogenous)	4.38	4.11		
	(5.15)	(4.55)		
PANEL (LFG exogenous)	4.22	4.23		
	(5.17)	(4.34)		
PANEL (LFG endogenous)	4.38	4.07		
	(5.15)	(4.34)		
Unobservable			0.0741	0.0461
			(0.1312)	(0.4871)
Observable			−0.0926	0.0490
			(0.1537)	(0.5061)
EDTG sample	$N = 1{,}745$	$N = 1{,}042$		
Biased	4.57	3.91		
	(6.91)	(4.71)		
Unconstrained OLS (LFG exogenous)	4.45	4.34		
	(4.71)	(3.88)		
Constrained OLS (LFG exogenous)	4.36	4.94		
	(4.87)	(4.01)		
2F PANEL (LFG exogenous)	4.45	4.33		
	(4.71)	(3.74)		

Notes: Probit equations include lagged values of LEVEL, STRA, and RELDIF. The "barebones" model includes KSG, LFG, and, in a smaller sample, EDTG. "Constrained" means that the coefficients on the arguments of the production function were constrained to 1.00. PANEL is OLS for dictatorships and 2F for democracies. "LFG exogenous" is based on the assumption that LFG is exogenous; "LFG endogenous" takes LFG at the observed mean of each regime.

the superiority of dictatorships in mobilizing savings for investment find no support in the evidence. Indeed, the input that grows faster under dictatorships is not capital but labor. The differences in the efficiency with which productive inputs are utilized are small. And, as a consequence, the selection-corrected average expected values of growth are almost identical....

Poor and Wealthy Countries

... [T]o test whether or not the results depend on the samples, we need to estimate production functions separately for different levels of development....

Poor Countries

In poor countries, the two regimes are almost identical, with observed rates of growth of 4.34 percent under dictatorship and 4.28 under democracy. The two regimes generate productive inputs at the same rate and use them in identical ways. They invest about 12.5 percent of GDP and increase capital stock at the rate of about 6 percent, and labor force at the rate of about 2.2 percent. An increase of 1 percent in the capital stock raises output by about 0.40 percent under both regimes, and an increase in the labor force by 1 percent augments output by about 0.60 percent.[15] Neither regime benefits much from technical progress, about 0.1 percent per annum; both get 2.8 percent in growth from an increase in capital stock, and 1.4 percent from an increase in labor force. With identical supplies of factors and their identical utilization, they grow at the same rate under the two regimes: The selection-corrected average growth rates are the same.

The idea that democracies in poor countries process pressures for immediate consumption, resulting in lower investment and slower growth,

seemed persuasive at the time it was advanced, and it was not implausible. There appear to be good reasons to think that people in poor countries want to consume more immediately: They cannot afford to make intertemporal trade-offs if they cannot expect to live to benefit from their short-term sacrifices. It is also plausible that unions, particularly if they are decentralized, and political parties, competing for votes, would push forward demands for immediate consumption. Yet, as likely as that view may seem, it simply is not true. Perhaps this only means that democracy is not very effective at processing what people want; perhaps developmental goals are not any more attractive to people under dictatorship than under democracy; perhaps poverty is so constraining that even dictators cannot squeeze savings out of indigent people.

The last explanation is most plausible....

Thus, poverty constrains. Whatever the regime, the society is too poor to finance an effective state....

Poor countries cannot afford a strong state, and when the state is weak, the kind of regime matters little for everyday life. In a village located three days' travel away from the capital, often the only presence of the state is a teacher and occasionally roving uniformed bandits.[17] ...

In sum, poor countries are too poor to afford a strong state, and without an effective state there is little difference any regime can make for economic development. Investment is low in poor democracies, but it is not any higher in poor dictatorships. The labor force grows rapidly in both. Development is factor-extensive: Poor countries benefit almost nothing from technical change. Clearly, this does not imply that all poor countries are the same or even that regimes may not make a difference for other aspects of people's lives; indeed, we show later that they do. But not for economic development in poor countries.

---

15. This is a constrained estimate. Constrained estimates are cited in the rest of this paragraph.

17. The best portrayal of life under a weak state is by Alvaro Mutis (1996).

Wealthy Countries

Once countries reach some level of development—somewhere between \$2,500 and \$3,000, that of Algeria in 1977, Mauritius in 1969, Costa Rica in 1966, South Korea in 1976, Czechoslovakia in 1970, or Portugal in 1966—patterns of economic development under democracy and dictatorship diverge. In countries with incomes above that threshold, regimes do make a difference for how resources are used, for how much people produce and how much they earn. . . .

Dictatorships appear not to change their ways whether they are in poor or wealthy countries. Although in more-developed economies they rely somewhat less on growth of the labor force and somewhat more on the growth of capital stock, they use the inputs in almost the same way and get little benefit from productivity growth. Democracies, in turn, exhibit different patterns in poor and wealthy countries. Their capital stock grows somewhat slower, and the labor force much slower, when they are affluent; they use labor more productively and benefit more from productivity growth. As a result, the patterns of growth are different in wealthier dictatorships and democracies.

Note . . . that the factors that differentiate wealthy dictatorships from wealthy democracies are the patterns, not averages. Corrected for selection, the average rates of growth of income are again almost identical under the two regimes. Although the observed rates of growth are higher under dictatorships, if the two regimes had used the same inputs in production, they would have grown at the same rate. But they would have grown in different ways.

Growth under wealthy dictatorships is labor-extensive. The labor force grows at a much faster pace under dictatorships, at 2.03 percent, than under democracies, where it grows at 1.32 percent. And whereas the elasticity of output with regard to labor is about 0.56 under dictatorship, it is 0.68 under democracy. Wealthier dictatorships benefit little from technical progress, 0.33;

they get most of their growth from capital, 3.05, and in spite of employing many more workers, they get less of it from labor, 0.85. Wealthier democracies benefit from technical progress, 0.91, get less growth out of capital, 2.20, and more from the labor input, 1.04, even though they employ fewer additional workers. . . .

. . . [G]rowth under wealthier dictatorships is both labor-extensive and labor-exploitative. The labor force grows faster under dictatorship, the marginal worker produces less, and the average worker much less, than under democracy. Even if they were matched for capital stock and labor force, workers would produce less under dictatorship. And labor earns less under dictatorship. Some of this difference is attributable to lower output, but a large difference remains even when we account for differences in factor endowments and even if we assume away differences in productivity. Democracy entails the freedom for workers to associate independently of their employers and the state. And strikes are three times more frequent under democracy than under dictatorship: 0.2434 per year under the former and 0.0895 under the latter. Because, in addition, under democracy workers also vote, these results are not surprising. Dictatorships repress workers, exploit them, and use them carelessly. Democracies allow workers to fight for their interests, pay them better, and employ them better. . . .

References

Barro, Robert J. 1989. Economic Growth in a Cross Section of Countries. In *NBER Working Paper no. 3120*. Cambridge, MA: National Bureau of Economic Research.

———. 1990. Government Spending in a Simple Model of Economic Growth. *Journal of Political Economy* 98(5): 103–125.

———. 1997. *Determinants of Economic Growth*. Cambridge, MA: MIT Press.

Barro, Robert J., and Xavier Sala-i-Martin. 1995. *Economic Growth*. New York: McGraw-Hill.

de Schweinitz, Karl, Jr. 1959. Industrialization, Labor Controls, and Democracy. *Economic Development and Cultural Change* 7(4): 385–404.

Drèze, Jean, and Amartya Sen. 1989. *Hunger and Public Action*. Oxford University Press.

Findlay, Ronald. 1990. The New Political Economy: Its Explanatory Power for LDCs. *Economics and Politics* 2(2): 193–221.

Galenson, Walter. 1959. *Labor and Economic Development*. New York: Wiley.

Huntington, Samuel P. 1968. *Political Order in Changing Societies*. New Haven, CT: Yale University Press.

Huntington, Samuel P., and Jorge I. Dominguez. 1975. Political Development. In *Macropolitical Theory*, edited by F. I. Greenstein and N. W. Polsby, pp. 1–114. Reading, MA: Addison-Wesley.

Kaldor, Nicolas. 1956. Alternative Theories of Distribution. *Review of Economic Studies* 23: 83–100.

Mutis, Alvaro. 1996. *Adventures of Maqroll: Four Novellas*. New York: Harper-Collins.

North, Douglass. 1990. *Institutions, Institutional Change, and Economic Performance*. Cambridge University Press.

Olson, Mancur. 1982. *The Rise and Decline of Nations: Economic Growth, Stagflation, and Social Rigidities*. New Haven, CT: Yale University Press.

———. 1991. Autocracy, Democracy, and Prosperity. In *Strategy and Choice*, edited by R. J. Zeckhauser, pp. 131–157. Cambridge, MA: MIT Press.

Pasinetti, Luigi. 1961. Rate of Profit and Income Distribution in Relation to the Rate of Economic Growth. *Review of Economic Studies* 29 (October): 267–279.

Przeworski, Adam. 1975. Institutionalization of Voting Patterns, or Is Mobilization the Source of Decay? *American Political Science Review* 69: 49–67.

———. 1990. *The State and the Economy under Capitalism*. Chur, Switzerland: Harwood Academic Publishers.

Rama, Martin. 1993. Empirical Investment Equations for Developing Countries. In *Striving for Growth after Adjustment: The Role of Capital Formation, Regional and Sectoral Studies*, edited by Luis Serven and Andres Solimano, pp. 107–143. Washington, DC: World Bank.

Rao, Vaman. 1984. Democracy and Economic Development. *Studies in Comparative International Development* 19(4): 67–81.

Robinson, James. 1995. Theories of "Bad Policy". *Policy Reform* 1: 1–17.

Sah, Raaj K., and Joseph Stiglitz. 1988. Committees, Hierarchies and Polyarchies. *The Economic Journal* 98 (June): 451–470.

Sen, Amartya. 1994a. Freedoms and Needs. *The New Republic*, January 10–17, 31–37.

Democracy in America

Alexis de Tocqueville

... America is the only country in which we can watch the natural quiet growth of society and where it is possible to be exact about the influence of the point of departure on the future of a state. ...

When, after careful study of the history of America, we turn with equal care to the political and social state there, we find ourselves deeply convinced of this truth, that there is not an opinion, custom, or law, nor, one might add, an event, which the point of departure will not easily explain. ...

... [O]ne observation, to which we shall come back later, applies not to the English only, but also to the French, Spaniards, and all Europeans who came in waves to plant themselves on the shores of the New World; all these new European colonies contained the germ, if not the full growth, of a complete democracy. There were two reasons for this; one may say, speaking generally, that when the immigrants left their motherlands they had no idea of any superiority of some over others. It is not the happy and the powerful who go into exile, and poverty with misfortune is the best-known guarantee of equality among men. Nonetheless, it did happen several times that as a result of political or religious quarrels great lords went to America. Laws were made there to establish the hierarchy of ranks, but it was soon seen that the soil of America absolutely rejected a territorial aristocracy. It was obvious that to clear this untamed land nothing but the constant and committed labor of the landlord himself would serve. The ground, once cleared, was by no means fertile enough to make both a landlord and a tenant rich. So the land was naturally broken up into little lots which the owner himself cultivated. But it is land that is the basis of an aristocracy, giving it both roots and support; privileges by themselves are not enough, nor is birth, but only land handed down from generation to generation. There may be huge fortunes and grinding poverty in a nation; but if that wealth is not landed, one may find rich and poor, but not, using words strictly, an aristocracy.

Hence there was a strong family likeness between all the English colonies as they came to birth. All, from the beginning, seemed destined to let freedom grow, not the aristocratic freedom of their motherland, but a middle-class and democratic freedom of which the world's history had not previously provided a complete example. ...

... [A]ll the immigrants who came to settle on the shores of New England belonged to the well-to-do classes at home. From the start, when they came together on American soil, they presented the unusual phenomenon of a society in which there were no great lords, no common people, and, one may almost say, no rich or poor. In proportion to their numbers, these men had a greater share of accomplishments than could be found in any European nation now. All, perhaps without a single exception, had received a fairly advanced education, and several had made a European reputation by their talents and their knowledge. The other colonies had been founded by unattached adventurers, whereas the immigrants to New England brought with them wonderful elements of order and morality; they came with their wives and children to the wilds. But what most distinguished them from all others was the very aim of their enterprise. No necessity forced them to leave their country; they gave up a desirable social position and assured means of livelihood; nor was their object in going to the New World to better their position or accumulate wealth; they tore themselves away from home comforts in obedience to a purely intellectual craving; in facing the inevitable sufferings of exile they hoped for the triumph of *an idea*. . . .

The English government watched untroubled the departure of so many emigrants, glad to see the seeds of discord and of fresh revolutions dispersed afar. Indeed it did everything to encourage it and seemed to have no anxiety about the fate of those who sought refuge from its harsh laws on American soil. It seemed to consider New England as a land given over to the fantasy of dreamers, where innovators should be allowed to try out experiments in freedom.

The English colonies—and that was one of the main reasons for their prosperity—have always enjoyed more internal freedom and political independence than those of other nations; nowhere was this principle of liberty applied more completely than in the states of New England. . . .

All the general principles on which modern constitutions rest, principles which most Europeans in the seventeenth century scarcely understood and whose dominance in Great Britain was then far from complete, are recognized and given authority by the laws of New England; the participation of the people in public affairs, the free voting of taxes, the responsibility of government officials, individual freedom, and trial by jury—all these things were established without question and with practical effect.

These pregnant principles were there applied and developed in a way that no European nation has yet dared to attempt.

In Connecticut the electoral body consisted, from the beginning, of all the citizens, and that is readily understood.[30] In that nascent community there prevailed an almost perfect equality of wealth and even greater intellectual equality.[31]

At that time in Connecticut all executive officials were elected, including the governor[32] of the state.

Citizens over sixteen years of age were obliged to bear arms; they formed a national militia which appointed its officers and was bound to be ready to march at any time to the country's defense.[33]

In the laws of Connecticut and of all the other states of New England we see the birth and growth of that local independence which is still the mainspring and lifeblood of American freedom.

In most European nations political existence started in the higher ranks of society and has been gradually, but always incompletely, communicated to the various members of the body social.

Contrariwise, in America one may say that the local community was organized before the county, the county before the state, and the state before the Union.

In New England, local communities had taken complete and definite shape as early as 1650. Interests, passions, duties, and rights took shape around each individual locality and were firmly attached thereto. Inside the locality there was a real, active political life which was completely democratic and republican. The colonies still recognized the mother country's supremacy; legally the state was a monarchy, but each locality was already a lively republic. . . .

I have already said enough to put Anglo-American civilization in its true light. It is the product (and one should continually bear in mind this point of departure) of two perfectly distinct elements which elsewhere have often been at war with one another but which in America it was somehow possible to incorporate into each other, forming a marvelous combina-

---

30. Constitution of 1638 [*Code of 1650*], p. 17.

31. In 1641 the general assembly of Rhode Island declared unanimously that the government of the state was a democracy and that power resided in the body of free men, who alone had the right to make the laws and provide for their enforcement. Code of 1650, p. 70. [Should refer to p. 12.]

32. Pitkin's *History*, p. 47.

33. Constitution of 1638 [*Code of 1650*], p. 12. [The reference should read p. 70.]

tion. I mean the *spirit of religion* and the *spirit of freedom*.

The founders of New England were both ardent sectarians and fanatical innovators. While held within the narrowest bounds by fixed religious beliefs, they were free from all political prejudices.

Hence two distinct but not contradictory tendencies plainly show their traces everywhere, in mores and in laws. . . .

Far from harming each other, these two apparently opposed tendencies work in harmony and seem to lend mutual support.

Religion regards civil liberty as a noble exercise of men's faculties, the world of politics being a sphere intended by the Creator for the free play of intelligence. Religion, being free and powerful within its own sphere and content with the position reserved for it, realizes that its sway is all the better established because it relies only on its own powers and rules men's hearts without external support.

Freedom sees religion as the companion of its struggles and triumphs, the cradle of its infancy, and the divine source of its rights. Religion is considered as the guardian of mores, and mores are regarded as the guarantee of the laws and pledge for the maintenance of freedom itself. . . .

Tyranny of the Majority

. . .

I regard it as an impious and detestable maxim that in matters of government the majority of a people has the right to do everything, and nevertheless I place the origin of all powers in the will of the majority. Am I in contradiction with myself?

There is one law which has been made, or at least adopted, not by the majority of this or that people, but by the majority of all men. That law is justice.

Justice therefore forms the boundary to each people's right.

A nation is like a jury entrusted to represent universal society and to apply the justice which is its law. Should the jury representing society have greater power than that very society whose laws it applies?

Consequently, when I refuse to obey an unjust law, I by no means deny the majority's right to give orders; I only appeal from the sovereignty of the people to the sovereignty of the human race.

There are those not afraid to say that in matters which only concern itself a nation cannot go completely beyond the bounds of justice and reason and that there is therefore no need to fear giving total power to the majority representing it. But that is the language of a slave.

What is a majority, in its collective capacity, if not an individual with opinions, and usually with interests, contrary to those of another individual, called the minority? Now, if you admit that a man vested with omnipotence can abuse it against his adversaries, why not admit the same concerning a majority? Have men, by joining together, changed their character? By becoming stronger, have they become more patient of obstacles?[3] For my part, I cannot believe that, and I will never grant to several that power to do everything which I refuse to a single man. . . .

. . . In democratic republics the power directing[6] society is not stable, for both its personnel and its aims change often. But wherever it is brought to bear, its strength is almost irresistible.

---

3. No one would wish to maintain that a nation cannot abuse its power against another nation. But parties form something like little nations within the nation, and the relations between them are like those of strangers.

If it is agreed that a nation can be tyrannical toward another nation, how can one deny that a party can be so toward another party?

6. Authority may be centralized in an assembly, and in that case it is strong but not stable. Or it may be centralized in one man, and in that case it is less strong but more stable.

The government of the American republics seems to me as centralized and more energetic than the absolute monarchies of Europe. So I do not think that it will collapse from weakness.[7]

If ever freedom is lost in America, that will be due to the omnipotence of the majority driving the minorities to desperation and forcing them to appeal to physical force. We may then see anarchy, but it will have come as the result of despotism. . . .

---

7. There is no need to remind the reader that here, and throughout this chapter, I am speaking not of the federal government but of the governments of each state, where a despotic majority is in control.

Does Democracy Engender Justice?

John E. Roemer

Does, or might, democracy engender justice? Whether this question is interesting depends, of course, on the definitions we adopt of democracy and justice. I begin by arguing for particular definitions.

We must, I believe, insist upon a division of labor between the concepts of democracy and justice for the initially posed question to be interesting. Democracy should be defined as a set of institutions and practices whose intention is to implement a certain kind of equal participation of citizens in the political process. Justice, on the other hand, consists in a set of relations among persons, and between persons and goods, in a society. With this division of labor, the initial question becomes a scientific one: will a given set of institutions and practices bring about the particular set of relationships that justice requires? . . .

. . . I shall not investigate the general question one could pose here, but a special case: must democracy eventually generate justice conceived of as equality of condition among citizens? I cannot here digress to the intensely interesting, and controversial, issue of precisely what condition should be equalized under an egalitarian construal of justice. I will, however, take it that the various candidates for the equalisandum would all imply a much more egalitarian distribution of income than we observe in almost all countries today.[2]

I have already argued that democratic arguments take a universalistic form. The question is whether, over time, the constraint to argue universalistically will force democratically chosen policies to be increasingly egalitarian in their effects. There are, evidently, arguments for and against.

I begin with two arguments in favor. The first is that, with the development of social science (economics, psychology, sociology), experts will not credibly be able to differ significantly in the values they assign to the critical parameters of the socio-economic mechanism. All experts will converge to something near the true values of these parameters. Therefore, any policy which can credibly claim to increase the welfare of all must, in fact, do so. Now just because a policy increases the welfare of all does not mean it creates more equality of condition—it could create less. So I must make a stronger argument, that policies with universalistic appeal must claim to distribute benefits fairly, where fairness entails a decreasing inequality of condition. To argue that the conception of fairness will come to entail ever-increasing equality of condition is a major undertaking, and it is not one I can pursue here. I say, then, that the first argument would go by establishing three premises: (1) that democratic arguments are posed universalistically, (2) that, due to the development of social science, experts will not credibly be able to disagree a great deal about the values of parameters in the economic mechanism, and (3) that conceptions of fairness entail, or will come to entail, increasing equality

2. I take equality of income to be the salient equality, not equality of wealth. Unequal wealths should be significant, for an egalitarian, only if they generate unequal incomes, or unequal streams of lifetime income. If a society were characterized by unequal wealths, but those wealths never generated unequal streams of income, an egalitarian should have no complaint. This is not an absurd thing to imagine: there might be returns to scale in wealth holding, so that a small fraction of people should hold all the wealth, but the income stream from those holdings might be distributed in an egalitarian manner.

of condition[3] (for instance, that condition might be "opportunity for the good life").

The second argument is that the general population will become increasingly well educated as economic development continues, which will force political parties/candidates to be less demagogic, and stick closer to the truth. Essentially, this argument substitutes "the increased sophistication of the citizenry" for "the development of social science" above.

I proceed to present several arguments against. The first concerns the multidimensionality of electoral politics. It is commonly observed that the relevant issue space of electoral politics in the advanced democracies is (at least) two-dimensional (see Laver and Hunt 1992; Kitschelt 1994; Poole and Rosenthal 1991). One issue, characteristically, concerns redistribution, and the other concerns "values"—what Kitschelt calls the "authoritarian–libertarian" axis. It might not be far-fetched to say that the second issue reflects a good part of what makes up different religious views in the population. If most societies will always be characterized by a spectrum of religious views, or of views concerning what constitutes the good, then it is not unreasonable to think that electoral politics will always, in those societies, be multi-issued. . . .

In a recent paper (Roemer 1998b), I study the nature of electoral equilibrium when there are two parties, which represent different constituencies in the population, competing on a two-dimensional issue space. Call the first party Labour: it has pro-redistribution, libertarian preferences; call the second party Conservative: it has anti-redistribution, authoritarian preferences. The citizenry have preferences whose ideal points cover the issue space (that is, there are voters with all possible ideal points in the two-dimensional issue space), but the distribution of such ideal points (voters) can be very general. A political equilibrium consists of a pair

of platforms, each of which announces the two-dimensional policy that a party will seek to implement, if it wins the election, and which together constitute an equilibrium in the voting game.[4] . . .

The general result, of which I have reported an instance, which I am confident is quite robust (even though the instance I report is associated with a particular model of electoral politics), is that when politics are multidimensional, there is little reason to think that political equilibrium will entail a high degree of redistribution, in a polity which is characterized by a significant variation in preferences on other, nondistributive issues. In fact, the countries where we do see a high degree of redistribution (the Nordic countries) are characterized by a rare homogeneity on the "values" issue, due to the great degree of religious, ethnic, and linguistic homogeneity of their polities. . . .

So I claim that, in societies which are heterogeneous in regard to preferences on noneconomic issues, the democratic process may well not produce . . . considerable redistribution, which is to say, it will not tend to produce equality of condition. The key premise, here, is the heterogeneity of values, and I note that such heterogeneity is a key assumption of the Rawls–Cohen–Barry formulation of the problem of justice (in Cohen's case, of deliberative democracy). It is, indeed, this heterogeneity which motivates the central issue for these authors, whether or not the definition of justice they propose is indeed neutral with respect to heterogeneous conceptions of the good (see Rawls 1993).

Finally, the electoral equilibrium I have been discussing satisfies, it seems to me, the conditions of procedural, impartial justice. That citizens vote according to their own preferences, as they do in my model, does not violate Barry's requirements of impartiality.

---

3. I do not claim (3) is true, but that it is a premise of this argument.

4. Indeed, the result I shall describe holds for several definitions of equilibrium.

The argument just given assumes that citizens' preferences are self-regarding. Recently, Piketty (1995) has produced a fascinating argument showing that, even should voters be other-regarding in their preferences, and care about the unluckiest in society, democratic political equilibrium will not necessarily entail a great deal of redistribution from the rich to the poor. Thus, Piketty's argument shows that, even should citizens have internalized a Rawlsian kind of view, many may well not vote for redistributive policies.

The important premises of Piketty's argument are that: (1) the relationship between effort and income is stochastic and obscure, (2) individuals form beliefs in a rational way, and (3) they are other-regarding, rather than self-interested. The argument produces the unhappy result of possibly low redistribution even when there are no right-wing parties or media trying to twist the facts, and even when voters are other-regarding. Piketty's model is an instance of the general argument I made earlier: that, when parameters of the economic mechanism are obscure, it is possible that reasonable people will reach very different views as to their values. Piketty's model is, in one sense, more damaging to the prognosis of equality in a Scanlonian world than my earlier example, for the sharply differing views citizens come to have about economic parameters are not due to their having listened to experts who had, themselves, different ideological (or class) positions.[5]

---

5. One might argue against the salience of Piketty's model for our purposes, because it assumes that citizens can observe only their own effort. Thus, conditions of "full information" would require that citizens know the response of income to effort *generally* in society. But I say this would be to assume away the central problem, that economic parameters are, because of the complexity of the economic mechanism, obscure. Piketty's model captures that obscurity by the particular assumption that individuals observe only their own effort.

Conclusion

The reader will note that the arguments ... depend upon subsets of these three features of society: that there is considerable uncertainty about the (true) values of economic parameters, that there are heterogeneous conceptions of the good (values), and that there is a considerable spectrum of incomes or wealth before the degree of redistribution is chosen by the democratic process. I argued ... that it might well be possible for democracy to engender the kind of procedural, impartial justice that has been most recently elaborated by Barry (1995), and is advocated as well by Scanlon (1982 and 1988), Rawls (1971 and 1993) and Cohen (1996). But my conclusion was that the sufficient conditions for just procedures that these authors propose are incapable of guaranteeing the kind of equality of condition that they prize.... I asked whether democracy would indeed tend to deliver that kind of equality of condition; the two arguments I offered in favor of such a conclusion both depended upon the elimination of uncertainty about the values of economic parameters.

I take the last two arguments ... against concluding that democracy entails equality of condition, to be instances of a general phenomenon, that the kinds of uncertainty and heterogeneity postulated in this section's first sentence push against democracy's engendering justice conceived of as equality of economic condition. I do think, however, that the two pro arguments offered ... have some weight, and that, consequently, advanced democracies will, over time, come to be characterized by more equality of economic condition than they currently have. My conjecture is that that degree of equality will be considerably less than present-day theorists of equality of condition (Sen 1980; Dworkin 1981; Arneson 1989; G. A. Cohen 1989; Roemer 1998a) think of as necessary for distributive justice....

References

Arneson, Richard. 1989. "Equality and equality of opportunity for welfare." *Philosophical Studies* 56: 77–93.

Barry, Brian. 1989. *Theories of Justice*. Berkeley: University of California Press.

———. 1995. *Justice as Impartiality*. Oxford: Clarendon Press.

Cohen, G. A. 1989. "On the currency of egalitarian justice." *Ethics* 99: 906–944.

Cohen, Joshua. 1996. *Liberty, Equality, Democracy*. Cambridge, MA: Dept of Political Science, MIT (xeroxed).

Dworkin, Ronald. 1981. "What is equality? Part 2: Equality of resources." *Philosophy & Public Affairs* 10: 283–345.

Kitschelt, Herbert. 1994. *The Transformation of European Social Democracy*. New York: Cambridge University Press.

Laver, Michael and W. B. Hunt. 1992. *Policy and Party Competition*. London: Routledge and Kegan Paul.

Piketty, Thomas. 1995. "Social mobility and redistributive politics." *Quarterly Journal of Economics* 110: 551–584.

Poole, Kenneth and Howard Rosenthal. 1991. "Patterns of Congressional voting." *American Journal of Political Science* 35: 228–278.

Rawls, John. 1971. *A Theory of Justice*. Cambridge, MA: Harvard University Press.

———. 1993. *Political Liberalism*. New York: Columbia University Press.

Roemer, John E. 1998a. *Equality of Opportunity*. Cambridge, MA: Harvard University Press.

———. 1998b. "Why the poor do not expropriate the rich: an old argument in new garb." *Journal of Public Economics* 70: 399–424.

Scanlon, Thomas. 1982. "Contractualism and utilitarianism." In Amartya Sen and Bernard Williams (eds.), *Utilitarianism and Beyond*. Cambridge: Cambridge University Press.

———. 1988. "Levels of moral thinking." In D. Seanor and N. Fotion (eds.), *Hare and Critics*. Oxford: Clarendon Press.

Sen, Amartya. 1980. "Equality of what?" In S. McMurrin (ed.), *The Tanner Lectures on Human Values*. Vol. I. Salt Lake City: University of Utah Press.

Facing up to the American Dream: Race, Class, and the Soul of the Nation

Jennifer L. Hochschild

The preface claimed that America's racial situation threatened the future of the ideology of the American dream in two distinct ways. This chapter focuses on the first challenge—blacks' and whites' increasing divergence in their descriptions of and explanations for America's racial situation. The two races share an overwhelming support for the American dream as a prescription for their own and other Americans' lives. The races disagree only slightly when people consider the American dream as a description of their own lives, but they disagree considerably when people consider the dream as a description of others' lives. African Americans increasingly believe that racial discrimination is worsening and that it inhibits their race's ability to participate in the American dream; whites increasingly believe that discrimination is lessening and that blacks have the same chance to participate in the dream as whites. I call that finding the paradox of "what's all the fuss about?"

The American Dream as Prescription

Americans are close to unanimous in endorsing the idea of the American dream. Virtually all agree that all citizens should have political equality and that everyone in America warrants equal educational opportunities and equal opportunities in general. Three-fourths or more of both races agree that all people warrant equal respect, that skill rather than need should determine wages, that "America should promote equal opportunity for all" rather than "equal outcomes," that "everyone should try to amount to more than his parents did," and that they

Excerpted from: Jennifer L. Hochschild, *Facing up to the American Dream: Race, Class, and the Soul of the Nation*. Princeton: Princeton University Press, 1995. Copyright © 1995 by Princeton University Press. Reprinted by permission of Princeton University Press.

are ambitious themselves. Seventy percent of black, and 80 percent of white, Californians agree that "trying to get ahead" is very important in "making someone a true American." An even more overwhelming majority of black than white Americans endorse self-sufficiency as one of their primary goals. These views are, if possible, even more strongly and uniformly expressed now than four decades ago.[1] ...

Beliefs about One's Own Chances to Achieve a Dream

Whites and blacks resemble each other almost as much when the topic shifts from general endorsement of the American dream to interpretations of one's own particular life course....

The Second Tenet

... [F]rom the 1940s forward, majorities of both races have anticipated success for themselves and their families, just as the second tenet of the American dream prescribes. Members of both races are as sanguine now as they were four decades ago. Furthermore, the two races have been generally close to one another even on surveys that show unusually high or low levels of optimism. And when the races do diverge substantially, blacks are always the more confident.

In fact, African Americans' optimism persists even when they recognize their comparatively worse circumstances....

The Third Tenet

Blacks and whites also come close to agreement on the third tenet—that the key to success lies in

---

1. McClosky and Zaller (1984: 64–100, 116); Kluegel and Smith (1986: 112–13; GSS (1993: vars. 456, 464); Citrin et al. (1990: 1132)

one's own hands—when they consider their own lives. In the mid-1960s almost six in ten members of both races endorsed "plan[ning] your life a good way ahead" rather than relying on luck, and over eight in ten blacks (compared with slightly fewer whites) insisted that "no weakness or difficulty can hold us back if we have enough willpower." By the mid-1980s more African Americans were prepared to admit a partial role for fate, but still half (compared with two-thirds of whites) insisted that their life course reflected solely their own abilities.[10]

The First Tenet

These findings are especially surprising in light of divergence between the races in their beliefs about the existence and effects of discrimination. The point is easily made: whites see little and lessening discrimination, and blacks feel themselves to be the objects of a lot, even increasing amounts, of discrimination. A majority of blacks always report discrimination in their lives, and in 1970 a quarter experienced it "almost every day of my life." . . .

The Fourth Tenet

What gives the American dream its moral power is the fourth tenet, that success is justified because (and only when) it is associated with virtue. When they think about their own lives, both races, especially African Americans, are committed to this claim. In 1986 over two-thirds of whites and three-fourths of blacks agreed that good relationships with family and friends,

commitment to religious beliefs, and social utility are all "very important element[s] of success." . . .

Beliefs about Others' Chances to Achieve Their Dreams

. . . When Americans look at the prospects of others or at the overall pattern of racial interaction, African Americans are increasingly dismayed at the height of racial barriers to the American dream while whites are increasingly gratified by the decline of those barriers.[15]

The First Tenet

Let us begin with beliefs about the first tenet's claim of equal opportunity to pursue one's dream. African Americans are a little more skeptical of the claim in general, since about 10 percent fewer blacks than whites agree that "a worker's child has . . . some chance to get ahead" or that "chances for success are distributed fairly."[16] But blacks and whites diverge more sharply when they consider racial discrimination.

Blacks see more racial discrimination than do whites. Whites' perceptions of racial discrimination varied widely in the 1960s, and seldom do more than a third now believe that blacks continue to experience racist treatment in jobs, housing, the media, or the criminal justice system. Blacks saw it then and continue to see it now.[17] For example, only a handful of whites

---

10. Survey Research Center (1964: vars. 50a, 50n); Marx (1964: vars. 50a, 50h, 50m); Campbell and Schuman (1968: vars. 176, 178); Roper (1986: var. 36). More blacks than whites insist that they have "a lot" of control over their children's future (Harris 1986b: var. C9). Kluegel and Smith (1986: 94) show no difference between whites and blacks in their attributions for personal circumstances.

15. Hochschild (1988) formulates racial disparities in perceptions and beliefs somewhat differently.

16. Schlozman and Verba (1979: 167).

17. In 1946, 66% of whites but only 28% of blacks thought "most Negroes in the United States are being treated fairly" (Erskine 1962: 139). Four decades later, one-third as many whites as blacks thought being of the right race was crucial for getting ahead (GSS 1987: var. 507I). Whites' perceptions of women's opportunity "are more negative than are corresponding

think that more than half of whites share the attitudes of the Ku Klux Klan; a quarter of blacks see more than half of whites as Klan sympathizers. In that context it is not surprising that over half of blacks but only a quarter to a third of whites think our nation is moving toward two separate and unequal societies.[18]

Whites, in fact, are increasingly convinced that racial equality is growing in the United States. In the mid-1960s, 30 to 45 percent (depending on the year and the wording of the question) felt that the nation was making progress in solving its racial problems; by the 1970s, 50 to 70 percent concurred, and by 1988, fully 87 percent of whites believed that "in the past 25 years, the country has moved closer to equal opportunity among the races."[19] African Americans, meanwhile, are becoming increasingly discouraged on the same point. The proportion of blacks who

see increasing racial equality *declined* from between 50 and 80 percent in the mid-1960s to between 20 and 45 percent in the 1980s. In some surveys up to half claim that the situation of blacks has *worsened* since some referent point in the past.[20] ...

Most importantly, the races differ on the specific question, crucial to the first tenet of the American dream, of whether racial discrimination affects Americans' life chances. . . .

In the 1960s a majority, or at least a plurality, of blacks were optimistic about blacks' chances to succeed. Their conviction was exceeded only by whites' (if we can rely on one survey item). By the 1980s most blacks were *not* optimistic about blacks' chances to succeed. Whites remained much more convinced of blacks' equal chances, and throughout the three decades generally a majority of whites agreed that race did not impede blacks' attainment of their dreams.

These results are critical for the viability of the American dream. The first tenet is the foundation of our nation's faith in liberty and equality for all. Absent disparate views on this tenet, disputes over the rest of the American dream lose much of their racial edge. But given the disparate views . . . one cannot talk about the meaning or future of the ideology of the American dream without also talking about race. . . .

---

perceptions about blacks" (Kluegel and Smith 1986: 235–39; see also *NYT*/WCBS News 1985: var. 33; GSS 1987: var. 507L).

See also NORC (1944, vars. 01, 04, 05); Harris (1966a: var. 21a; 1966b: vars. 11D, 13.1–13.15, 14F, 14G, 16A, 18A); Campbell and Schuman (1968: var. 230); Harris (1978: 4–13, 26–34); CBS News/*NYT* (1978: vars. 10a, 11a, 12a, 13a, 20, 21, 25, 38, 39, 40); *NYT*/WCBS News (1985: vars. 20, 21, 32, 35b); Gallup (1987: 36; 1988: 23); Harris (1988: vars. A, D, F, G, N); Media General/AP (1988: var. RC06); Harris (1989b: 199–202, 213–20, 253–58); ABC News/ *Washington Post* (1989: vars. 22.1, 24.1–24.5; 1991: var. 37); Gordon Black (1989a: vars. 11, 17; 1989b: var. 19); NBC News (1989: vars. 44, 74, 75); Sigelman and Welch (1991: 77); *Los Angeles Times* (1991b: var. 49); Gallup (1991b: vars. 9, 34A); Yankelovich Clancy Shulman (1992: var. 6); CBS News/*NYT* (1992: var. R21); People for the American Way (1992: 70–74, 154, 157, 159); *Washington Post* (1992: vars. 3k, 6, 9); D. Garth Taylor (1993: 20, 22, 23, 28; 1994: 29, 32, 39); "Thirty Years After" (1993); *NYT*/WCBS-TV Channel 2 News (1994: vars. 25, 27); Welch et al. (1994: 28–30); National Conference (1994: 16–19, 22, 84–86, 100–102).

18. ABC News/*Washington Post* (1989: var. 19); Gallup (1992: var. 16); "Thirty Years After" (1993).

19. Erskine (1962: 138; 1969a: 156); Hutcheson (1973: 56); Harris (1978: 56); CBS News/*NYT* (1978: var. 17); Converse et al. (1980: 79); *Los Angeles Times* (1983: tables 86, 94); Media General/AP (1988: vars. RC02, RC03, RC10); McLeod (1988b: A4); ABC News/ *Washington Post* (1989: var. 17); *Los Angeles Times* (1991b: vars. 57, 58); Yankelovich Clancy Shulman (1992: var. 23); CBS News/*NYT* (1992: var. R29); People for the American Way (1992: 65–67, 155, 159); *Washington Post* (1992: var. 2).

20. In addition to the citations in the previous note, see Brink and Harris (1966: 222–31); Marx (1969: 5–11, 220); NSBA (1980: var. 1222); Joint Center for Political Studies (1984: table 2); Cavanagh (1985: 3); Schuman et al. (1988: xiv, 141–43); Brown et al. (1994: table 15.9); Gallup (1988: var. 4; 1994: var. 30).

The Second Tenet

It follows logically that those who think discrimination is slight, declining, and unimportant in its consequences would anticipate more success for the less favored race than those who think discrimination is great, increasing, and potent in its consequences. And data support logic, for a change; whites have always been convinced of rapid black economic progress. In 1966 over two-thirds of whites declared blacks to be "moving too fast" or "asking for more than they are ready for."[24] By the 1990s whites' main response to black aspirations had shifted from denigration to satisfaction, but their conviction that these aspirations were likely to be fulfilled had not changed.[25]

Blacks, however, have traditionally felt and continue to feel frustrated with the past and pessimistic about the future prospects of their race. For example, in 1989 only 45 percent of blacks (compared with over 70 percent of whites) thought opportunities for blacks had improved during the 1980s; a fifth of blacks but only a handful of whites thought opportunities had worsened. Roughly the same proportions were optimistic or pessimistic about prospects in the decade to come.[26]

The political arena resembles the economic arena: most whites but few blacks believe that blacks can reasonably anticipate political success. In the 1960s no more than 6 percent of whites thought progress in promoting civil rights was too slow, compared with over half of blacks. By 1988 the proportion of impatient whites had

risen to just over 20 percent, whereas a majority of blacks remained frustrated at the pace of civil rights progress.[27] More generally, whites have more faith than blacks that political officials can be brought to attend to the needs and wants of ordinary citizens.[28]

The Third Tenet

Blacks and whites differ as much over the third tenet—that the key to success lies in one's own hands—as over the first two when they focus on people other than themselves. We saw above that blacks are almost as likely as whites to attribute their own success (or lack thereof) to their own abilities. Nevertheless, they are less likely than whites to attribute the success or failure of other Americans to ability rather than to fate or birth. For example, from 1972 through 1991, up to 70

---

24. Harris (1966b: vars. 11B, 18I; 1970a: var. 12A; 1970b: 11A); Schuman et al. (1988: 118–19).

25. Harris (1966a: vars. 21D; 1966b: var. 14E); GSS (1982: var. 148A, 148B); *NYT*/WCBS News (1985: var. 49); Gallup (1988: var. 4); McLeod (1988b: A4); Harris (1988: vars. A, N); ABC News/*Washington Post* (1989: var. 25); GSS (1990–91: var. 621A, F, G, H); *Los Angeles Times* (1991b: tables 57, 58, 59, 64); Gallup (1992: var. 10).

26. Gordon Black (1989a: vars. 18, 19; 1989b: vars. 1, 2). See also citations in previous note.

African Americans perhaps see more polarization by class on the second tenet than do whites. On the one hand, more blacks believe that the number of rich Americans is increasing (ABC News/*Washington Post* 1990: var. 14). On the other hand, more blacks believe that "the lot of the average man [*sic*] is getting worse" (GSS 1973; 1974; 1976–77; 1983; 1984–85; 1987; 1988–89; 1990–91: var. 176B).

27. Brink and Harris (1966: 220, 258); Goldman (1969: 231); Schuman et al. (1988: xiii, xiv, 118–19, 146–47); Harris (1989b: 114, 208; 1989c: 79); NBC News (1989: var. 69); Gallup (1991b: var. 5). Over the past three decades, the modal white has shifted from concern about civil rights moving too fast to satisfaction with the pace, whereas the modal black has shifted from satisfaction with the pace to concerns about sluggishness.

The proportion of whites who agree that "civil rights groups are asking for too much" has risen since 1963 from 42 to 47%. (It also rose among blacks, but the order of magnitude is entirely different—from 3 to 7%) ("Thirty Years After" 1993).

28. Shingles (1981: 84); Carr and Hudgins (n.d.); Harris (1989b: 192, 196, 275, 279); Harris (1989c: 285, 297); National Conference (1994: 68).

percent of whites compared with 50 to 60 percent of blacks agreed that people get ahead through hard work rather than through luck or help.[29] Conversely, blacks are at least twice as likely as whites to claim that having wealthy or well-educated parents, having political and personal connections, or being of the right religion, region, political conviction, or sex are crucial for getting ahead in life. Blacks are almost three times as likely as whites to agree that "society gives some people a head start and holds others back" (although a majority of both races also agree that hard work is the chief determinant of success).[30]

... [H]owever, the two races disagree most sharply over the explanation for blacks' success or lack thereof.[31] ... [W]hites have always been more likely than African Americans to attribute racial inequality to flaws within individual blacks or in the black community. This is hardly surprising, if only because everyone is more likely to attribute others' failings to the others' rather than to their own flaws. (If surveyors ever asked parallel questions about the problems of whites, we would presumably see the opposite pattern in the responses.) Perhaps the only surprise in this table is that the racial gap is not larger. In some surveys up to half of blacks were willing to accept responsibility for their race's lack of success—perhaps the most persuasive indicator yet of the strength of the ideology of the American dream.

---

29. GSS (1972–73; 1974; 1976 77; 1980; 1982; 1984–85; 1987; 1988–89; 1991 92: var. 197). See also GSS (1984: vars. 69B, C, D, G); Schlozman and Verba (1979: 167); Verba and Orren (1985: 73–77); Kluegel and Smith (1986: 90–100); People for the American Way (1992: 151).

30. GSS (1987: vars. 507A–507M; 1993: var. 458).

31. This table focuses only on what are commonly called individualist explanations for racial disparities. Individualists, however, often give structural explanations as well (Kluegel and Smith 1986: 201; Sigelman and Welch 1991: 94–107).

The Fourth Tenet

Just as blacks are slightly more likely than whites to associate virtue with success in their own lives, they are a little more inclined to judge others' lives in moral terms. ...

Implications of Blacks' and Whites' Beliefs for the American Dream

The fact that more whites than blacks see blacks' failure as their own fault reinforces whites' belief that discrimination is slight and unimportant and that blacks can reasonably anticipate success. Conversely, the fact that more blacks see blacks' failure as due to forces beyond their control—or due to whites in particular—reinforces blacks' belief that discrimination is powerful and pervasive and that blacks cannot anticipate success. More analytically, the beliefs of each race about the first, second, and third tenets are internally consistent, but externally contradictory.

That finding implies a powerful challenge to the ideology of the American dream. Whites believe it works for everyone; blacks believe it works only for those not of their race. Whites are angry that blacks refuse to see the fairness and openness of the system; blacks are angry that whites refuse to see the biases and blockages of the system. If that disparity persists or worsens, as it has every appearance of doing, the American dream cannot maintain its role as a central organizing belief of all Americans.[35]

---

35. African Americans may be ahead of white Americans in understanding the racially based threat to American stability. We saw earlier that many more blacks than whites think that over half of whites share the views of the Ku Klux Klan. But it is also the case that more blacks (24%) than whites (17%) think that *blacks* hold "racist attitudes toward whites" (ABC News/*Washington Post* 1989. var. 20).

Whites' Quandary

But this is only the first challenge to the American dream. Adding the findings about how the dream applies to one's own life produces a curious inconsistency within each race that generates yet more challenges to it. Consider whites' quandary first: although whites are *more* sure than blacks that discrimination is not a problem (tenet 1), *more* sure that blacks are increasingly able to succeed (tenet 2), *more* sure that people's future lies within their own control (tenet 3), and *more* sure that they control their own fate (tenet 3), they are *less* optimistic about their own future (tenet 2).[36] These reasons combine to make blacks' continued complaints about glass ceilings or hiring biases ring false to whites. It is only a short step from here to the view, held by one-tenth to one-third of whites, that compared with whites blacks have more opportunities, are less vulnerable to economic upheaval, receive better health care, are treated better in the courts and the media, and are more likely to obtain good jobs and be admitted to good colleges.[37] It is only another short step, for a few, to global racial hostility....

Whites are left at an impasse, which possibly explains the emotional charge of some whites' racial views. *Something* is wrong with the American dream, and the problem is associated with blacks in some way. But identifying what is wrong and how blacks are implicated in it is a difficult and thankless task for which they receive almost no institutional support.[38] It is far easier

to cling to the dream, insist that it really works, and find someone to blame for the lacunae.

Blacks' Quandary

African Americans face the opposite quandary. They are *more* sure than whites that racial discrimination inhibits black Americans (tenet 1), *more* pessimistic about how much success blacks can anticipate (tenet 2), *more* convinced that blacks' life chances are not within their control (tenet 3), and slightly *less* confident that they control their own life chances (tenet 3). Nevertheless, African Americans remain *more* confident than whites about their own prospects (tenet 2). That quandary could be resolved simply by assuming that each optimistic black believes that "I am so special, talented, determined, or whatever that I will beat the odds even though other blacks cannot." That sentiment is initially plausible, since everyone sees themselves and their children as special. But in that case why are not whites equally optimistic for themselves? Alternatively, African Americans could believe that they personally are only reasonably talented and so forth, but that other blacks are for some reason especially unable to cope with the demands of American society. Thus "*I* can handle the challenge of the dream but others like me are too handicapped by racism, poverty, or whatever to do so." This sentiment is also plausible but unappealing to anyone with a sense of collective

---

36. Hochschild (1981: 241–42) demonstrates this quandary in one person's reasoning.

37. Harris (1978: 52); CBS News/*NYT* (1978: var. 21); Schlozman and Verba (1979: 169); Roper (1986: var. 38); Harris (1988: ques. 1C, 1D; 1989b: 198–202, 213, 271; 1989c: 47, 53, 56, 59, 94, 272); GSS (1990–91: var. 422); *Los Angeles Times* (1991b: vars. 49, 50); Sniderman et al. (1991: var. skin); People for the American Way (1992: 52, 72–74); *Washington Post* (1992: var. 3g); MCIC (1991–94: vars. 424, 425).

---

38. Thus only 55% of whites, compared with 77% of blacks, agree that it is "very urgent" that America "honestly faces the issue of race." These results are probably inflated for whites by the fact that the question comes at the end of a long interview about race in America (National Conference 1994: 36). Almost the only institution that provides an explanation of this quandary is white supremicist groups, which argue that secret cabals of Jews or African Americans (or Catholics, in an earlier era) are manipulating the system to deprive whites of their deserved rewards. With friends like this, the American dream does not need enemies.

identity. And African Americans have a strong sense of collective identity.[39]

Blacks are left at as much of an impasse as are whites. For them, too, *something* is wrong with the American dream that is vaguely but certainly the fault of the other race. Identifying what is wrong and how whites are implicated in it seems easy at first but more difficult as one probes further. Far easier for African Americans, too, to cling to the dream personally, doubt it collectively, and find someone to blame for the lacunae.

The Next Step

The paradox of "what's all the fuss about?" has several nuances. Most centrally, whites either do not understand or understand but reject blacks' claims that opportunities are racially biased and that blacks cannot control their own life chances. As whites become more and more satisfied with the trajectory of racial change in the United States, African Americans become less and less satisfied with it; on the few occasions when black gratification increases, so does white disapprobation. Within that central perceptual divide lie several other quandaries that complicate each race's beliefs about the dream and evaluations of each other. These external contradictions and internal puzzles would threaten any dominant ideology, but they are especially threatening to one as predicated on equality and on faith as is the American dream....

Adding comparisons within each race to comparisons across races reveals two additional paradoxes beyond that of what's all the fuss about? They are:

Succeeding more and enjoying it less: As the African American middle class has become larger, more powerful, and more stable, its members

have grown disillusioned with and even embittered about the American dream.[1]

Under the spell of the great national suggestion: As black poverty has deepened and become concentrated, poor African Americans have continued to believe in the American dream almost as much as poor blacks did thirty years ago. But that support is tenuous and under great pressure.[2]

In combination these paradoxes produce the surprising pattern that poor blacks now believe more in the American dream than rich blacks do, which is a reversal from the 1960s. But these paradoxes are more than merely surprising; together they point to the second threat posed by American race relations to the future of the American dream. If poor blacks and all whites follow middle-class blacks in their deepening disillusionment with the American dream, then the dream faces an even greater problem than the comparatively simple racial hostility depicted [earlier]....

The First Tenet

For African Americans to believe ... that everyone, even they, can participate in the search for

---

39. Dawson (1994); Gurin et al. (1989); Tate (1993).

1. I borrowed the construction from the cigarette advertisement with the tag line, "Smoking more and enjoying it less?" (via Aaron Wildavsky's description of the politics of American health care: "doing better and feeling worse").

2. The phrase comes from Myrdal (1944: 4): "The American Negroes know that they are a subordinated group experiencing, more than anybody else in the nation, the consequences of the fact that the [American] Creed is not lived up to in America. Yet their faith in the Creed is not simply a means of pleading their unfulfilled rights. They, like the whites, are *under the spell of the great national suggestion.* With one part of themselves they actually believe, as do the whites, that the Creed is ruling America" (emphasis added).

success, they must believe that the barriers of race, class, and (for half the population) gender have all been knocked down low enough for people like themselves to climb over them. . . .

. . . Although many if not most poor blacks[3] believe that African Americans continue to experience racist treatment,[4] relatively few report suffering from discrimination in their own lives[5] or see it as a dominant problem. . . .

Well-off African Americans see *more* racial discrimination than do poor blacks, see less decline in discrimination, expect less improvement in the future, and claim to have experienced more in their own lives.[7] . . .

Comparing perceptions of discrimination over time yields the most surprising results: in the 1950s and 1960s, well-off African Americans frequently saw *less* racial discrimination, both generally and in their own lives, than did badly-off African Americans. . . .

The same pattern of reversal in the most disaffected obtains in the more confrontational question about whether "most white people want to see blacks get a better break or . . . keep blacks down." . . .

The absolute level of African Americans' bitterness about white intentions varies across time and surveys, and probably any given set of numbers is not to be trusted. What matters here is that the relative degree of mistrust switched between the 1960s and 1980s. . . . [U]p until 1969, whenever the classes varied, lower-status blacks perceived *more* white hostility than did their higher-status counterparts. . . . [W]ith the excep-

---

3. When referring to survey data that I have analyzed, this book has precise meanings for the terms poor (badly off), well off (affluent, middle class), well educated, poorly educated, high status, and low status. "Poor" and "well-off" whites or blacks are those whose family incomes are in the lowest or highest thirds of their race, respectively, in the sample for a given survey. Poorly educated blacks or whites are survey respondents with less than a high school education; well-educated blacks or whites are respondents with more than a high school education. When I refer to high- (or low-) status people, I am indicating that both the highly (poorly) educated subset of the sample in a given survey *and* the richest (poorest) third of that sample hold a particular view. For more detail on how the surveys were categorized and why I made those choices, see appendix A.

4. *NYT*/WCBS News (1985: vars. 20, 21, 45); CBS News/*NYT* (1978: vars. 10a, 11a, 12a, 13a, 17, 20, 21, 38, 39, 40, 48); NSBA (1980: var. 368); Denton and Sussman (1981); Parent and Stekler (1985: 533); Gilliam (1986: 56); Brown et al. (1994: tables 15.7, 15.9); Gallup (1988: vars. Q20, Q22); Media General/AP (1988: vars. RC02, RC06, RC10); Adams and Dressler (1988: 760); Harris (1988: ques. D, N); Harris (1989b: 105–61 passim); Gordon Black (1989a: vars. 11, 12, 17, 29B); NBC News (1989: vars. 44, 74, 75); ABC News/*Washington Post* (1989: var. 22.1; 1991: var. 37); GSS (1990–91: vars. 395B, 396B); *Los Angeles Times* (1991b: vars. 50, 64); *Washington Post* (1992: vars. 1, 2, 3E, 9); Yankelovich Clancy Shulman (1992: vars. 6, 23); Gallup (1992: var. 12); CBS News/*NYT* (1992: vars. 29, 30, 31); Gallup (1994: var. 30).

5. Campbell and Schuman (1968: vars. 206–21, 225–27, 259–60, 262–64, 270–72); CBS News/*NYT* (1978: vars. 10b, 11b, 12b, 42); NSBA (1980: vars. 346, 512, 598, 736); Lewis and Schneider (1983: 13); *NYT*/

WCBS News (1985: vars. 26, 27); Adams and Dressler (1988: 760); Gordon Black (1989a: vars. 1, 4, 6, 7, 8, 9, 16); Marshall and Barnett (1991: 18); GSS (1990–91: var. 625H1); Gallup (1991a: vars. 16A–16D; 1991b: vars. 12, 34A); *Los Angeles Times* (1991b: var. 73); Yankelovich Clancy Shulman (1992: vars. 10, 11); CBS News/*NYT* (1992: vars. 20, 21).

7. See citations in notes 4 and 5, as well as People for the American Way (1992: 68, 71–72). For mixed results, see Schuman and Hatchett (1974: 58–59, 68–73); NSBA (1980: var. 1222); Sigelman and Welch (1991: 71–75). For counterevidence, see NSBA (1980: var. 1223); *NYT*/WCBS News (1985: vars. 26, 27).

A study of six ethnic groups (Jews, Irish, WASPs, blacks, Cubans, Dominicans, and Puerto Ricans) in New York City found that "among all groups, it is the middle-class respondents that tend to perceive ethnic bias in city government and their groups as the victims of this bias" (Robert Smith 1988: 183).

tion of a single year, that discrepancy was reversed by the end of the 1970s.[14]

Perceptions of discrimination, however, do not necessarily translate into rejection of the first tenet of the American dream. To make that translation, African Americans must see racial discrimination as not merely an annoyance but a serious impediment to their pursuit of success.

... [B]lacks do not always assume that discrimination keeps them from pursuing their dream....

Nevertheless, Americans' beliefs about the first tenet of the American dream are unquestionably colored by their perceptions of discrimination....

... In many of the 1960s surveys, middle-class blacks were at least as optimistic, or even more so, for their race as were poor blacks (the difference scores are positive).[17] In virtually none of the 1980s and 1990s surveys do the same results obtain; poor blacks were almost always more optimistic for their race than were affluent blacks (the difference scores are negative). Although the actual responses fluctuate considerably across surveys and are therefore not trustworthy, one can discern a general pattern from them that explains this reversal: both classes of African Americans were more optimistic for their race in the 1960s than in the 1980s, but affluent blacks' optimism has plummeted while poor blacks' optimism has declined more gently.[18] Thus the combination of the two paradoxes—succeeding more and enjoying it less and remaining under the spell of the great national suggestion—produces the results seen here....

... [I]n the 1980s whites have the same pattern of responses as blacks; poor whites are always more confident of blacks' chances than are middle-class whites (the difference scores are negative). The substantive meaning of this formally similar pattern is, of course, very different across the races. To blacks, these questions ask about their race's chances *despite* discrimination; to whites, these questions ask whether discrimination still exists....

... Middle-class blacks have become much more pessimistic; poor blacks have become slightly more pessimistic; middle-class whites are fairly confident of blacks' chances to succeed; and poor whites are very confident of blacks'

---

14. Similar sets of questions produce similar reversals over time. In 1968 fewer poorly-educated than well-educated blacks agreed that "few white people dislike Negroes." By 1983 more poor than well-off blacks thought that "most white people like [me]" (Campbell and Schuman 1968: var. 317; Lewis and Schneider 1983: 13). In 1968 more poorly-educated than well-educated blacks trusted no whites, but fifteen years later more poor than well-off blacks claimed to like white people (Schuman and Hatchett 1974: 64; Lewis and Schneider 1983: 13).

17. More specialized surveys reinforce my claim of middle-class optimism during the 1960s. For example, among blacks who had experienced discrimination in 1967, those with little education mistrusted the political system more than those with a lot (Aberbach and Walker 1970b). Three-fifths or more of seniors in traditionally black colleges agreed in 1968 that Negro college graduates were likely to get at least as good a job as whites in most professional settings (Harris 1968: records 55, 73). See also Searles and Williams (1962).

18. Academic writings about race also demonstrate plummeting optimism among the best-off. Until the 1960s, "studies by black scholars always tended to be more positive and optimistic [than those by whites] about the possibilities for improvement [in race relations] and advancement [of blacks' condition].... For most of these researchers, ... integration of blacks and whites was inevitable, despite the objections of most whites and some blacks. Therefore progress in breaking down barriers to black advancement through greater desegregation was a constant source of optimism" (Franklin 1985: 20, 22). Starting in the 1960s, black scholars became more pessimistic and skeptical of the desirability of desegregation than the rest of the black population or than most white scholars of race.

chances. All three paradoxes obtain[19] for the first tenet of the American dream.[20]

19. Judgments of chances for political success differ slightly from judgments of chances for economic success. Poor African Americans have always been much less satisfied than better-off African Americans with their *own* chance to influence the government (Matthews and Prothro 1961: var. 428; Langton and Jennings 1972: 63; Aberbach and Walker 1970b; Wright 1976: 141, 176–81; Campbell 1980: 655; Shingles 1981: 84; Brown et al. 1994: tables 3.3, 1984 and 1988; 3.4, 1984 and 1988; 11.10, 11.11, 11.12; GSS 1987: vars. 337, 340; Colasanto 1988: 46; Gurin et al. 1989: 294; Smith and Seltzer 1992: 56). But better-off blacks have always been less satisfied with *their race*'s chance for political influence. In particular, high-status blacks are more likely than low-status blacks to think that their race has too little, and whites have too much, political influence (Gallup 1961: var. 05C; 1964: var. 14C; NSBA 1980: var. 1217; GSS 1987, var. 353; Brown et al. 1994: tables 13.10, 1984 and 1988; 6.5, 1984 and 1988; 6.7, 1984 and 1988; 18.12; GSS 1990–91: var. 394; Dawson 1994b: 95; Reese and Brown forthcoming: tables 1–3). For possible counterevidence, depending on how one interprets the questions, see Brown et al. (1994: tables 3.7, 1984 and 1988; 3.8, 1984 and 1988; 3.11, 1984 and 1988). For clear counterevidence, see ibid. (table 3.9, 1984 and 1988).

20. The two paradoxes roughly obtain when African Americans consider the effects of class discrimination. In the 1960s middle-class blacks were more convinced than were poor blacks that even the poor could succeed (if we can rely on one survey), but from the mid-1970s on, middle-class blacks were no more and sometimes less convinced of class-based equality of opportunity (Huber and Form 1973: 91; Schlozman and Verba 1979: 168, 170; Roper 1986: var. 42, 46; GSS 1987: vars. 507A, 507B; GSS 1990–91: var. 387D; Brown et al. 1994: table 6.10). One survey (Harris 1989b: 193, 276; 1989c: 288) has the opposite finding.

Whites are less predictable. In the 1960s and 1970s middle-class whites resembled middle-class blacks in their relative confidence about the chances of the poor (Huber and Form 1973: 91; Schlozman and Verba 1979: 168, 170), but surveys in the 1980s show conflicting results (Roper 1986: vars. 42, 46; GSS 1987: vars. 507A, 507B; 1990–91: var. 387D).

The Second Tenet

... The ideology of the American dream specifies not only who may participate but also what they participate in—the search for success, which one can reasonably expect to attain. African Americans, like other Americans, do not always translate a clear-eyed view of the past into a hard-nosed evaluation of the future....

... Well-off blacks are, once again, disproportionately discouraged in general in the face of their own well-being, and poor blacks are disproportionately encouraged in general in the face of their own poverty and poor prospects.

Other surveys confirm these findings. From the 1950s into the 1990s, poor blacks almost always felt less pleased with their own progress from the recent or distant past than did well-off blacks. The discrepancies were sometimes as great as two to one....

Poor African Americans are similarly more discouraged than are well-off blacks about the United States as a whole and various groups within it. On the nation: in 1991, 30 percent of middle-class but only 6 percent of poor blacks thought the nation was in better shape than it had been a year earlier.[25] On women: in 1970, almost half of middle-class but only 40 percent of poor blacks thought women received more respect than a decade earlier.[26] On the poor: more affluent than poor blacks think poor Americans are doing well now, were doing well a decade earlier, or will do well a decade hence.[27] On "the average man": in three of four surveys

There are too few questions, with no clear trends, to say anything about how different race/class groups view the issue of opportunity for different genders (Roper 1986: var. 45; GSS 1987: var. 507L).

25. *Los Angeles Times* (1991a: var. 31; see also var. 30); see also Roper (1986: vars. 4, 9, 29) and table 4.3.

26. Harris (1970a: var. 1a; 1970b: var. 1a).

27. Lewis and Schneider (1985: 6, 7, 59); Roper (1986: var. 46).

in the 1970s, more poor than well-off blacks agreed that "the lot of the average man is getting worse."[28]

But despite this broad and deep pessimism, poor blacks are at present *more* cheerful about the past and future progress of their race than are their well-off counterparts. . . .

In short, the paradoxes of succeeding more and enjoying it less and remaining under the spell of the great national suggestion hold with regard to the second tenet of the American dream in two ways. First, although the best-off third of blacks became dramatically better off during the past three decades, they simultaneously became much more cautious about anticipating success for their race. As the worst-off third of blacks became relatively or even absolutely worse off, they simultaneously became only a little more cautious about the likelihood that members of their race would achieve their dreams. Thus the two classes reversed positions.

Second, the paradoxes hold for comparisons across substantive topics as well as across time. During the 1980s and 1990s, well-off African Americans were relatively gratified and optimistic for themselves, the nation, and other groups of Americans—but were worried for their race. Conversely, poor African Americans were less gratified and optimistic for themselves, the nation, and other Americans—but were more sanguine for their race.[30]

---

28. Since then, poor African Americans have become slightly less discouraged and well-off African Americans slightly more so, so the two groups have converged (GSS 1972–73, 1974, 1976–77, 1980, 1982, 1984–85, 1987, 1988–89, and 1990–91: var. 176B). See also Austin and Stack (1988: 363–66); Austin and Dodge (1990).

30. Despite their *relative* gratification, badly-off African Americans, like well-off African Americans, are generally skeptical about the prospects of success for their race. Thus neither income group contradicts the findings of chapter 3 that blacks do not much trust the second tenet of the American dream when it does not refer to them personally. See Schlozman and Verba (1979) for a similar analysis.

The Third Tenet

. . . [W]ithin each race, the higher one's status, the more one feels in control of one's own life. In 1962 almost half of low-status urban blacks, compared with only one-fourth of high-status urban blacks, demonstrated high "anomia."[32] Six times between 1961 and 1976, up to twice as many poor as well-off blacks agreed that "a person has to live pretty much for today and let tomorrow take care of itself."[33] In 1968 poorly educated blacks rated themselves less personally competent than did blacks in general, whereas highly educated blacks deemed themselves much more competent.[34] Twenty years later, fewer badly-off blacks than well-off blacks or whites

Both paradoxes recur in African Americans' evaluations of their race's chances for political success. In 1961 well-off blacks scored race relations in their community over the previous five years 4.1 out of 10. They predicted a score of 8.0 five years hence. Poor blacks scored past race relations higher (4.6) but future race relations lower (7.1) (Matthews and Prothro 1961: vars. 404, 406; see also Campbell and Schuman 1968: vars. 258, 265, 271, 318). But by 1976 twice as many poor as well-off blacks thought there had been a lot of civil rights change (Parent and Stekler 1985: 530; see also Gallup 1991b: var. 5). Similarly, in the 1960s more well-off than poor blacks were hopeful about white attitudes toward "Negro rights"; by 1984 slightly more well-off than poor blacks doubted that American blacks will "ever achieve full social and economic equality" (Brink and Harris 1964: 130; 1966: 258; Brown et al. 1994: table 7.6; Sigelman and Welch 1991: 76).

32. Killian and Grigg (1962: 663).

33. Matthews and Prothro (1961: var. 427); Marx (1964: var. 50L); Survey Research Center (1964: var. 50m); GSS (1972–73, 1974, 1976: var. 176A). See also Middleton (1963: 976); Campbell and Schuman (1968: vars. 176–78); Bullough (1972: 88). In all the surveys, whites showed the same class pattern but much lower levels of agreement.

34. Campbell et al. (1976: 453–54); see also Marx (1964: var. 50h); Survey Research Center (1964: var. 66b); NSBA (1980: vars. 72, 73).

of any class claimed that their situation was within their control rather than a result of luck or fate.[35]

However, poor African Americans are more inclined, and well-off African Americans less inclined, to hold *other* people responsible for their circumstances. Fully 90 percent of the former agreed in 1964 that "no weakness or difficulty can hold us back if we have enough will power," and almost as many agreed that if one tries hard enough, one will succeed.[36] In repeated questions since 1970, poor blacks usually agree more than do rich blacks that people get ahead mainly through hard work rather than luck.[37]

That reversal is even clearer when African Americans focus on explanations for racial disparities. On this topic, the higher one's status, the *less* likely one is to attribute blacks' situation to their own actions....

... Again we see racial differences within each class and class differences within each race.

... [W]ell-off blacks are least likely to hold African Americans directly responsible for their unequal status.[39] Thus the very group that seems to exemplify the success of the American dream believes less than any other racial/class group that the key to black success lies in black hands.[40] That view has not changed since the 1960s, so the fullest version of the paradox of

"succeeding more" does not obtain. Nevertheless it remains psychologically and politically very important that well-off African Americans use the third tenet to explain their own lives but not those of other blacks.

... [P]oor African Americans do precisely the reverse—they use the third tenet to explain the lives of fellow blacks, even though they recognize how little control they exercise over their own lives. Their faith in the American dream is as extraordinary, and in as much need of explanation, as is the lack of faith of the best-off in their race.

The Fourth Tenet

... This tenet changes the ideology of the American dream from a mere formula for getting ahead into an ideal that Americans have found to be worth dying for. But startlingly few survey questions probe it. The previous chapter showed that African Americans are arguably more committed to the pursuit of virtue (as well as to the pursuit of material goods) in their own lives than are white Americans, and that they are perhaps less likely to equate material and spiritual success. But given the indistinctness of these patterns, it is not surprising that class-based patterns within each race are even less distinct....

---

35. Roper (1986: var. 36); see also NSBA (1980: vars. 78, 79, 81); Hughes and Demo (1989: 146–47); Gloria Johnson (1989: 38–41).

36. Marx (1964: vars. 50a, 50m). Poor blacks may have simply been responding to the tautalogous nature of these assertions. If so, they were more observant than high-status blacks, of whom about 10% fewer agreed with each statement. See also Survey Research Center (1964: vars. 50a, 50n).

37. Poor whites are slightly *less* inclined than well-off whites to attribute success to hard work (GSS 1972–73, 1974, 1976–77, 1980, 1982, 1984–85, 1987, 1988–89, 1990–91: var. 197; 1993: var. 458; for counterevidence see Survey Research Center 1964: var. 50I).

39. See also Richard Allen (1994).

40. Explanations of class inequality show different patterns: among whites, more well-off than poor blame the poor and praise the rich for their respective circumstances. Among blacks, in the 1960s the well-off also blamed the poor and praised the rich more than did the poor. But by the 1980s that pattern had disappeared, and none has emerged to take its place (Survey Research Center 1964: var. 13C; Marx 1964: vars. 50D, 50H; Alston and Dean 1972: 15; Huber and Form 1973: 101, 106; GSS 1972–73: var. 197; Schlozman and Verba 1979: 168; Jackman and Jackman 1983: 56; GSS 1984: var. 68H; Lewis and Schneider 1985: 6–7; Kluegel and Smith 1986: 95–100; Harris 1986: table 5; Gallup 1988: var. 16; Harris 1989b: 164, 261; 1989c: 240; GSS 1990–91: vars. 197, 443A–C).

Implications of Affluent and Poor Blacks' Beliefs for the American Dream

We see now the outlines of the second threat to the future of the ideology of the American dream. Blacks and whites increasingly diverge in their evaluations of whether the American dream encompasses African Americans.... In addition, middle-class blacks are increasingly disillusioned with the very ideology of the dream itself, and poor blacks may not be far behind—that is the message of this chapter. By the 1990s well-off blacks have come to doubt the reality of the dream for African Americans. They have also become increasingly pessimistic about the future of the dream in general, and more embittered about American society than white Americans expect, given their class's improved standing. Poor African Americans are relatively less skeptical about blacks' chances to achieve their dreams, are only a little more pessimistic about the dream than they used to be, and are much less embittered about American society than white (and well-off black) Americans expect, given the deterioration of their circumstances. Still, they show hints of increasing despair.

The ideology of the American dream has always relied on previously poor Americans not only achieving upward mobility, but also recognizing that they had done so, feeling gratified, and consequently deepening their commitment to the dream and the nation behind it. That, very roughly speaking, has been the experience of most immigrants. But middle-class blacks are not following the prescribed pattern. They recognize their own mobility, they are pleased by it, but their commitment to the American dream is declining, not rising. That is an unprecedented risk to an ideology that depends so heavily on faith in its ultimate fairness and benevolence.[45]

It is a risk both because middle-class African Americans are themselves increasingly important in the political, social, and economic life of the nation and because blacks have always led the way for other Americans in beliefs as in behaviors. The convictions of (mostly middle-class) blacks and their white allies led to the incorporation of the ideal of equality into the Constitution in the mid-nineteenth century.[46] One hundred years later, the determination of (mostly middle-class) blacks and their white allies to make that ideal a reality led to an expansion of the political influence and legal rights of all women, children, and other previously excluded groups. But we cannot assume that African Americans lead other Americans only along paths that reinforce the American dream; they could as well show the way to suspicion and bitterness.

The relative lack of disillusionment of poor African Americans comprises the other threat to the American dream revealed by disaggregation. The ideology has historically relied not only on the gratification of the upwardly mobile but also on the pacification of the deeply poor. That is, for the American dream's vision of success for all to stabilize rather than destabilize American society, the poor must be enticed to believe in the same process of upward mobility, with the same consequent commitment to the nation at large, as the no longer poor. That, again very roughly speaking, has been the experience of most immigrants not favored enough to join the middle class. So far, that remains the experience of most deeply poor African Americans. But any nightly newscast suggests how fragile that continued commitment is for those subject to drive-by shootings and schools innocent of plumbing, let alone textbooks. Thus if middle-class African Americans may lead other Americans into disillusionment with the ideology despite their success, so a few poor African Americans may, with

---

45. For a similar alarm, absent my ambivalence about the value of the American dream, see People for the American Way (1992: e.g., 52).

46. Katz (1988).

even greater reason, lead other poor Americans into a rejection of the dream that will make affluent alienation seem trivial.

Let me repeat: whether one sees these threats to the American dream as a revelation of hypocritical class and racial domination or as an attack on "the last, best hope on Earth" (or as something in between) depends on one's judgment about Americans' potential to make their ideology live up to its own best values. It also depends on one's judgment about its likely replacement. But that subject comes later. . . .

Works Cited

Abbreviations

AJPS	*American Journal of Political Science*
AJS	*American Journal of Sociology*
APSR	*American Political Science Review*
ASR	*American Sociological Review*
NYT	*New York Times*
APSA	American Political Science Association
ASA	American Sociological Association
IRP	Institute for Research on Poverty
MWPSA	Midwest Political Science Association
NBER	National Bureau of Economic Research
USGPO	United States Government Printing Office

ABC News/*Washington Post* (1989) "ABC News/*Washington Post* 9/89 Poll," Sept. 28–Oct. 3.

——— (1990) "ABC News/*Washington Post* Poll: Omnibus-September 1990," Step. 20–24.

Aberbach, Joel, and Jack Walker (1970b) "Political Trust and Racial Ideology," *APSR* 64, 4: 1199–1219.

Adams, James, and William Dressler (1988) "Perceptions of Injustice in a Black Community," *Human Relations* 41, 10: 753–767.

Allen, Richard (1994) "Structural Equality in Black and White," *Howard J. of Communication* 5, 1–2: 69–91.

Alston, Jon, and K. Imogene Dean (1972) "Socioeconomic Factors Associated with Attitudes toward Welfare Recipients and the Causes of Poverty," *Social Service R.* 46, 1: 13–23.

Austin, Roy, and Steven Stack (1988) "Race, Class, and Opportunity: Changing Realities and Perceptions," *Sociological Q.* 29, 3: 357–369.

Austin, Roy, and Hiroko Dodge (1990) "Despair, Distrust and Dissatisfaction among Blacks and Women, 1973–1987," paper at the annual meeting of the ASA, Washington, D.C.

Brink, William, and Louis Harris (1966) *Black and White* (Simon and Schuster).

Brown, Ronald, et al. (1994) *The 1984–1988 National Black Election Panel Study [NBES]: A Sourcebook* (U. of Michigan, Institute for Social Research).

Bullough, Bonnie (1972) "Alienation in the Ghetto," in Charles Bullock III and Harrell Rodgers, Jr., eds., *Black Political Attitudes* (Markham), 83–96.

CBS News/*NYT* (1978) "The Kerner Commission— Ten Years Later," Feb. 16–19.

——— (1992) "May National Poll," May 6–8.

Campbell, Angus, and Howard Schuman (1968) "Racial Attitudes in Fifteen American Cities," for National Advisory Commission on Civil Disorders (U. of Michigan, Institute for Social Research), Jan.–March.

Campbell, Angus, Philip Converse, and Willard Rodgers (1976) *The Quality of American Life* (Russell Sage Foundation).

Campbell, Bruce (1980) "The Interaction of Race and Socioeconomic Status in the Development of Political Attitudes," *Social Science Q.* 60, 4: 651–658.

Carr, Leslie and John Hudgins (c. 1989) "Race, Class, and External Political Efficacy" (Old Dominion U., Dept. of Sociology).

Cavanagh, Thomas (1985) *Inside Black America: The Message of the Black Vote in the 1984 Elections* (Joint Center for Political Studies).

Citrin, Jack, Beth Reingold, and Donald Green (1990) "American Identity and the Politics of Ethnic Change," *J. of Politics* 52, 4: 1124–1154.

Colasanto, Diane (1988) "Black Attitudes," *Public Opinion* 10, 5: 45–49.

Converse, Philip et al. (1980) *American Social Attitudes Data Sourcebook, 1947–1978* (Harvard U. Press).

Dawson, Michael (1994b) *Behind the Mule: Race and Class in African American Politics* (Princeton U. Press).

Denton, Herbert, and Barry Sussman (1981) "'Crossover Generation' of Blacks Expresses Most Distrust of Whites," *Washington Post*, Mar. 25: A1, A2.

Erskine, Hazel (1962) "The Polls: Race Relations," *Public Opinion Q.* 26, 1: 137–148.

——— (1969a) "The Polls: Negro Philosophies of Life," *Public Opinion Q.* 33, 1: 147–158.

Franklin, V. P. (1985) "From Integration to Black Self-Determination," in Margaret Spencer, Geraldine Brookins, and Walter Allen, eds., *Beginnings: The Social and Affective Development of Black Children* (Erlbaum), 19–28.

Gallup, George, ed. (1987) *Gallup Poll: Public Opinion, 1987* (Wilmington: Scholarly Resources).

Gallup Organization (1961) "The Gallup Poll," June 23–28.

Gallup Organization (1963) "The Gallup Poll," May 23–28.

——— (1964) "Hopes and Fears," for Potomac Associates, Oct.

——— (1988) "Gallup/*Newsweek* Poll: Race Relations," for *Newsweek*, Feb. 19–22.

——— (1991b) "Gallup News Service Survey: June Omnibus, Wave 2," June 13–16.

——— (1992) "Gallup News Service Survey: May Omnibus, Wave 1," May 7–10.

——— (1994) "CNN/*USA Today*—Report Card #5," for CNN/*USA Today*, April.

Gilliam, Franklin Jr. (1986) "Black America: Divided by Class?" *Public Opinion* 9, 1: 53–57.

Goldman, Peter (1969) *Report from Black America* (Simon and Schuster).

Gordon S. Black Corporation (1989a) "*USA Today* Poll: Racism," for *USA Today*, Aug. 30–31.

Gurin, Patricia, Shirley Hatchett, and James Jackson (1989) *Hope and Independence: Blacks' Response to Electoral and Party Politics* (Russell Sage Foundation).

Harris, Louis (1986) "Yuppie Lifestyle Felt To Be Unattractive to Americans" (N. Y.: Harris Survey), Feb. 3.

Harris, Louis, and Associates (1966a) "Racial Survey: Black Sample," for *Newsweek*, June.

——— (1966b) "Racial Survey: Random Sample," for *Newsweek*, June.

——— (1968) "College Student Peace Corps Survey: Black Sample."

——— (1970a) "American Women's Opinion Survey [Women]," for the Virginia Slim Division of Liggett and Meyers, Aug.

——— (1970b) "American Women's Opinion Survey [Men]," for the Virginia Slim Division of Liggett and Meyers, Aug.

——— (1978) *A Study of Attitudes toward Racial and Religious Minorities and Toward Women*, for National Conference of Christians and Jews, Nov.

——— (1986b) "Children's Needs and Public Responsibilities," for Group W—Westinghouse Broadcasting Co., Sept.

——— (1988) "A Nation Divided on Black Progress," for *Business Week*/Harris Poll, Jan. 20–26.

Harris, Louis, and Associates (1989b) *The Unfinished Agenda on Race in America*, vol. 2, for NAACP Legal Defense and Educational Fund, June–Sept. 1988.

——— (1989c) *The Unfinished Agenda on Race in America* (unpublished tables).

——— (1990) "The View from the Trenches," June.

Hochschild, Jennifer (1981) *What's Fair? American Beliefs about Distributive Justice* (Harvard U. Press).

——— (1988) "The Double-Edged Sword of Equal Opportunity," in Ian Shapiro and Grant Reeher, eds., *Power, Inequality, and Democratic Politics* (Westview Press), 168–200.

Huber, Joan, and William Form (1973) *Income and Ideology* (Free Press).

Hughes, Michael, and David Demo (1989) "Self-Perceptions of Black Americans," *AJS* 95, 1: 132–159.

Hutcheson, John (1973) *Racial Attitudes in Atlanta* (Emory U., Center for Research in Social Change).

Jackman, Mary, and Robert Jackman (1983) *Class Awareness in the United States* (U. of California Press).

Johnson, Gloria (1989) "Estimated Reference Group Effects of Underemployment and Underpayment on Psychosocial Functioning among Working Men," *National J. of Sociology* 3, 1: 25–50.

Joint Center for Political Studies (1984) "JCPS Releases In-Depth Survey of Black Political Attitudes," press release, August 30.

Katz, Stanley (1988) "The Strange Birth and Unlikely History of Constitutional Equality," *Journal of American History* 75(3): 747–762.

Killian, Lewis, and Charles Grigg (1962) "Urbanism, Race, and Anomia," *AJS* 67, 6: 661–665.

Kluegel, James, and Eliot Smith (1986) *Beliefs about Inequality* (Aldine de Gruyter).

Langton, Kenneth, and M. Kent Jennings (1972) "Political Socialization and the High School Civics Curriculum in the United States," In Charles Bullock III and Harrell Rodgers, Jr., eds., *Black Political Attitudes* (Markham), 60–71.

Lewis, I. A., and William Schneider (1983) "Black Voting, Bloc Voting, and the Democrats," *Public Opinion* 6, 5: 12–15, 59.

Los Angeles Times (1983) Poll no. 71: "National Survey," Sept. 18–22.

—— (1991a) untitled, June 28–30.

—— (1991b) Poll no. 259: "Judge Thomas, Race Relations and Ronald Reagan," Sept. 21–25.

McClosky, Herbert, and John Zaller (1984) *The American Ethos: Public Attitudes toward Capitalism and Democracy* (Harvard U. Press).

McLeod, Ramon (1988b) "Different Views of Gains by Blacks," *San Francisco Chronicle*, Mar. 30: A1, A4.

Marshall, Nancy, and Rosalind Barnett (1991) "Race, Class and Multiple Role Strains among Women Employed in the Service Sector," *Women and Health* 17, 4: 1–19.

Marx, Gary (1964) "Negro Political Attitudes" (also titled "Anti-Semitism—Negro Oversample") (U. of California, Berkeley, Survey Research Center).

—— (1969) *Protest and Prejudice: A Study of Belief in the Black Community* (Harper Torchbooks).

Matthews, Donald, and James Prothro (1961) "The Negro Political Participation Study" (U. of North Carolina), March–June.

Media General/Associated Press (1988) "National Poll #21," June 22–July 3.

Middleton, Russell (1963) "Alienation, Race, and Education" *ASR* 28, 6: 973–977.

Myrdal, Gunnar (1944) *An American Dilemma* (Harper & Brothers).

NBC News (1989a) "R.A.C.E.—Racial Attitudes and Consciousness Exam" (N. Y.: NBC News).

National Conference (1994) *Taking America's Pulse: The Full Report of the National Conference Survey on Inter-Group Relations*, by LH Research (N. Y.: National Conference of Christians and Jews).

NYT/WCBS News (1985) "New York City Race Relations Survey," April 27–May 3.

NYT/WCBS-TV Channel 2 News (1994) "New York City Poll," June 12–15.

Parent, T. Wayne, and Paul Stekler (1985) "The Political Implications of Economic Stratification in the Black Community," *Western Political Q.* 38, 4: 521–538.

People for the American Way (1992) *Democracy's Next Generation II: A Study of American Youth on Race* (Washington, D.C.: People for the American Way).

Pettigrew, Thomas (1964) *A Profile of the Negro American* (Van Nostrand).

Reese, Laura, and Ronald Brown (1995) "The Effects of Religious Messages on Racial Identity and System Blame among African Americans," *J. of Politics* 57, 1: 24–43.

Roper Organization (1986) "The American Dream Survey," for the *Wall Street J.*, Oct.

Schlozman, Kay, and Sidney Verba (1979) *Injury to Insult: Unemployment, Class, and Political Response* (Harvard U. Press).

Schuman, Howard, and Shirley Hatchett (1974) *Black Racial Attitudes* (U. of Michigan, Institute for Social Research).

Schuman, Howard, Charlotte Steeh, and Lawrence Bobo (1988) *Racial Attitudes in America* (Harvard U. Press).

Searles, Ruth, and J. Allen Williams Jr. (1962) "Negro College Students' Participation in Sit-ins," *Social Forces* 40, 3: 215–220.

Shingles, Richard (1981) "Black Consciousness and Political Participation," *APSR* 75, 1: 76–91.

Sigelman, Lee, and Susan Welch (1991) *Black Americans' Views of Racial Inequality* (Cambridge U. Press).

Smith, Robert (1988) "Sources of Urban Ethnic Politics," *Research in Race and Ethnic Relations* (JAI Press), 5: 159–191.

Smith, Robert, and Richard Seltzer (1992) *Race, Class, and Culture: A Study in Afro-American Mass Opinion* (SUNY Press).

Sniderman, Paul, Philip Tetlock, and Thomas Piazza (1991) "Race and Politics Survey" (U. of California, Berkeley, Survey Research Center), Feb. 1–Nov. 21.

Survey Research Center, U. of California, Berkeley (1964) "Anti-Semitism in the United States," for Anti-Defamation League of B'Nai B'rith, Oct.

Tate, Katherine (1993) *From Protest to Politics: The New Black Voters in American Elections* (Harvard U. Press).

Taylor, D. Garth (1993) *1993 Metro Survey Report* (Metropolitan Chicago Information Center).

―――― (1994) *1994 Metro Survey Report* (Metropolitan Chicago Information Center).

"Thirty Years after 'I Have a Dream'" (1993) *The Polling Report* 9, 18 (Sept. 13): 2.

Verba, Sidney, and Gary Orren (1985) *Equality in America: The View From the Top* (Harvard U. Press).

Washington Post (1992) "*Washington Post* Poll: Race Relations," Feb. 28–Mar. 3.

Welch, Susan, et al. (1994) "Justice for All: Still an American Dilemma," *Challenge* 5, 1: 19–37.

Wright, James (1976) *The Dissent of the Governed: Alienation and Democracy in America* (Academic Press).

Yankelovich Clancy Shulman (1992) "Rodney King Verdict and the Los Angeles Riots," for *Time* and Cable News Network, April 30.

Beyond Tocqueville, Myrdal, and Hartz: The Multiple Traditions in America

Rogers M. Smith

Since the nation's inception, analysts have described American political culture as the preeminent example of modern liberal democracy, of government by popular consent with respect for the equal rights of all. They have portrayed American political development as the working out of liberal democratic or republican principles, via both "liberalizing" and "democratizing" socioeconomic changes and political efforts to cope with tensions inherent in these principles. Illiberal, undemocratic beliefs and practices have usually been seen only as expressions of ignorance and prejudice, destined to marginality by their lack of rational defenses. A distinguished line of writers, from Hector St. John Crevecoeur in the eighteenth century and Harriet Martineau and Lord Bryce in the nineteenth century to Gunnar Myrdal and Louis Hartz in the twentieth century serves as authority for this view. Today, leading social scientists such as Samuel P. Huntington, Walter Dean Burnham, and Ira Katznelson, legal scholars, historians, and cultural analysts such as Kenneth Karst, John Diggins, and Sacvan Bercovitch, and many others still structure their accounts on these premises. Virtually all appeal to the classic analysis of American politics, Tocqueville's *Democracy in America*.

Tocqueville's thesis—that America has been most shaped by the unusually free and egalitarian ideas and material conditions that prevailed at its founding—captures important truths. Nonetheless, the purpose of this essay is to challenge that thesis by showing that its adherents fail to give due weight to inegalitarian ideologies

Excerpted from: Rogers M. Smith, "Beyond Tocqueville, Myrdal, and Hartz: The Multiple Traditions in America." *American Political Science Review* 87, no. 3 (1993): 549–566. © American Political Science Association. Reprinted with the permission of the American Political Science Association and Cambridge University Press.

and conditions that have shaped the participants and the substance of American politics just as deeply. For over 80% of U.S. history, its laws declared most of the world's population to be ineligible for full American citizenship solely because of their race, original nationality, or gender. For at least two-thirds of American history, the majority of the domestic adult population was also ineligible for full citizenship for the same reasons. Contrary to Tocquevillian views of American civic identity, it did not matter how "liberal," "democratic," or "republican" those persons' beliefs were.[1]

1. The percentage varies according to whether one dates the United States from 1776, the Declaration of Independence, or 1789, the ratified Constitution. State policies prior to 1789 on the whole made nonwhites and women ineligible for full citizenship. Women could always formally be U.S. citizens, but they were almost universally denied the vote until 1920, making them clearly second-class citizens. Other overt legal discriminations on their political and economic rights continued through the 1960s. Naturalization was confined to whites from 1790 through 1868 and closed to most Asian nationals until 1952. By then, the national origins quota system of immigration restrictions, enacted in the 1920s, prevented most Asians and many southern Europeans from coming to the United States and becoming permanent residents or citizens, explicitly because of their original nationality or ethnicity. That system was not repealed until 1965. Despite formal constitutional guarantees enacted in the mid-1860s, blacks were also widely denied basic rights of citizenship until the 1964 Civil Rights Act and the 1965 Voting Rights Act (Higham 1975, 29–66; Kettner 1978, 287–322; Smith 1989). Thus, though the specifics changed, denials of access to full citizenship based explicitly on race, ethnicity, or gender always denied large majorities of the world's population any opportunity for U.S. citizenship up to 1965. That represents about 83% of the nation's history since the Constitution, 88% since the Declaration of Independence. If, controversially, one assumes that women became full citizens with the vote in 1920, then a majority of the

The Tocquevillian story is thus deceptive because it is too narrow. It is centered on relationships among a minority of Americans (white men, largely of northern European ancestry) analyzed via reference to categories derived from the hierarchy of political and economic statuses men have held in Europe: monarchs and aristocrats, commercial burghers, farmers, industrial and rural laborers, and indigents. Because most European observers and British American men have regarded these categories as politically fundamental, it is understandable that they have always found the most striking fact about the new nation to be its lack of one type of ascriptive hierarchy. There was no hereditary monarchy or nobility native to British America, and the revolutionaries rejected both the authority of the British king and aristocracy and the creation of any new American substitutes. Those features of American political life made the United States appear remarkably egalitarian by comparison with Europe.

But the comparative moral, material, and political egalitarianism that prevailed at the founding among moderately propertied white men was surrounded by an array of other fixed, ascriptive systems of unequal status, all largely unchallenged by the American revolutionaries.[2] Men were thought naturally suited to rule over women, within both the family and the polity. White northern Europeans were thought superior culturally—and probably biologically—to black Africans, bronze Native Americans, and indeed all other races and civilizations. Many British Americans also treated religion as an inherited condition and regarded Protestants as

created by God to be morally and politically, as well as theologically, superior to Catholics, Jews, Muslims, and others.

These beliefs were not merely emotional prejudices or "attitudes." Over time, American intellectual and political elites elaborated distinctive justifications for these ascriptive systems, including inegalitarian scriptural readings, the scientific racism of the "American school" of ethnology, racial and sexual Darwinism, and the romantic cult of Anglo–Saxonism in American historiography. All these discourses identified the true meaning of *Americanism* with particular forms of cultural, religious, ethnic, and especially racial and gender hierarchies.[3] Many adherents of ascriptive Americanist outlooks insisted that the nation's political and economic structures should formally reflect natural and cultural inequalities, even at the cost of violating doctrines of universal rights. Although these views never entirely prevailed, their impact has been wide and deep.

Thus to approach a truer picture of America's political culture and its characteristic conflicts, we must consider more than the familiar categories of (absent) feudalism and socialism and (pervasive) bourgeois liberalism and republicanism. The nation has also been deeply constituted by the ideologies and practices that defined the relationships of the white male minority with

---

domestic adult population became legally eligible for full citizenship then. This still means that a majority of domestic adults were ineligible for full citizenship on racial, ethnic, or gender grounds for about two-thirds of U.S. history (from either starting point).

2. Orren (1991), a major alternative critique of Tocquevillian accounts, shows ascriptive inegalitarian labor systems long prevailed even among white men.

3. From early on, many American intellectuals and politicians believed that "like the Chain of Being, the races of man consisted of an ordered hierarchy" (Haller 1971, 11; Russett 1989, 201–3). Some believed in a natural order of rank among the races, some that cultures fell into a higher and lower levels of civilization. Most thought race and culture linked. Scholars disagreed about the relative ranks of Asiatics, blacks, Native Americans, and other races and cultures, but these gradations mattered less than the supremacy of whites over nonwhites. Mulattoes, for example, were legally treated as an intermediate racial group in antebellum America, but by the 1850s whites began to reduce their status to that of "pure" blacks (Williamson 1980).

subordinate groups, and the relationships of these groups with each other. When these elements are kept in view, the flat plain of American egalitarianism mapped by Tocqueville and others suddenly looks quite different. We instead perceive America's initial conditions as exhibiting only a rather small, recently leveled valley of relative equality nestled amid steep mountains of hierarchy. And though we can see forces working to erode those mountains over time, broadening the valley, many of the peaks also prove to be volcanic, frequently responding to seismic pressures with outbursts that harden into substantial peaks once again.

To be sure, America's ascriptive, unequal statuses, and the ideologies by which they have been defended have always been heavily conditioned and constrained by the presence of liberal democratic values and institutions. The reverse, however, is also true. Although liberal democratic ideas and practices have been more potent in America than elsewhere, American politics is best seen as expressing the interaction of multiple political traditions, including *liberalism*, *republicanism*, and *ascriptive forms of Americanism*, which have collectively comprised American political culture, without any constituting it as a whole.[4] Though Americans have often struggled

over contradictions among these traditions, almost all have tried to embrace what they saw as the best features of each.

Ascriptive outlooks have had such a hold in America because they have provided something that neither liberalism nor republicanism has done so well. They have offered creditable intellectual and psychological reasons for many Americans to believe that their social roles and personal characteristics express an identity that has inherent and transcendant worth, thanks to nature, history, and God. Those rationales have obviously aided those who sat atop the nation's political, economic, and social hierarchies. But many Americans besides elites have felt that they have gained meaning, as well as material and political benefits, from their nation's traditional structures of ascribed places and destinies.

Conventional narratives, preoccupied with the absence of aristocracy and socialism, usually stress the liberal and democratic elements in the rhetoric of even America's dissenters (Hartog 1987). These accounts fail to explain how and why liberalizing efforts have frequently lost to forces favoring new forms of racial and gender hierarchy. Those forces have sometimes negated major liberal victories, especially in the half-century following Reconstruction; and the fate of that era may be finding echoes today.

My chief aim here is to persuade readers that many leading accounts of American political culture are inadequate. I will also suggest briefly how analyses with greater descriptive and explanatory power can be achieved by replacing the Tocquevillian thesis with a *multiple-traditions* view of America. This argument is relevant to contemporary politics in two ways. First, it raises the possibility that novel intellectual, po-

---

4. A tradition here is comprised by (1) a worldview or ideology that defines basic political and economic institutions, the persons eligible to participate in them, and the roles or rights to which they are entitled and (2) institutions and practices embodying and reproducing those precepts. Hence traditions are not *merely* sets of ideas. The liberal tradition involves limited government, the rule of law protecting individual rights, and a market economy, all officially open to all minimally rational adults. The republican tradition is grounded on popular sovereignty exercised via institutions of mass self-governance. It includes an ethos of civic virtue and economic regulation for the public good. Adherents of what I term ascriptive Americanist traditions believe true Americans are in some way "chosen" by God, history, or nature to possess superior moral and intellectual traits, often associated with race and gender. Hence many Americanists believe that non-

whites and women should be governed as subjects or second-class citizens, denied full market rights, and sometimes excluded from the nation altogether. My thesis—that an evolving mix of these traditions is visible in America's political culture, institutions, and the outlooks of Americans of *all* backgrounds—is indebted to Orren and Skowronek 1993.

litical, and legal systems reinforcing racial, ethnic, and gender inequalities might be rebuilt in America in the years ahead. That prospect does not seem plausible if the United States has always been essentially liberal democratic, with all exceptions marginal and steadily eliminated. It seems quite real, however, if liberal democratic traditions have been but contested parts of American culture, with inegalitarian ideologies and practices often resurging even after major enhancements of liberal democracy. Second, the political implications of the view that America has never been completely liberal, and that changes have come only through difficult struggles and then have often not been sustained, are very different from the complacency—sometimes despair—engendered by beliefs that liberal democracy has always been hegemonic.

I shall review and critique Tocqueville's account of the sources and dynamics shaping democracy in America, along with two of the most influential extensions of Tocquevillian analysis in modern social science, Gunnar Myrdal's (1944) *American Dilemma* and Louis Hartz's (1955) *Liberal Tradition in America*. I argue that Tocqueville himself was much more perceptive than his modern "Tocquevillian" followers, though not free from the problems identified here. I shall note how Tocquevillian premises continue to flaw recent scholarship, especially general works on American political identity and citizenship. Finally, I shall illustrate the merits of a multiple-traditions approach by showing how it offers more insight into the qualified but extensive creation of new systems of ascriptive inequality during the post-Reconstruction and Progressive eras.

The Tocquevillian Thesis

Tocqueville began *Democracy in America* by calling attention to the immense influence of one "basic fact" that was the creative element from which each particular fact—and, indeed, the whole course—of American society is derived,

namely, "the equality of conditions." This "fact" absorbed Tocqueville's interest because he saw a democratic revolution taking place in Europe, especially in France, breaking down the power of nobles and kings. In the United States this revolution seemed "almost to have reached its natural limits." Thus, by studying America, Tocqueville could draw lessons for the future of his own nation and all of European culture (1969, 9–12, 18)....

The impact of Tocqueville's thesis on modern American scholarship was magnified by two among many works applying his ideas to twentieth-century politics, though in ways that compounded his deficiencies.[5] Each stressed one aspect of Tocqueville's account of America's point of departure. First, Gunnar Myrdal's (1944) study of American race relations emphasized the ideals of Enlightenment "humanistic liberalism." Elaborated by revolutionary leaders to define and justify their cause, these beliefs became, in Myrdal's view, the tenets of the American Creed and represented to Americans the essential meaning of their struggle for independence. It thus served as the cement of the nation, written into all the basic documents comprising the highest law of the land. This democratic creed proclaimed the worth and moral equality of all individual human beings and their "inalienable rights to freedom, justice, and a fair opportunity." It also denounced "differences made on account of 'race, creed or color'" (pp. 3–4, 7–8, 25, 52)....

If Myrdal stressed Tocqueville's argument that early Americans were shaped by egalitarian Enlightenment ideals, Louis Hartz (1955) emphasized Tocqueville's account of America's relatively egalitarian and free economic and social conditions. Americans' lack of feudal institutions, classes, and their lived experience of "atomistic social freedom" made the U.S. a liberal society. Hartz viewed the presence of

---

5. Other major Tocquevillian works include Daniel Boorstin's (1953) *Genius of American Politics* and S. M. Lipset's (1963) *First new Nation*.

"the liberal idea" among early Americans as important, but he did not think it was consciousness of a specific ideological heritage that made Americans liberal. Most were instinctive—even "irrational"—Lockeans, all the more so because they had no real awareness of any alternatives. Their comparatively nonascriptive, nonhierarchical conditions led most Americans to regard liberal beliefs in individual rights and liberties, petit bourgeois democracy, and Horatio Alger myths of economic mobility as self-evident. Far more than Myrdal and even more than Tocqueville, Hartz bemoaned the fixed, dogmatic character of this liberalism born "of a liberal way of life," seeing it as a tyranny of unanimity that went much deeper than mere tyranny of the majority. He believed the absence of any real sense of class and the wide regard of middle-class values as natural supported McCarthyite antisocialist policies in domestic and foreign affairs in the early 1950s (pp. 6–23, 35–36, 46, 51, 58, 62–63, 66, 284–309). . . .

Thus, Tocqueville, Myrdal, and Hartz differed mildly in their accounts of just why American political culture was pervasively liberal democratic and more significantly in their assessments of the desirability of that culture. But collectively, their arguments powerfully reinforced beliefs that the United States' core values should be so described. Yet all wrote at times when the nation was still denying most persons access to full standing within the American political community on racial, ethnic, or gender grounds. Their ability to stress the democratic nature of American values despite these facts is vivid testimony to how their focus on the absence of a European class system led them to minimize the significance of other types of ascriptive inequality. Each of them did, however, take some notice of America's exclusionary practices and beliefs, again in influential ways. . . .

On close analysis, then, Tocqueville showed a rich awareness of how limited democracy was in America. But like his successors, he still frequently wrote in unqualified terms about America's supposedly egalitarian conditions; he

relegated blacks and Native Americans to the status of "tangents," however important; and he obscured the intellectual respectability of racism, deeming it only prejudice. Worst of all, he claimed to reconcile the inferior civic status of women with democracy by accepting their confinement to domestic roles as natural. Hence he made America seem much more fully a liberal democracy than it was. The less comprehensive analyses of Myrdal and Hartz intensified all these failings.

Both were completely silent on women. . . .

Hartz's mature answer . . . was closer to Myrdal's. Despite the contrary judgments in his earlier book, it turned out that American defenses of racial inequality were structured in liberal terms after all. And on liberal premises, Americans could only justify racial inequalities by denying the humanity of blacks.

This response remained wholly inadequate. It did not begin to account for why, even after constitutional recognition of the humanity of blacks, Americans created new systems of racial inequality affecting not only blacks but all nonwhite peoples and maintained them through much of the twentieth century. Hartz's appeal to recent civil rights struggles left too much history unexplained. That shortcoming reflected the deeper failure of his whole analysis: If "European ideologies" such as liberalism did not know race, where did the category of "race" come from that they had to take into account? Why had this "unknown" (and biologically indefensible) classification been a "central conscious preoccupation" throughout U.S. history? The answer is that it had been burned into American minds by prestigious intellectual traditions, most of them inarguably nonliberal, that defended subjugation of nonwhites by contending that humanity was naturally divided into hierarchically arrayed "races." There had always been much in America's basic institutions, popular sentiments, and moral orthodoxies that rendered those traditions compelling. . . .

In an era marked by controversies over multiculturalism, one might expect the limitations of

Tocqueville, Hartz, and Myrdal to have long since been superseded. But for many in the social sciences and the humanities, these Tocquevillian arguments still provide the deep structure within which they debate real but lesser differences.[6] ...

None of these mainstream approaches to American politics has given prominence to the racial, ethnic, or gender makeup of the American citizenry, though neither have they wholly avoided those issues. In the last three decades, however, many other scholars have greatly enriched understanding of the ethnocultural dimensions of American life. Much of this research provides evidence for a multiple-traditions account of American politics. But few of these scholars have addressed the significance of their findings for general views of America. And, perhaps because of the real if partial truths grasped by the Tocquevillian orthodoxy, those who have done so have usually tried to accommodate it, not to challenge it. ...

Above all, recognition of the strong attractions of restrictive Americanist ideas does not imply any denial that America's liberal and democratic traditions have had great normative and political potency, even if they have not been so hegemonic as some claim.[9] Instead, it sheds a new—and, in some respects, more flattering—light on the constitutive role of liberal democratic values in American life. Although some Americans have been willing to repudiate no-

tions of democracy and universal rights, most have not; and though many have tried to blend those commitments with exclusionary ascriptive views, the illogic of these mixes has repeatedly proven a major resource for successful reformers. But we obscure the difficulty of those reforms (and thereby diminish their significance) if we slight the ideological and political appeal of contrary ascriptive traditions by portraying them as merely the shadowy side of a hegemonic liberal republicanism.

At its heart, the multiple-traditions thesis holds that the definitive feature of American political culture has been not its liberal, republican, or "ascriptive Americanist" elements but, rather, this more complex pattern of apparently inconsistent combinations of the traditions, accompanied by recurring conflicts. Because standard accounts neglect this pattern, they do not explore how and why Americans have tried to uphold aspects of all three of these heterogeneous traditions in combinations that are longer on political and psychological appeal than on intellectual coherency.

A focus on these questions generates an understanding of American politics that differs from Tocquevillian ones in four major respects. First, on this view, purely liberal and republican conceptions of civic identity are seen as frequently unsatisfying to many Americans, because they contain elements that threaten, rather than affirm, sincere, reputable beliefs in the propriety of the privileged positions that whites, Christianity, Anglo–Saxon traditions, and patriarchy have had in the United States. At the same time, even Americans deeply attached to those inegalitarian arrangements have also had liberal democratic values. Second, it has therefore been typical, not aberrational, for Americans to embody strikingly opposed beliefs in their institutions, such as doctrines that blacks should and should not be full and equal citizens. But though American efforts to blend aspects of opposing views have often been remarkably stable, the resulting tensions have still been important

---

6. As a full survey of pertinent works is impossible, I shall note some broad categories of scholarship in which most participants employ a misleading Tocquevillian framework, focusing on recent general discussions of American political culture and citizenship, where the limits of Tocquevillian premises are most damaging.

9. I also agree that tensions between liberal and democratic ideas and institutions have been vital factors in American history, visible, for example, in the great struggles between the defenders of property rights and populist and labor movements. Those conflicts have, however, also always involved battles over the nation's racial, ethnic, and gender ordering.

sources of change. Third, when older types of ascriptive inequality, such as slavery, have been rejected as unduly illiberal, it has been normal, not anomalous, for many Americans to embrace new doctrines and institutions that reinvigorate the hierarchies they esteem in modified form. Changes toward greater inequality and exclusion, as well as toward greater equality and inclusiveness, thus can and do occur. Finally, the dynamics of American development cannot simply be seen as a rising tide of liberalizing forces progressively submerging contrary beliefs and practices. The national course has been more serpentine. The economic, political, and moral forces propelling the United States toward liberal democracy have often been heeded by American leaders, especially since World War II. But the currents pulling toward fuller expression of alleged natural and cultural inequalities have also always won victories. In some eras they have predominated, appearing to define not only the path of safety but that of progress. In all eras, including our own, many Americans have combined their allegiance to liberal democracy with beliefs that the presence of certain groups favored by history, nature, and God has made Americans an intrinsically "special" people. Their adherents have usually regarded such beliefs as benign and intellectually well founded; yet they also have always had more or less harsh discriminatory corollaries.

To test these multiple-traditions claims, consider the United States in 1870. By then the Civil War and Reconstruction had produced dramatic advances in the liberal and democratic character of America's laws. Slavery was abolished. All persons born in the United States and subject to its jurisdiction were deemed citizens of the United States and the states in which they resided, regardless of their race, creed or gender. None could be denied voting rights on racial grounds. The civil rights of all were newly protected through an array of national statutes. The 1790 ban on naturalizing Africans had been repealed, and expatriation declared a natural right. Over the past two decades women had become more politically engaged and had begun to gain respect as political actors.

Confronted with these developments, what would Tocquevillian analysts have predicted for the next half-century of American life? Louis Hartz would have insisted that so long as the humanity of blacks, other races, and women was publicly acknowledged, the United States would have to grant them equal access to full citizenship. Myrdal, Karst, and Fuchs would have anticipated that surviving prejudices might produce resistance to implementation of the new legal expressions of the American Creed; but they would expect this opposition to be gradually, if painfully, overcome. Tocqueville on the other hand, would have been too pessimistic. He would have deplored the intrusion of women into politics, expected Native Americans to continue toward extinction, and foreseen deepening conflicts between whites and blacks that would probably end in some sort of destructive cataclysm.

None would have had the intellectual resources to explain what in fact occurred. Over the next fifty years, Americans did not make blacks, women, and members of other races full and equal citizens, nor did racial and gender prejudices undergo major erosion. Neither, however, were minorities and women declared to be subhuman and outside the body politic. And although white Americans engaged in extensive violence against blacks and Native Americans, those groups grew in population, and no cataclysm loomed. Instead, intellectual and political elites worked out the most elaborate theories of racial and gender hierarchy in U.S. history and partially embodied them in a staggering array of new laws governing naturalization, immigration, deportation, voting rights, electoral institutions, judicial procedures, and economic rights—but only partially. The laws retained important liberal and democratic features, and some were strengthened. They had enough purchase on the moral and material interests of most Americans to compel advocates of inequality to adopt contrived, often clumsy means to achieve their ends....

In sum, if we accept that ideologies and institutions of ascriptive hierarchy have shaped America in interaction with its liberal and democratic features, we can make more sense of a wide range of inegalitarian policies newly contrived after 1870 and perpetuated through much of the twentieth century. Those policies were dismantled only through great struggles, aided by international pressures during World War II and the Cold War; and it is not clear that these struggles have ended. The novelties in the policies and scientific doctrines of the Gilded Age and Progressive Era should alert us to the possibility that new intellectual systems and political forces defending racial and gender inequalities may yet gain increased power in our own time.

The civil rights reforms of the 1960s and 1970s are not as seriously threatened today as were the civil rights measures of the 1860s in the 1890s. Yet leading scholars like Richard Epstein now argue that the nation should eliminate all race-conscious laws, even the 1964 Civil Rights Act, in favor of programs of black self-help in the marketplace—precisely the position many nineteenth-century "liberals" used to justify abandoning Reconstruction (Epstein 1992). Also like these nineteenth-century predecessors, Epstein ultimately grounds his laissez-faire views not so much on a doctrine of human rights as on evolutionary biology, undaunted by how others then and now have used such views to explain racial as well as economic inequalities (Epstein 1985, 341, n. 19; Fairchild 1991). But though this blend of economics and sociobiology has disturbing precursors, some influential contemporary black leaders, such as Justice Clarence Thomas and economist Thomas Sowell, like Booker T. Washington before them, are aligned with such "self-help" views.

Racial, nativist, and religious tensions are also prominent in American life, as the Buchanan and Duke campaigns, the Christian Coalition,

the Los Angeles riots, the English-Only agitation, the popularity of anti-Japanese novels, renewed patterns of residential segregation, and the upsurge of separatist ideologies among many younger minority scholars all indicate. The discourse about the "ethno-underclass" is particularly striking, for as Lawrence Fuchs notes, poor urban minorities are often portrayed as historically and socially conditioned to possess foreign moral values (1990, 487–89). The political message that these accounts convey often resembles, however unintentionally, that of Lodge's similar characterizations of undesirable "races": these groups appear so irreparably different and dangerous that they do not merit equal status in the political community.

It is too early to assess the significance of these aspects of current American life. The achievements of Americans in building a more inclusive democracy certainly provide reasons to believe that illiberal forces will not prevail. But just as we can better explain the nation's past by recognizing how and why liberal democratic principles have been contested with frequent success, we will better understand the present and future of American politics if we do not presume they are rooted in essentially liberal or democratic values and conditions. Instead, we must analyze America as the ongoing product of often conflicting multiple traditions.

References

Boorstin, Daniel. 1953. *The Genius of American Politics.* Chicago: University of Chicago Press.

Epstein, Richard A. 1985. *Takings: Private Property and the Power of Eminent Domain.* Cambridge: Harvard University Press.

Epstein, Richard A. 1992. *Forbidden Grounds: The Case Against Employment Discrimination Laws.* Cambridge: Harvard University Press.

Fairchild, Halford H. 1991. "Scientific Racism: The Cloak of Objectivity." *Journal of Social Issues* 47: 101–115.

Fuchs, Lawrence H. 1990. *The American Kaleidoscope: Race, Ethnicity, and the Civic Culture*. Hanover, NH: University Press of New England.

Haller, John S. Jr. 1971. *Outcasts from Evolution: Scientific Attitudes of Racial Inferiority, 1859–1900*. Urbana: University of Illinois Press.

Hartog, Hendrik. 1987. "The Constitution of Aspiration and 'The Rights that Belong to Us All.'" In *The Constitution and American Life*, ed. David Thelen. Ithaca: Cornell University Press.

Hartz, Louis. 1955. *The Liberal Tradition in America: An Interpretation of American Political Thought Since the Revolution*. New York: Harcourt, Brace & World.

Higham, John. 1975. *Send These to Me*. New York: Atheneum Press.

Kettner, James. 1978. *The Development of American Citizenship, 1608–1870*. Chapel Hill: University of North Carolina Press.

Lipset, Seymour Martin. 1963. *The First New Nation*. New York: Basic Books.

Myrdal, Gunnar. 1944. *An America Dilemma: The Negro Problem and American Democracy*. Rept. 20th Anniversary ed., 1962. New York: Harper & Row.

Orren, Karen. 1991. *Belated Feudalism: Labor, the Law, and Liberal Development in the United States*. New York: Cambridge University Press.

Orren, Karen, and Skowronek, Stephen. 1993. "Beyond the Iconography of Order: Notes for a 'New Institutionalism.'" In *The Dynamics of American Politics: Approaches and Interpretations*, ed. Lawrence C. Dodd and Calvin Jillson. Boulder: Westview Press.

Russett, Cynthia Eagle. 1989. *Sexual Science: The Victorian Construction of Womanhood*. Cambridge: Harvard University Press.

Smith, Rogers M. 1989. "'One United People' Second-Class Female Citizenship and the American Quest for Community." *Yale Journal of Law and the Humanities* 1: 229–293.

Tocqueville, Alexis de. 1969. *Democracy in America*. Ed. J. P. Mayer. Garden City, New York: Anchor Books.

Williamson, Joel. 1980. *New People: Miscegenation and Mulattoes in the United States*. New York: Free Press.

9 DEMOCRACY AND THE GLOBAL ORDER

Perpetual Peace
Immanuel Kant

How Democracy, Interdependence, and International Organizations Create a System for Peace
Bruce Russett

Dirty Pool
Donald P. Green, Soo Yeon Kim, and David H. Yoon

Democracy and Collective Bads
Russell Hardin

Representation and the Democratic Deficit
Pippa Norris

The Transformation of Political Community: Rethinking Democracy in the Context of Globalization
David Held

Perpetual Peace

Immanuel Kant

Second Section

Which Contains the Definitive Articles of a Perpetual Peace between States

A state of peace among men living together is not the same as the state of nature, which is rather a state of war. For even if it does not involve active hostilities, it involves a constant threat of their breaking out. Thus the state of peace must be *formally instituted*, for a suspension of hostilities is not in itself a guarantee of peace. And unless one neighbour gives a guarantee to the other at his request (which can happen only in a *lawful* state), the latter may treat him as an enemy.*

Excerpted from: Immanuel Kant, *Perpetual Peace*. In *Kant: Political Writings*, edited by Hans Reiss. Cambridge: Cambridge University Press, 1991. © Cambridge University Press, 1991. Reprinted with the permission of Cambridge University Press.

*It is usually assumed that one cannot take hostile action against anyone unless one has already been actively *injured* by them. This is perfectly correct if both parties are living in a *legal civil state*. For the fact that the one has entered such a state gives the required guarantee to the other, since both are subject to the same authority. But man (or an individual people) in a mere state of nature robs me of any such security and injures me by virtue of this very state in which he coexists with me. He may not have injured me actively (*facto*), but he does injure me by the very lawlessness of his state (*statu iniusto*), for he is a permanent threat to me, and I can require him either to enter into a common lawful state along with me or to move away from my vicinity. Thus the postulate on which all the following articles are based is that all men who can at all influence one another must adhere to some kind of civil constitution. But any legal constitution, as far as the persons who live under it are concerned, will conform to ~~one of the three following types:~~

(1) a constitution based on the *civil right* of individuals within a nation (*ius civitatis*).

First Definitive Article of a Perpetual Peace: The Civil Constitution of Every State Shall Be Republican

A *republican constitution* is founded upon three principles: firstly, the principle of *freedom* for all members of a society (as men); secondly, the principle of the *dependence* of everyone upon a single common legislation (as subjects); and thirdly, the principle of legal *equality* for everyone (as citizens).† It is the only constitution

---

(2) a constitution based on the *international right* of states in their relationships with one another (*ius gentium*).

(3) a constitution based on *cosmopolitan right*, in so far as individuals and states, coexisting in an external relationship of mutual influences, may be regarded as citizens of a universal state of mankind (*ius cosmopoliticum*). This classification, with respect to the idea of a perpetual peace, is not arbitrary, but necessary. For if even one of the parties were able to influence the others physically and yet itself remained in a state of nature, there would be a risk of war, which it is precisely the aim of the above articles to prevent.

† *Rightful (i.e. external) freedom* cannot, as is usually thought, be defined as a warrant to do whatever one wishes unless it means doing injustice to others. For what is meant by a *warrant*? It means a possibility of acting in a certain way so long as this action does not do any injustice to others. Thus the definition would run as follows: freedom is the possibility of acting in ways which do no injustice to others. That is, we do no injustice to others (no matter what we may actually do) if we do no injustice to others. Thus the definition is an empty tautology. In fact, my external and rightful *freedom* should be defined as a warrant to obey no external laws except those to which I have been able to give my own consent. Similarly, external and rightful *equality* within a state is that relationship among the citizens whereby no-one can put anyone else under a legal obligation without submitting simultaneously to a law which requires that he can himself be put under the same kind of obligation by the other person. (And we do not need to define the principle of *legal* dependence,

which can be derived from the idea of an original contract, upon which all rightful legislation of a people must be founded. Thus as far as right is concerned, republicanism is in itself the original

basis of every kind of civil constitution, and it only remains to ask whether it is the only constitution which can lead to a perpetual peace.

The republican constitution is not only pure in its origin (since it springs from the pure concept of right); it also offers a prospect of attaining the desired result, i.e. a perpetual peace, and the reason for this is as follows.—If, as is inevitably the case under this constitution, the consent of the citizens is required to decide whether or not war is to be declared, it is very natural that they will have great hesitation in embarking on so dangerous an enterprise. For this would mean calling down on themselves all the miseries of war, such as doing the fighting themselves, supplying the costs of the war from their own resources, painfully making good the ensuing devastation, and, as the crowning evil, having to take upon themselves a burden of debt which will embitter peace itself and which can never be paid off on account of the constant threat of new wars. But under a constitution where the subject is not a citizen, and which is therefore not republican, it is the simplest thing in the world to go to war. For the head of state is not a fellow citizen, but the owner of the state, and a war will not force him to make the slightest sacrifice so far as his banquets, hunts, pleasure palaces and court festivals are concerned. He can thus decide on war, without any significant reason, as a kind of amusement, and unconcernedly leave it to the diplomatic corps (who are always ready for such purposes) to justify the war for the sake of propriety....

---

since it is always implied in the concept of a political constitution.) The validity of these innate and inalienable rights, the necessary property of mankind, is confirmed and enhanced by the principle that man may have lawful relations even with higher beings (if he believes in the latter). For he may consider himself as a citizen of a transcendental world, to which the same principles apply. And as regards my freedom, I am not under any obligation even to divine laws (which I can recognise by reason alone), except in so far as I have been able to give my own consent to them; for I can form a conception of the divine will only in terms of the law of freedom of my own reason. As for the principle of equality in relation to the most exalted being I can conceive of, apart from God (e.g. a power such as Aeon), there is no reason, if I and this higher being are both doing our duty in our own stations, why it should be my duty to obey while he should enjoy the right to command. But the reason why this principle of equality (unlike that of freedom) does not apply to a relationship towards God, is that God is the only being for whom the concept of duty ceases to be valid.

But as for the right of equality of all citizens as subjects, we may ask whether a *hereditary aristocracy* is admissible. The answer to this question will depend entirely on whether more importance is attached to the superior *rank* granted by the state to one subject over another than is attached to *merit*, or vice versa. Now it is obvious that if rank is conferred according to birth, it will be quite uncertain whether merit (skill and devotion within one's office) will accompany it; it will be tantamount to conferring a position of command upon a favoured individual without any merit on his part, and this could never be approved by the general will of the people in an original contract, which is, after all, the principle behind all rights. For it does not necessarily follow that a nobleman is also a *noble man*. And as for a nobility of office, i.e. the rank of a *higher magistracy* which can be attained by merit, the rank does not attach as a possession to the person, but to the post occupied by the person, and this does not violate the principle of equality. For when a person lays down his office, he simultaneously resigns his rank and again becomes one of the people.

How Democracy, Interdependence, and International Organizations Create a System for Peace

Bruce Russett

For nearly half a century the United States and its allies carried out a policy of containment during the cold war, to prevent the spread of Communist ideology and Soviet power. That policy succeeded, spectacularly. Now it must be replaced by another policy, one designed to consolidate the new acceptability of free institutions around the world. The new century presents more than just the passing of a particular adversarial relationship; it offers a chance for fundamentally-changed relations among nations....

Three Principles for a Peaceful International Order

... Contemporary policy needs a similar central organizing principle. That principle should build on the principles which underlay the rhetoric and much of the practice of containment, rooted in beliefs about the success of free political and economic systems. Those principles are democracy, free markets—especially on the argument that economic interdependence promotes peace as well as prosperity—and international law and organization. Each makes a contribution to peace, and in many instances they reinforce each other (and are themselves reinforced by peace) in "virtuous circles" or feedback loops....

A vision of a peace among democratically-governed states has long been invoked as part of a larger structure of institutions and practices to promote peace. In 1795 Immanuel Kant spoke of perpetual peace based partially upon states sharing "republican constitutions," which is essentially what we now mean by democracy. As the elements of such a constitution he identified freedom, with legal equality of subjects, representative government, and separation of powers. The other key elements of his perpetual peace were "cosmopolitan law" embodying ties of international commerce and free trade, and a "pacific union" established by treaty in international law among republics.

Woodrow Wilson expressed the same vision for the twentieth century.... His 1917 war message to Congress asserted that "a steadfast concert of peace can never be maintained except by a partnership of democratic nations." This vision emerged again after World War II, animating the founders of what became the European Union. It has since been taken up among countries of South America. At the beginning of a new century, it is newly plausible.

Democracies Rarely Fight Each Other

Democratization is key to this vision for two reasons. First, democracy is a desirable form of government on its own merit. It both recognizes and promotes human dignity. Democracy is not perfect, and should not be forced upon peoples who do not wish it. But for many countries it is better than the alternatives under which they have suffered.

Second, we now have solid evidence that democracies do not make war on each other. Some of it can be found in my book, *Grasping the Democratic Peace*, and in many more recent works.[1] In the contemporary era, "democracy"

Excerpted from: Bruce Russett, "How Democracy, Interdependence, and International Organizations Create a System for Peace." Adapted from a chapter in *The Global Agenda*, sixth edition, edited by Charles Kegley and Eugene Wittkopf. New York: McGraw-Hill, 2000. © 2000 The McGraw-Hill Companies, New York. Reproduced with the permission of The McGraw-Hill Companies.

1. Bruce Russett, *Grasping the Democratic Peace: Principles for a Post–Cold War World* (Princeton, NJ: Princeton University Press, 1993). There is an enormous body of more recent scholarship on this matter,

denotes a country in which nearly everyone can vote, elections are freely contested, the chief executive is chosen by popular vote or by an elected parliament, and civil rights and civil liberties are substantially guaranteed. Democracies are not always peaceful—we all know the history of democracies in colonialism, covert intervention, and other excesses of power. Democracies frequently resort to violence in their relations with authoritarian states. But the relations between stable democracies are qualitatively different.

Democracies are unlikely to engage in any kind of militarized disputes with each other or to let any such disputes escalate into war. They rarely even skirmish. Pairs of democratic states have been only one-eighth as likely as other kinds of states to threaten to use force against each other, and only one-tenth as likely actually to do so. Established democracies fought no wars against one another during the entire twentieth century. (Although Finland, for example, took the Axis side against the Soviet Union in World War II, it engaged in no combat with the democracies.)

The more democratic each state is, the more peaceful their relations are likely to be. Democracies are more likely to employ "democratic" means of peaceful conflict resolution. They are readier to reciprocate each other's behavior, to accept third party mediation or good offices in settling disputes, and to accept binding third-party arbitration and adjudication.[2] Careful statistical analyses of countries' behavior show that democracies' relatively peaceful relations toward

each other are not spuriously caused by some other influence such as sharing high levels of wealth, or rapid growth, or ties of alliance. The phenomenon of peace between democracies is not limited just to the rich industrialized states of the global North. It was not maintained simply by pressure from a common adversary in the cold war, and it has outlasted that threat.

The phenomenon of democratic peace can be explained by the pervasiveness of normative restraints on conflict between democracies. That explanation extends to the international arena the cultural norms of live-and-let-live and peaceful conflict resolution that operate within democracies. The phenomenon of democratic peace can also be explained by the role of institutional restraints on democracies' decisions to go to war. Those restraints insure that any state in a conflict of interest with another democracy can expect ample time for conflict-resolution processes to be effective, and democracies' political decision-making processes are relatively transparent. These two influences reinforce each other. The spread of democratic norms and practices in the world, if consolidated, should reduce the frequency of violent conflict and war. Where normative restraints are weak, democratic institutions may provide the necessary additional restraints on the use of violence against other democratic states.

To the degree that countries once ruled by autocratic systems become democratic, the absence of war among democracies comes to bear on any discussion of the future of international relations. The statement that in the modern

---

largely confirming or extending the principle, but some of it critical. See especially James Lee Ray, *Democracy and International Conflict* (Columbia, University of South Carolina Press, 1995; Spencer Weart, *Never at War: Why Democracies Will Not Fight One Another* (New Haven, CT: Yale University Press, 1998); Bruce Russett and John R. Oneal, *Triangulating Peace: Democracy, Interdependence, and International Organizations* (New York: W. W. Norton, 2001), chs. 2, 3.

2. Russell Leng, "Reciprocating Influence Strategies and Success in Interstate Bargaining," *Journal of Conflict Resolution*, 37, 1 (March 1993): 3–41; William Dixon, "Democracy and the Peaceful Settlement of International Disputes," *American Political Science Review*, 88, 1 (March 1994): 14–32; Gregory Raymond, "Democracies, Disputes, and Third-Party Intermediaries," *Journal of Conflict Resolution*, 38, 1 (March 1994): 24–42.

international system democracies have almost never fought each other represents a complex phenomenon: a) Democracies rarely fight each other (an empirical statement) because b) they have other means of resolving conflicts between them and therefore don't need to fight each other (a prudential cost-benefit statement), and c) they perceive that democracies should not fight each other (a normative statement about principles of right behavior), which reinforces the empirical statement. By this reasoning, the more democracies there are in the world, the fewer potential adversaries we and other democracies will have and the wider the zone of peace will be.

The possibility of a widespread zone of democratic peace in the world exists. To turn that possibility into a policy two fundamental problems must be addressed: the problem of consolidating democratic stability, and the prospects for changing basic patterns of international behavior....

Strengthening Democracy and Its Norms

... Probably most of the conditions affecting the success of democratization arise from circumstances internal to any particular state. But this list of possible conditions from outside is impressive also. Favorable international conditions may not be essential in every case, but they can make a difference, and sometimes a crucial one when the internal influences are mixed.

With economic conditions so grim in much of the developing world, eastern Europe, and the former Soviet Union, and the consequent dangers to the legitimacy of new democratic governments, external assistance—technical and financial—is especially important. New democracies will not survive without some material improvement in their citizens' lives. As a stick, aid can surely be denied to governments that regularly violate human rights, for example of ethnic minorities. A military coup or an aborted election can be punished by suspending aid. As

to the carrot of extending aid on a conditional basis, broader goals of developing democratic institutions require creation of a civil society. Recipients may see multilateral aid, with conditions of democratic reform attached, as a less blatant invasion of their sovereignty than aid from a single country.

It would be a terrible loss if the richer and older democracies did not make serious efforts— a loss to themselves as well as to the peoples of the struggling democracies. Any solution requires external assistance and protection to aid and speed transitions to democracy. It also requires devising institutions, and nurturing norms and practices, of democratic government with respect for minority rights. The creation of institutions, norms, and practices to protect minorities has never been easy. But it presents the fundamental challenge of world political development in this era. It is worth remembering that the most terrible acts of genocide in this century (from Turkey's slaughter of the Armenians through Hitler, Stalin, Pol Pot, and others) have been carried out by authoritarian or totalitarian governments, not democratic ones.[4]

Understanding that democracies rarely fight each other, and why, has great consequence for policy in the contemporary world. It should affect the kinds of military preparations believed to be necessary, and the costs one would be willing to pay to make them. It should encourage peaceful efforts to assist the emergence and consolidation of democracy. But a misunderstanding of it could encourage war-making against authoritarian regimes, and efforts to overturn them—with all the costly implications such a policy might imply.

Recollection of the post-1945 success with defeated adversaries can be both instructive and misleading. It is instructive in showing that democracy could supplant a thoroughly discredited

4. R. J. Rummel, *Death by Government: Genocide and Mass Murder in the Twentieth Century* (New Brunswick, NJ: Transaction, 1994).

totalitarian regime. It can be misleading if one forgets how expensive it was (Marshall Plan aid for Germany and Italy, and important economic concessions to Japan), and especially if one misinterprets the political conditions of military defeat. The allies utterly defeated the Axis coalition. Then, to solidify democratic government they conducted vast (if incomplete) efforts to remove the former elites from positions of authority. But they had something to build on, in the form of individuals and institutions from previous experiences with democracy. The model of "fight them, beat them, and then make them democratic" is no model for contemporary action. It probably would not work anyway, and no one is prepared to make the kind of effort that would be required. Not all authoritarian states are inherently aggressive. Indeed, at any particular time the majority are not. A militarized crusade for democracy is not in order.

Sometimes external military intervention against the most odious dictators may make sense. With a cautious cost-benefit analysis and with the certainty of substantial and legitimate internal support, it might be worthwhile—that is, under conditions when rapid military success is likely and the will of the people at issue is clear. Even so, any time an outside power supplants any existing government the problem of legitimacy is paramount. The very democratic norms to be instilled may be compromised. At the least, intervention cannot be unilateral. It should be approved, publicly and willingly, by an international body like the UN or the Organization of American States. When an election has been held under UN auspices and certified as fair as happened in Haiti—the UN has a special responsibility, even a duty, to see that the democratic government it helped create is not destroyed.

Under most circumstances, international bodies are best used to promote democratic processes when the relevant domestic parties are ready. Peacekeeping operations to help provide the conditions for free elections, monitor those

elections, and advise on the building of democratic institutions are far more promising and less costly for all concerned than is military intervention. The UN experienced highly publicized troubles in Somalia and the former Yugoslavia as it tried to cope with a range of challenges not previously part of its mandate. Nonetheless, its successes, though receiving less attention, outnumber the failures. It was a major facilitator of peaceful transitions and democratic elections in places like Cambodia, El Salvador, Mozambique, and Namibia. Its Electoral Assistance Unit has provided election monitoring, technical assistance, or other aid to free electoral processes in over 70 states.[5]

Economic Interdependence and International Organizations

Ties of economic interdependence—international trade and investment—form an important supplement to shared democracy in promoting peace. Analyses that show how rarely democracies used or threatened to use military force against each other also show a similarly strong peaceful effect when states trade heavily with each other. The effect of economic interdependence does not supplant, but supplements, the effect of democracy, and like democracy its effect remains even when alliances and economic growth rates are controlled for in the analysis.[6]
. . .

The role of international law and institutions, and the need for strengthening them, constitutes the third element of the Kantian/Wilsonian vision. As expressed by former UN Secretary-General Boutros Ghali, the UN has a new mission of "peace-building," attending to democratization, development, and the protec-

---

5. The scope of these efforts is evident in Boutros Boutros-Ghali, *An Agenda for Democratization* (New York: United Nations, 1996).

6. Russett and Oneal, *Triangulating Peace*, ch. 4.

tion of human rights.[8] It is newly strengthened and, paradoxically, also newly and enormously burdened. The UN and other international organizations promote democratization and peace directly as well as indirectly. As noted above, democracies are much more likely to use international institutions for peacefully resolving disputes among themselves than are dictatorships. . . .

The effects of these three Kantian influences can be found throughout most of the twentieth century, both before the cold war era and in the first few years after it. Two kinds of pairs of countries are especially likely to have reasons for violent conflict, and the ability to fight each other: geographically contiguous countries, and pairs of states in which at least one is a major power, with long-range military capability. Among these pairs during the past century, high levels of shared democracy and of economic interdependence both reduced the chances of a militarized dispute by more than 40 percent, and shared IGO memberships did so by about one-third. And in periods when levels of democracy and interdependence are generally high throughout the international system, the norms and institutions that go with them seem to have some restraining effect even on countries that are not very democratic or interdependent.[10] Common perceptions can be misleading: actually, the number of international wars worldwide has dropped precipitously since the 1980s.[11] . . .

Can a Wider Peace Be Built?

New democracies should be supported financially, politically, militarily, and morally. Successful transitions to democracy in some countries can supply a model for others. A stable and less menacing international system can permit the emergence and consolidation of democratic governments. International threats—real or only perceived—strengthen the forces of secrecy and authoritarianism in the domestic politics of states involved in protracted conflict. Relaxation of international threats to peace and security reduces the need, and the excuse, for repressing democratic dissent. . . .

A Kantian peace would be sustained by an interacting and mutually supporting combination of democratic government, economic interdependence, and international law and organization. Such an international system—an international society as well as a collection of sovereign states—might reflect very different behavior than did the previous one composed predominantly of autocracies. The West won the cold war, at immense cost. If we should now let slip this marvelous but brief window of opportunity to solidify basic change in the international order at much lower cost, our children will wonder why. Some autocratically-governed states will surely remain in the system. In their relations with states where democracy is unstable, or where democratization is not begun at all, democracies must continue to be vigilant and concerned with the need for military deterrence. But if enough states do become stable democracies in the next century, then we will have a chance to reconstruct the norms and rules of the international order. A system created by autocracies centuries ago might now be re-created by a critical mass of democratic states, economically interdependent with peaceful relations facilitated by international institutions. . . .

11. Monty Marshall, *Third World War* (Lanham, MD: Rowman, Littlefield, 1999); Peter Wallensteen and Marareta Sollenberg, "Armed Conflict, 1989–99," *Journal of Peace Research* 37, 2 (September 2000): 635–649.

8. *An Agenda for Peace* (New York: United Nations, 1993), paragraph 81.

10. Russett and Oneal, Triangulating Peace, ch. 5.

Dirty Pool

Donald P. Green, Soo Yeon Kim, and David H. Yoon

The quantitative study of international relations is dominated by analyses of pooled cross-sections. When analyzing dependent variables, such as the occurrence of a militarized dispute or the level of trade between two nations, researchers tend to work with panel data sets of NT observations, where N is the number of dyads (pairs of nations) and T is the number of time points (typically years). Thus, for example, when sixty nations are observed annually over the span of forty years, the pooled cross-sectional data set consists of 1,770 dyads × forty years = 70,800 observations. These data are said to be "pooled" in that no distinction is made between observations in time and space. A datum is a datum, and one can draw inferences with equal certitude across dyads or across years.

Concerned that the effective number of observations is less than the nominal NT, a great deal of methodological attention has recently focused on problems of interdependencies among the observations; unobserved factors that cause the United States to go to war with Japan in 1941 also cause it to go to war with Italy and Germany.... [W]e believe that the problems associated with standard pooled cross-sectional estimation run much deeper.[2]

We contend that analyses of pooled cross-section data that make no allowance for fixed unobserved differences between dyads often produce biased results. By "fixed unobserved differences" (or fixed effects, for short) we mean unmeasured predictors of the dependent variable that would cause each dyad to have its own base rate, or intercept. For example, year after year, trade levels between India and China fall below what one would expect based on a regression model that takes into account population size, gross domestic product (GDP), and shared borders. Because such a model fails to take note of the Himalayas, economic endowments, linguistic dissimilarity, and diplomatic relations, this model repeatedly overestimates bilateral trade between India and China, just as it consistently underestimates trade between Belgium and Switzerland. Pooling data implicitly assumes that the independent variables eliminate these persistent cross-sectional differences or render them uncorrelated with the predictors in the model. In this example, the fact that India-China differ in unmeasured ways from Belgium-Switzerland makes this assumption implausible. Given the vagaries of measurement and model specification in statistical studies of international relations, the statistical assumptions that underlie pooling are generally suspect.

... To demonstrate the importance of this issue to students of international affairs, we present two empirical examples of how statistical results change when fixed effects are taken into account. The first example concerns bilateral trade; the second, militarized interstate disputes. In both cases, we find dramatic changes in the size and statistical significance of the parameter estimates. For example, democracy, which seems to be a leading predictor of peace in a pooled cross-sectional analysis, has no effect on militarized disputes when the data are examined longitudinally. We conclude by discussing the implications of our results for methodological practices in the field....

Data

Using a panel of dyads for the period 1951–92, we examine two dependent variables: bilateral

Excerpted from: Donald P. Green, Soo Yeon Kim, and David H. Yoon, "Dirty Pool." *International Organization* 55, no. 2 (spring 2001): 441–468. © 2001 by the IO Foundation and the Massachusetts Institute of Technology. Reprinted by permission.

2. On count data, see Beck, Katz, and Tucker 1998; on sequential decisions, Signorino 1999; on simultaneous equations, Kim 1998; and on rare events, King and Zeng forthcoming.

trade volume and the presence or absence of a militarized interstate dispute.[9] For bilateral trade volume, the independent variables include the standard gravity model terms—log of *GDP*, *population*, and *distance* between capitals, and in addition, *alliance* and *democracy*. *Alliance* is operationalized as the absence (0) or presence (1) of a formal alliance; *democracy* as the lower of the net democracy scores within the dyad.[10] Trade data are from the *Direction of Trade Statistics* of the International Monetary Fund.[11] Data for GDP and population were obtained from the Penn World Tables, version 5.6.[12] The democracy variable was computed from the May 1996 version of the Polity III data set.[13] Data for contiguity, capability ratio, and alliance were obtained from the Correlates of War Project (1995).[14]

The model of militarized interstate disputes features a set of commonly used regressors: *alliance, democracy, geographical contiguity*, the absence (0) or presence (1) of a shared land border; *capability ratio*, the ratio of the higher to lower capabilities indexes of the countries in the dyad, in logs; *growth*, the lower three-year average growth in per capita GDP within the dyad; and the lower *bilateral trade-to-GDP ratio* within the dyad.[15]

We have chosen to include in our analysis all dyads for which twenty or more observations were available, a criterion that admits over 93,000 of the approximately 117,000 cases in our data set. The reason for this restriction is that dynamic models are biased when estimated on short time-series. Note, however, that the coefficients we report are not changed appreciably when we admit all of the observations or, conversely, just those for which complete time-series data are available.[16]

In the interest of drawing an exact parallel between pooled-regression and fixed-effects regression, we include the same set of regressors in both models. Note that in the context of a fixed effects analysis, regressors such as contiguity and distance vary only insofar as countries divide or change their capitals over time. Just sixty dyads experience change in contiguity over time, but none experience change in distance. Distance is therefore a constant that is absorbed into the intercept associated with each dyad. Fixed-effects regression turns a blind eye to such time-invariant regressors; to learn about their effects, one must either study them in a cross-sectional context, braving the usual threats to causal inference, or investigate particular historical instances in which observations vary over time.

Results

We begin our panel analysis by modeling a continuous dependent variable, the total volume of trade between two states (in logs). Our specification includes the three components of the "gravity model"—log of the two states' total GDP, the log of the two states' total population, and

9. See Bremer 1996; and Jones, Bremer, and Singer 1996.

10. For three large states (United States, USSR/ Russia, and Canada), the shortest distance from their main ports/capitals is used. The ports include New Orleans and San Francisco for the United States, Vladivostok for USSR/Russia, and Vancouver for Canada. This measurement approach follows Bliss and Russett 1998; and Gowa and Mansfield 1993.

11. IMF 1997.

12. Heston and Summers 1991.

13. Jaggers and Gurr 1995.

14. Singer and Small 1994.

15. For a summary of the capability index, see Singer 1990.

16. In an earlier draft of this article, we reported results from a "balanced panel," which is a panel restricted to just those dyads with complete data for the entire time span (1961–89). The coefficients were similar to those reported here, but the loss of observations made for larger standard errors. Despite a sample of more than 29,000 observations, no predictors of militarized disputes were significant at the 5 percent level in a regression that controlled for fixed effects.

Table 9.1
Alternative regression analyses of bilateral trade (1951–92)

Variable[a]	Pooled	Fixed effects	Pooled with dynamics	Fixed effects with dynamics
GDP	1.182**	0.810**	0.250**	0.342**
	(0.008)	(0.015)	(0.006)	(0.013)
Population	−0.386**	0.752**	−0.059**	0.143*
	(0.010)	(0.082)	(0.006)	(0.068)
Distance	−1.342**	Dropped: no within-group variation	−0.328**	Dropped: no within-group variation
	(0.018)		(0.012)	
Alliance	−0.745**	0.777**	−0.247**	0.419**
	(0.042)	(0.136)	(0.027)	(0.121)
Democracy[b]	0.075**	−0.039**	0.022**	−0.009**
	(0.002)	(0.003)	(0.001)	(0.002)
Lagged bilateral trade			0.736**	0.533**
			(0.002)	(0.003)
Constant	−17.331**	−47.994**	−3.046**	−13.745**
	(0.265)	(1.999)	(0.177)	(1.676)
	N = 93,924	NT = 93,924	N = 88,946	NT = 88,946
		N = 3,079		N = 3,079
		T ≥ 20		T ≥ 20
Adjusted R^2	0.36	0.63	0.73	0.76

Note: Estimates obtained using *areg* and *xtreg* procedures in STATA, version 6.0.
a. GDP, population, distance, and bilateral trade are natural-log transformed. Method of analysis is OLS and fixed-effects regression.
b. Lower value within the dyad.
** $p < .01$.
* $p < .05$, two-tailed test.

the log of the distance between the two states.[17] As Jeffrey H. Bergstrand cautions, this model offers reasonably accurate predictions of trade volume but lacks firm theoretical foundation.[18] Political scientists have treated the gravity model as something of a baseline, appending additional

17. See Tinbergen 1962; Linneman 1966; Leamer and Stern 1970, 145–70; Anderson 1979; and Deardorff 1984, 503–504.
18. Bergstrand 1985, 474.

political variables. We follow current practice in the spirit of examining the consequences of different modeling assumptions. We include as regressors the democracy and alliance measures from the previous analysis. Table 9.1 presents both pooled and fixed-effects models, each with and without a lagged dependent variable as a regressor. We find no support whatsoever for the null hypothesis that all dyads share the same intercept. For the nondynamic case, $F(3078, 90841) = 23.68$, $p < .0001$; when lagged trade is introduced as an independent variable, $F(3078, 85862) = 4.43$, $p < .0001$....

With large data sets it is sometimes possible to reject parsimonious regression models in favor of somewhat more complex models that produce substantively identical results. That is manifestly not the case here. The two regressions paint markedly different pictures of bilateral trade. In the pooled analysis, population has a strong negative effect on trade. A one-unit change in the log of population *reduces* the log of trade by .39 units. The tiny standard error associated with this estimate produces a T-ratio of epic proportions, -39.7. Not in a million years could these data have been generated by a true parameter of zero or more. Yet, look at the fixed-effects regression results: population has a positive coefficient (.75) and a T-ratio of 9.2. As two countries' populations grow over time, other things being equal, they trade more.[19] Alliance and democracy undergo similar turnabouts. In the pooled model, democracy encourages trade. In the fixed-effects model, dyads trade less as the less-democratic partner becomes more democratic. In the pooled model, alliance inhibits trade. In the fixed-effects model, the formation of alliances is associated with much higher levels of trade.

Similar turnabouts occur when we introduce a lagged dependent variable and focus on the short-term influences of the independent variables. Again the Hausman test indicates that the pooled cross-sectional regression is biased (a test against a null hypothesis of random effects produces $\chi^2(5) = 14,754.0$, $p < .0001$), and we see dramatic changes in the magnitude of the slope estimates associated with population, alliance, and democracy. As expected, the pooled model overestimates the effect of the lagged dependent variable. The coefficient that the pooled model assigns to the lagged dependent variable blends the true parameter with the parameter of unity that should be assigned to its (omitted) intercept. Because the effect of the lagged dependent variable is overestimated, it appears that perturbations to trade levels reequilibrate more slowly than they actually do.[20] In sum, assumptions implicit in different regression models greatly shape how one thinks about the determinants of bilateral trade.

To illustrate further the importance of fixed effects, we turn our attention to a nonlinear estimation problem. Table 9.2 reports the results of alternative logistic-regression models of militarized disputes. The pooled analysis suggests that the likelihood of disputes increases when dyads are contiguous and decreases as the less-democratic member of the dyad becomes more democratic. Alliances decrease the risk of war, whereas differences in military capabilities increase it. These results are in line with published research.

These estimates change markedly when fixed effects are controlled. Democracy's effects become negligible and statistically insignificant, whereas military capability and alliance prove much more influential. Consider, for example, what the fixed-effects regression results tell us about a dyad with a 5 percent chance of war. If the less democratic of the two nations becomes fifteen units more democratic, the risk of war decreases to 4.8 percent. The pooled regression would lead us to expect this risk to drop from 5 percent to 2.2 percent. Conversely, the formation

---

19. As noted earlier, the causal interpretation of coefficients growing out of the gravity model is problematic. Leamer and Stern (1970, 155) argue persuasively that population change may reflect a variety of unmeasured variables, such as technological change and changing health care. Note also that the gravity model makes no distinction between imports and exports, which might be differentially affected by trade volume. For these reasons, we are loath to say what constitutes the "right" sign for the population coefficient.

---

20. Results similar to the fixed-effects regression obtain when we use an alternative estimator that makes allowance for the fact that lagged trade is an endogenous regressor. This alternative estimator uses the Anderson-Hsiao methodology (instrumental variables) described in Hsiao 1986 and Greene 1997. These results are available from the authors on request.

Table 9.2
Alternative logistic regression analyses of militarized interstate disputes (1951–92)

Variable	Pooled	Fixed effects	Pooled with dynamics	Fixed effects with dynamics
Contiguity	3.042**	1.902**	1.992**	1.590**
	(0.092)	(0.336)	(0.120)	(0.375)
Capability ratio (log)	0.102**	0.387**	0.125**	0.350*
	(0.024)	(0.139)	(0.028)	(0.151)
Growth[a]	−0.017	−0.059**	−0.026*	−0.062**
	(0.011)	(0.012)	(0.013)	(0.013)
Alliance	−0.234*	−1.066*	−0.013	−1.090*
	(0.097)	(0.426)	(0.118)	(0.526)
Democracy[a]	−0.057**	−0.003	−0.053**	0.0004
	(0.007)	(0.015)	(0.008)	(0.016)
Bilateral trade/GDP[a]	−0.194*	−0.072	0.028	0.084
	(0.087)	(0.186)	(0.075)	(0.217)
Lagged dispute			4.940**	1.813**
			(0.102)	(0.103)
Constant	−5.809**		−6.274**	
	(0.090)		(0.108)	
N	93,755	93,755[b]	88,752	88,752[c]
Log likelihood	−3,688.06	−1,546.53	−2,530.31	−1,299.53
χ^2	1,186.43	75.75	3,074.67	380.40
Degrees of freedom	6	6	7	7
Prob $> \chi^2$	<0.0001	<0.0001	<0.0001	<0.0001

Note: Estimates obtained using *logit* and *clogit* procedures in STATA, version 6.0.
a. Lower value within the dyad. Method of analysis: Logistic and fixed-effects logistic regression.
b. 2,877 groups (87,402 observations) have no variation in outcomes.
c. 2,883 groups (82,932 observations) have no variation in outcomes.
** $p < .01$.
* $p < .05$, two-tailed test.

of an alliance decreases the risk of war from 5 percent to 1.8 percent, not 4.0 percent, as implied by the pooled regression. Controlling for fixed effects changes the way one views the relative importance of regime type, bilateral accords, and military capabilities. . . .

Having cautioned the reader against placing undue faith in fixed-effects models, we nonetheless believe that testing for fixed effects will put the quantitative analysis of panel data in international affairs on a path toward more robust and informative models. Many years after Stimson's watershed essay on the analysis of panel data in political science, it seems clear that the assumptions underlying pooled cross-sectional analysis of trade and conflict are suspect.[23] Dyads differ systematically in ways that are not captured by the measures used to gauge constructs such as "capability," "democracy," and the like. Pooling data under these circumstances leads to biased estimates. Yet analysts of international relations seem unaware of this problem or unwilling to come to grips with it.

The persistence of fixed effects in the cases examined here should be seen as a challenge to future scholarship on trade or interstate disputes: find new regressors that capture these cross-sectional differences. As Stimson points out, fixed effects are merely placeholders awaiting substantive explanation.[24] Scholars rising to this challenge may then judge their handiwork according to whether their revised regression models succeed in transforming any remaining dyad-specific intercepts into random noise, as gauged by a Hausman test. This approach, if successful, could resuscitate the cross-sectional component of panel analysis and turn pooled regressions into the kinds of conditional random-effects models envisioned by Simon Jackman.[25]

Until then, analysts of pooled cross-sectional data should proceed with caution, and consumers of this research should begin to demand that scholars consider potential problems arising from unmodeled fixed effects. . . .

References

Anderson, James E. 1979. A Theoretical Foundation for the Gravity Equation. *American Economic Review* 69(1): 106–116.

Beck, Nathaniel, Jonathan Katz, and Richard Tucker. 1998. Taking Time Seriously: Time-Series-Cross-Section Analysis with a Binary Dependent Variable. *American Journal of Political Science* 42(4): 1260–1288.

Bergstrand, Jeffrey H. 1985. The Gravity Equation in International Trade: Some Microeconomic Foundations and Empirical Evidence. *Review of Economics and Statistics* 67(3): 474–481.

Bliss, Harry, and Bruce Russett. 1998. Democratic Trading Partners: The Liberal Connection, 1962–1989. *The Journal of Politics* 60(4): 1126–1147.

Bremer, Stuart. 1996. Militarized Interstate Disputes, 1816–1992. Version 2.1. Available at ⟨http://pss.la.psu.edu/MID_DATA.HTM⟩. Accessed June 1997.

Deardorff, Alan V. 1984. Testing Trade Theories and Predicting Trade Flows. In *Handbook of International Economics*, edited by Ronald W. Jones and Peter B. Kenen, 467–517. Amsterdam: North-Holland.

Gowa, Joanne, and Edward D. Mansfield. 1993. Power Politics and International Trade. *American Political Science Review* 87(2): 408–420.

Greene, William H. 1997. *Econometric Analysis*. 3d ed. Upper Saddle River, N.J.: Prentice Hall.

Heston, Alan, and Robert Summers. 1991. The Penn World Table (Mark5): An Expanded Set of International Comparisons, 1950–88. *Quarterly Journal of Economics* 106(2): 327–368.

Hsiao, Cheng. 1986. *Analysis of Panel Data*. Cambridge: Cambridge University Press.

Jackman, Simon. 1999. In and Out of War and Peace: The Statistical Analysis of Discrete Serial Data on International Conflict. Unpublished manuscript, Stanford University, Stanford, Calif.

---

23. Stimson 1985. It is noteworthy that Stimson is cited by Wang 1999 and Zahariadis 1997, two . . . works . . . that introduce fixed effects into their international relations models.

24. Stimson 1985.

25. Jackman 1999.

Jaggers, Keith, and Ted Robert Gurr. 1995. Tracking Democracy's Third Wave with the Polity III Data. *Journal of Peace Research* 32(4): 469–482.

Jones, Daniel M., Stuart A. Bremer, and J. David Singer. 1996. Militarized Interstate Disputes, 1816–1992: Rationale, Coding, and Empirical Patterns. *Conflict Management and Peace Science* 15(2): 163–213.

Kim, Soo Yeon. 1998. Ties that Bind: The Role of Trade in International Conflict Processes, 1950–1992. Ph.D. diss., Yale University, New Haven, Conn.

King, Gary, and Langche Zeng. Forthcoming. Logistic Regression in Rare Events Data. *International Organization* 55(4).

Leamer, Edward E., and Robert M. Stern. 1970. *Quantitative International Economics*. Boston: Allyn and Bacon.

Linnemann, Hans. 1966. *An Econometric Study of International Trade Flows*. Amsterdam: North-Holland.

Signorino, Curtis A. 1999. Strategic Interaction and the Statistical Analysis of International Conflict. *American Political Science Review* 93(2): 279–297.

Singer, J. David. 1990. *Models, Methods, and Progress in World Politics: A Peace Research Odyssey*. Boulder, Colo.: Westview Press.

Stimson, James A. 1985. Regression in Space and Time: A Statistical Essay. *American Journal of Political Science* 29(4): 914–947.

Tinbergen, Jan. 1962. *Shaping the World Economy*. New York: Twentieth Century Fund.

Wang, T. Y. 1999. U.S. Foreign Aid and UN Voting: An Analysis of Important Issues. *International Studies Quarterly* 43(1): 199–210.

Zahariadis, Nikolaos. 1997. Why State Subsidies? Evidence from European Community Countries, 1981–1986. *International Studies Quarterly* 41(2): 341–354.

Democracy and Collective Bads[1]

Russell Hardin

Supporters of democracy might take special pleasure in noting how well democratic decision-making, even as messy as it typically is, has handled several problems of the generation of collective bads, such as air and water pollution.[2] Many autocratic states, which are often thought to have advantages in pushing through difficult policies, have been environmental disasters while Western democracies were actually improving their environments even while continuing economic growth. At the same time, democratic states—especially, but not only, the United States—have been relatively poor at handling distributive issues such as poverty and equal opportunity. These contrary results are inherent in the nature of democracy and the kinds of problems at stake. This fact bodes ill, oddly, for international handling of collective bads.

Democracy is particularly good at handling problems of coordination, sometimes including relatively difficult problems of coordination within the context of standard collective actions. It is generally poor at handling more conflicted issues, such as, especially, straight distributional issues. The regulation of many collective bads in our time falls on both sides of the democratic divide. In so far as these problems are purely domestic, as in the pollution of, say, Lake Tahoe, they are relatively easily seen as coordination problems by at least the bulk of the relevant population. In so far as they are very substantially international, as in the destruction of the ozone layer or acid rain, however, they often have massive distributive implications that would make their resolution difficult even in domestic politics but that make resolution extremely difficult in international politics. In domestic politics, they could, in principle, be handled by simple voting or by majoritarian representative legislation. In international politics, they must be handled through voluntary cooperation on the part of many states and, thus, they face the standard problem of the logic of collective action. Even worse, they face that problem in a normative context in which fairness as well as mere cooperation is often thought to be at issue.

Although there might be good abstract arguments for the use of democratic procedures to serve the general interest of each citizen, in actual democratic decisions it is almost invariably the case that some are losers while others are winners. A rare exception to this aspect of democracy as it actually works is the choice of whether to defend a nation under attack from outside. At least in the logic of the interests at stake, another very broad class of exceptions is, or may soon be, the general losses that all might suffer from such collective bads as environmental degradation. If collective action to overcome the generation of collective bads must be spontaneously, voluntarily motivated, we generally can expect such action to fail. In general, we expect

Excerpted from: Russell Hardin, "Democracy and Collective Bads." In *Democracy's Edges*, edited by Ian Shapiro and Casiano Hacker-Cordón. Cambridge: Cambridge University Press, 1999. © Cambridge University Press, 1999. Reprinted with the permission of Cambridge University Press.

1. Prepared for presentation at the conference, "Rethinking Democracy for a New Century," Yale University, 28 February–2 March 1997. Work on this paper has been supported by New York University, the Guggenheim Foundation, the Center for Advanced Study in the Behavioral Sciences, and the National Science Foundation (grant # SBR-9022192). I am grateful to all of these splendid agencies for their support. I am also grateful to the participants in the Yale conference and in the Rational Choice Seminar at the Center for Advanced Study for comments on an earlier draft and especially to Susan Hurley, Susan Moller Okin, and Steven Weber, who wrote lengthy comments.

2. On air pollution in the United States, see, e.g., *Scientific American* (1977).

it to succeed only for very small groups and for groups, such as labor unions, that have sanctioning power, to some extent, just as states have. When, however, it is determined by democratic vote with the backing of government to enforce the collective choice, we should often expect most individuals who vote to vote for enforcement, just as they might be expected to vote to defend their nation from attack.

Again, in the larger international system in which individual nations are unable to secure themselves against collective bads, however, the problem of collective action might be replayed at the higher level of states, because it may not be in the interest of a single nation independently to adopt self-regulative policies. I wish to investigate the nature and logic of democratic incentives in the face of such nested collective action problems of overcoming collective bads. In general, one might suppose that geographically very large nations, such as the United States, Russia, Brazil, Canada, Australia, and China, might have greater interest in regulation directly for their own benefit, so that domestic politics might suffice for some regulation in these nations, as it also might for the new European Union. Of course, even in these cases the levels of regulation that would be popularly chosen would likely vary with levels of prosperity. Contemporary Chinese would presumably be willing to suffer a larger trade-off of higher rates of pollution for higher rates of economic growth than would contemporary Americans.

Most nations in the world, however, could not plausibly justify the expense of certain environmental regulations merely for their own benefit, because almost all of the benefit would accrue to the people of other nations. This is most conspicuously true, perhaps, for the use of ozone-depleting chemicals. Ozone depletion is almost wholly internationalized, although nations such as the United States and Australia can reasonably see the problem of ozone depletion as particularly costly to their citizens, many of whom, with their fair skins and nearly tropical loca-

tions, may be especially susceptible to harms from the increased ultraviolet radiation that comes through the depleted ozone layer.[3] But other problems of, for example, ocean and air pollution are also predominantly internationalized for many nations that contribute to these problems. . . .

International Collective Bads

There is a peculiar difference between the traditional problems of securing collective goods and at least some of the contemporary problems of blocking collective bads. The latter are often inherently not national problems—they cross borders, they even straddle hemispheres. Democratic theory has virtually always been conceived at the level of relatively small populations in well-defined areas. Its expansion to cover large nations has been an evolutionary result in the older democracies and a move by analogy rather than by reinvention in such newer democracies as that of India with its population of, now, about a billion people. In our time there are two contrary forces underway that either expand or shrink the scope of democracy. The growth of ethnic politics has led to the splitting of nations into smaller units, as most dramatically in the case of the former Soviet Union, while the growth of concern with the benefits of larger markets and their efficiencies has led to the union of nations into larger blocks, as most dramatically in the case of the European Union (EU).

Pooling decisions at higher levels, as in the European Union, is what the international regu-

---

3. The seriousness of this problem may be less than has been supposed until recently. The worst implication of increased UV radiation exposure has been thought to be an increase in melanoma, a deadly cancer, an association that has been questioned by some findings. The lesser harm of superficial skin cancers, which are generally treatable, is far less ominous than a dramatic increase in melanoma.

lation of contemporary collective bads requires. The pooling of the EU, NAFTA, GATT, and similar supranational unions is designed to overcome institutional barriers to better results, barriers that get in the way of economic and other activities that would spontaneously happen if those barriers were not in the way. This is fundamentally a coordination problem rather than a problem of the provision of a collective good. Indeed, to date, successful resolution of international problems has typically been resolution of coordination problems. Contemporary collective bads will require institutional devices to motivate changes in action by individuals and institutions. It will require creation of stronger, international institutions rather than the weakening of extant, national institutions.

Arguably, the European Union entails an overall reduction in governmental power to the benefit of individual and corporate actors. The standard debate over the Union refers to the growing strength of government in Brussels, as though the issue were an old libertarian issue of the growth of government. The actual implication of that Union, at least for the short term, however, is the weakening of national government controls over individuals and nongovernmental corporate bodies.

There would be grievous conceptual and measurement problems in determining whether the EU gains more or less power than the individual national governments, taken together, lose. But a simple and compelling indicator of who loses and who gains is that individuals and corporate actors gain substantially, both economically and in other ways such as freedom to travel and live and work at will throughout the nations of the Union. It seems implausible that overall governmental control over individuals—which is the core concern of libertarianism—has grown. Surely it has been reduced. This is not to say that the power that individual nations had over individuals was beneficial to anyone or was deliberately exercised for some nationally beneficial reason. Much of it was almost certainly not. It

was often like the power of the bureaucrat, which, according to a joke that is too true to be entirely funny, is no power but the power to deny any reasonable request. Nations essentially just got in the way of individuals and corporations to make certain actions harder than they need have been.

Again, the change entailed in regulating contemporary international collective bads has virtually the opposite character: it seems likely to involve intrusions to block individual actions of many kinds. At the very least, it involves the creation of artificial incentive structures to alter behavior relatively unobtrusively.

At the international level all environmental problems are similar to the US national problem of auto pollution, whose principal harms are borne by Americans, who must bear the costs of reducing those harms. Of course, some of the harms are externalized to the larger world, especially the larger world of the northern hemisphere, and some of the regulatory costs are also externalized through the standardization of automotive design in the international market so that, say, Singaporeans drive cleaner cars and have to use more expensive fuel in them irrespective of whether they would want to do so. If each nation is responsible for reducing its industrial emissions, some nations cannot sensibly be thought to see it as their interest to bear the costs of the reduction even if that means no other nation reduces emissions either.

Hence, it is not conceivable to defend any international policy on reduced emissions without making interpersonal comparisons of the evaluation of the costs and benefits of such reductions. Straightforward policies are not likely to be Pareto improving. In some abstract sense, we might be convinced that there are policies that would be Pareto improving in that they would reduce pollution for virtually everyone without imposing costs on anyone that outweighed that person's own benefits from the reduction. But standard results in choice theory suggest that we cannot expect to reach agreement on the conclusion that any actually proposed policy is Pareto improving. It would be in the interest of, say, Brazil or China or the United States to assert that its own interest would be harmed by any given policy that allocated costs in a particular way.

Moreover, only in a world of relative equality could we suppose that such claims must be specious. Even without strategic misrepresentation of evaluations, we cannot expect to resolve the international problems with easy agreement because of deep inequalities. For example, suppose the Chinese economy is soon generally a market economy, with a small government role in the actual production of ordinary goods and services. Also suppose the government insists that its people do not value clean air enough to stop using coal in antiquated generators that are especially polluting. Finally, suppose that cleaning up the environment means, at least in large part for the short term, buying new equipment from abroad and using other fuels that would be internationally marketable, so that, whether they are imported or merely not exported, their use involves substantial losses of Chinese capital. Among the chief financial losers from any policy to clean up the environment would be various industrialists, but Chinese workers could also lose if the displacement of capital reduced rates of economic growth.

One might suppose that the transition of poorer nations to higher productivity could be subsidized by wealthier nations in ways that would benefit both. It would benefit the wealthier nations by reducing the externalities they would suffer from dirtier economic production in the poorer nations—but this is likely to be a chimera at present costs of technologies for environmental protection. The population of Africa alone is almost twice, and those of India and China are each almost four times, that of the United States. The wealthy nations of North America, Europe, Japan, and Australia have a small fraction of the population of the poor nations now hoping for rapid economic growth.

Substantial per capita subsidies to the poorer nations would require massive per capita contributions from the wealthier nations....

"Property Rights" in International Pollution

In a tradition that is not merely Lockean, it is commonly supposed that those who stake out an area first have a strong normative claim on it thereafter. The notion of national sovereignty, which is primarily a concern of the third world, is a variant of this principle of the rightness of prior ownership. In part, such a principle could be seen as essentially a convention that settles issues that would otherwise be destructively in conflict, so that, on the whole, all are better off from the stability of expectations and reduction of conflict that follows from virtually any form of property rights.

There is a sense in which the advanced industrial nations staked out a claim on the world's atmosphere and water during the past two centuries and that they have left little of these resources for those who come after them who wish to use the atmosphere and water of the world in similar ways. In John Locke's (1963 [1690]: paras. 27 and 33) argument for the normative derivation of claims of ownership from prior use, there is a condition, the Lockean proviso, that, if taken very seriously, cannot be met in our world. The proviso states that I have the right to some property if, after my appropriation of it, there is enough and as good left for others. Those who staked out claims to farmland in Iowa cannot be said to meet this proviso because there is very little farmland as good as Iowa. Similarly, those who put substantial pollutants into the air and into major water resources, including international rivers and the seas, left little further carrying capacity in those resources for others to use after them.

If the Chinese and Indians pollute at per capita levels today that rival the per capita levels of the United States in the era 1880–1960, they must bear huge burdens domestically and must externalize huge burdens to the rest of the world. Except for the massive problems of polluting energy sources, they might be expected to accomplish industrial growth at earlier American levels without polluting at American levels because technology has improved and become much cleaner. But since the scale of their current combined populations is roughly twenty times that of the United States at the beginning of its industrial growth, they probably cannot be expected to match American levels of growth without polluting far more in absolute terms than the United States did, especially if they rely on using abundant supplies of cheap coal for energy.

Naturally, Americans and Europeans concerned with overburdening the environment tend to focus relatively heavily on the responsibility of nations for their rates of population growth. Poor nations focus rather on national responsibilities for per capita rates of energy consumption and pollution. Population is treated more nearly as a domestic problem by poor nations and as an international problem by wealthy nations. It is both, but the difference in emphasis is essentially a distributional issue. Again, democracy is not good at handling distributional issues, and international democracy, which is exceedingly weak, cannot be expected to handle international distributions except in so far as wealthy nations choose to act more or less altruistically toward impoverished nations.

Concluding Remarks

As the problem of collective bads has not been a major concern of democratic theory, so too the problem of nested collective actions has not been addressed in democratic theory, perhaps because democratic theory has not yet gone international. When applied to a domestic population, democracy seems to yield relatively easy results of uniform policies on such issues as collective

bads and occasional collective goods. We stipulate that cars will meet various anti-pollution standards and then let individuals freely decide, within this constraint, what cars they buy. We do not necessarily have to enforce the policies against individuals to change their behavior. The central problem of nesting collective actions at different levels is that this relatively easy resolution is not possible at the higher level of international politics. When the issues have differential effects, especially distributional effects, at the international level, we cannot simply vote by some kind of majority decision procedure and then expect every nation to follow through as virtually every US citizen might be expected to follow through on Environmental Protection Agency directives.

The creation of larger, supranational governmental bodies such as the European Union may, however, make environmental regulation easier because such unification "domesticates" some of the relevant problems of collective bads. Instead of seeing its own polluting activities as largely internationalized, each nation of the Union can increasingly see its problem as merely the general problem of the larger Union, and at that level democratic choice might relatively easily reach consensus on regulation. A side advantage of supranational organizations intended for the resolution of simple coordination problems in economic activities may be to domesticate some problems of collective bads enough to make them consensually, democratically resolvable. This prospect should give many western European leaders greater incentive to broaden the Union by including the polluting states of eastern Europe—because much of the cost of the eastern pollution is visited on the western nations. In the short term, however, economic differences might make such resolutions harder by making them seem redistributive, because levels of economic development differ substantially from east to west.

Note that this resolution of the European problems of collective bads is far from creating a generally powerful supranational government. The nations could merge little more than economic policy, although there are likely to be, as there have been, more or less inseparable social issues that the Union might be forced to address. But it would not require a supranational police force to control compliance with environmental policies, because these could be coupled with other economic policies that have beneficial consequences. The bad to be regulated would be collective and its regulation would require more or less universal endogenous changes in behavior. But the policing of those changes in behavior would be done by each domestic government, and each domestic government would have its policies dyadically enforced by negotiation with each member state of the larger Union rather than by centralized directive, for which there might be no authority.

Not to couple environmental and other economic policies would inherently undercut the point of the Union, which is to make internal trade and production efficient across all the nations of the Union. Very dirty production in one nation would allow that nation to externalize its costs of production to the other nations, through pollution that crosses borders, thus lowering its production costs and increasing its benefits from marketing its production more competitively. National leaders who suppose that their nation must yield economic advantages in submitting to a Union whose members are not all equally advanced and productive have reason to temper their nationalist inclinations with concern for gaining ways to control the generation of collective bads in the less developed nations of the Union.

As argued above, the focus of collective action problems in international politics is distinctively different from that of domestic politics. Collective bads that are endogenously generated and that must be endogenously regulated are now, and for the near future of a generation or more, the main concern in the international politics of collective action. In a democratic political order

with sanctioning power, consensus that some pattern of behavior produces a severe bad implies good prospects for regulation of the bad. In a quasi-anarchy of states with only dyadic rather than centralized sanctioning power, a similar consensus may be less effective in motivating regulation. The best hope for regulation may lie in regional and other supranational organizations of states to address issues of economic relations.

These organizations form relatively successfully because their central problem is merely coordination. Although there are conflictual issues at the edges and in the details of the coordination, coordination is the modal incentive structure. Once such organizations are established, they can effectively use the value of coordinating with them as a dyadic sanction against those who do not join in resolutions of other issues that are not merely coordination. By increasing the geographical reach of policies on various issues, they can come much closer to domesticating collective bads that cross borders and that, therefore, would allow member states to externalize the burdens of the bads they produce to other states. At the regional level, there might therefore be consensus on regulating some bad that none of the member states would have an interest in regulating on its own. A moderately anarchic world of geographically very large nations and large regional organizations of nations might therefore be expected to handle international collective bads relatively well, even if perhaps not as well as could a functioning democracy with central power.

References

Locke, John. 1963 (1690). "The second treatise of government," in *Two Treatises of Government*. Edited by Peter Haslett. Cambridge: Cambridge University Press.

Scientific American. 1977. April: 27.

Representation and the Democratic Deficit

Pippa Norris

Introduction

Processes of political representation have to be understood within the context of the constitutional framework of the Union. These reflect a number of fundamental but unresolved controversies: whether the EU should be an *intergovernmental* organisation of sovereign states or the top level of a *federal* European state; how decisions should be made and powers allocated among EU institutions; whether the EU should develop as a wider and looser association or a closer and more integrated unit; and how the people should be represented and the "democratic deficit" cured. This last issue is particularly critical. The electorate influences the EU through two channels: *indirectly* through their choice of governments in national elections, and *directly* through elections to the European Parliament....

Indirect Channels of Representation via National Governments

Despite the substantial growth of Union powers, national institutions continue to retain the primary responsibility for ensuring democracy and accountability in the Union (Kirchner 1992; Keohane & Hoffman 1991). The most important law-making body remains the Council of Ministers, essentially an *intergovernmental* negotiating forum representing member states and acting behind closed doors. National governments also choose who is nominated for the European Commission, which exercises executive powers. Those who want to retain the intergovernmental

Excerpted from: Pippa Norris, "Representation and the Democratic Deficit." *European Journal of Political Research* 32 (1997): 273–282. Reprinted by permission.

emphasis of EU institutions seek solutions to the democratic deficit in improving national supervision, for instance through strengthening channels of consultation and information between the Commission and national parliaments, or by increasing the transparency of decision making in the Council.

Governments acting in the Council of Ministers remain accountable on a day-to-day basis to their own national parliaments, and at regular intervals, via elections, to their citizens. In this respect the Council of Ministers is similar to other intergovernmental organisations like the United Nations, NATO or UNESCO. We would not expect the public to have a direct say in issues such as whether the UN deploys peacekeeping forces or economic sanctions. Yet if there is a popular backlash, for example if the American public becomes angry about heavy losses for US forces deployed in UN missions, then at the next election they can hold their political leaders responsible, and "throw the rascals out." In this regard retrospective evaluations of government performance are critical for accountability.

In the same way, it can be argued, following G. A. Almond (1950) and V. O. Key (1961), that there existed a "permissive consensus" over Europe so that governments were authorised to negotiate detailed European policies over complex issues like CAP, EMU and border controls within the Council of Ministers. Surveys consistently confirm that the general public is rarely attentive to, or informed about, the arcane details of highly technical and complex issues in foreign policy. But if the public becomes dissatisfied with the outcome of decisions with clear domestic consequences, for example if they blame the EU for rising levels of unemployment or cuts in the welfare state, *and* they blame their government for EU policies (a critical step in the chain of accountability), citizens always have recourse to the ballot box. In foreign policy, therefore, governments may pay little attention to public opinion towards technical issues like the Common Fisheries Policy, since these attitudes may well be ill-informed and weakly rooted. Nevertheless in their negotiations ministers may pay closer attention to the *anticipated* reaction of their citizens to the outcome of these policies, and how opinion leaders may judge the actions of ministers on the final day of calling. Therefore domestic elections provide an indirect mechanism to link the decisions by the Council of Ministers to the preferences of citizens in member states.

Yet there are a series of problems with this model. The lack of transparency about "who said what" in negotiations behind the closed doors of the Council of Ministers, and the complexity of relating policy outputs to outcomes, makes it extremely difficult for the public to evaluate the actions of their government within Europe. Moreover the dominance of domestic issues in national elections means that foreign policy is usually of low saliency on the public agenda. Lastly, the major parties rarely offer voters clear alternative policy options concerning the major issues of European governance. Domestic elections are therefore an extremely blunt instrument for citizens to express policy preferences. Nevertheless retrospective judgements about government performance within the European Union may produce a rough justice: if the EU is blamed for economic conditions, excessive bureaucracy or extravagant agricultural spending, all governments may sink or swim together.

Direct Channels of Representation via the European Parliament

Yet much of the EU is *federal*, meaning that certain powers are transferred to European bodies above national governments (see Pinder 1991; Pryce 1987; Nicholl & Salmon 1990; Kirchner 1992; Keohane & Hoffman 1991). The European Commission, a rule-making institution, is essentially a supranational body, as is the independent Court of Justice; organised interest groups are consulted through the Economic and Social Committee, and the European Parliament is chosen through direct election. Among federal bodies, in the original treaties the European parliament was envisaged as the institution which directly represented the voice of the people, but with relatively weak powers. The original treaty gave the parliament only a consultative role in the adoption of EU legislation and the budget, and limited scrutiny over the Commission. The powers of the parliament were increased in a number of steps (see Duff 1994; Jacobs 1992; Pinder 1991). Yet because states (notably the UK) have been reluctant to allow any further erosion of national sovereignty, the Council of Ministers remains the dominant decision-making forum. While direct elections to the Parliament were envisaged, it was not until 1979 that they took place (see Lodge 1982). Moreover, there is almost unanimous agreement that these elections have been almost wholly lacking in public interest: typically they are described as second-order national elections (Reif & Schmitt 1980).

All the core institutions play a part in EU decision making. While decision making is generally labyrinthine in its complexity, the institutions involved do have different constituencies and, in principle, accountability is possible through the relationship between each institution and its constituency. Articles within this Special Issue focus on central aspects of one such relationship, that between the public and the European Parliament. They all address whether weak linkages between voters and the European Parliament, and flaws in the electoral and parliamentary mechanism of political representation, contribute significantly to the democratic deficit within the European Union.

The Breakdown of the "Permissive Consensus"?

The problem of the "democratic deficit" is whether these direct and indirect channels are effective in connecting the preferences of citizens to the outcome of EU decisionmaking. During the early years of the Community the technocratic and diplomatic elite determined the direction of European development, much as they controlled bodies such as NATO, with the tacit approval of a permissive consensus among mass publics. The idea of a "permissive consensus" implies general support within public opinion, with passive approval which is widespread if shallowly rooted, and which may allow future government action (Key 1961: 32–35). But there was always concern that public opinion about the future of Europe was somewhat fragile. Given limited popular participation in, and identification with, the European Union, decisions might easily be made by elites that would neither reflect, nor be seen to reflect, popular wishes.

The breakdown in this consensus first became evident in the early 1990s. The defeat of the proposal to adopt the Maastricht Treaty in the Danish referendum of 1992, and then the "petit oui" in France, produced a realization that at least some governments might be significantly out of touch with their electorate (Franklin, van der Eijk & Marsh 1995; Franklin, Marsh & McLaren 1994). The backlash against Maastricht and the ratification crisis were attributed, at least in part, to a lack of public engagement and popular debate about integration (Baun 1996). The period from 1991–92 saw a sharp fall in public support towards the European Union, across the standard indicators in the Euro-Barometer (Niedermayer & Sinnott 1995: 58–59). This fall was not just confined to opinion polls, as it occasionally found expression in violent actions, such as opposition by intense minorities to farming and fisheries policies. Problems of EU legitimacy were further under-lined by the June 1994 European elections, with record apathy in voter turnout, and gains for anti-Maastricht protest parties in France, Denmark and Spain (van der Eijk & Franklin 1996).

In 1996 these strains to the system were exacerbated and dramatized by the economic difficulties of achieving the strict convergence criteria for European Monetary Union, resulting in severe cuts in the welfare state in France and Italy. This was compounded by the political problems of persuading the public to abandon the familiar German Mark, French Franc and Pound Sterling in their pockets for the unknown Euro. The problem of the democratic deficit, given these stresses, is not just marginal to the enterprise, but central to the European project. . . .

Public Confidence in the Union

How serious is the crisis of public confidence in the Union? Is this merely a passing phase, triggered by temporary discontent with particular policies, or a more serious erosion of faith in European integration? . . . The dilemma facing the European Union, along with many emerging and consolidating democracies in divided nation-states, is how to build public support simultaneously across both levels. If there is widespread confidence in the underlying constitutional order, and a strong sense of identity with the community, then it becomes easier to resolve particular policy conflicts. But if the legitimacy of the basic political system remains under question, if European leaders are largely invisible to the public, and if there is little "glue" provided by a sense of European identity to hold disparate countries together, then it becomes more difficult to resolve substantive policy conflicts. Moreover many decisions about specific issues—like European Monetary Union, border controls, or the European Social Chapter—have significant ramifications for national sovereignty, and therefore cannot be decoupled from the constitutional framework. In this context the rules of the game are under dispute, as well as the division of spoils.

Although pressing, the difficult problems of institutional reform have consistently taken a back seat to substantive issues of European integration. Maastricht was essentially about the projects on EMU, common foreign and security policy, and enhanced cooperation in policing and justice (Duff et al. 1994; Baun 1996). Problems of institutional reform are part of the agenda of the Inter-Governmental Conference (IGC), which first met in March 1996. In his opening address to the European Parliament the President, Klaus Hansch, emphasized that the conference would be crucial in injecting more democracy into existing procedures, and in making decisionmaking institutions more effective. The basic decisionmaking structures were adopted by the Treaty of Rome, in 1957, when the Community had six members. By 1996 the EU has fifteen member states and, with more envisaged, the complicated decisionmaking process threatens to become grid-locked.

... Yet recently politics within the Union has focussed less on institutional reform than on the serious problems of fiscal discipline, and cutbacks in government spending, raised by the attempt by countries to meet the strict convergence criteria required for European Monetary Union in 1999.

Conclusions

If institutional reforms are to prove effective, they must be based on a clear grasp of how the representative mechanisms in the Union function at present. The conclusions from this Special Issue is that there are a variety of channels of representation, and some are more effective than others. Thomassen and Schmitt analysed the responsible party model of representation, to see whether European party groups are developing distinct and coherent policy positions on the major issues facing the Union. Some argue that

these groups are weak umbrella organisations, at best (Pedersen 1996). Nevertheless Thomassen and Schmitt provide evidence for the roots of an evolving party system in the European Parliament. Their study analyses how far the political attitudes of candidates and voters are constrained by the European party group with which their national party is associated. By comparing the position of candidates and voters towards the issues of a single European currency, unemployment policy and national borders, as well as left-right self-placement, the study found that the roots of a European party system is evident among candidates, and, to a lesser extent, among the electorate. This embryonic party system is based on the familiar left-right ideological cleavages which serve to shape so much of European domestic politics. Nevertheless there remains a large and significant gap between the attitudes of mass and elite on these issues, with political leaders far more in favour of European integration than the general public. This suggests that the emerging party system in Parliament needs to be strengthened further—organisationally, programmatically, and financially—to increase representation via responsible parties.

Social representation presents other problems for the legitimacy of the European parliament. Norris and Franklin consider how far the parliament "looks like a mirror of European society." As in most legislative bodies, there are clear social biases which mean that the European parliament underrepresents women, the younger generation, and working class socio-economic groups. This study considers how far we can explain this pattern is terms of a model of "supply and demand." The paper concludes that supply-side factors proved more strongly related to candidates gaining winnable seats—and thus election to the European parliament—than demand-side factors. In other words, the resources and motivation which candidates bring to the recruitment process are the primary factors explaining why some aspirants succeed while others fail. Equally important, the results confirmed that women's representation was strongly influenced by institutional structures, including the electoral system, party system and political culture. More women are elected in protestant countries, countries with strong left-wing parties, and countries with proportional list electoral systems, than elsewhere. This suggests that the European parliament, in common with most legislative bodies, will continue to remain socially unrepresentative for many years, although parties can take effective action in their recruitment processes to make sure that their ticket includes candidates from more diverse social backgrounds.

The roles which MEPs adopt may have important consequences for other types of representation, including functional linkages with interest groups, and service work with individual problems. Richard Katz explored the significance of these role orientations for members of the European Parliament. Looking at the priorities given to different tasks, Katz found that three roles clearly predominated among candidates. Some saw themselves in an intergovernmental view of the Union as representing *national interests*, stressing the importance of loyalties to national parties. The second group saw themselves primarily as constituency *agents*, giving priority to helping people with particular problems and service activity. The last group perceived their roles as *"trustees,"* using their own judgement about public policy rather than following national or European party policies. Katz goes on to consider explanations for these differences in role priorities, and to explore their consequences for legislative behaviour. Even if parties remain weak, this suggests that through casework for individuals or local groups MEPs who prioritise this activity may provide an effective conduit between citizens and the complexities of the European decision making process. We need to go further to understand the origins of these role perceptions, and how new MEPs

are socialised into prioritising activities during their early careers in the European Parliament.

The paper by Michael Marsh and Bernhard Wessels goes further by analysing candidates and members as territorial representatives, defending national interests within the European parliament, rather than being bound by party discipline. The study compared the attitudes of candidates, MEPs and publics within each country, to analyse the degree of policy congruence between them. Marsh and Wessels confirm the pattern noted earlier that the elite are far more strongly in favour of European integration than the electorate. But, interestingly, the gap between mass and elite was far greater in some countries than others. The paper concludes that these cross-national differences are due, at least in part, to different electoral and party systems. In particular, more proportional electoral systems and the inclusion of smaller parties produce MEPs who are closer to their general publics on the European issues under comparison. This has important implications, not just for the European parliament, but also for broader debates about the consequences of constitutional designs on political representation.

Lastly, we can turn to behavioural indicators of public attitudes towards the European Parliament by comparing turnout in European elections. Voting participation is commonly regarded as one major indicator of the health of a democracy, reflecting trust and confidence in the political system, although systematic studies suggest a complex relationship between attitudes and behaviour. Blondel, Sinnott and Svensson consider why there is such cross-national variance in the turnout to European elections. On average 58.5 percent of the European electorate voted in 1994, but the proportion was far lower in some countries like the UK, the Netherlands and Portugal. The study concludes that institutional factors played a major role in explaining these differences. The effects of compulsory voting and concomitant national elections are obvious, yet also very important. Other institutional variables, including proportional electoral systems and Sunday voting, also proved significant although the effects of these factors are not wholly straightforward. Lastly Blondel et al. conclude that as well as improvements to the practical arrangements for elections, turnout could be boosted by more effective mobilisation campaigns by parties, and by a more positive image for the European Parliament, the Union, and European integration. Voters were somewhat more motivated to go to the polls if they felt involved with, and knowledgeable about, European affairs. The results suggest that the problems of representation in the European Union could be addressed by a series of alternative steps and that, unless reforms are implemented, the problems of linkage between citizen and the Union ... can only be expected to become more evident under the stresses of broadening and deepening the European Union.

References

Almond, G. A. (1950). *The American people and foreign policy*. New York: Praeger.

Baun, M. J. (1996). *An imperfect Union: The Maastricht Treaty and the new politics of European integration*. Boulder, CO: Westview Press.

Duff, A., Pinder, J. & Pryce, R. (1994). *Maastricht and beyond*. London: Routledge.

Easton, D. (1975). A reassessment of the concept of political support, *British Journal of Political Science* 5: 435–57.

van de Eijk, C., Franklin, M. et al. (1996). *Choosing Europe? The European electorate and national politics in the face of the Union*. Ann Arbor, MI: The University of Michigan Press.

Franklin, M., Marsh, M. & McLaren, L. (1994). Uncorking the bottle: Popular opposition to European unification in the wake of Maastricht, *Journal of Common Market Studies* 32(4): 455–472.

Franklin, M., van der Eijk, C. & Marsh, M. (1995). Referendum outcomes and trust in government: Public support for Europe in the wake of Maastricht, *Journal of West European Politics* 18(3): 101–117.

Jacobs, F., Corbett, R. & Shackleton, M. (1992). *The European Parliament*, 2nd edn. Harlow: Longman.

Key, V. O. (1961). *Public opinion and American democracy*. New York: Alfred A. Knopf.

Keohane, R. & Hoffmann, S., eds. (1991). *The new European Community: Decision-making and institutional change*. Boulder, CO: Westview Press.

Kirchner, E. (1992). *Decision-making in the European Community*. Manchester: Manchester University Press.

Lodge, J. (1982). *Direct elections to the European Parliament*. London: Macmillan.

Nicholl, W. & Salmon, T. (1990). *Understanding the European Community*. Hemel Hempsted: Philip Allan.

Niedermayer, O. & Sinnott, R., eds. (1995). *Public opinion and internationalized governance*. Oxford: Oxford University Press.

Norris, P. (1997). *Electoral change since 1945*. Oxford: Blackwell.

Pinder, J. (1991). *European Community: The building of a Union*. Oxford: Oxford University Press.

Pryce, R., ed. (1987). *The dynamics of European Union*. London: Routledge.

Reif, K. & Schmitt, H. (1980). Nine second-order national elections: A conceptual framework for the analysis of European election results, *European Journal of Political Research* 8: 3–44.

The Transformation of Political Community: Rethinking Democracy in the Context of Globalization

David Held

This chapter focuses on the changing nature of political community in the context of globalization—in brief, the growing inter-connectedness, and intensification of relations, among states and societies. The chapter has a number of parts. In the first part, I explore the changing forms of political association and, in particular, the rise of the modern nation state as a background against which modern conceptions of democracy developed. With this in mind, I examine some of the key assumptions and pre-suppositions of liberal democracy; above all, its conception of political community. In the second part, I explore changing forms of globalization. In my view, globalization has been with us for some time, but its extent, intensity, and impact have changed fundamentally. In the third and final part of the essay, the implications of changing forms of globalization are explored in relation to the prospects of democratic political community. A particular conception of democracy is elaborated, a form of transnational democracy, which, it is argued, is more appropriate to the developing structure of political associations today. The future of democracy is set out in cosmopolitan terms—a new democratic complex with global scope, given shape and form by reference to a basic democratic law, which takes on the character of government to the extent, and only to the extent, that it promulgates, implements, and enforces this law. This is by no means a prescription for the end of the nation state or the end of democratic politics as we know it—far from it. Rather, it is a recipe for the enrichment

Excerpted from: David Held, "The Transformation of Political Community: Rethinking Democracy in the Context of Globalization." In *Democracy's Edges*, edited by Ian Shapiro and Casiano Hacker-Cordón. Cambridge: Cambridge University Press, 1999. © Cambridge University Press, 1999. Reprinted with the permission of Cambridge University Press.

of democratic life (see Held 1995 and 1996). It is argued that only by buttressing democracy, within and across nation states, can the accountability of power in the contemporary era be strengthened....

Built, as it was, upon an emerging conception of the modern nation state, the development of liberal democracy took place within a fairly delimited conceptual space (cf. Walker 1988; Connolly 1991; McGrew 1997). Modern democratic theory and practice was constructed upon Westphalian foundations. National communities, and theories of national communities, were based on the presupposition that political communities could, in principle, control their destinies and citizens could come to identify sufficiently with each other such that they might think and act together with a view of what was best for all of them, that is, with a view of the common good (Sandel 1996: 202). It was taken for granted that, bar internal difficulties, the demos, the extent of the franchise, the form and scope of representation, and the nature and meaning of consent—in fact all the key elements of self-determination—could be specified with respect to geography: systems of representation and democratic accountability could be neatly meshed with the spatial reach of sites of power in a circumscribed territory. Moreover, as a consequence of this, clear-cut distinctions could be elaborated—and national institutions built upon—the difference between "internal" and "external" policy, between domestic and foreign affairs. The vast majority of the theories of democracy, liberal and radical, assumed that the nature and possibilities of political community could be elaborated by reference to national structures and national possibilities, and that freedom, political equality and solidarity could be entrenched in and through the nation state. This became the cornerstone of modern democratic thought....

... [T]he theory of democracy, particularly as it emerged in the nineteenth and twentieth centuries, could take for granted the link between the demos, citizenship, electoral mechanisms, the nature of consent, and the boundaries of the nation state. The fates of different political communities may be intertwined, but the appropriate place for determining the foundation of "national fate" was the national community itself. In the contemporary era the key principles and practices of liberal democracy are associated almost exclusively with the principles and institutions of the sovereign nation state. Further, modern democratic theory and democratic politics assumes a symmetry and congruence between citizen-voters and national decision-makers. Through the ballot box, citizen-voters are, in principle, able to hold decision-makers to account; and, as a result of electoral consent, decision-makers are able to make and pursue law and policy legitimately for their constituents, ultimately, the people in a fixed, territorially based community. Accordingly, the heart or "deep structure" of the system of democratic nation states can be characterized by a number of striking features, which are, broadly: democracy in nation states and non-democratic relations among states; the entrenchment of accountability and democratic legitimacy inside state boundaries and pursuit of reasons of state (and maximum political advantage) outside such boundaries; democracy and citizenship rights for those regarded as "insiders," and the frequent negation of these rights for those beyond their borders.

Changing Forms of Regional and Global Enmeshment

At the centre of the dominant theoretical approaches to democratic politics is an uncritically appropriated concept of the territorial political community. The difficulty with this is that political communities have rarely—if ever—existed in isolation as bounded geographical totalities; they are better thought of as multiple overlapping networks of interaction. These networks crystallize around different sites and forms of power—economic, political, military, cultural, among others—producing diverse patterns of activity which do not correspond in any simple and straightforward way to territorial boundaries (see Mann 1986: chap. 1). The spatial reach of the modern nation state did not fix impermeable borders for other networks, the scope and reach of which have been as much local as international or even global. Modern political communities are, and have always been, locked into a diversity of processes and structures which range in and through them. The theory and practice of the democratic sovereign state has always been in some tension with the actuality of state sovereignty and autonomy. National political communities do not always make and determine decisions and policies simply for themselves, and governments do not always make policies and decisions exclusively for their citizens (see Offe 1985). The freedom of action of particular political communities has always been, to varying degrees, constrained. How should one understand these patterns of interconnections, and their changing form over time? And how should one understand their political implications, in particular, for sovereignty, autonomy, and the democratic political community?

The term "globalization" captures some of the changes which shape the nature of the political and the prospects of political community; unpacking this term helps create a framework for addressing some of the issues raised above. Globalization can be understood, I believe, in relation to a set of processes which shift the spatial form of human organization and activity to transcontinental or interregional patterns of activity, interaction and the exercise of power (see Held, McGrew, Goldblatt, and Perraton 1999). It involves a stretching and deepening of social relations and institutions across space and time such that, on the one hand, day-to-day activities are increasingly influenced by events happening on the other side of the globe and, on the other, the practices and decisions of local groups or communities can have significant global reverberations (see Giddens 1990). . . .

Globalization is neither a singular condition nor a linear process. Rather, it is best thought of as a multidimensional phenomenon involving domains of activity and interaction that include the economic, political, technological, military, legal, cultural, and environmental. Each of these spheres involves different patterns of relations and activities. A general account of globalization cannot simply predict from one domain what will occur in another. It is extremely important, then, to keep these distinctive domains separate and to build a theory of globalization and its impact on particular political communities from an understanding of what is happening in each and every one of them. . . .

Against this background, the meaning and place of political community, and particularly of the democratic political community, needs to be re-examined. At least two tasks are necessary in order to pursue this objective. First, it is important to illustrate some of the fundamental alterations in the patterns of interconnectedness among political communities and the subsequent shifts in the structure and form of political community itself. Secondly, it is important to set out some of the political implications of these changes. In what follows, I start by illustrating some of the transformations which have brought a change in the organization and meaning of political community. Clearly, these are indicative transformations only; they obviously fall short of a systematic account (see Held, McGrew, Goldblatt, and Perraton 1999).

(1) Among the significant developments which are changing the nature of political community are global economic processes, especially growth in trade, production, and financial transactions, organized in part by rapidly expanding multinational companies. Trade has grown substantially, reaching unprecedented levels, particularly in the post–World War II period. Not only has there been an increase in intraregional trade around the world, but there has also been sustained growth among regions as well (see Perraton, Goldblatt, Held, and McGrew 1997). More countries are involved in global trading arrangements, for instance, India and China, and more people and nations are affected by such arrangements. If there is a further lowering of tariff barriers across the world, these trends are likely to continue and to further the extension, intensity, and impact of trade relations on other domains of life. The expansion of global financial flows has, moreover, been particularly rapid in the last ten to fifteen years. Foreign exchange turnover has mushroomed and is now over 1.2 trillion dollars a day. Much of this financial activity is speculative and generates fluctuations in prices (of stocks, shares, futures, etc.) in excess of those which can be accounted for by changes in the fundamentals of asset values. The enormous growth of global financial flows across borders, linked to the liberalization of capital markets from the late 1970s, has created a more integrated financial system than has ever been known.

Underpinning this economic shift has been the growth of multinational corporations, both productive and financial. Approximately 20,000 multinational corporations now account for a quarter to a third of world output, 70 percent of world trade, and 80 percent of foreign direct investment. They are essential to the diffusion of skills and technology, and they are key players in the international money markets. In addition, multinational corporations can have profound affects on macroeconomic policy. . . .

Against this background, the traditional claims of democratic theory—above all, the claims to the possibility of a circumscribed, delimited self-determining community of citizens—begin to appear strained.

It is easy to misrepresent the political significance of the globalization of economic activity.

There are those, earlier referred to as the "hyper-globalizers," who argue that we now live in a world in which social and economic processes operate predominantly at a global level (see Ohmae 1990; Reich 1991)....

But the claims of the hyper-globalizers and their critics misstate much of what is significant about contemporary economic globalization for politics. Nation states continue to be immensely powerful, and enjoy access to a formidable range of resources, bureaucratic infrastructural capacity, and technologies of coordination and control. The continuing lobbying of states by multinational corporations confirm the enduring importance of states to the mediation and regulation of economic activity. Yet it is wrong to argue that globalization is a mere illusion, an ideological veil, that allows politicians simply to disguise the causes of poor performance and policy failure. Although the rhetoric of hyper-globalization has provided many an elected politician with a conceptual resource for refusing political responsibility, globalization has significant and discernible characteristics which alter the balance of resources—economic and political—within and across borders. Among the most important of these is the tangible growth in the enmeshment of national economies in global economic transactions (i.e., a growing proportion of nearly all national economies are involved in international economic exchanges with an increasing number of countries). This increase in the extent and intensity of economic interconnectedness has altered the relation between economic and political power. One shift has been particularly significant: "the historic expansion of exit options for capital in financial markets relative to national capital controls, national banking regulations and national investment strategies, and the sheer volume of privately held capital relative to national reserves. Exit options for corporations making direct investments have also expanded ... the balance of power has shifted in favour of capital *vis-à-vis* both national governments and national

labour movements" (Goldblatt, Held, McGrew, and Perraton 1997: 74). As a result, the autonomy of democratically elected governments has been, and is increasingly, constrained by sources of unelected and unrepresentative economic power. These have the effect of making adjustment to the international economy (and, above all, to global financial markets) a fixed point of orientation in economic policy and of encouraging an acceptance of the "decision signals" of its leading agents and forces as a, if not the, standard of rational decision making. The options for political communities, and the costs and benefits of them, ineluctably alter.

(2) Within the realms of the media and culture there are also grounds for thinking that there is a growing disjuncture between the idea of the democratic state as an independent, accountable centre of power bounded by fixed borders—in this case, a centre of national culture, able to foster and sustain a national identity—and interlinked changes in the spheres of media and cultural exchange. A number of developments in recent times can be highlighted. English has spread as the dominant language of elite cultures throughout the world: it is now the dominant language in business, computing, law, science, and politics. The internationalization and globalization of telecommunications have been extraordinarily rapid: international telephone traffic has increased over fourfold between 1983 and 1995; there has been a massive increase in transnational cable links; there has been an explosion in satellite links; and the Internet has provided a remarkable increase in the infrastructure of horizontal and lateral communication capacity within and across borders. Moreover, substantial multimedia conglomerates have developed, such as the Murdoch empire and Time Warner. In addition, there has been a huge increase in tourism—for example, in 1960 there were 70 million international tourists, while in 1994 there were nearly 500 million. And in television and film there are similar trends.

None of the above examples, or the accumulative impact of parallel cases, should be taken to imply the development of a single global, media-led culture (consider the impact of Star television in India), but certainly, taken together, these developments do imply that many new forms of communication media range in and across borders, linking nations and peoples in new ways. The creation and recreation of new forms of identity—often linked to consumption and the entertainment industries—are not to be underestimated. In this context, the capacity of national political leaders to sustain a national culture has become more complex and difficult....

(3) Environmental problems and challenges are perhaps the clearest and starkest examples of the global shift in human organization and activity, creating some of the most fundamental pressures on the efficacy of the nation state and state-centric democratic politics. There are three types of problems at issue:

a) the first is shared problems involving the global commons, i.e., fundamental elements of the ecosystem—among the most significant challenges here are global warming and ozone depletion;

b) a second category of global environmental problems involves the interlinked challenges of demographic expansion and resource consumption—pressing examples under this heading include desertification, questions of biodiversity, and threats to the existence of certain species;

c) a third category of problems is transboundary pollution such as acid rain, or river pollutants, or the contaminated rain which fell in connection with Chernobyl.

In response to the progressive development of, and publicity surrounding, environmental problems in the last three decades, there has been an interlinked process of cultural and political globalization as illustrated by the emergence of new cultural, scientific, and intellectual networks; new environmental movements with transnational organizations and transnational concerns; and new institutions and conventions such as those agreed in 1992 at the Earth Summit in Brazil. Not all environmental problems are, of course, global; such an implication would be entirely false. But there has been a striking shift in the physical and environmental conditions—that is, in the extent and intensity of environmental problems—affecting human affairs in general.... Thus, questions are raised both about the fate of the idea of political community and about the appropriate locus for the articulation of the democratic political good. The proper "home" of politics and democracy becomes a puzzling matter.

(4) Changes in the development of international law have placed individuals, governments and non-governmental organizations under new systems of legal regulation. International law recognizes powers and constraints, and rights and duties, which have qualified the principle of state sovereignty in a number of important respects; sovereignty *per se* is no longer a straightforward guarantee of international legitimacy. Entrenched in certain legal instruments is the view that a legitimate state must be a democratic state that upholds certain common values (see Crawford 1994). One significant area in this regard is human rights law and human rights regimes....

In international law, accordingly, there has been a gradual shift away from the principle that state sovereignty must be safeguarded irrespective of its consequences for individuals, groups, and organizations. Respect for the autonomy of the subject, and for an extensive range of human rights, creates a new set of ordering principles in political affairs which can delimit and curtail the principle of effective state power. Along with other international legal changes (see Held 1995: chap. 5), these developments are indicative of an alteration in the weight granted, on the one hand, to claims made on behalf of the state system and, on the other hand, to those made on behalf of an alternative organizing principle of world order, in which an unqualified state sovereignty no longer reigns supreme.

(5) While all the developments described so far have helped engender a shift away from a purely state-centered international system of "high politics" to new and novel forms of geogovernance, a further interesting example of this process can be drawn from the very heart of the idea of a sovereign state—national security and defense policy. There has been a notable increase in emphasis upon collective defense and cooperative security. The enormous costs, technological requirements, and domestic burdens of defense are contributing to the strengthening of multilateral and collective defense arrangements as well as international military cooperation and coordination (see Held, McGrew, Goldblatt, and Perraton 1999: chap. 2 for an elaborate discussion). The rising density of technological connections between states now challenges the very idea of national security and national arms procurement. Some of the most advanced weapons-systems in the world today, e.g., fighter aircraft, depend on components which come from many countries.[1] There has been a globalization of military technology linked to a transnationalization of defense production. And the proliferation of weapons of mass destruction makes all states insecure and makes problematical the very notions of "friends" and "enemies."

Even in the sphere of defense and arms production and manufacture, the notion of a singular, discrete, and delimited political community appears problematic. Indeed, even in this realm, any conception of sovereignty and autonomy which assumes that they denote an indivisible, illimitable, exclusive, and perpetual form of public power—embodied within an individual state—is increasingly challenged and eroded.

---

1. I am indebted to Anthony McGrew for this point.

Democracy and Globalization: In Sum

At the end of the second millennium, as indicated previously, political communities and civilizations can no longer be characterized simply as "discrete worlds"; they are enmeshed and entrenched in complex structures of overlapping forces, relations, and movements. Clearly, these are often structured by inequality and hierarchy, but even the most powerful among them—including the most powerful nation states—do not remain unaffected by the changing conditions and processes of regional and global entrenchment. Five central points can be noted to help characterize the changing relationship between globalization and democratic nation states. All indicate an increase in the extensiveness, intensity, and impact of globalization, and all suggest important points about the evolving character of the democratic political community.

First, the locus of effective political power can no longer be assumed to be national governments—effective power is shared, bartered, and struggled over by diverse forces and agencies at national, regional and international levels. Second, the idea of a political community of fate—of a self-determining collectivity—can no longer meaningfully be located within the boundaries of a single nation state alone. Some of the most fundamental forces and processes which determine the nature of life-chances within and across political communities are now beyond the reach of nation states. The system of national political communities persists of course; but it is articulated and re-articulated today with complex economic, organizational, administrative, legal, and cultural processes and structures which limit and check its efficacy. If these processes and structures are not acknowledged and brought into the political process themselves, they will tend to bypass or circumvent the democratic state system. Third, there is a growing set of disjunctures between the formal authority of the state—that is, the formal domain of political authority that states claim for themselves—and the actual practices and structures of the state and economic system at the regional and global levels. These disjunctures indicate that national communities do not exclusively program the action and decisions of governmental and parliamentary bodies, and the latter by no means simply determine what is right or appropriate for their own citizens (see Held 1995: chaps. 5 and 6; cf. Offe 1985: 286ff).

Fourth, it is not part of my argument that national sovereignty today, even in regions with intensive overlapping and divided political and authority structures, has been wholly subverted—not at all. But it is part of my argument that there are significant areas and regions marked by criss-crossing loyalties, conflicting interpretations of rights and duties, interconnected legal and authority structures, etc., which displace notions of sovereignty as an illimitable, indivisible, and exclusive form of public power. The operations of states in increasingly complex regional and global systems both affects their autonomy (by changing the balance between the costs and benefits of policies) and their sovereignty (by altering the balance between national, regional, and international legal frameworks and administrative practices)....

Fifth, the late twentieth century is marked by a significant series of new types of "boundary problem." If it is accepted that we live in a world of overlapping communities of fate, where the trajectories of each and every country are more tightly entwined than ever before, then new types of boundary problem follow.... In a world where powerful states make decisions not just for their peoples but for others as well, and where transnational actors and forces cut across the boundaries of national communities in diverse ways, the questions of who should be accountable to whom, and on what grounds, do not easily resolve themselves. Overlapping spheres of influence, interference, and interest create fundamental problems at the centre of democratic thought, problems which ultimately concern the very basis of democratic authority....

Rethinking Democracy in the Context of Globalization

In the liberal democracies, consent to government and legitimacy for governmental action are dependent upon electoral politics and the ballot box. Yet the notions that consent legitimates government, and that the ballot box is the appropriate mechanism whereby the citizen body as a whole periodically confers authority on government to enact the law and regulate economic and social life, become problematic as soon as the nature of a "relevant community" is contested. What is the proper constituency, and proper realm of jurisdiction, for developing and implementing policy with respect to health issues such as AIDS or BSE (Bovine Spongiform Encephalopathy), the use of nuclear energy, the management of nuclear waste, the harvesting of rain forests, the use of non-renewable resources, the instability of global financial markets, the reduction of the risks of chemical and nuclear warfare? National boundaries have traditionally demarcated the basis on which individuals are included and excluded from participation in decisions affecting their lives; but if many socio-economic processes, and the outcomes of decisions about them, stretch beyond national frontiers, then the implications of this are serious, not only for the categories of consent and legitimacy but for all the key ideas of democracy. At issue is the nature of a constituency (how should the proper boundaries of a constituency be drawn?), the meaning of representation (who should represent whom and on what basis?), and the proper form and scope of political participation (who should participate and in what way?). As fundamental processes of governance escape the categories of the nation state, the traditional national resolutions of the key questions of democratic theory and practice are open to doubt.

Against this background, the nature and prospects of the democratic polity need re-examination. I have argued elsewhere that an acceptance of liberal democratic politics, in theory and practice, entails an acceptance of each citizen's equal interest in democracy; that is, a recognition of people's equal interest in self-determination (Held 1995: part III). Each adult has an interest in political autonomy as a result of his or her status as a citizen with an equal entitlement to self-determination. An equal interest in political autonomy requires, I have also argued, that citizens enjoy a common structure of political action. A common structure of political action entails a shared enjoyment of a cluster of rights and obligations. This cluster of rights and obligations has traditionally been thought of as entailing, above all, civil and political rights and obligations. Again, elsewhere, I have argued that this cluster has to bite more deeply than civil and political rights alone; for the latter leave large swathes of power untouched by mechanisms of access, accountability, and control. At stake, in short, is a recognition that a common structure of political action requires a cluster of rights and obligations which cut across all key domains of power, where power shapes and affects people's life-chances with determinate effects on and implications for their political agency.

I think of the cluster of rights and obligations that will create the basis of a common structure of political action as constituting the elements of a democratic public law. If power is to be held accountable wherever it is located—in the state, the economy, or cultural sphere—then a common structure of political action needs to be entrenched and enforced through a democratic public law. Such a notion, I believe, can coherently link the ideas of democracy and of the modern state. The key to this is the notion of a democratic legal order—an order which is bound by democratic public law in all its affairs. A democratic legal order—a democratic *Rechtstaat*—is an order circumscribed by, and

accounted for in relation to, democratic public law.

The idea of such an order, however, can no longer be simply defended as an idea suitable to a particular closed political community or nation state. We are compelled to recognize that we live in a complex interconnected world where the extent, intensity, and impact of issues (economic, political, or environmental) raise questions about where those issues are most appropriately addressed. Deliberative and decision-making centres beyond national territories are appropriately situated when those significantly affected by a public matter constitute a cross-border or transnational grouping, when "lower" levels of decision-making cannot manage and discharge satisfactorily transnational or international policy questions, and when the principle of democratic legitimacy can only be properly redeemed in a transnational context (see Held 1995: chap. 10). If the most powerful geopolitical interests are not to settle many pressing matters simply in terms of their objectives and by virtue of their power, then new institutions and mechanisms of accountability need to be established.

In the context of contemporary forms of globalization, for democratic law to be effective it must be internationalized. Thus, the implementation of what I call a cosmopolitan democratic law and the establishment of a community of all democratic communities—a cosmopolitan community—must become an obligation for democrats; an obligation to build a transnational, common structure of political action which alone, ultimately, can support the politics of self-determination.

In this conception, the nation state "withers away." But this is *not* to say that states and national democratic polities become redundant. There are many good reasons for doubting the theoretical and empirical basis of claims that nation states will disappear. Rather, withering away means that states can no longer be, and can no longer be regarded as, the sole centres of legitimate power within their own borders, as is already the case in diverse settings. States need to be articulated with, and relocated within, an overarching democratic law. Within this framework, the laws and rules of the nation state would be but one focus for legal development, political reflection, and mobilization. For this framework would respecify and reconstitute the meaning and limits of sovereign authority. Particular power centers and authority systems would enjoy legitimacy only to the extent that they upheld and enacted democratic law....

Thus, sovereignty can be stripped away from the idea of fixed borders and territories. Sovereignty would become an attribute of the basic democratic law, but it could be entrenched and drawn upon in diverse self-regulating realms, from regions and states to cities and local associations. Cosmopolitan law would demand the subordination of regional, national, and local sovereignties to an overarching legal framework, but in this framework associations would be self-governing at different levels. A new possibility is anticipated: the recovery of an intensive and more participatory democracy at local levels as a complement to the public assemblies of the wider global order; that is, a political order of democratic associations, cities, and nations as well as of regions and global networks. I call this elsewhere the cosmopolitan model of democracy—it is a legal basis of a global and divided authority system, a system of diverse and overlapping power centres, shaped and delimited by democratic law (Held 1995 and 1996). However the model is specified precisely, it is based upon the recognition that the nature and quality of democracy within a particular community and the nature and quality of democratic relations among communities are interlocked, and that new legal and organizational mechanisms must be created if democracy is to prosper.

In this system of cosmopolitan governance, people would come to enjoy multiple citizenships—political membership in the diverse political communities which significantly affect them. They would be citizens of their immediate political communities, and of the wider regional and global networks which impacted upon their lives. This cosmopolitan polity would be one that in form and substance reflected and embraced the diverse forms of power and authority that operate within and across borders and which, if unchecked, threaten the emergence of a highly fragmented, neo-medieval order.

It would be easy to be pessimistic about the future of democracy. There are plenty of reasons for pessimism; they include the fact that the essential political units of the world are still based on nation states while some of the most powerful socio-political forces of the world escape the boundaries of these units....

But there are other forces at work which create the basis for a more optimistic reading of democratic prospects.... Today, we live at another fundamental point of transition, but now to a more transnational, global world. There are forces and pressures which are engendering a reshaping of political cultures, institutions, and structures. First, one must obviously note the emergence, however hesitatingly, of regional and global institutions in the twentieth century. The UN is, of course, weak in many respects, but it is a relatively recent creation and it is an innovative structure which can be built upon. It is a normative resource which provides—for all its difficulties—an enduring example of how nations might (and sometimes do) cooperate better to resolve, and resolve fairly, common problems. In addition, the development of a powerful regional body such as the European Union is a remarkable state of affairs. Just over fifty years ago Europe was at the point of self-destruction. Since that moment Europe has created new mechanisms of collaboration, human rights enforcement, and new political institutions in order not only to hold member states to account across a broad range of issues, but to pool aspects of their sovereignty. Furthermore, there are, of course, new regional and global transnational actors contesting the terms of globalization—not just corporations but new social movements such as the environmental movement, the women's movement, and so on. These are the "new" voices of an emergent "transnational civil society," heard, for instance, at the Rio Conference on the Environment, the Cairo Conference on Population Control, and the Beijing Conference on Women. In short, there are tendencies at work seeking to create new forms of public life and new ways of debating regional and global issues. These are, of course, all in early stages of development, and there are no guarantees that the balance of political contest will allow them to develop; but they point in the direction of establishing new modes of holding transnational power systems to account—that is, they help open up the possibility of a cosmopolitan democracy.

References

Connolly, William. 1991. "Democracy and territoriality." *Millennium* 20(3).

Crawford, James. 1994. *Democracy in International Law*. Cambridge: Cambridge University Press.

Giddens, Anthony. 1985. *The Nation-State and Violence* (Vol. II of *A Contemporary Critique of Historical Materialism*). Cambridge: Polity Press.

———. 1990. *The Consequences of Modernity*. Cambridge: Polity Press.

Goldblatt, David, David Held, Anthony G. McGrew, and Jonathan Perraton. 1997. "Economic globalization and the nation-state: shifting balances of power." *Soundings* 7: 61–77.

Held, David. (ed.) 1993. *Prospects for Democracy: North, South, East, West*. Cambridge: Polity Press.

———. 1995. *Democracy and the Global Order: From the Modern State to Cosmopolitan Governance*. Cambridge: Polity Press.

———. 1996. *Models of Democracy* (2nd edn). Cambridge: Polity Press.

Held, David, Anthony McGrew, David Goldblatt, and Jonathan Perraton. 1999. *Global Transformations: Politics, Economics and Culture*. Cambridge: Polity Press.

McGrew, Anthony G. 1992. "Conceptualizing global politics." In Anthony G. McGrew, Paul G. Lewis *et al.*, *Global Politics*, pp. 1–30. Cambridge: Polity Press.

———. (ed.) 1997. *The Transformation of Democracy?* Cambridge: Polity Press.

Mann, Michael. 1986. *The Sources of Social Power*, Vol. I. Cambridge: Cambridge University Press.

Offe, Claus. 1985. *Disorganized Capitalism*. Cambridge: Polity Press.

Ohmae, Kenichi. 1990. *The Borderless World*. London: Collins.

Perraton, Jonathan, David Goldblatt, David Held, and Anthony McGrew. 1997. "The globalization of economic activity." *New Political Economy* 2(2): 257–277.

Reich, Robert. 1991. *The Work of Nations*. New York: Simon and Schuster.

Sandel, Michael. 1996. *Democracy's Discontent*. Cambridge, MA: Harvard University Press.

Walker, Robert B. J. 1988. *One World, Many Worlds*. Boulder, CO: Lynne Reinner.

Appendix: Observing Democracies

Political scientists and sociologists have developed a number of ways to assess empirically whether a country is democratic.

One of the first and most influential systematic attempts to identify specific attributes of democratic regimes is due to Dahl (1971). He developed a measure of "polyarchy" based on what he considered to be the two main dimensions of democratization: opportunities to participate in elections and opportunities to compete for political power. With data for 1969, he used ten indicators of what he considered to be the seven institutional requirements for democracy.[1] With these data he produced a scale that placed countries on a continuum ranging from the least to the greatest opportunity for participation and contestation. This measure was later extended for 1985 by Coppedge and Reinicke (1990).

Although these measures of democracy cover a large number of countries, they are limited to one or two years.[2] Today, there are three different measures of democracy that cover most, if not all, countries for a relatively large number of years. These are the measures that are used by most political scientists, sociologists, and economists who study empirically the causes and consequences of democratic regimes. They are:

• The Polity IV measures of political regime characteristics and transitions, which cover 1800 to 2000 (found at http://www.bsos.umd.edu/cidcm/inscr/polity/).

• The Freedom House (FH) measure of political and civil liberties, which covers all countries of

the world between 1973 and 2002 (found at http://www.freedomhouse.org/).

• The classification of democracies and dictatorships developed by Przeworski et al. (2000) in *Democracy and Development* (DD), covering all countries in the world between 1946 and 1999 (found at http://pantheon.yale.edu/~jac236).

Although similar in that they cover a large number of countries for a relatively large number of years, these measures differ in at least three important ways:

• the conception of democracy that underlies each of them;

• the nature of the data used to assess political regimes; and

• the type of measurement they develop.

As illustrated by the selections in chapter 1, conceptions of democracy differ in terms of whether they adopt a strictly procedural view as opposed to a more substantive one. In the first case, democracy depends exclusively on the presence of certain institutions, with no reference to the kinds of outcomes that are generated by their operation. Thus, the authors of DD state that "'democracy' is a regime in which those who govern are selected through contested elections" (2000:15). Since they are interested in studying the relationship between democracy and normatively desirable aspects of political, social, and economic life, they need to define democracy narrowly so that they can avoid the tautology that a broader definition might imply (2000:14).

In substantive conceptions of democracy, institutions are seen as necessary but not sufficient to characterize a political regime. Although it may be that no democracy exists that does not have contested elections, not all regimes that are based on contested elections may be called democratic. What matters is that, through these elections, something else happens: the public

---

1. These requirements are: freedom to form and join organizations, freedom of expression, right to vote, right of political leaders to compete for support, existence of alternative sources of information, free and fair elections, and institutions that make government policies depend on popular votes.

2. A similar limitation applies to the measure developed by Bollen (1980). Originally constructed for 1960 and 1965, it has been extended to 1955, 1970, 1975, and 1980, but not for other years.

good is achieved, citizen preferences are represented, governments become accountable, citizen
participation in political life is maximized, economic equality is enhanced, rationality is implemented, economic conditions improve, and so
on. Those who use FH, therefore, believe that
the measure of "freedom" it offers can be used to
indicate "democracy." Similarly, Polity IV conceives of democracy as the presence of institutions that allow citizens to choose alternative
policies and leaders, in combination with "institutionalized constraints on the exercise of power
by the executive" and "the guarantee of civil
liberties to all citizens in their daily lives and in
acts of political participation" (manual, p. 12).
Finally, Bollen (1980:372) defined democracy as
"the extent to which the political power of the
elite is minimized and that of the nonelite is
maximized." In a later formulation, he stated
that "it is the relative power between élites and
nonélites that determines the degree of political
democracy. Where the nonélites have little control over the élites, political democracy is low.
When the élites are accountable to the nonélites,
political democracy is higher" (Bollen 1991:4).

A second difference between the measures of
democracy has to do with the type of information that is used, or required, to assess a political regime. Most measures are based on data
that require largely subjective judgements by the
coder. Thus, FH requires answers to the following questions, with no clear attempt to define
what the relevant terms or qualifiers mean: Are
there *fair* electoral laws, *equal* campaigning opportunities, *fair* polling, and *honest* tabulation of
ballots? Are voters able to endow their representatives with *real* power? Do minorities have
reasonable self-determination, self-government,
autonomy, or participation through informal
consensus in the decision-making process? Are
the people *free from domination* by the military,
foreign powers, totalitarian parties, religious
hierarchies, economic oligarchies, or any other
powerful group? Are there *free* and *independent*

media? Are there *free* trade unions and other
professional organizations, and is there *effective*
collective bargaining? Is there *personal autonomy*? Is there *equality of opportunity*? Similarly,
the Polity IV democracy scale requires one to
decide whether constraints on the chief executive in any given country are close to *parity*, face
substantial limitations, or are located in one of
two possible *intermediate* categories.

The Polity IV approach contrasts with the one
adopted by the authors of DD, who classify democracy on the basis of four observational criteria. Thus, for them, in order to be a democracy
a regime has to have an elected executive, an
elected legislature, elections in which two or
more political parties compete, and incumbents
who have lost power at least once. These rules
unambiguously classify the vast majority of regimes in all countries in every year since 1946.
They do not, however, account for a small proportion of cases (8.6 percent between 1946 and
1999) where history has not yet provided the
necessary information to apply the rules. Rather
than creating "intermediate" categories to accommodate these cases, they decide to keep them
separate and allow each user to decide how or
whether to use them in their analysis.

Finally, measures of democracy differ as to the
level at which they make the observation. Most
measures are either continuous or, although categorical, transformed into a continuous scale.
This is true of both Polity IV and FH. The former offers separate indices of democracy and
autocracy (each ranging from 0 to 10), which are
often combined into a 21-point scale for democracy (with high values indicating higher levels of
democracy). The latter provides separate indicators of civil and political liberties (ranging from 1
to 7), which are often combined into a single
measure of the degree of democracy, ranging
from 2 (highest levels of democracy) to 14 (lowest levels of democracy). In contrast, DD classifies political regimes simply into two categories:
democracies and dictatorships.

Among the debates that have engaged those who study democracy empirically, this is probably the one that has generated the highest level of controversy. The most forceful proponents of a continuous measure of democracy have been Bollen and Jackman (1989) who assert "the inherently continuous nature of the concept of political democracy" (p. 612) and claim that "since democracy is conceptually continuous, it is best measured in continuous terms" (p. 612) and that "democracy is always a matter of degree" (p. 618).

A different argument states that measures that allow for gradation should be preferred over dichotomies because they will contain more information, and that even though dichotomous measures may contain less error than continuous measures, they are less sensitive to variations in the underlying concept of democracy (Elkins 2000).

This issue has probably been blown out of proportion. The matter is not whether one should adopt a continuous or a categorical measure of democracy that is observable across all political regimes. The issue is whether there is a natural zero-point that divides democracies and nondemocracies. Even those who develop and use categorical measures of democracy may agree, given some appropriate criteria to use as a yardstick, that democratic regimes can differ as to how democratic they are, and that some measure to assess their degree of democracy may make sense. Note, however, that this refers to democratic regimes, as opposed to nondemocratic regimes. It assumes that some regimes fail whatever minimum requirement there is for them to be called democratic.

The belief that democracy is an attribute that can and should be measured over the spectrum of cases leads to assertions that may be absurd, for example, the claim that the level of democracy in Albania in 1950 and 1955, under the communist regime of Enver Hoxa, was, according to the Bollen scale, about 24 out of 100. The

level of democracy in North Korea in 1960 and 1965 was about 21 according to Bollen, and it went down to 11 in 1980. The average score for Cuba between 1960 and 1999 was −7 in the Polity scale (which, as we know, has a minimum of −10). The level of democracy in Chile between 1974 and 1980, according to Bollen was a low, but positive, 5.56; it averaged −7 according to the Polity scale and 11.6 according to the combined Freedom House scale. Singapore was more democratic than Cuba, scoring −2 as opposed to −7. Zaire under Mobuto, although almost close to the bottom, was not *at* the bottom of the Polity scale: often it scored a −9, but sometimes things improved and it scored −8; and according to the FH scale, its score ranged from the least democratic 14 to the somewhat more democratic 11. According to FH, South Africa under apartheid had scores that were similar to Russia since 1993, the Dominican Republic in the 1990s, postcommunist Albania and Romania, and Sri Lanka in the 1990s. Thus, if one believes that democracy can be continuously measured over all regimes, one has to be prepared to argue that it makes sense to speak of positive levels of democracy in places like Albania under Hoxa, North Korea and Chile under Pinochet; that it makes sense to speak of a change from one value to another along these scales; and, finally, that we can meaningfully interpret scores across countries.

As for the informational content of different measures, it is not true that a continuous scale will necessarily contain more information than a dichotomous classification of political regime. The informational content of a measure depends on the way in which it is conceptualized and observed, at least as much as it depends on the level of measurement. What kind of information is being conveyed when we say that the level of democracy in Singapore in 1965 was 76.94 according to the Bollen scale? Or that the Burmese junta scored a −6 in the Polity scale? Which measure conveys more information: the one that says that North Korea scored 21.04 in Bollen's democracy scale in 1965, or the one that says that North Korea was a dictatorship in 1965 because leaders were not selected on the basis of contested elections?

Measures are only as good as their components. Consider the FH scale. It is based on answers to 8 questions for the political liberty scale and 14 for the civil liberty scale. Given the nature of the questions and information required, as seen above, these answers often require highly subjective judgement on the part of coders. Coders assign "raw points" ranging from 0 to 4 for each of those questions, for a maximum of 32 political rights points and 56 civil liberties points. Countries are then distributed into one of the seven categories that make up the final political and civil liberties scales according to the number of raw points they received. For example, a country with 28 to 32 raw political rights points is placed in category 1 of the political rights scale; with 23 to 27 points, it is placed in category 2; and so on.

What needs to be true for the FH scale to convey meaningful information? For one, it is necessary that each of the 22 items that compose the checklist of political rights and civil liberties be sufficiently defined. Adjectives such as *equal, fair, honest, reasonable* and so on that appear in the description of the checklist items must have been sufficiently defined so that one may separate the cases of *unequal, unfair, dishonest, and unreasonable* practices that take place across countries. Then, there must be rules that allow one to decide when a practice related to political or civil liberty deserves a 0, as opposed to a 1, 2, 3, or 4 in each of these items. Not only must these items make sense, but one must be able to distinguish the levels in which they materialize. Moreover, it must also be true that different constellations of attributes that add up to the same number be equivalent. Having "personal autonomy" with no "equality of opportunity" must be equivalent to the opposite. Finally,

assuming that one knows what to do once one has the facts, one still has to get the facts about each of these items. What is needed is information about the policymaking activities of both executive and legislative bodies, political campaigning, political parties (both in government and in opposition), trade unions, professional organizations, the judiciary, the military, religious organizations, economic oligarchies, and so on.

If these conditions are met, indeed the FH scale will convey more information than a dichotomous measure based simply on whether or not contested elections took place. However, if these conditions are not met, then at each step of the process the numbers that are generated make less and less sense. One is left with a scale that is more refined than a dichotomy in the sense that it contains more categories and allows for more values, but certainly not because it conveys more information about the political regime in each country. It is possible that what they convey is information about the subjectivity of those involved in generating the scale.

So which measure should one use to study democracy? As with anything else, the best measure is a function of the question being asked and of its conceptual clarity. The measures of democracy, however, are all very highly correlated, thus making it irrelevant which measure one uses. Indeed, the correlation between Polity IV and FH is -0.91. Polity IV predicts correctly 94 percent of the cases classified as democracies by DD and 95 percent of those classified as dictatorships. FH predicts 88 percent and 95 percent, respectively. But continuous scales of democracy have a bimodal distribution, with a high concentration of cases at the low and high ends of the scales: 56 percent of the cases are classified in the three lowest and highest categories of FH's 13-point scale; 73 percent of the cases have scores that are -7 and lower or 7 and higher in the 21-point Polity IV scale. If one excludes the extremes of the democracy scales, the correlation among the different measures is considerably reduced. The correlation between Polity IV and FH becomes −0.75. Polity IV predicts 70 percent of the democracies in DD and 83 percent of dictatorships, whereas these numbers are 67 percent and 81 percent for FH. Thus it is the uncontroversial cases that drive the high correlation among different measures of democracy: No measure is likely to produce very different readings for, say, England, the United States, Sweden, North Korea, or Iraq. The problem arises with "difficult" cases, such as Mexico, Botswana, Malaysia, Peru, Guatemala, and scores of other countries that do not easily fit into the categories that make up existing measures. These countries are "difficult," however, not necessarily because they represent intermediate instances of democracy, thus calling for measures that allow for gradations; rather, they are difficult because the rules we have to sort the types of political regimes are not good enough to distinguish all the cases we encounter in the world. Perhaps rather than gradations of democracy, what we need is simply better rules for identifying democratic regimes.

None of this is necessarily an argument for the use of a dichotomous measure such as DD over scales such as FH, Polity, or Bollen. But given that once we get to these difficult cases—the cases that populate the middle of the distribution in these scales—no consensus seems to exist across measures, *the choice must be made on conceptual grounds and on the basis of the amount of error each measure may contain*. If we can make sense of what it means to be 4, or to move from 4 to 5 in the Polity scale, then one should probably use it. If one cannot make sense of what this means, and, for this reason, doubts the process that generated this number, then one might be better served by using a "cruder" measure, but one that has some theoretical and empirical meaning.

Table A.1
Distribution of democracies across regions, 1946–1999

Region	Country-years	% democratic	% democracies	% parliamentary	% mixed	% presidential
Sub-Saharan Africa	1730	10.23	6.01	36.16	33.90	29.94
South Asia	305	44.26	4.58	88.15	11.85	0.00
East Asia	263	9.51	0.85	4.00	48.00	48.00
South-East Asia	425	16.00	2.31	50.00	0.00	50.00
Pacific Islands/Oceania	242	59.50	4.89	83.33	0.00	16.67
Middle East-North Africa	612	19.12	3.97	100.00	0.00	0.00
Latin America	1026	52.83	18.40	0.00	0.37	99.63
Caribbean/Non-Iberic America	395	77.72	10.42	91.86	5.54	2.61
Eastern Europe/ Ex-Soviet Union	696	22.99	5.43	48.13	32.50	19.38
Industrial countries	1339	94.92	43.14	74.04	13.69	12.27
Oil countries	277	0.00	0.00	0.00	0.00	0.00
All	7311	40.31	100.00	59.57	11.30	29.12

In what follows we use DD to characterize the distribution of democracies in the world across regions and over time since 1946. Table A.1 presents the frequency of democracies in each region of the world between 1946 and 1999. These figures refer to 199 countries that either existed in 1946 or became independent after that year. The second column in the table presents the number of country-years observed in each region. For instance, as indicated in the note to the table, there are 19 countries in Latin America, each of which was observed since 1946, yielding a total of 19 countries times 54 years = 1,026 country-years for the region. Sub-Saharan Africa is composed of 50 countries. However, since most of them became independent after 1946, we do not observe them for the full 54 years that comprise the period between 1946 and 1999. Therefore, there are 1,730 country-years in this region.

The second column in table A.1 presents the percentage of country-years in each region that was spent under democracy. As we can see, the variation is large across regions. Only a small proportion of the time in sub-Saharan Africa, East Asia and the Middle East/North Africa was spent under democracy. The opposite was true for the Caribbean and the industrial countries, where most of the time was spent under democracy. Latin America is unique in that it experienced democracy and dictatorship in equal proportions.

The third column in table A.1 shows how the democracies that existed between 1946 and 1999 were distributed across the regions. As we can see, there is a clear regional pattern. Almost half of all democratic regimes existed in the industrial countries, with a significant but much smaller proportion occurring in Latin America and the Caribbean. No oil country has ever been a democracy.

Finally, the last three columns in table A.1 present the distribution of different types of democracy—parliamentary, mixed, and presidential—in each region. Recall that systems in which governments must enjoy the confidence of the legislature are parliamentary; systems in which they serve at the authority of the elected president are presidential; and systems in which governments respond both to legislative assemblies and elected presidents are mixed. As we can see, regional patterns are, again, very clear. Most democracies in the industrial countries are parliamentary. The same is true of the relatively few democracies that exist in South Asia, the Pacific Islands, the Middle East, and the Caribbean. Latin America, on the contrary, is overwhelmingly presidential, whereas the democracies that exist in sub-Saharan Africa tend to be equally split among the three types.

Figure A.1 presents the evolution of democratic regimes since 1946. As we can see, the postwar evolution of democracies can be approximated by a U-shaped curve. The proportion of democracies was relatively high at the end of the 1940s, when it started to decline, reaching a low of only 28 percent in 1977 to 1978. Since then the proportion of democracy in the world has been increasing, reaching almost 58 percent in 1999, the highest level since 1946. This pattern should not be immediately interpreted as evidence that democratization happens in waves, as argued by Huntington (see chapter 2). As Przeworski et al. (2000) argue, the pattern we observe in figure A.1 is not so much the product of democracies becoming dictatorships and vice versa. Rather it is because many countries have entered the world, that is, have become independent, in the 1960s and 1970s, and they did so as dictatorships. The proportion of democracies and dictatorships in countries that existed prior to 1946, as they note, has remained mostly constant, and the variation that we observe is almost entirely due to regime changes in Latin America.

Figure A.1 also presents the proportion of democracies that are parliamentary, mixed, or presidential. The most striking feature in this picture is the recent increase in the proportion of democracies that have adopted a mixed system,

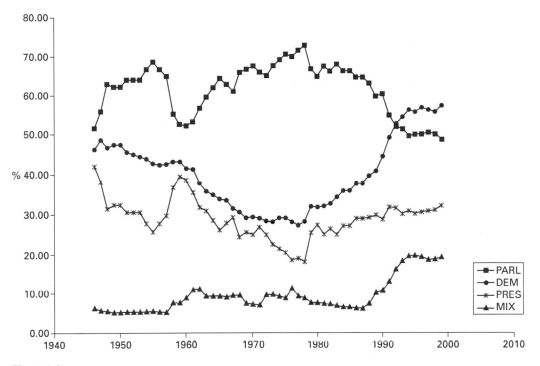

Figure A.1
Democracy over time, 1946 to 1999.

that is, one in which the government is responsible to a directly elected president and to a legislative majority. We know very little about the way these regimes operate, and the category in fact masks a large amount of variation in the way governments are actually formed and dismissed. There is no doubt, however, that this is an increasingly popular form of government among new democracies, one that needs to be studied more carefully.

References

Bollen, Kenneth A. 1980. "Issues in the Comparative Measurement of Political Democracy." *American Sociological Review* 45(3): 370–390.

Bollen, Kenneth A. 1991. "Political Democracy: Conceptual and Measurement Traps," in Alex Inkeles, ed., *On Measuring Democracy: Its Consequences and Concomitants*, pp. 3–20. New Brunswick: Transaction Books.

Bollen, Kenneth A., and Robert W. Jackman. 1989. "Democracy, Stability, and Dichotomies." *American Sociological Review* 54(4): 612–621.

Coppedge, Michael, and Wolfgang H. Reinicke. 1990. "Measuring Polyarchy." *Studies in Comparative International Development* 25(1): 51–72.

Dahl, Robert A. 1971. *Polyarchy: Participation and Opposition*. New Haven: Yale University Press.

Elkins, Zachary. 2000. "Gradations of Democracy: Empirical Tests of Alternative Conceptualizations." *American Journal of Political Science* 44(2): 293–301.

Marshall, Monty G., and Keith Jaggers. *Polity IV Project. Political Regime Characteristics and Transi-*

tions, 1800–1999. Dataset Users' Manual. University of Maryland, College Park. Accessed at www.bsos.umd.edu/cidcm/inscr/polity.

Przeworski, Adam, Mike Alvarez, José Antonio Cheibub, and Fernando Limongi. 2000. *Democracy and Development: Political Regimes and Economic Performance in the World, 1950–1990.* Cambridge: Cambridge University Press.

Index

Abortion, 254
Accountability, in deliberative democracy, 19, 22, 39
Acquired Immune Deficiency Syndrome (AIDS), 522
Acquired regulation, 393–397
Africa, 170f.
African Americans
  disaffection of in inner cities, 162, 487
  disillusionment among middle class, 469, 471–474,
    475
  poor blacks and the American dream, 469
  proposal to solve underrepresentation of, 153, 154t.
African National Congress (ANC), 99, 103–106
Agrarian sector
  elite-alliances with, 67–68 (see also Landed elites)
  "labor repressive" vs. "market" agriculture, 68, 69t.
  landed peasantry, 65
  peasant revolutionary potential, 68–70, 69t., 70n.25
  role of in bourgeois revolutions, 66, 67–68, 70, 75
AIDS, 522
Airline industry, 393
Air pollution, 504, 505, 507
Ake, Claude, 142
Albania, 94
Alger, Horatio, 129
Alienation, 38, 162
Allocative efficiency, 448, 449–450
American Civil War, as a bourgeois revolution, 66
American dream
  conflicting racial perspectives on, 46n.2, 463, 467,
    469–472, 475–476
  paradoxical aspects of, 485–486
  of social fluidity, 129–130, 131
"American exceptionalism," 174
"Americanization," 179
American political system, 93, 365–366
  based in material wealth of the land, 129–130
  citizenship and voting policies, 480–483, 480n.1,
    482n.4
  class analyses lacking in, 130, 131, 383, 384, 391,
    484
  electoral college, 324–325
  governability and interest intermediation in, 398,
    399–401
  historical factors, 66, 486, 487
    early-American homogeneous political culture, 480–
      483
    egalitarianism based in small homesteads, 129–130
    European struggle against the ancien regime not
      present in, 130–131, 483

manhood suffrage, 93, 131, 456, 484
    new petit-bourgeois/worker hybrid a facet of, 129,
      130, 131
    Puritan heritage fueling egalitarianism, 445–447,
      480–481, 482
  leftist parties not viable in, 59, 129
  multiple traditions analysis of, 482–483, 485–487
  political alliances in, 249–250
  problems of or critique of, 19, 38, 39, 51, 382–384
  separation of powers in, 193–194
  values differ from those of other modernized nations,
    170f., 173–174, 176f., 177f., 179
American Revolution, 66
Anarchy/disorder, 81, 425, 436–437
Ancien regime, 130–132, 483
Anomia, 473
Antipopulism, 321, 325
Apartheid, 153, 154t.
  in South Africa, 99–100, 102–103, 242n.71
Arab world
  democracy and Islamic religious culture, 36, 95, 96–
    97, 185, 187, 188t., 189t.
  liberalization of in early 1990s, 94
  oil countries, 531t.
  values associated with culture area, 170f., 175, 176f.
Arbitrary exercise of power, 252, 255
Argentina, 76, 83, 87n.54, 170f., 176f., 298, 299,
  299n.70, 303
Armenia, 170f., 176f.
Arrow, Kenneth, 321, 326
Arrow's Theorem, 317–320, 321, 324–325
Asia, 36
Assemblies. See Legislatures
Associations, 2, 367–369. See also Interest groups
  as potential interest groups, 366, 367–369
Ataturk, Mustafa Kemal, 97
Australia, 59, 63, 170f., 176f., , 335t., 343, 354
Austria, 59, 143, 146, 170f., 176f.
Austria-Hungary, 66, 74
Authoritarianism, 74, 427
  bureaucratic authoritarianism, 112–113
  capitalist authoritarianism, 433–434
  democracy compared to in terms of development,
    436, 444–446
  elections under, 90–91
  genocidal acts and, 494
  GNP per capita a predictor of, 186t., 187t., 188t.,
    189t.
  international threats tending to increase, 496